N'DIGO®

LEGACY
BLACK LUXE

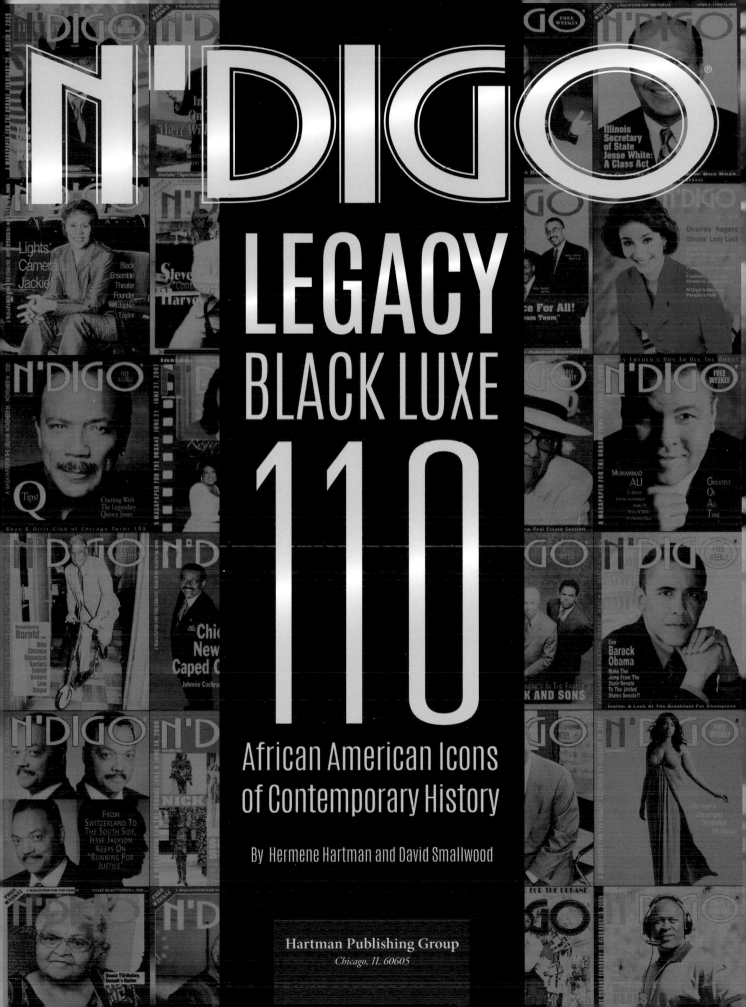

N'DIGO

LEGACY
BLACK LUXE
110

African American Icons
of Contemporary History

By Hermene Hartman and David Smallwood

Hartman Publishing Group
Chicago, IL 60605

Hartman Publishing Group, Ltd.
1006 S. Michigan Ave., Suite 200
Chicago, IL 60605

©Hartman Publishing Group, Ltd.

Library of Congress Cataloging-in-Publication data available.

ISBN: 978-0-578-18967-3 (regular edition)
ISBN: 978-0-578-19722-7 (limited edition)

10 9 8 7 6 5 4 3 2 1

ACKNOWLEDGEMENTS

Art Director/Graphic Designer: Jody Levitan
Assistant Graphic Designer: Jerald Miller
Editorial Assistants: Adrienne Brown & Julie Roberts
Operations: Sylvester Cosby
Research: Chicago Historical Society
Marketing and Production Management:
L&L Graphic Solutions, Elk Grove Village, IL 60007
www.llgraphicsolutions.com

Printed in the United States of America

WRITERS

Veronica Anderson
Rod Atkins
Derrick Baker
Ingrid Bridges
Ronald Childs
Donna Gist Coleman
Paul Davis
Monica DeLeon
Bonnie DeShong
Kai EL' Zabar
Tracey Robinson English
Hermene Hartman
Donna Hodge
Zondra Hughes
Ngina James
Iman Jefferson
Rae Jones
Barbara Kensey
Allison Keyes
D. Kevin McNeir
Sabrina Miller
Sergio Mims
James Muhammad
Simone Nathan
Sandra Jackson Opoku
Glenna Ousley
Ken Parish Perkins
Walter Perkins
Cheryl Jenkins Richardson
Keith Robbins
Mark Ruffin
Barbara Samuels
David Smallwood
Robert Starks
Chinta Strausberg
Rita Coburn Whack
Charles Whitaker
Jean Williams
Marcia Reed-Woodard
Alfred Woods
Conrad Worrill
Wanda Wright
Rosalind Cummings-Yeates

PHOTOGRAPHERS

Michelle Agins
John Beckett
Warren Browne
Ernest Collins
Chris Griffin
Michael Gunn
James Hollis
David Jenkins
Brent Jones
Paul Mainor
Darlene Martin
Jason McCoy
Reginald Payton
Victor Powell
Howard Simmons
Victor Skrebneski
Beverly Swanagan
Jason Thomas
Doyle Wicks
Jennifer Williams
Calvin Woods

ADDITIONAL PHOTOS COURTESY OF OR SHOT BY:

Muhammad Ali Estate
Mitchell Canoff
Chicago Bears
Clear Channel Radio
D/E Entertainment
DVA Agency
Chaz Ebert
Essential Photography
Final Call Newspaper
Ed Gardner Family
Laura Hamm
Dr. Mae Jemison
Quincy Jones
Living Word Christian Center
NASA
National Association
   of Broadcasters
Operation PUSH Wall
   Street Project
Premiere Network
John Smierciak
Harold Washington Library
Jesse White

Dedication

Mildred
Bowden

Doyle Wicks

Starting a business is more than a notion. It is a family affair every step of the way, like it or not. This book is dedicated to my parents.

My father, Herman Hartman, was a pioneer with the Pepsi-Cola Company. He was the first African-American Pepsi distributor in the country, starting in 1935. When he sold to Pepsi in 1969 he was still the lone African-American distributor.

On a frigid winter day, he went to get his first 20 cases of pop. He pawned his overcoat as collateral for his first load. Then he sold all of the pop and went back to get his coat. The company never outsold him in the areas he developed. I have heard his entrepreneurial stories all of my life. He was masterful on the concept of "branding."

When I started *N'DIGO*, my father was up in age and ill, but we had some of the best business conversations on Sundays. He taught me so much about distribution. He told me the most important thing about a product is distribution.

Pepsi-Cola was started and built on the South Side of Chicago. From his early Pepsi days, my dad taught me how to map the various locations in which to distribute my paper and his model is still effective. He was a mastermind on the South Side of Chicago. He helped me build the distribution route. His insights and experiences were educational.

My mother, Mildred Bowden, thought I was crazy because I had left the security of a tenured position at the City Colleges of Chicago to become an entrepreneur. She has been from the very beginning a great source of support, with appealing marketing ideas that I didn't know she knew. She has been a real strength for me to solve problems and to keep it moving.

My aunt, Bernice Hamilton, was an extra eye on the street. She diligently visited *N'DIGO* sites to see if the paper had been delivered properly. She gave me weekly reports that were just between she and I. She was on it.

Doyle Wicks was an invaluable asset to *N'DIGO*. Doyle was a brilliant, artistic photographer, a catalog photographer for Montgomery Ward at one time. He was one of the first people I talked to about the paper. I wanted him to be the photographer, exclusively to produce beautiful covers.

He suggested that there were a lot of photographers in town and we should showcase as many of them as possible. Doyle became the manager for distribution. He was a jack-of-all-trades. Doyle could do anything and I needed him for everything.

He was the rock of *N'DIGO*. He distributed the paper with timely precision and built a quality team of distributors. He was eyes and ears on the street at every level. Doyle continued in photography as he saw fit. He was one of the finest people I have ever known, true to the cause with firmness and compassion. Doyle passed away in 2016 and I will always be indebted to him.

Contents

N'troduction

My foray into publishing grew out of frustration. Allow me to explain.

began my career as a college professor, and then became a college administrator. My first media job was as a television producer and later, a newspaper publisher during one of Chicago's most racially divisive periods in media.

In 1983, biased media coverage had reached its racist boiling point following the election of Chicago's first Black mayor, Harold Washington.

With Harold's unprecedented victory, Chicago emerged as the political epicenter that the rest of Black America turned to for inspiration.

The significance of the election of Harold Washington as mayor of the "City of Big Shoulders" reverberated across the nation and spawned the push for Black mayors in other American cities, including New York and Philadelphia.

It lent encouragement to the budding movement for a serious Black presidential candidate. Thus, The Reverend Jesse Jackson entered the 1984 Demo-

"*The Greatest Generation.*" They are the ones who had fought in World War II, manned the frontlines of the civil rights struggle throughout the 1960s, and made the clarion call for Black political empowerment.

They are the ones who lived with segregation and turned it into integration. The Black economic infrastructure – composed of national and local Black-owned businesses and commercial establishments – was successful because it grew and developed in harmony with the emerging Civil Rights Movement.

Racially Insensitive Media

Yet, with all of its political and economic power, leadership and growth, the Black middle class had a burgeoning image problem, exacerbated by a race-insensitive media.

In this era, the mainstream media thrived on a steady diet of bare-knuckle politics, and newsroom

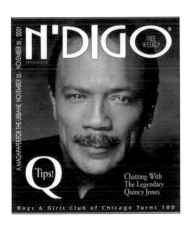   

cratic primary and eventually helped to change the nomination rules that paved the way for yet another political Chicago story, the election of Barack Obama as the first Black president of the United States.

Black Chicago in 1983 had the benefit of the leadership of the men and women of what journalist Tom Brokaw in his best-selling book labeled

racism had a firm grip on Black Chicago's image, vilifying Blacks in some publications and ignoring them altogether in others.

The papers were particularly brutal to Harold Washington and Eugene Sawyer; these Black men were racially bashed before, during and after their mayoral races and tenures on the fifth floor of City Hall.

The sudden death of Mayor Harold Washington on November 25, 1987 ignited a firestorm of negative media coverage that began the process of dismantling the Black political infrastructure and continued the propagation of negative Black images. Too often, Black leaders, politicians, and other civic figures were taken out of context and held to another standard; too often, they were under attack.

I was sick and tired of the way Black folks were cast in the media. If newspapers are the first blush of history, we were being unrecorded. We were always violent, ignorant. We were mostly buffoons and "less than."

The mass media did not show our full flavor and it was evident that the media gap on Black reality was wide and loud. Witnessing this skewed coverage was my awakening.

The Black middle class viewpoint was missing in action. Absent. I often asked myself, what was the Black perspective and insight on local, national and international issues? Where was our perspective? At that point, with all the race-bashing surrounding Harold, never before was the city more in need of an alternate point of view.

There certainly were very few African-American reporters, editors and gatekeepers working in mainstream media who could help promote our perspective in newspaper and magazine pages and on TV news screens.

We had opinions and viewpoints on things, and it was time for some new news about Black folk.

We presented a *Vogue*-like cover; we captured people at their best – in their splendor, if you will. And we wanted to shoot the absolute best pictures with the best photographers. Glamour all the way.

The cover story profiled people who have made a difference; that was the defining criteria for coverage. We were of style and substance and we showcased the diversity, the talent and the achievements of legends, emerging folks, the unknown, the accomplished and the newbies. We presented an authentic view of our community, Chicago, America's Black Mecca.

Many of my associates and colleagues – culled mostly from my involvement in the civil rights community – were also eager for a positive perspective.

Some people say, "Why doesn't it exist?" while other people say, "Why doesn't it exist…and why not be the first to do it?" That's me. I said, "We can do this," and that's what we set out to do with passion.

With a fistful of dollars, energy and loads of creative talent, we were on our way. My creative juices were on fire. I gathered friends who were photographers, graphic artists, writers and other media types to discuss the idea of a new publication and requested their input and involvement.

I provided a vision. We needed new news. I did not want to be like other Black papers, printing press releases. I strived for independence. We needed to author our story, history and contemporariness as it was happening in real time. We needed to tell the

  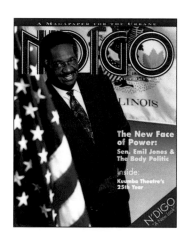 

An Authentic Perspective

I was interested in changing the concept of "minority" into "majority" and making our human interest stories real. We required a mainstream authentic view that was unapologetic and appealing to a progressive population that I label the urbane.

Urbane is metropolitan, cosmopolitan, sophisticated urban. It's inclusive, like jazz; I call it the Miles Davis model. *N'DIGO* developed as a magnificent hybrid of a magazine look with a newspaper feel – we call it a "magapaper."

stories that had been untold, mistold and needed to be retold.

Birth of "Indigo"

David Smallwood, Derrick Baker, Rae Jones, Doyle Wicks, Kai El' Zabar and Alfred Woods were among the initial group who sat with me one Saturday morning in an office on Hubbard Street in River North to listen to this new idea.

We created a progressive paper with broad appeal

and spoke to a Black cosmopolitan sensibility with authority and authenticity. I asked my friends to join me in writing about politics, fashion, art and education as we profiled our people and redefined ourselves. They all agreed and we decided that we would name this publication "*Indigo*."

In the Yoruba culture, color has sacred meaning and indigo blue to them conveys "trust" and is the common dye for the "outer image." Further, Indigo just sounded right – it had the correct sentiment and a hip array of Blackness, just like Duke Ellington's *Mood Indigo*.

But there was a problem. We couldn't use the name Indigo.

My legal counsel, Mark Jones and Mitchell Ware, doing an intellectual property check, discovered that Richard Pryor's production company was named Indigo and that there also was another publishing company using the name.

Hard lesson learned, because I had already spent a lot of money – all I had – on materials using the "Indigo" brand. The original logo, even "Indigo" business cards.

I was devastated until my mother, Mildred Bowden, proposed a solution. She said, "Stop crying and just spell it differently. Try 'N'DIGO,' and you'll have a creative way of spelling it that also gives it signature." So we spelled it uniquely and with creative license and the revised *N'DIGO* brand took root.

The original printed version of the paper was a whopping 11x19 inches. Poised on the very first

In The Vanguard of Journalism

For many years, beginning in the early 2000s, *N'DIGO* was the largest-circulated African-American weekly newspaper in the country, second only to *Jet* magazine in weekly readership. *N'DIGO* was born at the beginning of the end of the Black political zenith and has documented, analyzed and projected the lasting impact of this political transformation over the last 28 years, through almost 1,100 issues of the magapaper.

From the very beginning, this publication has been a leader in innovative journalism. Our unique approach to coverage of events – from our contemporary Black urbane perspective – has placed *N'DIGO* in the vanguard of journalism in the city and made it a sought-after voice for analysis and direction.

We've been in-depth; we've conducted insightful interviews with politicians and elected officials; we've looked at people behind the scenes; and we've analyzed the linkages between economics, politics, education, and religion. We even covered the parties.

N'DIGO has affirmed and validated the African-American experience, contribution and predicament. We write with a Black sensibility and we have contributed to racial enlightenment and cul-

N'Digo's first cover featuring the Reverend Willie T. Barrow.

cover was a regal Reverend Willie T. Barrow smiling sweetly, knowingly. The late civic rights icon and The Reverend Jesse Jackson confidant was billed on that first issue cover as "The Little Warrior." The inaugural issue – in December 1989 – announced The Reverend Barrow's retirement and was launched at her grand retirement party.

We put a copy of this brand new paper called *N'DIGO* on every seat at The Reverend Barrow's big banquet…and everyone was trying to figure out, what is this?

tural, social, and political enterprise in Chi-Town, by reaching a readership that includes the movers and shakers of all colors in the city, not just African Americans. People want our take, our cover, our story, our voice.

I am grateful to the *Chicago Sun-Times* and *Chicago Tribune* for their early business support of *N'DIGO*. In the beginning, I went to the *Sun-Times* requesting to do a Black History Month special insert for them. It was on the Black church and was the forerunner of what came to be *N'DIGO*. I provided the content and they did the rest.

After we began officially publishing *N'DIGO*, eventually the *Sun-Times* began to distribute us in their paper in targeted zip codes and they prepared the layout. They made an offer to purchase us, but we were not ready to be acquired.

The powers at the *Chicago Tribune* noticed us at a Black Expo Convention at McCormick Place and we began to meet. Both dailies were looking to supplement their coverage of African Americans. *N'DIGO* in its original form was designed to be a supplement to a daily paper.

We developed a strategic alliance with the *Tribune* that included funding, training and access to the executive level of management. I went to "*Tribune* school," so to speak, and made lifelong friends. I am forever beholden to them for teaching us some of the ropes of the newspaper business from their perspective and sharing their wisdom.

N'DIGO And The 44th

In 2003, *N'DIGO* published a cover story on an up-and-coming young man named Barack Obama, and as the 44th President of the United States noted in his book *The Audacity of Hope*: "(It was) a Black-owned weekly magazine, *N'DIGO*, that first featured me on its cover." Indeed, we were the first publication to write a major story on Barack, long before he hit the national stage. We saw him coming.

Obama's words forced *N'DIGO* into the fishbowl

were Chicago. Their question was, how did we see Barack Obama first?

A young female reporter from Hong Kong came to visit me and Bob Starks, our political writer. Her interview was to last for a few minutes, but it turned into a 30-minute special that won awards in her country. We took her by the hand to Hyde Park and showed her the President's community. She came back to visit with us, showing us the award-winning program with an Asian translation. Bob and I watched in awe.

At that moment, I got it. *N'DIGO* Magapaper, the publication that I envisioned and invested in almost 30 years ago, has left its footprint.

So, how did we see Barack Obama first? It was because we knew the community. We saw a rising star, and we paid attention to him. We recorded a special history. We were the first to do it because that's what we do…and that's what the mainstream media still continues *not to do* when it comes to covering the Black community, almost 30 years later.

And that was the point and purpose of *N'DIGO* Magapaper from day one.

This volume is a collection of 110 of our best and most interesting cover stories over the past three decades, noteworthy stories of people associated with Chicago who have made a difference.

Since the Al Capone days of the Roaring 20s, Chicago is famous for being a gangster town. President Donald Trump often refers to the statistical data about the city's outrageous crime rate and gun violence.

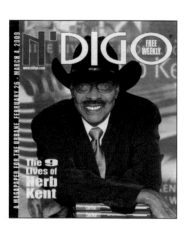   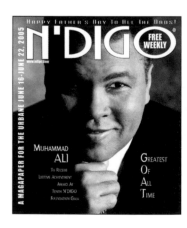

after he became the first Black American POTUS in 2008, when the media of the world converged on *N'DIGO*'s headquarters to trace his political roots.

It was the international media's interest and embrace of *N'DIGO* that really opened my eyes to the changing face of race and how our magapaper for the urbane is viewed abroad. The media had changed and we changed with it.

When the press from Hong Kong, Africa, the United Kingdom and Denmark visited *N'DIGO* following Barack's election, we weren't Black; we

Not to deny this history or these facts, but there is another Chicago. Good people, great families and people who have achieved high levels of success. Many of these people come from the same place, the South Side and the West Side of Chicago.

These are people who have made a difference, overcome obstacles, are educated and who have supported great causes from Dr. Martin Luther King, Jr. to President Barack Obama. These are some of the stories from the pages of *N'DIGO*, providing new news that some forgot to cover. Enjoy!

Editor's Note

This book is a testament to the momentous achievements of Black Chicagoans from roughly the 1930s through the first decades of the 21st Century, concluding with the administration of the first African-American President of the United States.

It was during this period that Chicago became the Black political capital and the Black business mecca of the entire nation.

This is not a general history, however, but a specific one, told through the lengthy and meticulously detailed profiles of 110 historic Black icons that appeared as cover stories in *N'DIGO* for nearly a 30-year period, from 1989 to 2017.

These icons, though Chicago based, by no means provide only local stories. Indeed, many of these individuals impacted the nation and the world. Consider some of the heroes featured in this book that have Chicago roots:

• The one and only, the Greatest of All Time, The Champ, Muhammad Ali.

• "His Airness" Michael Jordan, profiled with his mother, no less.

• Our own "Hidden Figure," Dr. Mae Jemison, the first African-American woman in space. Jemison is now in charge of a program to make interstellar flight outside of our solar system a reality within the next hundred years.

• August Wilson, whose entire cycle of 20th Century plays was first produced by Chicago's Goodman Theatre.

• John H. Johnson, the legendary publisher of *Ebony* and *Jet* magazines.

• Lovie Smith, the first Black NFL coach to lead his team to the Super Bowl.

• Funny fellows Bernie Mac and Dick Gregory,

who launched their careers here, and Steve Harvey, who first went on radio in Chicago. Other radio legends in the book are The Fly Jock Tom Joyner and the late Herb Kent "The Cool Gent," who held the Guinness World Record for the longest radio deejay career, and the creator of "Urban Radio," Marv Dyson.

• Music icons include Quincy Jones, Ramsey Lewis, Jennifer Hudson and Frankie Knuckles, the inventor of "house" music.

• Johnnie Cochran started a law firm here with Jim Montgomery; together these two lawyers tried more police abuse cases than any other attorneys in the world.

• The legal dream team of Eugene Pincham, Lewis Myers, Andre Grant and Berve Power. When seven- and eight-year-old Black boys were charged with rape and murder in 1999 – making them the two youngest murder defendants in American history – these four lawyers proved the boys' innocence.

• Mamie Till-Mobley, the mother of Emmett Till, whose murder by racist whites in Mississippi in 1955 was a primary catalyst for the Civil Rights Movement.

• Two of America's most significant Black leaders, The Reverend Jesse Jackson and Minister Louis Farrakhan.

• The first Black mayor of Chicago, "Here's Harold!" Washington.

• The first female deputy solicitor general in the country, Jewel Lafontant-MANkarious, who held positions with three U.S. presidents and was arguably the most powerful woman in America in her day.

• The first Black female United States Senator, Carol Moseley-Braun.

• The senior advisor to the President of the United States and presidential assistant, Valerie Jarrett.

• The first Black President of the United States, Barack Obama.

N'DIGO was the first publication to run a cover story on Obama; this was in March 2003, while he was still a state senator looking toward making a run for U.S. Senator from Illinois in March 2004.

Shortly after that story appeared, I saw Barack leaning against the wall of a North Side Walgreens smoking a cigarette, appearing to be waiting for someone inside – maybe Michelle and the kids. Noting his proclivity early in his political career to seeking higher office, I asked Barack, "What's next, running for the White House?" He looked at me and simply said, "Why not?"

"Why not?" That's the stance that the icons of this book took as they pursued their destinies. These are cowboys and cowgirls, risk takers who thought big and bold; visionaries who would let no one limit or define the scope of their dreams; pioneers and trailblazers who wouldn't take no for an answer to questions that had not even been conceived.

For almost everyone profiled in this book, there was no way they were supposed to accomplish what they did, and yet they did.

Filling Needed Niches

I think of the subject of our very first cover story, in December 1989, The Reverend Willie Barrow, the renowned civil rights leader known as "The Little Warrior."

Barrow began her fight for racial equality at the tender age of 12, when she organized a bus boycott in 1936 in her hometown of Burton, Texas, protesting Black students having to walk miles to school while their white classmates were bussed.

Barrow's boycott was successful, fueled her passion to remain a lifelong participant in the movement, and found her heading a major civil rights organization in Operation PUSH.

Barrow's story is like so many others in this book – what they accomplished was not necessarily planned;

it came about mostly out of need after someone stepped up and accepted the mantle of trying to facilitate positive change.

N'Digo staff 1990.

Banks wouldn't lend to Black businesses in Chicago, so a group of Black entrepreneurs pooled their funds and along with door-to-door solicitations, funded Seaway Bank, which became the largest Black-owned bank in the nation.

There were no media outlets to tell Black stories, so John Johnson founded the largest Black publishing company in the world to do so.

Blacks were not allowed in the construction trade, so Paul King made it his mission to lead that fight. Black Chicago obviously needed a Black mayor to represent Black interests, so a Black grassroots movement swept Harold Washington into office.

Emil Jones became President of the Illinois Senate to make sure Black communities and institutions received their share of the state's pie. Abena Joan Brown and Jackie Taylor worked to make sure Black theater thrived in the city.

Dr. Blondean Davis and Tim King are making sure that 100 percent of Black students graduating from high school are accepted into colleges and universities. And Father Michael Pfleger, the only white icon in this book, has dedicated his life to eradicating racism and gun violence in the city.

It's good that these heroes did what they did, because their significant accomplishments have given N'DIGO a reason to be in business – our

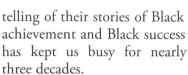

telling of their stories of Black achievement and Black success has kept us busy for nearly three decades.

The successes of the icons that we profile are breathtaking in scope, covering nearly every area of human endeavor, including: politics, theatre, fashion, music, media, law, economic ministries, social ministries, financial services, business ownership, the corporate suite, sports, education, the arts, history, civil rights, and institution-building, and portray these icons as power couples and strong Black families.

These are not 110 separate stories, but one book that shows how these people interconnected to construct one of the most crucial, productive periods of Black

Above right: N'Digo staff in 1993. Below: N'Digo staff in 1996. It takes a team to produce a paper.

success in American history.

Within this tome, the icons move within one another's stories. Warner Saunders exclusively covered Nelson Mandela's release from a South African prison for his TV station, but it was The Reverend Jesse Jackson who took Warner to Mandela's house to meet him. Then Warner pops up in Jackson's profile on the occasion of Jesse's 40th anniversary as a civil rights leader.

Jacoby Dickens rose to prominence as head of Seaway Bank, but may not have been in business at all if not for a business loan he received from Continental Bank, courtesy of its loan officer at the time Roland Burris, who would become a leading Illinois politician.

Jewel Lafontant, as U.S. Special Ambassador, traveled to Israel to make sure the Black Israelite settlement there in Dimona, whose residents were primarily from Chicago, received the necessary assistance from the Israeli government to survive in that land.

The stories in this book are lovingly told by 43 different Black writers, now spread around the country, but who called Chicago home at the time the articles were originally written. The stories run as they were originally published, but edited for length and updated to explain what has happened to these icons since.

In addition, the stories are illustrated through the work of 21 photographers commissioned by *N'DIGO* specifically to shoot these covers and the photographs show our icons as they were, in their full glory.

A Reminder for Today

There's a lot of manpower involved. It takes a lot of effort to "do" a cover story on someone – writers, photographers, graphic artists, makeup and fashion artists, not to mention on the administrative side; the sales executives and office support people, the circulation people who make sure *N'DIGO* gets into the hands of our readers.

It takes a lot, but we made the conscious decision all those years ago to do it because the people whose stories we tell deserve it. They deserve the public recognition we are honored to bestow upon them.

It's a safe bet that more than 100 of the icons in this book never ended up on any magazine covers other than *N'DIGO*, not because what they've accomplished didn't deserve attention. It's just that it is the nature of mainstream media in this country not to pay much attention to Black success.

And it's not because the people in these stories trudged the paths to their success – and those have been extremely difficult paths in most cases – looking for any pat-on-the-back or media notoriety. They haven't.

But it has been our honor to recognize and validate their accomplishments, their hard work to succeed always against the odds, in the way that we do; to give them the public "atta-boys/girls" that they truly deserve, and to preserve a public record of what they did.

To that degree, this book, *N'DIGO Legacy*, is both an elegant coffeetable book, AND an important contemporary history book that we anticipate sitting on

N'Digo staff 2000

library shelves and in family homes generations from now, long after we've all gone.

This book, the icons in this book, represent a sort of Golden Age of Black Achievement that was extraordinary to behold in its time. Because of societal changes, their likes may never be seen again.

Their "age" is definitely not the reality of Black Chicago today in 2017, where as we publish this book, our community is a mere shell of what it used to be. The leadership, the pioneers in all of the areas in which these icons excelled, are few and far between today.

To produce hope on the horizon, maybe we can learn lessons from the way these Black people succeeded, pay attention to the grit they displayed, and heed the wisdom of the one factor that almost all of them have in common – no matter what area they chose to make their mark in, almost every single one of these people went to college or pursued some advanced form of specialized education.

This book, *N'DIGO Legacy: Black Luxe*, is much needed – damn near mandatory – to remind the Black community of today and the near future of what Black achievement looks like.

What does Black achievement look like? It looks like this book, and the faces you'll find herein.

African American Icons...

Never compromise your goals: You must believe in yourself and then others will begin to believe in you as well. If you push yourself and say, 'I can do, I will do, soon you will be saying, 'I am doing.'

— Desiree Rogers

When I was growing up, we were poor, but we didn't feel like that because we had goals. People talked to you and you didnt feel trapped.

— Cirilo McSween

When you come from where I've come from, you don't want to go back. I've been poor and I've been rich, and I can tell you, rich is better.

— John H. Johnson

I wanted to control the images and help people understand who we are. We aren't all dope addicts; we aren't all prostitutes. We have done a lot for this country and our stories should be heard.

— Jackie Taylor

We are trying to rebuild a community where families get transformed from welfare to work, from being dysfunctional to functional, from being semi-literate to literate, and where children receive support to get to the point where they can compete successfully.

— Dr. Leon Finney

When I think about our community and the issues that confront us, the most formidable weapon that we have is education.

— Michael Scott

We have been left without any compensation for our centuries of free labor. We have never been given any official, legal, or economic consideration for what our ancestors sacrificed and died for in slavery, or for the racial injustice that has existed since slavery.

— Dr. Conrad Worrill

I firmly believe that the greatest addiction we have in this society is racism. To me, there's nothing that's a greater evil than that.

— Father Michael Pfleger

You have to organize and do something if you want change. You can't just sit around and complain.

— John Sengstacke

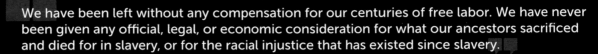

...of Contemporary History

I taught my children to work for a better America, that the kind of job one holds is not a measurement of self-worth. What matters is, are you a decent person? Are you doing good things?

— Mrs. Jacqueline Jackson

I especially encourage women and minorities to pursue careers in science and to use their own energy and innovation to push the boundaries of any field that truly draws their interest.

— Dr. Mae Jemison

I'm a sucker for the kids selling candy and magazines on the street; that's where the entrepreneurial skills start.

— Leon Jackson

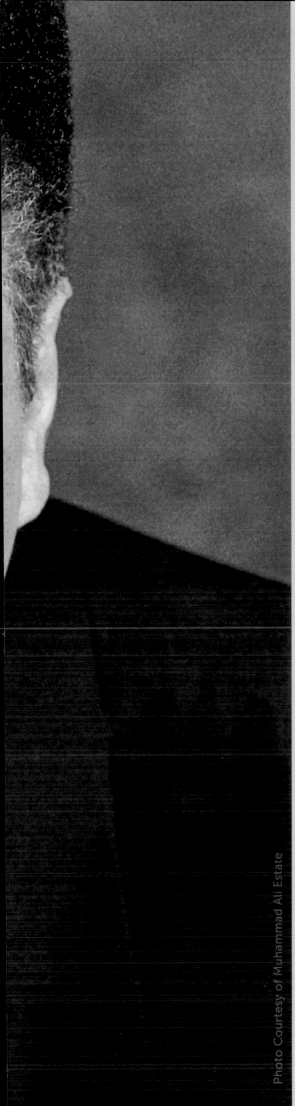

preface Ali

Muhammad Ali was known as "The Louisville Lip" for his verbosity and quips. Here in no particular order are some of Ali's wisest and most famous quotes:

"The word 'Islam' means 'peace.' The word 'Muslim' means 'one who surrenders to God.' But the press makes us seem like haters."

"Float like a butterfly, sting like a bee. Rumble, young man, rumble!"

"I hated every minute of training. But I said, 'Don't quit. Suffer now and live the rest of your life as a champion.'"

"I wish people would love everybody else the way they love me. It would be a better world."

"Hating people because of their color is wrong. And it doesn't matter which color does the hating. It's just plain wrong."

"I am The Greatest! I'm a baaaaaaad man!"

"I figured that if I said it enough, I would convince the world that I really was the greatest."

"I never thought of losing, but now that it's happened, the only thing is to do it right. That's my obligation to all the people who believe in me. We all have to take defeats in life."

"I had to prove you could be a new kind of Black man. I had to show the world."

"I should be a postage stamp because that's the only way I'll ever get licked."

"It's not bragging if you can back it up."

Muhammad Ali

By Hermene Hartman & Cover Photo Courtesy of Muhammad Ali Estate | *Originally Published June 6, 2016*

With the passing of Muhammad Ali, the world has lost a champion of a man. He was magnificent, awesome, a stallion. Ali not only changed the sweet science of boxing, but also had enormous impact around the globe and was considered the most recognized human being on the planet.

He had presence like no other, a prince prancing, a boxer dancing and the king of the jab. He could give a punch, he could take one, and he was a mastermind at psyching out his opponents to the point of embarrassment.

Ali said he was pretty and he was, but he also had a little nasty streak in him as he belittled, teased, angered, and ridiculed his opponents all in the name of promoting his fights. Sometimes it was personal, as in the cases of Floyd Patterson and Ernie Terrell, whom he beat mercilessly while shouting, "Uncle Tom, what's my name?"

Ali was a fighter full of confidence, a man assured of himself and his power. He was The Greatest, with no hesitation or reservation – in his own words, and everyone else's. A graceful and powerful, demanding, commanding giant, Ali changed the game as he broke every rule on the way to becoming a legend.

> **Thanks Champ, for showing us how to fight in life's ring.**
>
> — Hermene Hartman

In or out of the ring, Ali was the same. A jokester, a promoter, a marketing dream, witty and a street poet. He was a hell of a guy, by all measure.

He was serious and disciplined and practiced his craft all the time. Ali was a perfectionist. I saw him once in an exhibition at Navy Pier. His movement was magnificent; his grace was like a butterfly; and his body was perfectly sculpted. He used to run in Washington Park early mornings. I used to see him doing his roadwork as I was going to work.

Objecting To Vietnam

Ali was much more than the greatest boxer, the greatest sportsman of our time. When it was time to be drafted in 1967 to fight in Vietnam, he flatly refused.

At the time, Ali declared to white questioners at a press conference: "If I'm going to die, I'll die now, right here fighting you. You're my enemy; my enemy is the white people, not the Viet Cong.

"You're my oppressor when I want freedom. You're my oppressor when I want justice. You're my oppressor when I want equality. You won't even stand up for me in America because of my religious beliefs, and you want me to go somewhere and fight, when you won't even stand up for my religious beliefs at home."

He added of the Vietnamese, "They never called me nigger; they never lynched me; they never put no dogs on me; they never raped or killed my mother or father."

He thus summed up the Black man's position. White media crucified him for it, but Ali stood firm and tall in the confrontation.

The Lost Title

The politicos and the boxing commission stripped him of his title, however, for refusing the draft and they did it at the height of his career. He didn't fight for three years, during the apex of his prime.

He was also broke, being deprived of his livelihood, so Ali toured the college circuit, making speeches. He rose to the occasion. His title was gone, but his manhood was intact.

He told the boxing commission to come get the belt that was encased in the living room in his bungalow on South Jeffery Boulevard here in Chicago.

White America was angry, of course, at the audacity of this uppity Black man. Mainstream press hammered him. It was pretty much old white men who were extremely critical and sometimes brutal to young Ali.

The likes of a Black man standing up like Ali did not fit the docile attitude they were used to in their Negroes. He was arrogant, strong, angry and right and he challenged America's power structure.

The greatest boxer in the world saying, "I refuse to fight the Viet Cong; they are not my enemy." He was clear on who he was and where he was. A hero was in the making, speaking to the common man.

Black America and others embraced him. Black America was watching a Black man stand on principle. He said he would go to jail before going to the army to kill other brown folks, poor folks.

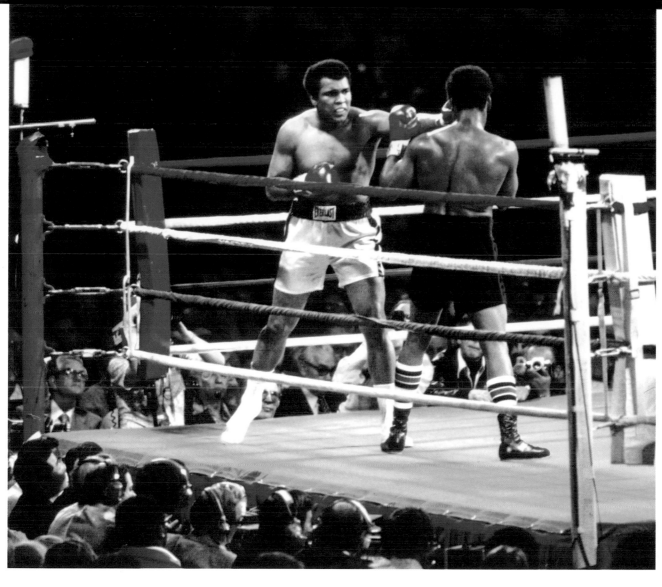

Muhammad Ali takes on Leon Spinks February of 1978.

He meant it. This was the making of his greatness outside of the boxing ring.

The Black Muslim Experience

Ali stood up for his beliefs and was a conscientious objector. Part of the objection was his religion. Ali was a member of the Black Muslims, under the strict guidance of The Honorable Elijah Muhammad. Major media referred to them as a "Black separatist group," and white America considered them a potential terrorist organization.

The Black Muslims were disciplined, focused and serious in bow tie uniforms, looking like an army. Ali followed his religious order and made the world respect him.

It was when he joined the Nation Of Islam that he dropped what he called his "slave name," Cassius Clay, to re-brand himself as Muhammad Ali, a new man.

The white news media, particularly his broadcasting friend Howard Cosell, joked with him about it. Ali would give Cosell an exclusive interview on ABC-TV and play with his toupee, making Cosell hold onto his head. Eventually the media and the world took Ali seriously as he proclaimed his new name.

The world will study The Champ's record for years to come – 56 victories, 37 by knockout, and five defeats. He is the only boxer to have won the heavyweight title three times. His legendary fights,

the Thrilla in Manila with Joe Frazier and the Rumble in the Jungle with George Foreman, were brilliant extravaganzas.

The Champ Of Chicago

In 2005, the N'DIGO Foundation, at our 10th scholarship gala celebration, presented Muhammad Ali with the Lifetime Achievement Award at the newly opened Millennium Park in downtown Chicago.

We had tried for three years to bestow such an honor on Ali, working with his team of Troy Ratcliff, Cleve and Belvon Walker, and Ali's wife Lonnie. I realized that Ali had almost never before been honored in Chicago because of prevailing racism, and religious and political maneuvers.

Mayor Richard J. Daley did not want the increasingly popular Ali to be recognized in his Chicago. He blocked Ali from fighting here in the city where he lived – despite the revenue such an event would bring.

Daley also tried as much as possible to block any awards to Ali that would attest to his credibility in any way. Ali was too popular for Daley's taste, but more importantly, Daley was not fond of the very well disciplined religious organization – the Black Muslims, headquartered here in Chicago – that was behind Ali.

The Daley mindset of dealing with such characters and situations was to stifle them before they could take hold and rise to become a political force.

Daley was successful with his political cohorts, but Ali was the champion of the people. He was rooted in the community. He walked the streets of the South Side of Chicago like a pied piper.

He went to the clubs, like the Dog House and Tiger Lounge. He went to the Muslim mosque on Stony Island and the Muslim restaurant on 83rd and Cottage Grove. Ali played with the kids on the playground and the cats on the corner.

Crowds gathered as he shadowboxed and preached. He went to Operation Breadbasket regularly with Rev. Jesse Jackson. He was rooted as a Black man. No excuses. No explanations. He was Ali and he was not confused.

Muhammad Ali and Barack Obama

His N'DIGO Gala Honor

When we were preparing for the 2005 Gala, he and Cleve visited the N'DIGO office every day for two weeks to help. One Tuesday, which is the day our newspaper goes to print, they came by and I said, hey guys, we are working for real today.

Ali said he came to help. Steve Johnson, our art director, began to hand him proofs. We had him reading proofs, looking for typos and corrections. He loved looking at the pictures we were running that issue. They stayed with us until we put the paper out . Amazing.

They came back the next day at lunchtime. We all had lunch and Ali told us jokes and did magic tricks. We were in awe.

I told him he was handsome. He said, "No I'm not, I'm pretty…and so are you." "Are you flirting?" I asked him. "Yes," he said smiling. "I'm still The Champ, you know, and women love me."

He was slower, his speech quieter, his steps measured and deliberate. But he was Ali. That day, after they left, I cried like a baby. He was now great, in another way. Life changes, but the essence of his real greatness remained very much intact.

I was happy that we were honoring him. The next day, he and Cleve came to work. Dolores Elliott, the coordinator of that year's event, suggested we plan some actual Gala work for Ali. She said, give him something to do.

I asked them to go sell tables. They did, and for the next few days, they had luncheons with their sports buddies and business types, sold tables and sought donations. Cleve and Ali were hosting meetings in Chicago's private clubs.

One day, Ali brought us a huge picture book of himself in the boxing ring. It was one of the largest books ever, and he said it would be very valuable one day.

That book, *GOAT, The Greatest of All Time*, cost $1,000. It was a gift. He signed some pages to add value. Then the next day, he and Cleve bought us red boxing gloves that he signed. He told me they would be very valuable. They were sold to news anchor Cheryl Burton at the Gala at a very hefty price.

Ali and Cleve decided that we should have a Muhammad Ali Scholarship. It started as one scholarship, but grew to four. Troy Ratcliff assisted to make it happen with kids from the Better Boys Foundation. Ali had rules, though. The scholarships had to go to bad boys from the West Side. That was his stipulation. We complied.

The night of the Gala, Sunday, June 19, 2005, was glorious. The weather was Chicago summer beautiful – a perfect day for an outdoor event to honor a champ, and Ali was excited. When he came to the stage, the crowd roared, "Ali, Ali, Ali!" He loved it.

International press was in attendance. Rev. Jackson stepped up to raise Ali's arm in championship fashion. Ali was the champ again – champion of the people. He was loved. He was always the champ, no matter what.

Barack and Michelle Obama were the Gala Chairs that year. They met Ali for the first time. Backstage, Ali was boxing with everybody and taking photos. He was having a ball. He boxed with then Senator Obama, Rev. Jackson, and fellow honoree Michael Scott.

They went to Gladys Knight's dressing room – she was the Gala entertainment that year – and totally disrupted her while she was getting ready to perform.

Ali flirted with all of the women. He took pictures; he shook hands. He was warm and receiving and funny. He was a riot. We loved him, and he loved everybody. He gave me a hug after it was over and I cried. He said, let's go back to the hotel and party. And we did.

Viva Ali! He will live forever. He is the stuff of legend and we probably will never see another like him in our lifetime. Bravo, Ali! The Greatest. Thanks Champ, for showing us how to fight in life's ring.

Respectfully submitted,
Muhammad Ali, A.K.A.
Cassius Marcellus Clay Jr.
CASSIUS MARCELLUS CLAY, JR.
a/k/a MUHAMMAD ALI
Special Field Minister
The Lost Found Nation of Islam

Muhammad Ali at Angelo Dundee's
5th Street Gym, Miami, FL

preface Barrow

Update: Rev. Willie Taplin Barrow hung up her marching shoes at the age of 90. She passed away on March 12, 2015. Flags in Chicago were flown at half-mast in her honor.

The Little Warrior's work took her to Cuba, Vietnam, Russia and Nicaragua, and she was in South Africa the day Nelson Mandela walked out of prison.

Rev. Barrow mentored more than 100 men and women whom she called her "godchildren," including a young Barack Obama, long before he became President of the United States.

Cover Photo by Kenneth Wright

Reverend Willie Barrow

By Chinta Strausberg & Photography by Calvin Woods | *Originally Published December 1989*

On December 7, Reverend Willie Taplin Barrow will be 65 years old, yet she remains on the frontline of the battlefield continuing her fight for economic, social and political justice for minorities across this nation.

Standing less than five-feet tall, this buxom and attractive civil rights leader affectionately known as "The Little Warrior" has walked with kings, met with presidents, traveled around the world and mingled with the poorest our nation has to offer.

She has marched miles for freedom and justice in the thick of enemy territory while her younger followers sat by the wayside, tired. Once a $10-an-hour laborer, Barrow began her fight for racial equality at the tender age of 12.

> When you witness history, the pain, agony and injustice, you want to become a part of it. I went to one march, and I have been in the movement ever since.

Protesting Deep In The Heart Of Texas

Coming from good stock, Barrow was born in 1924, and reared on a 120-acre farm in Burton, Texas, the fifth of seven children of Nelson and Octavia Taplin. Her father was a Baptist minister, her mother a Methodist who, upon marriage, converted to her husband's religion.

Barrow respected the earth and grew up close to God. At the break of dawn and sometimes before, she milked cows and fed chickens and hogs. She chopped sugar cane and picked cotton. After her chores were done, Barrow had to walk 12 miles down a dirt road to a one-room schoolhouse. "I grew up with animals people today go pay to see," she says. "And I've always had tired feet!"

Tired of being called "nigger" by white students riding by on buses instead of walking on their way to school, Barrow said, "I got mad and decided to fight back. This just wasn't right." So she led what became a protracted protest of 200 Black kids who, because of their large numbers, successfully stopped the buses.

"We wouldn't let them by. They would hang out of the windows and call us 'niggers' and tell us to walk," Barrow recalls. The game warden would come and the children would disperse and run, but they would come back and throw rocks at the buses. The buses represented injustice and the process was unfair, to the children's way of thinking.

Frightened of their boldness during a time when most Blacks accepted unequal treatment from whites as a matter of course, Barrow said her parents told her white students didn't want to attend her school – that they wanted their own. That, to Barrow, wasn't a good enough or valid enough reason to force Black children to walk miles to school while whites rode in comfort.

"I remember, there was a Black home economics teacher who understood the level of our frustration," Barrow says. "She took up our fight and protested right alongside us."

Their boldness paid off and the Black kids received their buses, but the inequity registered in Barrow's young mind and served as a catalyst for her involvement in seeking social change ever since.

"I went back home about 15 years ago," Barrow says, "and my sister-in-law is now driving the bus for all the people. That just goes to show that if you wait long enough and keep on fighting, your time will come."

"The Little Warrior" at the age of eight began reading the Bible and playing the piano in her daddy's church. Her leadership qualities surfaced at a young age. By 10, she was playing leading parts during the church's Easter programs and reciting famous speeches.

On The Road To Her Future

At 17, Barrow left home for Houston, Texas for high school and upon graduation, went to live with an aunt in San Francisco because her parents couldn't afford to send her to college.

Working as both a Woolworth store clerk and a hotel maid, Barrow applied for admission to the Warner Pacific Seminary in Portland, Oregon. She says that at the age of 16, she had been called to the ministry.

In Portland, during World War II, she found a job as a $10-an-hour welder at the Kaiser Shipyard where she worked from 1941-43. In 1945, she married Clyde "Honey" Barrow, himself a welder at the shipyard. Having become an evangelist, Barrow was dismayed that there were no Black churches in Portland, so she started one with two associates and a dozen congregants.

The Barrows moved to Los Angeles for a brief stint, but then Willie got called to Chicago by Rev. S. P. Dunn to be a youth minister.

To make ends meet in Chicago, she held various jobs, including the post office and as a laborer at a hairpin factory, and she did domestic work for wealthy whites that lived around 87th and Stony Island.

"At that time," she said, "that was the dividing line – where you better not be caught after dark." Today, Barrow has marched on stores on 87th Street demanding economic parity and equal employment.

Her "big job" came when Addie Wyatt, associate minister of Vernon Park Church, recommended her for a job at a meat cutters' union. It was around 1951 and Barrow began making almost $5 an hour packing sausage and bacon at 39th and Wallace. Wyatt later became a labor leader of nationwide recognition, and she and Willie have been inseparable since they met.

Barrow had joined forces with Dr. John Porter, who ran an extension of the Montgomery Improvement Association, and Porter sent her to Selma, Alabama, to march. "They had to sneak us in," Barrow says, referring to the 130 multi-racial group of civil rights activists that had been summoned by Dr. Martin Luther King Jr.

She and her group were met at the airport in Selma by a man driving a truck. "We had to lay on our stomachs on the floor of the truck," Barrow recalls. "They covered us with quilts because if the white police had known we were inside, we could have been shot."

Barrow said helmeted, club-swinging policemen lined the road in Selma and she called what she saw there "terrible." She saw children, women and men beaten. The planned one-day trip spilled into a week. "We had to wash our dresses every day," says Barrow, who was among scores arrested for attempting to march.

But it was a turning point in Barrow's life. She went back home, got some more clothes and came back. "When you get there and witness history, the pain, agony and injustice, you want to become a part of it," Barrow says. "I went to one march, and I have been in the movement ever since."

The Reverend Jesse Louis Jackson

As a field worker for Dr. King, Barrow made $25 a week. "We would train people in the non-violent method. We were the advance people, and when Dr. King came North, we began setting up Operation Breadbasket," says Barrow. Rev. Jesse L. Jackson took up the helm of the northern division operation.

Barrow began attending political meetings, often accompanied by the late activist Rev. "Ma" Houston. "They thought I was a secretary," Barrow mused. Spearheading a Toledo, Ohio youth rally, she invited

Rev. Jackson. Some 10,000 people attended.

Her organizing skills impressed him so much that Jackson asked her to become an organizer and work with him. Barrow said Rev. Jackson told his peers, "I don't know what it means to you having a woman work with you, but I want her to be a project worker as well as on the negotiating team. Anyone who can organize 10,000 people is qualified."

Barrow has been with Jackson ever since and is considered one of his closest and most trusted allies. "There is a bond there," Barrow confirms. "A marriage, but we had to go through a series of adjustments."

Barrow has never been a person to give blanket agreement or endorsement to anyone or anything, and she will speak her mind about it. Sometimes, she admitted, she would get so angry she would leave, but before exiting would say, "I'm not quitting. I'll be back." Later, she and Jackson would talk about what went wrong, each apologizing to the other.

A great achievement came when Jackson appointed her as chapter coordinator and she traveled around the country. "That was the delight of my life," Barrow says.

When he decided to run for President of the United States in 1984, Jackson made Barrow his deputy road manager, in charge of media and security. "It was a tremendous challenge and an experience I shall never forget," she said.

Barrow marveled at the way Jackson related to people of all ethnic backgrounds and walks of life, yet never forgot his roots. "He was able to deal with all of them," she says. "It was a strange and rewarding experience. Jesse is a genius, and now he is a super-genius."

Barrow said she could not have gotten that kind of human and political experience at Harvard or any other university. She said it has made her a "broad-based human being" and that the experience is "worth more than dollars."

There is no question that Barrow's mentor on this earth is Rev. Jackson, and reflecting on the civil rights activist and orator, she says, "My role in Jackson's career is one you could look at as growing up with a big brother or sister, or the role a mother has with her son. I was there in his weakness, in his strength. I was there when he needed me most, and I will be there when he needs me most, wherever I am.

"Once you grow up with a man and that person respects you, there is no such thing as growing out of touch. We will always be in tune with each other, and if we are not in tune with each other, we will have the capacity to tell each other of our weaknesses and our strengths…and not tell the press," Barrow chuckled.

An Impressive Body Of Work

The Little Warrior's work has spanned several decades. She has been a field and chapter coordinator and manager of special projects, which has enabled her to organize nationwide as well as internationally.

"The doors of opportunity have been opened in connecting politically and economically with Africa, Central America, and the Middle East," she says. "The learning experience of working with all of God's children no matter from what background they come – I have found out that there are cultural differences, yes…but people are the same everywhere."

She says that she is grateful to have participated in electing the first Black mayor of Chicago in Harold Washington, to have seen the success of what she calls Dr. King's "lieutenants" like Andrew Young, who become a mayor and an ambassador, "and to see eight or 10 Black mayors that our efforts have been instrumental in helping get there," Barrow says.

Looking back over her years in the struggle, she adds, "There is a core of Black people who started and have gone upstairs to be involved in local elections – running for themselves, raising money – who have become mayors and now know how to run departments…voter registration drives that have taught us how to win elections and field the right candidates."

With her recent weight loss, Barrow is looking particularly petite and spunky. And she buries any rumor that she will retire. "I will never retire, retire," Barrow says. "But I am going upstairs…I have earned the right to just be a consultant."

But many wonder whether the Little Warrior can ever hang up her marching shoes – even when she becomes 90 years old. What was it she said earlier…"when you get involved, you just want to be a part of history?"

Barrow is the first female to be chief executive officer of any civil rights organization. She has gone from being a 12-year-old child protester to one of the nation's most powerful female political organizers in modern times. And God is not through with her yet.

preface Bates

Update: Today, from her sprawling design studio in Chicago's South Loop, Barbara also operates her charity, the Barbara Bates Foundation, which supports inner-city high school students and promotes breast cancer education and awareness.

Barbara Bates

By Kai EL' Zabar & Photography by Darlene Martin | *Originally Published May 30, 1996*

No designer has creatively sculpted leather, as far as color treatment and style are concerned, as successfully as the former corporate secretary who now heads Bates Designs.

Barbara Bates hit the scene like a surge of lightning. The timing was right and the leather forecast stormed runways, making it the most desirable skin next to one's own. It was the early '80s. Barbara was working a 9-to-5, earning $18,000 a year, but she dressed like a high-powered executive and caught the eye of her colleagues.

On the side, she expressed her creative talent by designing fashions that she asked others to make; Barbara sold them out of her home and from the women's restroom at work. Leather was her forte and it never looked better than when her fashions were molded to her clients' bodies.

But suddenly, she was celebrating her 30th birthday. "It hit me, I'm 30-years-old and I hate what I'm doing. I hate sitting behind a desk," Barbara recalled.

What you wear should be an extension of yourself. Have you ever seen a garment wear the person? Major fashion mistake.

Small, shapely, statuesque, spirited, revved of energy and power while remaining poised and reserved, she continued, "I was the employee who did just enough to get by. So I knew there was no future for me in corporate America. But also, my mother would remind me that there were no Black designers out there succeeding on a big level."

Leap of Faith

But 10 years later, the tables turned when her mother, noting that Barbara had successfully designed and sold her clothes in spite of the obstacles, urged her to go for it, or else she'd regret having missed her opportunity.

"I've always had a passion for fashion," Barbara said matter-of-factly. "But I never thought I'd be doing this, I really didn't, though I wanted to do it.

"I guess you can say that my mother is my muse. My mother and her sisters, who were well-dressed women, inspired me. My mother's emphasis on appearance made me realize that it is an important part of one's character."

In high school, Barbara had taken her first entrepreneurial step by buying fabrics and patterns and taking them to friends who would sew her fashions. The unique way she combined fabrics with her personal sense of style won her the Best Dressed Senior title in her graduating class.

In April 1986, when she decided to pursue her fashion endeavor, she understood the importance of satisfying the customer because they were her only source of marketing and advertising other than herself.

Bates admits that she quit her corporate job with no business plan, no real money, only 20 loyal customers, and no idea of how she was going to do it.

"I didn't even know what kind of sewing machines to buy," she says. "I didn't sew. I've never done the sewing. I don't know the first thing about how to sew on a machine. If a button falls off, I have to give it to one of the tailors to repair."

It Was a Very Good Year

Barbara opened her first workspace at 1006 South Wabash. A partner put up an initial investment of $5,000 in start-up capital, which mushroomed to $28,000 after two months of being in business. The 750-square-foot space was used for production as well as a retail outlet.

After one year she bought out her partner, who wanted out, and shortly thereafter, picked up Michael and Juanita Jordan as clients. Basketball star Sam Perkins had become a client before Michael. Now the former partner wanted back in, but Barbara declined. "You see," she chuckled, "Michael Jordan as a client brought me so many new clients because, well, everybody wants to be like Mike."

Her clientele took off as other sports stars noticed Jordan's Barbara Bates-designed suits and admired the fit and style. Scottie Pippen and other Bulls came on board around the same time, which was in 1987.

Since then her clientele has grown to encompass a wide spectrum of athletes, entertainers and other

Barbara Bates

professionals, including Sinbad, Steve Harvey, Bernie Mac, Rev. Johnnie Colemon, Barbara Burrell, Tyrone Davis, Mike Tyson, Kool Moe Dee, Eddie Murphy, Tom Joyner, Herb Kent, Shaquille O'Neal, Eddie and Gerald Levert, Desiree Rogers, Hermene Hartman, and members of the Chicago Bears. Today, Barbara Bates Design has at least one client on each NBA team, and superstar client Whitney Houston stops by whenever she's in town.

Her Fashion Concept

Bates says she doesn't fit comfortably in the fashion designer pattern because she didn't go to school, study with the masters, apprentice under the tutelage of fashion gurus, or work with a couture house or for a designer label.

"I'm an artist," she clarifies, but swears she's not deep. "I'm not a mystic. I just have an affinity for texture." It emotes and inspires her. She explains that her talent has always been the ability to distinguish what fabric is good for what design. After her touch-and-feel test, Bates selects the material and takes it to the studio to play with and let it "talk" to her.

"Fabrics have spirit just like people and what I try to do is match the spirit of the fabric to the spirit of people or personality types," she explains. "What you wear should be an extension of yourself. Have you ever seen a garment wear the person? It's a major fashion mistake."

Barbara reveals that she used to design for the individual client, but today, she creates with a certain market in mind and allows clients to select their choice of fabric that she recommends for certain garments and then tailors it to them. Barbara thinks in terms of form, function and structure and designs for the working person, whatever their profession, male or female.

The garment has to be an attainable idea. According to Barbara, people want to look good, but clothing has to work for them. She says, "I'd never put anything outrageous on the runway. I think first, 'Will it sell?' No fantasy designs for me. It's just not practical. Special requests? Maybe."

On The Cutting Edge

According to Barbara, making something simple is far more challenging than making something that is very complicated. In her lifetime pursuit of her passion for fashion, she has quietly fused the outlandish with subtlety, sophistication with color, flair with structure, and the unlikely leather and suede with corporate.

"I am not really attracted to color," she says. "Texture drives me. I prefer black and white. But my clients like color, so I work with colorful textured fabrics." She explains that even the simplest design in black suddenly has a new identity as a strong graphic fashion element. "That's why working with black is exciting because of the endless possibilities. Black has the amazing capacity to look new in fresh designs," Barbara says.

The mother of two works a seven to nine hour day, seeing clients, interfacing with the head tailor, buying fabrics, sketching designs, conferring with consultants and overseeing the overall running of the business.

Her profession allows her a platform for her interests, from art to travel to talking to teenage mothers who need encouragement from a role model who's been there, done that and proved that life indeed goes on.

Barbara shares, "My whole family cried when they learned I was pregnant. My mother had such high hopes for me because I had been a good student at Simpson High." Fortunately she never dropped out, but attended an alternative school for pregnant girls, which enabled her to return to Simpson and graduate with honors at the age of 16.

Barbara almost didn't go to Bethany Hospital to speak to 15 young pregnant teenage girls one year. But at the last minute she did and when she finished talking, they were crying, she was crying, and she left having promised to make prom gowns for all who made graduation.

Barbara unassumingly gives, making donations to individuals who may need their rent or tuition paid, and she thinks of her contributions as just "a pair of shoes or two" that she won't get. She says, "At a certain level of success, you owe it to share."

Bates believes that she has been blessed because she has done all that she's accomplished for the right reasons. She does what she loves and still enjoys coming to her office everyday, seeing people wearing her designs, creating new collections and touching fabric.

Barbara says, "I want people to know that they can't get any better than what I do for the prices I offer. I want them to know that there is an alternative to Donna Karan or Escada!"

preface
Beavers

Update: William Beavers was 7th Ward alderman from 1983 to 2006, when he became a Cook County Board Commissioner representing the 4th District. His daughter Darcel was appointed to his 7th Ward aldermanic seat. Beavers remained a Cook County Commissioner until 2013.

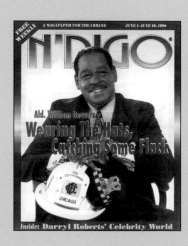

William Beavers

By Robert T. Starks & Photography by Calvin Woods | *Originally Published June 4, 1998*

The Honorable William M. Beavers was elected alderman of the 7th ward in 1983 and committeeman in 1984. For the past 15 years, he has presided over the sprawling Southeast side ward like a modern day political baron. The 7th Ward runs roughly from 71st and Yates to 103rd and Paxton and on over to 95th and Stony Island.

Beavers is always well dressed. Most of his colleagues share the opinion of 6th Ward Ald. Freddrenna Lyle, who, upon passing him in the lobby of City Hall last week, remarked, "Alderman Beavers, you are by far the best dressed alderman in the Council."

Beavers has a broad smile, a commanding voice and a proud gait, while his charm and wit have earned him the respect both of his colleagues and of those who totally disagree with him politically. It's all because of his ability to survive and prosper when everything and everyone around him seems to be doomed.

> **I have used my position as Chairman of Police and Fire to bring about reforms in those departments. I will continue to do that.**

Beavers often recalls his predicament following the death of Mayor Harold Washington. Initially, Beavers sided with the supporters of Mayor Eugene Sawyer, however, after considerable lobbying, phone calls and letters from grassroots organizations, he announced that he would support Ald. Timothy Evans.

There's a school of thought that says Beavers played both sides on this issue, so he was able to survive and avoid condemnation by grassroots leadership.

Beavers sums it up this way – "I have always tried to stay on the side of the people who elected me to office; I am here to serve them and represent their interests."

It was this perception that enabled Dr. Alice Palmer to marshal supporters in the ward in 1988 to defeat Beavers for committeeman. Beavers, however, points out that immediately after Palmer moved on to the state senate to succeed retiring Sen. Richard Newhouse, he returned to his committeeman's position, has been re-elected, and intends to run again in the year 2000.

Rising From "The Low End"

Alderman Beavers attributes his longevity in politics to his background. He proudly points out that he is from "the low end" – the 39th Street area, where he attended Oakland Grammar School and Phillips High School. He boasts, "I am from the 'hood, I am from the 3rd Ward, I grew up across the street from the old Abraham Lincoln Center."

After working as a go-fer in the 3rd Ward organization of Ald. Ralph Metcalfe, he became a member of the Third Ward Young Democrats. He remembers Harold Washington in those years because Harold, too, was a member of the Metcalfe organization.

In 1962, Beavers joined the Chicago Police Department because he says it was the best paying job he could find at the time. He worked his way up the ranks to the vice division, where he met his life-long friend and fellow policeman Lorenzo Chew. Beavers and Chew served out of the old 48th Street Second District station and later in the infamous West Side Fillmore district.

It was during this period in the late 1960s that Beavers came to the attention of Mayor Richard J. Daley and was assigned to City Treasurer Joseph Bertrand in the position of driver and bodyguard. Under Bertrand, Beavers learned the nuances of machine politics and developed a healthy interest in elective office.

Move Into Politics

In 1983, after Bertrand was redistricted out of his 7th Ward seat and placed in the 5th Ward, Bertrand lost the election to Ald. Larry Bloom. That left the 7th Ward with an open seat. Several candidates announced their intentions to run, among them police officer William M. Beavers.

Beavers recalls, "After running with Joe Bertrand for all of those years, I learned the ropes and I met lots of people. Joe taught me a great deal." As a result of his relationship with Bertrand, Beavers had the blessings of the Bertrand organization and sought the support of the grassroots community.

He subsequently met with and was interviewed by Lu Palmer of CBUC-BIPO, (Chicago

Black United Communities, and Black Independent Political Organization), the leadership of the Task Force for Black Political Empowerment, and other grassroots groups. He was given support over all of the other candidates with an endorsement that was conveyed to Mayor Washington. Beavers subsequently won the election.

Early on, it was clear that Beavers had a gift of gab. Further, and most importantly, he demonstrated a willingness to work with and support Mayor Washington. He was a team player. "Mayor Washington and I understood each other and respected each other. I never did or said anything to the press before checking with the Mayor personally," Beavers said.

His constituents have considered him at least a decent representative of the ward. He has never portrayed himself as a revolutionary, leftist or anti-Daley alderman. He has prided himself as an alderman who has been able to work within the political system of the city and the Democratic Party to deliver for his community.

He cites his four straight electoral aldermanic victories against an increasing number of challengers as proof of his solid support in the ward based on his ability to deliver.

Beavers argues that he is able to deliver because he knows the system, he knows the players and he is a skilled trader. "I fight for my ward and my people; that is what they sent me here for," he declares.

As the first African-American chairman of the Police and Fire Committee in the City Council and the City Chairman of the Cook County Democratic Party, he is at least structurally connected to the levers of power.

Uses Of Power

Within this context, Beavers is quite vocal concerning his latest efforts to bring economic development and stability to his ward. The alderman listed several projects, including three new nursing homes being built (at 71st and Coles and 73rd and 75th and Exchange) that will produce construction jobs and 600 permanent jobs.

Commercial development includes a $12 million, 200,000 -square-foot shopping mall at 95th and Stony Island Avenue that will be built by three

Black construction companies and financed by U.S. Equities. A Jewel-Osco store will be the anchor for this project.

Beavers also has on the drawing boards: a $4 million expansion of Trinity Hospital; a new Aldi Foods store; a new Metra station at 71st and Exchange; a state of the art $5 million fieldhouse at Rainbow Beach that will include an indoor swimming pool, banquet hall, full size gym and improvements on the beach and the grounds; and the rehab of almost 100 units of housing.

All of this development and redevelopment will be done by Black contractors and subcontractors. The alderman has stressed his desire to bring South Shore and the 7th Ward back to the glory and glamour of their heyday.

After listing the above plans, Ald. Beavers said, "Need I say more? Who do you know who is doing this much in their ward?"

Beavers cites the efforts he has made to assure the fairness of testing for hiring and promotion of both police and fire candidates.

He says that as Chairman of the Police and Fire Committee, he has some input in the selection of the police superintendent and the fire commissioner, as well as some of the top ranking personnel in each department.

It is through these avenues that Beavers has assured positive change in the character and performance of these two departments. Only last week, in fact, Beavers sponsored a bill in the City Council to require random testing of fire fighters.

The alderman says, "I have used my position as Chairman of Police and Fire to bring about reforms in those departments. I will continue to do that!"

Alderman Beavers plans to run again in 1999 for Alderman and in 2000 for Committeeman. The representative of the 7th Ward is a formidable opponent. Most observers see him as the ultimate survivor.

Rev. Al Sampson sums up this view when he says, "The strength of Ald. Beavers is that he can sing this song in my church on any Sunday morning: 'I've been through the storm and the rain, but I made it. You ask me how…I don't know, but I made it.'"

William Beavers

110 African Americans of Contemporary History

preface
Ben Israel

Update: In 2003, the Hebrew Israelites were granted permanent residency status in Israel; in 2009, the first Black Hebrew gained full Israeli citizenship, 40 years after the group arrived in Dimona. The year 2017 marks the 50-year anniversary of the original group first leaving American shores for Liberia.

Prince Asiel Ben Israel

By David Smallwood & Photography by David Jenkins | *Originally Published February 1991*

n this modern era, where merely escaping damage to life, limb or property on any given day is akin to hitting the lottery, there exists a community of Black Americans remarkably untouched by the social ills that plague the rest of us.

For more than 20 years in this Black community, there have been no murders, rapes, stabbings or assaults. There are no drug dealers, perverts or wife-beaters; no school dropouts, or youth gangs to terrorize the citizenry. Teen pregnancy, venereal disease and cancer are non-existent. There are no locked doors and even cavities have been eliminated.

Such are the benefits of life for the Hebrew Israelite community, commonly known as the Black Hebrews, who have forged a 2,500-member strong new society in southern Israel.

To wake up and not be a minority or inferior or called Negro, colored or Black, but to wake up with their God, their language and their culture, has given our children a sense of purpose and dynamism that words cannot express.

The Black Hebrews are African Americans, mostly former Chicagoans, who left this country for the Holy Land, where they have since 1969 settled primarily in the city of Dimona on the outskirts of the Negev Desert.

The rather idyllic social situation they enjoy is not a matter of luck; it is the result of a profound experiment that would make any sociologist or humanist proud.

The charter group of 350 Blacks that left America to eventually settle in Dimona wanted to prove that given the opportunity, proper surroundings and control of their own destiny, African Americans have the ability to create attractive alternatives to the problems confronting America's urban centers.

By creating a new standard of living in an environment of safe neighborhoods, strong family units, spiritual and physical vitality and economic viability, they intended Dimona to be a prototype for positive development in communities around the world.

Not only have the Black Hebrews succeeded in developing their model community, they have made history as the largest mass movement of American Blacks to settle outside of this country's shores. Theirs is a story of vision, integrity and survival.

How The Movement Grew

Prince Asiel Ben Israel is Ambassador Extraordinaire Plenipotentiary of the Black Hebrews – the foreign minister who handles the community's dealings outside of Israel and explains to the world who and what the community is.

His story is fairly typical of how and why so many Blacks united in a movement that would eventually take them half-way around the world – a movement born in the 1960s, when Black awareness was surging, counter-culture became the culture and people searched for their "thing."

Asiel was Chicagoan Warren Brown, in his mid-20s and fast-tracking his way toward the American dream. He owned a business, his wife was a teacher and his kids were in private school. They owned two cars and a house in Pill Hill, only the third Black family on the block. Asiel drank champagne, hung out in all the slick joints and was part of the jet set that went to Vegas and the Bahamas whenever they wanted.

"But every Sunday after those long weekends, I'd wake up unfilled," he remembers. "I'd have money in my pocket and would hang out with the boys at the frat house, but if our conversations weren't about money, they were about women. Something was definitely missing."

He was not into religion then, feeling that it didn't relate to Black people and especially not to the needs of young Blacks of the time. "We enjoyed the singing, but the message of the minister sort of left us empty," Asiel says.

With both his Black awareness and discontentment growing, Asiel eventually met proponents of the Hebrew movement, which he says has been in America since the end of slavery, with up to 2.5 million Blacks practicing some form of Judaism.

Asiel and what he calls other dissatisfied young Black "revolutionaries" in Chicago were looking for an answer to the "Black question" –What should a people do when they find themselves enslaved, denigrated and without a land, language or culture?

They gravitated to the Hebrew movement, which teaches that Scripture indicates that Black Americans are descendants of biblical Israelites, whose destiny is that at the appointed time, like the children of old Israel, they would have to leave the land of their captivity and return to their original land.

Meeting on a regular basis in Chicago, the group began to analyze why past Black liberation movements in America had failed, studying the cases of Marcus Garvey, Nat Turner, Bishop Turner, Denmark Vesey and even such modern "failures" as the NAACP, the Urban League and the fractured Nation of Islam immediately following the death of The Honorable Elijah Muhammad.

"We reasoned that these great individuals and organizations failed because in the land of their captivity, they could never be free themselves," Asiel says. "Nowhere in history has an enslaved people ever become the equal of the master in the land of their captivity."

In 1966, Black Hebrew member Ben Ammi, then a Chicago bus driver named Ben Carter, had the vision that it was time for the group to begin the Black Hebrew exodus out of America.

On To Liberia

The group believed the Scriptures directed them to return to their original land of Israel, but they were not prepared, so they planned to first go to Monrovia, Liberia to get ready for Israel.

Liberia was chosen because its constitution guarantees automatic citizenship to any person of African descent, meaning there would be no immigration hassle for the group. Liberia was to be the site for a shaking-out process.

"Remember, we were American whiskey drinkers, smokers, fools, clowns and disorganized," says Asiel. "We needed to purge ourselves of this slave mentality and our slave characteristics."

The members of the group were from all stations of life and held a variety of philosophies, so they had to figure out how to govern themselves. They also had to work for themselves, grow their own food, make their clothes, deliver and educate their children and be self-contained.

"It takes a certain kind of discipline and mind to be able to do that," Asiel says, "especially when you're under pressure at the same time from other forces. Our family and friends didn't understand what we were doing; the larger Jewish community didn't understand; plus, we were doing on-the-job training. It's pure hell trying to function on three or four different levels at the same time."

Asiel says that a lot of good people left, not because they didn't believe, but because they couldn't take that

pressure. In fact, 200 of the original group of 350 returned to America, but the remaining 150 became the core group that felt themselves ready to enter Israel and stay for the long haul.

After two and a half years, they had adjusted well in Liberia, opening small businesses and restaurants – they took the first Tastee-Freeze franchise to Africa – and showing films in the Monrovian bush. They even created alternative energy systems to provide for the first time electricity and cooking fuel for rural African villages.

The group pooled their money from these enterprises and had enough to leave for Israel in December 1969, but the trip used all their funds. The Hebrew Israelite community arrived in the desert town of Dimona, Asiel says, with no money, and "with virtually the rags on our backs."

The challenges of the sojourn in this West African wilderness would be many, as the pioneers faced searing heat, poisonous snakes, driver ants by the millions and a rainy season of monsoon proportions… all while living in tents and thatched-roofed dwellings, and forced to fend for themselves.

Life In The Community

But they knew the kind of society they wanted to live in and created it from scratch.

Asiel explains that the Black Hebrew community's culture is rooted in the Word of God and based on truth, righteousness and doing right by each other.

"Principally, we ought to respect and love one another, and that love grows into every aspect of what we do," he says. "We value the human being as opposed to anything material, so our value system does not permit our kids to kill each other for gym shoes and gold chains.

"We use as a fundamental foundation the commandments that Moses brought, but we interpret them with a higher understanding of what they mean in this day and time."

The society is governed by a Council of 13 men, headed by Ben Ammi. Under the Council are Ministers of departments, such as economics. Under them are "Crown Brothers and Sisters," who deal with the everyday problems facing the group. Then there are Men and Women of Color, working in official governing bodies that deal with the social, political and economic problems of the community.

Economically, in a collective, cooperative setting, there are enterprises established in clothing and shoe manufacturing, jewelry making, construction and music, and there is a health and natural food industry that stresses the development of organic farming methods using non-chemical fertilizers. They abide by a vegetarian diet and regular exercise is stressed for individuals of all ages.

There are three types of criminals to the community's way of thinking: one who commits crime out of need; one who thinks that is the way to get ahead: and one who chooses to be a criminal.

Punitively, the offender of the first type has his needs taken care of so that he won't have to commit crime: if he steals out of hunger, he is fed. The second type is counseled that committing crime is not the process for advancement in the community. The criminal who makes a profession of it is offered a chance at rehabilitation and then kicked out of the community if he doesn't change.

"We are based on an understanding that you just don't do certain things because there is no need to," Asiel says. "We have begun to see each other as truly our brothers and sisters and everything we own belongs to everybody."

A marital system was introduced known as "divine marriage," or a "righteous relationship," in which a man can have up to seven wives, though a woman can have only one husband.

All of the wives are equal: there is no pecking order and the wives consider themselves "sisters." In cases of multiple marriages, there is but one family unit and the husband is responsible for all the wives and children.

After 20 years in Israel, the Black Hebrew educational system produces children who, by their teen years, speak four languages – English, Hebrew, Arabic and French. They receive a "divine education," meaning that, woven into everything, they are taught the principles of morality, character formation and integrity – everything taught is geared to enhancing life and furthering peace. "We don't teach law to a child so that he can lie or teach him accounting so that he can learn to juggle books," Asiel says.

The children, schooled in vocational training, math philosophy, the arts, agriculture, home management and life sciences, enter manhood and womanhood training at age 13. By the time they're 18 or so, they can make all their own clothes, from shoes to garments, and have mastered the ability to take care of themselves anywhere in the world.

After 20 years, more than 700 of them, called the children of Dimona, have been born in Israel since the Black Hebrews arrived. They are children raised in an atmosphere free of vice and negativity, Asiel explains, children who have never seen their parents fighting, who don't know about broken homes, who have never been introduced to drugs.

"They're actually growing up in a new kind of society where they are in control," Asiel says. "To wake up and not be a minority or inferior or called Negro, colored or Black, but to wake up with their God, their language and their culture has given our children a sense of purpose and dynamism that words cannot express.

"That's not to say that we don't have minimal problems as it relates to growing up, because teenagers are teenagers. But they have grown strong and wise and we think it is this generation and the children whom they produce who will perfect the vision of Dimona."

The Black Hebrews work with groups like AfriCare and the International United Black Fund on programs that will lead to economic and technological development in African countries.

They also operate a chain of Boutique Africa shops and Soul Vegetarian restaurants in Chicago, Washington, D.C., Los Angeles, Atlanta, Cleveland and Bermuda. Chicago's Boutique Africa and Soul Vegetarian restaurant are located at 203 and 205 East 75th Street.

Prince Asiel is now a personally fulfilled man, joyous at having been involved in what he calls an experiment to prove that the African in America is not forgotten by God and that he does not need to hold on to his former slave master for his life.

For the Hebrew Israelite Community, the years have been fraught with hardships, doubt, and fear because of the enormity of what they were trying to do. But Asiel says they never got to the point where they were going to quit. "There was always enough progress to say, well, let's see what the end's going to be," he says.

Apparently, for the Black Hebrews, because of their faith, strength and volition, all's well that ends well.

preface
Bennett

Update: Bennett spent over 50 years with *Ebony* before he finally retired to write more books.

African America's Journalist Historian Confronts Race Issues with Power of the Pen

Lerone Bennett

By D. Kevin McNeir & Photography by Chris Griffin | *Originally Published February 28, 2002*

Lerone Bennett Jr. is one of those rare people who moves effortlessly between the worlds of journalism and scholarship. And while he has sometimes been challenged – even criticized – for his perspective, he has always remained determined to tell "the real deal," basing his books, news stories and essays on historical data.

In the process, he has used his dual roles of historian and journalist to educate, enlighten and enkindle his readers, sometimes to the point of evoking a change in the way they view the world and/or themselves.

Bennett is the executive editor of *Ebony* magazine and author or co-author of 14 books, including his seminal work, *Before the Mayflower: A History of Black America*, and the most recently published and controversial, *Forced Into Glory: Abraham Lincoln's White Dream*.

> I always wanted to read, convinced that I could find the answer to my question, 'Why are Black people treated so badly in America?' I'm still looking for the answer.

"I think of myself as a *witness participant*. You can't find truth simply by reading and watching – you have to get involved," Bennett says of his work. "So, I have not only written about the struggle for equality and racial issues in America, but I've marched, boycotted and organized from Mississippi and Atlanta to Chicago."

The Early Years, Southern Style

The Clarksdale, Mississippi native was born October 17, 1928, and somehow survived the hostility and prejudice that were part of daily life for Blacks of the time young and old.

While it wasn't easy being a Black boy living in the South in his formative years during the 1930s and '40s, Bennett said his childhood memories center around the support and protection of two loving parents (Lerone Sr. and Alma), and an insatiable appetite for reading that still remains a significant part of his character.

"I can remember disappearing for hours and someone from the family being sent to find me," he said with a smile. "They knew that wherever I was, I had a book in my hands. Ever since I can remember, I always wanted to read, convinced that I could find the answer to my question, 'Why are Black people treated so badly in America?' I guess you could say I'm still looking for the answer – or maybe, a way to cause a change for the better."

Bennett graduated Phi Beta Kappa from Morehouse College in 1949, where he was a classmate of a then unknown "teen wonder" from Atlanta's middle-class community of Auburn Avenue...Martin Luther King, Jr.

Bennett remained in the city, beginning his journalism career as a reporter and city editor for the now defunct *Atlanta Daily World*. He stayed for almost four years, until he received a call from an up-and-coming magazine publisher from Chicago ... John H. Johnson.

The Ebony Years And The Black Press

Bennett is proud of *Ebony* magazine's recognition as the number one Black-owned magazine in the world for 55 consecutive years (since its founding in 1945). He said that while working alongside hard-nosed and highly-respected John H. Johnson, *Ebony's* publisher, chairman and CEO, for 49 years, he has seen the world change in a very significant way, adding that, "but without the perspective readers receive from the Black press, this would be a very different world, at least for Blacks."

Johnson originally hired Bennett as an associate editor at *Jet* magazine in 1953, but soon promoted him to a more challenging position as associate editor for *Ebony*. And there Bennett has remained, becoming senior editor in 1958 and executive editor in 1987 – the position he holds today.

He muses, "Naturally, *Ebony* and *Jet* have changed over the years, but it's the test of a great magazine or newspaper that they maintain their relevancy and importance to their readers by changing with the people whom the articles address."

Bennett says his "love affair" with the Black press started when he was just a child, running the streets of Mississippi.

"I used to hang around the offices of the two Black newspapers that served the Clarksdale community (the *Mississippi Enterprise* and the *Jackson Advocate*)," he said. "And I sold papers. But I had no idea that I would one day become a newspaper writer myself.

"Then one day, the editor for the *Mississippi Enterprise* said since I was always around, maybe I'd like to write the back-to-school editorial. That was my first newspaper piece – and I was hooked."

When Bennett moved to Atlanta, he actually began working as a stringer (freelance reporter) for the *Atlanta Daily World* (also Black-owned) before being offered the position as reporter. He said right from the start he knew that he would only be satisfied by working for the Black press.

"I made a deliberate decision," Bennett says. "I knew I wanted to work for the Black press. Now, we as Black reporters have a duty to manage and work in the industry everywhere, so I'm not criticizing those who work for White-owned publications. I was just committed to doing my work for a Black-owned publication and I remain so."

Bennett's other role – as an educator and historian – has also been of great benefit to him, particularly in his reflections about and articles on the impact of the Black press.

"It is my belief that if the Black press did not exist today, it would now be necessary to invent it," he says. "We need it (the Black press) as much as we ever did, especially now that we have entered into this age of mystification and confusion."

Each of Bennett's books has been published by Johnson Publishing Company. His collection of essays, *The Negro Mood*, published in 1964, is an example of the Black press at its best — a probing analysis of issues like the failed integration of Blacks into American life and the ways in which African Americans are denied the fruits of society.

In reflections that most likely would not be given voice by White-owned publications, Bennett takes aim at the White liberal establishment for ignoring the accomplishments of African Americans and for just mouthing the words of racial justice, rather than performing the actions that might remedy it.

But it is his first published work, *Before the Mayflower* (1962), which continues to be one of the most requested books ever dealing with the topic of Black history. Bennett is currently working on an updated edition that will take readers from the original text's coverage – from the African past to the civil rights movement – and will add a new section on Black America's history over the past 25 years.

In the preface to the first edition, Bennett shared the story of how *Before the Mayflower* developed from an idea to reality.

"This book grew out of a series of articles which were published originally in *Ebony* magazine," he wrote. "The book, like the series, deals with the trials and triumphs of a group of Americans whose roots in the American soil are deeper than the roots of the Puritans who arrived on the celebrated *Mayflower* a year after a 'Dutch man of war' deposited 20 Negroes at Jamestown. This is a history of 'the other Americans' and how they came to North America and what happened to them when they got here."

Who Was Abraham Lincoln?

In his highly provocative *Forced Into Glory: Abraham Lincoln's White Dream* (Johnson Publishing Company, $35), Bennett asserts that far from the myth that America has created about this revered man, Lincoln was far from interested in the lives of Black folk, often invoked the "N-word," and never intended to free Negroes from slavery.

The book examines why the most famous political act in American history never happened and why the Emancipation Proclamation did not actually free African-American slaves.

Bennett says his intention in writing the well-documented book was not to cast Lincoln as a racist. Instead, he wanted to understand why America had sought to re-invent history and why, since his childhood, he had been told a lie.

"Lincoln is one of the keys to the American character – he's an industry, a religion, a secular saint," Bennett says. "It's clear in his recorded speeches that he believed that Blacks and Whites could never live in equality in the United States. His solution to the race problem was to return our forefathers to Africa and make America a place 'free for White people everywhere.'"

Few Black authors have written historical pieces on the life of Abraham Lincoln. Bennett surmises that it's because we (African-Americans) have always known – or sensed – the truth about "Honest Abe."

And here in Chicago, just a few miles from Springfield, where Lincoln first set up camp following his victory in the presidential campaign of 1860, one better have plenty of ammunition if they intend to present an alternative view of the revered president and his motivations.

But Bennett's book is filled with just that — historical references from eyewitnesses like Henry Villard, anti-slavery leader John F. Hume, Secretary of State William Henry Seward (the number two man in Lincoln's administration) his crony, Henry Clay Whitney, and a host of others.

"In a carefully devised plan, Lincoln's Emancipation Proclamation was itself only a promise of freedom," Bennett said. "Even J.G. Randall, called the 'greatest Lincoln scholar of all time,' said the Proclamation itself did not free a single slave. And Horace White, the *Chicago Tribune* correspondent who covered Lincoln in Illinois and in Washington, said it is doubtful that the Proclamation 'freed anybody anywhere.'"

Was The Emancipation Proclamation A Scam?

So how did such a scheme work? According to Bennett – and something we checked out by reading the Proclamation for ourselves – the document did not free a single Negro (it would take the 13th Amendment to legally carry out that process), because it excluded all Negroes within Lincoln's "military reach."

Upon closer examination of the document, it is clear that Lincoln only "freed" those persons held as slaves within states that were in rebellion against the United States – begging the question, "How could he free people in a place over which he had no control?"

"All Whites in 19th Century America were racist," Bennett said. "And while I find no joy in saying so, Lincoln was among that number. Now what we need is a dialogue between members of the Academy and others with different visions of Lincoln.

"His record shows that far from being an able leader, he was a man on both sides of the fence, a waffling, equivocating person who one local columnist said reminds her of current President George W. Bush.

"But I believe the real damage from which all Americans still suffer is that through this myth about Lincoln, we have refused to deal with the deep-seated problems of our country that are a direct result of slavery."

Bennett's book was at first boycotted by the White press and he remembers some people calling him crazy for putting together such a book. But he adds that once he presented his evidence to Johnson and the Johnson Publications staff, he had their support.

Some people, Bennett says, don't want to believe, while others are even fighting not to believe, but "as an historian and journalist, I have the responsibility of uncovering and then sharing the truth with my readers, and it's an awesome task."

Bennett concluded, "Carter G. Woodson, the man who first started us on the road to celebrating Black history with a day in February (which became a week and later the entire month), was a historian who felt compelled to uncover and then share the truth. And that's the lifelong mission that I still travel today."

preface Bowen

Update: Bowen retired from public life in 2004 and now pursues his passion for collecting African and African-American art.

Chuck Bowen

By Charles Whitaker & Photography by Calvin Woods | *Originally Published April 17, 1997*

Chuck Bowen exists in the seams of Chicago politics. He is one of the durable yet inconspicuous threads that help hold together the delicate fabric that cloaks racial discord in the city.

In the genteel parlance of bureaucrats, he is a "facilitator," one who quiets political storms by promising – and more often than not, delivering – spoils, both large and small, on behalf of Mayor Richard M. Daley.

Officially, his title is Executive Assistant to the Mayor, a position described in Bowen's abbreviated city-issued bio as "liaison for the religious leadership."

Ostensibly, Bowen is Daley's link to the powerful African-American ministers of the South and West sides, a coterie of feudal lords whom the astute mayor knows he must appease to maintain political control. It is a mistake, however, to assume that Chuck Bowen's influence extends only to Black churches.

> I'm there as an advocate for the Black community to let the mayor know how we see things.

As important as his connection to the pulpit is, Bowen's role in the Daley administration looms much larger. For the past six years, he has been, to a great degree, Daley's sounding board and troubleshooter for a variety of issues and causes relating to Black Chicagoans.

He has weighed in to calm criticism of everything from what many believed to be the administration's tepid response to the killing of Dantrell Davis, to the CTA's cavalier decision not to re-open several West Side stops along the newly refurbished Green Line.

Though Bowen controls no budget and makes no hiring or policy decisions, his position as the gateway and gatekeeper to the mayor makes him one of the most powerful players in City Hall.

Tough Job, Somebody's Gotta Do It

To exercise that power, Bowen walks a precarious tightrope each day. On one hand, he is the lieutenant in the Daley administration responsible for mollifying the residual resentment over the decline of Black clout in City Hall since the death of Harold Washington.

On the other, he is one of the chief conduits through which Black Chicagoans gain access to the mayor, and as such, helps determine the administration's agenda on many racial matters.

It takes deft maneuvering and a good deal of political acumen to accomplish such a difficult balancing act. But Bowen loves the work. And it is no wonder.

He is, after all, a voracious political animal that cut his teeth in the jungle that was Chicago's machine politics of the 1950s and '60s. He feeds on the endless negotiating, wrangling and cajoling that are part and parcel of maintaining the illusion of "the city that works."

Unlike many of the dismissive baby boomer bureaucrats who populate government, Bowen, 63, has a gracious, avuncular manner that is perfectly suited for his current post.

"You know why I love my work?" he asks. "Because there is not one day that I don't leave my office when someone doesn't say 'thank you' for something I've done. That's a great feeling."

Here's a small example of Chuck Bowen's handiwork: A few years ago, a group of disgruntled teenagers from the Englewood community were demanding restitution from the mayor's office for a campaign they'd undertaken to clean up litter and graffiti in the neighborhood.

A would-be community organizer had told the young people they were to be part of a city-sponsored jobs initiative. The only hitch was that the city had no such initiative, and finding the money to fund a haphazardly administered and already completed cleanup campaign, no matter how noble the effort, would be a political nightmare.

Still, Bowen felt the youths' efforts should be rewarded and supported. Rather than take the problem to the mayor, he presented it to a group of Black business owners who agreed that the teenagers should be compensated and encouraged. So at Bowen's urging, the businessmen rounded up the money to pay the kids.

"That was one of my proudest achievements," Bowen says, looking back on the incident. "It was the first time that the Black business community really stepped up to the plate and took responsibility for a situation. And it showed the mayor a lot about the Black community's ability to mobilize and willingness to do for ourselves."

The quick, unceremonious resolution of what could have turned into a prickly public relations conundrum was classic Chuck Bowen. He sees his job as making and maintaining the alliances that will keep Black Chicagoans involved in City Hall.

"I'm there as an advocate for the Black community," he says, "to let the mayor know how we see things. But what people have to remember is that there are other people in other positions in City Hall who are there vying for their own communities, too.

"So while I want to convince the mayor that it's necessary to have African Americans in management jobs in the administration, because it makes my job easier, I have competition for that. And the mayor – who has to be the mayor for all of the city – has to listen to all of us."

Something In Common

Bowen is hesitant to say that he is part of Daley's inner circle of advisers. ("I'm not really sure that with this particular mayor there is an inner circle," he says.) But he allows that he and the mayor have a bond that enables them to communicate in the same language, a sort of political shorthand that each learned in their formative years as apprentices in Chicago's old political machine.

In fact, the trust that Daley and Bowen share may result from the fact that their political – and to some extent, personal – upbringings are similar. Both are lifelong Catholics, which is quite ironic given Bowen's connection to the overwhelmingly Protestant Black clergy of Chicago.

Both got their political schooling at the elbow of powerful machine bosses: Daley by his father, the late Richard J. Daley, and Bowen by the late U.S. Congressman, William L. Dawson.

"There are very few students of the business of politics," Bowen says, "and Mayor Daley is one of those. He and I are pretty much contemporaries. When he and I sit down and talk, of course we reminisce about how things were in the old days and what they are now. And if there is something happening outside that I have not been involved in, he will call me in and say look at this, and get my opinion on what's going on."

Though times have changed radically since the days when the elder Daley and Dawson held sway over the city with iron fists that delivered patronage jobs to the machine faithful, one can see a slight parallel between the elder Daley's relationship with Dawson and the present-day Daley's relationship with Bowen.

Dawson was the elder Daley's channel to the Black community, the role Bowen plays for the younger Daley today. But while Dawson was a high-profile elected official with a seemingly impregnable

patronage network under his control, Bowen has little more than his considerable powers of persuasion to win friends and influence people.

Fortunately, he has the sort of disarming personality that makes his job that much easier. "Generally, I set the tone for what it is I'm doing and working on. I'd guess that 90 percent of the things that come to me, I never even have to take to the mayor," Bowen said.

"They're things where people just need creative thinking applied to the problem and I can handle those right from my desk, though I will let the mayor know that we've worked on it."

In many ways, Bowen's current job is the culmination of the more than 40 years he's spent in business and politics. There is hardly an association or connection from his past that he has not called upon to settle a dispute or solve a problem.

How It All Began

Born in Atlanta – he moved to Chicago with his family at age 6 – Bowen is a chauvinistic Chicagoan with a deep affinity for the Bronzeville district of the city's South Side, an area that was once the cultural, social and political cynosure of Black Chicago. He attended Corpus Christi elementary and high school, and left Chicago only briefly for a short stint at Clark College (now Clark University) in Atlanta.

Upon his return, he began what became a rather precipitous rise in Democratic Party circles. It all began quite by accident. Young and unemployed, Bowen sought a job with the CTA as a bus driver, but he is color-blind and couldn't pass the vision test.

Dispirited, he turned to the place where any knowledgeable Chicagoan would turn when seeking a city job – his precinct captain, the venerable Edison Love of the second ward's 89th precinct.

Love would become Bowen's professional mentor. He enlisted his new recruit in the Young Democrats, a group that at the time included up and coming Black politicians like Harold Washington, Cecil Partee, Gus Savage and John Stroger.

Bowen was the baby of the group, but he was a firebrand and quickly caught Dawson's eye. At age 21, he was named captain of the seventh precinct of the second ward. In the ensuing years, he gained party recognition and perks for his ability to get out the vote.

He did it with patronage and political favors, of course, but also with a human touch that recognized the residents of the precinct as more than stepping stones on the road to political success.

"We did things like provide a line of credit for residents who had our card at the local stores," he recalls. "And people would pay the money back because they were appreciative of what we did and they didn't want to mess it up for the next person who needed help."

The people skills he learned in politics enabled him to make a successful segue into the private sector. For 23 years, Bowen worked his way up through the ranks of Somerset Importers, one of the world's leading producers of alcoholic beverages. "I did the same thing for Somerset that I do for the mayor," he said. "I was their liaison for the NAACP, the Urban League. I helped them make connections to groups like the Black Airline Pilots Association."

Bowen returned to politics in the late 1970s, serving a four-year appointment as deputy clerk of the Cook County Board of Commissioners before being elected to a four-year term on the County Board in 1982. The hallmark of his tenure in elective office was spearheading the county's first-ever minority set-aside program, which established a 30 percent floor for participation by women and minorities in all county contracts.

That taste of elective office on the county level was enough to cure Bowen once and for all of any higher political aspirations, however. "I would never want to stand again for elective office," he says emphatically.

"When you are an elected official, people expect that you can do things that you can't. I do twice as much, 10 times as much, than most elected officials can do because I'm in a position where I'm speaking for the mayor."

It's hard imagining when Bowen will call it quits in politics. Clearly he's enjoying himself. "It takes a long time to get to really know and understand how politics works," he said. "I like where I am now because I understand how this system works and I'm able to help it work better for people."

preface Brazier

Update: Bishop Arthur Brazier passed away in 2010 at the age of 89 after leading his church for 48 years. His congregation grew from 100 to 20,000. His son, Dr. Byron Brazier, assumed pastoral duties after his father retired.

Legend Retires, Son Accepts Leadership Mantle

Bishop Arthur Brazier

By James Muhammad & Photography by Victor Powell | *Originally Published July 10, 2008*

At age 86, Bishop Arthur Brazier breezes through the wide hallways of Apostolic Church of God (ACOG) with the sway of a man 30 years younger. He's dressed in a crisp, gray suit and matching tie that could have come straight off the store racks, but because he wears it so well, one would automatically think it was custom made.

Most people in the church this afternoon greet him before he can utter a word. He seems to draw them to him. And all offer to do something – anything – for the man they refer to simply as "Bishop." The reverence is appropriate.

Brazier has led this congregation for 48 years and has been a stalwart of leadership in this South Side community. Congregants' respect and concern is heightened by the recent announcement of his retirement and last official sermon as pastor from the church pulpit on June l, 2008. His retirement is against his doctor's orders.

"My primary physician advised me not to retire," Brazier says. "He told me to just cut back because most men my age as active as I am, when they retire, they don't last too long.

"I did cut back," he continues, "but it was hard, so I finally decided the best thing to do is to retire. If I don't retire now, then when?"

> **Jesus said to first seek the Kingdom of God and other things will follow.**

The problem was that Brazier was doing just as much in his "cut back" mode as he did on normal days. Even in retirement, his days will be just as full as he focuses on a myriad of civic duties that he also has performed over the years. He'll still commit to returning all his phone calls within 36 hours and will continue to set his own schedule and appointments.

"I want to stay close to the people," he says.

Apostolic's Long And Rapid Growth

Born and reared in Chicago, Brazier accepted the call to lead ACOG on June 1, 1960 — and fittingly, he chose June 1 to preach his last official sermon as pastor.

Brazier was preaching at the Universal Church of Christ when members of ACOG approached him to lead their church. The combined congregations totaled 100 members.

The church grew quickly; these are the days the bishop refers to as his happiest. At the church location at 6344 South Kimbark, he expanded the seats from 144 to 200. In 1978, he entered the edifice at 63rd and Kenwood with 500 members.

By 1992, he built the current church at 63rd and Dorchester that seats 3,000 people for a 20,000-member congregation.

"I entered this church thanking God that I wouldn't have to preach two sermons from now on, but I've been preaching two sermons every Sunday," to accommodate the overflow crowd, he says.

The church has since added a television studio, a 400-seat banquet facility and a family and youth center, complete with a basketball court, classrooms

Above right:
Dr. Byron Brazier

and dance studio.

At one time, Brazier worked for the U.S. Postal Service. He went to night school at Moody Bible Institute and has lectured at University of Chicago Law School, Northwestern University Law School, and Harvard University.

He is the founding president of The Woodlawn Organization (TWO), one of the city's most effective community groups, and he also founded the Woodlawn Preservation and Investment Corporation and the Fund for Community Redevelopment and Revitalization.

Brazier has authored three books, *Black Self-Determination, Saved by Grace and Grace Alone,* and *From Milk to Meat,* as well as *the Empowerment Tools* series.

The most troubling time in Brazier's life came in the 1960s when TWO received a grant to do gang intervention work. The group provided gang members with job training and education opportunities, but things didn't go well.

"We thought we had the support of the power structure, but we didn't," Brazier recalls. "The program floundered. It was probably the worst time I've ever had, but I think we did some good."

It turned out that members of one gang were taking stipend checks from some of the young people and signing them. The group was accused of funneling money to gangs. There was an IRS investigation and Senate hearings, Brazier says.

The First Lady of Apostolic

Through it all, he thanks God for the companionship of his wife of 60 years, Isabelle.

"When you decide to take the marriage vows, I tell people to close the divorce door and lock it," he says. "As long as an opportunity to split is there, the temptation to do it is always there." In fact, a couple once asked if they could write their own marriage vows, but when he heard them say, "As long as love lasts," he rejected it.

"Some young people go into marriage without the idea that it's a life-long commitment," he says.

An Army veteran who has also marched the civil rights battlefield with Dr. Martin Luther King Jr., Brazier is a staunch supporter of Barack Obama, though he is careful to keep his politics and the church separate.

Brazier points to Obama as an example of progress

The Brazier Family

Bishop Arthur Brazier and Dr. Byron Brazier

in America. He reflects on days when it was impossible for a Black man in America to get a job and when he had to ride in the back of the bus.

"That is not the America of today," Brazier says. "Things have changed." Comparing present day America for Blacks to "the Promised Land," he debunks the concept that such a place is where you sit around eating pomegranates and honey.

He explains: "When Israel entered the Promised Land, the first thing they had to do was fight. It means you're still in the struggle, but you are not in the wilderness."

Not afraid of controversy, Brazier acknowledges that he has been severely criticized by some for his strong support for Chicago Mayor Richard M. Daley.

The Bishop says he's never received favors from the city in return for his support, nor has he received discounted prices for the housing units he has erected. He supports Mayor Daley simply because "he's the best mayor the city's ever had," Brazier says.

"I look at politicians as men and women who are supposed to serve the community. Mayor Daley has spread the largess around. He has made the city better," says Brazier, noting that the late Mayor Harold Washington never got the chance to really function.

The Spiritual Foundation Of The Church

Brazier is a pastor who preaches for the poor. His motto is the people come first. And that's where the rub comes for him with the so-called "prosperity gospel." He is saddened by the emphasis placed on material wealth and the thought that if you serve the Lord you will be prosperous.

"There are people who don't serve the Lord who are very prosperous," he points out. He believes there is a place in the ministry for preaching about prosperity because America is a capitalistic society and everybody has a desire to earn enough money to live comfortably. "But Jesus said to first seek the Kingdom of God and other things will follow," Brazier argues.

"(The prosperity) message doesn't work if your church is in the heart of the Robert Taylor Homes," he says, referring to the recently torn down Chicago housing projects. "We're getting it backwards when we first seek the other things."

As he turns over the reins of church leadership to his son Byron, the Bishop is comforted that his institution remains in good hands.

Byron Brazier, 56, worked for years in Corporate America and owned his own company before answering the call to the ministry in 1992. He was invited by his father to join the church staff as administrator in 1995.

Several years ago, the church's executive board decided that the younger Brazier would assume his father's role when Bishop retired.

The younger Brazier plans to stay the course his father set. "The church has a great foundation. There is no reason to try to build a different foundation," he says.

Byron Brazier's three goals, as he assumes leadership, are to stabilize the congregation's comfort and trust; maintain the church's economic stability; and continue to invest in young people. His actions with parishioners will be based on the premise of building spiritual identification with Jesus Christ, and building spiritual character and vision.

Bishop Brazier says he has advised his son not to change the message – that Jesus Christ is Lord, that the people must be saved – and not to get caught up in phases or church fads. But Byron Brazier says his father's best advice has come through example, not words.

"When I came to the church, it didn't matter if I would be pastor or not," the younger Brazier explains. "Being a pastor isn't an ambition, it's a calling.

"When people ask me if I'm ready, I say, 'Yes,' because the Lord has given me what I need to be ready," ACOG's new pastor says. "If you believe that God has been with you and he opens an additional door, it's not arrogance, but spiritual and Godly confidence that pushes you through."

Apostolic Church of God, 6320 South Dorchester

preface Brooks

Update: Pastor Corey Brooks spent more than 90 days on the roof of an abandoned motel across the street from his church, until a $100,000 donation from filmmaker Tyler Perry helped him reach the goal of raising money to purchase and demolish it. For the next phase, Brooks walked across America to raise funds to build the $15 million community and economic development center for kids under the auspices of Project HOOD. The project is still soliciting funds as it rehabs the building in which the center will be housed.

Pastor Corey Brooks

By James C. Muhammad | Photography by Jason Thomas | *Originally Published January 12, 2012*

n November 2011, Pastor Corey Brooks pitched a tent on the roof of a vacant motel across the street from his New Beginnings Church on 66th and King Drive and vowed to stay there as a protest against senseless street violence among youths.

Two months later, he had only come down from that roof three times to preach at funerals for young people killed by senseless street violence.

"Nobody should get comfortable with preaching at funerals for young people," Brooks said, sitting under his rooftop tent with two friends visiting one unusually warm January evening. "I'd much rather be developing a community center than to become a professional mourner."

Brooks took the drastic action on November 22, 2011, shortly before Thanksgiving. Earlier that week, he was preaching at a funeral for a boy killed in the streets when gunshots rang outside his church even as he spoke.

> It was a scary and depressing night. Scary because I never heard so much gunfire in my life; depressing because I couldn't believe all these people in our community have guns.

Brooks says, "After 10 funerals in one year, I couldn't take it anymore. After gang members, in broad daylight, began to shoot at the attendees of the funeral of a 15-year-old gun victim, right in front of the church as they were entering the building, I knew something had to be done. In order to bring awareness to the gun violence issue in our community, I chose to live in a tent on the rooftop of an abandoned motel right across the street from my church."

Brooks, founder of Project H.O.O.D. (Helping Others Obtain Destiny), contemplated the incident that night as he lay in bed reading the book of Habakkuk in his Bible. A chapter in it describes a vision of the prophet going upon a watchtower amidst violence in the nation and awaiting God's instructions.

Brooks' church already had a contract to purchase the motel and plans to build a community center in its place. Sensing that violence will continue as long as young people don't have positive alternatives, Brooks announced he wouldn't come down from the roof until the $450,000 needed to buy the property was raised.

On many evenings since, men of the church and the community have marched through the streets chanting for the violence to end. Passing cars honk in support and people young and old watch from the sidewalks.

The rallies and the pastor's rooftop vigil have attracted international attention and contributions had risen to more than $225,000 at N'DIGO press time. And, yes, Brooks says he has seen change.

"I think more people are optimistic that change can come about. I see a more diverse group of people who are more conscious and aware of what's going on in the community. People are behind the effort to make things better," he says. "Change will come, but change will be gradual."

Case in point: There have been several high profile killings in nearby communities since Brooks began his protest. He preached at the funerals of some of them. And there was the brazen robbery of a community food store where an off-duty police officer was shot and killed with semi-automatic weapons.

On New Year's Eve, Brooks contemplated coming off the roof because he knew that people would be firing weapons into the air in celebration and thought his stay at that point might be foolhardy and counterproductive. He decided to stay after talking to two visitors – young men who had spent time in solitary confinement in federal prison.

"The more I talked to them about coming down, I saw how broken they became. Finally, one of them said, 'If you go down you will be letting everybody down.' They were coming to be encouraged, but ultimately they encouraged me," Brooks says. That night, he turned his futon over like a barricade and slept under it.

"It was a scary and depressing night," Brooks recounts. "Scary because I never heard so much gunfire in my life; depressing because I couldn't believe all these people in our community have guns, and not just single-shot guns.

"I believe in the right to bear arms," Brooks continues, "but not illegally and not if you're not trained. I understand that people may feel they need a gun to be safe, but I don't understand why they need a semi-automatic. The only purpose I can see is to shoot at people."

Answering A Calling

Brooks grew up in Muncie, Indiana. He accepted his calling to preach at the age of 19, but only after doing everything he could think of to avoid it.

The seeds of his future planted in him by his mother finally germinated, however, and he received his first assignment at Mt. Moriah Church in Richmond, Indiana, at the age of 23.

At age 27, Brooks pastored at West Point Church on Chicago's South Side before founding New Beginnings at 6620 South King Drive in 2000. The church currently houses a K-8 school, a fitness center and music studio. It is a place that young people can be found most evenings.

When Brooks' wife, Delilah, first heard the pastor's idea about staying on the roof, she didn't take him seriously. But the idea quickly sank in and his four children embraced the mission, even though they had to spend the holidays without him.

"At first, a group of us thought it was a joke," Mrs. Brooks says. "But it became serious and our children understand that their dad is a man of God. I'm much more aware now of what's going on and it has caused me to reach out to some mothers who have lost their children."

The motel courtyard that Brooks overlooks every morning is littered with old mattresses, broken bottles, and other debris left by years of abandonment, illegal drug use and other activities that have taken place there.

Like the cluttered courtyard, Brooks said the debris in the Black community – mis-education, lack of economic development, and the social and spiritual illnesses – can't be cleaned up until Black leaders find ways to collaborate and build trust among themselves to address the problems.

Brooks says his seven weeks of nightly solitude, along with a 30-day liquid fast, have caused him to grow spiritually. He's more patient, less stressed, and has an increased sensitivity "toward the things of God," he says.

The pastor spends a lot of time on the exercise bike erected in a corner of the roof and does other calisthenics to stay in shape. But mostly, Brooks' days are consumed with studying, discussions with church employees, whom he meets under the tent, answering endless phone calls and text messages, and posting to Facebook and Twitter.

His visitors must ride a rented construction lift to get to him, and even elders have no gripes about the bending and twisting movements they have to perform to get off the lift.

One visitor offered a matching $50,000 donation that the church met. Another – an architect from Sweden – invited the pastor to come to his country to view community centers his company has constructed.

Numerous others have come to offer words of encouragement and contributions. Surprisingly, most of the visitors have been young people from the community who also want the violence to stop.

"They want to help and I send them back to tell their peers to squash the violence," the pastor says, rubbing a quarter-inch beard that has grown in seven weeks.

A Center for the Community

The community center Brooks wants to build will house a recreation center, theaters for arts and music, a computer center, and counseling and educational facilities.

A rooftop greenhouse garden will be named in honor of Sylvia Sobolik; in whose name the matching grant was donated. There will also be parts of the facility named for others – living and deceased.

During one of the rallies outside the church, State Senator James Meeks, pastor of Salem Baptist Church in Roseland, questioned why more resources aren't coming to cities and organizations to help curb violence. He cited more than 425 killings in the city in 2011.

"We did a lot as a nation to protect the bald eagle. The bald eagle is no longer an endangered species, but the African-American male between the ages of 18 and 30 is the new endangered species. Let's do as much for the African-American male as we did for the bald eagle," Meeks said.

He suggested that obtaining the building would be easier for New Beginnings if the City of Chicago sold it to Brooks for $1. It's a suggestion that Brooks appreciates and understands, but he'd rather raise the money the old fashioned way and earn it.

"Sometimes you think everybody feels the same way you do about a situation," Brooks says, explaining he didn't think it would take so long to raise the money. "People have responded, just not as much as I expected.

"But if the city gives you anything, you are going to owe the city eventually," Brooks cautioned. "If you give us anything, you've got to know that there are no strings attached. God is telling me you can't get upset because it don't come the way you want it to come. God puts us in a position so He gets all the credit," Brooks says.

Pastor Corey Brooks lived on a rooftop for 90 days begining November 2011 to protest the violence in Chicago's Black communities.

preface Brown

Update: The mother of Chicago's Black arts movement, Chicago native Abena Joan Brown was a graduate of Roosevelt University and had a master's degree from the University of Chicago's School of Social Service Administration. She passed away in 2015 at the age of 87, after running eta for 40 years until 2011.

Abena Joan Brown

By Kai EL 'Zabar & Photography by David Jenkins | *Originally Published September 1991*

As president and CEO of eta Creative Arts Foundation, one of Chicago's few Black-owned and operated professional training and performance centers, Abena Joan Brown is a leading lady.

Her track record is amazing. She is petite, but the power of her presence is mesmerizing. When she steps outside her professional mode and falls into the enigma of the magic woman she is – speaking always in her most charming voice, while her eyes peer deep into your psyche, reading you as only a cross examiner does – suddenly you find yourself disarmed.

Skeptics warned Diva Abena Joan Brown that her vision of a theatre company wouldn't work on the South Side. But, with the faith of a roots worker, she ignored them and simply acted upon her faith.

As a result of her fundamental belief in people, and confidence in knowing of the need for theatre in the African-American community, eta (deliberately spelled all lower-case) Creative Arts Foundation, came to life in 1971 and established its home at 7558 S. South Chicago Avenue.

> **By positioning itself in the African-American community, eta meets a deep longing for African Americans to see ourselves in some authentic ballad doing what we do, in the ways only we can, with all the nuances and unique idiosyncrasies reflective of our ethnicity.**

Abena has often said that the impetus for starting eta was her own inability to find work as an artist. eta was preceded by a group started in 1969 called Ebony Talent Associates, formed by Abena, Okoro Harold Johnson, Al Johnson and Archie Weston to increase work opportunities for Black actors and to train them at their craft.

The 16,000-square foot building that houses eta was originally a storm window factory until eta's renovation in 1988. Brown used her own money to secure a bank loan to complete the renovation. There is now a 200-seat theater, a library, community room, art gallery, a workshop and office space.

The modern day diva says, "Everything about eta proves that by positioning itself in the African-American community, it meets a deep longing for the African-American to see him/herself in some authentic ballad doing what we do in the ways only we can with all the nuances and unique idiosyncrasies reflective of our ethnicity."

Magic, Past And Present

Art and theatre patrons have always associated the "magic" of eta with the alluring, almost mystical quality of its unique blend of art and culture with the practical. eta is committed to the concept of "magic for the multitudes."

Brown describes it best in the eta Magic Storybook, which says, "The ancient Kushites (Egyptians) defined 'magic' as knowledge and power. The 'magi' or magicians' were the wisest, most resourceful and most esteemed individuals.

"They were called upon to perform astoundingly prodigious metaphysical feats on a grand scale. The 'magician' or theatrical organization as in our case, must be cognizant that 'magic' (knowledge and power) is never an end in itself; rather it is a conscious attempt to achieve a specific goal."

The application of knowledge and power took eta from its humble beginnings in 1971 with an annual operating budget of $12,500 to a budget of $630,000 over 20 years later.

Growth and development are all a part of eta's mission. "We've discovered playwrights who had not showcased their work before," Brown says. In fact, 98 percent of the plays that eta presents are world premieres and the others are those seldom produced.

She emphasizes, "It is a policy. We do original works by African-American playwrights and about African-Americans. It is an extension of our mission in colloquial terms to tell our own story in the ways that Langston Hughes indicated we ought to in the 1930s. In fact, W.E.B. Du Bois spoke in the 1920s of the Negro Arts Movement needing to be by, for, about and near the Negro people."

She continues, "I think historically that some of us have thought that the answer was in 'being downtown,' but the fact that we are in the context of a community is a commitment to the neighborhood, to accessibility. We also know that the arts leverage economic development. The reality is that this is not limited to Chicago, but around the nation. eta's position in context to an African-American community has impacted business."

In addition to offering plays, eta also showcases the art of premiere African-American artists like Dr. Jeff Donaldson and Calvin Jones. "It has been our experience that people see something they like and take it home with them," says Abena Joan Brown. "I think that in doing the exhibits, we have set the ground for creating a 'real gallery' just as we built the 'real theatre' in terms of community respect and the actual physical space."

She is adamant in expressing, "I think that in presenting the full spectrum of the visual artist it increases the opportunity to have art work in our own homes to reflect ourselves. We push the concept that every African-American family ought to have one piece of kente cloth, one piece of handmade jewelry, and an original art piece in their homes. It is consistent with what theatre means to us."

The Playwright

Looking at ways to enhance opportunities in the arts community is eta's priority. One such initiative is the development of the playwright. Understanding the importance of the playwright is often overlooked.

Directors most often do not meet playwrights to discuss the script. Actors have even fewer opportunities than the director to meet the playwright and therefore depend on the director's interpretation. eta feels a responsibility to elevate the playwright and put into focus the status of the African griot.

"We feel that the playwright must be developed the same as are performing or other visual artists," Brown says. "Actors, dancers, musicians, painters, directors, technicians, and the like are all trained. Playwrights must take part in a training process if they are to become viable storytellers."

eta does this in several ways, one being the Reader's Theatre that allows the playwright the opportunity to showcase his/her work. The playwright receives critiques of his/her work from the public, and eta's artistic personnel. He/she also has the chance to hear and see the particular work and get some idea as to how the work can be made into a producible piece.

An extension of the Reader's Theatre is the opportunity for budding writers to work closely with seasoned playwrights to discuss specifics: how the structure can be changed, how a scene can be strengthened, or how the dialogue can be developed, etc.

Abena expresses that "eta is examining the whole question of what needs to be done to develop a body of dramatic African-American literature." And a question of images emerges. She addresses concern for traditional Black stock characters.

"They are either caricature, or stereotypical which makes a negative statement about us," Abena says. She is convinced that if asked to identify stock African-American characters, most people would rattle off "pimp, prostitute, addict, drug dealer." She says that eta is determined to introduce new stock characters.

African Americans have internalized the established negative stock characters as have others. We have to think about who the stock characters really are. She points out that we have aunts, uncles, and stepfathers who have reared families after divorce, separation or death. We have grandmothers. The point is, we know that all of these characters exist in our oral literature, but the need is for them to come into life in our written works.

Abena says, "We are concerned with developing a formal process for bringing them out – introducing them to the world."

Inner Vision

The eta lady says, "It's my goal to plan for five years from now as far as mentoring and preparing leadership to carry on. Staff is in training. We are fortunate that our board and staff have longevity. This makes for a wonderful sense of commitment and continuity. If I left today, I feel confident that eta will go on to thrive and flourish.

"Let it go on record once and for all; I had a vision, as opposed to a dream, of what eta has become and is evolving to become. I was very awake when I made a conscious choice to share my professional skills and knowledge in service to my community.

"I am happy to say that eta is an example of what the artist can do in collaboration and in coalition with the brightest and competent ones from various other disciplines. It's true the artist cannot be in isolation because the art is about all of us. After all, darling, this is theatre!"

preface Bunch

Update: Bunch was Chicago Historical Society director from 2001 to 2005. He left to return to the Smithsonian as the founding director of the National Museum of African American History and Culture, the first national Black museum, which opened in September 2016 in a ceremony led by the first Black President of the United States, Barack Obama.

Lonnie Bunch

By Jean A. Williams & Photography by Jennifer Williams | *Originally Published December 30, 2001*

His great love for history has been the passion and the driving force in Lonnie Bunch's life since he was five years old.

While reading a book to his grandson, Bunch's grandfather came across a photo of students taken in the 1870s with a caption that read, "unknown school children."

"My grandfather said something like, 'Isn't it a shame that people could live their lives, die, and yet, be unknown?'" Bunch says. "That question always fascinated me, so in essence, my whole career has been about trying to make the invisible visible and give voice to the anonymous."

His present position as President of the Chicago Historical Society (CHS) provides Bunch with the opportunity to fulfill his life's mission.

Lonnie G. Bunch III has the honorable distinction of being the first African American to head the 145-year-old historical institution. He is one of only two African Americans in the country to head a museum that is not racially or ethnically specific. In effect, he has made history.

> **I have never met a people that care about history like Black folks, who recognize that their lives today are shaped by experiences of the past.**

"For years, I have pushed and prodded the profession of museums to be as diverse in their leadership as is the country, because I realized how few people of color are leading these institutions. So when this opportunity came my way, I felt an obligation to take this on. I wasn't unaware of the symbolic value," says Bunch.

As CHS president, he guides and oversees development of the museum's exhibitions, programs, research collections and publications.

The unanimous decision of the Historical Society's board of trustees to select Bunch as president was arrived at undoubtedly because of his extensive background and over 20 years of experience as a historian, curator, and documentary filmmaker.

He comes to Chicago from the Smithsonian's National Museum of American History, where he served as curator, Associate Director for Historical Resources, and most recently, as Associate Director for Curatorial Affairs.

He also served as an adjunct professor of museum studies at George Washington University, American University, and the assistant professor of American and Afro-American history at the University of Massachusetts at Dartmouth.

One of the most rewarding positions Bunch has held is that of Senior Curator of History for the California African American Museum in Los Angeles.

"I helped to open the museum in 1980 with a major exhibition on the history of Blacks in the Olympics," he recalls. "This was the first state-funded African American museum in the country, so it was really an important symbol and I remember coming to the opening and experiencing the wonderful feeling in the room."

Another gratifying experience for Bunch was the collaborative work he did on the Smithsonian's exhibit called "The American Presidency: A Glorious Burden."

This popular and highly acclaimed exhibition was of unprecedented size and scope and brought together for the first time objects that represented the lives and times of the country's then-42 previous presidents.

"This exhibit allowed me to put together smart people in order to craft a major exhibition that millions of people enjoyed," Bunch said. "I've been really lucky because there have been a lot of projects that have allowed me to learn things, allowed me to be successful." This exhibit was his swan song at the Smithsonian before coming to Chicago.

Finding Out What Makes Chicago Tick

Bunch, a family man who glows when speaking of his wife and two daughters, was born in New Jersey in 1952 and earned his bachelor's, master's and doctoral degrees in American history and African history at American University.

"My family and I are community-driven," he says. "We do a lot in the community, so my hope was that Chicago would be a community that we could be a part of. I discovered that it is."

The leadership of Chicago's African-American

Lonnie Bunch

cultural institutions helped to ease Bunch's transition by hosting a reception at the DuSable Museum.

Antoinette Wright, then DuSable's CEO and President, believed it was important to welcome and acknowledge Bunch as the first African American to head CHS.

"We are pleased and happy to see growth in our colleagues as they lead an institution of note," Wright says. "It demonstrates something to our youth, that a career in museums can take you into leadership positions."

In his exploration of Chicago, Bunch observed several things about this city that every Chicagoan knows. It is a city of neighborhoods, a city that is open and friendly, and a city whose residents are really proud to be Chicagoans.

"I find that fascinating. There is a genuine desire among Chicagoans to understand the city, celebrate the city, and make the city better. That appeals to me a great deal," Bunch said. His fascination, enthusiasm, and fresh eye are what he believes will bring a new perspective to the exhibits and programs of CHS.

Chicago is an historian's dream because, in Bunch's estimation, much of what is celebrated here is the city's history.

"When I listen to the Mayor (Richard Daley) talk about his vision for the city, it's about history. It's about a past we should be proud of, about Chicago's role as the great city of the Midwest. So what appeals to me is that this is a city that is shaped by its history, that is ripe with history, that embraces history," Bunch noted.

Learning this has helped to shape his vision for the Historical Society. "I've been telling staff, 'Look, we're history. This is what the city loves. Let's be bold as we create exhibits and share stories,'" Bunch said. "Ultimately, I want people to see the Society as a place that has some resonance for them in their daily lives."

Stimulating Black Involvement

Therein lies his greatest challenge. According to Bunch, while most people, especially African Americans, care a great deal about history for the most part, they don't visit the CHS.

"I have never met a people that care about history like Black folks," Bunch says. "Black people care about the past and recognize that their lives today are shaped by experiences of the past. The legacy of slavery, Jim Crow America, and segregation still float out there. For African Americans, history isn't dead."

So, for those African Americans who aren't familiar with the Chicago Historical Society, he wants to build bridges, and for those who are, Bunch believes that they should be encouraged to take ownership of it.

In a joint effort to bring African Americans into the Historical Society and the DuSable Museum, both museum presidents have agreed to collaborate on future exhibitions. "We are excited about the partnership and what it will bring, not only to the African-American community, but to the community at large," Wright said.

Overall, Bunch's efforts are aimed at reaching out and letting people know that the stories CHS tells really have a meaning and are accessible. He believes the best way to do this is to increase the Society's visibility.

"I'd like to plan a series of major, important exhibitions that will get visibility," he says. "With that in mind, next year on President's Day, we're going to open the show that I did at the Smithsonian on the American Presidents. Right away, that will send a message that we're a national player that tells local as well as national stories."

Within a year after that exhibit, the CHS President plans to do a major history on sports in Chicago which will not only touch on the most familiar stories, but will also tell the story of sports as a cultural tool used for Chicago's identity.

"Then," he says, "I want the third show to be a major history of what it's like to be a teenager in Chicago told by Chicago's teenagers.

"I want to craft an educational project and an exhibit that will allow us to look at rites of passage, ethnicity, and fundamental similarities in the lives of teenagers from as early as the 19th century until now."

He also plans to redo all the permanent exhibitions so that within five years, every permanent exhibit will be new.

It is clear to Bunch that history is the most vibrant thing we have, but it's not usually thought about, taught, or presented in that manner.

Bunch recalled, "When my daughters first walked through the museum, they said, 'it's quiet.' But history is messy, full of noise, full of music, full of laughter. So I want to create programs that bring people back in to listen to music, hear stories, and laugh."

preface
Burrell

Update: Thomas J. Burrell retired from his agency in 2004. In 2010, he wrote a critically acclaimed book titled *Brainwashed: Challenging the Myth of Black Inferiority* that confronted the negative images of Blacks throughout American history.

Thomas Burrell

By Ronald E. Childs & Photography by Warren Browne | *Originally Published June 13, 1996*

The images are unforgettable, indelible slices of African Americana. Images that first helped to define, and then decidedly elevated the science of creating effective, impactive Black print and broadcast advertising to an accomplished art.

Take for example the scene of the Grambling University marching band, high-stepping to the chant of "Coke Is It!" Or the young Black girl proudly presenting her winning grade-school essay about one day growing up to be a single parent — "just like my daddy." Consider the vignette of a Black man savoring the taste of a Big Mac, while in the background Barry White coos "My, My, My" in his throaty, trademark baritone.

Whatever the creative imagery, be it the soft radiance of former Miss USA Kenya Moore showing what Pantene Pro-V shampoo and conditioner does for her hair, or the confident smile of "Calvin," the young man who quickly ascended the ranks to become a member of McDonald's restaurant management team, each of these concepts and volumes more are the priceless work of Chicago's very own Burrell Communications Group (BCG).

In 1971, visionary Thomas J. Burrell founded the agency, which is acknowledged as America's premier Black-owned, full-service advertising, marketing, public relations and consumer promotions firm. The innovative and award-winning shop has become one of the most respected institutions in the African-American community.

Given the absence of accurate, inclusive depictions of Blacks and our culture when the agency was formed, it could be argued that necessity mandated BCG's existence, that Burrell sensed the void.

Ranked as high as 16th on *Black Enterprise* magazine's annual listing of the Top 100 Black Businesses, BCG is revered industry-wide for the extent to which its pioneering, positive images of African Americans has changed the face of advertising.

Its founder's long-standing philosophy of "positive relevance" has enabled Burrell to attract and build upon an impressive roster of blue-chip clientele, including such household names as McDonald's, Coca-Cola, Comcast, Toyota, General Mills, American Airlines, Disney's Dreamers Academy, Quaker Oats, Procter & Gamble, NYNEX, Nabisco, Sara Lee, Kraft Foods, Polaroid, Mobil Oil, and Sears, among numerous others.

Thomas Burrell prides himself on his team's ability to effectively reach the Black community using well-developed, targeted marketing communications. Still another element of Burrell's success is its people, and the firm's genuine, demonstrated sense of corporate responsibility.

It is his brand of forward, pro-active thinking that makes Burrell "an American Institution" as he has been declared by *ADweek Magazine*. Similar accolades include his induction into the Chicago Business Hall of Fame, being honored as "Ad Person of the Year" by the Chicago Advertising Club, and being bestowed the prestigious Trumpet Award by Turner Broadcasting of Atlanta.

Burrell spoke with *N'DIGO* about BCG's years of delivering fair and authentic images of African Americans in advertising.

N'DIGO: *After you started the company, what was the initial reaction of African Americans to seeing themselves fairly depicted in advertising?*

THOMAS BURRELL: Actually, it was really amazing. You don't realize the impact of people seeing themselves on the TV screen realistically portrayed, and you don't imagine how significant it is until you see it. You're talking about a positive response that was based simply on people seeing themselves for the first time in advertising — and almost for the first time in media period — being positively and accurately portrayed.

This was after having been characterized for generations as either comic relief, or as acceptable exceptions. But just to see Black people being themselves and doing what people do, jumping double-dutch or going to church on Sunday? It was amazing the kind of response we got from that.

N'DIGO: *Is it true that in your youth you never really anticipated accomplishing all that you have?*

> "You don't realize the impact of people seeing themselves on the TV screen realistically portrayed, and you don't imagine how significant it is until you see it.

TB: As a child I didn't have anything specific in mind as far as this business was concerned. I knew I wanted to achieve something, but I didn't find out anything about advertising until I was 17, when a teacher told me that I should pursue it.

When I started BCG, I had no intention of being its leader. I simply set it up and named a president and a creative director, the two key jobs within the agency.

The person I selected to be president balked at the last minute, so I became president that way. And then about three years later, the creative director left, and then I became the creative director. That's the way it was for a couple of years.

You just evolve into the job and then you say, "Hey, I'm leading something here." You wake up one day and realize that you've got something going. I realized very quickly that the agency was growing and that I'd better get a handle on it. And that's basically what I've done.

So I didn't really start off saying, "I've got to do something great," or "I've got to achieve." As a matter of fact, going through childhood, I cannot remember a single thing that I was good at. You know?

Some people know how to flop on sleds. I couldn't flop. Some people can throw a baseball. Some people are nerdy, or in a book all of the time. I didn't do anything that said, "This is what I do." I basically just made it through until I gained consciousness at about the age of 18. Better late than never, of course.

N'DIGO: *You were once told to be realistic, "that it would be difficult for you as a Black man to achieve success in advertising." How is it that you were not dissuaded?*

TB: The instance you're talking about was when this psychologist tested me because I was having problems with my academics. As a result of the test, he said that I should just forget about finishing college because I wasn't capable of doing so, and that what I should do was try to get a job.

He felt that I could possibly pass the post office exam, but that I should not entertain any thought of finishing college because I was not intellectually capable. He actually told me that, and that is a pretty harsh sentence.

You're definitely damaged by that kind of thing, but you say to yourself, "Well, I'm going to see if I can fool people into thinking that I'm smart." And so you go about the business of trying do that, but all the time there's this doubt in the back of your mind about why.

When you achieve success, you think, "I'm not really worthy of this success, but I must be pretty skilled at fooling people." And then you get to a point where after people tell you that you are smart, and that you did this well, you think, "Wait a minute, maybe he was wrong! Maybe what they say about me

now is the truth. Maybe I am smart."

And then you gain a little bit more confidence as you gain more of that attitude. I am certain at this point, all these years later, that that guy was wrong!

N'DIGO: *How pivotal has the work of BCG been to the term "general market"?*

TB: I think that the industry is beginning to narrow its use of the term. "General market" was essentially a euphemism for White advertising, or non-Black advertising. With the development of segmented marketing overall, the general market, as in mass market, is becoming a relic.

Given the competitiveness and the complexity of the marketplace today, marketers have to basically decide what sub-segment of the market they're going to pinpoint and to own that so as to keep someone else from owning it.

N'DIGO: *You've said that it's easier to effectively reach a predominantly White audience through Black-oriented advertising than the reverse. Why is that?*

TB: Because of the emulative pattern that exists between the races. Many of the things that exist in this society in terms of behavior, language, dress, pop culture, music, even forms of art, start in the Black community. So Black people are a major influencer of culture.

We are creators; that's what we do. We created the blues, and we created jazz and we created various dances. The dances that country and western folks do? That line dancing all started with us. I mean, that's what we do.

So when you're doing advertising aimed at the Black consumer market, basically what you're doing is cutting-edge, or forward-thinking advertising for the general market. Because whatever it is that we're dealing with today, the general market's going to be dealing with tomorrow.

Plus, it's easier for us Black folks to do advertising that is inclusive of White values and White perspectives because we understand the White market better than the White market understands us. And the reason we understand it better is because we've had to, because we are living in a White world and have to survive.

We have to understand White culture almost to the same extent that White people understand it, whereas most White people can live their total lives having zero exposure to the various things that make up a Black life. That's why we can do a better job of talking to them than they can do talking to us, as a general rule.

preface Burris

Update: Roland Burris lost his race for governor in 1994, but was appointed to fill the seat as United States Senator from Illinois in 2009, succeeding Barack Obama, who resigned the position to become the first Black President of the United States in 2008. Burris served in that capacity as the only African-American member of the U.S. Senate until November 2010, when he retired to practice law.

N'DIGO

February 17- March2, 1994

Roland Burris, Illinois' Next Governor?
Inside:
The Economics of Slavery
Ski School - Taos Style
Black Politics Defined

Roland Burris

By David Smallwood & Photography by John Beckett | *Originally Published February 17, 1994*

Roland W. Burris wants to be the next governor of Illinois. Should he succeed in becoming the state's first Black chief executive, he will have hit an historical trifecta.

Burris became the first African American in Illinois history to be elected to statewide office when he won the office of Comptroller in 1978. He entered the record books again in 1990 upon being elected as only the second Black Attorney General, and the first Black Democratic one, in the nation. (The first Black Attorney General was Republican Edward Brooke of Massachusetts.)

A third history-making political endeavor would stroke his ego – and he does have an abundance of self-esteem.

But it's hard not to give Burris his due when it comes to knowing government and having hands-on experience in making it work, after his 21 years of residing in the upper echelon of state government in significant fiscal, legal and administrative positions.

His first real political foray was serving as Director of General Services in the Cabinet of Gov. Dan Walker from 1973 to 1977. In that position, Burris was in charge of purchasing, the Architect's Office, all the construction for a while, the vehicles, printing and the telephone system.

"People depended on my office to get what they needed to service the public, so I was like the administrative vice president of a corporation. And I had to deal with all the agencies," he adds, "so I became very knowledgeable about state government."

When he became Comptroller in 1978, Burris had to redesign the office's entire computer system. "It was taking up to five weeks for an ordered check to be written, but within two and a half years, we had reduced the check processing time down to a 24-hour turnaround. Unheard of," Burris says.

As the state's chief fiscal officer, he also prepared the first balance sheet in the history of Illinois listing all assets and liabilities. After leading the nation in government accounting and reporting through disclo-

sure information on government financial statements, Burris was named president of the National Association of Auditors, Comptrollers and Treasurers.

He was also named vice president of the National Association of State Comptrollers, which increased under his tenure from 10 members to about 48, representing almost all states in the nation.

As state comptroller, Burris was a leader in the fight to establish a comptroller for the federal government, which had never had a real one, and to require a comptroller in every major agency. "Government accountants feel so strongly about me that today I am a trustee member of the Financial Accounting Foundation, which oversees all the accounting standards for industry and government," Burris says proudly.

State's Top Prosecutor

When he won the Attorney General's post in 1990, making him the state's top prosecutor and senior democratic constitutional officer, Burris campaigned on four themes: consumer protection; environmental enforcement; fighting crime and drugs; and advocacy, and adds, "I can report very positive accomplishments in every area."

To combat crime and drugs, legislation was passed that for the first time gave the Attorney General's office its own statewide grand jury to use for indictments in drug prosecutions in the state.

And he hastily assembled a legal team to respond to any legal challenges that might delay the execution of John Wayne Gacy after the Illinois Supreme Court scheduled May 10, 1994 as the murderer's day to die.

His office also instituted a gun turn-in day in Chicago that Burris says amassed 142 guns, the largest number of weapons collected during any such program in the country that offered no cash reward.

"In terms of consumer protection, you name it and we've been on it, from pantyhose to games," Burris says. "We sued mattress companies for false advertising, auto companies for not following regulations, contractors for taking peoples' money and either not doing the work or doing shoddy work.

"On the advocacy side, I promised we would set

up women's and children's advocacy divisions and we have. That was important because violence against women and children is really a big thing. We held hearings and the testimony we got as a result was used to improve the domestic violence statute."

Burris' $28 million, 254-lawyer Attorney General's office has also been aggressive clamping heavy fines on polluters, administering laws regulating charities and charitable fund-raising, enforcing tax laws and recovering monies owed the state.

"We have been able to accomplish all kinds of things in three years in the Attorney General's office, even while facing tough fiscal problems, basically without having any money," Burris says.

> ## If we as a race of people are going to get anything in this society, we're going to have to have lawyers and elected officials that are responsible and responsive.

"But I still had to keep the office moving forward and institute new programs. It was my administrative skills, leadership skills and fiscal knowledge of how finances in Illinois work that did it, because without that knowledge, we would not have been able to do what we were able to do or get done what we had to get done."

Burris smiles contently at his accomplishments as Attorney General and admits that he likes the office. "If my political clock wasn't running out, I'd probably stay here another term," he says. "But I see my skills being needed now at a higher level."

Motivating Factors

In a land where racism either steels a Black man to succeed or beats him down, Roland Burris is partially who he is and primarily what he is because of it. In his downstate hometown of Centralia, where his family lived for four generations, Burris, as a 15-year-old high school sophomore, had an experience in 1953 that changed his life.

A swimming pool had been opened in the town in 1937 that Blacks had never been allowed to swim in. That summer his father, a laborer and businessman, along with the president of the local NAACP, decided to integrate the pool.

Burris' father traveled to Chicago to try to find a lawyer to assist in the effort. No one would come. His dad eventually found an attorney in East St. Louis and paid him a $100 retainer – roughly a month's wages for the senior Burris.

When the day came to integrate, young Burris, his brother and three friends from another family went to the pool, and swam with no incident. His father was dejected, however, because the attorney failed to show up.

"My father said to me that 'if we as a race of people are going to get anything in this society, we're going to have to have lawyers and elected officials that are responsible and responsive,'" Burris recalled.

"That stuck with me. From that incident, I decided I wanted to be a lawyer and a statewide elected official. I figured that statewide was where you could make the decisions that would help my people." From that point on, pursuing those two goals became his destiny.

Burris completed his undergraduate studies as a political science major at Southern Illinois University in Carbondale. That's also where he met Berlean Miller, whom he married in 1961. Their union resulted in two children and now Dr. Berlean Burris is Vice Provost at National Louis University.

After Southern, Roland Burris studied international law at the University of Hamburg in Germany and then earned his law degree from Howard University Law School.

Burris returned to Chicago to join Continental Illinois National Bank in 1964. "At the time, racism was so thick at Continental that you could cut it with a knife," Burris recalls.

Though he was a lawyer and the first Black professional the bank hired, he was stuck in the back room in the Trust Tax Division, where he stapled tax returns together for his first four months while White law students were put into training programs to learn how to administer estates.

Burris says he asked his boss why he was put in the back room while others progressed. His boss could not answer. "Finally, a vice president looked at me very nonchalantly and said, "Roland, I didn't create racism in this society and I as an individual cannot change it. If you're going to make it at this bank, you're going to have to be 10 times better than your White counterpart.'

"He didn't bat an eyelash. I went home and cried with my wife and baby, cried myself to sleep, said my prayers and asked the Lord to give me some guidance and direction. And he did. I woke up the next morning, got the red out of my eyes.

"I didn't go and leave the bank, or picket or throw a brick through the window and get mad. I went down and kicked butts and took names. I became 10 times better. They didn't know I'd turn out to be one of the best tax consultants the bank ever had," Burris says.

In two years, he was teaching all the tax classes and was head consultant on the complicated tax returns, including Harlem Globetrotters founder Abe Saperstein's estate and the disposition of the King Ranch in Texas, one of the largest in the country.

"And I set another goal. I gave the bank five years to make me an officer and after four years and eight

months, they did," he adds.

Burris rose through the ranks to the level of vice president in charge of a division of seven people responsible for minority and government guaranteed loans.

All the while at Continental he kept his fingers in politics and his eyes on his goal of becoming a statewide elected official. Burris' reputation as an achiever with various community and political organizations grew. He made his first run for office as an Illinois State Representative in 1968, but lost.

In Pursuit of "Statewide"

Despite being a banking success, he chucked corporate life to join Dan Walker's Cabinet in 1972. When Independent Walker ran for reelection in 1976, Burris was slated on the Independent ticket for the office of Comptroller. The Independents were wiped out by the regular Democratic contenders, slated by Mayor Richard Daley.

But then the old Daley died, statewide elections were held again in 1978 through ruling of the revised

Illinois Constitution of 1970, and Democratic Party Chief George Dunne opened the candidacies to anybody with credentials.

Burris, who had gone to work as Executive Director of Operation PUSH and directed William Cousins' successful aldermanic campaign in 1977, joined the Regular Democratic Organization through the auspices of then 6th Ward Alderman Eugene Sawyer.

Through the political maneuvering of mainly Sawyer and Alderman Wilson Frost, Burris was slated for Comptroller in 1978, the office he won to make history and fulfill his ambition of attaining statewide office.

There had been skepticism about Burris' ability in that election to capture votes outside of Chicago, but in what has become one of his most remarkable political attributes, he was able to capture as many votes throughout Illinois as his white counterparts.

It's a scenario that has played over and again in his subsequent elections and one that he feels will propel him into the governor's seat this year.

preface
Burroughs

Update: Dr. Margaret Burroughs, who bowled and took up roller-skating in her 80s, passed away in 2010 at the age of 95. Her DuSable Museum of African-American History remains the oldest museum of Black culture in the United States. She said it was "the only one that grew out of the indigenous Black community. We weren't started by anybody downtown; we were started by ordinary folks."

In 2016, The DuSable Museum was granted affiliation status by the Smithsonian Institution in Washington, D.C. The distinction signals the beginning of a long-term collaborative partnership between the DuSable and the world's largest museum and research complex. It is only the second arts, culture and education facility in Chicago to receive Smithsonian Affiliate status; the other is Adler Planetarium.

Dr. Margaret Burroughs

By Alfred L. Woods & Photography by David Jenkins | *Originally Published March 1991*

Dr. Margaret Taylor Goss Burroughs, founder of the nationally recognized DuSable Museum of African American History, wears more titles of distinction, more hats of achievement, and more vivid cloths of community and self-awareness than a park full of people wear in a lifetime.

United States presidents, governors and mayors have all proclaimed her achievements. She has been named International Woman of the Year. Magazines, colleges, universities, and institutions have bestowed honors upon her, including a Doctor of Humane Letters degree from the Art Institute of Chicago, in recognition of her life achievements.

She wears the title of Vice President of the Board of Commissioners of the Chicago Park District. But regardless of what she wears, whether it is a title, position, opinion, or presence, Margaret Taylor Goss Burroughs wears it well.

Margaret went through three decades jumping, dancing, singing, painting, marrying, birthing, divorcing, and marrying again, educating, directing and founding. When asked how she managed to do so much, she simply replied, 'When I got tired of doing one thing I would rest by doing something else.'

Margaret was born in 1917 to Alexander and Octavia Pierre Taylor in St. Rose, Louisiana outside of New Orleans. She was born the same year the first European war was declared. After World War I, southern Blacks seeking jobs in the industrialized north moved to Chicago at an overwhelming rate. Margaret's family joined that move to Chicago in 1922, to a Black community by then of more than 100,000 people.

In June of 1929, Margaret graduated from Carter Elementary School and then Englewood High School in 1933. At the time, unemployment in the United States ballooned to more than 8 million people. This was the Great Depression era. By the time Margaret graduated from high school, she had already experienced world-shattering events socially, racially and economically.

The Activist Artist

Growing up, she was active in the arts, crafts, and recreational activities. She was never an "Ivory Tower" artist – she refers to herself as a community or grassroots artist.

Anchored and active in the community, she shared community concerns. While still in high school, Margaret joined the youth division of the National Association for the Advancement of Colored People (NAACP).

At the time, organizations like the NAACP that spoke out for human rights and an end to segregation were popularly considered subversive and un-American. Several years after joining the NAACP, while she was still in her twenties, the FBI opened a file on Margaret Taylor that it maintained for more than 40 years.

In art, as in life, events or things do not occur one at a time or in any perceived order, and because Margaret is an artist, the canvas of her life is a canvas of simultaneity. While she was working with the NAACP, she was also dancing with her friend, Rosalie Dorsey Davis, at the Abraham Lincoln Center.

During that same year (1933), she sang in the James Mundy Youth Choir of 100 voices at the celebration of Chicago's 100th Anniversary, The Century of Progress Exposition. The Exposition ran for one year and attracted 38 million visitors to the city.

In 1936, Margaret tried out for the Olympics in the high jump event. She missed the qualifying jump by only two inches. Had she qualified, she would have been on the same Olympic team with international track stars Jesse Owens and Ralph Metcalfe. One can only speculate what history would be like if Margaret had gone with them to Germany to face Hitler.

Undaunted by not qualifying, Margaret tried out for a role in Langston Hughes' play, *Do You Want To Be Me?* It played at the Parkway Community Center at 51st and King Drive. It was there as an understudy that she met the author Richard Wright.

About her early childhood and young adult life, Margaret remembers two things distinctly. She remembers her mother losing $2,000 in the Binga

State Bank when it was closed in 1930. And she remembers there was absolutely no space for artists to exist and exhibit.

Margaret had no control over the bank, but felt she could provide an outlet for artists. Thus, appeared "Little Bohemia I" at 45th and King Drive and "Little Bohemia II" at 63rd and Vernon.

In her marriage to Bernard Goss, himself a renowned artist, and after their divorce, Margaret lived in a coach house that she opened to artists. At her parties came artists and writers like Gwendolyn Brooks, Cyrus Colter, Elizabeth Catlett, Eldzier Cortor, Charles Sebree, Robert Davis, Alain Locke, Charles White, Gordon Parks and Langston Hughes.

Great Mother of African-American Consciousness

It was during this period that Margaret finished her formal education and began to teach. In 1945, she first appeared in print in *Time* magazine. In 1947, she published her young readers book *Jasper The Drummin' Boy*.

Her most famous poem, *What Shall I Tell My Children Who Are Black?*, written in 1968, has been translated into African languages, Russian, Chinese, Arabic, and Spanish. Some 3,000 phonograph records

of her reading her poems have been produced.

In the visual arts, she wears the mask of a printmaker, oil painter, sculptress, and pen and ink artist. Her work has been exhibited in galleries, art fairs, exhibitions, colleges and universities in the United States, Mexico, Poland, Germany, and China. She has made more than twenty trips to Africa and traveled on four continents.

Noted musician Phil Cohran says of Margaret, "She is the great mother of African-American consciousness and a great artist; therefore, the medium in which she expresses herself is the appropriate medium for eternal consideration."

Margaret was from working class people and did not seek to know prominent people. The people that she calls her friends are the people from her childhood. They are friendships that span 60 years. But like Margaret, they became prominent.

Margaret entered Chicago Teacher's College as one of two Blacks admitted. After completing course work for her teaching certificate, she did substitute teaching while working towards her Baccalaureate Degree from the Art Institute of Chicago.

In 1946, she began teaching at DuSable High School, where she remained until 1969. While at DuSable, she also taught at Barat and Kennedy-King colleges, practiced her craft as an artist and writer, maintained

her home, and founded and served on the boards of several historically significant arts organizations.

Margaret went through three decades jumping, dancing, singing, painting, marrying, birthing, divorcing, and marrying again, educating, directing and founding. When asked how she managed to do so much, she simply replied, "When I got tired of doing one thing, I would rest by doing something else."

The Founder

Margaret attributes most of her administrative skills to her experience while working with the board of directors at the South Side Community Art Center (SSCAC), which she and other artists helped start.

The SSCAC was a program of the Works Progress Administration (WPA), an agency of the U.S. government created in 1935 to provide useful public work for America's unemployed. In its eight years of operation, it employed 8.5 million people at a total cost of $11 billion.

The WPA's art project paid artists to produce paintings, drawings, sculpture, and more than 2,500 murals and it created eight community centers. The South Side Community Art Center at 3831 South Michigan Avenue was one of the eight and today, it is uniquely the only surviving art center created by the WPA.

Over the years, the mission of the Center has been focused on the African-American artist. Margaret was the first recording secretary and before she left the board, she would have served in every capacity including chairman.

In 1952, while she was employed by the Board of Education, "someone" called the Board of Education and accused Margaret of being a communist.

It was at the height of McCarthyism, that period in the history of the United States when U.S. Senator Joseph McCarthy launched an anti-communist reign of terror campaign that lasted from 1950-'54.

The Board of Education called Margaret in for questioning. She denied being a Communist, saying she was opposed to the ideas that would keep one group under another for the profit and exploitation of the ruling group.

The Board of Education suggested that she take a sabbatical. She went to Mexico for one year to study with Leopoldo Mendez, then returned and resumed teaching at DuSable High School.

Margaret started the Lake Meadows Art Fair in 1959 and the Chatham Art Fair in 1964. She was a member of the local and state committees that later became the Chicago Office of Fine Arts and the Illinois Arts Council. In 1990, she was instrumental in inaugurating the art gallery at the South Shore Cultural Center. She even served as art director and columnist for the *New Crusader,* a community newspaper, in 1960.

Margaret attributes the idea for the DuSable Museum to her association with the *New Crusader,* but the germ of the idea might have been planted as far back as 1938 when she was a guide at the Negro Exposition. In that Exposition were exhibits on the local Black community, and dioramas depicting historical achievements of the African American in education, music, art, and literature.

Committee meetings to found the DuSable Museum were conducted in the kitchen of Margaret's greystone mansion. The museum opened in 1961 in three rooms on the first floor of the Burroughs home.

The staff consisted of six volunteers and Charles Burroughs was one of them. The furnishings were given to them by libraries, other institutions, and individuals. The library was housed in a pantry.

In 1967, with a grant from the National Endowment for the Arts, Dr. Burroughs interned at the Field Museum of Natural History. In 1972, the DuSable Museum of African-American History moved to its present location in Washington Park at 740 East 56th Place.

Margaret's Multiple Faces

After 40 years of looking at the many faces of Margaret Burroughs, the FBI closed its file on her. After 40 years of looking for the face of a subversive character conducting un-American activities, they saw the face of an organizer with vision.

They saw the face of resilience and fortitude. They saw creativity and determination. It is a face of confidence and independence. They saw an African-American woman investing not in just tomorrow for her own children who are Black, but a woman investing in generations of the world's children.

Through her writings, art works, teachings, the organizations she has founded, Margaret has influenced millions around the globe. The economic impact of what she has created is still to be evaluated.

In 1933, Margaret, the visionary, wrote the conclusion to this article when she wrote in her yearbook, "I would like for the world to be a better place to live because I have been here." That is the face of commitment.

preface Butler

Update: : Jerry Butler has remained a Cook County Board Commissioner since his first term in 1985 and always wins re-election by overwhelming margins. As a singer, the Ice Man has recorded more than 50 albums in his career and was inducted into the Rock and Roll Hall of Fame in 1991 as a member of the Impressions.

Jerry Butler

By Derrick K. Baker & Photography by John Beckett | *Originally Published January 1993*

To call Jerry Butler, he of the eight gold records, a cool Cook County Commissioner wouldn't be a misstatement. Nor would it be an egregious error to dub him a thinking man's man or political bridge-builder.

Interestingly enough, Butler does admit to trying "not to be easily excited," but he can be either as calm as a comatose hospital patient or as gregarious as a five-year-old in a candy store.

As a matter of fact, contrary to his "Ice Man" nickname, Butler is animated and frequently answers questions with an infectious guttural guffaw. He's prone to using his hands to make a point, often using them more than a frisky 16-year-old boy on his first real date.

At the same time, Butler says he's at peace with himself, with a successful political career still spiraling towards its zenith and the recent release of his latest album *Time & Faith*.

> **Entering the political arena was a natural transition for me. I had the one thing politicians would die for, and that was name recognition.**

The legendary singer, who has one of the most distinctive voices in music, began his career in 1958 when he and Curtis Mayfield formed a group in Chicago called the Roosters, later known as the Impressions. He says that all things considered, he's satisfied with the way his life has panned out. Which is to say that Butler, who still performs around the country, has accomplished much and isn't finished… not just yet.

The Content Butler

"I probably could say that I'm happy to be able to do both of these things at the same time," he explains. "To be able to be a performer and provide what I feel as a political person is a service to the community."

When he says, "My long marriage to my wife Annette (who is one of his backup singers when he performs) is still working," a smile creases Butler's face. He explains, "In the entertainment area, that's a difficult thing to do. My kids are both grown (he has twin sons) and they're off doing their own thing.

"As far as music, I am still fairly active because county commissioner is a part-time position by law, so on Fridays, Saturdays, and Sundays I get the opportunity to steal away someplace and perform." Because Butler rarely does extended engagements these days, like some sort of singing Superman, he's back behind his desk Monday morning.

If politics and music are mutually exclusive, then how has Butler been able to mix the two? What would his critics and supporters say about that unusual combination?

"From a political point of view, if there was going to be a criticism, it might be that I'm not visible or active enough. The best thing they might say is that I work real hard at what I do, trying to understand the issues and what the questions are and how my constituents would want me to vote relative to those issues," he says.

"From a musical point of view, I guess the best thing they could say is that, 'we still enjoy going to see him and he always gives us a good show.'" And in an exhibition of self-deprecating humor that often isn't synonymous with entertainers, Butler laughingly adds, "Probably the worst thing that could be said is that, "he has not given us a hit record in about 10 years."

Is *Time & Faith*, his most recent release, going to break that dry spell? Why record another album instead of concentrating on surviving Chicago's predatory political arena?

"Because old singers never die," Butler rues. "They just look for the next hit record. You always think you can just walk back into the studio and make this music." And although he's proud of the new album, Butler raises questions about its marketability.

"The problem I have with the album is I'm not sure who wants to play it," he says candidly. "It's not a blues album. It's not a rhythm and blues album. It's not a hip hop album. It's not a jazz album. It is a Jerry Butler album of songs that Jerry thought were the kind of songs that he would have written if he had time to write them."

Realistically, Butler has a little difficulty defining his audience, for whether it's *Ain't Understanding Mellow, Never Gonna Give You Up, Western Union Man,* or *Only The Strong Survive*, his classics can still be found in more than a few and varied record collections.

And he does marvel at the longevity of his career. "When I started recording in 1958, a record company usually signed an act to a three- or five-year contract and that was supposed to be the extent of your marketability," he explains.

"There were a bunch of artists who never made it to the three or five years. They had one hit record and no one ever heard of them again. I could have easily been one of them, and oftentimes I wonder, why wasn't I? What did I do to sustain me past that one hit?"

Butler answers his own question: "I'm fortunate to have been the writer of the songs that I've had the most success with. I've been fortunate to sing songs that were not caught up in the heat of the moment. They were not songs that were just going to be relevant in a particular time frame."

For example, Butler recalls a man who told him his song *Only The Strong Survive* helped him and his buddies through the Vietnam War. And "people tell me about *For Your Precious Love*," he says. "They say, 'I got married to this song.'"

On Today's Music

Noting that musicians, songwriters and poets have a tendency to reflect society, Butler says, "What I see in the music today is a reflection of how loose our society has become in terms of its moral fiber. I remember when Hank Ballard recorded a song called *Annie Had A Baby, She Can't Work No More* and it was X-rated. Today, the lyrics are so explicit and the videos are even more explicit than the lyrics.

"The music has become so physical, so from the waist down. When we were singing love songs it was about the heart. 'I love you, I love you.' But now the lyrics are, 'I want to hump you.' It's not left up to the imagination. It's all so blatant and upfront and in your face."

Back in the late '50s, not long after Butler started performing solo, George Woods, a Philadelphia disc jockey, gave him the "Ice Man" nickname. Woods took it upon himself to coin nicknames for everyone who performed at the renowned Uptown Theater in Philly.

Butler recalls, "One day George said, 'This guy is so cool, we're going to call him the Ice Man,' and it stuck. Part of the reason I got the nickname was because Jackie Wilson and James Brown were very exciting dancers and I was trying to be a modern-day version of Nat King Cole. I wanted to stand there and sing love songs. I wanted to do it with so much style and so much class that I didn't have to do all this other stuff to make it palatable."

So well known is Butler's nickname that he included it on the ballot back in 1985 when he ran for a slot as a Cook County Commissioner. He even owns the trademark for the moniker, which he uses in the name of his publishing company, Ice Man Music. The nickname also was part of his beverage distribution firm, which several years ago ceased operations.

The Political Butler

Butler was sort of goaded into making his foray into Chicago politics. A conversation back in the mid-'80s with his former beverage distributing partner about local politics was the catalyst for the singer to turn to politics. Rather than complain about the state of local politics and politicians, his partner contended, "Why not run yourself and do something about it?"

Prior to running for a seat as a Cook County Commissioner, Butler says he never considered politics, although, "I always found myself involved with people and causes, usually in a lead role," he says.

Like other popular Black entertainers during the civil rights movement of the '60s, Butler often used his influence and fan support to champion the push for equal rights for Black America.

"It was the entertainers who were always raising the money to make it possible for Martin Luther King Jr. to speak or to send the Freedom Riders to different places," recalls Butler. "It was the entertainers who were called when the Black politicians – and white politicians, too – wanted to get a good group of Black citizens to come and hear what they had to talk about.

"So," Butler adds, "entering the political arena was a natural transition for me. And what I found out after getting involved was that I had the one thing politicians would die for, and that was name recognition.

"People knew Jerry Butler, had known him for 25 or 30 years, had grown up listening to his music. I had been fortunate enough to keep a fairly respectable name. And so when my name came up as running for a seat on the Cook County Board, I, myself, was surprised at the number of people who came out in support of that proposition."

The Philosophically Honest Butler

Butler's segue from music to politics begs the question, "What do the two fields have in common?" As usual, he answers as forthrightly as a man under hypnosis.

"There is this ego thing. There's a certain vanity, certain arrogance," he says. "I would venture to say that sometimes it's probably more prevalent in the political arena than it is in the entertainment arena. Entertainers have bodyguards around them basically because they don't really know how to deal with fans and stardom. Politicians, on the other hand, kind of want that to help them look important."

So, what's the difference between politics and music? "The entertainment piece deals with making folks feel happy for the moment, like a good Chinese meal. But in politics, you don't get that instant gratification," he explains.

For example, while campaigning for his first election to the county board, Butler pledged to work for single-member districts to replace at-large races in county board elections. And although his dream was realized, it won't take effect until the next election.

"That's eight years since I first said I'd vote for single-member districts until it becomes a reality. Politics is long and drawn out," says Butler, who chairs the Cook County Board's Health and Hospitals Committee.

Political Butler, musical Butler, entrepreneurial Butler. Here's what jovial Jerry Butler believes people will say about him after he is gone: "He had a great sense of humor and loved to laugh. He got a thrill out of being able to help people."

In the end, whether it's politics or music, or business or social consciousness, one thing remains for sure: The Butler did it.

preface Cage

Update: Founded in 1977, Cage Memorial Funeral Home has provided sterling funeral, memorial and cremation services with distinction from the South Shore community for 40 years.

Augustus Cage

By David Smallwood & Photography by Warren Browne | *Originally Published October 2, 1997*

s it conceivable that Black funeral parlors could ever go out of existence? After all, they would seem to have a continuous source of business, as well as a captive clientele, within our community.

Historically, Black morticians burying dead Black people has been a surer combination than red beans and rice. The overwhelming majority of all African Americans who ever lived have been buried by somebody who was Black. That's been about as certain as death itself.

But now a threat looms against the Black funeral home industry which could shake that certainty to the core and send Black funeral homes the way of Black-owned hotels and the dinosaur – into extinction.

The threat comes from several large, White-owned conglomerates that are reshaping the $7 billion-a-year death industry by snapping up ownership of previously independent funeral homes and cemeteries to create chain operations on the level of a McDonald's or Domino's. The leading conglomerates each own several thousand funeral homes and cemeteries.

> **Because of the nature of what we do, it makes it a very special, unique, almost sacred position that we hold in the community. We embrace Christian doctrine and it's our belief and faith that's at the very core of how we do what we do.**

These large White firms have recently begun encroaching on the African-American consumer market, "in recognition that we represent some economic substance," says Augustus Cage, owner of Cage Memorial Funeral Home at 76th and Jeffrey on the South Side of Chicago.

The conglomerates have started to move into Chicago's Black market. Initially, they have passively tried to acquire Black funeral homes – apparently to judge the level of interest in this approach – but at this point, they've been met with staunch resistance.

Spencer Leak Jr., of Leak & Sons Funeral Homes based at 79th and Cottage Grove, acknowledged that his family has been approached with multi-million dollar offers by the White chains. The business was founded 85 years ago and it has since become one of Chicago's oldest and largest Black funeral operations, conducting more than 1,000 services a year.

"We would never consider it. I would rather drive by 7838 South Cottage Grove (where Leak is located) and see the place bordered up than sell it to a White-owned conglomerate. That will never happen," Leak Jr. said. Cage, who also admits to having been approached, concurred with Leak's sentiment.

"Not everything is for sale," Cage said. "You can't buy a person's legacy, or character, or their blood, sweat and tears of history. You can sell your name for the right price, I guess, but in this case, if funeral directors are considering it, selling their name is about the same as selling their souls."

Cage warned that over time, with their aggressive marketing practices, the conglomerates could "slowly induce individuals and families into pre-arranged contracts, which are as binding as sharks' jaws in many instances, so they'll have the (Black) market locked up from that standpoint and the individual Black funeral home operator will die on the vine."

Affecting the Black Economy

That means, he continued, that an important segment of the African-American economy could be in danger.

"The Black church and the Black funeral business are the two areas in the Black community that remain independent, unencumbered and unattached to the White mainstream," Cage said. "The funeral businesses started from meager beginnings, but have developed to the point that they are not only viable, but considered stalwarts in the Black economic scheme of things."

The issue is that independent minority ownership of the funeral businesses brings about re-investment in the local economy. Being indigenous to the local community, they invest in the community. It may be difficult to find African Americans who make Cadillac limousines for hearses, but there are Black distributors, mechanics, and gas stations for the funeral home operators to patronize.

They have to go to the majority community for some things, but still find African Americans who produce caskets, chemicals, services, and they use local Black banks. In a Black community that has been built on local business enterprise, any erosion that occurs that hurts one part of the community ultimately hurts all the community. So they see any threat to their survival as independent Black funeral home directors as one that hurts everybody.

The one saving grace Chicago's Black funeral operators cling to is the bond between them and the Black community. "It's been pretty loyal both ways, and that's our advantage," said Leak. "We feel the families' needs, we see their needs, just a little bit more and we can give the kind of service that White conglomerates never could. If there's a problem, the family talks to the owners – me and my family in the office right next door. They don't talk to a regional manager. I think that giving the best possible service is what's going to sustain us."

Life After Life

"We make a difference with people at important times in their lives," Cage agreed. "Things you do for them, the way you do those things, can have a significant consequence in how they are able to get on with their lives after the loss of a loved one. At Cage Memorial, we call it the Life After Life concept," he explained.

"The rite of passage we call a funeral, acknowledging that a person has made a transition from a physical realm to a non-physical one, ought to be celebrated because it allows people to come together and bind each other up emotionally, to reflect in a memorable way, to pay tribute. It enables people to get on with their lives and what we call a 'good grief recovery.'"

Cage Memorial offers a Visitation Reception Room, which provides the traditional catered reception that it might be too difficult for the bereaved family to have at home.

"It really helps. The family appreciates the support and the coming together of friends and relatives they haven't seen in years," Cage said. "It allows them time in a prescribed setting to vent their grief, to have tears of sorrow and laughter, and to ultimately recognize that what has happened is not necessarily a bad thing. It hurts because there's a wound, but a wound properly treated not only heals, but closure comes together even stronger."

Cage embraces the spirituality of the business that he's in and calls it a type of ministry in terms of dealing with people who may be "churched," but may still be a little weak or shaky in terms of a real spiritual foundation. He added that it takes something spiritual for funeral home operators to be part of it all.

A Unique, Sacred Position

"If people pursued this profession just for dollars, they wouldn't be able to stay," Cage mused. "There aren't enough dollars to pay us to day-in, day-out, deal with the drudgery of people's grief and the ugly manifestations of physical death. Yet, we are charged with the responsibility of restoring and presenting back to the family a pleasing last memorable picture.

"Because of the nature of what we do, it makes it a very special, unique, almost sacred position that we hold in the community. We embrace Christian doctrine and it's our belief and faith that's at the very core of how we do what we do.

"If we were not grounded spiritually, it would be very hard to pass on in a compassionate, sincere way to someone who's just lost a child, a spouse, a sibling, a parent, that weeping may endure for a night, but joy cometh in the morning."

Cage entered the funeral business after a successful career as a Chicago banker. His parlor averages about 350 funerals a year – sells about the same number of pre-packaged funerals – and his clientele tends toward the more middle-and upper-class segments of the community.

Making A Life's Difference

Cage founded his business, he said, because his grandparents and aunt and uncle had little parlors, doing maybe two funerals a week. "But they were such remarkably nice people and so well thought of. They provided a sensitive and caring service and the community held them in such high regard," Cage recalled.

"I was smitten and got into the business because everybody, at some point, would like to feel they contribute something to their fellow man, that your living hasn't been in vain and that in some ways, you've made a difference."

While Cage expressed concern about the inroads White firms are attempting to make in his industry, he acknowledged that up to 95 percent of Black people are still buried by Black funeral home directors and most still want to be. That's partly because of the racial conditions they faced while here on Earth.

"Deep down, all of us recognize that no matter how far in the socio-economic strata we've risen, at the very core of us, we have flashbacks and deja vu of all the hits and knocks and slings we took – be it in school, the military, the business sector, wherever – as we were getting in and moving along.

"So when it comes time for final rites, it's an intrinsic motivator to seek out those who we feel would

have more empathy and understanding of what we need," Cage said.

"Besides," he noted, "the White conglomerates only want a certain segment of our business. They don't want to deal with the clientele in the projects; they just want the Pill Hill, Jackson Highlands, Hyde Park and Lake Meadows folks – the more affluent, upscale and better educated – and they'll leave the rest for the Black funeral director, who is

obligated to take all types of situations – and who does so with pride and honor."

Cage concluded, "All we're saying is that Black consumers should take caution before buying any funeral-related products or services before talking to their funeral director. The consumer needs to know what the differences are from a pricing standpoint, so shop around, ask a lot of questions, price compare... in short, just let the buyer beware."

preface Cave

Update: Cave's work has traveled the world and been featured in *Vogue* Magazine. Some of his soundsuits now sell for six-figures. Cave became the first recipient of a professorship chair at The School of The Art Institute in 2016.

Nick Cave

By Barbara Samuels & Photography by Chris Griffin | *Originally Published June 8, 2006*

To simply describe Chicago-based genius Nick Cave as "an internationally-acclaimed, multi-dimensional artist and teacher" is to lift the term "gross understatement" to new heights.

Nick Cave possesses an artistic stream that flows through his body like hot lava. His creativity and ingenuity have garnered accolades from prestigious museums from around the world.

According to art activist Greg Cameron, Associate Director of Chicago's Museum of Contemporary Art, "Cave is attentive to process, and uses common materials. He also paints, draws, sews, constructs, designs, prints, sculpts, performs, photographs, and films. He is a Renaissance artist working in the 21st Century; he gives pleasure to our senses while nourishing our souls."

The Famous Soundsuits

The artistry of Nick Cave is on display at the Chicago Cultural Center in an incredible exhibit called *Nick Cave: Soundsuits*.

Thirty of his creations symbolize the pain and glory of being a Black male in America, and many of them depict aspects of his life from boyhood to the present. Cave constructed his first soundsuit in response to the Rodney King beating.

> **I don't set out to create masterpieces. Being fearless is the fuel that keeps me going. Being a Black American male is my major resource.**

The soundsuits encompass family collectibles, flashy fabrications, and "found" items that reflect religion, racism, and remnants of nature.

Visitors to the exhibit are greeted by the sight of two massive wall hangings that are almost hypnotic in their beauty. Each one measures approximately 18 feet in diameter, and each carries its own message.

One consists of astral pieces on a black background; the other is almost blindingly bright. The contrast between the two is mesmerizing. A pair of video presentations shows Cave at work and in performance. Upon entry into the main section of the gallery where the suits are mounted, you won't believe your eyes or the direction your mind will take while viewing the collection.

What do the soundsuits represent? Observers see myriad expressions of race, gender, sexuality, oppression and the freedom of mind, body, and spirit. Some find the suits confusing at first, but they eventually "get it." Everyone is immediately struck by their unique beauty and incredible workmanship.

Cave, who has a master's degree in textile design, crafts his soundsuits of deconstructed vintage apparel, twigs, bottle caps, corks, lint, mirrors, sequins, wood, and anything else he finds on his material-gathering forays. Many of the suits are layered, and several natural and creative elements are at play.

This exhibit is all about a stunning array of textures that combine to create a multi-dimensional effect. Remarkably, many of the soundsuits were crafted this year in anticipation of Cave's show at the Jack Shainman Gallery in New York City later this year.

Says Cave, "My art reaches a level of consciousness that exceeds the norm. I want observers to come face-to-face with their inner selves. I want people to sense an aura of commitment, desire, and passion while experiencing a connection to something extraordinary."

Walking His Journey

Cave is deeply spiritual. Every day when he wakes up, he thanks God for his life and the profound pleasure of being surrounded by art of all sorts, and also the gift of expressing his unique creativity. He feels that on one's pathway in life, in spite of obstacles, one must stand in his or her own light or glory and make a difference.

"We all walk on our own journey, and we all go to the other side alone," he believes.

Cave finds himself spending more time in preparation for the personal, emotionally draining process he goes through when creating yet another masterpiece.

"I don't set out to create masterpieces," he says. "Being fearless is the fuel that keeps me going. Being a Black American male is my major resource. I can secure myself, as opposed to being anchored. If my work can inspire a positive change in someone, then

I've reached my goal on that piece."

Cave can be extremely gregarious, but he can jump back into his private space in a nanosecond. That's when he can shut out all of the noise, the conversations, the music, or any other distraction on the premises, making one wonder what goes through his mind during those times.

In addition to being attracted to Cave's art, people are also attracted to the physical being of the man. Cave is handsome, and he possesses a body build that's honed by his private gym, his diet, and the discipline he achieved as a dancer with the Alvin Ailey dance troupe. He has a piercing gaze, and he doesn't miss a thing.

Family Ties

Cave credits his family – especially his mother, Sharron Kelly, for instilling her values to her six sons. "We never had any conflicts. We weren't judged, and we were given the privilege of finding ourselves and knowing we were loved unconditionally, regardless of our choices in life," Cave says.

"My mother worked hard to better our situation, and she sacrificed her own dreams in order for her children to achieve theirs. She still gives us that same level of support. I am very close to my brothers; we're all different, and it doesn't matter."

He remembers a particular incident that symbolizes his mother's ingenuity. Says Cave, "We never had to struggle – that we knew of, anyway. In spite of the fact that my mother also fed a neighboring family, I never thought we were poor.

"One day my mother came in and announced that we were going to have a popcorn party. We ate popcorn and had fun, not realizing there was no other food in the house."

Cave admits that he would drop everything immediately, no matter what he was involved in, to race to his family's rescue. His family is extremely close and supportive of each other's efforts.

Nick Cave is a firm believer in "giving back" to, and investing in, the Chicago art community. In addition to his artistic endeavors, Cave is the Chair of the Fashion Design Department at the prestigious School of the Art Institute. He also is a patron and mentor to several artists of Gallery 37, as well as talented "starving artists."

preface Clark

Update: Frank Clark maintains a very full schedule in the philanthropic and for-profit worlds. He is President of the Chicago Board of Education, Chairman of the Board of BMO Financial Corporation, and sits on the boards of Aetna, Waste Management, and boards that provide grants for the arts, social services, and education in the greater Chicago area.

He is heavily involved with the DuSable Museum, the Museum of Science and Industry, and Metropolitan Family Services, and he co-founded the Rowe-Clark Math & Science Academy, a charter school on the West Side, along with John Rowe.

Frank Clark

By Monica DeLeon & David Smallwood & Photography by Victor Powell | *Originally Published May 16, 2002*

n an age when such loyalty and long-term commitment to a single company is almost unheard of, Frank Clark stayed with the power utility Commonwealth Edison Company for 46 years. From his position working in the mailroom when he was hired in 1966 to heading up the whole joint by the time he retired in 2012, Clark became ComEd's first Black president in 2001 and CEO in 2005 and remained in those positions until his departure.

ComEd is Illinois' largest utility. The Exelon company delivers electricity to 3.8 million customers over 11,400 square miles, has over 6,700 employees and annual revenues totaling more than $15 billion.

On his climb from the bottom to the top of ComEd, as he shattered glass ceilings, Clark held positions in a variety of departments, including Information Technology, Communications, Human Resources, Labor Relations, Distribution Services, Customer Service, Marketing, Sales, Regulatory and Community Affairs.

> I will do everything I can to support African-American leaders and African-American businesses because we don't have enough of them. And we don't have enough success stories in our community for people to look up to.

He held the position of executive vice president before being hired as president of ComEd and became a civic stalwart in Chicago during his nearly half-century of impressive service to the company.

He's got quite an impressive vitae for someone who was just a regular guy trying to make ends meet starting out.

"I worked at a Catholic bookstore – Thomas Moore Bookstore – when I finished Hirsch High School in 1963. I was an avid reader and you could not have pulled me away from that place, I was so happy there. Working there was ideal for me, until I got married," Clark begins with a chuckle.

Vera and Frank had been sweethearts since the sixth grade before getting married in 1965. "My wife felt that there was no future at the bookstore,"

Clark continued. "It was a small company, but they made me a supervisor and I had three or four people working for me, so I was in second heaven.

"But she was right. Like many young spouses, Vera was very persuasive and insisted I go look for a better job. Reluctantly I did. Turns out I had a friend who worked at ComEd who told me they were hiring. But the only job they would hire me for at ComEd, even though I had two years of college, was in the mailroom.

"I was at Loop College at the time and went back and told my wife I wasn't going to take that job; I didn't want to work in a mailroom because I was supervisor at my other job and thought it was below me.

"She only asked one question: 'How much does it pay?' Well, the mailroom paid $80 more, so that was it! I dug in for a little while, but let me put this in a delicate way – I was newly married, very young, and women have immense capabilities in getting your attention. I reported to work two weeks later…and was happy to show up! I've only had two jobs in my life – that book store and ComEd."

Not A Lot Of Options

Clark said that back then, at his ComEd beginning, "there were two-three other Black guys and myself, but everyone else in the mailroom was White, including all the leadership. In the rest of the company at the time, there may have been two Black guys who had managing positions of any note.

"This was 1966; the only other job options for Black folks then were the post office, the military, and Chicago public schools for Black middle-class opportunities. That was it. Utilities weren't hiring that many of us at the time."

Even making more money, Clark still wasn't the happiest camper at the time. "In the mailroom back then, there was no technology. You literally pushed a cart to get bags of mail," he says. "In 1966, ComEd was located at Clark and Adams, and I pushed a cart from the nearby post office to ComEd's mail room. I hated it.

"I had to be there by 5:45 a.m., and I am not an early riser by nature, so that was brutal. Plus, I was terrified that I'd run into somebody from my alma mater, Hirsch High School, while I was pushing this wooden cart. It just didn't seem very glamorous. When I ran into friends while at work, I was embarrassed to confess that I worked in a mail room," Clark confides.

But he says his mother's teaching kicked in. Clark was encouraged by his mother early on in life to achieve challenging goals. One of eight children, he was raised by a single mother who while putting herself through school as an adult, instilled in her children the belief that they could accomplish anything they set out to do.

"My mother didn't believe in obstacles; she saw them as something to pass through, not something that should stop you from being and achieving your best," Clark says. "So not liking my job in the mail room had nothing to do with it, according to my mother's philosophy. To her, if this was how you earned your living, then do it well. And also, do it with sort of a joyous heart, because this is your income.

"So, I did. I was a very good mail carrier and got to meet some executives here who saw my positive attitude and they tended to look favorably on me."

Clark's position as mail clerk ended up being a very helpful step in his path to higher future positions in the company, as it taught him about the ComEd's resources and the job opportunities that existed within. And another corresponding life experience shaped him in another way.

"I worked in the mail room for a year before I got drafted to serve in the military in 1967, and I spent two chilling years of duty," Clark continued. "I was shipped overseas and you get into some really horrible situations and you begin to appreciate things in a different way."

Diligent Application

When he got out of the service, Clark's job at ComEd was protected. "The manager of the treasury department at the company was especially respectful of veterans. He paid attention to me and transferred me to a higher clerical job," Clark says.

"When I came back, I diligently applied myself. I spent seven years working non-professional jobs while attending classes at night at DePaul University. I earned a Bachelor's degree in business, and went on to earn a law degree at DePaul Law School," Clark explains as he thoughtfully remembers his sinewy career path.

Clark received his law degree in 1976 when he was 31, but thought more about pursuing opportunities related to his studies of business than about a career as a lawyer. He didn't have specific ambitions with respect to a career in law, but the General Counsel of ComEd insisted that he take the bar exam, and Clark recalls the counsel testing him to see if he would pass.

"I had a very good memory and passed," Clark says with a shrug. "I passed the bar and at the time, it made me the only Black attorney at ComEd."

After that, he worked in the Commerce Division, and became even more noticed – people took an interest in him, and he was given weightier assignments. At the time, ComEd had six divisions – two in the city, and four outside of Chicago. Clark was given commercial responsibility of the Western Division, the largest one outside the city.

Next he was called to do governmental regulatory work, to negotiate issues in Springfield proposed by the Illinois Commerce Committee. Through his work, Clark managed to raise electricity costs for residents in order to cover the high rates required to run nuclear plants from which consumers benefited as an energy source.

"Utilities thrive off ratemaking and we had an awfully good track record under me. That brought revenues into the company and they liked that, so I got a lot of other opportunities to head up different areas," Clark explains.

"What happened is that people increasingly couldn't deny that I had a certain set of skill sets and more than anything else, I got things done that were complicated."

The Corporate Minority

There were few minorities in all of the management positions in the company at the time; Clark says there were no minority executives and not many women either at ComEd until the 1970s.

In October of 2001, ComEd hired Clark, at the age of 54, as the first Black president in the company's history. To that he says, "What I have seen over my time here is a conscious and progressive effort by a team of executives, including Tom Ayers, James O'Connor, and most recently John Rowe, to build diversity as a part of the company's business goal.

"And they mean it; it's remarkable," Clark continues. "Most companies don't have space for minorities. There aren't many opportunities for minorities, and it's hard for anyone to get to these (high-level management) jobs.

"But you also have to be careful to remember that minority or not, you're valued by the company for your contribution that allows for the company's profitability, and for work that ensures an increase for shareholders."

Clark became senior vice president of corporate and governmental affairs in the 1990s before moving on to become ComEd's executive vice president in 1998 when Jim O'Connor left. John Rowe, brought in to replace O'Connor, selected Clark and others as his "first team," a senior team to help manage the company's affairs.

"I am pleased to have been John Rowe's top lieutenant and to be the one he turned to for information and recommendations. It was because of his confidence in me and my performance that I was

selected to become president of ComEd," Clark says with an air of modesty.

"When I took over as president, I forget what our earnings were, but they were in the single digits and very low. There were a lot of issues in the utility world then, but I was able to take those earnings and get them up to levels that were at least equal to or superior to most of the industry. Success makes people feel good about you."

The Next Chapter

Leaving ComEd was bittersweet, as Clark noted of his last days with the company. "You see right away that life goes on, the sun comes up, decisions get made good, bad, or otherwise, and things go on — without you," he said.

"That helps you deal with the reality of it. It also helps to have things that you like to do that you can continue doing. And I'm very fortunate in that

regard. I did not retire to do nothing. I'm not that kind of person."

Outside of family and friends, Clark's top priorities are his work in education and with social service agencies. "Education is what brought me from the mail room to the boardroom and the city's social service resources have helped me," he says.

Possibly because of the support and guidance that he received from loved ones and mentors alike, Clark also puts a large effort into human development, and works hard to help others reach their personal best and achieve their goals.

Clark is also very involved in the lives of his two sons, Frank, "who is a carbon copy of his dad," Clark describes; and Steve, who is like his mother, Clark's wife Vera.

Vera Clark has been instrumental in encouraging Frank Clark to achieve his own personal best. As he puts it: "If it weren't for her persistence and goal to make my life better, I wouldn't be where I am today."

preface Cochran and Montgomery

Update: Attorney Johnnie Cochran, who represented such Black notables as Michael Jackson, Sean "Puffy" Combs, Jim Brown, Tupac Shakur, Todd Bridges, Riddick Bowe, Marion Jones and Snoop Dogg, in addition to O.J. Simpson in his career, passed away in 2005 at the age of 67. After his passing, Cochran, Cherry, Givens, Smith and Montgomery evolved into The Cochran Firm, which handles civil plaintiff and criminal defense work in 15 states.

Attorney James Montgomery remains managing partner of James D. Montgomery & Associates, one of the nation's top personal injury and civil rights law firms. In 2013, Attorney Montgomery was inducted into the Trial Lawyer Hall of Fame, and he serves as a board trustee for the University of Illinois.

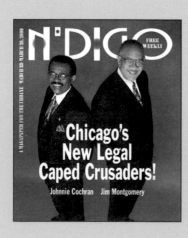

Cochran and Montgomery

By Derrick K. Baker & Photography By Reginald Payton | *Originally Published March 22, 2000*

As the immaculate white stretch limousine slowly pulled up on Franklin Street and in front of Sears Tower, more than a few passersby slowed their swift lunchtime pace and craned their necks to catch a glimpse of who would be so important to require travel in such a vehicular behemoth.

Seconds later, the stern-faced driver pulled open the curbside door and out came a tall, dignified man with the confident countenance of a professional's professional, but with an expression that concurrently said, "I'm enjoying myself immensely" to all who looked into his fatherly face.

Next emerged his traveling companion, a man with an internationally familiar face. A sartorially splendid man with a thick mustache and equally thick sense of self and freedom. And as they stood together, waiting to be led to a private gathering inside the Tower, passersby now stopped dead in their tracks. Many flashed toothy smiles and inconspicuously glanced; others flat out gawked and several more tried in vain to look without actually looking.

> **"You could not go any place in the world and find two attorneys who have tried more police abuse cases than me and Jim.**   — Johnnie Cochran

The impressive sight? Famed attorneys, old friends, and new partners Johnnie Cochran and Jim Montgomery, Chicago's newest and community-conscious law partners who were making a splash on a concrete street this brisk March day, and making friends out of strangers and the curious alike.

The New Firm

Now professional partners after first meeting socially several years ago as a result of their affiliations with the prestigious International Academy of Trial Lawyers, Cochran and Montgomery were on a mission in the Windy City to spread the word that they've joined their substantial forces and resources to form the law practice known as Cochran, Cherry, Givens, Smith and Montgomery. The other principals are Samuel A. Cherry Jr., J. Keith Givens and Jock M. Smith.

The firm, located at 111 West Washington Street, specializes in personal injury, medical malpractice, airplane crashes, wrongful death, and product liability cases.

Equally far reaching is the undeniable fact that the firm represents a symbolic renaissance, so to speak, of top-flight legal representation, power, and influence in the African-American community. With sister offices in Atlanta, New York, Washington, D.C., Montgomery, Alabama, and Los Angeles, the Cochran, Cherry, Givens, Smith and Montgomery firm is an integral part of the largest personal injury law practice in the country.

On this brisk March day, Chicago was forced to stand up and take notice of, as Cochran phrased it, the arrival of the "caped crusaders." In other words, Cochran and Montgomery can rightfully boast of practicing law, franchising the disenfranchised, and speaking for the voiceless for more than 80 collective years between them.

With their "arrival" in Chicago, Cochran and Montgomery instantly became the city's most talked-about attorneys for what their union represents to their colleagues, Chicago's legal community, and current and potential clients. The partnership represents the culmination of discussions Cochran and Montgomery began in April last year, as Cochran was interested in coming to Chicago, and Montgomery already was a veritable giant in a city of giants.

To make matters better, both men understand well that the absence of tort reform in Cook County means plaintiffs can collect a full measure of punitive and compensatory damages in personal injury cases filed here. The new firm accepts cases on a contingency fee basis.

As a matter of fact, it might just be kismet that the two now are partners, given their separate yet corresponding roles in two high profile cases that speaks volumes about their lifelong commitment to justice and to the Black community.

To wit, both men made names and reputations for themselves by representing members of the Black Panther Party – Montgomery as lead counsel in the 18-month civil rights trial involving the December 1969 murders of Illinois Black Panther Party leaders

Montgomery

Fred Hampton and Mark Clark; and Cochran as counsel and confidante to Elmer "Geronimo" Pratt, who was freed 27 years after being incarcerated on murder charges (a judge ruled Pratt didn't receive a fair trial).

Furthermore, a combination of providence and tragedy has brought the two attorneys to the limelight in Chicago, as even before they agreed to partner, Cochran took on representation of the family of Robert Russ – the unarmed Northwestern University football player who was killed by police in June 1999 during a traffic stop. Montgomery is representing the family of LaTanya Haggerty – who was also killed by Chicago police in the same highly publicized and controversial shooting as Russ.

The Soul of Jim Montgomery

As the managing partner of the new firm, the fiery but mild mannered Jim Montgomery brings to the table a legal mind and courtroom expertise that blazed a trail for his own successful firm, James D. Montgomery & Associates, Ltd., which specializes in plaintiffs and defense personal injury, wrongful death, and white collar criminal defense.

"We want to effect change in the community. We can give back something to the same community that has allowed us to be successful. Our careers pretty much match each other. We're both here in Chicago trying to fight oppression and police misconduct," explains Montgomery.

"We have practiced law and tried cases in the vineyards of every degree of complexity and kind, and yet there is a mentality about that that says, 'Your ice is not as cold as somebody else's.' I thought partnering with Johnnie would go a long way in dispelling the notion lawyers get because of the Calhoun character from *Amos 'N Andy*."

A conscientious and ambitious attorney who started with a "wig" practice – meaning "whatever I get" financially – Montgomery remains committed to supporting young African-American lawyers to fill gaps in the community and plug them before they form.

"The scarcity of law practices in the African-American community is highly evident," notes Montgomery, who has practiced for 44 years, including distinguishing himself from 1983-86 as Chicago's corporation counsel in the late mayor Harold Washington's administration. "You have to train people in the way you do things, in the thoroughness of the way you work, making sure you're totally up to snuff on the issues.

"That was one of the best decisions I've ever made in my life," is how he remembers agreeing to join the Washington administration because of its history-making role in the administration of the city's first Black mayor.

"In 1983, I was in the middle of a deposition in Las Vegas when I got a call about becoming corporation counsel," Montgomery recalls. "I was finally earning a substantial income and I had no interest in government and cutting my income. However, the 'Council Wars' fed into the warrior in me. I got a charge out of it. I was completely apolitical. I found out I was not a political animal. I was a lawyer."

A sought after teacher and lecturer, Montgomery is a graduate of the University of Illinois College of Law, and a member of several professional organizations, including the American Bar Association, Chicago Bar Association, Cook County Bar Association, Federal Bar Association, and the Illinois State Bar, where he was recently inducted as a Laureate in its first class of the Illinois State Academy of Lawyers.

"The Lord has blessed me with excellent health," says Montgomery, when talk turns to him enjoying the fruits of his stellar career. "I have a dozen books in my head, and I want to write about the experience of being a Black lawyer and growing up in America."

In the meantime, when the former assistant U.S. attorney for the Northern District of Illinois wants to take a break, he heads straight to his yacht, Jim's Toy 2, for quality quiet time.

"I find it's a place to relax and enjoy good music, or go to read or visit with friends. I have always been a family man, (Montgomery has six adult children, three of whom followed in his ample footsteps to become attorneys). The only time I have trouble 'turning it off' is when I'm in a trial. Then, I'm not available to my family or anyone until it's done."

Johnnie Cochran Has Come To Town

Cochran's storied career mirrors philosopher Henry David Thoreau's statement that "There are a thousand hacking at the branches of evil to one who is striking at the root."

And now with Montgomery at his side, the country's most celebrated trial lawyer soundly contends that, "You could not go any place in the world and find two attorneys who have tried more police abuse cases than me and Jim. I'm a trial lawyer. I love that. I am not an administrator."

So why bring his passion for trying cases to Chicago – besides harboring fond memories that date back to April 1996 when 1,200 people, the largest turnout ever, flocked to a meeting of the Cook County Bar Association to hear Cochran speak?

"I have often said that if you want to practice law, you have to come to Chicago, and who better to partner with in Chicago than Jim Montgomery, a man of great stature, of integrity, and ability," Cochran says.

"Together, Jim and I are dedicated to doing something to bring about change and justice in this community. We're like the caped crusaders. We have seen a need to bring our level of advocacy regardless of race, and help people receive some measure of justice."

Cochran has practiced law for the past 37 years, and is the only attorney in the history of Los Angeles to receive both the Criminal Trial Lawyer of the Year and Civil Trial Lawyer of the Year awards.

Although both renowned and reviled for his successful role as the lead defense attorney in the O.J. Simpson murder case – which he rarely brings up unless asked – Cochran's legendary career comprises dozens of professional affiliations, accomplishments, professional appearances, lectures, and a multitude of awards and honors.

A graduate of Loyola University School of Law, his career has spanned from the 1966 founding of the law firm of Cochran, Atkins and Evans, where he handled a substantial volume of civil and criminal cases, to celebrating the 1998 dedication of the Johnnie L. Cochran Jr. Academy of Legal Studies and Community Service in East Orange, New Jersey.

Cochran has served as deputy city attorney for the city of Los Angeles, assistant district attorney of Los Angeles County, and in 1979 he was the founding chairman of the Domestic Violence Council of Los Angeles County.

He has been repeatedly honored as one of the nation's top trial attorneys. *Time* magazine designated him "Headliner for 1995," and Cochran is a member of the exclusive Inner Circle of Advocates, which comprises the top 100 plaintiffs' lawyers in the United States. His 1996 autobiography, *Journey to Justice*, was a fixture on several bestseller lists.

Now a legal and social force to be reckoned with in Chicago, Jim Montgomery and Johnnie Cochran firmly believe they've joined forces in the right place and at the right time. And with scant doubt, Chicago had better be prepared for these crusaders who have hit the ground running in search of truth, justice, and the American way for people from all walks of life, and especially African Americans.

preface
Colemon

Update: Reverend Dr. Johnnie Colemon passed away on December 23, 2014 at the age of 94. She retired as active head of Christ Universal Temple in 2006.

Reverend Johnnie Colemon

By Sandra Jackson-Opoku & Photography by Doyle Wicks | *Originally Published April 1990*

Meeting Reverend Dr. Johnnie Colemon can be a daunting experience. Her approach is entirely no-nonsense. Her handshake is firm. Her bearing is regal. Her attire is elegant. Her expression and features strong, almost stern – that is, until she smiles a welcome, and the charm and charisma that is Johnnie Colemon shines through.

Of course, Colemon is one competent, capable individual. One wouldn't expect less from the founder and builder of the nation's largest New Thought church. But there is also another side, and it explains her widespread appeal as the city's most popular minister.

So both sides of the coin make Johnnie Colemon the person that she is: the shrewd, tough-minded professional woman and the caring, compassionate spiritual leader.

> **Thoughts are things. You are the thinker that thinks the thought that makes the thing. If you don't like the thing, then change your thoughts. Make it what you want it to be...I will not think poor. I think rich and I therefore express the richness of God.**

From her stylishly appointed modern offices, Johnnie (as she is affectionately known) presides over the Christ Universal Temple complex at 11900 South Ashland Avenue.

The stunning architectural showplace campus is set in a former industrial park and includes a building which houses a 4,000-seat auditorium, classrooms, a print shop, offices, a bookstore, prayer rooms, and many other components.

The Annex, a banquet facility, is situated at the east end of the property and the grounds also boast a "Garden of Stars" that honors patrons who helped make the dream of the Christ Universal Temple complex a reality.

Finding Her Path

Reverend Johnnie Colemon is celebrated as the first lady of America's religious community. It is only natural to wonder about what brought her to this position in life.

Many ministers speak of having had a moment of divine inspiration when they heard the call to preach. Although Colemon came from an old-fashioned, Southern, churchgoing family, she maintains that the way of the cloth was the furthest thing from her mind when she was a young woman in the early 1950s.

"I had no desire to be a minister," she says. "The reason I'm a minister is because of an incurable disease that doctors said I had. They said I would only live six months. When that kind of situation faces you, you find God. In finding God, I also found many other gifts. I realized that if I could find the healing power and presence within me and receive a complete healing, then I had to tell other people."

Born February 18, 1920 in Centerville, Alabama, and raised in Columbus, Mississippi, where she was the class valedictorian of her high school; Coleman graduated from Wiley College in Marshall, Texas. She then taught in Mississippi, before moving to Chicago and teaching in the public schools.

Following her recovery from her health crisis, she attended the Unity School of Christianity near Lee's Summit, Missouri, where she was the first African American to live on campus. Colemon was trained in New Thought, a philosophy that combines Christian teachings with metaphysics and focuses on positive thought, meditation and healing.

Johnnie still hadn't accepted the ministry as a way of life and considered eventually becoming a teacher or counselor. But she met people with needs and found that she could help them to help themselves.

"There were people facing the same kind of challenges that I had, many people who had been told by doctors that they had illnesses they couldn't do anything about, people walking through lack and poverty because they thought that's what they were supposed to have; that it was God's will," Colemon says.

"I found myself with people wanting to do something better with their lives and I wanted to teach people how to understand themselves and live better lives. There's a very thin line between being a teacher and a minister. I realized that I had a congregation and I became a minister."

A Church Is Born

That was in October 1956. In the years since she opened the doors of her first church, then Christ Unity Temple, which met at a YMCA, Coleman's congregation has grown from 35 people to over 10,000.

The church moved three times, outgrowing each of its meeting places, until Johnnie found four lots at 86th and State Street upon which she erected the first New Thought church built in the City of Chicago.

By the early 1980s, it was obvious that Christ Universal Temple, as it had by then been titled, had again outgrown its facilities. So Johnnie, once again, began to look for property, and that was the beginning of the Christ Universal Temple complex, built in 1985.

In addition to housing a church, it is the headquarters of an institution called the Universal Foundation for Better Living. That is a denomination Colemon founded herself, which has 20,000 members in churches located across the country, and in Canada, the Caribbean, and South America. Its components include a teaching arm, The Johnnie Colemon Institute, and a telephone prayer ministry.

Coleman prides herself on the success she has attained as an independent woman minister. She says, "No man in the city of Chicago, bar none, has done what I've done in the religious field without having political help. I've had no help from anybody. The largest money that anybody has ever given us is $10,000. And that was from a minister friend."

When it comes to playing politics, as many Black ministers do, she is decidedly apolitical.

"I do not get involved with any particular political movements," Colemon says. "No politician speaks in my church, because people who come to my church are coming to learn how to live a better life.

"People are free to vote for anybody they wish to vote for, because they have an instructor inside of them to tell them where to go and what to do. You're free. You know it's time for elections. I can't dance by anybody's music, but God's."

Her Religious Philosophies

Reverend Colemon recently reflected with *N'DIGO* on her guiding spiritual beliefs.

N'DIGO: *Please explain the principles of New Thought.*

REVEREND COLEMON: God is the only presence and the only power in the universe. God is all there is; there is absolutely, positively nothing else. Example: fire is good. You can cook with it, but you can also take that same fire and burn up your house. There is only one power, and that power can be used for your highest good, or you can use that same power for negative things.

Where is the power? Not on the outside, but within. If you're unhappy it's not your husband's fault, or your children's fault. It's your own fault. And because you have caused the situation that you are in, the exciting thing is you can change it. And you change it with your own thoughts.

Thoughts are things. You are the thinker that thinks the thought that makes the thing. If you don't like the thing, then change your thoughts. Make it what you want it to be. But first you've got to know yourself.

What do you want? Many of us do not know what we want. And when we do decide what we want, then we expect somebody to hand it to us on a silver platter. It doesn't work that way.

God has already given us everything that there is and He's waiting for you to discover what has already been created. There's plenty for everybody. My having plenty does not take anything away from you. I draw to me according to my own consciousness, my own awareness: my friends, my money, my health, my joy, and my peace.

N'DIGO: *You say that prayer is not an act of begging, but of "claiming your divine inheritance."*

RC: Prayer is really communion with God. You do not have to be in a certain position, you do not have to have a certain form. Prayer is just talking to God like you would any other friend.

I pray constantly. I pray without ceasing. Every thought is a prayer. I pray driving to work. When I get up in the morning, my first prayer is, "Thank you, God, for this beautiful day."

You don't have to beg God for anything. It's already yours. You've just come back from the store and put a quart of sweet milk in your refrigerator and closed the door. Later on that afternoon you decide you want a glass of milk. Would you stand in front of the refrigerator and beg for a glass of milk? You know it's in there. All you have to do is open the door and get the glass of milk.

The same thing with God. He has created everything and he wants you to have it. Why? Because he's my Father, I am his child and he doesn't know anything about poverty. All he knows is an abundance of every good thing. An unlimited supply. God is the source of my supply. So, I don't have to beg, I don't have to get down on my knees and plead.

I had always been taught that you were expressing God when you did not have. Surely, if you were a Christian, you were not supposed to have nice shoes, nice clothes, a nice automobile. You were not supposed to have any of those things.

But it's here for you and if you don't have it, then that's your business. If you suffer, you suffer because you cause yourself to suffer. My God is not a punishing God. God is love, but God is also law. When you misuse the law, then you set the law in motion for or against you. So God does not punish anybody, you punish yourself.

N'DIGO: *The concept of "the consciousness of prosperity" is certainly an interesting one for the African-American community. How has thinking poor as a race made us poor?*

RC: Because of old beliefs and concepts. We have been taught these things for years and so, we have accepted them. We believe we're supposed to be in poverty. We believe we're not supposed to have as much as the White man. And what you believe is what you receive.

In my book, *It Works If You Work It*, I speak of the prosperity principle as a "consciousness of abundance." If you live and practice this principle, you will be blessed with rich ideas, rich results, from expected and unexpected ways.

There's no Black money, there's no White money, there's not Black awareness, there's not White awareness. There's only one "awareness," and it's God awareness.

Unless African Americans learn how to place their faith in God as the source of their supply and not the job, not the husband, not the paycheck, and know that those things are just the channels through which the source, God, is bringing them whatever it is that they need, they'll always be poor.

I will not think poor. I think rich and I therefore express the richness of God. And when I say rich, I'm not just talking about money. I think rich health, rich happiness, and I think big and I think a lot of it. I don't want a small little bit of nothing.

But nobody has been bold enough to say it to Black people: "You've got everything everybody else has got. You can have as much as you want to have. But you've got to want to do better and be better and move up

preface
Compton

Update: James Compton remained as President and CEO of the Chicago Urban League until his retirement in 2006. He has been a member of several boards, including ComEd, DePaul University, Ariel Mutual Funds, eta Creative Arts Foundation, Morehouse Research Institute, and Seaway Bank. Compton has been Board President of the Chicago Public Library and the Chicago Board of Education and is a Life Trustee of the Field Museum of Natural History.

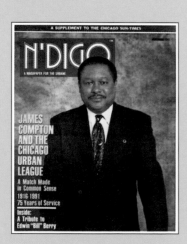

James Compton

By Derrick K. Baker & Photography by David Jenkins | *Originally Published November 1991*

Take a drive to 45th Street and Michigan Avenue on Chicago's South Side. On the southwest corner, you'll find a large, stately looking mansion, partially covered with red and green leaves.

Directly to the south of it, you'll see another building, but this one is as new as its neighbor is old. Foot after foot of glass wraps the second building: the white concrete holding the place together reminds of a company's corporate headquarters more than an agency of some sort.

And therein lies the contradiction and success of the vaunted Chicago Urban League, which as the local affiliate of the National Urban League, has been working since 1916 to improve the quality of life for Black people, white people, yellow people and brown people. In other words, anyone who is "in a state of disadvantagement."

> **The basic mission of the organization is the same as since we started in 1916. We're trying to bring about the elimination of discrimination and segregation based on race.**

The League is one of the city's greatest resources and advocates for equality and fairness for all, but traditionally for African Americans. It's a resource that the Windy City couldn't live without. And if you're not sure that's exactly true, just ask James R. Compton, president and CEO. He'll tell you.

"I think we enjoy a positive reputation in Chicago," says Compton. "That does not mean that everyone agrees with us on every single thing at all times, but that doesn't bother me either because I don't try to put the organization in a popularity contest.

"We're trying to fulfill our mission, and that means at various times some people will be irritated. But in the main, given where we have started and where are, we are a valuable institution, a valuable resource in this community."

Continuing, he says, "We have been the most consistent, dependable, constant entity in bringing about equality education for all children in Chicago. Others have come and gone, but we have been there for the long haul and continue to be there. We have

been able to keep up the pressure on and I think kept the educational situation from getting worse than it is."

Guided in part by one of his mentor's sayings – "When you wake up, get up and when you get up, do something!" – for the past 19 years, Jim Compton has put his commitment to civil rights, education and equality to the test leading the ship called the Chicago Urban League.

With about 150 people currently on staff, he continues to guide the organization in efforts to "bring about the elimination of discrimination and segregation based on race."

Like a first-time father, Compton is proud of what the League stands for, what it has accomplished, and what it means to Chicago. As example, he says: "When you move around and ask people how they got their first jobs, quite a few of them will tell you, 'Through the Urban League.'

"Harold Washington said that; I've even heard some white people say that," Compton notes. "The League is for all people who need help, although historically our largest clientele has been African American. But if you go to other parts of the country, that wouldn't necessarily be true."

In The Beginning

Compton completed high school half a year ahead of his class at East Aurora High in the western suburb, "not necessarily because I was so intelligent, but because I didn't want to stay there," he says.

Between that time and going back in June to graduate, one of his teachers encouraged him to go and hear Dr. Benjamin Mays, then president of Morehouse College in Atlanta, speak at a nearby college.

After hearing Mays' speech, Compton decided to attend the famed men's college. "I was so impressed with Dr. Mays that I prepared myself to learn more about what I was going into," he says. For that reason, Compton remembers being "better prepared than most of my fellow students."

He recalls, "It was a highly competitive environment. The expectations were always that you would not only be productive, but you would excel. You were always reminded that you had to be the best."

He later decided to major in political science, and chosen to serve as chauffeur for Dr. Mays, capitalized on the opportunity of having the legendary educator as a captive audience.

That chance, coupled with the whole "Morehouse experience," prompts Compton to say, "Every Black youngster who is willing and able to undertake the philosophy and the academic rigor should go to Morehouse. It's a school that is first about building men and then building men for leadership."

In 1959, Compton was one of seven students selected by the U.S. State Department to participate in a cultural exchange program with the U.S.S.R. He spent that summer touring and speaking in the likes of Poland, Czechoslovakia, and the Soviet Union.

He was also awarded a coveted Merrill Fellowship, which enabled him to attend the University of Grenoble in France, miles and miles away from Chicago. There he earned a diploma in French literature before returning and graduating from Morehouse in 1961.

After graduation, he taught in the Chicago public schools for a few years before being recruited into the civil rights movement in general and the Urban League in particular by his uncle, Whitney Young, who was then executive director of the National Urban League.

During his first year with the Chicago Urban League, he met fellow Morehouse man Dr. Martin Luther King Jr., who, like Dr. Mays, was another source of inspiration for the neophyte civil rights worker.

Working with another of his mentors, the late, legendary Edwin C. "Bill" Berry, Compton began with the Chicago Urban League in 1965 as a counselor and employment representative for the League's On-the-Job Training Program.

But a few years and positions later, he left Chicago to take the job of executive director of the Broome County Urban League in Binghamton, New York.

Then in early 1972, Compton was named acting executive director of the Chicago Urban League after its former leader departed.

Compton's business prowess and problem-solving talents were just two of the reasons that led the League's board of directors in 1972 to remove "acting" from his title and officially hand him the agency's top position.

The Task At Hand

What did the former Chicago public school teacher think of the job before him? He recalls, "I was not personally overwhelmed. I regarded it as a challenge and a job to be done and felt that it was going to be done.

"There was an appropriate and necessary place for the organization in Chicago and we sold the League on the proposition that if there was not an Urban League, you would have to create one."

Research and publication of numerous studies examining such significant issues as election reform, school segregation, community involvement, economic development, consumer prices and housing has long been a hallmark of the League and the integrity of that information cuts to the organization's very core.

"Something that I've always tried to put forth in the Urban League," Compton stresses, "is that our research must be irrefutable. Our efforts in the delivery of service must be such that there is no question about the effort. Our posture on issues must be such that it cannot be challenged as to its merits and its honesty.

"You can have excellence," he notes, "and not have integrity." How? "You can be an excellent thief," Compton answers.

The More Things Change...

Has the League changed over the years? "In some ways, it has not changed," he says ruefully. "The basic mission of the organization is the same. We're trying to bring about the elimination of discrimination and segregation based on race.

"We're putting more emphasis on advocacy and less on the delivery of direct services that we once did, although we continue to deliver some services out of absolute necessity, but we do recognize that we'll be in the service delivery business forever if we did not try to bring about systemic and institutional change.

"So, our real thrust is to try to alter a culture and to change the way society and institutions and individuals behave and respond to African Americans and other minorities and the poor."

What is the League's biggest accomplishment? Compton summarizes: "The consistency in our mission and purpose and the interracial nature of our organization. We've always tried to bring people of all persuasions together to try to reach some commonality and understanding."

Can institutions be changed?" We don't consider it an impossibility," he ponders. "We obviously know what the obstacles are based on our experience. We've been around since 1916 fighting some of the same battles, but we've also recognized some change," Compton says.

"The institution of slavery is gone. Legal segregation has been abolished. Rural peonage in the main is gone, so the obstacles and the hurdles have reached a more advanced state, and often time, it's much more subtle and covert."

If his long years of working toward achieving quite a few lofty goals almost necessitates having some regrets, Compton says except for one or two,

he doesn't play Monday morning quarterback.

"We might have done better in restricting the expansiveness of the program," he says. "We had been trying to address all the ills we're called upon to address instead of just focusing in on a few.

"Because of who we are, we're called upon to try to deal with every need and every request from the community. We get calls from poor and rich to do something on their behalf. But we're trying to keep our agenda where the impact will be much more viable and more measurable.

"Now we're focusing just on education, community development and economic empowerment. There was a time when we tried to have programs for people from the cradle to the grave. But with limited resources, you run into a dilemma as far as the impact you can have on addressing everything."

Black In Chicago
As chief of a leading social services agency in a racially conscious big city, what's it like for James Compton to be a Black man in Chicago?

"It means you're always faced with the challenge of acceptance and acceptability as other people define it. I personally don't concern myself with that, even though I know it's ever present," he says.

"There is the realization, however, that there are situations that exist that are not necessarily open to you. We must continue to challenge those obstacles in opening the doors, particularly for the youth and the children who must be prepared to walk through them."

Despite the League's innumerable tangible and intangible effects on Chicago, Compton says the city is still one of the most segregated in the country.

He warns, "That is something we really need to come to grips with because physical segregation not only fosters discrimination, it also has a very detrimental psychological and intellectual impact on the human psyche and spirit, which then manifests itself in behavior. There's no question in my mind that segregation in Chicago has to be eliminated."

Is that possible? "There's some degree of breakdown in that regard," Compton responds. "But we've still got a lot of work to do."

preface Coney

Update: Les Coney became executive vice president and senior managing director of Mesirow Financial Holdings Inc. in 2006 and has also served as a major bundler and corporate liaison for President Barack Obama's election campaigns. He is now a Life Trustee for the Goodman.

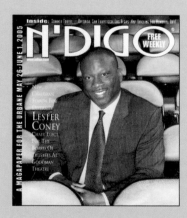

Lester Coney

By Rosalind Cummings-Yeates & Photography by Reginald Payton | *Originally Published May 26, 2005*

Lester Coney emanates energy.

On the one hand, he gives a warm, personable kind of feeling that puts people at ease. On the other hand, that vitality is channeled into the dynamism that earns well-placed positions and cuts shrewd deals.

Both sides of this quality come in handy for anyone involved in a corporate setting, but as the newly named Chairman-Elect for the board of trustees of the prestigious Goodman Theatre, Les Coney will really put them to good use.

"It's important as an African American to take the knowledge we learn from non-African American environments and pass it on," says Coney.

As Senior Managing Director for Aon Corporation, he has mined the opportunities he's earned, and transported them to an impressive list of community organizations, from DuSable Museum, to eta Creative Foundation, to Congo Square Theatre Company. Now, as the first African American named to a prestigious Chicago cultural board, Coney stands poised to contribute on many more levels.

> ## Once you get on one board, people have a confidence in you and want you to join their cause, too.

Community Involvement

Historically, the board of trustees for high profile cultural organizations has been filled with the same affluent, well-connected, White Anglo-Saxon Protestants that such organizations generally serve.

Boards target high-powered movers and shakers who can use their resources in support of the institution. They look for people who will fit into the institution's culture and help retain the status quo. They also tap potential members who can donate or raise large sums of money.

People of color have been mostly excluded from prestigious board membership because of these lofty expectations. According to a recent poll by *Crain's Chicago Business*, 85 percent of the members of Chicago's cultural institutions are White, even though African Americans represent 53 percent of the city's population.

It's a statistic that Coney has been working to change for a decade.

In 1995, Coney accepted his first board position for the Juvenile Diabetes Research Foundation. He had no idea how much this involvement would alter his life.

"A close friend, James Tyree, the CEO of Mesirow Financial, is a diabetic; he invited me to join the Foundation since they had never had an African American as a director. I thought, diabetes affects us just as much if not more than everybody else, and my mother is also diabetic."

So Coney joined the board and kick-started his journey as a trail-blazing trustee. "Once you get on one board, people have a confidence in you and want you to join their cause too. It's like dating … when people see you with somebody else, they all want you. But nobody is interested when you're by yourself, trying to get a phone number."

Currently, Coney is a member of a whopping seven boards: the Goodman, DuSable Museum of African American History, Roosevelt University, Aurora University, City Year, Athletes Against Drugs, and Congo Square Theatre Company.

He cautions that such community involvement requires more than just lending your name to press releases and showing up at fundraisers. "You're giving of your time, resources and energy. After a 50-hour work week, you're looking at maybe 65 hours with volunteering."

Appreciating Culture

Growing up in Philadelphia during the 1960s and '70s, Coney says he learned his work ethic from his father, and community involvement from his mother.

"My father taught me about hard work and rolling up your sleeves. My mom was very involved with the Boys and Girls Clubs," he says.

Coney and his three siblings were always instructed to appreciate culture and he remembers attending plays and going to museums. "I saw theater as a young person, but I didn't grow up in a wealthy family. There wasn't much opportunity to go spend $60 or $70 for theater tickets," he says. "I saw plays through educational programs and sponsorships. I really developed my interest in theater over the last 10 years."

It was six years ago when Peter Bynoe, an attorney and chairman of the Goodman Executive Board, invited Coney to a reception for Pulitzer Award-winning playwright August Wilson. "I was very impressed with August, and afterwards Peter called to see if I was interested in joining the Goodman board," Coney recalls.

"I had never been to a Goodman production, so he took me to see *A Christmas Carol* and a few other plays. I did some research and found that the Goodman has a long commitment to diversity and quality. I was impressed by that. When I joined, there were three other board members of color, now there are 13."

Indeed, the Goodman's track record for diversity outdistances not only all of Chicago's prominent cultural institutions, but the rest of the country as well.

As Chicago's oldest and largest non-profit theater, the Goodman was one of the first major theaters to employ non-traditional, color-blind casting with the opening of the annual holiday production *A Christmas Carol* 27 years ago.

Over the years, the theater has showcased luminaries such as James Earl Jones in *Othello* in 1968, Paul Winfield in *An Enemy of the People* in 1980, and Harry Lennix in *A Raisin In The Sun* in 1993.

In addition to producing August Wilson's cycle of plays about the African American experience throughout the decades, the Goodman hosts a Latino theater festival and boasts such revered African American theater professionals as director Chuck Smith, actor/director/playwright Regina Taylor, and Harry Lennix as an artistic associate.

"When you look at the cultural institutions in Chicago, I think it's important that they represent the population of the city," says Coney. "You take the Goodman's eight productions in a season, and there will be something that represents most of the population."

Coney was instrumental in ensuring that Chicago's African-American population was represented in a holiday production with the inception of Langston Hughes' *Black Nativity* last year.

"I helped to found Congo Square Theatre's board, and I try to expose them to everything I'm doing," he says. "When I was in D.C., I heard about *Black Nativity* and I asked Derrick (Sanders, the artistic director for the company) why aren't we doing this? He said, we can't afford it. I said, give me the numbers, we'll get it."

After crunching those numbers, Coney drummed up Target as a corporate sponsor, and got the production a plum location in the Goodman's Owen Theater. The production sold out and garnered rave reviews, ensuring that the lavish, soul-drenched play, also scheduled for this year's holiday season, is on its way to being another Chicago holiday tradition.

Diversity

Although he's excited about his duties as the Goodman's Chairman of the Board of Trustees, Coney doesn't particularly care for the title. "I never liked the title Chairman because it implies more power than it entails," he says. " Basically, I make sure that the 80 trustees raise money, and that the organization is fiscally sound. I don't sit with Bob Falls (Goodman's artistic director) and decide on what productions to have."

However, Coney will help decide how to increase diversity and recruit younger board members. At 46, Coney has obtained a high-profile position that typically goes to people decades older.

"I'd like to see us make a commitment to the 28- to 42-year-old population … those are the future leaders, the future chairs," he says. "They are just getting comfortable in their careers and organizing their lives. We need to tap into this group early."

In terms of diversity, for four years Coney has been hosting "diversity nights." He gets a block of 100 tickets, hands them out to community members, and invites them to a reception with the artists after the production.

"As a trustee, I personally bring a group with me to a play," he explains. "We do it during pre-production, and that group spreads the word about the play."

Coney believes that theater is the key to broadening experiences and developing sensitivity to other people. "The only thing bigger than seeing it on stage is living it," he says.

"Theater gives the public a peek into the lives of another person. A White person from the North Shore can see a Chuck Smith play and get an exper ience that they may never have the opportunity to witness."

As the father of two teens, Coney considers his community involvement as the most important thing he does besides being a good parent.

"If I die tomorrow, I don't want people to say, he was a good insurance guy. I'd like to be remembered for helping the Goodman with diversity, for helping establish a small theater company like Congo Square. It's the community involvement that counts."

preface
Daniels

Update: Daniels closed his West Side music room several years ago to concentrate on the airport store at 5700 South Cicero. Because of his vast selection of music-related paraphernalia, he has maintained his business comfortably even as brick-and-mortar record stores are no longer a primary source to buy or hear music. Daniels left his Midway location in 2017 to relocate to Navy Pier, one of Chicago's premier tourist destinations.

George Daniels

By Mark Ruffin & Photography by Jennifer Williams | *Originally Published July 26, 2001*

Thousands of visitors to Chicago can now take a piece of Lawndale with them when they board their jets to return home. That's because the rapidly expanding Midway Airport – a gateway into and out of our beautiful city for millions – has opened its own version of George's Music Room.

The affable and always dapper owner of the venerable West Side institution, George Daniels has taken his operations global by doing business with his feet planted on the ground and his heart in his neighborhood. He didn't beat out all the giant music chains with back door dealing or cut-rate bidding, but rather by just being himself.

Who he is, is the two-time winner of the National Retailer of the Year Award, and the only African American on the very influential board of National Association of Recording Merchandisers (NARM).

He has made his store at 3915 West Roosevelt as important to record companies as any of those other big-name outlets.

We're known for having what's hot!

"The Midway store will be a great symbol of Lawndale," Daniels said, sitting at his desk in the back of his flagship store. "But truthfully, I never thought about something of this magnitude. In all my years of business, I never even applied for a business loan, until now. Obviously, I've grown through the years, and want to continue, but I never thought this big."

The 52-year-old storeowner didn't dream of expanding beyond Roosevelt Road at all until a fateful day almost two years ago. Now Daniels is basically moving to a beautiful new store as a reward for "supporting the Lawndale community when everybody else was running."

In the early fall of 1999, in what he thought was going to be a small ceremony, the city honored him for 30 years of business at his current address. The press conference included Cong. Danny Davis, Ald. Michael Chandler, Police Supt. Terry Hilliard, and Mayor Daley himself.

"I was really surprised. Right in front of my store, they brought out the official city podium and the whole nine yards," said the man who, now that he owns the block, likes to tell the story of his eviction from the premises decades earlier.

"It was quite an exciting day for the city to recognize that I stayed here and built a little business for myself," he proudly beamed.

The local political muscle at that event must've felt dwarfed when they walked in his store afterwards and realized the national might of their honoree. Between the dizzying number of posters, cards, and placards marketing popular music in George's Music Room, there was ample evidence that they were in the midst of a giant in the music industry.

Every major record company, and a few local ones, has awarded Daniels multiple gold and platinum plaques for helping them sell records. Many of them are scattered throughout the store, along with an impressive photo gallery of Daniels posing with African-American music and film powerhouses that's so star-studded, it's easier to list whom he hasn't mingled with.

"Once the ceremony was over, Mayor Daley was looking around at all the awards and the basic layout of the store," Daniels remembered. "He turned to me and said, 'I think I have an idea for you, I have something I know you'll like.'"

Maybe it was the picture with Quincy Jones and Daniels, or maybe the photos with Shaquille O'Neal, or with Toni Braxton that swayed the mayor. Or maybe it was when Daley looked up at the image of Daniels and country singer Clint Black, that he turned to his assistant and told him to schedule an appointment with the entrepreneur.

In any case, a week later, Daniels was in City Hall sitting down with the mayor one-on-one, and he had no idea why.

"He initially made reference that there were no record stores at the airports, and my stomach started bubbling. I'm thinking, 'Oh my god, I know he isn't going to ask me about the airport.'

"I recovered and got enough nerve to correct him," Daniels remembered. "I said, 'Your Honor, I know there's none at Midway, but there is a chain at O'Hare.'"

Daniels said Daley dismissed that as of little concern, and went straight to the heart of the matter, asking him if he could get the support together to open a store at Midway.

The mayor went on to explain the application process of permits and licenses involved, and how George's Music Room would be partnered with another major retail chain that does business with the city.

"Even before all of this, I admired this mayor, because he had to earn (the Chicago Black population's) respect and trust," Daniels exclaimed. "Then, to give a small retailer like myself an opportunity to do business next to major international chains, in a place like the airport, is a tremendous gesture."

The Makings Of The Music Room

As a young man, Daniels moved to Chicago from New York City just in time to service his first musician, his high school sweetheart, the late, great vocalist, Minnie Riperton.

"Back in '65, George was one of Minnie's first boyfriends," reads the liner notes to the recently released 2-CD, 35-song retrospective titled *Petals: The Minnie Riperton Collection*. George escorted Minnie to her senior prom at the original McCormick Place.

It was the legendary multi-octave singer who helped Daniels land a job as a janitor at Chess Records, where she was a receptionist. As she moved up to background singer under the tutelage of Chess behind-the-scenes wizard Billy Davis, young George got more opportunities.

"I was a utility man," Daniels said with his ever-ready laugh. "I'd be sweeping and Billy would say, 'George, put that broom down and come in here. I need some hand claps.'"

One day Davis called asking if George would be the driver for one of the hottest acts on Chess, a physically huge singer from Washington named Billy Stewart. He was known for his hits, *I Do Love You*, *Sitting In The Park*, plus others, and for one six-month tour, a 17-year-old Daniels was his chauffeur.

"But Billy Davis never asked me if I had a driver's license," Daniels remembered. "I drove all around the country and never got caught. But I sweated every time I saw a police car."

It was at Chess Records where Daniels fell in love with the record business. He called his stint at the legendary company his "first-hand look at a record company plantation." He said he regularly saw Muddy Waters, Ramsey Lewis, Etta James, the Dells, Howlin' Wolf, and many others.

"There were all those Black folks working, but when the boss came around, it was two White guys," Daniels said. "They were harvesting some of the greatest Black music in the world."

After leaving Chess, Daniels moved into the wholesale side of the record business. He began by selling records out of the trunk of his car to small record stores and bowling alleys. He started his unique brand of personal service back then by

volunteering to help his clients on some weekends when they were swamped.

"You have to remember that this was a time when the record business had literally, 80 to 90 percent of (Black people's) entertainment dollars," said Daniels. "There were no theatres in our neighborhood, and the cheapest form of entertainment was to buy some 45s or an eight-track and hit the liquor store. We were partying at home.

"On some Friday and Saturday nights, those record stores, which usually had no employees other than the husband and wife, would be swamped," he continued. "So, I'd hop behind the counter and help them out. I learned from some of the finest independent retailers in the world."

Daniels credits Ernie Leaner, a historically important Chicago record executive, as his mentor in the record business. However, his father, a man he says is the sharpest man he's ever met, was his business model. Daniels said he gets both his penchant for sartorial splendor and customer service from the elder Daniels, who owned a restaurant in the Bronx in New York.

George's Music Room first opened December 12, 1969. "I started here a week before my 21st birthday, and a year after the Dr. King riots devastated Lawndale," Daniels remembered. "Then open housing hit in Austin and Oak Park like the plague. The businesses that had flourished after the riots and many homeowners left the area.

"The opportunity for me to run my own business was right here at hand, and I wasn't going to abandon the community."

Building A Business

Daniels insists that he built his business by knowing his customers and knowing what they want, and sometimes when they want it.

Through the years, with changing styles and musical trends, the constant has been that the record business still caters to younger audiences. The result for Daniels has been serving generations of customers who have used a trip to George's Music Room as a family outing.

Kids, of course, have changed. So has George's Music Room. The majority of his inventory is hip-hop and urban pop, but he keeps a wide variety of all forms of Black music, including jazz, blues, reggae, gospel, and R&B dusties.

He loves the changing trends, and has contributed to the success of a number of young Black Chicago stars, including R. Kelly, Public Announcement, Do or Die, Soldiers At War, Common, and others.

"Plus, we're known for having what's hot," he said on a day when a White and an Asian DJ from the

North Side shopped at the store.

It was one of his young customers that helped make George's Music Room at Midway possible. He is Robert Steele, the son of West Side politician Bobbie Steele.

"Both Robert and his brother were customers of mine for years," Daniels said, explaining Steele's involvement.

Reasoning that the aspect of meeting with architects, designers, the city itself, and the red tape at the airport could be a bit intimidating, Daniels reached out to Steele, who heads the Lawndale Business and Development Corporation.

"I'm not so big that I can't admit what I don't know," he exclaimed. "Just because people give you the opportunity doesn't mean you're qualified.

"I started seeing things and experiencing things

that I was just not familiar with, and I've seen so many people attempt to expand, and they not only lose what they're attempting to do, but they lose what they had.

"By no means did I want to gamble to lose what I built for some 30-odd years," said the man who also insisted on using his neighborhood financial institution, the Community Bank of Lawndale, for financing.

"These people have literally held my hand all through this process, and I can honestly say if it wasn't for Robert Steele being my project manager, I probably would've backed out of this thing."

Instead, a piece of Lawndale is going global, with a sleek, stylish new extension of their neighborhood, George's Music Room at Midway Airport.

preface Davis

Update: Dr. Blondean Davis was the subject of a 2016 resolution from Richton Park Village acknowledging her many contributions to education, citing her vision and leadership in raising student achievement levels and in the reform of education.

Around the same time, she was honored by the National Alliance of Black School Educators for her personal and professional sacrifices in the advancement of education for African-American students.

And Dr. Davis was cited by the trustees of Tougaloo College, for her tireless work on behalf of the United Negro College Fund.

Dr. Blondean Davis

By David Smallwood & Photography by John Smierciak | *Originally Published January 9, 2003*

n her profession of education, Matteson School District 162 Superintendent and founding CEO of Southland College Prep Charter High School, Dr. Blondean Davis is the gold standard. Named Illinois Association of School Administrators Superintendent of the Year in 2008, she could just as rightfully receive that honor every year as well.

With years of experience in the profession, Davis knows education and knows how to make it work. Her place is right up there in the pantheon of legendary Chicago educators that includes Marva Collins and Barbara Sizemore and her achievements through the years border on the miraculous.

Davis became superintendent of the south suburban Matteson school district in 2002, overseeing six elementary schools, a middle school and some 2,900 students.

When she arrived, only 55 percent of the district's students met or exceeded the proficiency goals of the Illinois Standards Achievement (ISAT) Test.

> **With these children, what's significant is the concept that you have the potential, and we can make whatever it is that you want happen.**

In five years under her leadership, those scores increased by almost 50 percent. After just three years, in 2005, one of the schools was named among the top elementary schools in the south suburbs based on its composite ISAT score.

By 2008, all of Davis' schools had received the Illinois Academic Improvement Award and several have become Illinois Spotlight Schools. In 2009, Arcadia, which serves kindergarten through third grade students, earned the coveted National Blue Ribbon School designation by the U.S. Department of Education.

At the end of the 2011 school year, Sauk Elementary School in Davis' district was honored by Scholastic Books as being the first school in the nation, if not the world, in the number of minutes the students spent reading.

The 500 Sauk students read more than 1.5 million combined minutes during the school year. Sauk was one of only six schools to hit a million minutes and spurred Matteson SD 162 on to leading all other school districts in the country in time spent reading that year.

A Different Kind Of High School

Davis' high school – Southland College Prep Charter School in Richton Park – opened in 2010 and has graduated just four classes, but 100 percent of those graduates have been accepted at four-year institutions of higher learning.

More than $70 million in merit-based scholarships have been offered to students in those classes, with the 2016 class awarded more than $24 million. The 117 graduates in the 2017 senior class received more than $25 million in scholarships.

In 2016, honor student and volleyball playing senior Morgan Brunson received $600,000 in college scholarship offers and chose to attend Jackson State University to major in business marketing and management. She graduated from Southland with a 4.13 grade point average on a 4.0 scale.

Southland graduates have been accepted by more than 300 colleges, including every major four-year university in Illinois, 12 of the 14 "Big Ten" schools, 38 of *U.S. News & World Report*'s Top 50 Colleges, and seven of the eight Ivy League schools, plus Stanford – after only four graduating classes.

Southland was conceived after area parents approached Davis about creating something a little better than the local high schools in the district, which were struggling with declining test scores and climbing dropout and suspension rates.

Southland became the first charter public high school approved by the Illinois State Board of Education in the Chicago suburbs. Niche.com, which analyzes neighborhood schools across the United States, ranks Southland number two among the 29 charter high schools in the Chicago metro area in 2017.

The secret to her success, Davis says, is that "I know what is necessary to run a good school. I know why schools don't work for kids. I know that whether you call it – charter, or Catholic, or whatever you call the entity that educates our children – that we as an

African-American community simply wants the best for our kids."

Much of that learning of "what is necessary to run a good school" took place in the Chicago Public Schools (CPS), where Davis worked for 31 years.

Rooted In Chicago Schools

A product of the Chicago public schools herself, Davis, an Englewood High School graduate, earned her Bachelor's, Master's and doctorate degree, all in Education, from Loyola University Chicago.

In 1970, she joined CPS and through the years functioned as a teacher, counselor, assistant principal, principal, district superintendent and deputy chief education officer.

Then, from 1995 to 2001, she served as Chief of Schools and Regions for CPS. As one of the top generals for Schools CEO Paul Vallas, Davis was responsible for the daily management of seven regions and 601 schools.

Dr. Davis left the Chicago Public Schools in August 2001 to briefly become Associate Professorial Lecturer at Saint Xavier University, where she trained prospective school principals.

Then she accepted the superintendency of Matteson School District 162 in 2002 with a vision of how she wanted to do things. Her aim was directed along two lines – acceptance of new levels of responsibility by administrators, principals, faculties, parents, students and community leaders to produce a true learning family, and implementation of a more rigorous curriculum and instructional program.

The curriculum is more than rigorous, especially at Southland. There, during an European-Asian model, nine-hour, 8 a.m. to 5 p.m. school day – which is even before the extracurricular activities begin – students take four years of foreign languages, math, science and the arts and graduates earn credits for more than a full year of courses taken by most other Chicago area high schools students.

In addition to the academic preparation, Southland offers every student an extensive, personal college counseling approach under its central premise that students have unlimited possibilities and unlimited potential.

"We have an excellent college conference with each student, a three- to four-hour individual family conference during the summer where anybody that has anything to do with the child comes – grandparents, whoever you are – and explains what your wishes and dreams are, and then we analyze who this child is and figure out the best place for them," Davis says.

"We tell them you're applying to this and that college, but in the end, you're going to have to go to the school that gives you the best education with the best financial package because we do not emphasize college loans."

Reinforcing Core Values

A third crux of Davis' educational vision is discipline. "I know that our children want structure and that in our community, the values that we had over the years have disappeared," she says.

So Davis begins every morning at Southland with the students reciting a creed that reaffirms their values and positive actions, including the notions that "the strong should take care of the weak, the students of today are the leaders of tomorrow, learning is the key to ultimate success, we give 100 percent every day, we act in a way that earns the trust of others, we are role models for other students, we act in a way that leaves a lasting impression."

Davis says, "The reason we start with it and the reason I don't have monumental discipline problems is because after a while it becomes a part of you." She cites maybe two to three discipline problems during the course of a school year and says when that happens, "that means I bring the family together."

That's literally the whole family – whoever works in the building, whoever goes to school there, whatever parents may be in the building at the time – they all gather together "and we talk about the problem and I tell them what we're going to do," Davis says.

"We talk about our values, who are we. I know that you have to get in the heads of these kids, to let them know that we don't behave as you do on the streets; that there are some things that just cannot be permitted within the family.

"I tell them why I'm doing what I'm doing, why we can't do this. All of this is based on concepts that really are not so much religious as much as what this country is supposed to be about.

"I know these children and their families really want this – they want their children to be successful, and to be successful, there are certain kinds of common experiences and values that have to exist."

She adds that, "Even coming out of Chicago, I was always very strong on the character side of who you are because I think integrity and determination are very important. With these children, what's significant is the concept that you have the potential, and we can make whatever it is that you want happen. You just have to do your part."

Davis

A Mighty Family

When Davis says "the family," she says she means that "the whole village is involved – the teachers, clerks, the lunchroom people. The family is about 4,000-strong." That includes the 2,800 students and 600 adult workers in District 162 schools, and the 530 students and 40 adult employees at Southland College Prep.

"The family" works together and takes care of each other. When the Southland students in college come back for the summer, Davis hires them as tutors in her elementary schools because summer jobs for them are scarce, but also because, "Who better to teach the smaller children?" she asks.

"Then, instead of bringing in outsiders to clean the buildings, a lot of the young men work under our janitors and they strip the floors, do the toilets, do the painting.

"After our first two graduating classes at Southland, we had 116 of them working within the family. They painted these walls, they cleaned the carpeting; they painted the other schools.

"In return, at their graduation, I tell them that for four years, we're going to stick with you through college. Your diploma means we have an obligation to make sure you're successful. You come home during the summer; you come here, this is your home. It will be okay.

"You have a problem away at school or anywhere, this is the phone number that you call. Somebody will answer it right away. And we send our people to check up on them at school."

Because of the nurturing family atmosphere, Davis says, "Our students are not angry about anything. They're not fighting in the halls. They're waiting around for the next good thing to happen to them.

"The children feel that something wonderful is on the verge of happening to them; that something is going to happen here that will give them opportunity like other American kids who have opportunity, too. And usually something does happen to them that makes that a reality."

Southland serves students, 99 percent of whom are minorities, from middle-class to high-poverty families in Country Club Hills, Flossmoor, Hazel Crest, Homewood, Matteson, Olympia Fields, Park Forest, Richton Park and Tinley Park, in a three-story building on an eight-acre site at 4601 West Sauk Trail in Richton Park. It compares favorably academically to the acclaimed Marian Catholic High School in the area, but without the exorbitant tuition cost.

Proof of Davis's excellence as an educator is in the fact that for all of Southland's enormous success, it's a non-select school. It doesn't skim the cream of the crop of the best area students; admission is by random public lottery, so whichever 130 student names pop up first, comprises the next freshman class.

The Southland family doesn't know if these lottery-selected students have individual education plans so they need special education services, doesn't know if they've been in 20 fights, doesn't know if there's a no-parent household or if they're homeless –they don't know, and they don't care.

"We say whoever you are, welcome, we'll see you for the freshman scholars program and get you ready for your four years and then everybody's going to college," says Dr. Davis.

About her tremendous success and achievements, the educator says, "It's very interesting what can be done and thinking about why it's not done. We don't have a lot of money; we don't get any more than the other high schools in the district. But if we can do this, you know that it can be done. It can be done in Chicago; it can be done in Detroit. It can be done."

preface Davis

Update: The freshman Congressman is still on the job 20 years later, a member of the 115th Congress that convened January 3, 2017, as President Donald Trump began his administration. In the Congress and throughout his West Side District, Davis has maintained an intense focus of issues of job creation, poverty, healthcare, education, youth, anti-gun legislation and criminal justice reform.

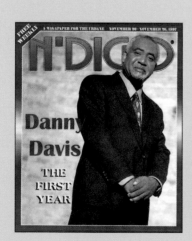

Danny Davis

By David Smallwood & Photography by Calvin Woods | *Originally Published November 20, 1997*

Danny Davis is in a good place. Since being elected new Congressman of the 7th District last November, he's shed about 25 pounds and is happily participating in democracy on the world stage.

The weight loss trick involved a three-prong combination. 1) Sticking to a low-salt, low-fat, low-sugar diet, which makes eating a bore "because there isn't a lot of stuff to eat in those categories that tastes good," Davis says. 2) Walking as often as possible, which he claims "amounts to a pretty decent piece of exercise, along with not having a lot to eat." 3) Drinking tons of water and juice – "flushing all this stuff out of your system, running to the bathroom, it's just good for you," he says.

"I've never been a water drinker and have to force myself, but when I do, I really don't feel like eating. So I'm going to try my best to keep it up because it's so healthy... but it's hard," Davis chuckles. You sense he'd really like to go somewhere and chow down.

> **I'm into this democratic activism thing. If you can bring people together and have them play a rightful part in what's going on, you can accomplish a lot.**

You'd also think that being a much in-demand speaker on the rubber chicken dinner circuit, the freshman Congressman would have added pounds, not taken them off. Davis explained that his Congressional schedule is so tight that once he gets to a dinner, there's usually no time to eat. "You run in and generally don't stay longer than half an hour," he notes. "You say your piece and leave because you have somewhere else to go – there's that much to do."

And Davis has pretty much been a nonstop whirlwind of motion in his first year, putting as much on his plate as he can. On a recent, brief appearance on the Oprah Winfrey Show, for instance, Davis, who is "Oprah's Congressman," answered her question about why you should know who your Congressional representative is.

Even as he delivered his answer – "because you can't know if the person is representing you if you don't know who the person is," – he was moving off-camera, telling Oprah he was running to catch a plane to cast a vote for her in Washington, D.C.

Before becoming a Congressman, the Parkdale, Arkansas native born in 1941, was Alderman of the 29th Ward for 11 years, then a Cook County Board commissioner for six years. He has a bachelor's degree in history from Arkansas AM&N College, a master's in guidance from Chicago State University and a PhD in public administration from the Union Institute in Cincinnati, Ohio.

Where He's Coming From

In his first year, Davis has cast more than 500 roll call votes and signed his name as co-sponsor to more than 250 pieces of legislation. The legislation and the votes cover the quintessence of the true liberal philosophy involving social issues.

He's for improvements in healthcare, public education, assistance to senior citizens, the environment, women's rights, etc. He's against NAFTA and Fast Track – efforts that take needed jobs away from poorer segments of American communities.

Davis has remained true to his position as a decidedly progressive liberal – "liberal" in the best sense of that term, before it was turned into a dirty word by forces who have little compassion for real human needs. That's why Davis was one of the few representatives who voted against this year's historic, bi-partisanly supported federal budget, which will balance out in 2002.

He feels that the package of tax cuts required by this budget slashed too deeply and that the balance will be made on the backs of the poor. "It took away every human service safety net from the people at the bottom of our country," Davis said.

"We're cutting spending on the most vulnerable in our society, cutting Medicare by $115 billion, but still giving $150 billion in corporate welfare. We cannot have a great civilization or humane nation without paying the cost. If all we do is cut, cut, cut, all we will get is blood, blood, blood."

A Voice on the Floor

Davis has taken to the floor numerous times in this 105th Congress to voice similar concerns about social legislation. He has spoken elegantly against school vouchers and in defense of the Women, Infants, and Children's program when it was targeted for cuts.

Davis has also been outspoken in his efforts to get more stringent laws in place aimed at regulating handgun manufacturers and distributors. "Face it, the only real purpose of handguns is to kill somebody," he says. "You don't hunt with them, or sport shoot, and it's crazy to think they're useful for self-defense.

"In the meantime, homicide by guns is the leading cause of death for young African Americans. We must continue the effort to reduce the number of handguns on our streets, especially in inner-city communities, and the only way to do that is to keep pushing the idea that Joe Blow just does not need a snub-nosed revolver."

Davis, a loquacious orator, has spoken from the House floor on all kinds of issues and expresses some "surprise and amazement at the level of opportunity that has existed to effectively participate." But it was one of the reasons he wanted to go to Congress, where he says the "pulpit is more expansive and influential, and the arena you play in is bigger."

Davis has had the chance to assert some influence on the two committees on which he sits, Government Reform and Oversight – which is investigating the current hot-button issue of campaign finance reform – and Small Business. The Freshman Congressman authored an amendment to "correct" the fact that very little Small Business Administration (SBA) loan money actually gets to inner-city ethnic minorities.

While the amendment didn't pass, it stirred enough debate to warrant the Small Business Committee to conduct full hearings on the matter last month. "As a result," says Davis, "I'm almost certain we're going to get some changes in the way SBA operates."

That's just one of several significant accomplishments of his short tenure. Davis was also able to take the lead in getting his district declared a federal disaster area after massive flooding from the rains of August. More than 31,000 Seventh District residents have applied for relief and obtained more than $29 million in grants and $7 million in loans so far.

Davis was also able to lobby Veterans Secretary Jesse Brown to prevent any of the three veterans hospitals in the 7th District from being closed due to downsizing. And he played a pivotal behind-the-scenes role in causing the Justice Department to decide to investigate police brutality in Chicago following the Jeremiah Mearday incident.

Davis' office has announced an $8 million grant for the Sinai family health centers; a $600,000 grant for Haymarket House; and money has been obtained for an AIDS clinic. A job fair his organization sponsored attracted more than 1,000 people and was a huge success. Currently, Davis is working with schools trying to actively recruit students to sign up for the nation's military academies, which are offering scholarships worth $100,000.

A People's Coalition

The Congressman administers his efforts through the People's Assembly, a grassroots consortium involving

a wide spectrum of district residents who help provide direction. The Assembly meets about twice a month at Edna's restaurant, and the core group of 75-100 can nearly quadruple in size as people easily flow in and out of these lobbying, and planning sessions.

The Assembly is a vehicle for brainstorming with people across a broad range of professions. More than 20 subcommittees have been established in such areas as public health, tax reform, unemployment, education, the environment, and youth and women's issues. These committees present policy positions to Davis, which he eventually plans to sponsor as legislation. The education committee, for instance, has actually written two bills that the Congressman expects to introduce shortly.

His reliance on the Assembly is rooted in the same reasoning that is the basis for the more than 30 town hall meetings Davis has hosted across the breadth of the district, involving everyone from school kids to church and business leaders – to update, give-and-take, and stay in touch with the constituency.

"I'm into this democratic activism thing," Davis explains. "I've learned there's not a lot an individual can do in terms of public policy-making, but there are a lot of things groups of individuals can do working together. If you can bring people together and have them play a rightful part in what's going on, you can accomplish things."

On reflection, Davis expressed happiness about his first year. "What I don't like about Congress is that you don't have as much of an opportunity or time to nurture intimate relationships," he assessed.

"I might see my wife on Monday and not again until Friday. And I went to see my daddy on Labor Day cause I hadn't seen him but once this year. Friends and associates — you don't have as much time for them.

"But that's the only down side. On the up side, Momma Hawk's kids made a beautiful piece of art for me. You get to see so much good and be a part of it. And you play a part on the world stage.

"I want to see the same thing for people throughout the world that I want to see for my constituents on the West Side of Chicago, especially those who are poor and oppressed and in need of technical help and resource development. You can't think of yourself in an isolated way, you've got to see yourself as part of a larger whole.

"Yep," Davis ended conclusively, smiling introspectively, "we've been able to deliver goods and to become a more influential player in the process. Without acting like Tarzan and beating the chest or anything, we've been quite pleased over a very productive first year."

preface
de'Alexander

Update: Quinton continues to design fabulous couture clothing and produce fashion shows. In 2013 he started the 'We Dream in Color' project. In 2017 the project became a foundation. They provide gourmet dining for the homeless. They provide clothing and toys for cancer patients during the holiday season, and he encourages makeovers for women undergoing life challenges, particularly cancer, domestic violence and substance abuse.

Quinton de' Alexander

By Barbara Samuels & Photography by Reginald Payton | *Originally Published May 10, 2001*

Fashion innovator Quinton de' Alexander is famous for many things – his imposing 6'6" height, an unerring attention to detail, and his jaw-dropping "drama dresses."

As CEO of Chez de' Alexander, he is an award-winning designer whose fashions have graced runways from coast to coast. He strongly believes in the words of Helen Keller, that "life is either a daring adventure, or nothing."

"No other quote expresses my philosophy better," he admits. "I put my all behind my projects. You must continually reinvent yourself and take risks. One should always make time to give back to the community; I have done so throughout my career."

de' Alexander gives back in a big way. He is Chairman of the Ellis Foster Excellence in Performance Arts Scholarship Foundation; a board member of Concerned Citizens, Inc./Mother's House; a volunteer for the City of Hope and Celebrating Life Foundation's study of breast cancer facilities; the Illinois Chapter of the Lupus Foundation; Orchid Village; and he works closely with the DuSable Museum.

> He justifies owning over 300 suits by saying, "I don't think a designer should be seen wearing the same outfit twice."

Quinton produces fashion shows. His most notable was one called Spring Sensations. He says, "A production like Spring Sensations proves that a variety of artisans can work together for a common cause. There are enough clients out there for all of us. I want to further the careers of other designers, as well as my own. I even recommend others to my clients, and the gesture is reciprocated."

de' Alexander shakes his head as he talks about the planning processes behind the Sensations show. "I have a reputation for being difficult to work with," he says. "I suppose that's true when you're mounting a hopefully flawless show that people will enjoy long after the curtain has gone down."

"But I'm not hard to work with; I just want things to work the right way. My shows are avant-garde, and every scene is designed to be a showstopper. There's no time for chaos or hurt feelings. Some people just don't like to take directions."

de' Alexander deSigns

He doesn't draw the line when it comes to creating apparel. de' Alexander sews for men, children, and women of all sizes. He sews for anyone who can afford his prices, but don't look for bargains if you see something you like.

Gowns are created from the most fabulous and expensive fabrics he can find. Add in the cost of solid crystal trims, opulent finishes, and just the drama of sewing yards of ruffles and other refinements, and you'll understand why his gowns are expensive.

His prices range from $500 to $5,000 on less elaborate gowns. An exquisite hand-beaded couture gown can range from $5,000 to $15,000. A simple prom dress can cost under $500 depending on the design and fabrication.

In spite of the large amount of press coverage and exposure he has received, de' Alexander's manner is down-to-earth and warm. He is quick to laugh, and uses animated gestures throughout his conversation. He is passionate about his work, and freely expresses his concern and compassion for the "underdog."

Along with top professional models, he is known for including a few amateurs who don't have the self-confidence the pros possess. "Nothing makes me happier than to see a model who started out with low self-esteem come to life and blossom on the runway," Quinton says. "I love to use older or larger models, along with the 5'10", size 6's and 8's."

Another fine point: he does not make clothes that show lots of skin. He feels that women should show their natural beauty. "Everything does not have to hang out," he says.

de' Alexander's designs have appeared in major newspapers and magazines across the United States. He has been seen on the Danny Bonaduce television talk show. His styles were featured on-stage in the Ebony Fashion Fair fashion shows, and in *Harlem*

Suite, starring Stephanie Mills and Maurice Hines; *Beauty Shop III*; *Song Diva*; and *The Spiritual Revolt of Nathan Branch*.

His latest honor came when the 2001 Mrs. Illinois/USA Pageant Finalist Nicole Wondrasek won the "Most Original Design" award, wearing a cardinal red glitter gown bedecked with Austrian crystals created by Quinton.

The designer is inspired by the texture and glow of a fabric. The fabric actually "speaks" to him. "I carry my sketchbook in my head. When I am inspired, I mentally 'see' a design," he says. "For detailing, I use paper. Sometimes I can dream of a design. I keep a notepad beside my bed. I normally wake myself up and sketch out basic ideas and details."

Admiration, Contribution, Vision

Quinton is busier this year than he's ever been — and that's going some. He is creating gowns for a variety of social events, including the 2001 *N'DIGO* Awards Gala on June 16th. He is also working on his Fall and Holiday lines.

In the midst of all this, de' Alexander is formulating a plan for his largest event yet. "Creativity United" will be an all-star coalition of nine of the top designers in Chicago. Acclaimed dancer Joel Hall will choreograph the event, and he is looking forward to working with the impressive list of designers who have expressed an interest in participating.

According to de' Alexander, "There is no reason why nine highly visible couturiers with different design philosophies can't pull together to make the event a success." Former New York supermodel Peggy Dillard Boone (now a national fashion and beauty columnist) will also play a major part in the presentation.

"In order to grow, we must learn to work together — exclusive of race. People say I am striving to be the best. That is not true. I want to be one of the best. When you're the best, there's nowhere else to go," Quinton declares.

Moving forward, de' Alexander has designed an eye-catching denim collection for fashion-forward men and women called "DEEZ JEANS."

These are denims with a difference. Trimmed with snakeprint and bold graphics, the line will be carried at Mario Uomo in late July. "I design everything I wear, from T-shirts to tuxedos, and I greatly enjoy what I wear," Quinton says.

He justifies owning over 300 suits by saying, "I don't think a designer should be seen wearing the same outfit twice. Everyone expects us to look good and different all the time."

He is not so involved in his creativity that he cannot name others that he greatly admires in the fashion industry. He respects the artistry of Valentino of Rome, and Maria Pinto of Chicago.

He also names Ken Owen, who consults with Mrs. Eunice W. Johnson in the preparation of the Ebony Fashion Fair show. He rounds out his list by naming local talents Herbert VanStephens and Barbara Bates.

If he were not so immersed in fashion, de' Alexander would choose to work in the mental health field. He volunteers some of his time helping people who are mentally incapacitated. Of all the volunteer work he performs in the name of charity, he considers his mental health activities among the most important.

"Shelters and hospitals need much more funding than they receive," he says. "Patients should have safe, clean facilities where they can get the kind of help they need for recovery."

He has envisioned owning a boutique that will have a French feeling as far as décor is concerned.

The showplace will be upscale, hung with crystal chandeliers, and furnished with fine antiques.

preface Dee

Update: Merri Dee was a journalist for WGN-TV from 1972 to 1983. She was Director of Community Relations from 1983 until she retired in 2008. Merri has since been inducted into the National Association of Black Journalists' Hall of Fame and is currently the Illinois State President of AARP, which has 1.7 members statewide.

Merri Dee

By Rita Coburn Whack & Photography by Victor Powell | *Originally Published September 27, 2001*

Vintage wines, classic literature, and well-seasoned marinades all operate on the principle that if one starts with a good creation, maintains it and holds onto it over time, the natural end result will be better, much better, than its beginnings. This is what I am thinking about as I watch Merri Dee look over the golf greens at the Flossmoor Country Club.

Once again, there is an outing, a fund-raiser and a need for a speaker, a motivator, and an icon. Once again, there is a cause and those who can give will give, but their resources need to be tapped, and they need to be entertained and enlightened. In the process, a bridge must be built.

While Merri Dee is many things, most notably Director of Community Relations for WGN-TV, the elegant face and manicured nails that pull the winning numbers several times a week for the Illinois State Lottery, a national speaker, a self-confessed doting grandmother, and an undisputed class act whenever she simply walks out the door, many don't realize that she is an architect of sorts.

> **Walking into the room with Merri was like walking with royalty.**

Educated as an engineer, it was natural beauty that placed her career cornerstone in the community as the first Black female to become a spin model for the auto show held at McCormick Place in the late 1960s.

Dee says, "You were hired and given the script a week before. You had to know the interior and exterior, all about the motor, and we weren't allowed to talk to the people passing by." That included those who marched by with inflated chests, straightened backs and coifed afros whispering or proclaiming, "Get it girl." "Look, a sister is up there." It was big time.

From a profession where she was not allowed to speak to passersby, Dee discovered her broadcast voice as "Merri Dee the Honey Bee" for WBEE radio. Entertainers like Tim Reid, Cannonball Adderley, Ramsey Lewis, Sammy Davis Jr., Tom Dreesen, and Nancy Wilson fostered relationships and some became life-long friends.

After the race riots of the 1960s, when television stations decided to play fair, or more accurately, began the process of hiring African Americans as reporters, Dee was hired by WGN as a TV newscaster, announcer, and also a radio show host. After she became the television talk show host for the station's public service program, *Heart of Chicago*, Dee was offered the position of Director of Community Relations.

Twenty-nine years later, having outlasted all her original counterparts in the market, she has survived and flourished under nine management teams. One former general manager, Dennis FitzSimons, describes a day in the community with Dee.

"Shortly after I became general manager of WGN-TV, I attended a Chicago community event with Merri Dee," he says. "Walking into the room with Merri was like walking with royalty. I knew Merri had a great relationship with the community, but I didn't realize the full extent of the goodwill Merri generated from her years of volunteer work."

Early on, Dee's unquestioned strength in the Black community opened opportunities to serve a larger public. Crossing race, color, gender and political lines in greater Chicago, throughout Illinois and speaking on a national level seemed like an effortless move.

A Childhood In A Simpler Time

As the National President of the National African-American Speakers Association, drifting back to her South Side beginnings, Dee says she has always been a talker and a helper.

"I remember being like this when I was little at seven, eight and nine. I was going to the grocery store for the senior citizens, helping kids draw hopscotch on the sidewalk," says Dee, who attended Englewood High School and is a graduate of Xavier University with a degree in business administration.

"It was a neighborhood of churches. Reverend Cobb's church was across the alley and we would sit on the steps in the evening at sundown and all the kids would talk about the problems of the world.

"It was a neighborhood of basement stores where you could get not penny candy, but five for a penny candy. It was a neighborhood of smells, we could smell the Silvercup Bread Bakery." She makes a face quickly followed by a smile, "you could smell the stockyards."

These humble beginnings sent Dee on a journey that would cross its own version of fresh baked bread and stockyard smells. The bitter with the sweet, the good with the bad, and a dark shroud of ugliness – the well-publicized shooting incident that left one man dead and Merri Dee with two gunshot wounds to the head.

Dee is never far away from the memory, the drive out to the Flossmoor Country Club, the pass by Beaubien Forest Preserves, she says.

Shortly after becoming host of *Heart of Chicago*, Dee was kidnapped along with a man who had been a guest on the show that day. They were taken to the forest preserve; both were shot in the head. The guest died and Dee eventually crawled to the highway. Even then, after flagging down cars, finally arriving at a hospital, she was still questioned at length before being given medical treatment.

Dee recalls her teenage daughter growing up overnight, rushing to the bedside of a mother in a coma and never again feeling that they should be separated for long periods of time.

Dee says her care was hampered by racism, but she also recalls the will to live for her daughter and her own love of life. Still, there are other reminders, like the chronic pain in the head she has learned to live with on a daily basis, coupled with a periodic loss of feeling in her face.

One benefit of the incident was a law Dee fought to change once she found out her assailant had been released from prison without her knowledge. Successful lobbying in the Illinois legislature now helps prevent others from the surprise of a convicted offender being released without the victim's knowledge and allows an impact statement by the survivor of the crime.

And there are other poignant reminders: "I'm out in the community all the time and somebody's kid gets shot and somebody calls me and they think that I can bring up the rear and heal the world because God has blessed me," Dee notes.

"I had to stop going to children's funerals because there seems to be no evening out of murders.

I stopped because it became too emotional for me. You cannot do that over and over again and not feel anything. You feel it every time. You see the pain that comes to families."

Unbelievable Drive

That concern for children became another station hat for Dee to wear when she was given the additional title of Manager of WGN-TV Children's Charities.

Her positive energy and earned popularity have helped raise money to offer children and their families services that impact a wide range of programs, among them adoption, education, physically challenged care needs, and the arts.

"I have helped raise about $19 million for children," Dee says. "When I add in the United Negro College Fund – this is my 23rd year doing the telethon – I would probably add another $20 million to that easily."

What drives a woman to arrive at WGN's North Side station most mornings shortly after dawn, attend a business meeting, rifle through paperwork and meet with community leaders, go in front of the camera for the Lottery pull before heading out the door to a charity luncheon, stop by corporate headquarters downtown, return to her desk, head to the studio to record some public service announcements, meet with advocates of a new community program, head off to speak at a business dinner, then appear as the emcee at another event and head home for a few hours of shuteye, only to arrive literally just after dawn the next morning to embark on a similar day, which will lead to another, often a jaunt out of town during the week and back for more work on at least one day of the weekend?

It's a drive that makes some people feel a bit lax, even jealous. "I find myself putting out a disclaimer in some groups: Don't let me drive you crazy with all this energy. Unless you are ready to work real hard, then maybe you shouldn't have me in it," she says.

"I feel kind of crazy sometimes, like I should slow down to be normal. But I am a happy camper, living in the light and loving it. I love what I do and have no intentions of stopping anytime soon."

Merri Dee

preface Dickens

Update: One of the most prominent African-American financiers in Chicago for over five decades, Jacoby Dickens passed away in 2013 at the age of 82. He distinguished himself as much for his philanthropic efforts as for his entrepreneurial successes.

In addition to the community outreach programs developed through Seaway, Dickens designed a loan and scholarship program at DePaul University named in his honor. As a director of Chicago State University, Dickens donated more than $1 million to the institution. In 1995, the Chicago State University gym was renamed the Jacoby Dickens Physical Education and Athletics Center in his honor.

Jacoby did remarry, in 1998, and when he passed, his wife Veranda Dickens assumed chairmanship of the board of Seaway, making the bank the largest Black-owned, woman-owned bank in the nation at the time, with assests of over $378 million and 220 employees. Seaway Bank was sold in 2017.

Cover photo by David Jenkins

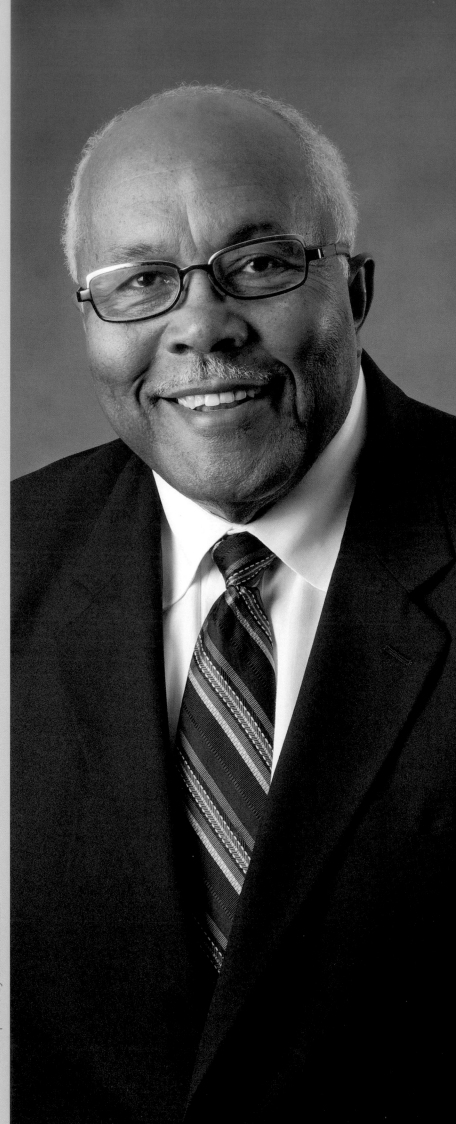

Jacoby Dickens

By Derrick K. Baker & Photos by Essential Photography | *Originally Published May 1990*

Engaging in a one-on-one conversation with Jacoby Dickens, chairman of Seaway National Bank of Chicago, and listening to his seemingly endless anecdotes and philosophies, is like talking to several different people – all at the same time.

Dickens is a deep well of experiences, insights and explanations, all of which helps one understand more about the introspective man that leads Seaway National Bank, the largest African American-owned bank in the country.

To learn of his stature in Chicago's business and civic communities is to be duly impressed. To listen while the thoughtful bank executive, who was once told he should become an undertaker, relives his years as a young adult is to understand the meaning of perseverance and persistence. And pride. And respect.

In short, to know Jacoby Dickens, the man and the banker, is to like him.

Born in 1931 in Panama City, Florida, population 36,000, Dickens came to Chicago at the age of 15 and enrolled at Wendell Phillips High School. That was the first of a few sojourns at the likes of Roosevelt University, Wilson Junior College (now Kennedy-King College) and the U.S. Army, where Dickens served for two years as a dental lab technician.

> As chairman of Seaway, I'm more sensitive to the needs of the community because it was a stroke of luck for me to find someone so sensitive to recognize *my* needs.

Despite his stints at several schools, he never actually earned a degree ("I started making money too soon," he explains). It was in 1954 that educators at the University of Chicago told Dickens that his future was in the undertaking business.

"I was determined, if nothing else, to make the University of Chicago wrong," he now says from his small, tastefully appointed office overlooking 87th Street.

Although he didn't immediately set the business world on fire, Dickens did venture down another career path, this time in the warehouse at Goldblatt's department store. There he worked for about a year before taking on a second job as a night janitor at the University of Illinois Dental and Medical School.

Almost miraculously, Dickens worked both jobs – full-time, no less – for the next five years while also attending night school. It was then that his business acumen began to rear its ingenious head, for during those five years, Dickens never cashed a single payroll check from his second job. By depositing each check in his savings account, he was able to buy his first apartment building in 1959.

Dickens went into business as a real estate developer in the same South Side neighborhoods where he was raised. He was able to purchase, renovate and lease apartment buildings in key areas of the city during the peak of the Northern Migration. At the height of this enterprise, Dickens managed more than 100 apartments.

Not one to wear out his welcome, nor his body, Dickens tired of working 16 hours every day and after five years of doing just that, in a bold move, he resigned from both jobs on the same day. He did so knowing that he had already passed the Chicago Board of Education's engineers exam, which is one of the positions at the board in which he worked for the next 13 years. He actually started as a janitor and then became a fireman, and finally was promoted to engineer.

Bowling For Bucks

In 1969, Dickens made the first of several major business acquisitions. Armed with experience in organizing and overseeing bowling leagues on the South Side, he joined forces with his friend, legendary radio disc jockey Daddy-O-Daylie, as an investor to purchase Starlite Bowling Lanes on East 87th Street. Ironically, Starlite is located a few hundred yards from Seaway, the bank he would later lead to prominence.

Dickens explains that the headache that he and Daylie went through to secure a $260,000 loan to purchase Starlite is one that indelibly impacted the way in which he now runs Seaway.

After being rejected by nine banks, he and Daylie applied for a loan from Continental Bank and worked with a loan officer who also had designs for his own future. His name? Roland Burris, now comptroller of the state of Illinois.

Once the $260,000 loan was approved under a Small Business Administration program, Dickens and Daylie each presented a check for $13,000, which represented the 10 percent they thought was needed as a down payment.

However, says Dickens, "They told us, 'We're going to take your two checks for $13,000 each and deposit them into your checking account because you're going to need this as working capital.' From that day forward, we've never had a (financial) problem because we went in properly financed," explained Dickens. "As a result of that, I've never had to be concerned about my bank balance.

"As chairman of Seaway, I'm more sensitive to the needs of the community because it was a stroke of luck for me to have someone that sensitive to recognize my needs," adds Dickens, peering out of his office window toward Starlite. "Continental's sensitivity is what got me here." (As an aside, the $260,000 loan was the largest at that time ever given to a minority in the SBA Program.)

Once the bowling alley belonged to Dickens and Daylie, business was so prosperous that they were able to pay off the seven-year loan in five years. In 1975, they took out another loan from Continental, this time for $300,000, to refurbish the business. "I called Continental and the only trip I made down there was to pick up the check," he says. That loan was also settled early.

Dickens ran the day-to-day operations of Starlite. In 1975, he ventured out on his own and purchased Skyway Lanes on 99th and South Torrence Avenue, one of the largest African American-owned bowling alleys in the country.

With his Donald Trump-like penchant for acquisitions still brewing, four years later, in 1979, Dickens and a group of investors purchased an NBC television affiliate in Rhinelander, Wisconsin. In 1983, that same group purchased another television station, this time an ABC affiliate in Bangor, Maine.

How does Dickens explain his impressive business resume? "I had an insatiable thirst to succeed. I spent 17 to 18 hours a day, seven days a week in the bowling alley. There was nothing more important to me than that business. I only left to go to sleep. There was no way I could fail," he says with both confidence and rebelliousness. "My whole life was in that place. Not having been in business before, I didn't have the ability to delegate. I thought I had to do everything.

"I'm not suggesting that you have to go to those extremes, but I didn't know when to quit or when to go home. I had and still have the toughest boss I know – me."

However, as successful as Dickens was in the bowling business, he understood two realities. First,

that despite the superhuman effort and hours he put in at Starlite, there was still the chance that it would fail. For that reason, he held on to his job at the Board of Education for the first three years after buying Starlite. Secondly, he understood that even he couldn't be in two places at the same time.

"The long hours remained until I bought the second business in 1975. It taught me what I needed to know about delegating. That was my growth," he says.

Like most successful entrepreneurs, the road Dickens traveled was paved with pitfalls. It cost his first marriage, which ended in divorce in 1968. "I didn't have the luxury of having a wife during that time," he says. "It was me against the world and I liked it that way." As fate would have it, exactly one year to the day after his divorce, Dickens and Daylie finalized their purchase of Starlite.

He joined Seaway as a director in 1978 and became chairman of the board in 1982. Four years later, in 1986, Dickens, who served as chairman of the late Mayor Harold Washington's re-election campaign, bought out Seaway's largest stockholder, Ernest Collins, which, he says, "took the cover off. People then knew I was of some means."

"My goal in life," he says ruefully, "was to be a millionaire and not have anybody know about it. I blew that a long time ago."

At Seaway, Dickens has boosted the bank's outreach and community development programs, giving assistance to neighborhood churches and sponsoring African-American teenagers through high school and college. He has made loans available to small businesses on the South Side that previously had trouble securing credit.

Mirror, Mirror

If it's at least partially true that the way in which a person thinks of himself impacts others' opinions of him, then Dickens' associates and employees probably like and respect him. Often times, the two are mutually exclusive.

"Why do you respect someone?" he asks rhetorically. "Because you like something about them. The business community usually respects people who are successful, whether they deserve the respect or not, although success doesn't say too much about you as a person.

"My customers say I'm tough, no nonsense, frugal. They say I'm not willing to give the product away. I'm not going to walk in the (bowling alley's) bar and buy everybody a drink, but I think they respect me.

"I don't know my customers like I used to," he continues, speaking of the clientele at Starlite. "There may be some resentment because of that. I used to be able to call every customer by name. I knew

something about them and their families. I made that a vocation because it was important.

"I'm God-fearing and proud. I love life and people. I don't smile as often as I should and some people think I'm mean. But that's the way I am. We are what we are."

Dickens, who recently lost 60 pounds to get into better shape, also has the admiration and respect of other executives in the city, as illustrated by his membership and participation in a number of organizations.

They include the boards of the Chicago Urban League, Museum of Science and Industry, DePaul University, United Way, Florida A&M University's School of Business, Chicago Economic Development Commission, Chicago State University, and the Economic Club of Chicago. Dickens sits on the finance committee of the village of Olympia Fields, were he owns a home and he also has a second home not far from Seaway, as well as a home on Fisher Island in Miami.

Despite all of his noteworthy business accomplishments, civic affiliations, power, prominence and personal wealth, Jacoby Dickens, the banking executive who doesn't have a secretary ("I like to answer my own phone," he says), in his seat as chairman of a multi-million dollar financial institution, remains humble and grateful.

What makes him happy? With the look of a kid in a candy store, he says with a laugh, "As long as you spell my name right, I'm happy."

preface Dyson

Update: Marv Dyson celebrated his 50th year in radio in 2017. In his amazing career, he discovered popular on-air talent Doug Banks, who passed away in 2016, and he also gave Steve Harvey his first break in the radio broadcasting industry.

In 1998, Dyson received a Lifetime Achievement Award from the March of Dimes and in 2003, was named the Broadcast Advertising Club of Chicago's Person of the Year. By then, WGCI was owned by Clear Channel Radio, along with other stations including WVAZ/V103, and Dyson was head of the entire Clear Channel cluster.

He retired from WGCI in 2003 and became a founding partner of Urban Radio Broadcasting Group, the second largest Black-owned radio company in the country, which owns 17 radio stations in Mississippi, Alabama and Ohio.

He also became, in 2004, director of operations at WKKC-FM, Kennedy-King College's urban radio station on Chicago's South Side. Dyson is a director emeritus of the Illinois Broadcasting Association.

Marv Dyson

By Derrick K. Baker & Photography by Jason McCoy | *Originally Published June 2, 1995*

Visit the bustling Michigan Avenue headquarters of radio station WGCI/107.5-FM and you'll witness a motley crew of people: excited listeners bouncing in to collect prizes, men and women scrambling about, and disc jockeys in the halls and on the air. Yep, the joint is jumpin'.

Listen to the city's best music station and you quickly understand why Chicagoans feel like 871,600 weekly co-owners, which, of course, is a marketing boon to advertisers. Add to the equation a highly energetic, eyes-on-the-prize staff and you have a recipe for big-time success.

Ask 15-year 'GCI veteran Marv Dyson, the station's president and general manager, to size up his job and he'll emphatically declare: "I'm ecstatic. I love my job. I have, without a doubt, the best job in America. To be running the No. 1 radio station in your own hometown, that is the ultimate ego trip."

> We are the No. 1 radio station in Chicago and we are worth as much as any non-Black radio station in this market.

Dyson is effusive in his praise for the almost 80 account executives, support staff, supervisors, deejays, engineers, producers, etc. who make 'GCI what he calls "the epitome of urban radio," as illustrated by the following:

- The station consistently ranks at or near the top in the major demographic categories: 18-34 years, 28-59 and 25-54. The quarterly race for the ratings crown usually is a two-horse race between WGCI and WGN-AM. On a given day, between 250,000 and 500,000 people tune in.

- Last year, WGCI's billings topped $20 million, up from $2 million in the last year before Dyson took over.

- The station has sponsored successful fundraisers for families and causes and even "stops the hits" whenever it's necessary to discuss such crucial matters as gang violence, teen pregnancy, or HIV/AIDS.

- Other successful station efforts have included voter registration drives, fundraisers for families in need, and the WGCI Music Seminar, which attracts more than 1,000 aspiring singers, musicians and music business executives.

Anatomy Of A Winner

WGCI, with its 33,000-watt signal reaching parts of four states, is Chicago's leading trailblazing urban contemporary radio station and reflects the city that it's in. It is also a heritage radio station, a generation radio station, meaning that a 45-year-old mother would enjoy 'GCI and her 18-year-old child would enjoy it as well.

"I think WGCI is perceived by a lot of Black people as the station they listen to and are proud of, and they feel as if it belongs to them," explains Dyson. "I hear that a lot: 'It's my radio station.'

"Black people take radio very seriously and to heart. Talent, in terms of on-air talent, is probably the most crucial thing that makes us No.1. And I have to give that to Tom Joyner and Doug Banks as our principal anchors, as well as the support staff around them."

At 2 p.m. during the week, all hell breaks loose as Doug Banks, lovingly referred to as "Dan Ryan Head," flies without a net. A nine-year 'GCI veteran, Banks has the proverbial bird's eye view of why the station that's synonymous with his name is also synonymous with No. 1.

"This radio station is not your average radio station," Banks offers. "All the personalities here are like members of your family. It has warmth and the personality is so strong. People who listen day in and day out know what to expect from us.

"They know they are going to hear a good time. But they also know that if there's something wrong in this town, nine times out of 10, they can turn on 'GCI and we're going to talk about it. One of the reasons 'GCI will maintain its position in this market is because it's focused on the community."

Banks, who once had his sights set on an entertainment law career, says, "Chicago is the greatest radio market in the country," and "I have the greatest job in the world." However, his highly successful ten-

Marv Dyson

ure in the Windy City will come to a halt at the end of this year when he moves to Dallas to broadcast a nationally syndicated afternoon radio program.

But, "Chicago is a wonderful place to be. This will always be my home," promises the Detroit native. "This is a town that is very personality-oriented when it comes to radio.

"When I have people come up to me and say, 'I just had a really bad day at work today and listening to you brought me out of a very deep depression,' that means that I've had a good day, as well," says Banks. "Next to the birth of my child and my marriage, that's the best feeling because you know you're helping people."

The Best Station, Period

Being the voice of the community that people turn to for information and direction, Dyson says that the station is not so big and established that it can't try something different.

Over the years, that trying something different has taken the form of playing 10 songs in a row; splitting the mid-day slot between two deejays, and debuting "The Fly Jock" Tom Joyner, who made headlines with his daily commute between radio jobs in Chicago and Dallas.

The one chance they took that really didn't work well was an April Fool's joke a few years ago when the station played country music all day. People did not seem to get the humor in that at all and wanted their station back in their format. Dyson says he sometimes enjoys listening to country music on radio.

He adds to the reasons for GCI's success by noting, "Consistency is the No. 1 thing, as well as an inner drive on the part of everybody at this radio station to be the best in Chicago. Not the best Black station; the best station. I suppose a lot of that probably comes from me because when I took over the reins 15 years ago, I told everybody my goal was to be the No. 1 station in Chicago.

"A lot of people looked at me like I was crazy," recalls Dyson. "But if I'm going to work in my hometown and I'm running a radio station, my ego and my friends would not allow me to be last. I just could not fathom that.

"I told everybody that being good at radio was not brain surgery and that you didn't need to be a nuclear scientist to run a good radio station, because

I'm certainly neither of those things.

"But 15 years ago, when I came in, we thought of ourselves as a Black radio station and our mindset was not getting what we were worth in terms of charging for advertising. That mindset has now changed," says Dyson, a self-proclaimed loner who says he prefers solitude and who calls his "walk-around" management style loose and laid back.

"Now we believe we are the No. 1 radio station in Chicago and we are worth as much as any non-Black radio station in this market. We now ask for the money and if we don't get it, more often than not, we will just walk away from that business."

Always Radio

Dyson was born and raised in the radio business in Chicago, the son of Richard and Florence Dyson, both radio announcers themselves. Marv, however, is quick to credit John Johnson, publisher of *Ebony* and *Jet* magazines, for the opportunity to really learn radio and the opportunity to fail.

Dyson joined WJPC-FM radio here in Chicago in 1968, and soon became president and general manager. "Mr. Johnson had a daytime radio station and he let me run it. I was learning as I went and he understood that," Dyson says.

"We parted ways (in 1978) because he wanted to go in a different direction and I came to WGCI. But he paid me for a year after I left simply because we had a verbal agreement, and I thank him to this day. He literally pushed me to become successful."

Dyson joined 'GCI in 1978 as an account executive, then worked himself up to general manager of the station in 1981 and president in 1994 after leading the station to Chicago's highest audience ratings. He studied Communication and Media Management at The Wharton School in the Class of 1986.

Dyson's short-term goal is for 'GCI to be No. 1 for an entire year (the station already has racked up consecutive three quarters victories and other first-place ratings victories). Even loftier, he has his sights set on 107.5 FM entrenching itself as Chicago's top station for 10 straight years.

Dyson says determinedly, "Most people would be surprised at how serious I am about the success of this radio station."

Actually, looking at and listening to the media giant known as WGCI, no they wouldn't.

preface Ebert

Update: Roger Ebert wrote his best selling memoir in 2011 called *Life Itself*, which was made into a biographical documentary in 2014 after Ebert passed away in 2013 at the age of 70. Chaz Ebert is the publisher of RogerEbert.com and a regular contributor to the site, writing about film, festivals, politics, and life itself.

Cover Photo by Chris Griffin

Chaz Ebert

By Bonnie DeShong & Photos Courtesy of Chaz Ebert | *Originally Published June 27, 2007*

Meet Chaz Hammelsmith Ebert.

Her husband Roger is the most famous, admired, feared and respected American film critic and historian in the world. With the flick of his trademarked thumb, Roger Ebert can catapult an unknown filmmaker to soaring heights – or bury a Hollywood studio's chances at a box office hit.

Roger Ebert has been the film critic of the *Chicago Sun-Times* since 1967 and won the Pulitzer Prize for criticism in 1975. Ebert's reviews are now syndicated in more than 200 newspapers in the U.S., Canada, England, Japan and Greece. He is the only film critic with a star on the Hollywood Walk of Fame and won the Lifetime Achievement Award from the Screen Actors Guild.

> We have never gotten much flack for being in an interracial marriage and we never think about it. But I have seen the privilege and I have also seen how I am treated differently when I am not with him, so I do know the difference.

"One thing I've discovered is that I love my job more than I thought I did," Roger Ebert says. "And I love my wife even more!"

The best onscreen romance would pale in comparison to the tender, unscripted, love story of Roger and Chaz, who married in 1992. In an *N'DIGO* exclusive, Chaz draws the curtains and gives us a peek into the charmed life of a beautiful Black girl from Chicago's West Side who conquered a Hollywood kingmaker – without losing her sense of self.

Bonnie DeShong/N'DIGO: *Chaz, tell us about your childhood.*

CHAZ EBERT: I grew up on the West Side of Chicago; I lived on Roosevelt Road and Racine. I have four brothers and four sisters. There were actually 11 of us, but two died very young. Dad worked at the stockyards as a butcher. He was a quiet man, but he took care of his family. We knew he loved us and I always felt very secure as a child.

Mother was the kind of woman that when she walked into a room, she brought the sunshine with her. She was such an optimist; I think that is where I get my optimism.

Bonnie: *As a little girl, what did you want to be when you grew up?*

CHAZ: From the time I was six years old, I always had three dreams: I wanted to be a lawyer; I wanted to make an entrée into international diplomacy; and I always wanted to be a philanthropist.

Bonnie: *What is your educational background?*

CHAZ: I went to John H. Smith Elementary School and Crane High School. I went to the University of Dubuque in Dubuque, Iowa. I received my master's degree from the University of Wisconsin and my law degree from DePaul. I was always either the president or vice president of the class or National Honors Society or some group.

In college, I was the Chair of the Black Student Union – it was called the Black Presidium – and at law school at DePaul, I was the president of the Black American Law Student Association.

Bonnie: *Leaving Chicago and attending college in Iowa had to be culture shock for you.*

CHAZ: When I first went to school in Dubuque they still had signs on the cash registers about not cashing Negro checks. Growing up on the West Side of Chicago, I could go blocks and blocks without seeing a White person, we were so segregated, and yes, it was a major adjustment.

Bonnie: *You became a mother and then a wife as a teenager. How did you manage to stay on track with your schooling and dreams of becoming a lawyer?*

CHAZ: My children were born in the early 1970s, so I took them to class with me. I also had the support of

my mother and my aunt. My biggest fear was I didn't want to bring shame on my family.

But my family gathered around me and was so nurturing. My then-husband's family loved our children and was very supportive of us. We didn't have much money growing up, but I felt so fortunate to be a part of this wonderful family.

Bonnie: *What kind of mother are you?*

CHAZ: I am a "Helicopter Mother," one that hovers over her children. I am very over-protective. My son and daughter are in their thirties now and I still hover.

Bonnie: *Tell us about Chaz, the lawyer.*

CHAZ: I have always done civil litigation. I've done civil rights work. I worked at the EEOC. I enforced discrimination laws; fighting for the underdog has always been my passion.

Bonnie: *So why did you stop practicing law?*

CHAZ: When Roger and I decided to get married, I knew I could not continue to practice law and travel with him. He traveled all the time. When we started dating, I didn't know how much traveling he did and I thought it would be temporary.

But I discovered that's his life, with the film festivals and speaking engagements and his natural love of traveling. We found that I was well suited and very much qualified to look out over the whole enterprise of the Ebert Company, so I became the vice president of the Ebert Company.

Bonnie: *How did you and Roger meet?*

CHAZ: Ann Landers and Roger were very good friends and they were out at a restaurant. Roger saw me and wanted to meet me. I was at a table with people they both knew and Ann brokered an introduction. I guess, as they say, the rest is history.

Bonnie: *How did you know he was the one?*

CHAZ: I noticed that, even at the first dinner, there were other people at the table and when conversations stopped, he and I kept talking. I knew he was interesting to talk to and very bright. I like very smart men and he is a great storyteller and very funny, and he made me laugh. Also, my mother liked him a lot.

Bonnie: *How did Roger propose?*

CHAZ: He proposed in Monte Carlo. It was during the Grand Prix and we were in Monaco sitting out by the harbor. He didn't know that he was going to propose to me that day. There was a lull in the action because the cars weren't going around.

We were sort of sitting there and he said, "I would like to spend the rest of my life with you." He then said, "Should I get down on my knee?" and I said, "No, that isn't necessary. Let me think about it." It was very, very sweet.

Bonnie: *What have you brought to Roger's life?*

CHAZ: He said that I was one of the most optimistic women he has ever met, one of the smartest, and he says that he never knows what I am going to do. Every day is a mystery. He also loved the fact that I am so family oriented and he said I was very balanced and sane and secure. That comes from growing up with a mother and father who loved me.

Bonnie: *What has Roger brought to your life?*

CHAZ: One thing I love about Roger is that he lets me be me. I'm a very complex character and everyone who knows me knows it. I also love that he reads as much, really more than I do, and we can talk about a lot of things. He has a big curiosity about the world and he has the biggest heart for humanity and people, which is very important to me.

Chaz Ebert

Bonnie: *After 15 years of marriage, how do you keep it fresh?*

CHAZ: It sounds like a cliché, but every day is a new day. We both are very curious and we both want to see what's going to happen tomorrow. We don't take each other or anything for granted. We are both tremendously interested in politics and our grandchildren. There is just always something new going on in the world and we are very good friends.

Bonnie: *How do you keep from being eaten up in the Roger Ebert frenzy?*

CHAZ: I'll tell you something very funny. When Roger and I were first dating, before we were engaged, if people knew I was just a girlfriend, they would almost sweep me aside to do interviews with him. Or women would run up to give phone numbers to him.

I was like, wait a minute, no, no this cannot happen. I don't know what other people were used to, but this was not something that I could allow. I told him he had to control that situation and he was the one to teach people how to treat me. I love him for that.

Bonnie: *Do you and Roger feel any flack for being an interracial couple?*

CHAZ: Quite frankly, to be truthful about it, we have never gotten much flack for being in an interracial marriage and we never think about it. He's Roger and I'm Chaz.

I did realize that there are some areas – geographical, cultural and political areas – that I have been privy to that I wouldn't be if I were alone or if my husband was an African American. I have seen the privilege and I have also seen how I am treated differently when I am not with him, so I do know the difference.

Bonnie: *What do you do for fun?*

CHAZ: My all-time favorite thing to do is being with family. We may rent a house in Jamaica, or a villa in Tuscany or take a barge through the French locks in Burgundy. But the most important part of it is having several generations together.

Bonnie: *Are you a spiritual person?*

CHAZ: I was tremendously humbled when my husband was sick. He was in the hospital for eight months. I was there by his bedside and I saw things I have never seen before. I do believe in miracles, today I do believe in miracles. I saw a miraculous healing of him.

So many people came and held my hand and we held prayer circles. Not only for him, but also for everyone in need. I called out to the religious community from all faiths and they came and we prayed. People reached out from all over the world telling me about their dreams and prayers. I learned how to pray in a way I never knew I could pray before and I won't stop praying for people.

preface
Evans

Update: Reverend Evans and Lutha Mae have been married for more than 60 years. He led Fellowship until 2010, when he retired. The Rev. Clay Evans Archives, chronicling his 91 years of life and work, will be exhibited at the Harold Washington Library, Chicago's main library branch, in 2017. A musical legend, Rev. Evans has had 11 albums chart on the Billboard Gospel Albums list since 1984.

Reverend Clay Evans

By Wanda Wright & Photos Courtesy of the Chicago Public Library, Special Collections, Rev. Clay Evans Archives | *Originally Published December 12, 1996*

Under the authority of every good man lies a good woman...not as a doormat, neither as an accessory, nor as a partner of "convenience." Rev. Dr. Clay Evans, as a good man, selected the prettiest girl in Brownsville, Tennessee to share his dreams and life with. Fifty years and five talented children later, Lutha Mae (nee Hollinshed) Evans is still the girl of his heart.

How do you keep the music playing that long? Especially above the moral cacophony through which America's been howling since they first met? The Evans' formula for a long and happy marriage is extraordinarily simple. In fact, most of us have a copy of their guidebook in our own homes.

It's God's Word, the Bible, and in it, Proverbs 31:10-31 personifies this couple's credo in the classic section that glorifies the virtuous wife whose price is far above rubies. Rev. Evans goes to war, Lutha Mae keeps the homefires brightly burning.

Blessed With Strong Character

Both were reared in religious homes, where love, respect and genuine care were daily legislation. Rev. Evans reflects on his early character-building years with frequent references to the lesson taught by his mother. "With strong character, you have something that no one can ever challenge. It belongs only to you, and no one can ever remove it," Evans says.

> God has made provisions...I just pray for guidance.

"Giving someone a small measure of respect is so rewarding. I still have no problem saying, 'Yes, Ma'am,' and 'No, Sir.' After all these years, the response from that kind of recognition remains warm and is passed on."

Trained as a mortician through Worsham College of Mortuary Science, Evans tried to ignore a louder voice. But obeying the call to the Ministry, he assumed the cloak of Founder and Pastor of Fellowship Missionary Baptist Church.

After he was ordained in 1950, the young couple built a huge following from humble beginnings. But they have never been impressed with the material aspects that have come from managing their flock.

"God has made provision," smiles Rev. Evans. "I just pray for guidance."

The church is housed in a beautiful building that recently added a school facility. It sits as a modern edifice, built from faith, at 45th Place and Princeton Avenue, amid the demarcation of neighborhoods that reflect despair and poverty. By choice they remain here to make a difference in lives. Rev. Evans wants to restore souls in America.

Restoring Damaged Souls

During a religious convention in Chicago, Evans told his colleagues: "Damaged souls are a result of the constant pressures of police brutality, sick education and political institutions that have drained our spirits. The Samaritan woman who met Jesus at the well was a victim of racism.

"She is indicative of the thirst of the soul that exists among all people when one's inner source of renewal and hope has dried up. Our resilience is flimsy, our guards are down and our defenses weak when our souls are empty. We as ministers must provide the soul transplant."

The Evans phone rings around the clock for advice, assistance and support. Lutha Mae fiercely supports her husband's leadership choices and remains at his side to fit in whenever she is needed.

But she avoids the spotlight, choosing to maintain a haven – an inviting and warm refuge for a taxing ministry that now spans 10 states.

Halls behind the sanctuary are loaded with history that embraces people of all color. Photos of Dr. Martin Luther King Jr., co-pastor Rev. Jesse Jackson, Al Raby, Father George Clements, Nelson Mandela, Mayor Daley Sr. and Jr., and former U.S. presidents line the walls.

There are also elegantly framed thank you and commendation letters, declarations from clergy, governors and heads of state. There is a framed thank you from Operation PUSH that honors Rev. Evans for seeing fellow board members and the organization through rough financial times.

Fellowship has been one of the main churches selected for visiting by many celebrities and dignitaries.

Reverend and Mrs. Clay Evans
at a diner, circa 1945

Vice President Al and Tipper Gore stopped by and selected Evans to officiate during this year's Democratic National Convention.

Celebrating The Golden Anniversary

During the Evans' Golden Anniversary recently, luminaries, clerical and city officials were front and center to hand deliver wishes of happiness to the couple. Rev. Dr. and Mrs. Evans graciously received all guests with the same amount of enthusiasm.

It is no secret that Rev. Evans holds tremendous political clout, clout that sometimes raises eyebrows in the community. Here today, gone tomorrow, this minister believes that all things eventually pass away. His support of Mayor Daley for hiring people from his congregation received public thanks and spirited rhetoric.

But he praises all efforts to unite the disenfranchised, including those of Minister Louis Farrakhan. "Anybody who can gather more than one million African American men for a positive, healthy exchange of information, deserves credit," says Evans, who doesn't believe that he has any power, save the Grace of God and looks to no one to define who he is.

Much of the history he has lived is contained in his autobiography, *From Plough Handle to Pulpit: The Life Story of Rev. Clay Evans.* Or in the music that has come from the collective efforts of the African American Religious Connection.

As a bottomline, he tries not to personally influence anyone with anything but the Gospel, and answers to no one, except the good Lord and Lutha Mae. Mrs. Evans runs the household. Once Reverend steps across the threshold, she's the Boss and Prayer Warrior.

Both partners agree that their happiness and successful union is based on respecting boundaries. Whether husband Clay is called across the state or continent to consult on world issues, or rushes tirelessly out to console the sick or needy, Lutha Mae takes care of her children and the household.

Navigating The Ship

Any church business is handled by a well-trained core of parishioners or employees and remains the territory of the parish. They have seldom if ever had an argument. Her mission is accomplished through the power of prayer, a faithful commitment to God, her husband, and traditional family responsibilities.

"Captain" Clay Evans and Lutha Mae have been soul mates for years, and although she would like to see her 75-years young husband retire, she realizes that he navigates the "Ship" with love and concern for all. As Pastor, he is still trying to raise the emotions and intellect to free those who cannot lift themselves from mental enslavement.

With quiet strength and honor, Mrs. Evans wears not only the clothing, but the crown of a "good woman," exemplifying the strength of a role model – one from whom we can all learn valuable lessons about holding a marriage together for endless years of happiness.

Left: Reverend Clay Evans at the opening day of the New Fellowship Missionary Baptist Church building, April 8, 1973.
Below: Operation Breadbasket ministers watch Dr. King sign a covenant.

preface Farrakhan

Update: Founded in 1930 by Master Wallace D. Fard Muhammad and led to prominence from 1934 to 1975 by the Honorable Elijah Muhammad, the Nation of Islam continues to positively impact the quality of Black life in America.

Today, Minister Farrakhan's Nation of Islam is alive and well with tens of thousands of well-organized followers in over 120 cities in America, Europe, and the Caribbean, as well as missions in West and South Africa.

In 1993, Minister Farrakhan penned the book, *A Torchlight for America*, which applied the guiding principles of justice and goodwill to the problems perplexing this country.

In 1995, Minister Farrakhan and the Nation of Islam enjoyed a banner year with the successful "Million Man March" on the National Mall in Washington, D.C., which drew nearly two million Black men. Minister Farrakhan was inspired to call the march out of his concern over the negative image of Black men perpetuated by the media, which focuses on drugs and gang violence and being less than real men.

Cover photo by Michael Gunn

Minister Louis Farrakhan

By Hermene Hartman & Photos Courtesy of *The Final Call* | Originally Published November 1993

The Honorable Minister Louis Farrakhan. The mere mention of his name provokes America's strongest emotion – racism.

He is one of the country's most misunderstood men. He is as feared as he is revered. His words ignite. It is commonplace for Black leadership to be called on to denounce him. His is a lone militant voice in the Malcolm X tradition. To say that he is controversial is an understatement.

He is also a contradiction. The media scolds him constantly, yet he generates stadium-sized crowds to his speeches like rock star concerts. He attracts thousands, more than any other Black leader in America.

> **Elijah Muhammad saw more in me than I saw in myself (but) Malcolm X was the father that I never had, the big brother that I never had, the male image in my life that I never had, and therefore I was to Malcolm like a child is to a parent that the child adores.**

He filled New York's Madison Square Garden to capacity. A crowd of 80,000 heard his fiery words. Sixty thousand came to Atlanta's Dome. More people packed Farrakhan's stadium than the World Series.

He is today's most respected voice among Black youth. They say he understands. They say he hasn't sold out.

The Honorable Minister Louis Farrakhan cannot be overlooked or ignored – this mild-mannered man is always elegantly attired, this perfect polite gentleman groomed in the best of British manner, who says "Yes, sir," and "No, ma'am."

He is a most gracious host, allowing those to dine at his table who are afraid to make their associations with him known publicly. Farrakhan has criticized Black leadership, likening their treatment of him to a prostitute. He has said, "You visit me in the night and are afraid to be caught with me in the daylight."

Looking far younger than his years, he works out daily as a result of being diagnosed in 1991 with prostate cancer that has since been cured. He is a devoted husband with nine children and a grandfather to 23.

He lives in a palace in the old moneyed neighborhood of Kenwood. His home originally belonged to his mentor, the late Honorable Elijah Muhammad; now the Nation of Islam owns the home.

Who is Louis Farrakhan? What does he represent? What does he mean? Does he represent Black America's enlightened self-interest? These are some of the questions we raised in a rare interview with the man.

His Garvey-Inspired Background

Born Louis Eugene Walcott in the Bronx, New York on May 11, 1933, and reared in a highly disciplined and spiritual household in Roxbury, Massachusetts, his mother was a beautiful, proud West Indian woman from St. Kitts who was on the fringe of the Marcus Garvey movement. His father, whom he never knew, was also a Garveyite.

His mother instilled in her child a love and pride of being Black. She introduced him to the NAACP's *Crisis Magazine*, where he read the writings of the famed scholar W.E.B. Du Bois. He read about lynching and other horrors in the *Afro-American* and *Pittsburgh Courier* newspapers.

The Minister recalls a memorable occasion at age 11 that made a lasting impression. While visiting his uncle's home, he saw a picture of a Black man on the living room wall. He stood on a chair to get a better view and questioned his uncle as to who this man was.

The man was Marcus Garvey, his uncle told him. "He's the man that came to unite Black people." Little Louis asked, "Where is he?" When told that he was dead, Louis cried.

But his uncle reassured him that though the man died, his movement lived on. Farrakhan says the picture on the wall of a proud Black man in a Black home was significant for him – his mother's home had a picture of the King and Queen of England and a White Jesus.

Farrakhan's mother also introduced him to the love of his life, music. At an early age he began to play violin, but was discouraged by his teachers from becoming a classical violinist. He had the talent, but that opportunity was not afforded a Black man, or so the prevailing thinking went.

Farrakhan was raised in Boston, where he attended high school and prep school. He traveled south for the first time in his life to attend Winston-Salem Teachers College in North Carolina. He married his childhood sweetheart in September 1953.

Turning his attention to popular music, he became a popular Calypso singer and dancer and won the competition on the Ted Mack Amateur Hour TV show. He was popularly known as "The Charmer."

Becoming A Muslim

It was in Boston that Farrakhan met his spiritual teacher, Malcolm X. Malcolm, recently released from prison, had been appointed by the Honorable Elijah Muhammad and was organizing for the Black Muslims in Boston.

Farrakhan says, "In between show performances, I was introduced to this tall, imposing man that I was kind of frightened of. He had on a brown tam, brown shoes, brown gloves. I shook his hand and got away as quickly as I could. I was 19 years old. But my friends had already told me about 'The Messenger' (Elijah Muhammad)."

In February of 1955, while appearing on Chicago's Rush Street in the Calypso Follies, the young musician was invited to attend the Nation of Islam's National Saviour's Day Convention, at 53rd and Greenwood on the South Side.

At the event, Farrakhan listened to the man who would shape his adult life, Elijah Muhammad, with reservations.

Farrakhan recalls, "I didn't understand everything that he said and I don't know whether I necessarily agreed with everything that he said, but most of what he said that I understood, I was in agreement with.

"You know, he didn't speak very eloquently. So, when he began to speak, I said, 'Oh, this man can't even talk.' And when I said that, he looked up in the balcony where I was sitting, like he heard.

"He said, 'Brother, I didn't get a chance to get that mighty fine education that you got. When I got to the school door, it was closing. Don't pay no attention to how I'm saying it, you pay attention to what I'm saying. And then you take it and put it into that fine language that you know. Only try to understand what I'm saying.'"

Farrakhan's wife and uncle had accompanied him and his uncle became irritated with him. When the altar call came, Farrakhan's wife jumped to her feet and joined the mosque. His uncle told Farrakhan, "Get up."

Farrakhan continues, "I went back to Boston and then moved to New York. A year later, I went to the mosque and heard Malcolm X speak, and that was it. After I heard Malcolm, I did not need to hear any more. I wrote my application letter to join and my wife and I both got our 'X' in October

1955." (Upon becoming a Muslim, it is customary to change your name. Taking on the X is the first order of the process.)

Making A Life Choice

Because of Muslim rule, Farrakhan was forced to choose between show business and religion. It was a hard decision for him. Harry Belafonte had appeared on the scene and the Calypso sound was becoming even more popular.

But just as his show business career was about to take off, Louis decided to devote his life to the teachings of The Honorable Elijah Muhammad. His life changed drastically.

His next job was as a dishwasher in a New York restaurant at $35 a week. He peeled potatoes, mopped the floor and loaded trucks. But he was a disaster as a laborer, so he moved back to Boston to work in the garment district making $45 a week.

Farrakhan recalls, "I was trying hard to be a Muslim. I wrote a play and titled it 'Orgena.' It is 'a Negro' spelled backwards. The story is about the White man on trial for his sins."

It played at Symphony Hall in Boston, Carnegie Hall in New York, and the Tivoli in Chicago. Elijah Muhammad saw the show in Chicago at Dunbar High School.

"There was a scene where I sang acapella and the audience cried," says The Minister. "There was a part where a woman played a prostitute and a brother played a homosexual. I was showing how the teachings of Elijah Muhammad cleaned us up.

"Mr. Muhammad asked me to come by his house. This was in 1961. He said to me, 'Brother, I don't want our women playing prostitutes, because in order to play such a role, they have to get into the mind of such a role.'

"He acknowledged my song as wonderful and drew me real close to him and said, "I know that you love music and you think your music is your great gift, but your spiritual gift is greater than music. So, I'm asking you to give up your music altogether and concentrate on the spiritual.'

"I never played again publicly. I never sang again. I never wrote another song. I played my violin for him at his request, always in private. Elijah Muhammad saw more in me than I saw in myself."

Minister Malcolm's Student

Malcolm X was Farrakhan's hands-on mentor. He recalls, "Malcolm was the father that I never had, the big brother that I never had, the male image in my life that I never had and therefore I was to Malcolm like a child is to a parent that the child adores.

Minister

"I studied Malcolm. I learned from Malcolm. He was an inspiration to me. We became friends and companions. He was always the greater and I was the lesser. He was the teacher and I was the student."

Malcolm was the first to recognize Farrakhan's gift as a speaker. It's hard to believe that this renowned orator once stammered and stuttered as a young boy. He never talked except to close friends.

In a regular Wednesday Muslim meeting, where the brothers held "bearing witness" sessions, the young Muslims would speak about what Islam had done for them. One night Malcolm called on Farrakhan and the spirit of his speech touched the people.

Malcolm, realizing his potential, made Farrakhan an assistant minister. In the organization of the Nation of Islam, his first assignment was to organize the mosque in Boston.

In May of 1965, three months after the assassination of Malcolm X, Farrakhan was appointed Minister of Temple No. 7 in New York City. The atmosphere was hostile because of the allegations of Muslim involvement in the death of Malcolm.

Restoring The Nation of Islam

The Nation's founder Elijah Muhammad died in 1975. As if the Nation was suffering from cancer, there was internal turmoil, and the Nation was slowly dying from within.

Mr. Muhammad's son, Wallace D., brought many changes about, many contrary to his father's teachings. Property was being lost. The once prosperous businesses that supported the Nation's independence were closing. There was chaos.

Farrakhan agonized and eventually decided to assume a leadership role. In 1978, he began to resurrect the original teachings of The Honorable Elijah Muhammad. He moved to Chicago and his mission began.

Minister Farrakhan restored many of the businesses and institutions created at Elijah's helm. He followed Mr. Muhammad's blueprint. His headquarters were on the South Side in an old funeral home on 79th Street.

In 1979, he founded the newspaper *The Final Call*, which was patterned after his predecessor's paper *Muhammad Speaks*, which in its day was the country's most circulated national Black newspaper.

In 1988, Farrakhan repurchased, refurbished, reopened and rededicated Mosque Maryam, located on South Stony Island Avenue, Chicago Black Muslim's home mosque. He also opened the University of Islam, which provides a traditional Muslim education.

Farrakhan received national media attention in 1984 when, for the first time in the history of the Nation of Islam, Muslims became involved in a presidential campaign.

Farrakhan provided protection for Rev. Jesse Jackson through the Fruit of Islam, the military arm of the Nation of Islam community, when Jackson made him aware that the FBI had informed him that there were 100 real threats on his life as he was legitimately running for president in his first campaign.

Farrakhan says, "I felt that Reverend Jackson's boldness in standing up to be the nominee of the Democratic Party to be President of the United States was one of the boldest steps a Black man could take. Just saying it, meaning it, and doing it would free forever thousands of little Black children from the idea that they could only be sports figures, firemen or policemen."

In Elijah Muhammad's Nation, the main recruits were ex-convicts transformed and disciplined into productive citizens. Today, you will find doctors, lawyers and other professionals among the Muslim ranks.

Farrakhan himself lectures throughout the world. Internationally, he travels like royalty and is received as a head of state in African and Arab countries.

The Controversy Of Farrakhan

Privately, he is humble, elegant, soft-spoken and even demure. His public stage presence is commanding. About his controversial perception, Minister Farrakhan comments, "Whenever any Black person, male or female, rises to speak against that norm that we have accepted as truth, it creates what you call controversy.

"So, Marcus Garvey was controversial. Booker T. Washington was controversial. W.E.B. Du Bois was controversial. Malcolm and Martin were controversial. The press helps to create the controversy by distilling what I say. They use language that they feel represents what I say."

The Honorable Minister Louis Farrakhan will continue to be a torchlight or a blowtorch whether he is accepted or not, whether he is liked or not, whether he is understood or not.

Louis Farrakhan

preface Finney

Update: Dr. Leon Finney is pastor of Metropolitan Apostolic Community Church, a former Marine criminal investigator who worked in counter-intelligence, and he has taught at the University of Chicago, Northwestern University, the University of Illinois, and the Lutheran School of Theology. As of 2010, TWO and WCDC had $190 million in real estate investments.

Dr. Leon Finney

By Keith D. Robbins & Photography by Brent Jones | *Originally Published October 21, 1999*

No sooner than you can ask, "What are they building now?" ground will be broken to begin construction of 13 spacious, elegant single-family townhomes that will make up the new Homes at Blackstone residential community at 63rd Street and Blackstone Avenue on the city's South Side.

And when the project begins in a brief matter of time, nowhere in Chicago will the revitalization of a community be more evident, exemplary and eye-opening than the continuous renewal of the Woodlawn community.

Moreover, interested observers and skeptical cynics alike will be equally – if not more –hard-pressed to find people who are bursting with more pride and commitment to the rebirth of a community than urban development and public housing expert Rev. Leon D. Finney Jr., chairman of The Woodlawn Organization (TWO) and its sister agency, the Woodlawn Community Development Corporation (WCDC).

For not only is TWO the driving force behind the luxurious Homes at Blackstone, as well as a number of other residential properties, but the renowned organization that comprises 115 organizations, including block clubs, churches, tenant councils and other civic and institutional interests, is setting a national model by literally and figuratively changing the South Side's physical and demographic landscapes.

As an advocate, community developer and human services provider, TWO is in a league of its own, but in a league in which it invites other players to join, if they bring with them resources and a commitment to the vision.

Dr. Finney and his staff can point to TWO's pioneering role of virtually creating the concept of mixed-income housing in the 1960s, and being the first organization to mix the concept of social services with housing development.

> We are trying to rebuild a community where families get transformed from welfare to work, from being dysfunctional to functional, from being semi-literate to literate, and where children receive support to get to the point where they can compete successfully.

Given that TWO has evolved from a protest organization to a major community developer speaks volumes about the perseverance of those who remained committed to restoring the community's rich past and ensuring an even brighter future.

TWO is in charge of a property management portfolio that comprises 4,150 units of housing on Chicago's South Side and all of the Chicago Housing Authority's scattered site public housing located in an area bounded by 22nd Street on the north, the Dan Ryan Expressway on the west, Lake Michigan to the east and south to 138th Street.

Those responsibilities make TWO the largest non-profit African-American housing management company in the United States.

Woodlawn's population peaked at 80,000 in 1960, and the area once boasted of more than 800 businesses that in years past were patronized by an ethnically diverse population. With their sights set squarely on continuing to break new ground – pun intended – throughout Woodlawn, TWO is the high-octane fuel in the engine driving redevelopment.

They do so by providing a litany of services for their constituents – holistic services including infant, day care and head start centers, alcohol and substance abuse counseling, HIV/AIDS support, job training, crisis intervention for mentally ill adults and a state-of-the art welfare-to-work program, to name just a few.

All of which means the TWO alliance is demonstrating how an inner city community should be – actually, must be – strategically revitalized to attract and keep middle-class families and provide affordable housing to create what Finney calls "communities of choice," where people of all races want to live and prosper.

"Plain and simple, the future of any community is directly tied into its ability to build houses and stimulate home ownership," explains Finney, a former CHA board member, who for years has been affiliated with a number of civic and community organizations.

"We are creating a process through which families get transformed from welfare to work, from being dysfunctional to functional, from being semi-literate to literate, and where children receive support to get to the point where they can compete successfully.

"We are trying to help rebuild a community to

help the city of Chicago become a city of choice. We are about building communities because nobody can be an island unto themselves," says Finney, who shares the name that his father, Leon, Sr., has made synonymous with the barbecue business in Chicago.

The Homes At Blackstone

With no doubt and even less equivocation, Finney is staunchly committed to transforming 63rd Street between Cottage Grove Avenue and Stony Island Avenue from a commercial area to an attractive residential community for people from all walks of life and income levels.

Expected to serve as the gateway for the revitalization of East 63rd Street by offering "gracious living in the heart of the city," the Homes at Blackstone have already attracted buyers of the 13 units, which sell between $225,000 to $269,000.

Buying into TWO's plan as a partner with a shared vision is Lakeside Bank, whose chairman and CEO, Victor Cacciatore, ironically and appropriately was a graduate of Mt. Carmel High School, which is a stone's throw from the Homes at Blackstone. Lakeside Bank provided TWO with financing in the form of a $1.3 million loan to begin construction of Phase I; Phase II will mean 22 more homes.

"Lakeside Bank is proud to be associated with The Woodlawn Organization (TWO) and Dr. Finney. There are committed, dedicated and very competent people in the TWO organization. Lakeside Bank works under the theory and unequivocal belief that we are all colorless," said Cacciatore.

"The only way that this city and the country are going to go further is to remain that way. It's through developments like this that we are going to bring about true integration, through the exchange and togetherness of ideas and values. We want to be involved with TWO into the future. To be doing things that are so significant in the revitalization of a community is important to us. We're tickled pink."

Exceeding The Boundaries of Woodlawn

Ready, willing and able to continue leading the charge in its role as a community developer, TWO owns and manages property located in 13 communities and dispersed throughout nine Chicago wards: the 2nd, 3rd, 4th, 5th, 7th, 9th, 10th, 17th and 20th. TWO's diverse management portfolio includes an array of planned and existing properties, including:

- Edwin C. "Bill" Berry Manor — a seven-story, 59-unit senior and physically handicapped housing development at 727 E. 69th St.;

- Father Martin Farrell House — a five-story, 60-unit senior and physically challenged housing development at 1415 E. 65th St.;

- Park Shore East Cooperative — 148 two-story townhouses that are racially and economically integrated and located at 6250 S. Park Shore East Court;

- Jackson Park Terrace — a 322-unit, integrated, high rise, garden and townhouse development at 6040 S. Harper Ave.;

- Woodlawn Gardens — a 504-unit residential development for low-income families located along South Cottage Grove Avenue;

- South Park Plaza — which is the new name for the Prairie Courts development at 26th Street and King Drive; the new project will include 160 units of mixed income housing;

- Woodlawn Park Homes — single family homes and duplexes — are slated for construction on 63rd Street between Ingleside and Kenwood avenues, and

- Anchor House—a two-story, 115-unit multi-family residential facility that provides an array of services for families on the verge of becoming homeless.

Regarding Anchor House, which is located in his ward at 76th Street and Racine Avenue, Ald. Terry Peterson (17th) couldn't be happier with this one-of-a-kind facility, and with TWO's pursuit of its vision.

Peterson says, "The thing I like about Dr. Finney's vision is that he's attempting to provide housing for people of all income levels. As far as I know, he was the first in the city to develop a safety net for families like this. Dr. Finney is doing things that other people aren't doing, but should be doing."

In The Beginning

What TWO is doing these days is rooted in its well-documented beginnings when it organized boycotts, marched, protested against slum landlords and used other legal forms of action to prompt change for its constituents.

Social and economic discrimination in the 1950s greatly limited opportunities for advancement for African Americans in Chicago who had made the trek from the South. And as Woodlawn changed from a historically White population to a mostly Black one, disinvestment and White flight followed.

Then came the 1960s, when businesses sold inferior products at inflated prices. Absentee landlords did little to improve the community's housing stock, and city agencies reduced delivery of essential public services. Gang warfare escalated and ripped the fabric of the community. The despair was obvious.

However, through the efforts of block clubs and religious leaders, including Dr. Finney, community organizer Saul Alinsky and Bishop Arthur M. Brazier, whose Apostolic Church of God now is a highly influential mainstay in Woodlawn, a coalition of more than 100 neighborhood associations, religious institutions and civic organizations mobilized to fight back. As a result, TWO was founded to enable residents to build and exercise responsibility over the various influences that have affected their lives.

Since then, TWO and WCDC have grown to the point where they touch the lives of more than 18,000 people each day. The services are provided by TWO's 350-person staff, and the 27-year-old WCDC, which has 157 people on staff. All of which makes TWO an economic factor in Chicago as well, what with its annual $15 million payroll and tentacles that support constituents from the cradle to the grave.

And when it comes to funding, TWO stands on its own feet, as less than five percent of its funding comes from city government and less than one-half of one percent comes from the private philanthropic community. Rental income, state contracts and funds from its development activities are the cornerstone to the organization's financial foundation.

Led by Dr. Finney and his multi-faceted vision for creating a community people want to live in, TWO and Woodlawn are destined to continue recapturing families. Woodlawn's future, as Dr. Finney sees it, will be realized and captured much in the way ground was recaptured, in a manner of speaking, to construct the Homes at Blackstone.

"What we stand for is making Chicago whole again, so that people and families don't run from each other, and low, and moderate and middle-income people can live and recreate together and people of different ethnic backgrounds can also live together. We wouldn't have it any other way," Finney says.

Finney

preface Foster

Update: The never boring Stella retired from the *Chicago Sun-Times* in 2012 after 43 years. Her retirement ended an era of one of the city's most popular columns. She continues her "Stella in the City" dishing on her Facebook page.

Stella Foster

By Sabrina L. Miller & Photography by Victor Powell | *Originally Published May 20, 2004*

The first thing you need to know about Stella Foster is that she is a Leo. She is a textbook, astrology guide Leo – extroverted, creative, confident, generous, larger-than-life, loyal, dominant, and a born leader.

Her Leo personality comes out in her leopard print shirts, her pink pen with the feathers shooting from the top, the gold hoop earrings and gold chain with her name stenciled in them. Stella's annual August 6 "Divas" party, which brings together women from all over the city for networking while celebrating her birthday at the same time, is also a testament to her Leo personality.

So, too, was her recent, lively "Stella in the City" party at a West Loop nightclub to celebrate her twice-weekly *Chicago Sun-Times* feature, "Stella's Column." It debuted following the death of her boss of 34 years, legendary *Sun-Times* columnist Irv "Kup" Kupcinet in November 2003.

Stella is a woman with one of the biggest contact databases in the city, who prides herself on never meeting a stranger. "She has one of those personalities that everybody loves. Everybody thinks they're her best friend, just about everybody I know loves her," says Melody Spann-Cooper, president of WVON radio, one of Stella's closest friends and herself a Leo.

I owe it to my readers not to bore them to death and I put out a damn good column, if I say so myself!

Hundreds of Chicago's "who's who" packed the club, cha-cha sliding, taking pictures, eating and drinking through the entire evening. Media types like Warner Saunders, Art Norman and Bill Kurtis, business types like John Rogers, civic figures like Judge Arnette Hubbard and Ald. Walter Burnett, sports figures like Norm Van Lier, and the activist minister Rev. Michael Pfleger, were among the many minglers there. Camera news crews from most of the local stations showed up to document the event.

Her friends and loyal subjects alike agree that what draws people to Stella, in good or bad times, is her "aw shucks," just-plain-folks demeanor that makes celebrities and non-celebrities alike eager to dish to her.

"Many of us have known that she was laboring quietly behind the scenes for many years for Kup. We always knew that she was the wind beneath his wings," says NBC-5 newsman Art Norman. "So it is absolutely fitting that she is now in the spotlight and coming into her own as a columnist. It is absolutely where she belongs."

The Sun-Times Job

Stella was Kup's assistant and trusted confidant for more than three decades, working his phones, and generally keeping his operation as the premier gossip columnist in Chicago for that era in impeccable order. As Kup's health began to deteriorate, Stella began quietly "co-writing" the column.

Which leads to the second thing you need to know about Stella Foster: She never had any intention of becoming a newspaper columnist.

"I never aspired to be a Kup-Etta, never wanted to be a columnist, never did. My thing was always being behind the scenes, making sure that we put out a good product. It was not a matter of me sitting back waiting for him to croak so I could take over, that was never, ever, ever anything in my mind that I wanted to do," Stella says, with trademark candor.

"I never wanted to be a writer. Ever. I've never had any inclination toward being a journalist. It was just not that appealing to me. I never studied journalism, never intended to be a journalist, any of that," she says. "Everything I've learned I've learned from doing it."

Estella Mae Foster grew up in Englewood on Chicago's South Side, the middle daughter of Mamie and Peter James Foster, who were the popular owners of Foster's Variety Store at 431 West 81st

Place. Stella graduated from Calumet High School, then attended Chicago State University "for about a minute" she says, with aspirations of becoming a physical education teacher.

She enrolled in night school at the Central Y, working at Illinois Bell during the day. Back then, she says, "if you could type or if you had shorthand, you could get a really good job."

Stella went through a series of jobs at Illinois Bell, the Palmer House Hotel, LaSalle Bank, and Beatrice Foods when her sister Jamie Foster Brown (now publisher of *Sister2Sister Magazine*) found out through her boss, a close friend of Kup's, that Kup was looking for an assistant. Stella interviewed with Kup on August 4, 1969. Two days later, on her birthday, Kup, himself a Leo, born on July 31, told her that she had the job.

The girl from Englewood admits to initially being intimidated by the offer. "Kup was really in full bloom in terms of his popularity at the time, doing six columns a week and a television show," Stella remembers. Kup's old assistant was going on maternity leave, "and I had to hit the ground running. I had a lot to learn," Stella said.

The job turned out to be as demanding and exciting as she thought it would be. "I had to handle the phones, take news items, take them down accurately because he'd put them right into the paper, make his reservations – and back then he was heading to the Oscars every year and covering galas and always out at night at the restaurants, he and Essee," she says.

"It was exciting, but it was also a lot of hard work. Putting together six columns a week was no joke. It took a lot of time and energy and know-how, really."

Taking Writing To The Next Level

Stella's transition into writing was quite unplanned, but something she ultimately had been prepared for her entire life, according to her sister Jamie.

Jamie says that the lessons that have carried all of the Foster children to successful careers started at home with her parents. Jamie and Stella have a younger sister, Shirley Hunter, who is a speech therapist. Their older brother, Warren, died in 1984.

"I remember so clearly that we used to sit on the sofa every Sunday, and our father had us read the newspaper. He was the one who always drilled in us to work hard, to be kind to people, don't run in a pack, be indispensable to your boss," Jamie says. "We all benefited from those lessons."

Both sisters find it amusing that they've built careers in media although neither, initially, had the background or interest in doing it. *Sister2Sister* – a title Jamie came up with based on her many marathon phone calls with Stella about pop culture events of the day – is full of Black celebrity gossip

that many find a guilty pleasure to read.

"It's funny…neither of us started out with any intention of being writers or doing columns, and now we're like Dear Abby and Ann Landers," Jamie says. "Who would have thought it? We laugh about that all the time."

Stella's real "training" as a writer came from the urging of Jamie's husband, the late Lorenzo Brown, who urged her to write a column for *Sister2Sister*.

"My brother-in-law told me that what was special about my writing is that it reads like I talk. It's easy to understand, and very conversational," Stella says. "He used to say, 'I have writers here who went to school for it, and I spend more time editing their copy than yours!'"

So by the time Kup's health began to fail, and the luster of his column eventually began to fade – from being published six times a week to three, and then finally two – Stella was prepared to jump in.

In assuming the bulk of the writing duties, she also was able to expand Kup's audience. When Kup's column began giving shout-outs to folks like Jay-Z and R. Kelly, the touch was unmistakably Stella.

"I haven't missed a beat because I was already doing it, I was already used to fact-checking, double-checking everything," she says. "Writing the column for me…it's like, ok, now my name is on top, that's the only difference.

"The column is still a very multi-cultural, multi-ethnic thing, very much in the tradition of Kup. I'm telling you where the charity events are, where the galas are, where people are eating, who's coming to town, what movies are being filmed here, what the politicians are doing, what is going on in the sports world," she says. "It's a very complete column. I owe it to my readers not to bore them to death.

"I put out a damn good column, if I say so myself. I work late. I do whatever it takes to get the job done. I have maintained Kup's audience, but also expanded it. I don't care what the other columnists necessarily are doing. I just don't want to put out the same information," says Stella, who stresses to her sources that the information they are giving her are exclusives.

Her job is not always easy, however, and friend Melody Spann-Cooper says, "A lot of people don't realize that Stella is very sensitive. She's lost a couple of good friendships over her column, and she keeps on going because you have to, but it hurts her."

Stella says, "You know, Kup had people who fell out with him from time to time, but they'd always come back on board. I think as long as you know you didn't tell a lie and it's accurate, you can't sit back and apologize. I'm a fair reporter. I'm a fair journalist.

"Kup was not known for character assassination and neither am I," she says. "We were both very much

Stella Foster

oriented to trying to be kind to people. That's how you get sources. That's how you get information, but you still have to report the news. You try to treat a situation that is negative with a delicate glove."

Which leads to the last thing you need to know about Stella Foster: She is fiercely loyal to her family and friends.

She is very close to her sisters, and considers Jamie's two grown sons so close to her that, "I might as well have given birth to those kids myself.

"I always had long-term relationships, but I never wanted to be married, never necessarily wanted to have children. I've been engaged three or four times, and I was the one responsible for breaking up with all of them. So I'm about three diamonds in the hole," she confesses, laughing. "I'm still good friends with them, I'm just not a desperate woman."

For as public as her life is, Stella says she's just as comfortable staying holed up in her North Side condo watching television or catching a movie alone. "I have to watch myself because I could very easily become a recluse," she says. "I really do enjoy my own company."

She could, but her friends, family, and sources won't let her.

preface
Freeman

Update: Judge Freeman served as Chief Justice until January 1, 2000. He ranks as the senior member of the Illinois Supreme Court, and after being re-elected in 2010, his current term does not run out until 2020.

Justice Charles Freeman

By David Smallwood & Photography by Warren Browne | *Originally Published June 4, 1998*

The next time a child contemplates a Black man running the court, he can think beyond Michael Jordan driving to the basket, tongue a-wagging. Now, joining "His Airness" as a role model for children and adults alike, is "His Honor," Charles Freeman, who shakes and bakes on his own court.

Let history show that on May 12, 1997, Charles E. Freeman was selected as Chief Justice of the Illinois Supreme Court. That makes him team captain on the highest court in the state. Freeman is the first and only African American to serve on the Illinois Supreme Court, and thus, the first African American to be chosen as its Chief Justice.

Freeman's selection was made by the Court's seven justices to replace James Heiple – the former Chief Justice who stepped down as leader of the Court earlier in May after being censured by the Illinois

> **If I can help the public have a better understanding of the court system – the possibles and impossibles of the system – I think I will have accomplished something.**

Courts Commission for behavioral impropriety.

Seniority-wise, as Freeman was next in line to be elevated to the top spot – the vote was basically a no-brainer – the situation would only have become controversial had he not been selected.

So the tenure of Judge Freeman on the Illinois Supreme Court, which he was elected to in 1990, remains historic. As its Chief Justice – the first among equals – Freeman is charged with controlling the Court's $240 million budget and managing the operations of the lower courts in Illinois.

Moving On The Administrative Front

It's on the administrative side of his responsibilities that Freeman hopes to have more of a major impact than anything that might happen judicially.

"We're about to go into another century and I think the Court should start doing some things administratively that reflect the times. I hope that I can act on that because this is the perfect time," the Judge says.

The timing is indeed perfect for Freeman to lead the Illinois courts system into the next century, as his tenure as Chief Justice literally expires on December 31, 1999. His 10-year term as a member of the Court then terminates in December 2000.

Administratively, Freeman plans to draw from what he calls "a wealth of material sitting and waiting for us" in the form of studies and reports done by law groups over the years.

"Some very top-rate people from all over this state have involved themselves in the diverse issues that face the court system and how it is administered," Freeman said. "I think mainly of the *Solovy Report*, which contains a lot of great suggestions. That report has been on the back shelf for a while now, but it would be very helpful for us to look at it again and try to move on some of the suggestions."

Specifically, the new Chief Justice wants to expand the Court's Judicial Education courses, which have been cut back recently. He also wants to establish a statewide mentoring program for new judges coming into the courts – particularly for those newly elected judges who do not have to submit themselves before the Chicago Bar Association to receive a "qualified" rating, which they would have to do if they were appointed instead of elected.

"We're getting some fine people – there's no question about that – and I'm not in the position to evaluate those who have been elected, I'm just concerned about the public's perception of those who have been elected," the Judge maintained.

Under Freeman's mentoring program, new judges would be assigned to an older judge to be their immediate source of support, guidance and development. "Not that that judge would make decisions for them," Freeman said, "but the transition from being in a private practice or other public sector job to the judiciary is just a tremendous change.

"It takes some time and preparation and I think a good mentoring program would help. We have a host of good judges all over the state who are willing to participate in helping new people adjust to the bench."

Freeman also wonders if a statewide Inspector General for the courts might be in order, not to ferret out corruption, but to identify problems for the Court to deal with.

"Court watchers note there are a lot of vacant courtrooms," Freeman said. "There are things that could be done with the assignment of judges, and shifting of loads in various counties that could help us utilize the judges and the courts better. That's where an Inspector General could come in – to identify areas where we could make changes."

Mostly, Freeman's biggest intent as Chief Justice is to have more people know more about the court system in order to restore their confidence in it.

"If I can help the public have a better understanding of the court system – the possibles and impossibles of the system, I think I will have accomplished something," he says.

Joining History Making Forces

Of the very many people who so very often evoke the name of Harold Washington, Judge Freeman is one of the few who can do so without taking that name in vain.

A historymaker himself, Freeman just happened to be very good friends with two other African American history makers – Douglas Wilder, who in 1989 in Virginia became the nation's first elected Black governor, and Harold Washington, who became Chicago's first Black mayor in 1983.

Freeman was born in Richmond, Virginia, in December 1933 and attended high school and college with Wilder. "I started two years behind Doug and I think I finished before him. I was smarter than he was!" Freeman quipped of his childhood friend, adding that they didn't have much of a clue as to the monumental success that both would later achieve.

"I was a little different then," the Judge admits. "I had other things of more importance on my mind. Doug had begun to develop political friends in Richmond, but I couldn't care less, I was worried about where the nearest beer garden was. (Nonetheless) Doug was always at the beer garden when I got there, but he was focused and knew where he was going."

After graduating from Virginia Union University in 1954, Freeman landed in Chicago at John Marshall Law School, where he received his Juris Doctor degree in 1962. Deciding to become active politically, he joined Ralph Metcalfe's organization, where he was befriended by Harold Washington.

"Harold, too, had some wild excursions, but I was married then and couldn't hang out as much, but boy, he could have a good time! Until he changed. He just suddenly changed," recalled Freeman, who shared an office on 63rd and Peoria with Washington for 10 years.

"During most of that time, Harold wasn't practicing law and people would come to him, but he didn't care anything about money, so he would refer the business to me. Harold wanted nothing. His father left him a lot of property, which he just abandoned," Freeman said.

"Those things were not important to him, but Harold had books on the legislature all over and he was always working – Harold was the hardest working guy I've ever seen." Years later, his friend Harold selected Freeman, then a Circuit Court judge, to swear him in as Mayor of Chicago.

The Route Taken

Following his own historic route, after earning his law degree, Freeman became successively an Illinois Assistant Attorney General, Assistant State's Attorney in Cook County, and an Attorney with the Cook County Board of Election Commissioners. He served as an arbitrator with the Illinois Industrial Commission from 1965 to 1973, when he was appointed by the Governor to the Illinois Commerce Commission.

Freeman was elected to the Circuit Court of Cook County in 1976, then to the Illinois Appellate Court in 1986, and four years later, to the Supreme Court of Illinois. He enjoyed a meteoric rise through the judiciary.

After just one year on the bench, Freeman moved to the Law jury Division of the Circuit Court, which handles heavy money cases like injuries, medical malpractice and product liability.

"Going to law jury that fast was almost unheard of," Freeman noted with pride. "But I had a good background, working at the Industrial Commission hearing workers compensation claims, so I was up on my game. It wasn't political contacts."

There are two reasons for his success, Freeman maintained. One is his family – his wife of 55 years, Marylee, and their son Kevin, an attorney.

Freeman's other key to success is productivity. "I believe in doing my work and I'm prepared," he said. "In the Law Division, I produced almost more than anyone else for the eight years I was there. I turned over cases fast and lawyers began to ask for me on both sides.

"In Chancery, I worked hard and went to the Appellate Court," he continued. "Part of my campaign for the Supreme Court was that I led the Appellate Court as a newcomer for two years in case disposition, with figures that I don't know are being matched today."

As a Supreme Court justice, Freeman is best known for writing the recent decision that reversed the conviction of Rolando Cruz for the murder of little Jeanine Nicarico. He also wrote the dissenting brief in the case of Guinevere Garcia. Freeman's heartrending words were used by anti-death penalty advocates, including Bianca Jagger, to help influence Governor Jim Edgar to commute Garcia's execution last year.

The public can look for more interesting opinions from Justice Freeman in the following years. Unlike most chief justices, who are allowed to cut back on their caseloads to assume more administrative responsibilities, Judge Freeman doesn't plan to follow suit.

"It's a lot of extra work, but there are some good, interesting cases coming down and I want my share of them. I want to say what I have to say," he said.

An African-American Presence

There's no doubt that Justice Freeman is a presence on the Court and he plans to make that presence felt. In that sense, he feels that his background is a plus. He noted that "judges come from various backgrounds and various exposures to people and sometimes they don't react or interact too well. And they will say things, not really appreciating the hurt that attorneys and litigants may suffer because of what they say," Freeman said. He added that he will attempt to provide some type of sensitivity education for people in the system of that disposition.

"In those kinds of areas, administratively, being African-American can have an effect, I think," he said. "Judicially, when you have a different background and exposure, there are just life experiences that you talk to people at the table about, which could affect the way decisions might go.

"So I hope I can impact upon the image of the Court not only by being there, but by increasing the Court's visibility and sensitivity, doing that very soon, and letting the public know what we're doing," Judge Freeman concluded.

preface Gardner

Update: Gardner authored another bestselling book in 2009 called *Start Where You Are: Life Lessons In Getting From Where You Are To Where You Want To Be*. He was also named the Ambassador of Pursuit and Happyness for AARP, which has nearly 40 million members worldwide, and has since exited the brokerage business to focus on philanthropic pursuits and motivational speaking projects.

Chris Gardner

By James G. Muhammad & Photography by Victor Powell | *Originally Published May 18, 2006*

You would think that Chris Gardner is on top of the world.

He runs a multi-million dollar investment company, Gardner Rich LLC, that sits in the shadow of the Chicago Board of Trade.

His autobiography, *The Pursuit of Happyness*, was recently published and is already a *New York Times* and *Washington Post* #1 bestseller. A movie based on the book starring Will Smith hits the silver screen at the end of the year.

So how does Gardner feel?

"I'm still climbing," he says. "But it's like climbing Mt. Everest. As much as you have climbed and as steep as it has been, the second you're ready to ascend, it goes like this."

Gardner raises his arm from a 45-degree incline to a 90-degree, straight up and down angle. Sitting on the second floor loft that overlooks the office cubicles in his glass-enclosed building, he smiles: "You're dealing with the struggle and there ain't no oxygen, but you still have to climb."

> ## Chris is a credit to African-American men who did not let circumstances determine who he'd become.

Chris is still climbing and probably will be forever. But for now, Gardner has reached a plateau where he can marvel at the landscape laid out before him.

The book and movie both take you through Gardner's tough times as a homeless man with an infant son living in the streets and subways of San Francisco and Oakland.

Smith plays Gardner and Smith's son, Jayden, plays Chris Jr. Gardner is thrilled with the book and movie, and doesn't intend to be distracted by the glare of the high profile attention that is sure to come.

"I'm going to stay in the light that doesn't go out. The light of God," Gardner says. "Folks have started hating already. But what can you do but stay focused? God got me to this point."

Making A Difference

The tall bald Gardner is a spiritual man who easily could have gone into modeling. He quietly advocates for the homeless and education, donating to various causes, particularly Glide Memorial United Methodist Church in the Tenderloin district of San Francisco.

It was there under the watchful eye of Rev. Cecil Williams that Gardner got his life on track, and it was in that area that the movie was filmed. Gardner was happy to employ dozens of homeless men and women as extras in the movie, some of them earning the first paycheck they've had in years.

Gardner is a jet setter who can travel to as many as five cities in a day. At 52, he realizes he needs to be in shape to continue his grueling schedule.

He has changed his diet and exercise habits, losing 49 pounds so far and developing "a six-pack instead of a 40-ounce," he says, referring to rippling muscles developing in his abdomen.

There's another vice he's proud to be overcoming. He pulls out a case that holds only eight cigarettes. That's down from a pack a day. As a result of his weight loss, Gardner has had to clear out his wardrobe, and gave away 200 tailor-made suits and accessories to the homeless.

"A few weeks ago, I saw a man in (Glide Memorial) church wearing suede Gucci loafers. I couldn't resist asking where he got those. He said the reverend (Williams) gave them to him. Those were my shoes. That's cool," he says. "I'm at a point now that I want to be part of what's making a difference. I ain't got to have my picture hanging all over the place. I got to get used to it, but that ain't my thing."

In Pursuit Of The Dollar

Gardner's downward spiral started unexpectedly. Right after high school, he joined the Navy and served in the medical corp. Upon discharge, he served as a research assistant in San Francisco to a Navy doctor he had served with.

He soon grew tired of the low pay and began a job as a medical supply salesman. Disenchanted with that job, he stumbled upon the idea of being an investment broker one day when he saw a man driving a red Ferrari.

Gardner stopped the man and asked two questions: What do you do, and how do you do it? When the man told Gardner he was a stockbroker making

Chris Gardner

$80,000 a month, Gardner began his pursuit of a job as a stockbroker.

Things were going well until the day he quit his sales job for a job at an investment firm. As luck would have it, the man who hired Gardner had been fired and when he showed up, nobody there knew Chris Gardner.

Now out of work and living with his girlfriend and child, Gardner struggled doing odd jobs. Eventually, his family left him, and on that same day he was arrested for having $1,200 in outstanding parking tickets.

After spending 10 days in jail, Gardner showed up at a previously scheduled interview at Dean Witter wearing the same clothes he wore in jail. The scene was so bizarre, he says, that he couldn't think of a lie good enough to tell the boss, so he told him the truth.

Gardner got the job and was working as a stockbroker trainee while living in a boarding house, when his girlfriend showed up and dropped his son off to Gardner – for good.

Since the boarding house didn't allow children, Gardner was forced to leave. He wound up in cheap motels frequented by prostitutes who would see him going back and forth with his child.

The women occasionally would give the baby money, in their own way admiring Gardner for his commitment to his son, and knowing the man was in desperate need of funds.

But even living at the motel was a strain on funds, so Gardner and his son took to the streets. He'd work during the day, pick up his son in the evening, and prepare for the next day in the subways, bathing his son in bathroom sinks before putting him to bed on a mat of rags.

"I'll tell you something about those people. Twelve percent of them have jobs and go to work everyday," Gardner says, citing statistics from the National Coalition for the Homeless.

"That's an invisible class. People just say 'the homeless,' but 12 percent of them have jobs that don't pay them enough to have a place to call home. That was me."

Gardner's fortunes turned around for good when he visited a shelter for single mothers run by Rev. Williams. The pastor allowed Gardner to stay, and that allowed him to focus on his work, earn his broker's license, and move into an apartment.

The rest is a fairy tale ending to a story of trials and tribulation: He worked in New York for Bear Sterns before leaving to start his present firm in Chicago. In January of 2003, the news show 20/20 did a segment on his life that attracted a lot of attention, which brings us to today.

"Chris has taken all his opportunities and turned around a really hard situation," says close friend Mellody Hobson, president of Chicago's Ariel Capital Management. "The circumstance he has come through makes him extra sympathetic to people."

Marilyn Stewart, (former) president of the Chicago Teachers Union, whose pension fund Gardner's firm manages, said, "Chris is a man of integrity and a credit to African-American men who did not let circumstances determine who he'd become. His story speaks volumes about what you can do, and that education is the way out. You can use your brain instead of your muscles."

Mom's Inspiration

Gardner credits his success to the words of his mother. One day while watching a basketball game, a young Gardner predicted that one of the players would make a million dollars. His mother scoffed and told him that he, too, could one day make a million dollars.

"Until my mother said that, I never thought for a second that I could. I couldn't dance, I couldn't sing, I couldn't run and catch balls," he says.

His formula for success: "There ain't no secrets. It's the basics – blocking, tackling, practice, practice, practice. But beyond that, find something that you love, that you're passionate about. Find something that the sun can't come up quick enough because you want to go do your thing. The money will come. And even if it don't come, it's more important to be happy."

Sitting in Gardner's office loft, there are two things you notice immediately – statues of elephants, and biographies of great men on bookshelves and strewn across the floor. Elephants because Gardner goes after the big game in the cutthroat world of investments; biographies because "I want to know how they did it."

How did Che Guevara lead a revolution? How did Muhammad Ali become "The Greatest?" And his favorite topic: How did Nelson Mandela survive prison to become President of South Africa?

Gardner had a chance to find out in 1993 when he traveled to South Africa to help develop an investment plan for the country, and met with Mandela for 45 minutes.

"The first time I met him, he shook my hand and said, 'Welcome home, son.' At 45 (years old) I never had a man say that to me, and for that first man to be Nelson Mandela, I cried like a baby," says Gardner.

preface
The Gardners

Update: Ed and Bettiann Gardner started Soft Sheen Products, a black hair company, in their South Side home in 1964. The family business grew into a major enterprise. They sold the company to L'Oreal in 1998. The Gardners have been major supporters of community causes. Nowadays, Ed and Betty spend their days remaining active in community concerns, puttering in their garden, doting on their seven grandchildren, and reveling in the success of their four children.

Ed and Bettiann Gardner

By Melody M. McDowell & Photos Courtesy of the Gardner Family | *Originally Published June 28, 2012*

Ed and Bettiann Gardner's lives can be measured in moments that are undergirded by a love for their community, their fellow man, their family and their God.

In decades of moments, the couple has scaled and reached the summit of business success and are idolized as entrepreneurs, philanthropists, political activists and humanitarians.

They founded Soft Sheen Products, Inc. in 1964, and for 34 years, presided over the growth of this family-run enterprise into a business model worth studying, emulating and applauding.

Their parallel devotion to politics made them an iconic force behind the election of Chicago's first Black mayor Harold Washington and others aspiring to higher office. They continue to leave their marks on Chicago's cultural and educational landscape and give generously to organizations and entities whose missions mirror the Gardner ethnic.

> To stop the violence, more police aren't always the answer. You need a loving family that is concerned with one another and is aware of their responsibility to make life better for one another.

All totaled, Ed and Betty have touched, impacted, and enriched thousands upon thousands of lives. With such a portfolio of greatness, it is understandable why the husband-and-wife duo is now basking in the afterglow of their lives…and relishing the moments.

This composite of moments has elevated them to iconic status across a broad swath of sectors, including having a street named after them near where Soft Sheen Products thrived.

A Stellar Pair

The Gardners are the model of grace and dignity. They marvel at their journey and speak with gratitude of the moments that make up the texture of their lives. They share nuggets of their 67-year marriage, and even slyly flirt with one another.

Gardner is quick to point out that their odyssey began humbly.

"I come from an African-American family with modest means whose parents only had a grade school education," he recalls wistfully. What his parents lacked in creature comforts, they made up for in the values they taught Ed and his late brother Frank.

"They provided guidance on how to help others," he said. "This is the responsibility we accepted. We have been given an awful lot and we continue to provide examples for young families. That is one of the most successful things we have done…to show by example the responsibility of the African-American family."

Their narrative has become part of Black business lore. Early on, Ed Gardner was an eighth-grade teacher at Carver and later an assistant principal at Beethoven Elementary.

However, his growing family was straining his educator's salary. With four children to support, he began peddling hair care products for a beauty supply company.

While on his beauty shop rounds, stylists confided to him about what the customers liked. With that information, he figured he could develop a formulation that customers craved.

With the support of his wife, he began "stirring the pot" and mixing a formula from out of their basement. Through several trials and errors, he came up with a product that beauticians wanted.

In 1964, he was hawking products that he formulated. The operators told him to "keep bringin' those products" and told him not to "mess with" the formula because he'd gotten it "just right."

Family Business

What is remarkable about this saga is that the Gardners created a product without the benefit of a chemistry background or the business savvy to configure a business empire. So, in spite of what "they" say is required to succeed in business, Soft Sheen Products was born.

Central to the company's success was Ed and Betty's decision to involve their children. "They sacrificed play dates because they loved working in the business. Later, when they got older, they got involved with their degrees and brought in new ideas," Gardner explains.

During the family's run of the company – the manufacturer was sold to L'Oreal in 1998 – Ed headed Soft Sheen and presided over the day-to-day management. Eventually, eldest son Gary brought his business savvy to the firm and later headed the company while Ed remained chairman.

Gary's wife, Denise, led the marketing arm. Spin-off businesses were created to handle the various company needs: daughter Terri presided over Brainstorm Communications, the advertising agency. Son Guy has an aptitude for engineering and played a key role in building the factory. Youngest child Tracy rounded out the company.

The Gardners also founded Perfect Pinch, a seasoning company, and Shop Talk, a hair care trade magazine whose publisher was Betty.

Soft Sheen eventually moved its corporate headquarters and manufacturing operations to 1000 East 87th Street. The company became a major employer and economic engine and a hub from whence community and political movements were spawned.

Because Soft Sheen became a source of pride, power and a launching pad for the community's aspirations, it was lovingly billed as "The Miracle on 87th Street."

Deeply Rooted

At its height, Soft Sheen employed thousands and had operations worldwide, including in Africa. Among its hallmark brands were Carefree Curl, Miss Cool and its signature Soft Sheen brands.

Despite the heights they reached, Ed and Betty remained rooted in the community. Betty was reared in Bronzeville and attended school there.

Ed's parents bought a home in the Chesterfield community and he and Betty settled into the neighborhood where Ed was raised. From this haven, they raised their children. Being in the thicket of the city's goings on, Ed and Betty kept their pulse on the community and often drove the dialogue.

In the early 1980s, the community was clamoring for a Black mayor and reached out to then state senator Harold Washington as their candidate of choice.

But Washington let it be known that he would accept the draft only if an inspired campaign could be mounted that would both spark voter registration and

raise the funds that would assure a serious mayoral bid.

In a moment of clarity, son Gary suggested that the money Soft Sheen used for advertising be funneled into a campaign to get Harold Washington elected.

Drawing from everyone's talent bank, the Gardner braintrust launched a successful stealth campaign to spark voter registration and stimulate a get-out-the-vote campaign.

On the cultural front, Betty played a lead role in reviving the Regal Theatre. Her affinity for culture was DNA-earned from her French Creole grandmother who was her inspiration. This was evident in her board membership with the Chicago Sinfonietta.

While her influence at this fabled institution was renowned, she sought a venue where the halcyon days of the Regal on 47th and King Drive could be enjoyed. The couple had grown up with many of the artists who were part of the Regal narrative.

When the famed entertainment hub was shuttered, Betty suggested that the family acquire and restore the Regal Theater. Through delicate negotiations with the city, the Gardners acquired the name, and renovated and transformed the Avalon Theatre at 79th and South Chicago into a cultural mecca.

Acts like R. Kelly, Gladys Knight, and the Whispers journeyed to the Regal to delight inner-city audiences thirsting for a South Side location for quality entertainment. The couple eventually sold the theater, but reflect with pride on the days when they restored glory to the legendary venue.

Moments continued to define their lives. When Mrs. Gardner learned that Rev. T.L. Barrett's church needed stained glass windows, she generously donated the entire cost, making the Life Center Church of God a WOW-inspired cathedral to God.

Eventually, the couple became stockholders in the Chicago Bulls organization and broadened their influence as they strengthened their business empire.

Probably what most defines the Gardners' compassion are the circumstances that led to the founding of Black on Black Love, the anti-crime initiative. The organization evolved out of a single moment. A homeless woman had hunkered down in an alley behind the Regal Theater.

One day, she threatened to kill herself and a policeman brought her to Ed with the assurance that "Mr. Gardner can help you." She was crying about her life, which had spiraled downward.

Gardner sensed that hers was a plea for help rather than a suicide threat. He saw something in this young woman and took her under his wing. He introduced her to Frances Wright, then a Soft Sheen employee who shared Mr. Gardner's vision.

Together, they opened up an infrastructure of caring and located housing and clothing, identified agencies to help her, provided help for her children and set her on a path to dignity. Today, she is married and thriving and credits Gardner and Black on Black Love with saving her life.

Black on Black Love

The incident that strengthened the Gardner's resolve to get immersed in the anti-crime cause was when an employee of Perfect Pinch was shot in the chest during a robbery. Outraged, Mr. Gardner took pen to hand and paid for full-page ads decrying the Black on Black crime that was pulling down the community.

This letter writing sparked an overwhelming reaction from Chicagoans who applauded him for taking a stand. They urged him to capture this spirit in a full-fledged campaign. Again, up to the challenge, he fired up his creative team, which blanketed the community with the Black on Black Love appeal through a flurry of messages in a variety of mediums.

This indignation was the spark that led to the founding of Black on Black Love. Wright eventually assumed the helm of the organization. Even after Soft Sheen was sold, Black on Black Love continues to be a programmatic cocoon for realizing Gardner's vision to replace Black on Black Crime with Black on Black Love.

Now nearly 30 years old, Black On Black Love operates a number of programs. Its signature initiative, My Sister's Keeper, helps women who have been released from the correctional system lead productive lives. Since its founding, it has helped thousands of women successfully re-enter society.

Wright confides that she's seen Gardner weep when young lives are snuffed out so senselessly. Mr. Gardner says he has definite ideas of the problem and the fixes.

"More police aren't always the answer," he explains. "You need a loving family that is concerned with one another and is aware of their responsibility to make life better for one another."

This passion, and the Gardner's' willingness to invest in causes they hold dear, are part and parcel of the moments that make up the Gardner legacy.

preface
Gregory

Update: Dick Gregory still makes numerous national public appearances commenting on social issues of the day and has remained married to Lillian for 57 years. Dick Gregory passed away on August 19, 2017 at the age of 84.

Dick Gregory

By Kai EL' Zabar & Photography by David Jenkins | *Originally Published February 20, 1997*

One of the funniest men in our history is also one of the most political and certainly one of the most controversial.

In the 1960s, Dick Gregory brought a new perspective to the world of comedy. He went on to become even better known for his poignant political commentary, civil rights activities, and work as an athlete/health and diet guru.

He's also authored several books, including his autobiography, *Nigger*, and *Dick Gregory's Natural Diet For Folks Who Eat*: co-authored *Code Name Zorro*, a book about Dr. Martin Luther King Jr.'s assassination; and for another book on the same subject, written by Dr. King's convicted killer, James Earl Ray, Gregory raised some eyebrows by writing the foreword.

Gregory was a comedic pioneer. He took the art of making people laugh and not only utilized it as a teaching tool, but also as a means to bring up in the pop media culture situations that formerly had been off limits for Black people in public discussion.

Good evening, ladies and gentleman, I understand there are a good many Southerners in the room tonight. I know the South very well. I spent 20 years there one night.

Gregory always brings humor to the sublime and ridiculous when least expected. It is the stuff that made him the well-paid comedian he rose to become. Yet in the turbulent '60s, the more engaged in political activities he became, the less comedic work he got, until eventually his career ended.

Recently, though, Gregory has resurrected his stand-up comic act. He debuted his one-man show, *Dick Gregory Live*, on a small-off Broadway stage in Manhattan and took it across the country, playing to favorable critics and audiences.

Original Roots

His beginnings were humble. Born Richard Claxton Gregory on Columbus Day in 1932 in St. Louis, he grew up in poverty with his siblings and mother.

But poverty never inhibited him; he was a go-getter from the start. Gregory's natural instinct for survival put him on a winning course. As a child, he made money selling newspapers, shining shoes in a bar and scrubbing steps.

In order to make what he considered "real money," he lied about his age to work on the Mississippi River piling sandbags. An ingenious kid, when he was a teenager and frozen pipes prevented him from bathing at home, he made a deal with the high school band teacher to clean the band room in exchange for using the shower facilities.

His destiny was set in motion when he joined the track team. Subsequently, he won the Missouri state mile race in 1951 and 1952, which gave him notoriety as being quite an athlete and in 1953, earned him a scholarship to Southern Illinois University. He became a famous track star and that's when, Gregory explains, the White press changed his name from Richard to Dick.

College ended for Gregory when he quit and joined the Army, where he continued to run track and competed in talent shows. He had first heard comedians in the mid-1950's on Chicago's South Side and decided that he could do that.

His street sense motivated him to pay the Esquire Show Lounge master of ceremonies $5 for his first chance to make fun of processed/conked hair, outer space, "The Man," his dumb cousin and his mother-in-law. To his surprise, two weeks later he replaced the master of ceremonies.

Gregory packed the house at the Esquire, but left when they refused him a $2 a night raise. He opened his own club outside of Chicago, called the Apex, with money he acquired from a young woman from a small town in Ohio whom he'd met at the Esquire. He's been married to that woman, Lillian Smith, since 1959. She manages Gregory's finances, his hectic schedule and their 10 children.

The Apex closed after only six months as a result of a horrible Chicago winter that kept audiences away. So, Gregory worked a couple of clubs and washed cars to provide for his growing family.

Sitting On The Couch

One night in 1961, when White comic Professor Irwin Corey couldn't make a gig at the Playboy Club, owner Hugh Hefner called Gregory to fill in. Gregory walked 20 blocks in freezing weather and was told that the audience that evening was primarily made up of White Southern executives. Gregory, in his winning manner, politely told the manager that he was not leaving even if there was a lynch mob in the room. He walked out and greeted his audience:

"Good evening, ladies and gentleman, I understand there are a good many Southerners in the room tonight. I know the South very well. I spent 20 years there one night. Last time I was down South, I walked into a restaurant and this White waitress came up to me and said, 'We don't serve colored people here!' I said, 'That's alright, I don't eat colored people. Bring me a whole chicken.'"

In spite of a few hecklers and the terrified manager, Gregory managed to disarm the crowd and remained on stage for some two hours, rather than the scheduled 50 minutes. *Time* magazine ran an article with his photograph, proclaiming, "Dick Gregory, 28, has become the first Negro comedian to make his way into the nightclub scene big time."

The doors opened and Gregory stepped up to the plate. When he received an invitation to appear on the *Jack Paar Show*, he turned it down because he had been told that Paar never allowed Black entertainers to sit on the studio couch for an interview.

Gregory explains that even though he declined the show, he still cried thinking he had blown his big break. But as he was drying his eyes, he got a call. It was Jack Paar on the line wanting to know why Gregory had refused. Gregory explained, "because Negroes never sit down on your show."

Paar said, "Sammy Davis Jr., sits down." Gregory said, "No, Davis sits down when he fills in as a guest host." In the end, Paar got Gregory and Gregory got to sit on the couch. After that, Gregory's weekly salary skyrocketed from $250 to $5,000. By 1962, he was making $350,000 annually.

Politically, the climate was tumultuous and the Civil Rights Movement was in high gear, so the timing was perfect for Gregory's acerbic commentary. Comic Mort Sahl had just started to deal with social issues and Gregory became the first Black comic to do so.

Suddenly, he was asked to speak at benefits for the Congress on Racial Equality, the Student Nonviolent Coordinating Committee and the Southern Christian Leadership Conference. In 1961, Mississippi Civil Rights leader Medgar Evers asked him to speak at a voter registration rally in Jackson, Mississippi.

The comedian's new role became to inspire Blacks to vote, raise money and promote a movement that would make history. Gregory led a double life – traveling to and from rallies in the South and returning to the North to make people laugh at the travesties of racism.

Life and death faced him consistently as he continued to march and protest for civil rights. Gregory describes that time in this life as when he was just trying to make it. He spent months away from home entertaining and protesting and although his wife was concerned, she understood his situation.

Gregory got his first brutal beating by Sheriff Eugene "Bull" Connor's minions in Birmingham in 1963 and his work with the movement cost him $250,000 in earnings over a two-year period by 1964. But in the long run, he gained more than he lost.

He was privy to the great Black minds of the time and marveled at their genius and strength. "Both King and Malcolm X were special because they were consistent. They were the same on or off the camera," he says.

The Health Guru

Gregory smoked and drank and his diet was non-structured and not very healthy. He ate lots of starches and drank gelatin for protein and his weight ballooned from 132 to 365 pounds.

No longer streamlined or athletic looking, Gregory decided to fast for the first time in 1967 to protest the Viet Nam War. He dropped down to a very frail 97 pounds, but his romance with health and fitness began at this time.

In 1973, his newfound sense of health awareness caused him to stop performing in bars and clubs because smoking and drinking were allowed. That same year, he moved his family from Chicago to a 12-room farmhouse in Plymouth, Massachusetts.

By this time, Gregory was lecturing at least 20 days a month on a college tour. He spoke on his many conspiracy theories from the '60s, which put the late FBI Director J. Edgar Hoover at the forefront of the assassinations of John F. Kennedy, Medgar Evers, Malcolm X, and Martin Luther King, Jr.

Hoover's contempt for Gregory is captured in the 13,000 pages of FBI documents released in 1978. Among the notes is a memo written by Hoover, stating: "Chicago, as office of origin on Richard Claxton Gregory, also known as Dick Gregory, should develop counterintelligence measures to neutralize him. This should not be in the nature of an expose [sic], since he already gets far too much publicity. Instead, sophisticated, completely untraceable means of neutralizing Gregory should be developed."

The Popular Bahamian Diet

By 1984, Gregory's health sense had put him in another tax bracket. He developed the Slim Safe

Bahamian Diet, a weight-loss program, while trying to come up with a way to feed starving people. He learned that America lost more people to obesity than anything else. "I realized that being overweight is a form of malnutrition," he says.

The program's sales brought in about $30,000 daily and Gregory purchased a hotel (that he no longer owns) in Fort Walton Beach, Florida to use as a retreat for people who wanted to lose weight under supervision.

In 1987, he partnered with two others in a health food distribution company, Correction Connection, based in Philadelphia that *Black Enterprise* magazine named to its list of the nation's top 100 Black businesses. At the time the company's sales were $10 million.

Gregory stayed on his mission — fasting to call attention to the nation's drug epidemic and for statehood for Washington, D.C.; protesting against gangsta rap, apartheid and the Persian Gulf War; and running marathons to protest hunger and malnutrition.

He took on 1,000-pound man Walter Hudson and made headlines, as under Gregory's supervision, Hudson lost 400 pounds and was able to walk out of his home for the first time in 18 years.

But along the way, Gregory watched his favorite funny men, Bill Cosby, Richard Pryor, Robin Williams and George Carlin become superstars. Too many had forgotten Gregory as the great comedian he is and many never knew until producer Ashton Springer called and said, "Let's take your show to Broadway."

Gregory very humbly states that he's just happy to be back on the stage and in the mix because he has just as much fun as the audience does. But fun never cancels the activism – it's his mission to help make this a better world.

preface Harvey

Update: Steve Harvey continues to go nonstop as the hardest-working man in show biz. He hosts a daily nationally syndicated morning radio show that reaches six million listeners weekly, a daily nationally syndicated TV talk show, and is the host of the popular daily TV game show, *Family Feud*, in addition to being a best-selling author. Harvey was inducted into the National Association of Broadcasters Hall of Fame in 2013.

Steve Harvey

By Ken Parish Perkins & Photography by National Association of Broadcasters and Premier Network | *Originally Published May 29, 1997*

Sometimes the ways of fame boil down to the moment you open your head and your heart and your wallet and let brothers and sisters stroll in unchecked. You leap up with a handshake and a "let's-do-this-thing" and go about the business of doing what's right for you, for them, for Black folks.

After all, it's about us. It's about making it on your own without European money, influence and their philosophies getting in the way of creative change on the authentic cultural tip.

Steve Harvey likes to do business this way because he's gotten a piece of it and now can't let go. Won't let go. He remembers as a youngblood standup comedian trying to land gigs in places he wouldn't dare visit otherwise and wondering when he could move on.

He was far from the position he now enjoys, a lofty power player with enough juice to have his name in the title of a situation comedy, head TV's only Black weekly variety special, *Showtime At The Apollo*, and have the opportunity to sport that flat top fade on the big screen.

> Standup's the thing, dog. It's the funk. It's my high. It's gratifying to make the truth funny, to paint pictures in the mind.

But he is, and always will be, a "brother comic," and brothers in this country can't let their guards down, Harvey says, laughing. The odds are too high, the margin of error too small, the risks too many.

Not All Fun And Games

Times for Steve Harvey have been filled with mixed blessings. His has been a professional and personal life of ups and downs, of divorce and defeat, of triumph and tribulation.

When he bounces on stage for his standup routines, he talks about life, love and lessons, and the importance of staying real because he's been there and done that. He's won and he's lost and come out of it with the high-up fade clearly intact.

So the notion of hiding is moot. Harvey knows this but the perception is there and he doesn't like it. "One of the negatives of this whole fame thing," says Harvey, who grew up in Cleveland in modest surroundings but now owns property in Dallas, Beverly Hills, Cleveland and Chicago, "is that people think they know you. They see you on stage or on TV and swear you're exactly what they see.

"I'm not that way at all. I'm shy. I get in moods. You can be talking to me and I'd be looking out the window. I know you're there, but I'm in another world. And those around me know what's up. Time to leave me the hell alone."

To consider Steve Harvey, consider October 8, 1985, his first time on a comedy stage. "A friend of mine asked me to do it," says Harvey, who was selling insurance in Cleveland. "I just went on a Tuesday night to watch, just chillin' with some grapefruit juice watching the show. Someone put my name on the list to perform."

The next thing he knew, someone was calling his name. "So I go up on stage," Harvey says. "I just talk. Talk smack. Talk about life. My life. Other people's lives. I have only 10 minutes, but never once look at my watch. All I remember is this guy at the foot of the stage flashing this light in my face."

The people were cracking up, rolling in the aisles. He won amateur night. They bankrolled him a $50, and asked for a return to open the next week's contest. Harvey says he didn't know "you could tell the same jokes," so "I come back with all new stuff. I clean up again. That was it."

That was it. He quit his insurance sales gig for uncertain chaos. Within months, he was on the road, clocking more than 120,000 miles in his car, making the best of things in places like Vermillion, South Dakota, Rockingham, North Carolina and Addison, Texas, trying to win over the drunks and partiers and racists who weren't all that interested in his presence, let alone his thoughts.

But he kept moving. Kept driving. And what a training ground. Harvey wasn't all that interested in becoming the "brother comic" with no marketability or versatility. He'd stepped into his true passion and felt blessed.

A Young Man's Dream

"I'd always wanted to be a stand-up," Harvey says, sounding almost bashful. "I was eight when I watched TV and said, 'I want to do that.'"

But he made the mistake of telling his sixth grade teacher, who told him to sit down, be quiet and focus on attainable pursuits. Be a professional wearing a white shirt and carrying a briefcase. Comedy? Brother, please. At least she didn't say dig ditches. But she might as well have.

After that, "I kept my dream to myself," Harvey says. Didn't want the ridicule. Didn't want the negativity. Didn't want to know the odds.

He didn't even tell his father, to whom he owes his sense of humor and "third eye," as he calls it. Once he was caught secretly listening to his father's recordings of Rudy Ray Moore. Momma Harvey grounded him for months and his dad made him recite Moore's entire routine in front of his buddies, profanity and all.

Dad was too crazy, says Harvey. He was a coal miner who grew up in West Virginia, where Harvey was born. They moved to Cleveland when construction jobs for Black men opened in Cleveland. He did what he had to do to make life better.

"It's definitely genetic based," Harvey says of his comedic funny bone. "My father is hysterical. He just grew up at a different time. He would have been in show business had circumstances been different. But I learned from him to look at life in another way."

Yeah, through a third eye. "That means you see the black and white and gray area, which is usually where the comedy is hidden," says Harvey.

Until he was 15, he spent the school year in Cleveland and summers in West Virginia with his grandparents. He was a city boy on the farm. He fed hogs and chickens and horses, bailed hay, the whole nine yards.

It gave Harvey a breather from the congestion and madness of the city. In Cleveland, "I'd get in fights and things and the gangbangers were closing in the older I got," he says.

It's all there on stage. Harvey jokes about his childhood, coming

from a working class neighborhood, having older parents. The youngest of five, Harvey was born when his parents were well into their 40s. His humor related to life around the kitchen table, in the backyard, from the playground.

He had one act for White audiences and another, edgier routine for Black clubs. Within five or six years, he was headlining, earning $1,000 a week at big city comedy clubs in Chicago, New York and Dallas.

Soon he was bringing in $2,500 a week playing at resorts and performing regularly on pay cable standup comedy specials like *The Comedy Concert Hour* on The Nashville Network and *Comedy From the Caribbean* on Arts & Entertainment Network.

Ability To Move The Crowd

Early on, Harvey exhibited a rare talent: going with the mood of the crowd. "He has a way of connecting with both the intellectual snob and the culturally-deprived parasite," observes Stan Lathan, who produced *The Steve Harvey Show*.

"You don't know how hard that is until you've tried it. He does that with ease. It might have a lot to do with the fact that he was able to mix both his shows for White and Black audiences and find some kind of happy medium."

What's fascinating about Harvey's standup routines, says filmmaker and Chicago native Robert Townsend, "is that he pulls everyone in no matter their background.

"A lot of comics alienate some segment of the audience because they limit themselves to a certain segment. It's almost a natural. And these are good comedians. Steve doesn't appear to do that. By the end of the night, he's won everyone over. He's best at adjusting to his surroundings, I guess."

He had to adjust to radio when WGCI in Chicago called him. He'd substituted for Tom Joyner and Doug Banks and for other DJs across the country. He was funny and fluid and natural. "No thang," he figured.

Surprising even to WGCI General Manager Marv Dyson, who pushed hard to sign Harvey after losing Joyner and Banks to syndication deals, Harvey connected to the audience as a new breed morning personality.

Forget target audiences. Forget research. Butt naked radio, he called it. Raw. Without a tightrope. His audience was larger than Joyner's his first time out. Amazing.

Despite being a popular radio figure, Harvey says there's a certain type of music he won't play. "I don't give a damn about rap and I can't stand gangster rap," he says. "You can't expect me to go along with gangster rap that's talking about the murder and destruction of our people. Hell, that's nothing but Black on Black genocide."

When the WB approached him about a sitcom, which became *The Steve Harvey Show*, Steve laid out the rules. He wanted a Black producer and Black supervising producer. He wanted Black writers. He wanted the series to be set in a diverse high school. The "brother comic" got it all.

Harvey wants to show how, given the right application of perspective and brains, business can be a positive pulpit.

Not Hung Up On Fame

"I don't care for the public side of my job at all," Harvey says. "What's the Tupac line, 'All I want is the money, f--- the fame. I'm a simple man.' That's how I feel. I enjoy it when people applaud my art, when I'm on stage and I'm standing there giving people their money's worth.

"But when I get through, I revert back to the man I am. But standup's the thing, dog. It's the funk. It's my high. It's gratifying to make the truth funny, to paint pictures in the mind. There are times when I'm talking about stuff and Black folks stand and turn and run up four or five rows and come back because they're laughing so hard.

"At that point I feel like a preacher saving souls, getting them to come to the pulpit. I concentrate more, work harder, keep pressure on them until I say goodnight. I love doing that, love it. I love doing that for Black people. It's a feeling I don't want to give up."

preface
Higginbottom

Update: Elzie Higginbottom manages more than 12,000 residential units and several commercial properties, and has developed more than 3,500 units of housing across the Midwest.

Elzie Higginbottom

By Walter M. Perkins & Photography by Calvin Woods | *Originally Published September 4, 1997*

The real estate development and management business is a penny business. You have to save a penny here and there, and pretty soon you've got yourself a dollar. For the most part, it's a day in day out, four yards and a cloud of dust business."

So says Elzie Higginbottom, Chairman/CEO of East Lake Management and Development Corporation headquartered at 2850 South Michigan.

Higginbottom describes East Lake as a "multi-faceted business that manages company owned residential property and residential and commercial property owned by third parties. East Lake also does startup construction and rehabilitation of existing properties."

In business since 1975, Higginbottom started East Lake while working for real estate giant Baird & Warner, where he established and directed their government assisted Multi-Family Housing Finance Division. He began work for Baird & Warner following graduation from the University of Wisconsin in Madison where he earned a degree in economics, with a minor concentration in real estate, and was also an NCAA All-American in track and field.

There's a need for young people to provide services to our industry like painting, decorating, repair, carpentry, plumbing, heating and those kinds of things. When you drive through our community, you don't see those kinds of businesses.

Higginbottom credits John Baird with being an early mentor and helping him learn the real estate business. "That is one of the reasons I feel a strong need to nurture other strong people who might be trying to determine whether or not they'd like to be involved in real estate as their life's work," he says.

It doesn't take long to realize that you really don't want to be at the negotiating table with Elzie Higginbottom unless you're part of his team.

Seated in his conference room on South Michigan, Higginbottom's calm, confident manner engulfs the room. While gracious and friendly, he is every bit the corporate CEO. The difference here is that he seems to be a CEO with a corporate conscious and a concern about the neighborhoods he develops.

"I think that it is important as a developer to make sure that you leave some history or have that development associated in some way with its historical past. Especially in our community. I think that too much of our history has been lost."

While he was specifically talking about the planned renovation of the original historical Provident Hospital building, Higginbottom was also talking about his personal philosophy of development. Concern about neighborhoods, people and tradition permeate his conversation.

Going back to the Provident project he says, "We are in the planning stages to redevelop that building, either as a rental or assisted-living facility for seniors. I just saw that as a building that had too much history to be torn down. We intend to develop it in a way that will constantly remind people of the history that has taken place in that building."

Real Estate Rebirth

Asked about the reason for the current real estate boom in Chicago, Higginbottom credits the late Mayor Harold Washington with initiating the boom and Mayor Richard M. Daley with its continuation.

"Mayor Washington started it all with his neighborhood initiative program, which brought in more and better public services to the neighborhoods. People began to see a revitalization of these neighborhoods as a result of public sector involvement. That resulted in the private sector getting involved," Higginbottom said. "The initial focus was on rehabilitation of existing housing."

Of the current mayor, Higginbottom says, "To Daley's credit, he has continued the neighborhood initiatives. He has had enough foresight to see that they have been very good for the city. He has added to the neighborhood initiatives that were started by Mayor Washington, and the results of those actions are evident. You just have to drive through any neighborhood in the city, and you will see substantial changes, a real rebirth. You can see these neighborhoods are alive."

Not everyone is pleased with the flurry of real estate development going on in Chicago. Some say it is a case of already rich developers adding to their coffers. Others say the city is involved in a land grab and that there is no definite, cohesive plan for those displaced as a result.

These are intense political questions begging for answers. "We have very high unemployment in the Black community," Higginbottom says. "Redevelopment of areas where Blacks live means employment opportunities. Instead of being critical of redevelopment in those areas, we should be preparing our labor force and our business community to step in and take part in this development, which, I think, will strengthen our community all around. We must train our communities so they have the expertise to participate."

Concerning the issue of displacement of the poor he says, "I think we should be concerned about reducing the number of poor. If we expand employment opportunities, we will reduce the number of poor people, if we continue an economic development approach. Will the number of poor people ever be down to zero?" he continues. " Probably not. But we can make it smaller than it is."

More Than Just A Developer

Just as Higginbottom sees his role as a developer and nurturer of the communities he works in, he also plays a similar role with young people working at East Lake and those who express interest in the real estate business.

"They first have to learn to be patient," Elzie stresses. "You see some industries where young people have gone in overnight and made a lot of money, but the development business is a very slow and methodical business, although we do read about developers who have done a couple of big deals.

"The overall business climate in Chicago is very good," he continued. "I would like to see more minorities get involved in retailing and the service industry. If you go through our community, you will find there is a need for grocery stores, hardware stores, and dry cleaners.

"There's also a need for young people to get involved in businesses that provide services to our industry like painting, decorating, repair, carpentry, plumbing, heating and those kinds of things. When you drive through the community, you don't see those kinds of businesses. I think the youth and schools need to focus more on this."

The community and others have recognized Higginbottom's contributions to the quality of life in the city of Chicago. The U.S. Department of Housing and Urban Development thought so highly of his efforts, that they gave him their first Minority Entrepreneur of the Year Award in 1984. In 2000, he was inducted into the Chicago Association of Realtors Hall of Fame, the only African American to be included in that group.

Organizations ranging from Operation PUSH to Lewis University have honored him for his work. Higginbottom has also been recognized by Catholic Charities of Chicago; Lawndale Peoples Planning and Action Conference; the Midwest Community Council; Fellowship Baptist Church and others. In addition, he is currently a director of the University of Wisconsin's Alumni Association, Cole Taylor Bank, the Illinois Institute of Technology, and After School Matters.

Besides the Provident renovation, his company's current projects include, "a number of tax credit properties on the South Side of Chicago," he said. "We do a lot of partnering with neighborhood-based not-for-profit organizations. We are also doing a rehabilitation project with Grant Memorial Church Corporation. And, we are embarking on a historic tax credit property that is going to result in rehabilitation of an historical hotel building."

For fun, Higginbottom says his primary passion is boating, "although I haven't had much time for that lately. I also like to spend time with my wife, Deborah," he says.

Asked how he would like to be remembered, Higginbottom reflected, "I've been very fortunate to have been helped by many people who helped me get [to] where I am today. I would like to be remembered as a person who was always willing to give a helping hand to someone who was in need of a helping hand.

"The Black community is underserved from the standpoint of representation by the business community, and from the standpoint of not being able to employ its own residents. I would like it said that I was able to do a small part in expanding economic opportunities in my community as well as other communities."

Higginbottom

preface Hobson

Update: Mellody Hobson has had a different home address and phone number since she married *Star Wars* filmmaker George Lucas, with whom she has a daughter, in 2013. And she took on another job, as board chair of Dreamworks Animation.

Mellody sits on the boards of Starbucks, Estee Lauder and the Chicago Public Education Fund, and is chairwoman of After School Matters, the nonprofit that provides Chicago teens with out-of-school programs. Mellody was tabbed as chairman of the Economic Club of Chicago in 2017.

Mellody Hobson

By Jean A. Williams & Photography by Victor Powell | *Originally Published December 30, 2001*

Mellody Hobson is something of a study in contrasts. She has the poise and sophistication of a cosmopolitan woman who is running things, but on this blustery day in early December – with her hair pulled back into a ponytail and wearing a pullover top and a pair of brown pants covered in flowers – she also exudes a bit of school-girl flair.

Nevertheless, it's obvious that Hobson is a woman who knows her stuff and is, thankfully, happy to share her knowledge.

At 32, Hobson is the president of Ariel Capital Management and Ariel Mutual Funds, the oldest and largest African-American owned mutual fund company in the nation.

When asked to explain the fundamentals of mutual fund investing, Hobson is at the ready. She dashes over to a compartment behind her desk in her office on the 29th floor of the AON building in downtown Chicago. She returns to her chair with, of all things, a plastic freezer bag.

"I do this presentation all the time," Hobson says. She removes several pieces of cardboard, each emblazoned with the names of well-known products from the well-worn bag. She puts the cardboard pieces aside and displays the now empty bag.

We want to be the mutual fund company of Chicago and we also want to be the mutual fund of choice for Black investors.

"We're going to call this the Building Wealth Mutual Fund, because all of us are investing, hopefully, to build wealth," she says. Hobson then explains how a mutual fund is like a basket, and in her explanation she begins to use the terms interchangeably.

"You've also heard of this basket being called a portfolio," she says, adding a third term that she also uses interchangeably. "So the portfolio is empty right now. (At Ariel), we're money managers. We come in, in the morning, and we say, 'I'm going to buy some McCormick Spices for my portfolio.' Those shares go into the mutual fund." She places the McCormick Spices cardboard into her bag.

"We also say, 'I'm going to buy some Clorox for my portfolio,'" Hobson continues. "Those shares go into the basket – the portfolio, the mutual fund." She places another piece of cardboard in her, er, basket.

"We don't own this stock, but I'll give it to you as an example just because it resonates with people," she continues further. "The line at Starbucks seems very long. It seems like a great business. I'm going to put Starbucks into my portfolio. So that's in there."

After the bag is filled with the assorted cardboard businesses, Hobson says, "So that's what we do. The day is over. We're done. This is our portfolio."

The process happens again each day as the mutual fund/basket/portfolio is re-examined by highly skilled managers. As simplistic as her presentation may sound, it's an example of how flexible she has to be in her job.

One minute, she could be addressing a roomful of potential investors who are reluctant to buy because they don't really understand how mutual funds work. The next minute, she is addressing the board of directors or shareholders who may be as savvy as she. Hobson has to be prepared for every scenario.

A Fortuitous Meeting

Like the stocks in her example, you might say Hobson's career is securely in the bag as well. The youngest of six children, Hobson grew up on Chicago's South Side, where she felt as if she were practically an only child because all of her siblings were so much older. She honed an enviable work ethic at the knee of her mother, who was a real estate entrepreneur.

"I sort of had an odd thing," Hobson recalls. "I didn't go to pre-school. I just went right to kindergarten. Until I was five, I went to work everyday with my Mom. My earliest memories are being in her office when I was a little kid.

"She worked really, really hard, and she always had a very industrious way about her, and that certainly rubbed off on all of us. She was very demanding of herself because she had to be to take care of all these kids."

Like her mentor, Ariel founder and CEO John W. Rogers Jr., Hobson attended Princeton University. In fact, she first met Rogers, who spearheaded minority recruiting for his alma mater, during an acceptance dinner at the school. "He was nice enough to say if you're ever home for the holidays for vacation, just give me a call, it'd be good to stay in touch," Hobson says.

She took him up on the offer, contacting him when home for Christmas break during her sophomore year at Princeton, where she was studying international relations and public policy at the Woodrow Wilson School of International Relations and Public Policy.

"I had lunch with him and I asked him if he took interns at Ariel and he facilitated me getting interviewed by Eric McKissack, who's our vice chairman," Hobson says. "At the time, Eric was our director of research. It's really funny. When we moved our offices last December, we all were cleaning out and purging lots of files, and (McKissack) found the notes from my original interview, which I thought was hysterical."

But her stint at Ariel has been anything but laughable. On the contrary, it's been quite remarkable. After another stint in Baltimore as an intern at T. Rowe Price, Hobson earned a degree from Princeton and began her career at Ariel. She hasn't looked away since from the slow and steady journey of the tortoise – which is the company's logo, embodying the theme of patient investing through value stocks.

"Ariel was my first experience with investing – total – when I was an intern," she says. "I knew nothing about the stock market, didn't know anything about investing. I didn't grow up in a house where we owned stocks. We never talked about the stock market. We were very typical of our community.

"Ariel has done a lot of surveys about Black investing patterns, and I think our family would have been all the statistics – favored real estate over all other types of investments, very conservative. My knowledge of the investment world came 100 percent from working for Ariel that one summer."

Secret Of Her Success

Hobson and Rogers make up a mutual admiration club. Having worked her way up through the ranks of the firm, Hobson now has an office directly next door to her mentor's.

"From the very beginning, Mellody has always been very, very driven, and someone who has worked extraordinarily hard to accomplish her goals," Rogers says. "I noticed that in her college career, I noticed that when she came to Ariel. As the years went on, when she joined us full time, I came to appreciate her ability to get things done.

"I started to count on her judgment more and more and thought that she had the ability to think about things in creative ways. She helped me think through some of the tough issues that we have faced in this organization."

Hobson has long been key in the marketing of

Ariel. In some ways, she's like head cheerleader of the firm. "They're the factory," she says of Rogers and McKissack, who manage the funds. "And I am with our marketing team and our client-servicing group, the ones who are going out and making sure people understand the story: What is Ariel all about? And how can we crystallize that message so that in good or bad times, they know what to expect from us?"

Work she does outside of Ariel also sheds positive light on her role at the firm. Hobson is a regular guest on ABC's *Good Morning America*, where she imparts financial planning wisdom via a segment called "Mellody's Math." Her other media experiences include giving financial advice through the pages of *N'DIGO*, spending three years as a financial reporter on WGN's *Minority Business Report* and regular appearances on CNN and CNNfn.

Explaining her success, Hobson says, "It's really simple. I just worked hard. I think the greatest gift my mother gave me was to teach me the importance of hard work. She always used to tell me, try to make yourself indispensable, and I thought that the only way I could do that is to work really, really hard – work hard for our clients, work hard for other individuals here, work hard for myself. And I think that helped a lot. I think that's a big part of success in America and that's what America is all about."

Validating just how hard she does work for the firm, Ariel rewarded the former intern with the presidency of the company in May 2000. It was a title that Rogers himself had held before granting it to Hobson. Now Ariel is looking for Hobson's leadership and dedication in making it a robust brand.

"She's really been working extraordinarily hard over the years to build our brand name in Ariel Mutual Funds," Rogers says. "That is something that is critically important to the future of our company, and it's something that she'll continue to spend a lot of time focused on. That's a very important part of her responsibilities here, and she's done an excellent job at it."

Hobson is working hard to make Ariel Mutual Funds available through company retirement plans.

"We're trying to get corporations to add us to their investment lineup so that their employees can pick us," Hobson says. "That's something that's a big part of our marketing strategy. So right now we're in the 401(k) plan at the NFL. We're in the 401(k) plan at Coca-Cola. We're in the 401(k) plan, soon to be, at Mitsubishi.

"We're hoping people go out and say, 'Why isn't Ariel in my lineup?' And then we can be there, alongside Fidelity or T. Rowe Price or Vanguard or Janus."

Getting The Community Into Investing

Educating the community on the virtues of the stock market is part of the mission at Ariel. Hobson has

been at the forefront of those efforts. She would like to see the reticence of African Americans disappear when it comes to investing.

"We want to be the mutual fund company of Chicago and we also want to be the mutual fund of choice for Black investors," Hobson says.

"We have clients in our mutual funds all over the country, thousands and thousands of shareholders. But if we build a really strong base in our (primary) communities, both Chicago and the Black community, that will ultimately allow us to push out further in our marketing efforts as we get bigger (with) more name recognition."

As much as she has reflected on the trail that led her to the top ranks of Ariel Capital Management and Ariel Mutual Funds, Hobson can't imagine a future outside of the firm. "I certainly couldn't work in another industry," she says. "I had that revelation really early on.

"I was talking to a friend today from college and he was saying how I'm one of the few people in our entire graduating class of 1,100 people who has the same job.

"I have the same home and work phone number since I graduated. That kind of stability is really rare these days – that you find your calling really early. It's said that the average American has 11 jobs in their lifetime – I've only ever had one."

preface Hudson

Update: Jennifer won Oscars and Golden Globe Awards as Best Supporting Actress for her role in *Dreamgirls* and has gone on to garner worldwide acclaim as a singer and actress. She has won a Grammy for Best R&B album, has a star on the Hollywood Walk of Fame, and has performed at the Superbowl, the Academy Awards and for President Barack Obama's inauguration.

Sadly, in 2008, her mother, brother and nephew were killed in shootings in Chicago. Afterward, Hudson created the Julian King Foundation in honor of her nephew to provide stability for children of all backgrounds so they may grow into productive and happy adults.

Jennifer Hudson

By Iman A. Jefferson & Photos Courtesy of DVA Agency | *Originally Published December 21, 2006*

There's no business like show business, and Chicago native Jennifer Hudson knows that best.

After being voted off *American Idol* surprisingly early on in 2004, she became a household name as one of the fan favorites in *Idol*'s Season 3. But a year later, her time came in a big way.

When the Tony-award winning musical *Dreamgirls* was to be adapted as a motion picture 25 years after its Broadway debut, Hudson knew the film was hers. After beating out close to 800 singers and actresses, including Fantasia Barrino who beat her out for the top spot on *American Idol*, Hudson landed the coveted star role of Effie White.

"I just said if God gives me the opportunity, I promise I'll make it work," Hudson said of the movie that features an all-star cast of Beyoncé Knowles, Eddie Murphy, Jamie Foxx, Danny Glover and Anika Noni Rose.

Born In The Church

During *Idol*, guest judge Elton John was amazed by Hudson's vocal range and depth. Surprisingly, her six-octave range isn't from years of professional training, but from spending many Sundays at the Pleasant Gift Missionary Baptist Church on the city's South Side.

Singing since the age of seven, Hudson is quick to acknowledge her late maternal grandmother Julia Kate Hudson as the reason her voice is as powerful as it is.

> It's God, it's not me. I'm just the instrument.
> You can't do anything without Him.

"I started singing in the church. I was 'born in the church,' as we call it. My grandmother was the 'voice,' and that's where I got my voice from," Hudson said.

Growing up in the Englewood community, Hudson says her grandmother, a proud matriarch who was active in the church's choir, made sure Hudson was always singing, and honed Hudson's signature range.

Shari Nichols-Sweat, vocal director at Dunbar High School and Hudson's cousin, remembers Hudson's early days of singing in the junior choir in the church.

"Even when she was young, she had a nice voice and a great spirit about her singing. It moves people. She loved singing, and it always came out when she sang," Nichols-Sweat said.

As Hudson's voice continued to mature, she began performing at various events. Nichols-Sweat spoke about Hudson's dedication to being a singer.

"I remember when Jennifer was in the eighth grade, she told me she really wanted to go to Dunbar and sing in my Spirit Choir," she said. "We're not surprised by any of her accomplishments; she always had that determined spirit."

Even now with a busy schedule, Hudson still views the church as her home and center of strength. "It's still my favorite place to sing to this day," Hudson says.

From Englewood To Hollywood

When Hudson graduated from Paul Lawrence Dunbar High School in 1999, she went away to college. But after spending a semester at Historically Black Langston University in Oklahoma, Hudson realized her and Oklahoma were not a perfect match.

"I went for one semester. I called myself following my cousins, and honey it did not work for me," Hudson muses. "I didn't like the weather; it totally affected my voice and I couldn't sing, and anytime something affects my voice, I got to go."

Hudson returned to Chicago and enrolled at Kennedy-King College, where she took several courses. But once again, Hudson's commanding voice continued to garner attention and she ended up singing at graduations for the college, just as she did in high school.

Soon after, Hudson, 19 at the time, landed her first theater job at the Marriott Lincolnshire Theater playing in *Big River*. A little over a year later, she began working for Disney playing "Calliope," the head muse on their Disney Wonder cruise ships. It was while working for Disney that Hudson began seriously considering auditioning for *American Idol*. "When I decided to do it, I did it for the experience. It wasn't like 'oh, I want to be the *Idol*.' I like to do things for the experience," Hudson said.

She was in the first group of semifinalists, but wasn't voted into the final round. However, she won the wildcard, and it was *Idol* judge Randy Jackson

Scene from
Dreamgirls

that voted her in as a finalist.

Though one of Season 3's favorites, Hudson was continually ridiculed by judge Simon Cowell on her clothing choices and presentation. While Hudson was initially disappointed with her elimination, she now looks at her *Idol* time as prime exposure.

"Every bit of being on *Idol* was like 'wow, you get to touch that dream,'" Hudson said. "Now I'm glad I went that way."

Landing Effie White

Twenty-five years ago, *Dreamgirls* made its Broadway debut, loosely based on the rise of The Supremes. The story follows The Dreams, a singing trio (Hudson, Knowles, Rose) from Chicago and their shaky rise to fame. Hudson's character Effie is eventually dumped by her group, and her manager/boyfriend played by Jamie Foxx.

In 1981, Jennifer Holliday made Effie White a role longed for by singers and actresses everywhere. Her earth-shattering performance of the musical's climactic number, *And I Am Telling You I'm Not Going*, helped land her a Tony Award for Best Actress in a Musical.

When there was talk about the show being made into a movie, many wondered who'd fill the heels of the famous Effie White.

"I was in the process of working on a (music) project when I got the call to audition for *Dreamgirls*," Hudson said.

While researching the role of Effie White, Hudson noticed parallels between the story of the character and her own experiences during *Idol*.

"With me being on *American Idol*, it's like well, if she's one of the more 'talented' ones, then how is she eliminated, and if Effie is the talented one, then why is she put in the background and then kicked out of the group?

"Going through the whole journey and trying to survive after being kicked out the group … me trying to continue doing my thing after *Idol* and then still

rising back up again with *Dreamgirls* … and her doing her own thing with a solo career," Hudson said.

After initial screenings of *Dreamgirls* in New York and Los Angeles, critics everywhere praised Hudson's performance of Effie. Even Oprah Winfrey, after viewing Hudson's performance, sought to have her on her show, saying it was a "religious experience."

With a 100-watt grin, Hudson says, "It's God, it's not me. I'm just the instrument. You can't do anything without Him. This is what I happen to do, and the world happens to know about it. The goal is to hold on to me. I like to just be real and have people comfortable around me."

Her alma mater, Dunbar High School on the South Side, created the "Jennifer Hudson Room" there in honor of her involvement with the school's music program while a student and now her success as a performer. For Hudson, it definitely means a lot.

"That's amazing. I'm just glad that kids in the Englewood community and kids that go to Dunbar have someone to look up to. When I was back in school, anytime somebody who was anybody would come back and visit, it touched me and helped me see if I can touch it, that means I can achieve it."

Even with her trekking around the world, Hudson appears more as an old-fashioned girlfriend than superstar and her dreams continue to come true.

Despite all the accolades rolling in, the biggest honor is the one that deals with Hudson's original passion: singing. In November, Hudson inked a record deal with legendary Clive Davis of Arista Records under the Jive Records label. Arista is the home of icons Whitney Houston, Aretha Franklin, Dionne Warwick, and many more.

"My goal has been to sing and get a deal, so I'm just excited about it. This is what I worked for," Hudson said. She heads into the studio early next year to work on her debut album.

"I put all my focus into *Dreamgirls*. I refused to sing for anything else, and now I can do just that," Hudson said.

preface Jackson

Update: Jacqueline Jackson is the matriarch of the Jackson Family in a marriage that has now lasted some 54 years. She is former president of the Jackson Foundation and remains a lifelong activist against injustice. In 2000, she was arrested and spent 10 days in a federal prison in San Juan for protesting U.S. Navy bombing exercises on the island of Vieques in Puerto Rico.

Jacqueline L. Jackson

By Wanda Wright & Photography by Reginald Payton | *Originally Published May 2, 1996*

When America looks at the shattering of families, Black America is reminded of its matriarchal legacy. In our survival throughout history, African-American mothers have played strong, silent roles.

Mothering in general can be a difficult, thankless job. How then must it be for one who is highly visible?

Meet the other half of the "People's Movement," Mrs. Jacqueline L. Jackson, wife of Jesse, mother of five Jackson children. Her strength is honest, refined through generations.

What follows is a lesson from a Black sister who manages one of America's most successful families as she shares her recipe for childrearing.

I taught my children to work for a better America, that the kind of job one holds is not a measurement of self-worth. What matters is, are you a decent person? Are you doing good things?

People talked about her grandmother, Oronia Davis, who displayed her parasol, as well as a "high falutin" attitude, in the community of Fort Pierce, Florida. The granddaughter, Jacqueline Lavinia Brown, earned her role in family leadership as a whippersnapper. Her sharp wit, precociousness, sparkling personality and colorful language held people spellbound.

Bootleg Legacy

Jacqueline directed the family's bootlegging business starting around the age of six, but unlike the Kennedy family, which plied the same trade before son John F. Kennedy was elected President of the United States, Jacqueline's family's average customers were Black and Native-American.

In a stovetop town embroiled with inequity, murder and extortion, she learned style. Her cookbook legacy held a palate of sidebar samples, requiring her to study'n'sew, while shakin' and bakin' business with nearby tribes of Seminole Indians.

Today she beholds her vintage brewed – a full course complement of American family, delicately spiced with integrity, loyalty and self-respect.

Raised from a nest of strong, determined women, Jacqueline's male influence came initially from a caring stepfather, then minister, and eventually husband Reverend Jesse Louis Jackson.

Family circumstance forced early maturation on little Jackie. Gertrude Davis Brown, Jackie's mother who was orphaned at age 14, found herself a mother at 17, and determined to remove her babies from what she described as "the bottomless hole" of a Floridian ironclad caste system. Brown headed north to find better accommodations, leaving her children in the care of surrogate "Aunt Nita."

The Mulberry Tree

Here we go 'round the mulberry bush! But there was no singsong around this tree. Today, it stands as the meeting point for old men who played checkers. Stubborn and fearless, "Aunt Nita", sporting "fightin" short hair, declared emancipation upon this spot. Auntie refused to compromise her imposing 6-foot, 300-pound cocoa brown frame onto a field hand-crowded truck to go and pick tomatoes.

"By standards of what is lovely and charming, she was rejectable," tenderly laughs Jacqueline. "She spurned White people. Didn't like them. And they didn't like her! She felt it insulting to iron White peoples' shirts and believed in self-employment. During this time, the Black community found other ways to survive.

"Aunt Nita was the proprietor and bouncer of her own jook joint, so we saw prostitutes with their throats cut. But she also made sure we learned self-respect, religion and loyalty under supervision."

Jackson tells of a time when adults made sure that they were home to address the needs of their children. No latchkeys. No one ever admitted hunger outside of the nest, and of the respect they had for one another.

Recalling methods of survival when toilets were in the yard and the occasional stray chicken or duck meant a grand evening's supper, she explained how the lack of money meant no education and possibly no way out.

"Our race was at the bottom, economically," she whispers, wringing her hands. "No alternatives existed without education, and there were no scholarships.

"But we as a people were much too proud to be 'poor.' Everyone looked to better themselves. Self-employment was unique, very American and very elite. Self-employment was the goal. It meant becoming your own master."

College and Jesse

Moving to Newport News, Virginia, found Jacqueline and Aunt Nita riding on the back of a bus behind a curtain. She recalls carrying the "slop jar" to urinate in and looking forward to freedom.

She rediscovered prison in the home of her parents. Classmates teased Jacqueline about the "warden parentage" under which she lived. The Browns insisted on all-day participation in the Baptist Training Young Peoples Union on Sundays.

She was expected home at 3:30 p.m., with no after-school activities allowed. A brilliant student and accomplished dancer, Jacqueline enrolled in North Carolina AT&T College.

"During my day, you went to college to get an education, but you didn't leave without a husband. I was so glad to be free that I didn't care about a man, though," she admits. "Our campus was afire with excitement of change. The protests in Greensboro, North Carolina, drew the attention of the world press. The last thing I wanted was romance."

So how did she attract Reverend Jackson? Jacqueline insisted on being the most exciting personality on campus. She was a provocative speaker and smolderingly sexy. Still, she wouldn't let Jesse, whom she met in her freshman year, "get over" and he was mystified by her mixed signals.

Yes, she was bold, but there was no compromise of morals and values. Her sense of self-responsibility, duty, diligence and virtue were not negotiable. It drove him crazy.

"You marry based on care and need," she quips. "My husband loved me; I liked him. He adored me, chased me. It wasn't fun! I wanted him as a buddy. I didn't want a boyfriend. I had too much on my agenda.

"At the time Jesse Jackson was madly in love with me, I'd written my own fantasy. I thought that Sam Cooke, Marlon Brando or Elvis would ride up on their horse as I let down my 'Rapunzel' hair to ride off into fantasyland. Jesse didn't even have a red wagon," she smiles. "I didn't want to marry a Caucasian, but I wanted that life, a chance to sample a lifestyle that we saw on the silver screen."

Jesse and Jacqueline married on New Year's Eve in 1962. Years later, she tells of standing in line with her children during a tour of the Smithsonian Institute.

Coming to a section dedicated to the Civil Rights Movement, her mouth fell open. It contained a counter and stool from the Woolworth's that refused to serve Blacks in Greensboro.

"What an incredible feeling!" she breathed. "I was there with Jesse when they refused to let us in. I sat there, eventually ate there, and now this seat is a part of history.

"We were there at the Smithsonian as no one in particular. Nobody knew who we were. You can't imagine what that meant to me and my children. Glory without the ceremony, that's what I taught my kids."

She's also taught her brood several other basic principles, such as self-respect. No accolades or parties are given upon graduation from high school because this is an understood responsibility, an absolute demonstration of loyalty to self. She also stresses, "Handle your body with love. When you awake, brush, floss, bathe, and thank God for letting you rise – before you eat."

She's taught them the principle of deferred gratification. "You must be tolerant of the by-and-buy," Jackie says. "Waiting for the fur coat, waiting for that kiss, because that kiss is a reward for something you've done very well."

She offers, "God loves you unconditionally. God has that capacity. I don't, I know that I am not God. We're living in a country called America, where racism exists as a chameleon. Equip yourself to recognize it, even when it isn't apparent."

She tells a cautionary tale to illustrate her point: "After integration, when toilets were accessible to all, coin-operated admission cropped up. Many Blacks didn't have a dime to use the facilities. Always be on the lookout," Jackie advises.

All My Children

"A lot of people died in front of me in Florida," she recalls. "Jook joint murders, people tied to railroad tracks, people fed to alligators by Caucasians. Racial unbalance and violence were something my kids witnessed during the Movement.

"I learned early to defy fear and stand on my convictions. You can fight or take flight. We taught our children to stand their ground. We were young and committed to sacrifice for the good of all.

"My kids slept on floors, walked miles in picket lines, shared their meals. We never separated the kids from us. Not for sit-ins, dinners or fights. We shunned behavior that might taint them.

"Reverend's road trips were difficult," she mused. "I'd ask him to reinforce punishment, but he didn't like it. Fathers are traditionally good or bad guys. As mothers, we either threaten, or 'tell your father,' which means he's seen as the disciplinarian."

The "Jackson Five" – Jackie's and Jesse's children – represent academia, chemistry, entertainment, investment, banking, politics, law and theology. Their educative investment had to cost a fortune in time, patience and money.

Speaking of individual characteristics of each child, she declares "Santita the smartest, Jonathan the most compassionate and spiritually brilliant, Jesse Jr. the most dutiful and responsible, Yusef the rising star, and Jacki Jr. as the most eclectic and talented."

Jacqueline says her secret lies in her ability to teach a child to love him/herself, no matter the circumstance. But it's love stirred by more than embraces as she suggests a careful sprinkling of admonishment, along with the rod.

She feels our society is a mixture of reward and punishment. Jacqueline says, "Teach kids to make your word your bond. Your word will follow you to your grave. So many people say things today that don't mean a damn thing."

With these principles gently folded early in the elixir of life, lessons of constraint will distill themselves. Blend caring and loyalty with boundless amounts of love, she says, and loyalty then spills from love of self to love of your race.

"What I taught my children was to work for a better America," she says. "My children have learned that the kind of job one holds is not a measurement of self-worth. Neither are cars, clothes, or material possessions. What matters is, are you a decent person? Are you doing good things?"

It hasn't been easy holding such a large, high profile family together through the years, though, Jacqueline candidly admits. But she's proud that she has. "Many look to my family as an example of strength. I feel very grateful that we exist as examples of perseverance, sacrifice, compassion and tenacity," she says.

"When all the world said

no, we did! We are proof that families can make it. My marriage has survived decades of hardship. This has been the most difficult task of my life. It's difficult to live with yourself, much less other people. It's not clear sailing and requires a lot of love, sacrifice and prayer."

Supposing she had the chance to repeat her choices…would she decide otherwise? "Absolutely not!" she gushes. "Jesse Jackson is the most exciting individual in the United States – and, so am I! We're not perfect, but it's a match."

preface Jackson

Update: In 2016, The Rev. Jesse Louis Jackson celebrated 50 years of involvement in Civil Rights activities. In that time, he has played a pivotal role in virtually every movement for empowerment, peace, civil rights, gender equality, economic equity and social justice.

Often called the "Conscience of the Nation," challenging America to be inclusive and to establish just and humane priorities for the benefit of all, Jackson is known for bringing people together on common ground across lines of race, culture, class, gender and belief.

In August 2000, he was awarded the Presidential Medal of Freedom, the nation's highest civilian honor, by President Bill Clinton. Jackson continues to travel the world speaking, marching and protesting social justice issues and still holds weekly Saturday morning meetings.

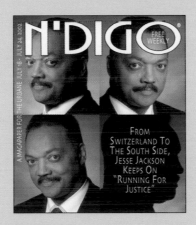

Reverend Jesse Jackson

By David Smallwood & Photography by Reginald Payton | *Originally Published November 16, 2006*

t's a cool drizzly Friday afternoon in October and the Rev. Jesse Jackson has made camp in the lounge area outside the second-floor grill of the East Bank Club, doing interviews, fielding phone calls, and taking care of who-knows-what-else other business.

He's seated alone at the last table in the back of the lounge, next to the glass partition separating the escalator, ostensibly to people-watch the comings and goings.

But his back and right flank are also protected in this particular seating pattern, probably an unconscious, reflexive security move triggered by decades of being a controversial public figure who witnessed the assassination of Dr. Martin Luther King Jr., and has visited some very dangerous places.

It's the day before a black-tie gala at the South Shore Country Club to celebrate Jackson's 65th birthday and 40 years of service in Civil Rights activities, and it's a surrealistic scene.

Jackson – the only African American in the lounge – sits quietly talking to Cliff Kelley on his cell phone for an interview that is streaming live in real time over WVON. He has no notes, just the tiny phone and an earpiece.

> I feel that I've made good use of my time. I sometimes wish I could have done more. But when I look back, I've helped to make the nation and the world better.

His fellow Caucasian loungers double-take when they realize it's Jackson, but quickly return to their own affairs, giving the celebrity in their midst his space.

NBC news anchor Warner Saunders is spotted by Jackson heading out the building, then comes over and apologizes for not being able to attend the Saturday celebration due to lingering throat problems.

A couple other acquaintances spot "The Reverend" and stop by to shake hands, but mostly, it's just Jackson solo, with no "handlers" nearby. Bespectacled and well dressed, he's seemingly older and wiser, contemplative, and at peace with himself.

He'd just given WVON listeners his birthday wish: "Cliff, I don't want any neckties; don't bring me any trinkets," he said. "What I need is for everybody to help just one person get into college, help just one person get to the polls and vote. That's all I want."

Jackson's sentiment was heartfelt, and in a way, summarizes what his life has been about. For the next hour, in an equally heartfelt conversation with N'DIGO, he reflected on what we tried to piece together as the 12 most significant moments of Jackson's life.

We came up with a "baker's dozen" of personal and professional incidents that have affected his character, development, understanding, and direction, or were hallmarks of his life.

Here's the list, according to Jesse, with his explanation as to why these are the moments:

1. *Being born into the climate that existed at the time.* "I was born during the Second World War under legal apartheid, in racially segregated Greenville, South Carolina," Jackson began. "It was illegal for Black people to make the same amount of money as White people. A second-class education for Blacks was the law. You couldn't apply to the state universities.

"My father was a veteran of World War II, came back home, and couldn't vote. I was born under conditions where we were not second-class people, but had second-class positions as a matter of law, a kind of state terrorism.

"I grew up resenting those conditions, and it made me want to be an odds-buster and improve beyond my circumstances."

2. *Being arrested in July 1960 with seven other students for trying to use the public library in Greenville.* Actually, this moment started Christmas of 1959, when Jackson, then a freshman football player at the University of Illinois, returned to his hometown for the holiday.

Over the break, he had to prepare for a speech with 25 annotated bibliographies, but Jackson says the "colored" library didn't have that many books, so the librarian sent him to the "White" library and called ahead that he was coming.

But the White librarian called the police, who arrived before Jackson, and when he got there, the librarian refused to give him any books. The police told him to leave.

"It was very painful and I cried because that hurt me," Jackson recalled. "I was hurt because I was humiliated, but that put in me a resolve to fight back."

The next year, Jackson transferred to North Carolina A&T State University in Greensboro, where he played football, became student body president, and started participating in sit-ins.

In July of that year, he and fellow students were arrested for trying to use public facilities in the library in nearby Greenville.

"They called us ignorant, but arrested us for trying to use the library," Jackson said, laughing at the irony. "That was my most daring act to that point.

3. *His decision to come to Chicago.*

"I had been indicted for disturbing the peace, so I came here to study, to step away for a while, and for a year I was able to do that," Jackson said. "While I was here, I was organizing in the Kenwood and Oakland neighborhoods, and helped pull together KOCO (Kenwood-Oakland Community Organization) as a combined group during that time."

4. *Being at Selma.*

The Selma to Montgomery marches for voting rights in March 1965 were a pivotal turning point in the Civil Rights Movement. Also, one of its bloodiest moments.

In the first march on "Bloody Sunday," March 7, nearly 600 marchers got only six blocks away to the Edmond Pettus Bridge, where state and local lawmen attacked them with billyclubs and tear gas, driving them back into Selma.

The brutality was witnessed by the entire nation on TV and drew 3,200 participants to the third and successful march on March 21. President Lyndon Johnson signed the Voting Rights Act of 1965 five months later.

Jackson took three carloads of seminary students to Selma for the marches, and began to work with Dr. King shortly there after in 1965.

5. *Working with Dr. King.*

"I was still in Chicago, and he came here in the later part of 1965 and I joined his staff," Jackson said.

"I found out that (the first Mayor Richard) Daley began to organize the ministers to turn against Dr. King and lock him out of pulpits in Chicago, then to have a press conference and attack him publicly.

"That's when Rev. Clay Evans stood up and gave Dr. King access to his pulpit at Fellowship Baptist Church, and he paid a great price for that because they cut off his money to build his new church for seven years."

Jackson says King asked him to work full-time in 1966 as his development director – they had begun to raise money – and as national director of Operation Breadbasket.

"I didn't want to leave school because I had another semester to go, but (his wife) Jackie said I should not refuse his request," Jackson sighed, his expression conveying that this was truly a monumental decision.

"It was highly risky," he continued, "because I had Jackie and two children. It was a $57.50-a-week job without any health insurance, a guaranteed high-risk job, and there was so much I had planned to do (otherwise)."

6. *The development of Breadbasket.*

Of course he took the job, and high-risk developed into high reward.

"Breadbasket was a great highlight because we opened all kinds of closed doors to businesses," Jackson said. "Putting Black products on shelves: Joe Louis Milk, Johnson Publishing Company magazines, Parker House Sausage.

"The barriers started collapsing. Got ads in Black newspapers – we got (Illinois) state treasurer Adlai Stevenson to make an adjustment in the law to put money in Black banks.

"What we did at Breadbasket became a method and model for all of urban America. So, working with Dr. King was a big moment in time and a lot changed in that moment."

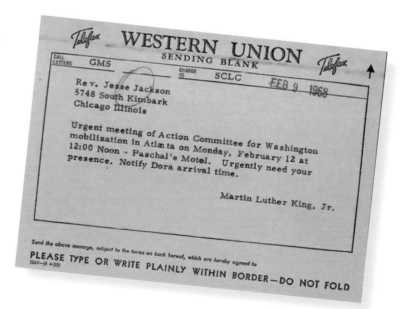

7. *Being in conversation with Dr. King when he was shot.*

"A traumatic moment – it was a world-changing moment for the entire Civil Rights struggle at that stage," Jackson recalled.

"But we were determined not to let one bullet kill the whole movement, so we didn't stop. At that time, Breadbasket had just exploded with interest and people and popular support."

8. *The ChicagoFest boycott in 1982.*
Rev. Jackson, Lu Palmer, and other Black activists in the city called for and successfully staged a weeklong boycott of then-mayor Jane Byrne's pet project, ChicagoFest, the forerunner of Taste of Chicago and other summer extravaganzas.

Byrne had riled the community by appointing White members to the board of the Chicago Housing Authority, whose developments were overwhelmingly populated by Black residents, and as head of the largely Black public schools system.

"Boycotting ChicagoFest was a big factor in Harold Washington's election in 1983, and was a turning point in Chicago politics," Jackson said.

9. *The decision to run for the President of the United States in 1984 and 1988.*
"A big decision!" Jackson whistled excitedly. "In 1984, we had no infrastructure, no money, no preparation, but Jane Byrne and (the second Richard) Daley had Harold running against them and (Democratic presidential contender Walter) Mondale supported them – it was important for them to defeat Harold. Suddenly, the liberalism in the Democratic Party was bankrupt, so we had to fight back.

"I tried to get Andy (Young) to run, and he wouldn't. I tried to get Maynard (Jackson). At some point, somebody said, 'Run, Jesse, run!' and I couldn't resist that challenge.

"Running for the presidency was a big deal because appearing on stage at those debates changed our collective minds about what was possible.

"We brought in six million voters. In primaries, I won New York in 1988; Dave Dinkins won (as mayor) in '89. I won in Virginia in '88; Doug Wilder won (as governor) in '89. Victory after victory came from those presidential runs and inspired more people to get involved in the political process.

"When I first ran for president, it seemed almost a joke," Jackson continued. "But because we were so successful, the Republicans said, 'The Democrats have Jesse Jackson, we can have Colin Powell – he's more qualified than Jackson!

"Then comes Barack (Obama). So what we did was to remove the roof as to what was possible. We've always had qualified Black people; we've just had an artificial and low-hanging roof. We're giants in holes and people simply couldn't grow.

"Before then, there were the questions: Should a Black run? Can we handle debates? Can we discuss foreign policy? The runs showed that we can move forward, that we can be Secretary of State, that we can be President."

10. *The decision to go get Goodman in Syria.*
In January 1984, Jackson made a successful freelance diplomatic mission to Syria to gain the freedom of Lt. Robert Goodman, a captured Navy flier being held prisoner there. It was the first of several prisoner releases Jackson brokered in Cuba, Iraq, and Kosovo in the '80s and '90s, and turned him into an accepted international diplomat.

11. *Living with Jr.*
"I got to live with Jesse Jr., who is now our Congressman and who was born while I was in Selma," Jackson said. "There's a valid connection between Selma and his running for the Congress. There's such a valid connection between his birth in that struggle and what he is doing now."

12. *Wife Jackie's protesting of the naval occupation in Puerto Rico.*
Jackson said it "brought out anxiety and maybe anger" in him because it started as a routine Civil Rights protest. "They decided to tighten up the reigns on her, and wanted her to go through a criminal process and invade her body, submit to a body cavity search. She refused to accept it," Jackson said.

"They put her in jail for 10 days in the hole, which was a frightening experience, but she ended up organizing the women in jail! Her coming out was a big deal – a lot of pride – because she came out unscathed, and it just reaffirmed her own mental toughness in terms of the struggle."

13. *Meeting on Saturdays.*
Jackson said it's probably something that's taken for granted, "but we have met every Saturday since 1966 – for 40 years – educating, inspiring, directing, and becoming a frame of reference for our struggle, and there's a whole generation of people who have benefited."

Explaining The Civil Rights Movement

Jackson tried to explain the different dimensions and evolution of the Civil Rights Movement by doodling a flow chart on a piece of paper.

In the first stage, "Civil Rights was a legal battle that involved confrontation with the law," he said. "We were confronting Bull Connor, Jim Crow, confronting the court system, fighting to change laws, fighting the brutality, fighting the structure.

"Once you win Civil Rights struggles, you win the battle to get into the University of Mississippi. Those who get through that door move on to the next stage,

which is civil responsibility. They are responsible for taking advantage of the door that got opened, and that's a little less confrontational.

"Then there should be a stage of civil behavior – show self-respect, don't self-degrade, avoid drugs, have good manners. That leads to civil opportunity. You won the Civil Rights battle; you went to school and learned through civil responsibility; you behaved in a manner that is civil; so now you have opportunity.

"Barack, Harold Ford, Jesse Jr., and all these guys – they have civil opportunity to run for office. They don't have the blood of this (the initial Civil Rights struggle, he pointed out on his drawing), but yet they are purged in the faith that the struggle does not stop.

"I'm delighted to see the oncoming generations continue to grow and push to new heights," Jackson beamed. "It was Dr. King's position that I may not get there, but we will get to the Promised Land."

And the Country Preacher is proud of his contribution to that, right?

"I am very proud of that!" he asserted, "because I feel that I've made good use of my time. I sometimes wish I could have done more. But when I look back, I've helped to make the nation and the world better," Jackson assessed.

"We battled to get Aristide back to Haiti in that bastion of poverty and violence; helped to get Mandela out of jail in South Africa; helped to define our role in foreign policy; helped to remove cultural assumptions about Black inferiority by running for president.

"And if you can run for president, you can surely run corporations. It's the evolution of the struggle."

preface Jackson

Update: Leon Jackson still operates Bill's Shades and went on to become the board chairman of The Woodlawn Organization (TWO) and The Woodlawn Community Development Corporation (WCDC).

Jackson was also board chairman of Teamwork Englewood, formed in 2003 to spearhead comprehensive community development of the Englewood neighborhood, including the construction of the new Kennedy-King College on 63rd and Halsted.

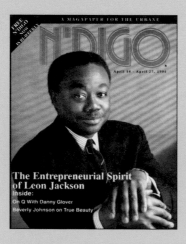

Leon Jackson

By Veronica Anderson & Photography by John Beckett | *Originally Published April 14, 1994*

A look at Leon Jackson's lengthy resume tells the story of how he's applied his formula effectively for several decades in the business community.

When Jackson first bought Bill's Shades and Blinds Service, Inc., the small contract window treatment company had annual sales of a few hundred thousand dollars. Since Jackson took over as president, the South Side business has grown to over $1 million a year in receipts, and employs 15 full-time workers.

Jackson also was the first entrepreneur to be granted a license to own and operate a Sara Lee Bakery shop. His two South Side stores – one in Chatham, the other in Evergreen Park – were the only two minority-owned businesses of more than 60 Sara Lee Bakery direct outlets around the country.

"Buying a little neighborhood business (like Bill's Shades and Blinds) is typical, but Sara Lee really was unique. They carved a niche in their business and made it available to me," Jackson says.

Not that the stores were handed over to him on a

> **I'm a sucker for the kids selling candy and magazines on the street; that's where the entrepreneurial skills start.**

silver platter. Getting the deal required a good dose of tenacity, he says, noting, "It was not easy for a Fortune 500 corporation to deal with an entrepreneur."

But what got him in on the ground floor was his 24-year affiliation with Chicago United, one of a number of local business networking groups in which Jackson is active, like the Cosmopolitan Chamber of Commerce and Black Contractors United.

"If I had not been a member of Chicago United, I would not have known Sara Lee was looking for a local entrepreneur to develop city locations in the Black community."

No matter how talented, successful entrepreneurs are the ones who also belong to groups like these, which can provide a wealth of contacts and timely information – an area where Jackson says Black businesses are routinely shut out.

"We simply don't have access to the information," he says. "Typically, when mainstream corporate executives know about something, they don't call somebody who's Black, they call somebody they know."

The Art of Networking

One place corporate executives did come together with the Black business community was at Chicago United, an organization that was founded in the 1960s at the height of the Civil Rights Movement. Its original mission was to build bridges between Black entrepreneurs and corporate America to improve economic, educational, and housing conditions for minority communities.

Chicago United proposed that Sara Lee Corp. make room for minority businesses in its industry. As Jackson recalls, Sara Lee did some research to find out how it could slice a piece of its business off and make it available to a minority-owned business. Once Sara Lee honed in on its bakery outlets as the vehicle for opportunity, Chicago United offered the networking structure for the company to recruit potential candidates.

"Sara Lee was looking for somebody to take advantage of an opportunity they had created to bring jobs and income to the inner city. Leon Jackson responded to this information and hung on pretty stubbornly until it panned out," says Charles Davis, president of public relations firm Charles Davis & Associates and a long-time member of Chicago United.

At first, Sara Lee turned down Jackson's proposal in favor of another candidate, whose deal fell apart sometime later. When that happened, Jackson didn't hesitate. "I again expressed my interest aggressively," he says.

This time when he presented his plan to Sara Lee, he was armed – with a lawyer, a bank president and a then co-chair of Chicago United. "They were impressed," Jackson says.

Still, it took six months to get a deal signed, and at least another six months to get the first store opened. It was like a "clash between two cultures," Jackson says. "They didn't know anything about operating a retail store in the city."

Jackson says the paucity of strip retail on the South Side meant he had to settle for a second-class location when he opened the first store in 1986. Later he moved the bakery to a better location, a new strip center at 87th Street and Cottage Grove.

Despite his successes, Jackson and others say racism is still a factor Black businesses have to reckon with. Says Charles Davis, whom Jackson calls a business mentor: "If you're on the outside, you know less than the folks on the inside. Chicago United has begun the communication process. But just being a member doesn't make you an insider."

Historically, Chicago has been a center for African-American business. Ironically enough, it was segregation and discrimination that gave rise to Black businesses in the first place. The hundreds of thousands of Blacks who migrated here from the South had to shop for goods and services somewhere, and the community had to develop its own resources to satisfy those needs.

Breaking The Mold

Seated behind his cluttered desk at the Bill's Shades plant, Jackson's smooth brown face and youthful grin belie his age. Jackson's father worked as a sharecropper to support the 12 children in his family and wanted more for his offspring.

"My father encouraged us to break the mold," Jackson says. "We grew up in an era when Black youngsters had three choices: teaching, a profession like the ministry or medicine, or menial jobs."

He moved to Chicago at 14 and later put himself through college by working 40-hour weeks at Mt. Sinai Hospital, while attending Roosevelt University. In 1971, he earned a Bachelor of Science degree in X-ray technology.

The following year, Jackson landed a job as a sales representative for Xerox Corporation. Getting a good, well-paying job didn't satisfy him, though — what he really wanted was to run a company of his own.

"Nobody encouraged me to go into business," Jackson remembers. On sales calls to companies in his north suburban territory, he shared his future plans with customers. "When I would say to people I was going to leave Xerox and go into business for myself, they thought I was crazy."

Most people figured he would open up a barbershop or some other service related business. Or if he was really thinking big, folks told him, he'd buy a McDonald's franchise.

Jackson did neither. After a couple of years at Xerox, he decided he wanted to buy into a suburban company that manufactured loose-leaf binders. Sheldon Rosenberg, whose family owned the business, remembers picking Leon out of a slew of prospective business partners.

"People were coming in with business degrees from Wharton and Harvard looking for an executive position in a business that would amplify their position," Rosenberg said.

"I was looking for somebody who was willing to go out into the marketplace and get business. Leon was a go-getter. Bankers didn't think Leon was prestigious enough, but I wouldn't do the deal without him."

Jackson put up 25 percent of the money for the business, then called Sales Tools Products. Investors put up the rest. One of the investors was Charles Davis, who remembers being impressed when he met Jackson back in 1974.

Jackson had been presented to a venture capital group of which Davis was a member. "We liked what we saw — intelligence, energy, confidence. We decided to invest," says Davis, and his group, Inner City Industries, put up about $50,000.

For the most part, it was a successful venture. As president, Jackson presided over a company that initially had $1 million in sales. In his years at the helm, sales increased tenfold. At one point, the firm made *Black Enterprise* Magazine's Top 100 list of Black-owned businesses. "It was a pretty high-profile company," Jackson says.

Philosophical differences with business partners led to his departure from the company, however. In his hunt for a new base of operations, he found what he was looking for and bought Bill's Shades and Blinds Service at 765 East 69th Place in 1984.

Maye Foster-Thompson, executive director of the Chicago Regional Purchasing Council, says Jackson makes it a priority to teach African-American youth to have a positive image of themselves. He's also helped adults to develop their career or business aspirations. "Leon is very good at spotting talent," she says.

One such talent is Keith Miller, president of Thumbs Up Lawn Care, one of four companies that recently won Tanqueray's Emerging Entrepreneur Award. In addition to a monetary grant, Miller was paired up with Jackson in a yearlong mentor-mentee relationship.

Jackson says he was impressed by Miller's commitment to go into a business that required physical labor. In fact, Jackson says he's thinking of throwing some business Miller's way. "I did my own lawn up until this year," he quips.

Closer to home, cutting the grass has inspired at least one of Jackson's three children to learn the value of keeping a promise in business relationships.

Eric Jackson, who managed his father's Sara Lee stores, remembers the time he received his regular allowance on a Friday, but didn't follow through with his required lawn mowing duties the following morning. Eric says he figured he'd do it later in the week. Leon Jackson saw things a bit differently.

"You collected the allowance, but you didn't cut the grass," Eric recalls his father saying to him sternly. Leon was not playing around. "I was out there at 10:30 at night cutting grass," Eric says. "It seemed

like a harsh thing to do – but I learned something from it. When you make a promise or sign a contract, you have to fulfill it."

Investing In Community

Jackson says he likes to support budding entrepreneurs. "I'm a sucker for the kids selling candy and magazines on the street; the reason I buy from them is because that's where the entrepreneurial skills start," he says.

Jackson's business success has not gone unrecognized by his business and civic peers. He has earned The Woodlawn Organization's Advocate Award. The Chicago Regional Purchasing Council bestowed its Minority Business of the Year honor on him. And Jackson has been designated by *Dollars & Sense* Magazine as one of "America's Best and Brightest."

Government officials have tapped Jackson to serve on local and state boards. Chicago mayor Har-

old Washington appointed him to the city's Private Industry Council. Jackson also was selected by form Governor James Thompson to serve a two-year term with the State of Illinois' Small Business Development Centers.

Despite his demanding business responsibilities, Jackson always finds time for volunteer work. He's involved with at least eight organizations, including the Chicago Urban League, Project Image, and Leadership for Quality Education, a group that monitors public school reform. He's also the chairman of the editorial board for *Catalyst*, a school reform publication.

Says Davis, "Leon Jackson is unique in his sense of civic and social responsibility. I don't think you'll find a great number of people like him. He gives a tremendous amount of time to the community."

But Jackson says his motivation for this is simple. "I want to do well by doing good. How I make a living does make a difference to me," he says.

preface Jarrett

Update: As Mayor Daley's deputy chief of staff in 1991, Valerie Jarrett hired away a woman from a private prestigious Chicago law firm named Michelle Robinson, who was engaged to a guy named Barack Obama, and they all became great friends.

After leaving the Department of Planning in 1995, Jarrett served as chair of the CTA board for 10 years, through 2005. Afterward, she was CEO of the Habitat Company, the real estate development and management firm. She was also a board trustee member of the Chicago Stock Exchange, the University of Chicago and the Museum of Science and Industry.

When her friends Barack and Michelle became President and First Lady of the United States in 2008, she joined them at the White House as Senior Advisor to the President and Assistant to the President for Public Engagement and Intergovernmental Affairs.

With the conclusion of the Obama Administration in 2017 after two terms in office, Jarrett returned to Chicago with an eye toward using her vast experience in Chicago and federal government and continue to work for the public good. Jarrett became a board member of Ariel Capital in 2017.

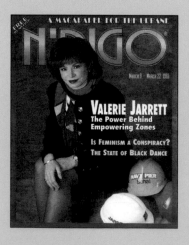

Valerie Jarrett

By Allison J. Keyes, David Smallwood & Photography by John Beckett | *Originally Published March 9, 1995*

Valerie Jarrett looks at Chicago through the eyes of a dreamer. But she's one of those rare people with the power to turn her vision into reality.

Jarrett, 38, is Chicago's Commissioner for the Department of Planning and Development. She is also the youngest, and highest ranking African American, in Mayor Richard Daley's administration.

Jarrett believes her office is making Chicago a better place by revitalizing communities that have fallen through the cracks and by sustaining existing healthy neighborhoods.

"This isn't the old urban renewal," she says. "This is about allowing residents to participate in a process that leads to a healthier community. It's about balanced development; it's about doing rehab; and, it's about providing opportunities for low-to moderate-income people.

> **I think that I take all of that wonderful training and experience and apply it in a way that helps people.**

"The city should be one big area where you've got community groups coming together with government, where we try to go out and bring together resources to make the community look the way it wants to look, and we're doing it with the residents who live there today," says Jarrett.

"The city's dollars are there to jump start. A healthy community is one that's self-sustaining – that's one of my biggest philosophies. A healthy community doesn't require long-term government subsidy; it has private investment," Jarrett explains. "What the government has to do is look at the community, with the community, and help figure out what the community needs to be self-sustaining."

SNAP Decision

That's also the main philosophy behind Jarrett's department – to actively promote community and economic development and create a one-stop shopping center to help neighborhoods and businesses get the resources they need.

The SNAP (Strategic Neighborhood Action Program) initiative is Jarrett's baby, and the type of program she says can turn a neighborhood around no matter how long it's been neglected.

SNAP targets investment in a specific geographic area. The city has four so far – the first in an area bounded by Damen and Western avenues, Van Buren Street, and Washington Boulevard.

"This community came up with a plan, their vision for the area, and that provided the blueprint for what we're doing in that area. What we did was get resources from four city departments for jump start money," Jarrett says.

The owners of the United Center in this area dealt with people displaced by the new stadium and built permanent housing to begin with. But next door to those beautiful replacement homes were abandoned houses that created an eyesore, so within two years, the city tore down 22 abandoned buildings.

"We resurfaced all the streets, planted trees, fixed the median along Madison Street and began assembly of vacant land for commercial development," Jarrett says.

"When you see a neighborhood that two years ago was really struggling and in a span of a very short time, considering how long it took to get to the point that they were in, you have all these resources and it is a different neighborhood today than it was – that's really what we're about," Jarrett says.

The city is also getting help from the federal government in a program Jarrett says is much like SNAP, but on a broader level, as Chicago has been named as one of four federal empowerment zones.

That brings with it $100 million in federal money, plus tax credits and waivers to attract business. The Chicago zone includes Kenwood-Oakland, Woodlawn, Washington Park, Pilsen, Little Village, and parts of the West Side, along Madison Street.

"Anything you need you can get through this program, along with the money and resources to do it. It's very exciting," Jarrett explains.

"The philosophy is to take people in need, areas with high unemployment, and link those people up to job opportunities. If a company hires someone that lives in this area, they get a $3,000 tax credit every year per employee over the life of the project.

"You're getting a linkage. You're not just trying to attract business to Woodlawn. You're telling the business I have tools to help you go there. It creates an incentive for local hiring. Moo & Oink wanted a second site, so we helped them find one on the West Side and they did all their hiring locally, creating 75 jobs."

Jarrett's department has also done a great deal of work in the South Side Kenwood-Oakland community and in Woodlawn. The area is bounded by 47th, 39th, Cottage Grove and Lake Park.

The Planning Department and community residents worked to come up with a comprehensive plan to redevelop the neighborhood. That included low-density, residential housing like single family and townhomes, as well as some multi-story development.

Jarrett says the plan has been to create an economically integrated community with a commercial hub at 47th and Lake Park. The 360-acre area has much vacant city-owned land.

"A lot of people look at vacant land as an eyesore, but when we own it, it's an advantage because we can make it available quickly for development that we want to see happen, as opposed to what the private sector wants to do," says Jarrett.

Parade of Homes

So the city did what's called a Parade of Homes – selling city-owned land to creative homes developers, then to residents after the houses are built.

Jarrett required 40 percent minority participation because the neighborhood is mostly African American. She also tried to address community concerns of outsiders coming in and making a profit off of the residents.

"Everybody recognizes a low-income community can't be healthy if everyone who lives there is low-income," Jarrett says. "And many of the homeowners in the area said, 'Look, we'd love to have an economic mix. We want to have the upscale homes and we also want to have the affordable homes.'

"So you give opportunities to low- to moderate-income people, and at the same time, stabilize the community by bringing in the people who can afford the upscale homes being built."

Ten homes ranging from $150,000 to $200,000 were built in the first phase, and 50 more are under construction. Under the New Homes for Chicago program, Jarrett's department got federal funding to build 50 homes ranging from $70-90,000 in the South Shore area.

She says her office, along with Bishop Arthur Brazier's development group, also helped build the first market rate housing in Woodlawn in over 30 years, including single family homes and a rehabbed multi-story building.

From Private Life To Public

Jarrett was born in 1956 in Shiraz, Iran, and lived there until she was five. Her father, James Bowman, ran a children's hospital under a program where American doctors and agricultural experts helped developing countries with their health and farming efforts.

Jarrett's great-grandfather was Robert Taylor, the first Black architect, the first Black student enrolled at MIT, and the guy for whom the Robert Taylor homes were named.

Jarrett's family lived in London for a year when she was six and moved to Chicago's Hyde Park neighborhood in 1963. As a child, she spoke Farsi, French and English.

In 1966, her mother, Barbara Taylor Bowman, was one of the creators of the Erikson Institute that teaches child development to teachers and other professionals working with young children.

Valerie earned her Bachelor's degree in psychology from Stanford in 1978 and then her law degree from the University of Michigan Law School in 1981.

After working as a commercial real estate attorney for several big law firms, she joined city government to be part of the movement the election of Chicago's first Black Mayor Harold Washington had created. Jarrett came in at the beginning of Harold's second term in 1987 as Deputy Corporation Counsel for Finance and Development.

Washington died in office just three months after she joined, but Jarrett felt her life was more rewarding doing public work than in the private sector, so she stayed in Chicago government through Harold's successor, Mayor Eugene Sawyer, and then Mayor Richard M. Daley.

Four years later, in 1991, Daley appointed Jarrett as his deputy chief of staff. Part of her job was reorganizing and streamlining various departments and finding a way to consolidate planning, economic development, and housing-related issues. Jarrett says getting things done had become a bureaucratic nightmare.

"You had economic development being handled on a case-by-case basis in one place, and planning dealing with broader community issues in another place, and you had the land, which is a major asset the city brings to the table for economic and community development, somewhere else," Jarrett says.

"There were horror stories – companies that spent six months working with one department thinking they have a deal and then they come over to another department and find the zoning wouldn't permit them to do what they wanted to do."

Multiple Viewpoints Of Government

Planning and Development merged in October 1991, and Jarrett was named Commissioner.

"There's a lesson here," Jarrett laughs, "Be good at what you do because you never know where you're going to end up. One of the things I would say about my time in government is I've now seen it from three very different vantage points. Each has been unique and I think given me skills to move on to the next scene.

"In the law department, you're kind of an advisor, performing a non-policy role. In the mayor's office, it was a major oversight role where you get to look at all of city government from (the mayor's) vantage point and see how all the pieces fit together. To take that experience and go into a department gives you a better sense of where you fit and that makes you a better department head. You don't come to it with tunnel vision."

Jarrett says she wishes more young people would see the value in public service, and the satisfaction they could get from giving something back to their community and the city in general.

"I think a part of what's wrong with our country is that we don't have enough young people who are committed to public service. One thing I have is enormous satisfaction and a sense of commitment and responsibility," Jarrett says of her public service work.

"When I was growing up, we were a society where if you could, you should, go to college. And if you went to college, then you should go on to something else. It was a sense that you were fortunate if you could, and you were lucky. People died so we could have these opportunities.

"I think that I take all of that wonderful training and experience and apply it in a way that helps people, and at the end of the day, there's nothing more gratifying than that."

preface Jemison

Update: Wanting to go far beyond merely colonizing Mars, Dr. Mae Jemison leads "100 Year Starship," a global initiative founded in 2012 to ensure the capabilities for human travel to another star outside of our solar system within the next 100 years, while transforming life on Earth at the same time.

In 1999, Jemison founded BioSentient Corporation to develop a portable device that allows mobile monitoring of the involuntary nervous system. She also founded the non-profit Dorothy Jemison Foundation for Excellence, which designs and implements STEM education experiences.

She serves on the board of directors for Kimberly-Clark, Scholastic and Valspar, and, recognizing her accomplishments, the Mae C. Jemison Academy, an alternative public school, was established in 1992 in Detroit, Michigan.

Dr. Mae C. Jemison

By Simone J. Nathan & Photography Courtesy of NASA and Dr. Jemison | *Originally Published May 4, 1995*

On September 12, 1992, Dr. Mae C. Jemison – who grew up on the South Side of Chicago – blasted into orbit aboard the Space Shuttle Endeavour, the first Black woman to go into space, and she stayed up there until September 20th.

Jemison was a Science Mission Specialist on the STS-47 Spacelab J flight, a joint eight-day American mission with Japan. She conducted experiments in life sciences and material sciences – 44 such experiments were undertaken – and was a co-investigator for the bone cell research experiment.

According to NASA, Jemison orbited Planet Earth 127 times during her flight and logged 190 hours, 30 minutes and 23 seconds in space.

Since that remarkable achievement, Dr. Jemison – chemical engineer, scientist, physician, astronaut and now entrepreneur – has been profusely honored across the country for probing outer space and for utilizing her own "inner space" and remarkable personal character to benefit the people of the world.

> I especially encourage women and minorities to pursue careers in science and to use their own energy and innovation to push boundaries of any field that truly draws their interest.

On a recent trip back to Chicago, Dr. Jemison was feted by the Chicago Chapter of the National Association of Women Business Owners (NAWBO), one of the organization's largest chapters in the country.

She was greeted by dozens of high school girls, more than a thousand members of Chicago's business leadership community, Mayor Richard M. Daley, Governor Jim, Edgar and hundreds of women business owners.

Jemison was returning to the place she remembers fondly. "You know that although I was born in Decatur, Alabama, I consider Chicago my hometown. I was raised in the city and attended Morgan Park High School," she says. "I always remember Michigan Avenue as one of the most beautiful boulevards in the big cities of the world, and I remember Chicagoans as practical, friendly, and down to earth."

A Lot Of Knowledge

Jemison was born in Alabama on October 17, 1956, the youngest of three children. Her family moved to Chicago when Mae was just three years old. At an early age, an uncle introduced her to the world of science and Mae developed interests in anthropology, archeology and astrology that she pursued throughout her early years.

Jemison graduated from Morgan Park High School in 1973, then enrolled at Stanford University at the age of 16. She received a Bachelor of Science degree in chemical engineering and a Bachelor of Arts degree in African and Afro-American Studies.

She earned her doctorate degree in medicine from Cornell University in 1981, and somewhere along the way, learned to speak fluent Russian, Japanese and Swahili! She also skis to relax, collects African art and took lessons in dance at the Alvin Ailey School.

Jemison credits Chicago's public school system for giving her what she calls an "excellent educational foundation."

Feeling very strongly about the American public education system, Jemison says, "It is critically important that U.S. public schools, open to all, must be kept viable. Across the country today, a lot of leadership in science, business, the arts, medicine and government, has come from this universal institution, the public school system.

"Open to all children who seek the basics upon which to build a life," she continues, "America's public school system has helped millions of children develop their basic interests and skills and led many children to mentors who fostered these budding strengths."

At Cornell University, where she got her medical degree, Jemison advanced her interest in and knowledge of Third World countries, and made the inner commitment to contribute in w ays that would be effective. She traveled to Cuba and rural Kenya, and spent a medical clerkship in Thailand at a Cambodian refugee camp. Altogether, she has practiced medicine on three continents.

With a background in both engineering and medical research, she has worked in the areas of computer programming, printed wiring board materials, nuclear magnetic resonance spectroscopy, computer magnetic

Dr. Mae C. Jemison

disc production, and reproductive biology.

Her work today combines her interests in computer science, nuclear magnetic resonance, spectroscopy, and tropical medicine.

Dr. Jemison completed her internship at USC Medical Center in July 1982 and worked as a general practitioner with INA/Ross Loos Medical Group in Los Angeles until December 1982. From 1983 to 1985, she served as a Peace Corps medical officer for Sierra Leone and Liberia in West Africa.

Jemison then returned to Los Angeles to resume her medical practice with CIGNA Health Plans of California. That's when NASA called.

She was selected for the astronaut program in June 1987 along with 14 other recruits and her assignments included launch support activities at the Kennedy Space Center in Florida, verification of shuttle computer software in the Shuttle Avionics Integration Laboratory, and Science Support Group activities.

She has said that as a child growing up in Chicago, she always knew she would go into space and that by the mid-1980s, "thought we'd be going into space like you were going to work." Since that didn't happen, she applied to be a shuttle astronaut, "instead of waiting around in a cornfield for E.T. to pick me up or something," she says.

Following her service with NASA – which she left in March 1993, six months after her space flight –

Jemison founded The Jemison Group, Inc. and began her adventure as an entrepreneur.

Current projects of hers include "ALAFLYA," a satellite-based telecommunications system to improve healthcare in West Africa, and "The Earth We Share," an international science camp for students ages 12 to 16 that utilizes an experimental curriculum to advance technology in developing countries.

New Explorer

Those who have followed her career have not been surprised by her accomplishments. "Mae was always a dreamer, never inhibited by a lack of role models," says Bill Kurtis, CBS and PBS-TV journalist, who observed her career from his own Chicago TV news days and developed a nationally televised special about her as part of his *New Explorers* series.

"It didn't matter that there was no footprint for her to follow," Kurtis says. "Her vital curiosity, energy, and the drive to excel arising from her innermost being were evident even in early years, and she was fortunate to have those around her who encouraged these characteristics and fostered her personal discipline and great strength of character."

But that is history. Today, Dr. Mae Jemison is dedicating her energies to encouraging children who seek science careers and assisting the fields of science and technology in efforts to represent full gender, ethnic and social diversity.

"I especially encourage women and minorities to pursue careers in science and to use their own energy and innovation to push boundaries of any field that truly draws their interest," says Jemison, whose own intense interest in science as a child was constantly rebuffed – even by her teachers – because she was a girl.

She says she was inspired to pursue her dream by the work of Dr. Martin Luther King, Jr. whom she says was "all about breaking down the barriers to human potential."

Jemison's words of encouragement to the students she works with are more than fluff stuff. "The curiosity, the intelligence, the spirit of collaboration shared by these children from around the world is energizing," says Jemison.

Her camp's curriculum, she explains, combines both "hard" science – input from the technological realm – and "soft" content that touches on the arts and culture of the young people involved. Physical and intellectual discipline are encouraged, but so is high-spirited, imaginative problem solving and future-orientation.

In addition to belonging to a plethora of scientific groups, Jemison has also appeared on an episode of *Star Trek: The Next Generation*.

"The next generation is exactly what this day is about," Deborah Sawyer said when Dr. Jemison visited her NAWBO group function. Sawyer, owner of Environmental Design International, an African-American environmental engineering and construction firm, added, "There are still too few of us exercising powerful role modeling for the next generation."

Certainly, the basics that Dr. Mae Jemison acquired in Chicago took her on an immense journey whose expanse continues to unfold unto this very day.

preface Johnson

Update: Mr. John H. Johnson passed away on August 8, 2005 at the age of 87. His wife Eunice died January 3, 2010. Daughter Linda Johnson Rice sold *Ebony* and *Jet* in 2016, ending its 71-year family run, but she retains a position on the board of the company that bought the magazines.

John Johnson

By Charles Whitaker & Photography by Darlene Martin | *Originally Published November 6, 1997*

He is both an icon and an enigma: an instantly recognizable American institution-builder, and one of the nation's most fiercely private public figures.

But he is also the affable, almost paternal, chief executive who knows the face, and practically every name of the more than 200 people who work in his South Michigan Avenue corporate headquarters; and whose reedy, whistle of a laugh is like an infectious breeze that cools and calms company storms.

He is the most successful Black entrepreneur of the century, perhaps of all time. Yet he remains a man motivated by a palpable fear of failure and a return to the poverty that marked his youth.

Such are the complexities and contradictions of 79-year-old publishing and cosmetics magnate John H. Johnson, the architect of one of the greatest success stories in African American history, in all of American history, in fact. He is a man we know all too well, yet hardly know at all.

Johnson's image and reputation are etched in bold relief across the African-American consciousness. We know him through the pages of *Ebony* and *Jet* – the publications he created to reflect and celebrate our triumphs and achievements in ways that other media did not.

And we know him through his best-selling autobiography, *Succeeding Against the Odds: The Autobiography of a Great American Businessman*, which chronicles his rise from indigence in Arkansas, to wealth, prestige and power in Chicago.

Still, for all we know, John Johnson remains, largely by design, something of a mystery. Though genial, almost garrulous with the few visitors to whom he grants an audience, he generally eschews the limelight. He prefers a quiet workaholic life in the 11-story concrete tower that is both his sanctuary and his bunker.

> **When you've come from where I've come from, you don't want to go back. I've been poor and I've been rich, and I can tell you, rich is better.**

Humble As Can Be

It is one of the ironies of his existence that this media baron prefers not to have his own life and work habits inspected and interrupted by media intrusion. He grants precious few interviews, and rarely allows the sort of "at home with ..." chats that are an *Ebony* staple.

The careful parceling out of his image, combined with a scrupulously low-key public persona, have afforded Johnson the sort of peaceful anonymity few in his sphere enjoy. Rarely are his day-to-day travels encumbered by the encroachment of stargazers, paparazzi or other hangers-on. He would have it no other way.

"I am usually not bothered by people when I go out," he says, "because I don't try to call attention to myself. The people who have to worry about being noticed and bothered are the ones who are doing things to attract that kind of attention. They have 12 bodyguards and an entourage, and they're wearing dark glasses and ducking and hiding. I don't do all that. When I go out, I usually drive myself. When I fly, I travel on commercial airlines. The people who do recognize me are very polite, so I don't have any problems."

He likes to tell the story about how shocked the occasional passerby is to find him casually perusing the produce aisles of the supermarket, doing his grocery shopping. "They'll ask, 'Mr. Johnson, why are you in the grocery store? Don't you have people to do that for you?' And I tell them, 'Yes, I could have someone do it for me. But I want to shop for myself. I like to do it.'"

Hardworking And Hands-On

And therein lies the key to John Johnson's success and his persona. He is the epitome of the hands-on manager who likes to do most things himself, his way.

Even though he's three months shy of his 80th birthday, he still involves himself in almost every facet of his $325 million empire. He also is a man of simple passions and singular focus.

Beyond grocery shopping, there is little that diverts his attention from the running of Johnson Publishing Company. He doesn't drink, smoke, play golf, tennis, bridge or badminton. Running the company is his job, and his joy; he's rarely away from it.

At the insistence of his wife, Eunice Johnson, he does take a three-week respite at their second home in Palm Springs, California, for the Christmas holiday. But Johnson confesses that all the while, his heart and soul remain at his true home in Chicago.

"This is what I like to do," he says. "I like to come to work. This is my fun."

When he is in town, he is at the office everyday, usually by 8 a.m. More often than not, he is among the last to leave. From his 11th floor suite – an expansive book and newspaper-strewn chamber with a gorgeous view of Lake Michigan – he sets the pace that keeps the company coursing along.

JPC President, Linda Johnson Rice – the Johnsons' only daughter – has emerged as the company's chief spokesperson and has taken charge of new initiatives such as: the company's internet site, its move to digital production and layout, and its link with mail-order retailers like Spiegel. John Johnson retains the title of Chief Executive Officer, and remains the heartbeat of the company.

His often-quoted management style is simple: "Delegate freely, but check on it every chance you get."

And so he meets almost daily with department heads – approving stories and cover art for all the magazines and spurring to action the advertising sales force, as well as the sales staff of Fashion Fair, the cosmetics wing of the company. No detail is too small to escape his notice. He is one of the few publishers of his pre-eminence who is not above making a sales call.

He doesn't have to work so hard at this juncture of his storied career. He does it because he loves it.

"I come to work because all of my friends are here," says Johnson, whose employees call him simply 'The Publisher' out of respect. "There are people in this building I've worked with for 30 or 40 years. I like being with them. I like what I do. So this isn't work for me. This is what I do to relax."

The pleasure he derives from being king of this dominion shows on his face. It is hard to believe that a Black man who launched a business more than a half century ago could appear so worry-free.

And the image is deceptive. Despite being the number one Black publisher for all 55 years that he has been in business, there are dark fears that gnaw at Johnson pressing him to keep up the pace.

As ridiculous as it sounds, it is a fear of failure, a fear of losing it all, a fear of returning to the impoverishment from which he so valiantly climbed. It is an unfounded fear, but a powerful and deeply moving force in John Johnson's psyche, nonetheless.

"When you've come from where I've come from," he says, "you don't want to go back. I've been poor and I've been rich, and I can tell you, rich is better."

Mr. Johnson in 1982 became the first Black person to make the list of Forbes 400 Richest Americans

History, Still In The Making

The up-by-my-bootstraps John Johnson story is deeply etched in African-American history. He was born on January 19, 1918 in Arkansas City, Arkansas, to Gertrude and Leroy Johnson.

His father was killed in a sawmill accident when he was eight years old. Though his mother married James Williams, a delivery man for a local bakery, the light of her life was clearly her only son, on whom she doted and for whom she was willing to make any sacrifice.

Because the Arkansas City Colored School System only went to eighth grade, Gertrude Williams decided she had to move to Chicago so that her son could further his education and make a better life for himself.

There were skeptics. "My stepfather told my mother, 'Gertrude, how do you know the boy can make anything out of himself?' People told her she was risking everything for a boy who might not amount to anything. But my mother knew she had to give me this chance. And I knew I couldn't let her down."

His mother's devotion has been another driving force in John Johnson's life. By now, everyone has heard the legendary story of how the 24-year-old publisher-in-the-making pawned Gertrude Williams' furniture in 1942 to start *Negro Digest*, the magazine that launched Johnson Publishing Co.

Johnson remained unfailingly dedicated to his mother's happiness and security until her death in 1977. The white-carpeted office with the alabaster furniture that he established for her in the company headquarters at 820 South Michigan Avenue, remains empty – a monument to her memory.

Johnson's work ethic was fueled by his mother's faith in his ability. From the moment he set foot in Chicago, he went about distinguishing himself. At Wendell Phillips High School, he became editor of the school newspaper and sales manager of the yearbook.

When Phillips was heavily damaged by fire, he transferred with the rest of the student body to the newly constructed DuSable High School. DuSable was, in many ways, the cauldron in which Johnson's desire to succeed was forged.

He was mocked and ostracized for being too "Black," too bowlegged, and too country. He responded by working and studying harder than all of his peers. By his senior year, he was elected president of his class. He seemed destined for something big.

Johnson is among the first to say that his success is the result of vision and hard work, for which, he says, there are no substitutes. "People used to say to me, 'Aw, you got where you are because you were lucky,'"

Johnson says. "But they weren't there when we were working hard and struggling to build this company."

If genius is, as Einstein said, 10 percent inspiration and 90 percent perspiration, then John Johnson had the formula right. He founded JPC because he saw in the publishing marketplace a void where stories of Black achievement and success were absent, even to other Black Americans.

The launching of *Ebony* in 1945 marked a new era in American journalism, one in which Blacks would at last see the full range of their achievements reflected in a glossy picture magazine.

The birth of *Jet* in 1951 signaled the entree of a Black publisher in the newsweekly war. Johnson has tried to capitalize on openings he perceived in the marketplace. Well before niche marketing was an advertising buzzword, Johnson was creating and promoting a niche – the Black consumer market.

Some of Johnson's brainstorms were born of necessity. When models in the renowned Ebony Fashion Fair – the clothing extravaganza produced and directed by Eunice Johnson – began mixing their own shades of makeup because White cosmetics manufacturers didn't make foundations that suited the spectrum of African-American complexions, Johnson created Fashion Fair Cosmetics in 1973.

The "Honorables" of JPC

Johnson acknowledges that his success is not entirely the result of his ingenuity. Eunice Johnson, his wife of 56 years, also has been an inspiration. It was she who came up with the name "Ebony" and in the process altered the American lexicon.

And Eunice Johnson's vision 39 years ago to create the world's largest traveling fashion show made the Ebony Fashion Fair a social and cultural institution, and proved to be a circulation boon for the magazines.

In recent years, death and retirement have thinned the ranks of the close lieutenants who have been at his side for the past 40 years. Of the men who for decades were part of his inner sanctum sanctorum, only Ebony Executive Editor Lerone Bennett remains.

"It's been sad, and we miss people like Bob Johnson (the *Jet* associate publisher who died in 1996) very much. But you have to move on, and we have."

One suspects, however, that it will be some time before John Johnson fully moves on from control of the company he birthed and nursed into the thriving enterprise it is today.

For the enigmatic executive is like the Energizer bunny: He keeps going and going, feeding not on fame, but on the charge he gets from betting the odds and remaining master of his own destiny. That may be all we really know of him. But in the final analysis, it may really be enough.

preface Jones

Update: After 10 years in Chicago, Earl Jones returned to Louisville as the new Market President for iHeartMedia's eight-station cluster in that market. Smooth Jazz station WNUA went off the air in 2009.

Earl Jones

By David Smallwood & Photos Courtesy of Clear Channel Radio | *Originally Published October 26, 2006*

Earl Jones didn't think he would play football in college. He didn't think he would be drafted to play pro football for the Atlanta Falcons for five years. And he didn't think that he would head one of the largest radio conglomerates in the third largest market in the country, as President and Market Manager of Clear Channel Radio Chicago.

But then again, he never thought that he wouldn't, or couldn't, either.

That's because of the simple, yet sage advice his grandmother instilled in him while Jones grew up on land she sharecropped in Tuscaloosa, Alabama back in the 1940's and '50s.

"My grandmother always stressed – don't put boundaries on yourself," says Jones.

Late last year, he was appointed regional vice president for Clear Channel stations in Chicago, as well as Milwaukee, Madison, and Eau Claire, Wisconsin.

> I'm the guy that you bring things to and I make a decision. I'm not afraid to look someone in the eye and tell it like it is...but I also have fun!

This summer, Jones was kicked up to president of the Chicago Clear Channel cluster, which consists of stations WGCI, V103, WNUA, WLIT, WKSC, and WGRB.

In both cases, he has been the first African American to hold these positions in the Chicago area for Clear Channel, whose stations generally garner about 23 percent of local radio listeners, which is the area's largest ownership share.

Ironically, much of Jones' innate business acumen developed as he watched his grandmother go about her business.

"Very few Black women were sharecroppers back then," Jones said of the woman who raised him. His mother was 19 when she had him and his mother and father never married.

Jones continued, "Instead of taking a job, grandma said, 'You give me some land and I'll farm it and give you a share, or I'll take my share and give you the rest.'

"She was only sixth-grade educated, but she wouldn't let anybody 'beat' her – you couldn't take (cheat) money from her and you couldn't out-count her," he recalled.

"She instilled in me that if you could get educated, you could really learn how to do good business, and do well in the business world."

The Road To Radio

So Jones knew he was headed to school. An only child, he used athletics as a way to stay on the good side of his peers, many of whom were from the Tuscaloosa projects.

"Athletics was a way for me to survive; it was esteem-building, and actually built me," says Jones. In high school he played basketball, ran track, and doubled up in the concert band and marching band.

"I was active and like my grandmother said, not putting boundaries on myself," Jones notes. "I didn't know it at the time, but I was positioning myself for whatever happened. It's about opportunities."

Those opportunities began to happen quickly. He was able to get enough grants to attend Norfolk State University, where he graduated in 1980 with a bachelor's degree in chemistry.

Norfolk's coaches tabbed him to play football, which he had never intended to play, and made him a defensive back, a position he had never played before.

He was a first year starter and played so well that the Atlanta Falcons selected him in the third round of the 1980 draft.

Jones had worked for the Portsmouth-based Virginia Chemicals Company for his last two college years, and when he got drafted, the company took a picture of him holding a volumetric flask in one hand and a football in the other and put it in their newsletter.

"They said, 'We know you're not giving up the NFL, so what do you want to do?' Jones said. "I told them I'd like to come back in the off-season and maybe work in sales. So they trained me in chemical sales."

Going into his fifth year, Jones got a knee injury and was replaced by a less expensive player. He decided to retire instead of coming off injured reserve, to pursue his other options.

Jones had met his wife, Dolores, to whom he's been married for 18 years – with three children – who was a national sales manager in radio.

"When she told me how much money she made in sales, I asked how long did it take to get to that point," Jones said. "She said you go from A to Z real fast. It would have taken me 30 years to do that in chemical sales, so I got into broadcast sales. And fortunately, as I was developing in it, my wife was the breadwinner all that time."

From 1985-'97, in his TV sales career, Jones worked for FOX, the WB, Paramount/Viacom stations in Atlanta and Washington, D.C.

In 1998, he switched to radio sales in Clear Channel's Atlanta group as director of sports marketing. Jones rapidly moved up Clear Channel ranks as general manager in Detroit, then market manager for Clear Channel Louisville and regional vice president for stations in the Louisville area, before coming to Chicago.

Radio In Chicago

When he arrived, Jones said he found radio here in general to be very slow to change, very much caught up in history, with the personalities, very nostalgic.

"Looking at that and looking at where the business is today and where we need to take it, you can take history into consideration, but some of the things that have been successful for most people for years, they see that as being successful for them 5-10 years from now, and that's not going to happen," Jones says.

"Things are changing so much, so fast, that our industry is being affected tremendously. You have so many more choices today than there were yesterday, as to where you spend your media dollars.

"We used to go right to radio or TV, now you have Ipods, podcasters, the Internet, on and on, so we have to be more competitive.

"I have to look at what's made these people historically great, the ones that are, and what's going to help them see the change in the coming years and create a 5-10-15 year plan on how we're going to continue to grow at the rate we have over the past years," he summarized.

As for the Chicago Clear Channel cluster itself, Jones said he first evaluated the systems, looking for ways to make them better, keeping good processes in place, improving on the ones that weren't.

Then he started looking at the stations individually, programmatically. "Are we doing the right things from a 'GCI to an 'RLL? Once I got that together, I said here are the people I have who can fit into these positions," Jones says.

"So, get the processes right, get the positions right, then put the people in the positions. There are some people better suited for other positions."

Jones cited Angela Ingram as an example, saying, "She was a station manager and in charge of marketing for the urban stations. Angela's job now is Vice President of Communications; she's my right hand. What comes out of my office goes through Angela.

"She's not just over the urban stations, she's over all the stations. And I've seen a tremendous success in her just making sure the word gets out the way it is and also opening us to the media, so that they can ask us questions.

"That's one of the positions that did not exist, that we created, and there are other situations like that.

His own position changed from regional vice president to Chicago president when Clear Channel took out a layer of management.

"They decided to put the best people in the best markets and have them focus on the best earnings potential," Jones explains. "They said I needed to focus just on Chicago. They did that across the country, so I report directly to the executive vice president, and can get a yes real quick or a no real quick."

Though Jones loves all his children, he admits to having a favorite station out of the cluster. "Oh WNUA, no question about it," he chirps. "I love jazz. We just signed Ramsey Lewis to another five years, not that I had any bias about that."

WVON, No Longer 1450!

One of Jones' most striking achievements in his short time in Chicago is the recent deal he brokered with Melody Spann-Cooper to allow WVON to lease the 1690 frequency from Clear Channel for five years with the option to buy. Moving the station to a stronger frequency has given WVON the opportunity to broadcast for 24 hours, a dream it has pursued for years.

Jones says, "That came about through the evaluation of the processes and stations we were talking about. You always look at what the revenue potential of a station is, and what the format should be.

"WRLL 1690 has a really good signal, but we were trying to fit the right format," he explained, suggesting that the oldies format wasn't working.

"If we put sports on it, maybe, but you'd be up against the Score and some other stiff competition. What else? Black talk?

"If we did that, it meant we would have been a competitor of someone who's been a good friend and confidant since I've been in this market – Melody Spann.

"I couldn't do that because I promised her that we wouldn't compete. Besides, could you read the headlines of Clear Channel creating a Black station

that's going to kill WVON?

"Then I said, wait, maybe Melody might want to take it over because the third alternative was to put on paid programming. Melody was delighted and it was a good business deal because (Clear Channel) makes some money off of it."

The Secret of Success

Jones, an impressive, down to earth man who clearly seems to enjoy his position, says that if there's any clear secret to his success, "It's that I have a great team.

"I've had great teams everywhere I've been. I always look at it like I'm building an NFL roster. In football, a good defensive back is very dependent on other guys like the linebackers and defensive line. If I took away my linemen and we played 7-on-7 out there, I'd give up more than I'd stop.

"It's the team in front that really makes me good. I could have all the God-given ability in the world, but if I'm alone on an island with the receiver, he's going to beat me 6 times out of 10. But if I have my defensive line, now I might beat him 6 out of 10 times.

"I have a team here at Clear Channel, guys in front of me who are really out in the trenches day to day. I'm the guy that you bring things to and I make a decision. I know just enough to ask the right questions, and if the answers don't make sense, ask another question and another question.

"What I think really sets me apart is that I'm not afraid to make a tough decision. Not afraid to look someone in the eye and say, 'You need to do better,' or, 'You're doing great.' I'm going to tell it like it is.

"But also I have fun, and I want people to know that we work hard first, but don't think you have to work hard all the time and not have any fun."

preface Jones

Update: Emil Jones retired from the State Senate in 2009, still as President, afterserving in the Illinois General Assembly for 36 years. He is President and CEO of Strategic International Group, a business and political consulting firm. In 2016, he donated the papers from his long and illustrious career to the University of Illinois at Chicago for research study.

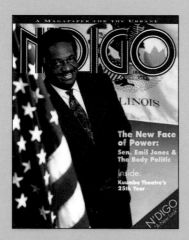

Emil Jones

By David Smallwood, Paul Davis and Robert Starks & Photography by John Beckett | *Originally Published November 2008,*

As sure as the sky is blue, without Emil Jones Jr., there would have been no President Barack Obama.

Before Obama ever ran for elective office, Emil Jones was the face of political power in Illinois. He was in the midst of a 10-year run as the State Senate's Minority Leader when Barack entered politics, and in 2003 Jones became Illinois Senate President.

When Obama won his first election as an Illinois state senator in 1996, Jones took Barack under his wing and guided his protégé as a political novice all the way through to his ambitious run for the White House in 2008.

Jones has known Obama for years, since Barack was only 24 years old, in fact, and he's one of the few people who actually remembers Barack as a community organizer.

"That's how I first met him; it was in 1985 shortly after he came to Chicago and worked as a community organizer," Jones verified. "We had a very, very good working relationship for about three years prior to him going to law school.

> **Having the power and not using it to help the people doesn't do you any good to have it. Basically, my role is making sure that my people receive a share or a slice of the pie.**

"It was meeting with ministers and community folks and dealing with their issues as far as high school dropout rates; setting up programs to deal with displaced workers because the steel mills in the area had begun to close down; on environmental issues in the Altgeld community. We worked together on all those initiatives."

Jones' take on early Obama is, "At the time I met him, he was young, very aggressive, and somewhat pushy, but he was very sincere in what he was pushing because he was sincere about what he was trying to get accomplished. In that sense, he was green, but he learned how to refine it," Jones says.

Entering Politics With A Mentor

When Obama became state senator, Jones said it helped that the two already knew each other. "I was the leader of the Senate Democrats and he came to me and said, 'You and I have worked together in the past. You know me, and you know I like to work hard, so feel free to hand me any tough assignments.' I did and Barack would do his level best to carry them out," Emil says.

"It's kind of unusual and refreshing to see a young man come up and actually have that kind of work ethic and want to do things. So, I took him at his word and we worked together on a variety of issues. Quite successfully."

For instance, under Jones' direction, Obama helped to craft legislation that spawned a prescription drug discount program for senior citizens and the disabled that became law.

Jones' support took into account other factors beyond Obama's legislative skills. He relates the story that in 2003 when Jones became Senate President, Barack came to him said, "You have a lot of power now."

Jones continues: "I said, 'What kind of power do you think I have?' He said, 'You have the power to make a United States senator.' I said, 'All that sounds good, do you know of anyone I could make?' He said, 'Me.' After further conversation I said, 'You know, that sounds very good — let's go for it!' That started the campaign."

That's when Jones said he developed a sense of Obama's real potential. "We were campaigning one Sunday for the U.S. Senate, and this little old lady in southern Illinois, first time she saw Barack, said, 'He's going to be president one day and I want to be around to vote for him.'"

Jones agreed. In an early March 2004 interview, a couple of weeks before the U.S. Senate election, Jones told N'DIGO, "An Obama victory in the March 16th Democratic primary would inspire countless Black boys to have the will to win in whatever career pursuit they may choose.

"Assuming he is elected to the Senate, he has a legitimate chance to be the President of the United States in our lifetime," Jones predicted. "He has the talent and intellect to do it."

After Obama's victory, Jones called him a coalition builder and said, "I knew he had the potential for attracting voters across the board. If one looked at how he won that primary for the U.S. Senate – he received strong support from all sectors of the state – they should have known then that he could attract a lot of White voter support."

For that reason, Obama's victory in Iowa, the first sparring contest of the Democratic primary when he ran for President in 2008, didn't shock Jones. "It didn't surprise me, but it may have surprised others, if you follow me," he says.

"I think to validate his candidacy for president – not for White folks, but for a lot of Blacks – Iowa was very critical to firm up in their eyes that Barack could get that support, which brought a lot of Black people on board. Iowa was very critical, no question about that," Jones says.

Supporting Our Own, Politically

He had to do a lot of arm-twisting, however, particularly with Black politicians, to get support for Barack throughout his various elective runs against status quo (read: White) candidates.

Jones really laid it on the line for Obama in February 2007, shortly after Barack announced his bid for the presidency, when he urged African-American members attending a Democratic National Committee meeting in Washington D.C. to support Obama at a time when it was assumed that Hillary Clinton would be the eventual Democratic nominee.

"I told them we have a very bright, intelligent, articulate, smart young man running for president of the United States and we should get behind him and support him. I said he is our son; he deserves our support. I said we don't owe anybody anything," Jones recalls.

"I never felt we would be better off siding with Hillary. Hillary hasn't done anything as far as we're concerned. Maybe her husband did something, but what he did, I always felt he was supposed to do since he got our vote.

"If we go through life continuing to think that we have to payback someone, pay someone, then our sons and daughters never get an opportunity. And here was a unique chance to give one of them an opportunity."

Jones notes that since becoming president, Barack has publicly acknowledged his support on several occasions.

"When I was in Washington for the Congressional Black Caucus weekend, he addressed the group and singled me out as his good friend from Illinois," the elder statesman says. "He's called me his political godfather who helped steer him through in order for him to be successful. He stood up in some meeting I was in and told folks, I wouldn't be here if it wasn't for Sen. Jones."

He beams about what Barack Obama being elected president does for young African-American children.

"It is inestimable," Jones said through a choked voice. "I was principal for a day at one of the schools before the election and these little kids in first grade and kindergarten – they knew the name Barack Obama. His election is something that's very needed for their self-esteem.

"Barack's ascendancy to the presidency – the impact it's going to have all across this nation, is that the 'Yes, we can,' is going to become 'Yes, you can!' and that piece alone is worth this whole effort. In that sense, this all goes far beyond Barack."

But the president's mentor added candidly, "What my support of Obama did, though, is it brought a lot of heat on me because the major media tried to destroy anybody closely connected to Barack."

The Real Emil Jones

But Emil Jones is a tough hombre who can stand the heat. Born October 18, 1935 in Chicago, Jones graduated from Tilden Technical High School in 1953. After graduating from Loop Junior College (now Harold Washington College), he attended Roosevelt University and majored in Business Administration.

After college, Jones worked in the insurance game and eventually became one of the top salesmen in the city. At the same time, he was a volunteer in politics where he worked on various campaigns and knocked on doors and became a precinct captain.

Later, he worked for the City of Chicago in various capacities. All of this political activity prepared him for his election to the Illinois House and the Senate.

His work as an insurance salesman was especially helpful in preparing him for a political career. "Walking the neighborhoods and going door to door talking to people was something that I have always enjoyed," says Jones. "I still like to do it. There is nothing more important than having personal contact with constituents and letting them know that you care about their issues."

Jones began serving in the State Legislature in 1973, when he was elected to the Illinois House of Representatives from a district that was only 20 percent Black at the time, and he served there until 1983 when he was elected to the State Senate.

In his time in the Senate, Jones has garnered more than $100 million for Chicago State University; Roseland and Mercy hospitals; the Pullman Historic Site; City Colleges of Chicago; the newly built Kennedy-King College; DuSable Museum; Muntu Dance Theatre; Women's Treatment Center; 111th Street YMCA; and the Chicago Convention Bureau, among others.

He has passed reforms to the criminal justice system that require videotaping of interrogations and for law enforcement agencies to keep records of the racial make-up of people they pull over in traffic stops. He raised the state's minimum wage twice, as well as the amount spent per child in public education in the largest single increase in state history.

Supporting Our Own, Economically

As President of the Senate – only the second time a Black held that position – Jones became the most politically powerful African-American in Illinois. In 2006, he pulled off a master political coup when he poured thousands of dollars into several downstate and southwestern suburban senate districts in an effort to win seats that were held by Republicans.

Victorious, he won five new Democratic seats that gave President Jones a 37 to 22 veto proof senate. In the Illinois Senate, it takes 36 votes – a super majority – to override vetoes and pass state construction bond issues, including building and reconstructing public schools. Jones' 37 votes controlled everything.

With his veto proof Senate, Jones became the only Illinois Senate President to serve in that position with a super majority. He also became the second most powerful elected official in the state.

Recognized for his outstanding legislative abilities, Jones has been elected to several national boards and committees. As a member of the Forum of Senate Presidents' Board of Directors and the State Legislative Leaders Foundation's Board of Directors, he is often in situations where he is the only African American in the room among the most powerful state legislators in the country.

But Jones says he views politics as a way of "getting things done," and that "having the power and not using it to help the people doesn't do you any good to have it."

"Basically, how I've always seen my role," he explains, "is making sure that my people receive a share or a slice of the pie, be it legislation, substantive issues, or money being spent for major projects. I do it because I'm in a position to get it done. My people have to be involved in it."

Jones says that when he was sworn in as Senate President, he was astounded at the number of African Americans who were on hand to witness the ceremony. He said he recognized then that people understood the significance of his position. The people are aware, Jones said, that he could help to effect change to improve their lives.

This Senate giant is a hero to African Americans for his dedication to building institutions within the Black community.

Evidence of this is his commitment to Chicago State University, to which he

has funneled tens of millions of dollars. Jones has led the funding of a construction boom on that campus that includes a new library, a dormitory, a conference center, a pharmacy department, and a new convocation center that bears his name.

He has also led the push for the funding of independent Black institutions such as the Little Black Pearl Arts Center, the Bronzeville Children's Museum and the Illinois Slave Trade Study Commission located at the Jacob Carruthers Center for Inner City Studies at Northeastern Illinois University.

For all of these reasons, President Jones remains not only the longest serving leader of Illinois State Senate Democrats in history, but also a community hero.

preface Jones

Quincy Jones continues to write books, produce music, television programs and raise awareness and money for global children's initiatives through his Quincy Jones Foundation. He is a musical mentor to many and continues to impact the world of entertainment.

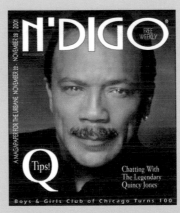

Quincy Jones

By Hermene Hartman & Photos Courtesy of Quincy Jones | *Originally Published November 22, 2001*

He is a creative genius, a music master. *USA Today* has recognized him as one of music's brightest minds. Friends call him "Q," a nickname bestowed by the legendary Frank Sinatra. *Time* Magazine named him one of the top 100 artists and entertainers of the 20th Century.

Quincy Delight Jones Jr., born in 1933 on the South Side of Chicago at 3633 South Prairie Avenue, since 1963 has won every music award you can name, for work beginning with Frank Sinatra and Count Basie's *I Can't Stop Loving You*, and continuing through Michael Jackson's best-selling album in history, *Thriller*.

"Q" has the golden touch. He produces musical magic and has received over 150 awards, including the Key to the City of Paris. He is the most nominated Grammy artist of all time with 79 nominations, of which he has won 27, and holds 26 honorary doctorates/academic awards from institutions as diverse as Morehouse College, Harvard and Hebrew Universities.

Quincy composed his first music for his elementary school graduation. A Hollywood insider and impresario, his 65-year career has seen him in the roles of composer, record producer, artist, film producer, arranger, conductor, trumpeter, record company executive, magazine founder and multimedia entrepreneur.

> **Quincy would call any cat at any time, even Jesus Himself, if he knew Jesus was in town and played E-flat baritone sax and could read music.**

As a master inventor of musical hybrids, he has shuffled pop, soul, hip-hop, jazz, classical, African and Brazilian music into many dazzling fusions, transforming virtually every medium, including records, live performance, movies and television.

At the age of 68 in 2001, "Q" wrote *The Autobiography of Quincy Jones*, which took a decade to write. The book chronicles his life and reveals a history of modern music, from be-bop and traditional jazz to hip hop, and his major role in all of those genres. The audio recording of the book earned Quincy his 27th Grammy Award in the

Best Spoken Word category.

Always writing, arranging or composing – at the dinner table, sitting poolside, or playing with kids, Quincy is humorous, spontaneous and gives everybody a nickname. He called Michael Jackson "Smiley"; Ray Charles was "Six Nine"; Barbara Streisand he calls "B. J." for Barbara Joan; and Oprah is "Baby Sister" – he also calls her "Sophia" for her role in the movie *The Color Purple*, which he co-produced and which introduced the world to Oprah, the actress.

Profound Beginnings

Quincy's mother, Sarah, suffered from schizophrenia, and as a young child he saw her put into a straitjacket. He remembers visiting her in Manteno State Hospital, a mental institution in Illinois.

This had a profound affect that would stay with Quincy for the rest of his life. These were bad memories that he totally blocked out until 1989, when he revisited the situation for a documentary on his life.

He says he has no concept of his mother. His father, Quincy Sr., a carpenter, and his brother, Lloyd, moved to Kentucky, where the Jones brothers lived with their grandmother. At the age of 10, his father moved them to Seattle.

His father remarried; a woman with three children, and Quincy had the typical childhood of a Black boy growing up in a Black neighborhood during the Depression. He shined shoes for five dollars a week.

One day, he peeped into a jook joint (nightclub) window, and then, at the age of 11, faced his life's calling – music. "I don't remember what I saw, nor do I remember what the band was playing," Quincy recalls. "I only remember the feeling that came out of that window.

"It hit my heart so hard, washing over me with such beautiful force, that I spent the next 55 years trying to get back to it – the darkness, the women, the laughter, the gambling, the dancing, the drinking, the joy, the funky blues that splashed across my face like rosewater. There was family in there. A family getting down. I knew I belonged there."

Quincy began to play piano and learned the trumpet from Clark Terry, whom he bugged to teach

him how to play at the age of 13. He visited Terry early in the morning before school and Terry says that even then, Quincy had a "beautiful embouchure." As a teen, "Q" met his best buddy Ray Charles, who taught him more music.

He says he wanted to be like Ray, whom he described as being "independent, talented, proud, fun-loving and lady-loving, with a 360-degree attitude about life." Ray even taught Quincy Braille.

An American Abroad

Music is Quincy's soul. It brought him solace. In his book he says, "Music was the one thing I could control. It was the one world that offered me freedom. When I played music, my nightmares ended. My family problems disappeared. I didn't have to search for answers.

"Music made me full, strong, popular, self-reliant and cool. The men who played it were proud, funny, worldly and dapper dressers. The New York cats and kittens that came through town were like kings and queens. Jazz gave Black men and women dignity."

Quincy joined vibraphonist Lionel Hampton's band at the age of 16 and stayed there briefly until Hampton's wife spotted him on the back of the bus. She put him off the bus and told him to go back to school. But some years later, he came back to Hampton's band as a trumpeter and arranger as they played the jook joint circuit.

His first marriage was to his high school sweetheart, Jeri Caldwell, when he was 19 and the struggling couple lived in New York as Quincy began his career.

He went to Paris in 1957, which proved to be a

life-altering experience. Quincy recalls, "In France, I was able to envision my past, present, and future as an artist and as a Black man: I took a wider view of the human condition that extended to both art and life, and later that helped me to take stock of global markets in business dealings. I became comfortable as a citizen of the world. France treated me like an artist. France made me feel free, and glad to be who I was."

While in France, he became a student of the noted Nadia Boulanger, who also tutored American expatriate composers Leonard Bernstein and Aaron Copeland.

While in Europe, Quincy formed a band and they traveled for 10 months as vagabonds, he says. There was no booking agent, no business manager, no travel agent, no publicist. It was all on Quincy and it was a great band, playing one-nighters, looking for the next gig. Quincy, only 25 at the time, said it was too much, too soon. Flat broke, the band broke up and everybody went home.

The Music "Business"

Returning to America, Quincy landed a job as Vice President at Mercury Records and his musical career changed from hard-core jazz to pop music. He signed Cannonball Adderley, Dizzy Gillespie, Gerry Mulligan and others to the Mercury label and he made great records – that didn't sell.

But this was the beginning of Quincy learning the music "business." He left New York for California to write movie scores, where he made Hollywood history as one of the few Blacks to score movies – he could write really good film music and write it fast.

Among his more notable movie scores were those for *In The Heat of the Night, In Cold Blood, Come Back Charleston Blue, The Pawnbroker,* and *The Wiz.* He would later write popular theme songs for such television programs as *Ironside, The Bill Cosby Show and Sanford & Son.*

His life elevated when Quincy met Francis Albert Sinatra. One of Sinatra's best recordings is with Count Basie and *Sinatra at the Sands* in Vegas, under "Q's" arrangement and direction.

Sinatra taught Quincy largesse and wouldn't permit him to be treated any way other than first class. Quincy says, "If you worked for him (Sinatra), you were out front with him. That's how he played everything – up front."

"Q" and Sinatra became great friends and today he wears Frank's pinkie ring, which Frank's daughter, Tina Sinatra, gave him, and which he cherishes.

Another dear friend was The King of Pop. Of Michael Jackson, Quincy says, "Michael was a total sponge, a chameleon. He had some of the same qualities as the great jazz singers I'd worked with: Ella, Sinatra, Sassy, Aretha, Ray Charles, Dinah Washington.

"Each of them had that purity, that strong signature sound and that open wound that pushed them to greatness. Singing crushed their pain, healed their hurts, and dissolved their issues. Music was their release from emotional prison."

On his gift for arranging, he says, "It is difficult work, but at its best, arranging is like painting. The final product is a beautiful thing to hear, a tapestry of different colors and textures and densities, but the meat and guts of arranging is sweatshop work, a blend of experience, architecture, soul and science."

Quincy works at a maddening pace. He buries himself into projects, often working three days at a time until burnout sets in. At one time, while working on an album, he had an aneurysm that almost killed him.

Two months later, he had a second aneurysm and his chances of survival were one out of a hundred. He was just 41 years old, and he survived.

No Finale In Sight

Quincy devotes a chapter in the book to his life with women. He has had several marriages, including his 14-year marriage to actress Peggy Lipton, formerly of the popular television program *The Mod Squad.* Quincy is the father of seven children by five women, which has produced him six daughters, a son, and many grandchildren.

"Q" suggests that many of his relationships have been rocky because of the influence of his parents' dysfunctionality. He comments, "The fact is, I love women – every touch, every whisper, every glance, every scent, every drop of them. To me, loving a woman is one of the most natural, blissful, life enhancing – and dare I say it, religious – acts in the world.

"I grew up in Seattle and Chicago, and not having a mother, it gives you a perspective on life and women that others simply don't have. I understand what it's like to live in an emotional vortex: giving love, using love, finding and losing love, and yearning to feel real love."

The legendary life of Quincy Jones hasn't been all roses, but it has been all real and Q has lived it his way.

"You need to improvise on life," he says. "It shapes how you deal with people, how you love people. It's about freedom, imagination. Inevitably there will be hardship – that goes with the territory – but you don't have to let suffering define your experience of life. You learn and grow from it – you teach your pain to sing."

He has made beautiful music along the way and he is happy. His impact is lasting. Music has shaped his world, Quincy has shaped the world of music, and he has no plans for giving it up.

"As far as I'm concerned, retirement is like sitting around waiting to die," he says. "Staying in touch with the world is about anticipating change – cultural, spiritual and technological – and embracing it."

Left: Quincy with
Frank Sinatra

Right: Quincy
with Count Basie

Left: Quincy Jones is the most nominated
Grammy artist of all time, with 79 nominations.
He has won 27 Grammys.

preface Jordan

Update: His Airness played 15 seasons of professional basketball before retiring in 2003. He now owns the NBA Charlotte Hornets.

Michael Jordan

By Charles Whitaker & Photography by Mitchell Canoff | *Originally Published September 21, 1995*

For a half-dozen or so years in the 1990s, the best professional basketball player in the history of the game operated the Michael Jordan Foundation in Chicago for kids.

Jordan and the directors of his foundation set their sights somewhere in the middle ground of youthful endeavor, that place where pretty good kids meet the wrong influences and go bad. It is in this murky territory where the battle for the hearts and minds of America's young people is less obvious, but no less important or difficult.

Jordan's goal was to reach and inspire children at that critical juncture where a bit of encouragement can make the difference between a lifetime of success or a lifetime of deferred dreams and perilous missteps.

> My parents are heroes, because they taught me, first of all, how to set goals for myself and see myself 10 years down the road and how to have dreams and strive for those dreams.

"I felt an obligation to give kids some guidelines to follow and to help less fortunate kids," Jordan told *N'DIGO*, explaining his rationale for starting the foundation and giving it the focus that it had. "I felt that if a kid coming from a small city didn't have the motivation, certainly he wouldn't have the dreams and the determination to achieve.

"I felt that we could give kids the opportunity to move from point A to point B so that they're not afraid to at least try. Through the foundation, we were able to give kids positive motivation and desires for improvement."

In essence, the Jordan Foundation was rooted in the work ethic and values that – along with a lot of God-given talent – made Michael Jordan the greatest player in the history of the National Basketball Association. One might also say that the foundation, like the man himself, was steeped in the traditions and values that Michael's parents, Deloris and the late James Jordan, instilled in their family.

Giving Heirness To His Airness

Deloris Jordan, the co-founder and President of the Foundation, was the moral compass and guiding light of the organization. It was she who pressed for the foundation's focus on family education.

"Within our family we have always stressed giving back," Mrs. Jordan says. "We began the foundation by simply trying to pool all of what Michael shares, gives and contributes under one umbrella. But after a while, we felt the need to focus on education and to create an organization that would help to get parents more involved with their children, because parental involvement is so important."

Parental involvement was the prevailing code in the Jordan household. During his youth in Wilmington, North Carolina, Michael, the second youngest of the five Jordan children (James, Deloris and Larry are the older siblings, Roslyn is the baby), always had the guidance and counsel of his parents, no matter what the activity.

"We were always involved in some sort of family activity," Mrs. Jordan recalls. "Whether it was baseball, softball, track or anything, Mr. Jordan and I always tried to be very involved in our children's lives. That is where the values and the motivation come from."

But even Michael's seemingly charmed life has been wracked by withering blows. The brutal and shocking murder of his father in 1993 – the incident that many believe prompted his premature retirement following the Bulls' 1993 Championship season – left an immeasurable void in both his world and ours. With Michael away from the game, off the court and out of the air, his absence was deeply felt.

"Just Do It"

Jordan's parents stressed that natural athletic talent was no substitute for hard work, especially where education is concerned. "They constantly reminded me of the value of education and what doors it can open up for me," Michael says. "As I moved up the ladder in age, I understood that, and I was able to motivate myself after the initial motivation of my parents."

Jordan calls his parents his heroes, "because they

taught me first of all how to set goals for myself and see myself 10 years down the road and how to have dreams and strive for those dreams."

But there's more to dreams than mere dreaming; one must act upon a dream in order to actualize it and bring it to fruition. First, one must have the need to accomplish the dream. Second, the desire and determination must drive one to do whatever it takes to get it done. Third, one must, "just do it."

Michael Jordan's success is a testament to that. It is this information that he wishes to convey to the young people with whom he works. Talent is just part of the equation. The rest is a combination of one's determination to accomplish and the preparation/discipline it takes to work toward one's goals.

But Michael is convinced that determination is first and also says that one of the chief fundamentals is for young people to accept and learn from even the most difficult endeavors. He cites his own setbacks as a case in point.

Remember, the Michael Jordan who led the Chicago Bulls to three consecutive NBA championships twice is the same Michael Jordan (give or take 12 inches and 80 pounds) who was cut from his high school basketball team. Still, he never gave up on his dream of one day playing in the NBA. "You have to try and put forth that effort even though you may not achieve that dream or goal," Michael says.

He even uses his brief and less than illustrious foray into professional baseball to motivate young people to reach for their dreams. "When I made the switch from basketball to baseball, I was at the top of my basketball game," he says, "but I wasn't afraid

to go to the bottom of another industry. I had a dream. I wasn't afraid to make that switch.

"When kids are dealing with any situation, they have to make an effort and accept that challenge. I wasn't afraid of the way I would be perceived as a baseball player. It felt true to my heart that this was what I wanted to do even if I wasn't going to be successful doing it. What came from that whole baseball experience is that I wasn't afraid to try something and I wasn't afraid to fail."

Don't Fail To Try

Truth be told, however, Michael Jordan knows that the only real failure is the failure to try. History tells us that the failure to go for the gold denies one the opportunity to push oneself toward the goal at which one is aiming.

If you fail to reach the moon, you still win because your experience in going for it has a lesson that in itself is rewarding. From those experiences, you develop strength and stamina. You learn so much about yourself. It builds character and discipline. Your loss may be the gold, but your win is knowledge and wisdom, both of which are invaluable.

So Michael didn't become a mega baseball star. Yet, his pursuit of a dream experience gave him another perspective that had he not tried, perhaps he would not have been privy to see. Did Michael fail in baseball? It's a matter of how you look at it.

For youth the world over, his actions demonstrated that you can do whatever you want. But you must first take the step to go for it. Many kids don't believe that they can even try out for team sports, whatever the level.

Now they know they can and it's okay if they don't become the all-star at it. So Michael may not have succeeded as much as he wanted at his personal goal, but he still won one for those who are afraid to try.

Not that "failure" is a word that could ever be appended with much significance to Michael Jordan's name.

Look at his accomplishments: Rookie of the Year; Five-time NBA MVP; Six-time NBA champion; Six-time NBA Finals MVP; Ten-time All-NBA First Team; Nine-time NBA All-Defensive First Team; Defensive Player of the Year; 14-time NBA All-Star; Three-time NBA All-Star MVP; 50th Anniversary All-Time Team; Ten scoring titles — an NBA record and seven consecutive, matching Wilt Chamberlain; Retired with the NBA's highest scoring average of 30.1ppg; Two-time inductee into the Basketball Hall of Fame.

And his global impact goes far beyond achievements, records, awards and championships. With those credentials, you could attempt to become the world's first six-foot, six-inch thoroughbred jockey and still come away looking like a winner.

Michael JOrdan

Chicago Bulls Legend
Michael Jordan

preface
Jordan

Update: Dr. Robert Jordan retired from WGN News after 43 years in September 2016. Karen Jordan co-anchors the number one rated weekend newscast in Chicago on ABC 7. Her husband Christian Farr joined NBC 5 News Chicago in 2009 as a general assignment reporter and fill-in anchor.

Robert & Karen Jordan

By Jean A. Williams & Photography by Brent Jones | *Originally Published October 30, 2003*

Long before national "Take Our Daughters to Work Day," WGN/Channel 9 veteran broadcaster Robert Jordan had his prepubescent daughter Karen on the job.

"That was my first exposure to going out and seeing the city," says Karen, now a grownup statuesque beauty, while sitting in her parents' elegant yet comfortable den in Lincolnwood.

"Of course, when I was six or eight years old, I didn't quite understand what it was that he was doing, the whole process that went into putting news together, but I remember riding around and seeing the news cars. Anywhere that he would go, I would go."

And we're not just talking cutesy feature story events. Baby girl was on the scene from rallies to murder investigations. "I wanted her to see what it was like, and see a lot of the different types of lifestyles in the city of Chicago," says Papa Jordan, sitting in an armchair across a coffee table from his daughter.

"She went along with me on a variety of things, from demonstrations to feature stories," Robert says. "She would ride with me and sit in the back of the car."

Young Karen, the only child of her parents – the other half of which is Sharon Jordan, a librarian at an Evanston elementary school – was deeply moved by some of what she saw and experienced.

"One of the reasons that I would take her to work was that I wanted to keep her grounded in the realities of life," Robert says. "I remember taking her to a demonstration in the Robert Taylor Homes, where the residents were complaining to the CHA about conditions and so forth.

"Karen was standing next to me, and I said just keep your eyes on where I am so that we don't get separated. While I was reporting, I kept watching her out of the corner of my eye."

On the return ride, Robert noticed that his daughter was a bit despondent. "I asked, 'Is anything wrong?' She said, 'I'm concerned about girls my age who live there.' And she sort of teared up. I told her, 'You know, Karen, until you see what conditions are

We grew up in a family where education and excellence were stressed, and every one did well.

like in all aspects of life, you don't really have the full picture. Sure, you live in a safe and secure home, but not everybody does.' She really teared up then."

Bit By The Broadcasting Bug

Ultimately, Karen would decide to follow in her father's footsteps and enter the world of broadcast journalism. She made the decision while studying for a Bachelor's degree in English at Spelman College in Atlanta. She initially had intended to give teaching a try.

"It was her sophomore or junior year," Robert says. "I think she said, 'You know, I'm thinking of applying to Medill for my Master's.' And I thought, 'Wow, Karen. Medill is not an easy school to get into.' But she had the grades and did well and got accepted. I was pleased."

In short order, Karen completed her studies at Northwestern University's Medill School of Journalism and then accepted her first reporting job in Rockford, Illinois.

"I was there for about a year and a half, then I went to Dayton, Ohio," Karen says. "I happened to meet my husband there. He's in the same business. We met there and got engaged right before he took a job in Philadelphia, which is his hometown, his home market.

"I was fortunate enough eight months later to also get a job in Philadelphia, and that's where we were living before we got married."

This summer, the Evanston Township High School graduate returned to home base when she accepted a position at ABC7-WLS, where she is weekend co-anchor.

Taking the job meant being reunited with her parents, while leaving her husband, Christian Farr, in Philadelphia for the time being. "We've been commuting for the past three months," she says.

On the streets of Chicago, fans often kid her about competing with her father. "I think they get a kick out of it," Karen says, laughing.

She and her father are mutual fans of each other. "He's on at 9 p.m. on the weekends, and I'm on at 5 and 10," Karen says. "So I watch her at 5, and when I get off at 10, I switch over and watch her at 10,"

Robert says. "And I watch him at 9 right before I go on at 10 p.m.," Karen continues.

Generations Of The Jordan Family

The Jordan family is one, in fact, that has always been very rich in resources. Born in Atlanta, young Robert Jordan would find himself of enviable pedigree.

His mother, Millicent, was a noted educator who taught English and Black studies at Spelman College, of which she was an alumnus, for more than 30 years. His father, Dr. Robert H. Jordan Sr., was a dentist with his own practice.

Though influenced by both of his parents, Robert has drawn closer parallels to his mother's legacy. As part of the Black intelligentsia, she brought amazing adventure into the household when he was coming of age with two brothers.

Esteemed writer James Baldwin was her friend and a visitor to the Jordan home, as was musical legend Cab Calloway. Gutsy Millicent traveled the world, making more than 22 trips to Africa, where she avidly collected art. Much of it was inherited by Robert, who later picked up the pastime.

Just as amazing, Millicent was the third of six daughters. Each of the Dobbs girls would prove to be extremely accomplished as women – all six earning graduate degrees and two earning doctoral degrees – as would each of their children.

In his private study and library, Robert, himself a Ph.D. in education with a minor in ethics, is proud to show off the varied volumes in his personal collection, and to relay the tale of these mavens of the South who ultimately wielded worldwide influence.

"This one is Mattiwilda, who was a Metropolitan Opera singer," Robert says, pointing to a sepia tone picture of his mother and her five siblings. "Marian Anderson was the first African American to sing at the Metropolitan Opera, but Aunt Mattiwilda was the first Black woman to sing a romantic role at the Metropolitan Opera. She sang all over the world."

His finger moves across the frame. "This is Aunt Irene, Maynard Jackson's mother – the first Black mayor of Atlanta, who just recently died," he says.

He points again: "Aunt June, who has a doctorate in sexology," he says. "She worked with Masters and Johnson for four years. She went to school with Dr. Ruth."

Along with his mother, each of his aunts attended and graduated from Spelman College, including his aunts Willie and Josephine, says Robert.

The academic legacy continued when Karen also attended Spelman College, as had her own mother, Sharon, who met future husband Robert when he was a student at Morehouse College.

"We grew up in a family where education and excellence were stressed, and everyone did well," Robert says. "It's amazing. Out of all of those sisters' kids, they've all excelled."

There's A Book About 'Em

Writer Gary M. Pomerantz chronicled the Jordan family story in the 1996 tome *Where Peachtree Meets*

Sweet Auburn: The Saga of Two Families and the Making of Atlanta, which is essentially a history of the city through the prism of two of its mayors, Ivan Allen Jr., who was White and served the city in the 1960s, and Maynard Jackson, who became the city's first Black mayor in 1973.

"Ivan Allen was one of the first progressive mayors of Atlanta," Robert says. "It traces Ivan Allen's family back to being slaveholders, and it traces Maynard Jackson's family back to being slaves.

"Peachtree is the main street that runs through Atlanta, and Auburn Avenue is the main street in the Black community, and where they meet, my grandfather was instrumental in renaming Auburn Avenue as Sweet Auburn."

Such a storied and accomplished family.

Now that Karen is living back in the Chicago area, the close-knit Jordans are reunited just like old times, but the unit will really be completed "once she gets her husband here to town," Robert says.

As Karen dashes off to work, she gives her dad a warm hug and good-bye kiss. Later, he expresses happiness that his daughter seems content. "I think the sky's the limit for her," Robert says.

preface Joyner

Update: Joyner followed his hunch about the future of radio and for the past several decades has been host of the *Tom Joyner Morning Show*, which is nationally syndicated daily in more than 100 markets. He is also the founder of Reach Media, the Tom Joyner Foundation, and www.BlackAmericaWebb.com.

Tom Joyner

By Allison Keyes & Photography by John Beckett | *Originally Published June, 1993*

Radio fly jock Tom Joyner, who jets across the country daily doing top-rated radio shows in Chicago, Illinois and Dallas, Texas, says he's the last of a dying breed.

"I'm a freak of the industry," says Joyner. "Radio deejays are dull these days. There's more music and less talk. That's what stations want, but you can't build a career that way, can't become a personality. And if you can't become a personality, there's no future.

"That's bad because Black radio was built on personalities. Black people in this town were brought up on personalities, people like me, and (fellow deejays) Doug Banks and Herb Kent. But now, disc jockeys are just voices, and you can't build a future on being a voice. You can't build a career like that."

Joyner has built quite a career for himself since starting in radio in 1970. But he says he is getting out of the business of splitting his life between two cities, which he's been doing for eight years.

"It's been great, but it's time to move on before things start slipping. I won't miss it," Joyner says. "It's been fun, but you get up one day and say, 'Do you really want to keep doing this?' I don't want to get burned out. I want to relax and do something cool."

> If I am in any way a role model for youth, I hope they try and emulate my work ethic. I've worked hard, and I think hard work and dreams can pay off. You can have your dream if you work hard, but mostly smart.

The Ham

Doing something cool has been a Joyner trademark ever since he started in radio in Tuskegee, Alabama. The "ham" with the distinctive voice did news in Montgomery, Alabama, but admits he went more for the sensational and bizarre than for the actual news value in his stories. Joyner says even then, he knew he wanted the power of sitting behind the mike for more than a five-minute news show.

"Everybody always knew the names and voices of the deejays, and I wanted that recognition. I would try to find ways to make my newscasts stand out.

For two years I did that, filling in when the deejay got sick. Then, I got an offer to go to Memphis, Tennessee, and presto! I was it!" Joyner says.

He stayed in Memphis six months, then moved to Dallas, for the first time, in 1972. He took Chi-Town by storm in 1977, starting out working for WVON-AM, then WBMX-FM, and then back to the AM side to work for WJPC, which is owned by Johnson Publishing Company.

Joyner recalls, "That was the turning point, because Mr. (John) Johnson decided to advertise the radio station in the *Jet* Magazine, which hadn't been done before. I was in there almost weekly. Black people think of *Jet* as a Bible...so I was a deejay god, when I was really just a deejay at a small station, an AM daytimer. But in *Jet*, JPC was 'the' station, and I was 'the' deejay, when in reality, I was nothing."

But those magazine sightings of Joyner made him a national phenomenon. In fact, that was one of the reasons Joyner "went crazy" and decided to give television a shot.

Joyner persuaded Johnson to let him become the first host of the *Ebony-Jet Showcase*, even though he knew nothing about TV. As host, producer, editor and salesman, Joyner admits his hands were a bit full, and the show was shut down after a year because of low ratings.

"My boss was a self-made man and he told me to go for it. He had known nothing about publishing before he created *Ebony* and *Jet*, so why shouldn't we be able to put on a TV show? He pushed me with his money, and oh, I messed up lots of money," Joyner laments. "He wanted me to go back to JPC, but AM was dying and it's important to go from one success to another."

For Joyner, that meant returning to KKDA-FM in Dallas. "I was this big star who decided to come home and work. I mean, they didn't realize I had failed miserably...I'd been in *Jet*. I had been in Chicago, and now, to them, I was back just kickin' it," Joyner says laughing.

It's A Bird, It's A Plane!

In the early 1980s, Joyner signed a two-year deal in Dallas, and then received what came to be a historic

phone call from WGCI's head honcho Marv Dyson in Chicago.

Joyner, never one to miss a chance to improve his lot in life, informed his Dallas employer that he had an offer to return to Chicago. He gave both stations a list of what he wanted in a contract, and to Joyner's surprise, both okayed his requests.

"And I went 'Bing! Maybe I can do both.' I checked out flight schedules and found one that fit me like a glove. Then I started trying to figure out if I could physically keep this up," said Joyner.

His on-air radio schedule in Dallas was 5:30 a.m. through 9 a.m., and in Chicago the hours were 2 p.m. to 6 p.m. Doctors and nutritionists told Joyner he could physically handle the schedule if he drank lots of water, cut out alcohol and cigarettes, exercised and could find a way to sleep six hours out of 24. Joyner thought, "Why not give it a shot?" So he signed both contracts.

"I was supposed to start at both stations in October, and each station thought they had me, but neither knew I had accepted both. When I told the guys at the stations, they were livid!" Joyner recalls. "They said, 'You can't do that; we'll find some legal way to stop you!'

"I might have been less than open, but I told them to trust me. After Marv got over being mad, he decided to make some lemonade out of these lemons and did a huge, planned promotion. I came to Chicago in October of 1985, with a high school marching band, limo and press conference, the whole she-bang. It was wild, but it was cool…and six months later the numbers were going through the roof."

Three years into the five-year deals he signed, Joyner re-negotiated for another five, making it eight years total. Even though he's the self-described "hardest working man in radio," Joyner says he's quitting the full-time, two-city deejay circuit because he decided he wanted his life back.

He says he wants to spend time with his family, spend his money and get some sleep. He quit working at the Dallas station a few months ago to give them a chance to find a good replacement for him and says it has been great.

Down To Earth

"I mean just going out again is a gas," he admits. "It's only been eight years, but it seems like another life. So regimented. Just work and resting, no life outside of my schedule. I like closing down joints, staying until the ugly lights come on."

Joyner admits that he didn't always live up to his "Fly Jock" nickname, noting that three years into the deal, he began doing his Chicago show by satellite one day a week so he could do a syndicated top hits countdown show. In fact, in the last three years,

Joyner says he's only been making the flight between the two cities three times a week.

"I'd be on the radio in the morning in Dallas when it's snowing in Chicago, goin', 'How am I gonna get to the airport tonight to get back here?' I did feel bad about it. I'd be in 70-degree weather getting off the air and going swimming, then heading for the snow. But on the other hand, being on top isn't forever, so when you're there you have to drive. I got the chance for the satellite show and took it."

He's been doing that countdown show for six years, and it airs in 100 cities nationwide. Joyner says syndication is the wave of the future for radio, and he intends to get more than just a piece of it.

"Networks will consume the best talent available.

They will also consume what's left of personality radio – not just in my format, but in all formats," Joyner says. "It'll be country. It'll be rock, and on down the line. Most radio networks aren't doing music yet, but that's where it's going," Joyner says.

"Satellites are cheaper," Joyner maintains, "and here come some people like (controversial talk show host) Howard Stern, in the big markets and successful as all get out. So as more stations pick up shows like that, and move to music, I'd like to be the first to do it in that format. Besides," he says smiling, "it'll be another publicity run."

Of his legacy, Joyner says, just because most Black youths know his name and voice, and many people in the city have grown up listening to his wry humor and political commentary, doesn't mean he wants to be a role model.

"If I am in any way, I hope they try and emulate my work ethic. I've worked hard, and I think hard work and dreams can pay off," he says. "If there's anything youth can emulate from me, I hope they learn you can have your dream if you work hard, but mostly smart.

"Another thing they could do would be to take some advice from my grandfather, who said, 'Get what you can while you can, and can what you can.' I've followed that prescription."

Joyner scoffs at those who might call him a legend. "I'm definitely not a legend. I'm just a guy who has fun on the radio. It's not that serious," he shrugs.

preface Kelley

Update: Cliff Kelley served as an alderman for 16 years. He has been a radio talk show host since 1993. He continues his three-hour afternoon drive Monday-Friday talk show on WVON and remains a much sought after commentator, speaker and analyst locally, nationally and internationally.

Cliff Kelley

By David Smallwood & Photography by Reginald Payton | *Originally Printed November 4, 2004*

On the heels of the most important presidential election in decades, Minister Louis Farrakhan and the Rev. Jesse Jackson are teaming in a rare joint appearance to discuss current conditions in America.

The historic conversation between these Black leaders will be broadcast live on The Cliff Kelley Show over talk radio station WVON (1450) AM.

Jackson, founder and head of the Rainbow/PUSH Coalition, and Farrakhan, leader of the Nation of Islam, will discuss the election results and their implications, the war in Iraq, leadership, and the state of Blacks in America, among other topics.

"It becomes sort of an African-American State of the Union Address," notes then-WVON Marketing Director Latrice Spann, who was given the idea for the program by one of the station's loyal listeners.

"The Cliff Kelley Show was doing one of our frequent live remotes with the Black McDonald's Operators Association at 87th Street near Stony Island, when this older gentleman – he must have been in his 80's – came up to me," Spann explains.

Wherever Black Chicago is on a conscious level as it relates to learning about the issues and being well-informed – that, in large part, is due to Cliff Kelley.

"He said, 'I want to commend you guys for what you're doing at WVON; you've been such a wonderful media outlet in the community. Let me give you a wonderful idea that if you do, I think will take the station to a different level.'

"He said that for all our Black leaders in the past, there's no real history of conversations they've had. Where's the archive of the conversation between W.E.B. DuBois and Booker T. Washington? There's no record of the conversation between Martin Luther King and Malcolm X.

"He said WVON needs to have the conversation with Minister Farrakhan and Rev. Jackson about what's going on in our community.

"That kind of sent chills through me," Spann remembers. "I thought, we have to do this, we can

do this. How often do you have a relationship with two of the biggest leaders in our community – global leaders, in fact – like WVON does? They've both been down to the station and I knew they would talk to Cliff."

Kelley, known as "The Governor Of Talk Radio" for the many years he's spent practicing the lively art of conversation over WVON, thought it was a great idea when Spann broached it.

"If you think about Dr. Martin Luther King and the Honorable Elijah Muhammad – and you can't get any people who have been more important to the Black community than that – Jesse and Minister Farrakhan are their successors," Kelley says.

"I thought to have the two of them together would be just fantastic when you consider from whence they come and the impact that their mentors had on the Black community, which we live every day. They are continuing the legacy, so to have them talk about where we are and where we ought to be going, I think, is extremely important."

To Kelley, there's an additional positive to this meeting.

"Not only is this an historic conversation," he says, "but you also have two very deep people doing election commentary, two of the very best analysts you could ever hope for. It's like a dream team to have these two men talk about this most crucial election and its impact almost immediately after it happens."

Farrakhan's Concerns

Kelley says he has a good relationship with both men and didn't think there'd be a problem getting them to do the show.

He's participated in a number of events with Farrakhan and says, "I love the Minister's humility."

Kelley admits to having a difficult relationship with Jackson many years ago, but says, "Jesse and I get along beautifully now. He calls into the show every week and we have these regular dialogues. I do his TV show a lot. He's great, he's family."

Though his good relations with Jackson and Farrakhan caused him to be optimistic about arranging the joint interview, Kelley marvels, "It was even easier than I thought. I felt maybe a couple of problems would come up, which I would have been willing to deal with. But there weren't any problems at all.

"They both said yes the first time I talked to them, and nothing's off-limits. The Minister was concerned about who was going to be there. I said, just the three of us and he said, no problem.

"In a way, I think it signifies growth on both their parts because at one time, this would have been difficult," Kelley opined.

"I think that each of them has understood that collectively, they can do more than they can singularly, and that they have the same goal of trying to increase the Black community economically, socially, and in every other way."

He also feels that the public pairing of the two men is a winning proposition all the way around.

"I think that progress in the Black community nationally since they are both national figures – will certainly be improved as a result of their working together," Kelley says. "Everybody is better off, and although they may have differences on some things, they put those aside and work together on the major issues."

"I truly believe that people appreciate the fact that they are getting along because I think Black folks want to see 'Black leadership' get along. There doesn't have to be a Black leader.

"I think the Black community likes the fact that there is more than one person who can represent their views. There are a number of Black folks out there and Minister Farrakhan and Rev. Jackson are two of them."

Count on Gus

The show may seem to be all-love on paper, but moderating a live two-hour conversation between the two hig-powered, explosive personalities may still be a high-wire act without a net for Kelley.

But he says he's handled any number of dicey situations during his 16 or so years in talk radio, which includes stints at WBEZ, WGCI and V103, in addition to WVON.

One of the more exhilarating experiences occurred when C-Span selected his WGCI show to review an annual segment they aired called *We Can Talk Radio*.

"C-Span covered us for three straight hours and it was unbelievable," Kelley recalls. "I started off with Gus Savage for the first hour and he scared me to death because Gus would go off on people!

"We were doing a segment about racism and an old White woman called in and said, 'Well, I'm here in Alabama and we got one colored family and they ain't got no problem.' I'm holding back Gus under the desk, waiting for him to go off and

call this woman all sorts of names! I told Gus, 'You're gonna blow my whole show and we've only been on 20 minutes.'

"Minister Farrakhan did the second hour and he was fantastic. He was so good. I was vice president of the City Club of Chicago at the time and all these White folks were saying, 'My goodness, the man talked so well on your show!' I said, yes, that's because I wasn't asking all these 'Do you still beat your wife?' type questions mainstream media asks him and I gave him time to respond."

"The third hour I had three former mayors on – Jane Byrne, Michael Bilandic, and Eugene Sawyer," Kelley continues. "It was so funny because I would ask Byrne a question and she would answer. I would ask Sawyer a question and Byrne would answer that, too. Then I would ask Bilandic a question, and nobody could understand what he was saying! But that was the best show! C-Span ran that show four times."

The Talking Drum

Kelley is a funny, story-telling raconteur who does the town – and fortunately for his 6 a.m. to 10 a.m. morning drive audience, doesn't require much sleep. He travels extensively and brings a wealth of knowledge about local, national, and international affairs to his listeners.

He is known to ask the hard questions, does not necessarily back the status quo, and is hardly humbled by the celebrity or power of the guests on his show.

A native Chicagoan and attorney, he's been active in the city's political arena for decades. As an alderman, Kelley became a regular guest on radio talk shows and always seemed to have an interesting point to be considered. He became a regular WBEZ panelist and was eventually sought out as a host by several stations.

With the passing of Lu Palmer and Vernon Jarrett, Kelley might be considered one of the deans of the Black journalistic scene in the city, except that Kelley doesn't consider himself a journalist.

"I'm not a trained journalist like Lu and Vernon were and there's nothing objective about me – I have an opinion about everything," Kelley says. "What I bring is a lot different, based on the experiences I've had related to international politics and from being a locally elected official.

"My whole point is in disseminating information, arming people with the knowledge to confront misconceptions. There are a lot of things I say that probably wouldn't be said to a lot of folks if I was a trained journalist, but there are a lot of things trained journalists won't say that I insist that our people know."

To that extent, Kelley says he prefers to interview guests whose opinions disagree with his because the listening audience gets more out of it with the back and forth of the conversation.

"With radio, I'm trying to serve the public in a way I couldn't do even when I was in politics because of my ability now to reach more people," Kelley explains of his work.

"I think I'm doing more at WVON in that regard than I could do as an elected official, when you think of all the kinds of people we bring in as guests and their points of view.

"The reason I do it is because the only way you can have a true democracy is to have an enlightened electorate. Somebody's got to do it, and if I am the one to do it, fine."

Latrice Spann offered a statement likely to be seconded by every one of the station's 150,000-plus listeners:

"WVON is a rare voice where Black folks can share their views, opinions, learn about who we are as a people, celebrate it, and not have it regulated by White folks," Spann said. "The Black community in this town, wherever we are on a consciousness level as it relates to learning about the issues and being well-informed – that, in large part, is due to Cliff Kelley."

preface Kent

Update: Herb passed away on Saturday, October 22, 2016, at the age of 88, just hours after completing his morning radio show on V103, still rated number one in his time slot. In all, he was on the air for 72 years, which landed him in the *Guinness Book of World Records* for longest career as a radio deejay.

Herb has a Chicago street named after him in Bronzeville, whose residents elected him "Mayor of Bronzeville" in 1998. In 2009, along with *N'DIGO* Editor David Smallwood, he co-authored his autobiography, *The Cool Gent: The Nine Lives of Radio Legend Herb Kent*, with a foreword written by former Chicago Mayor Richard M. Daley.

Cover Photo by Victor Powell

Herb Kent

By David Smallwood & Photography by Reginald Payton | *Originally Published June 27, 1996*

Like our sports teams, Lake Shore Drive, downtown's architecture, the newspapers, Bronzeville, and the smell of barbecue wafting on an early evening breeze, there are some signatures that make Chicago uniquely Chicago.

Herb Kent, jacking his "dusties" like a big dog on Saturday and Sunday afternoons over radio station WVAZ-V103, has enshrined himself as one of them.

Fittingly, Herb, a native Chicagoan, has made his mark the Chicago Way – by employing a strong and determined work ethic.

In the 1940s, his Northwestern University broadcasting professor told him, "It's so sad that you have the nicest voice in this class because it isn't going to do you any good. You're a Negro and you'll never get anywhere in this field."

Kent, who never got less than an "A" in college, replied, "Man, just give me my grade and I'll worry about the rest."

This year, Herb Kent, the nationally renowned Cool Gent, became the first Black disk jockey voted into the Broadcast Hall of Fame. And except for brief stints at stations in Gary and Milwaukee, he's spent his entire radio career working in the Chicago area.

> **I'm thinking all the time about the audience. Can they dig what I'm doing? Are they liking it?**

At his height, Kent was the most popular deejay at arguably the most popular Black radio station ever in America – the legendary WVON, broadcasting at 1450 on the AM dial from the '60s through mid-'70s.

Today, Chicagoans of all ages and colors tune him in on the car radio as they rush to the store during a Bulls or Bears half-time break. They listen to his "Battle of the Best" on Sundays over a late breakfast at the IHOP. They jam along to this Pied Piper's music while chilling along the lakefront.

He's also seen on Friday nights as host of Channel 7's popular *Steppin' At Club Seven*, the steppers dance program that airs at 1 a.m., "but is the most popular show in that time slot," Herb chuckles.

For 50 years, Chicagoans have been captivated by this most recognizable of voices, which Kent developed during his first radio experience as a 15-year-old Hyde Park High School student working at WBEZ.

He entered radio in the first place to distract him from the heartbreak of a failed teenage romance. The only Black student in Hyde Park's Radio Guild, Kent was elected its president.

While in the guild, he auditioned for WBEZ, which used high school students to tape educational bits that were played in the school system and aired as public service spots over local stations.

Herb was a soprano in grammar school, but at BEZ, he was taught how to articulate, enunciate, project and drop his voice at least half an octave. However, Kent says the voice that has served him so well has also been an occasional handicap.

He notes, "Sometimes you don't really want to be known." Like when standing in line in a crowded takeout joint and all eyes turn his way once he places his order. Or on even more awkward occasions.

"Once," Herb recalls, "I took this girl to a hotel and then heard all this scuffling outside the door. I heard a chambermaid say, 'It's Herb Kent! He in there, yeah he is!' and then all this running around as people came to the door!"

Back To The Day

If anybody knows about "Old School," it's Kent, who would have to be considered both the dean and head curator of that institution. He's witnessed Black and popular music change for six decades and can rattle musical history off the top of his head. Some of Herb's quick remembrances:

- "In the '40s, Nat King Cole's Trio was it.

- "In the mid-'50s there was this song *Honky Tonk* by Bill Doggett – a shuffle blues that you danced a little bop and jitterbugged to. James Brown did *Please, Please, Please* in 1956.

- "That was followed immediately by doowops, which were only here for three years, from 1956-'59. *Goodnight Sweetheart, Earth Angel* – good for slowdancing, grinding and stuff.

- "Early '60s...Dee Dee Clark, Ben King's *Stand By Me*, more James Brown. Then less emphasis on the group and more on the lead singer... Gladys Knight and the Pips, Diana Ross and the Supremes. Motown came in and dominated music all over the country.

- "Dances from the '60s – the Bristol Stomp, Roach, Watusi, Continental, Madison, Twist, Twine – I could do them all. They said I was the Uncle Willy champion!

- "In the '70s, Black music just exploded, really came into its own. In 1945, eight records went number one on the R&B charts; in 1975, there were 42 and a lot of them went pop, too.

- "Music since the '70s has been washed out and not as rich. There will never be another period like that, where it all came together like it did. But I don't get stuck in any one era because fortunately, a good song is a good song and if you find one, it'll be a good song forever."

Hanging Out

As one of the premier jocks in the country, Kent has had the privilege of hanging out with some of Black music's premier entertainers. When he recounts those times, it's not name-dropping, it's just recollection.

"I hung with Stanley Turrentine, Garland Green, Curtis Mayfield, the Impressions, the Dells, Walter Jackson, Patti LaBelle, Johnny Taylor, the O'Jays, James Brown, Bobby Womack," Kent briefly lists.

"Bill Withers came to my house when I had this 10-pound South American fish. Bill was a country boy at heart and never got over seeing such a big fish. Eddie Kendricks and I were really friendly. Smokey Robinson and I have remained friends. I went to his house in California a couple months ago, such a house you wouldn't believe.

"Smokey's doing great, playing golf all the time. He wrote so many songs that he must get a residual check for a few hundred thousand dollars every three months or so, but he's as friendly as ever. Just a nice guy who never changed."

Kent says, "'Hanging out' meant going to nightclubs, or sitting up all night with a drink talking about our careers, what we wanted to do, our problems. We went to parties together, hunted women together – all the stuff that young, red-blooded American guys do."

After this trip down memory lane, Kent assessed

The Cool Gent

his 50-year career and gave a startling glimpse into the personal side of a man who has entertained so many people for so long.

"I remember in the mid-'50s working at WBEE making $85 a week. I lived in Lake Meadows, had a car and a great looking girlfriend," Kent begins. "I was happy, but I didn't live that happiness because I was always waiting for that day when I was really going to get ahead and be great.

"I was always so driven to succeed that I didn't really enjoy things as much as I should have. Always looking to the next step, trying to get ahead, trying to get a foothold in this business, trying to be great at it. I've never gotten to that point where I could say to myself that I've succeeded, or that I'm great. Not even to this day."

Kent got his first paying job ($35 a week) in 1949 at a Gary, Indiana station doing a "race show," a Polish hour and a country-western hour. He moved on to WBEE for five years, where he developed an "oldies show" and created the term "dusty records."

The WVON Good Guys

Kent joined WVON in 1960, shortly before the station launched its "Good Guys" format featuring wall-to-wall, over-the-top radio personalities like Pervis Spann, E. Rodney Jones, Bill "Butterball" Crane, Ed Cooke, Joe Cobb and Richard Pegue. All of them talked non-stop smack.

"I've never seen a phenomena like it," Kent recalls. "The baddest station in the country. For almost 15 years, we 'broke' 90 percent of all the Black records. That means we were the first ones to play a record and make it popular so that it's picked up by other stations around the country."

Kent created popular, bizarre radio characters like the Wahoo Man and the Electric Crazy People. He made the Kappa Karnival at Southern Illinois in Carbondale a national success, held "hops" at every high school and college in the area, and created the immensely popular "Times Square" dance center.

Thanks to the Good Guys, WVON climbed to number one in the ratings, ahead of powerhouse WLS. "They had 50,000 watts and could be heard coast-to-coast. We could barely be heard past 95th Street," Kent recalls.

"When we became number one in the city – and this was mostly with a solidly Black audience on the South and West sides – WLS called and said, 'Who are you guys?'"

JAM-osity

Somehow, when he walks into a room full of old records, the sound just comes out differently than when other folks do it.

Herb tried to explain the secret to this "jam-osity," this ability of his to jam so hard that you fear he's gonna hurt himself one day. Yes, he says, there is a method:

"When I get on the air, I'm always ahead. I don't play one song and before it's over say, 'Gee, what's next?' I'm thinking three to five records as to where I want to go."

"When I follow Pam Morris on Sunday mornings, I like to put on a religious-type record or some old-time stuff, maybe an *Oh, Happy Day* by the Edwin Hawkins Singers and follow that with maybe a Staple Singers, so I hold onto some of her audience and ease into mine.

"Then I try to play an ear-catching record I haven't played before. Maybe it's *Flashlight*. My mind starts working like a computer: 'Ah, *Flashlight*...now let's have some Bootsy. Okay, Bootsy funked...now let's have some George Duke funk with *Reach For It*. And as long as we're funking, let's do some *Backstroking* by the Fatback Band.'

"Then I'm to a break and I come out of the break with a 1960s quiz – 'Who's the guy who used to girlwatch on 63rd Street and was earmarked to replace Otis Redding after he died?' That's Johnny Taylor, and I'll play an old one of his, say *Disco Lady*. Then, so as not to lose the younger audience, I come back with an '80s record that has the same beat – like *Dazz* by Brick and then cut to a BeeGees with the same sound.

"I'm thinking this way all the time and really working the audience so I don't lose anybody of any age group. Then I listen to what listeners say when they call in, and I play that and I blend it in and I play and I jam. I try to, anyway.

"I'm thinking all the time about the audience. Can they dig what I'm doing? Are they liking it?"

Apparently so. He must be doing something right to be on the air as long as he has. And after 50 years, Kent says, "I'm going to stay at this until I die. Hopefully, I'll drop dead at the mike. Some people think that's not funny. But for me," Herb says, "that's real."

preface
King & Brooks

Update: The dynamic duo left the cable business to enter the food industry. Marty King has developed a fast food seafood restaurant operation called the Crazy Crab with intent to franchise nationally, while Brooks is CEO & President of Hyde Park Hospitality, a food, facility and retail management company.

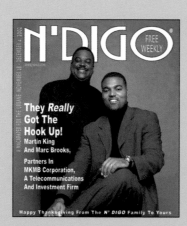

Martin King & Marc Brooks

By Kevin McNeir & Photography by Reginald Payton | *Originally Published November 28, 2002*

Sometimes the road to success begins with a dream or an idea, other times it starts with the kinds of examples we have around us.

For two successful Chicago entrepreneurs, Martin King and Marc Brooks, it was a combination of both – big dreams and positive role models.

But it takes more than just a good idea and a family of business-minded movers and shakers to make one's dreams come true. It takes hard work, perseverance and a belief in oneself.

And now these two childhood friends have parlayed their first business enterprise, Mar-Comm Wireless, into the recent purchase of WideOpenWest (WOW), making them part of the country's 12th largest competitive cable and internet providers. Not bad for a couple of brothers from the South Side of Chicago.

> **We grew up in an atmosphere where we were taught the way to handle a business, how to invest money, and how to make key connections.** — Martin King

"We believe this new venture is historical because only a few minorities in the U.S. have ever owned a piece of equity in the cable market," Brooks said. "We are building a bridge to the digital divide and are changing the playing field, as well as the structure of this company, so that the owners are beginning to look like the customer base to whom they provide service."

Both King and Brooks are quick to point out that their good fortune did not come about because they wished on a star and waited for something to happen. For them, it's been years of hard work, long hours and supportive families that have made this latest coup possible.

Still, it's an incredible achievement, particularly given the fact that they are both African American and only 33- and 34-years-old, respectively.

Mighty Oaks From Little Acorns

A company flow chart might actually be needed to understand the complexity and the business relation-

ships formed by King and Brooks, who back in 1997 started Mar-Comm Wireless with three Ameritech authorized cellular and paging stores on the city's South Side and in the South Loop.

Today, the co-founders of MKMB Corporation at 1623 East 95th Street are two of the hottest and most respected young businessmen this side of the Mason-Dixon and with good reason.

MKMB is the parent company of subsidiaries in the telecommunications business. One subsidiary, Urban Media Group L.L.C., provides urban marketing, consulting, and field sales for major telecommunications companies. Urban Media Group L.L.C. has also grown to become one of the largest distributors for U.S. Cellular.

A second subsidiary, Mar-Comm Wireless, was a distributor for Verizon Wireless before being sold back to the parent corporation in June 2001 – an amazing feat for any small business owner – and the transaction was made so that the two owners earned a significant profit.

"Yeah, we had kind of been called the South Side Cell Phone Guys," King says laughingly. "But a big part of our success was the homework we did. We studied the locations before we set up businesses.

"We knew our communities and we knew places like 87th Street, that had great foot traffic and a real market for cellular phone service. We didn't have as many stores as other distributors did, but we had the best locations. So, it's still true in business today – location is everything."

But the accomplishment which still causes King and Brooks to beam with pride is the May 2001 minority stake that they acquired in WideOpenWest L.L.C., a digital and broadband service provider that acquired SBC's cable unit, Ameritech New Media.

Not only are they minority partners, but both serve on the board of directors and handle the business's day-to day operations, with King focusing on governmental relations and Brooks handling sales and marketing.

"We wanted to make sure we were not only investors, but also key players in the company's daily operations," Brooks said. "For us, it's more than just owning a cable company. We want to keep working hard, grow the business, learn everything we can, and provide service to customers who remain satisfied. And we want to be able to provide employment opportunities for people from our community."

To put it in perspective, most African Americans are familiar with BET (Black Entertainment Television), but consider that that is only one cable station. By locating other investors interested in the WOW acquisition, and with the ability to raise the necessary capital, King and Brooks have gotten in on the ground floor.

Chicago's newest cable and Internet provider currently handles about 70,000 customers in Illinois and a total of 300,000 in the three-state region of Michigan, Ohio and Illinois.

One might justifiably ask, how do you come up with the millions of dollars needed to actually pull off such a purchase? King's response is, "It wasn't easy. The transaction was actually a couple of years in the making.

> **While I was playing college basketball, I realized that even if I could make it to the NBA, I could make a great deal more money owning the team.** — Marc Brooks

"We formed BTK Partners Fund L.L.C. and brought in a third partner, Stuart Taylor, so that we could create a minority fund to invest in WideOpenWest with other minority investors.

"Then we had the incredible fortune to connect with the majority partner – Oak Hill Capital – a multi-billion dollar investment company. They're the big boys in venture capital and it just doesn't happen often in big business that a minority partner gets such an opportunity.

"In addition, from the beginning (1997), we established a solid business relationship with Northern Trust Bank, who especially in this latest venture really stepped up to the plate and assisted us in accomplishing our goal."

Like Father And Father-Like Sons

Both men agree that Chicago is a mecca for African-American businesses. But they don't just cite successes like Oprah Winfrey or John H. Johnson.

"We grew up in an atmosphere where we were taught the way to handle a business, how to invest money, and how to make key connections with other like-minded individuals," King said.

"I remember when Jesse Jackson Jr. was successful in his first bid for Congress. A lot of other young Blacks here in Chicago wanted to immediately jump into politics because we were educated, trained, and believed we had something to offer.

"But it was conversations with people like *N'DIGO*

Publisher Hermene Hartman who said, 'Wait a minute, we're going to need some of you on the business side of the fence.'"

King's father, Kenneth King, was a self-made businessman who decorated and painted homes. According to the younger King, his tutelage into the world of business was an everyday encounter. In addition, King's grandfather, Hayward Bland, opened Pacific Coast Bank in San Diego in the early '70s.

Brooks, too, has a family that taught him the value of business, which he says, "lit a spark that has grown with time."

Besides his duties at MKMB, he also serves as vice chairman for Brooks Food Corporation, the parent of several companies that manufacture specialty food products for national restaurant chains. His father Frank initially founded that business as Brooks Sausage.

"My dad played a key part in my desire to own a business," Brooks said. "He never forced me to do that; he just exposed me to the possibilities. It was men like my father and Martin's who were living examples of excellence.

"But there were others – Cirilo McSween, George Johnson, Lester McKeever and Harold Washington – folks who paved the way for our generation and who made it possible for us to now be able to reap the benefits. The real key in all of this is passing it on to the next generation. That's what they did and that's what we intend to do."

King added, "Chicago's Black business leaders fought for economic justice, especially Rev. Jesse Jackson. I grew up as a 'PUSH baby,' always around doing something, anything, just to be involved and to learn.

"I had the great fortune of having Rainbow/PUSH support me financially through college. That's what being there for the youth in your community is all about. Now we have to start giving back."

King's dedication to PUSH was recently rewarded with his election last summer as chairman of the board of trustees.

"The thing about groups like PUSH is that they allow young people to get involved – to learn how to organize, to learn about our history and to develop healthy relationships," he said. "Some of us stayed for awhile, but others, like me, wanted to continue to learn. And I'm still learning."

Brooks says, "For me, with my dad and his close associates, it wasn't about trying to be like Mike, it was trying to be like my father. While I was playing college basketball, a lot of the lessons I had learned came to mind. I realized that even if I could make it to the NBA, I could make a great deal more money owning the team."

King says he, too, learned from an early age that the African concept of the village being responsible for the raising of its children was the key to his success.

"We had great business leaders and educators who took the time to let us see what the world – their world – was like," he said. "I wanted to meet Jesse Jackson, not Reggie Jackson. And I really believed, from my youngest days, that I could actually do whatever I wanted."

Words For The Next Generation

Both businessmen emphasize the importance of having a solid business plan and doing a good job every time you have a chance to do the job at all.

"People might look at the work we've done in the cellular wireless business (they recently struck yet another deal to reenter the field based on their solid performance), but none of this has happened overnight," King said.

"Hard work still pays off. We have had about 90 percent 'no' in terms of business transactions that we've attempted to complete and only 10 percent 'yes.' But that doesn't mean you give up. It means you remain persistent. That's critical."

"Confidence is important, too," Brooks adds. "On the other hand, you can't approach things like you know it all, either. What really matters is if one has the ability to get to the answer – it's about having access to individuals. And that starts with having a credible story to tell and a good track record."

preface King

Update: A prolific writer on contemporary issues, Paul King published the book *Reflections On Affirmative Action in Construction* in 2009.

The inventory of his early construction years, called "The Paul King Papers circa 1967-1997" and comprising 45 boxes and 22 linear feet, is archived in the Chicago History Museum.

King is a founding member of the Business Leadership Council, a group of African American corporate professionals and entrepreneurs who came together to support Black leadership in politics and business.

Paul and his wife Loann, a career educator, are advisors to the board of their son Tim King's very successful Urban Prep Academies, a charter high school network for Black males in Chicago, whose graduates have a 100 percent acceptance rate into college.

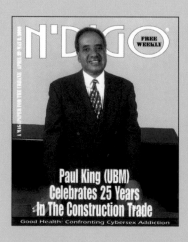

Paul King

By Rae Jones & Photography by Brent Jones | *Originally Published November 1991*

Something has gone terribly wrong in affirmative action and minority setaside programs. While fingers can be pointed in many directions, the fact remains – those who made the initial efforts and sacrificed the most for Black empowerment in the construction trade are not the direct beneficiaries of those efforts.

No one is more aware of this fact than Paul J. King. And, his frustration is evident.

King is Chairman and CEO of UBM, Inc., the largest African-American owned construction firm in Illinois. It is a multi-disciplined construction management consulting agency, a general contractor, and an engineering firm.

King was a primary player in the efforts of the 1960s-'70s that launched what grew into a local and national Black contractors movement.

Working under an unusually cooperative agreement with the city's three largest street gangs and some local community organizations, King helped shut down housing rehabilitation projects in 1969 on Chicago's West Side.

The gangs were used to intimidate workers into walking off the job. They had agreed to put aside the individual interests of each gang for the betterment of the larger community.

The combined group's strategy was to stop the construction projects to draw attention to the plight of Blacks in construction crafts. Because the projects were valued at millions of dollars, the strategy worked.

Representing a group of 80 Black building contractors under the umbrella of the West Side Builders Association, King and others sought to force union leaders to the bargaining table where the issue of opening unions to Blacks could be resolved. At the time, the unions were 97 percent white.

"We wanted our fair share of jobs, our piece of the pie," King says. "Blacks would pass construction projects in their neighborhoods and see nothing but white workers. It was a slap in the face – a daily insult.

> In trying to advance the Black contractor, we're talking about trying to stimulate an agent for the cause of Black economic development and empowerment. It is part of a process.

"Our strategy was to initially try to get jobs on a site, then move to being developer and owner of a site, and to gain control over business enterprises, jobs, and all the commerce that interfaces with those enterprises," King explained.

While the short-term strategy worked, the long-term plan didn't. King is frustrated that the early pioneers – the Black contractors – no longer are benefiting from the hard work and energy they put into that movement.

"It's a very saddening thing to note that all the proponents, the core, in 1969, were Black," he begins. "We pivoted off of a Black presence. We pivoted off of a Black commitment. We pivoted off of projects going on in Black communities. But, with all of this effort, if we look at statistics in employment alone, without even considering development and ownership, we are losing ground every day."

Noting that the number of "minority" apprentices has grown from less than four percent in 1969, according to U.S. Department of Labor figures, King is quick to caution a careful examination of the numbers. When broken down by race and gender, these numbers, he insists, do not bode well for Blacks.

"It is not that I am against any other ethnic group," King says. "It is that I believe that there should be a fair proportion going to the people who started all of this in the first place.

"When I think of the Black contractor, I am thinking about the Black businessman in the construction industry – an industry that is one of the biggest in the United States," King explains.

"At 10 percent of the Gross National Product, the construction industry represents one dime out of every dollar. One out of every seven jobs is in some way related to construction. It's a big, big business.

"So, in trying to advance the Black contractor, we're talking about trying to stimulate an agent for the cause of Black economic development and empowerment. It is part of a process."

Affirmative Action Pioneer

Unfortunately, that has not happened.

"We're at a crossroad," King says of today's affirmative action situation. "What we are experiencing is a total erosion in what we initially meant for setaside programs. The initial activists – those most in need, and most deserving – are not receiving full or near adequate benefits. We are being overlooked across the board and it has been justified by a change in the language of setaside legislation."

King knows what he is talking about. He has lived it and he has watched others suffer as a result of it. A prominent force behind the local and national push to institutionalize affirmative action setasides through legislation, King's efforts began early.

Former president of the National Association of Minority Contractors, he has traveled to more than 40 different cities in 24 states, speaking, writing, and having position papers published in various magazines on the plight of minority contractors. He also has been instrumental in securing governmental funding for minority contractor assistance programs in Chicago and nationally.

Working with Congressman Parren Mitchell's Black Business Braintrust, King wrote portions of the Public Works Act of 1976, which relates to a 10 percent Minority Business Enterprises (MBE) provision in construction. Later, in 1978, he testified before Congress on the effectiveness of that provision.

The result, the Local Public Works II Program, established $4 billion worth of local public works projects to provide stimulus to the economy and increase job opportunities and needed public facilities. The first legislation of its kind, it contained the unprecedented provision that at least 10 percent of each grant be spent with minority businesses, contractors or suppliers.

"But the situation now is a problem of conjunction," King commented. "We have watched the original language in affirmative action legislation go through various stages. It changed from 'Disadvantaged' to 'Minority or Women', then to 'Minority and Women.' Along the way, the word "Black" disappeared, and from where I sit, right now, white women are the primary beneficiaries."

King explains, "The billions of dollars of construction setasides that carried minority stipulation, with the whole intent being to have greater development of minority firms so that they would be competitive and be in a position to employ and train other people, hasn't happened as proportionately for Black people as it has for other ethnics."

The Chicago Plan

Born and reared in Chicago, King is especially sensitive to the Black construction effort here. Despite an early agreement for the implementation of employment of minorities in the Chicago building and construction industry, not much ever really happened.

Signed with much fanfare in 1970 by the Chicago and Cook County Building Trade Council, the Building Construction Employers Association of Chicago, and the Coalition for United Community Action (CUCA – an outgrowth of the 1969 West Side construction shutdown), the Chicago Plan committed to provide construction training and employment opportunities for 1,000 disadvantaged young adults.

King participated with the CUCA, which he helped form, in negotiations to develop the Chicago Plan. Within two years, it was clear that the Plan was a dismal failure.

Coalition leaders stated, "The Plan we signed has not worked because there exists no commitment from the various craft unions. It has not worked because the implementation device does not give the minority community proper decision-making power. It does not work because too many of those involved are not sincere."

Only a measure of success was achieved by a handful of minority contractors and UBM, Inc., was one of them.

Chicago Roots

King attributes his company's success to several factors, including his original partners, Sandra Giles and Sham Dabadghao, who have been just as committed as King and play major roles in the company. The continuity has helped.

"I think you must be willing to sacrifice," King says. "A successful business takes a lot more time and a lot more risks than a job. But the benefits are enormous, both from a sense of satisfaction and a sense of independence.

"Just because you don't work for someone else, doesn't mean that you don't work. It's a different attitude. You work harder. You can see and control the results of what you get. We have to associate our young people with a business zeal."

Fortunately for Paul King and others he has affected, the process started early. His own father was an entrepreneur. He owned a produce company and taught Paul at an early age the value of productivity.

"My father instilled in me a proper mode of conduct, of working long hours. My uncle taught me how to paint and how to work. He taught me how to perform a task," King says.

King graduated from De La Salle High School in 1956, studied chemistry at the University of Chicago, attended the University of Illinois for construction management, and did graduate work at Roosevelt University in political science.

He worked his way through college by doing paintwork he learned from his uncle and work was so plentiful that it became his full-time business. But

when he saw how Black contractors were routinely shut out of public contracts, he organized other Black construction tradesmen, and in 1969, became executive director of the United Builders Association of Chicago – a government funded organization that provided technical assistance to minority contractors.

The Super Contractor

As Chairman and CEO of UBM, he presides over a company with more than 50 employees and contracts worth a billion dollars. UBM has worked on – and won awards for – such large projects as the O'Hare Airport expansion, Great Lakes Naval Training Center, Gateway Foundation's West Side treatment center, James Thompson Center, University of Illinois Hospital, Goodman Theatre, Hyatt Regency McCormick Place Hotel, *Chicago Sun-Times* printing plant, Northern Trust Bank, Trinity United Church, Cineplex Odeon Theater in Lawndale, Cesar Chavez Elementary School, and the Stony Island Plaza anchored by Jewel-Osco at 95th and Stony Island.

Looking back on his monumental achievements, King notes, "I was very inspired, but I also was very naïve. I thought that when we got through with the construction piece, back in the '60s and '70s, we would get that under control, then we'd go after education. Then we'd go after the police. Then we'd straighten out transportation. I had no idea that these struggles would be lifelong.

"I never knew that we were operating without an agenda. There's no agenda about Black economic development, Black entrepreneurship, Black land ownership.

"But Black people have survived under the most terrible situations, so I am not truly depressed. We have to continue to beat the bushes and confront once and for all how we impact on the institutions that influence our situation.

"We need a collective will. We need some people to leap out there in given areas to be activists and advocates in areas of concern and action.

"But, that's the funny thing about Black people. Every time you're ready to throw up your hands, ready to give up, somebody leaps out there with something that will give you some enthusiasm."

And, that's also the thing about Paul J. King. Always ready to do something. He always has and he still is – doing something to help Black people.

preface King

Update: Tim King stayed at Hales for five years. In 2002, he and other Black civic, business and education leaders founded Urban Prep Academies, a network of three charter public high schools in Chicago serving all African-American males, mostly from low-income families.

The campuses are in Englewood, Bronzeville and the University Village/Little Italy area. The first school opened in 2006 and since then, with its first graduating class in 2010, 100 percent of Urban Prep graduates have been accepted to colleges and universities.

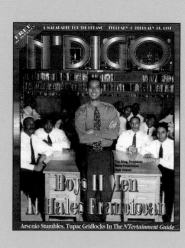

Tim King

By Derrick K. Baker & Photography by Darlene Martin | *Originally Published February 6, 1997*

From his austere, oblong office with barren walls, Hales Franciscan High School President Tim King has an obstructed view of the equally stark, mostly blighted neighborhood that encompasses his school; it's a neighborhood in need, but is, ironically, home to one of the most uniquely accomplished and meaningful schools in Illinois and the entire country, for that matter.

What makes the physical and socio-economic conditions of the community around 49th and Cottage Grove even more stark and contradictory – yet virtually meaningless to the students and staff who call Hales home – is that inside the school's four walls lives the personification of purpose, perseverance and pride.

For as the only historically Black Catholic, all-male college preparatory high school in the state, Hales Franciscan is more than just the ultimate feel-good story. It's an educational legend.

> I know that what we're doing is saving lives. And because we're saving lives, we're ensuring that there are going to be generations of strong Black men, their wives, their children, the people they touch.

Led by the youthful-looking King, who was appointed President in July 1995, the 330-student school continues its much-lauded tradition of success in turning Black boys to men, preparing them for college and the challenges of being a Black man, and broadening their horizons with academic trips to other parts of the world.

For example, last year, all 57 members of the school's graduating senior class were accepted into colleges across the national map. Moreover, in the first fiscal year of his tenure, King, with the support of Hales' 40-person staff and administration, benevolent benefactors and altruistic alumni, orchestrated:

- raising donations to nearly double the amount collected in any previous year;

- reducing the student attrition rate by some 30 percent;

- increasing student retention by 50 percent without compromising standards;

- developing "Hales Service," a day in which the entire school engages in community service; and

- reestablishing the Hales football team after a 25-year hiatus.

More Than Just A School

An unbridled bundle of energy, King prides himself on being able to help people along the way. "It's a tough thing to say without sounding paternalistic," he says, "but I think it's a great honor to be a part of someone's life. I'm actually honored to be able to make a definite contribution. I think everyone can make those types of contributions, but I don't think everyone realizes they can.

"I know that what we're doing at Hales – all of us – is saving lives. And because we're saving lives, we're ensuring that there are going to be generations of strong Black men, their wives, their children, the people they touch. The list goes on and on," King offers.

"In a more nebulous sense, though," he adds, "I want to try to make this world a little bit better and I think education is the key to doing that. To put people in an environment where they feel loved and nurtured and give them some 'stuff' to put into their brain is what's going to allow them to not only go to college, but to be productive in life. And that, in turn, will make the world better."

Speaking of the world, Hales boasts an impressive track record in exposing its charges to locales near and far, domestically and internationally. From Florida A&M University; Dartmouth College; the University of Chicago; Howard University to the University of Notre Dame, for years Hales graduates have continued their academic pursuits at schools across the country.

On a broader geographic scale, in his first year, King, who himself has studied at the European University Institute in Italy and the University of Nairobi in Kenya, implemented the Summer of Enlightenment program for achieving seniors.

Last year the program provided the opportunity

for 20 students to attend the likes of the Academie of Paris, Oxford University and Cornell University, and intern at investment asset and financial services firms Goldman Sachs, Morgan Stanley, and PaineWebber, among others.

Despite the inner-city neighborhood the school is located in, King says that while he realizes "perceptions are important," he doesn't "think they are primary to what we are trying to do here."

He explains, "I want people who are worried about the violence in the inner city and 'these Black kids in these gangs' to recognize that here's a school that's dealing with some Black boys who *aren't* going to get involved in that stuff.

"I want some Black business people to say, 'Here's a school that represents everything I'm trying to be about as a Black businessman or woman.' I want parents to recognize that if they want a high-quality education for their children, they don't have to be slaves to the public school system. There are other options."

The Road Less Traveled

King, 29, is younger than the 35-year-old institution he heads. But it's that same youthful vigor that allows him to bring to the table a necessary energy and vision to steer the Hales ship and keep it on course. His confluent dedication and spirit are precisely what propel King to provide Hales students with a background as diverse as his own.

"I'm a combination of different influences and people and obviously who I am has had an awful lot to do with my environment, upbringing, my parents and entire family who have been very significant in my life," explains the graduate of Georgetown University's Law Center. His parents are Chicago construction entrepreneur Paul King and educator Loann Honesty King.

"I don't think I could, or anybody could, define themselves in a sentence or phrase. More importantly, I'm still becoming. It's an evolutionary process, a work in progress. I like being able to help people along the way. I think it's important to be faithful to people and to causes. I am committed to my family. I'm committed to my community and to the world," King says.

"Specifically, I'm committed to this institution and the young men in this school. They need people who will love them and care about them and be there for them and support them and help them along the way."

Practicing what he preaches, King teaches a class at Hales titled "Social Justice" that addresses such contemporary social issues as racism, poverty and homelessness, and how students can effect change. King's law background, in part, keys his interest in such topics, and had he not taken the mantle at Hales, the legal community is where you would probably find him.

After completing his undergraduate degree at Georgetown University, King remained there to attend law school. While a law school student, one of King's former professors, who became president of an inner-city Catholic school in the nation's capital, asked King to teach a part-time history course.

Great Expectations

"I went on to teach other courses and I fell in love with it so much that I became a full-time teacher and part-time law student," King recalls.

After graduating, he took on additional tasks at the school and then in 1994, "finally made the decision that I wanted to be in Chicago with my family," he says. "I had every intention of practicing law and making a little money. But whatever I thought I'd end up doing, it was not getting involved in education."

The best laid (or malleable) plans often go awry, however. So, after agreeing to meet with a Hales board member about doing development work for the school, King was hooked.

"I fell in love with the institution and what it stood for and what it was founded for," he admits. That led to his post as Vice President of Administration and Development at Hales. Then the announcement that former Hales President Father Charles Payne would be stepping down led to King's appointment as President.

King's management style stresses clarity in purpose and message to his students and staff. "In my business, I think you have to be clear in terms of expectations and hopes and goals because the students and faculty and administrators need to know that it's my expectation that you're going to get A's and you're going to graduate from this school," King says.

"It's my expectation that you're going to stay out of trouble. My faculty needs to know it's my expectation that when you're confronted with a student who thinks he doesn't want to learn, you're going to find a way to make him realize he *does* want to learn."

Like a proud and protective papa, King's voice becomes even more robust when he says, "I want people to perceive the institution for what it is: an outstanding academic institution that is doing something that no other school in this city is doing, in my opinion.

"And that is taking some kids, most of whom are economically disadvantaged and come from single-parent households, most of whom don't score off the chart in standardized testing, who are not going to get a chance to make it in public school, and

meeting their needs."

For the work that has been done for three decades plus and continues to be done – that is, transforming uninitiated Black boys into productive, respectful Black men – Hales' motto, In Virum Perfectum, (Unto Perfect Manhood), is salient.

"I had no clue that this is what I was going to end up doing for this part of my life, but it's definitely a wonderful experience," King says triumphantly. "I know that, eventually, Hales will outgrow me and what I can do for the institution. Then it will be time for me to move on and make a contribution elsewhere."

preface
Knuckles

Update: The Godfather of House Music passed away on March 31, 2014. Upon his untimely death, Mayor Rahm Emanuel called Knuckles "one of Chicago's most treasured cultural pioneers."

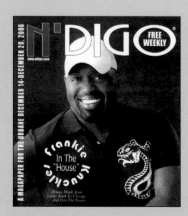

Frankie Knuckles

By D. Kevin McNeir & Photos Courtesy of D/E Entertainment | *Originally Published November 14, 2006*

One of the fascinating things about African Americans is the diversity within our own race. Consider music, for example. We make love to R&B, we groove to hip-hop, find inspiration for social and political movements in reggae, reflect on the vicissitudes of life when listening to the blues, and seek spiritual renewal through gospel.

And then there's *house music* – an eclectic style of electronic dance music whose roots can be traced right here in Chicago dating back to the early 1980s – that just makes you want to get up and … dance.

The name "house music" is said to be derived from the Warehouse – a popular Chicago nightclub where an up-and-coming DJ from the Bronx, Frankie Knuckles, was beginning to gain notoriety for his unique mixes of classic disco, soul, R&B lyrics, beats from the Philly International label and European synthpop recordings.

After a five-year stint at the Warehouse that started in 1977 when the club opened, sweeping young dance lovers off their feet, Knuckles attempted to establish his own club here, The Power Plant, which subsequently folded, leading him to return to NYC where he was quickly tagged as the resident DJ at The World, The Choice, and other popular New York clubs. As his career began to really take off, Knuckles focused his attention on producing, remixing, and recording.

> **House music in its truest form is deeply rooted in everything that is real about music.**

Today, as he nears 30 years in the business and is universally credited as a pioneer of dance music, Frankie is known around the world as "The Godfather of House Music," with a bevy of awards, including a Grammy, under his belt.

"House music is all about R&B beats and lyrics, and it's positive music," Knuckles says. "It makes folks want to get up and dance, and you don't need a partner to have a good time. When I started experimenting at the Warehouse on Saturdays, kids started coming out and staying until the club closed.

"Soon, one day wasn't enough for them, and so people started having parties at people's apartments and houses. And other clubs got into it, too, putting signs in their windows that said, 'We play house music.' When people talked about going to the Warehouse to party, they would say they were going to the HOUSE. I guess the name just stuck."

New York State Of Mind

Knuckles was born January 18, 1955 in the South Bronx and grew up on the tough streets of Harlem, but unlike many Black youth today, his dreams of stardom were not built on making it in the music industry.

Actually, he says he wanted to be a fashion designer, and remembers stringing beads for gowns for local drag queens with his best friend and "partner-in-crime," Larry Levan, before enrolling in classes at FIT in Manhattan where he hoped to study textile design.

As the story goes, one night he and Levan, both underage teens, snuck into the historic nightclub The Loft in New York and Knuckles' life would change forever. He met the club's resident DJ David Mancuso, who introduced the young man to a world that he had never experienced, drawing him into the art of mixing dance music like the Pied Piper of Hamlin, and developing his love for what would later be called "house music."

"House music in its truest form is deeply rooted in everything that is real about music," Knuckles said. "Maybe that's a vague statement, but let me clarify. What inspired house music in the beginning were the songs – great songs by incredible songwriters like Kenny Gamble and Leon Huff, Thom Bell and Linda Creed, Nick Ashford and Valerie Simpson.

"Songs that gave inspiration, songs that made you cry, songs that spoke to the heart and made you move your feet. Even some of the greatest gospel and inspirational tunes can be found in the history of house music. And then there were techy tunes from groups like Kraftwerk that helped bridge the gap between analog and digital music."

A Star Is Born

Chicagoans who began to pack the Warehouse once a week during its heyday (1977-1983) were a significant part of Knuckles' rise to fame, filling the small-framed nightclub because of his turntable artistry by the thousands – numbers unheard of for any DJ.

Many remain loyal followers of "The Godfather" through today and sometimes travel to places like New York's Sound Factory, Montreal's Club Stereo, and Pacha in Ibiza – popular nightspots where Knuckles is still regularly invited to perform his magic.

"I prefer to spin in front of an audience that is willing to hear what I have to offer, complete without judgment or criticism," Knuckles said. "I've never claimed to be technically perfect at mixing, but I do work hard to bring a message to what I do – to entertain folks and take them on a journey.

"And I don't really think I've changed all that much, my style that is, from the early days. In actuality, I think technology is what has changed the way music is made. Today dance/club music is more DJ-based, but back in the day, the music I started out playing was written by studio writers and producers. Those songs were produced to appeal to a wider audience."

Knuckles has crafted, remixed or produced original productions for Diana Ross, The Pet Shop Boys, Luther Vandross, Michael Jackson, Janet Jackson, and Toni Braxton. Particularly in the late

'80s and into the '90s, Knuckles developed into one of the most sought after DJs for mainstream artists who hoped to blend the pulsating drum beat of house music into their own sound.

Perhaps the zenith of his achievements was reached in 1997 when Knuckles was recognized for his comprehensive work as a producer, when he became the first DJ to receive the newly created Grammy Award for Remixer of the Year.

"When I moved back to NYC in 1987, I was brought onboard NARAS (The National Academy of Recording Arts and Sciences/The Grammys) as governor by Jellybean Benitez," Knuckles said. "The Academy wanted to bring dance music into greater focus at the Grammys. After two years as a governor, I was promoted to trustee because of all the charity work I did with MUSICARES and Grammy in the Schools.

"Many people on the voting body of NARAS were rooting for a new category, best dance recording, for many years and finally in 1996 we got the word that the category was to be announced and presented at the awards show the following year. And as a bonus, Best Remix (non-classical) was included. I had a very good year with two mixes for Toni Braxton (*Unbreak My Heart* and *I Don't Want To*), and a few other songs and … well, I won."

House Rules

While many claim that New York City is the "capital" of house music, Chicago natives argue that the Windy City is the real home of *house*. Even local political leaders have caught the "house music bug," effectively spread by Knuckles' mixing prowess.

In the shadow of the site where the Warehouse once stood and where Knuckles' career would really take off, Chicago Mayor Richard M. Daley officially declared August 26, 2004 "Frankie Knuckles Day" in the DJ's adopted home. And with the support of State Senator Barack Obama, an ordinance was approved that changed the name of the street where the legendary Warehouse once stood to "Frankie Knuckles Way."

"When I hear house music, I feel a sense of relief," says music fan Carl Triggs, 37, who lives in Oak Park. "I still see it as a Chicago phenomenon, and I remain an ardent fan of Frankie Knuckles. When I hear it, I feel like I'm listening to church music, because I'm able to get rid of all the pressure from a long week at work when I put on my house music every weekend and become one with the music and the sounds."

Given his success over a career reaching three decades, and with the constant challenge of younger artists, no one would blame Knuckles if he curtailed his transcontinental junkets and retired. But Knuckles isn't one to reminisce for long about the past, or rest on his laurels.

He emerged from the studio in 2004 with *A New Reality*, his first album of completely original material in seven years, with his song *Back in the Day* reaching number one on the *Billboard* chart. And he began this year (2006) with a new remix album and the launch of his own label.

Whether it's in the recording studio or in the DJ booth, Knuckles keeps waving his magical wand, continuing to contribute to the legacy of dance music that he helped create.

preface
Lafontant-
MANkarious

Update: Jewel passed away at her home in Chicago from breast cancer in 1997 at the age of 75. She held positions under six Presidents of the United States, making her the highest ranking woman of her day. Her grandfather, J.B. Stradford, owned a hotel in Tulsa, Oklahoma, and was accused of starting the Tulsa Race Riots in 1921. That happened when white racists burned to the ground the thriving Black community known as the Black Wall Street. Jewel was able to get her grandfather exonerated from the false accusation before she died.

Jewel Lafontant-MANkarious

By Allison Keyes & Photography by David Jenkins | *Originally Published February 8, 1996*

Ambassador Jewel Lafontant-MANkarious believes that everyone needs a place to call home.

In her three years as Ambassador at Large and the United States Coordinator for Refugee Affairs, Lafontant-MANkarious has tried to fulfill that philosophy on a global basis.

"It's so important that people know that others care…and the best people are your own. But if you don't have your own, anybody will do who'll take an interest," Lafontant-MANkarious says.

"I guess it's natural to want to go home, but when I went into this job, I was under the impression that everyone wanted to come to the United States. I found out that once peace is restored, refugees say they want to go back home. The normal thing is to want to stay home, if you can stay home peacefully and in dignity."

The Chicago native is the person who recommends to President George Bush the total number of refugees that will be allowed into the country each year, and where they will come from. She coordinates the efforts of several agencies to help the growing number of refugees in the world.

Lafontant-MANkarious works with the Department of Immigration and Naturalization, the State Department, Health and Human Services, the National Security Council and the United Nations.

Part of Lafontant-MANkarious' job is visiting refugee camps in other countries to see how inhabitants are being treated, and meeting with local officials to take care of nuts and bolts things like food, medicine and shelter. She also solicits help from international agencies like the Red Cross.

"It's hard to see the suffering in some places," she explains, 'but it's offset by the fact that you're saving lives, you're improving the quality of life. You see the sadness, but you also see what you can do to improve the situation."

In May of 1991, Lafontant-MANkarious visited the Iraqi-Turkish border to check on the Kurdish refugees.

> **Blacks should be in both parties so we can get the benefit of whatever goodies are offered, and can educate the people in power. There is danger in African Americans all being in one party.**

The Allied Forces did air drops of food and medicine, then brought them down from the mountains.

"Out of all the refugee camps I've been to, and that includes Africa, this is the first time that I've walked into a camp where people greeted us with open arms and said, "Thanks to America and President Bush. You've saved our lives. You've fed us and you've clothed us, but don't leave us here," she said. "Instead of using the camp as a permanent asylum place, they're prepared to go back home. They used the camp as a sort of a way station, and then they went back to their villages."

In March of 1990, Lafontant-MANkarious visited Malawi, where a good percent of the population consists of refugees from Mozambique, which is in the midst of civil war. Refugees are surviving on maize and ground nuts. Last year, after visiting Iraq, the Ambassador went to Moscow to press for passage of legislation that would allow people to leave Russia for other countries.

She then went to Israel and convinced the government to keep the schools in Gaza and the West Bank open, in order to make up for time lost during the Gulf War. The Ambassador intervened with the Israeli government to get water and access to schools for the Black Hebrew settlement of Dimona.

Lafontant-MANkarious initiated the Refugee Day program in 1990 that has since become an annual celebration. President Bush has proclaimed October 30 Refugee Day. It's an all-day conference with workshops designed to teach Americans and the international community about the plight of the millions of refugees in the world, and to find out what assistance can be offered.

The Subtext of Refugee Racism

The Ambassador explains that to be a refugee, one must prove to the INS that one is fleeing persecution in their own country, or one must have a reasonable basis to believe that one would be persecuted or put to death if one returned to their homeland.

She also says that politics sometimes affects the number of refugees allowed into America and from which countries they come. The United States expects to bring in approximately 142,000 refugees this year.

Sixty-two thousand are expected from Soviet Russia, 52,000 from Viet Nam, 6,000 from Africa and 3,500 from the Middle East. Another 2,000 refugees are expected from Haiti, and also a few thousand from Latin countries.

While Lafontant-MANkarious concedes that the United States has historically favored European refugees over other countries, she stops short of calling the immigration policy racist.

"I want to bring equity and fairness to the program, but when you look at it objectively, you see some things are unfair, inequitable, and not consistent in different parts of the world. But, you can't separate the refugee issue from the political issue," Lafontant-MANkarious says.

"Historically, our immigration laws have favored certain parts of the world over other parts of the world. But it's too easy to call it racism because vital interests have to be taken into consideration."

As an example, the Ambassador points to the situation of the Vietnamese refugees, saying though it seems they are favored over others, the rationale goes back to the Viet Nam War.

"We feel it's our responsibility to save these people, because they lived under a repressive regime and had to flee persecution. The same with the Amerasian people, who are a product of the mixing of our boys overseas with the Vietnamese.

"They cannot make a decent life in Vietnam because the purity of their race has been spoiled and they're looked down on in their own country," she explains. "And when we were fighting the Cold War, we were more interested in people who were fleeing communism. So, therefore, you favor certain parts of the world over others."

The refugees who make it to America go about carving out an interesting life for themselves, she explains. "We have found that some refugees who come here, though at first they may take advantage of social service programs like welfare, get off of welfare quickly, work hard and frequently start their own businesses," the Ambassador says.

"In little or no time, they are contributing to the tax base. You could go into all sorts of philosophical reasons why people who are fleeing persecution work harder than people who are born here, with the assumption that they will have certain things.

"In countries where there has been repression, it takes a lot of nerve and gall to get up and leave. When you know how bad it can be, you appreciate more and more what America has to offer. Instead of people being afraid of them (refugees) and resenting them for taking away what we have, they can be incentives to our own American citizens to do better."

Unprecedented Accomplishment

Lafontant-MANkarious is one of the most accomplished people to ever come out of Chicago – Black or White, male or female.

Born in April 1922 as Jewel Carter Stradford, and an attorney by trade, she has held positions under six presidents, dating back to Eisenhower. She was the first female deputy solicitor general of the United States and considered by President Richard Nixon as a nominee for the Supreme Court.

She's the daughter of C. Francis Stradford, who co-founded the National Bar Association. After earning a political science degree from Oberlin College, she attended the University of Chicago Law School in 1943 as the only Black woman in her class and was the first African-American woman to graduate from that school.

Afterward, she founded a law firm in Chicago in 1949 with her first husband, Tuskegee Airman John Rogers Sr. The couple had one child, John Rogers Jr., the Chicago business powerhouse who founded Ariel Capital Management investment company.

President Dwight Eisenhower appointed her as an assistant U.S. Attorney for the Northern District of Illinois. In 1961, she started a new law firm with her second husband Ernest Lafontant and in 1963 became the first Black woman to argue a case before the U.S. Supreme Court. Her case set precedent for the Miranda ruling, in which all arrestees must be read their rights.

In addition to sitting on the boards of Jewel Companies, TransWorld Airlines, Mobil and Revlon, in 1972, Lafontant-MANkarious was U.S. Representative to the United Nations, which is where she met President George Bush.

She explains: "I was having lunch with all the female delegates and a man went by and waved. I turned to the woman next to me and asked, 'Who was that man who just went by? He just waved at us.' And she looked and she said, 'Isn't he handsome?' and I said, "Yes.' And she said, "Isn't he charming?' And I said, 'Well, yes.' And she said, "That's George Bush, my husband.' We've been friends ever since!" Lafontant-MANkarious chuckles.

Eggs In All Baskets

She says those who criticize Bush for not doing enough to help the nation's poor and minorities are playing on the fears of the public rather than paying attention to the good things Bush has done.

The Ambassador says that when Bush was Vice President, he met regularly with a group of six African-American community and business representatives including her, so that he could keep up with the state of African Americans in this country.

Lafontant-MANkarious has been a Republican

since childhood, which is rather unusual for an African-American Chicago native from 49th and Washington Park Court. She says both political parties need Black input to educate them on what they can do to help our community.

"I am not a Republican just to be different. I actually believe in the tenets and philosophy of the party. But, I also never liked being bulldozed into doing certain things, or needing something so badly that I would have to follow like sheep follow each other," Lafontant-MANkarious says.

"I came up under the late Mayor Richard J. Daley regime and couldn't kowtow to his kind of control. The idea that you had to produce a certain number of votes in order to get a job never appealed to me.

"I believe that Blacks should be in both parties so we can get the benefit of whatever goodies are offered, and can educate the people in power. There is the danger of the brains of the African-American community all being in one party, currently the Democrats."

The Ambassador's business expertise got her an invitation to the Chicago Rotary Club when the U.S. Supreme Court ordered all-male clubs to admit females. That's how she met her third husband, international business consultant, Naguib S. MANkarious, who happened to be the Chicago Rotary Club Vice President.

"I went over there for lunch one day to check the fellas out, and they were all so nice, in a condescending way. Naguib was the nicest of all," she recalls, "and after a period of time, one thing led to another, and he proposed."

Of her son, John W. Rogers, Jr., the proud mother says, "I don't know what has made him as energetic and driven as he is, but like me, he rebels against control. It doesn't mean you are not disciplined – you are, you just make your own decisions.

"He's married to a lovely woman, and they have a beautiful daughter. We're so fortunate to have families. Some kids have no refuge, no place they can come to at the end of the day and say, 'Momma guess what happened?' Or have someone to put their arms around. So what do you do to make up for the refugee children?'"

preface
Leaks

Update: Still in business after 83 years, Leak & Sons Funeral Homes serves about 2,500 families a year at its two locations – on Chicago's South Side and in Country Club Hills.

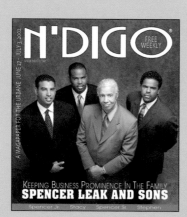

The Leaks

By Wanda Wright & Photography by Victor Powell | *Originally Published June 27, 2002*

Near the turn of the 20th Century, for many Southern Blacks, the bondage of economic slavery came to an end. It was time to go, especially for the 15th child of Jemiah and Archie Leak.

Amid what became a massive African-American migration north, came young Andrew Robert Leak, who eagerly went to work as a bathroom attendant and managed to save $500. He met and married Dottie, who inherited about the same amount from her father.

Their business venture began in 1933, weaving the fabric of Leak Funeral Homes into a tapestry of community, civil rights leadership, dedication and love for their neighbors.

Segregation abounded in those years, so economically, the creation of service industries for Black folk was positive. Out of necessity, to satisfy needs, groceries, drugstores, barber shops, restaurants, and funeral homes flourished, because Whites would not service Blacks.

Leak's struggle to define a place in African-American life and define authenticity for unshakable business principles, required thread spun from several sources.

One thousand dollars bought a lot in those days, but not enough to buoy a business dream or raise a family. Building trust, providing services, and maintaining consistency cost far more than the tools of the funeral business.

> ## You work harder in your own business than you will ever work on anybody's job.

For the next eight years, Leak would wash dishes at a restaurant, and work around the clock to service a growing family and community beyond the throes of death.

Segregation forged business to business relationships. True to the stimuli that led him to Chicago, Andrew and Dottie opened house to the community in 1959. This idea proved revolutionary and lessened the gruesome stigma of funeral homes.

With determination and intensity, Andrew Leak began to teach his four young sons the pride of teamwork. Edward, Andrew Jr., Leon, and Spencer took on regular chores around the funeral home and eventually completed their education in mortuary science.

During the early years of growth, Leak Funeral Homes offered a plethora of services, including transportation. There were no fire department ambulances, or integrated limousine services to serve Blacks. Leak provided transportation for both the sick and famous. Spencer Sr. recalls days of being chauffeur to Reverend Martin Luther King Jr.

Integrating Oakwood Cemetery

During those times, even death was unequal. This injustice came under fire in 1964, when then all-White Oak Woods Cemetery refused to cremate a client's mother. The closest facility to service African Americans was 50-60 miles away.

The angry mortician refused to make one more trip. With permit in hand, 10,000 protesters, including the full ranks of the NAACP, marched on the burial ground that lay nestled in the middle of Black communities. Policy admitting Blacks to the cemetery changed the next day.

Reverend Leak intensified his goal to create equality and entrepreneurship until his death in 1993, but before embarking upon new challenges, he handed the business to the best trained and licensed funeral directors he knew…his sons.

Spencer Sr. recalls the pride they all felt when his dad built "The Colonial House" on East 79th Street, then the only, largest banquet facility for Blacks on Chicago's South Side.

Spencer Leak Sr. says, "C'mon, my dad came to Chicago making $8 a week. He was motivated to never work a job forever. Besides, you work harder in your own business than one will ever work on anybody's job. He left us in charge so that he could help open doors for others."

Economic development was paramount to Reverend Andrew Leak because by investing in depressed areas, business grew and flourished. Business creates jobs, which lead to solidified, substantial communities. He felt that if Blacks are able to live in such areas, self-imposed reparation is established.

While each brother served for a time, Spencer

Sr., wife Henrietta, and his sons Spencer Jr., Stacy and Stephen, now run establishments in the North, West, and South Side neighborhoods of Chicago.

Despite the demands of education, school, responsibilities, and a family mandate to change the future by commitment through service, Spencer Sr. found time to fall in love.

There was never a secret about his gaze that fixed on the lovely young lady in the choir stand of Liberty Baptist Church. Henrietta Leak is partner and wife of the Dynasty of Leak, spreading support and compassion across Chicago.

She carves out time for her favorite pastime, which is caring for children, and serves on community action boards. It has been this unique combination of sacrifice and support by family that allows each of its members to remain rooted in the business, yet satisfy other aspects of career and personality.

Challenging The Criminal Justice System

Illiteracy, miseducation, and crime trouble Spencer Leak Sr. Spurred by his father's accomplishments in civil rights, and with an educational background in criminal justice and a supportive family, he decided to try and change a system that ignores the real problems of its clients.

Using education, experience, and earned influence, Spencer served as Executive Director of Cook County, Department of Corrections from 1987 to 1991. He went on to serve as Deputy Director, Illinois Department of Corrections 1993-1999, applying his background in criminal justice.

To fulfill a need to provide a greater degree of public service, Leak was bent on making a positive change. The criminal justice system needed someone who cared about soaring numbers of African Americans behind its bars.

As Leak watched thousands of young Blacks drop in and out of jail, he felt several factors were clear. "Without finishing high school, drug treatment or behavior modification, hope of a future would be destroyed. These weren't just some kids breaking windows or having fist fights," Leak says.

Lack of public awareness and concern have borne a new type of thug, he says, explaining that "veteran criminals, 10, 11 and 12 years of age are found guilty of arson, rape, murder, and armed robbery. After-care does not exist."

He feels that parole officers are not social service workers, but more like police officers themselves, some of whom use their position as a battering ram to harass kids and earn "brownie" points for their careers.

Spencer Leak Sr. was able to build "One Church, One Inmate," which spread to 15 states, and involves more than 800 ministries that adopt one inmate.

Though he contributed to the design of new jails, many of his suggestions were disregarded.

He provided alarming studies. Prophetically, the reports were precise and on target, but its principles remain ignored, and the prison industry continues to grow at the taxed expense of our race, "sending us back into slavery," Leak Sr., says.

The Paths of the Sons

Spencer Leak Jr., respectfully waits for his dad to finish, then adds, "My father and mother worked as a unit. Dad wasn't there to play baseball and basketball with us because of his intense work schedule. And although dad was not there, we understood the nature of his work, and that constant work was necessary, so that there would be something to pass on."

The Leaks have a reputation of running to the rescue of impoverished families consumed by fires, violence, and neglect, assuring proper services first and dealing with the financials later.

"If you noticed, our old sign has been removed. The new one reads: 'Founded by God in 1933, co-founded by Reverend and Mrs. A.R. Leak.' So, the poor little rich kid syndrome doesn't exist around here. You know God never sleeps and is always on time! We are constantly measured against the highest standards by our Father," says Spencer.

Completing the cycle of support he has been taught to utilize, Spencer Sr. has returned to the industry to extend opportunity for his sons to explore new avenues of education and interest. He has never insisted that his sons be a part of the business, believing that other avenues should always be investigated.

He offers, "I would have loved to have spent more time with my kids, though it's more fun for me now. Still I am proud of the way they have developed.

"Stephen remains politically astute, serving as Assistant to Senator Peter Fitzgerald. Spencer Jr. is a licensed mortician, starting his own family, and embarking into the study of law. My baby, Stacy, film director/producer, recently graduated from Columbia College. But they aren't spoiled little rich kids. A silver spoon doesn't bring the satisfaction of hard work. Especially us. We work 24 hours, 7 days a week.

"With that understanding, our business remains the foundation, no matter what other career or family choices arise. If I need help, the family comes as called, because they recognize that this is the education, foundation that nourishes and respects them. They learned early on, by getting to recognize, reach out, comfort and console families, friends that are bereaved. It is a part of who they are as men today."

Opposite page from left to right, Spencer Jr., Stacy, Spencer Sr., and Stephen Leak

preface Dream Team

Update: Floyd Durr was arrested for Ryan Harris's rape and murder in 1999 and after repeated trial delays, pleaded guilty to the charges in 2006. He received a life sentence, plus 30 years. The families of the accused boys sued the police department and the City of Chicago and won combined settlements of over $8 million. At the civil trial, Detective Allen Nathaniel admitted to never talking to the eight-year-old boy, though the boys allegedly "confessed" to the crime.

Judge R. Eugene Pincham passed away in 2008 at the age of 82. Lew Myers still practices and teaches law, particularly in the areas of civil rights and criminal defense. Berve Power Muhammad is now an attorney, religious scholar and book author with the Nation of Islam.

Shortly after the Harris case, in May 1999, Atty. Andre Grant successfully represented another falsely accused Black youth — a teenager who confessed after police interrogation to fatally stabbing a woman, who it turned out, had never been stabbed at all, but was strangled to death.

Atty. Grant continues his private practice of criminal law in Chicago. He represented the owners of the E2 nightclub tragedy in Chicago in 2003 where 21 people died in a stampede. Both Grant and Myers have taught criminal justice at Chicago State University.

The Legal Dream Team

By Derrick K. Baker & Photography by Reginald Payton | *Originally Published April 1, 1999*

With only a cursory knowledge of the facts surrounding the sensational July 28, 1998 rape and murder of 11-year-old Ryan Harris in the Englewood community, the irony of how four doggedly dedicated defense attorneys successfully opened the lines of communication with the two young boys charged in the homicide is not lost on even the most disinterested person. Not by a long shot.

The team of attorneys – assembled by an energetic young lawyer whose private practice is now growing by leaps and bounds – combined their considerable skill and outrage to demonstrate that murder charges should be dropped against the boys, ages seven and eight.

They did so by cleverly and paradoxically using the fictional Power Rangers live action figures to first ease the fears of the eight-year-old boy who was being questioned by Chicago police after Harris' body was found in a vacant lot.

This was perhaps this system's most wicked moment. It didn't take 10 minutes talking to them to realize these kids didn't have any idea of what all this was about. They basically had been seized by the police.

The sheer irony of it all: The "Dream Team" of attorneys – as they have been dubbed by the public – employed fictional characters to prove that murder charges against the two youngest murder defendants in United States history were equally fictional.

When you meet attorneys Andre Grant, architect of the Dream Team; the renowned former Circuit Court Judge R. Eugene Pincham; hard-driving civil rights attorney Lewis Myers Jr.; and the up-and-coming Berve Power, expect to meet four men whose appearances figuratively will be cloaked in black, green, red and blue – the magical colors of the Power Rangers.

The legal dream team has been lauded far and wide for righting a wrong in the internationally infamous Harris case.

The charges against the boys were abruptly dropped last September – after they had stood accused for al-most a month – when tests revealed semen on Harris' underwear. The specimen was linked to Floyd Durr, who currently is in custody for three attacks on girls in Englewood.

The Team has filed a civil lawsuit on behalf of the eight-year-old, seeking more than $200 million in damages.

The suit alleges that two Chicago police detectives, Allen Nathaniel and James Cassidy, intentionally framed the boys, who had been charged on the strength of their alleged confessions. The Team refers to two other homicides in which Cassidy obtained confessions under questionable circumstances.

Birth of the Power Rangers

Last July, Andre Grant received a phone call from one of his mother's closest friends, the grandmother of the eight-year-old boy who told Grant her grandson was in trouble.

"It really didn't sink in because I thought she had misinformation," Grant recalls. "I went to her home and saw a picture of this kid and it still didn't hit me until the morning when I got to the police station," recalls Grant, the father of a five-year-old son. "I walked back there and I saw this baby – and he's every bit of an eight-year-old – and I said, 'This child didn't do what they're accusing him of.'"

Joined by Atty. Berve Power, Grant met a scared little boy. "When I went into the lockup, this kid was just crying. I was trying to talk to him, but he wouldn't respond," Grant says. "I told him that I was his lawyer and that his grandmother had hired me.

"I asked him if he knew what a lawyer was and he said no. I asked him if he knew who I was and he said yes, 'You're another police.' This kid was looking like my child, so I knew I had to go straight into daddy mode to get to him."

Grant asked the boy if he liked the Power Rangers. "He looked at me kind of strange and that was the first time he really looked at me. He nodded yes.

"I know that boys like Power Rangers and I know that boys have a favorite Power Ranger," continued Grant. The boy told Grant the blue Power Ranger was his favorite. "I said, 'I'm the Blue Power Ranger.

I'm going to fight for you.' That was the first time he stopped crying."

Realizing that not only was the case "bigger than me, it wasn't even about me," Grant says, "I knew I needed firepower" to mount a full frontal assault on what Grant calls "a process that stinks." He reached out to Pincham and Myers, and the Dream Team was formed.

Grant encouraged the boy to decide which Power Ranger each attorney would represent. The coming together of the team "was almost magical" adds Grant, who highly praises his fellow attorneys. "We fought all the time, but when we walked into the courtroom it was one team. We were the Power Rangers."

"There was no physical evidence connecting the boys to the crime. The only thing they had connecting these children to this crime was their so-called confessions, according to a police officer who has a history of taking false confessions and framing children."

In claiming that the boys were framed, Grant notes, "We have bad lawyers, bad judges, bad doctors and bad police officers. This one happens to be an absolutely rotten one." He still cannot fathom the fact that "the officer who framed them, with his motive, his mindset, his sickness, is not under investigation," Grant says.

Grant vigorously derides the law enforcement, family and psychiatric experts who were quick to explain how and why two young kids could commit such a crime. "These children are not from broken families. They're poor, but both parents are in the home," Grant says.

"They had no involvement with the Department of Children and Family Services. The problem is if you begin with the wrong premise, you're going to end up with the wrong conclusion.

"A seven-year-old with a sex drive? It takes determination to assault a woman in such a way. A seven- and eight-year-old can't even clean off the table without leaving traces that they've been there. They can't clean up their room. They're not efficient like that. But you have seven- and eight-year-old kids who have the entire Chicago Police Department baffled? It was garbage from the beginning."

Grant says when he reflects on the case, "My first thought is outrage. I'm just mad as hell. The more we get involved in this case and the more information I get, the more obvious it becomes that these children were framed."

Pincham: The Black Power Ranger

Outspoken and no-holds-barred, former Appellate Court Justice R. Eugene Pincham is a living legend in Chicago's legal community, having distinguished himself as an astute judge, loquacious lecturer, talented trial and appeals attorney and committed community activist.

But when he talks about the Harris case, the terms "animated" and "angry" are apropos in describing his temperament; "apoplectic" even.

When he first heard about the case and before Grant requested his aid, Pincham says, "I said to my wife, 'I hope they don't go out in Englewood and find some mope, an ex-convict, homeless, no family support, with a low IQ, arrest him, question him for 40-50 hours and come out and say he confessed, that he knew things about the case that nobody would know but the murderer.' I was wrong. They arrested two children and said the same thing," starts Pincham.

"What cannot be ignored is the disdain and disrespect that the power structure has demonstrated for and against the Englewood community. First they go out and bring two children into a police station on a Sunday and interrogate these children for seven, eight hours without their parents being present.

"That would never occur in Kenilworth. That would never occur in Highland Park. Yet it occurred in Englewood," says Pincham, who served for 25 years as a trial and appeals attorney in the state and federal courts.

Pincham further argues that police overstated the height and weight of both boys, but "there's no way in the world you can make that kind of mistake accidentally." Given the smaller stature of both boys, "who didn't weigh 100 pounds together," Pincham says they weren't physically able to move Harris' body, which was 5' tall and weighed 103 pounds.

Pincham says, "The girl fought for her life and fought valiantly and it wasn't a seven- or eight-year-old child that did it. That just didn't happen."

Myers: The Green Power Ranger

A noted trial lawyer and civil rights and criminal defense attorney who once represented Black Panther Elmer "Geronimo" Pratt who was wrongly convicted of murder, Myers is revered for his untiring and lifelong fight for justice and equal rights.

That history, coupled with having a 10-year-old son of his own, prompted the Harris case to resonate loudly with the man who has represented the likes of Nation of Islam Minister Louis Farrakhan and Rev. Jesse Jackson.

"The first time I saw these kids was three days after they were arrested," Myers says. "I saw these two young babies surrounded by deputies standing all around, and as you look down you see these tiny children. I was instantly outraged and almost overcome with emotion. When I first saw them, I knew this was perhaps this system's most wicked moment.

"It didn't take 10 minutes talking to them to realize these kids didn't have any idea of what all this was about. I'm looking at those kids and seeing my own baby. At that moment, I realized we had to do everything within our power to free these children. They basically had been seized by the police."

Myers, whose resume includes litigation experience in school desegregation, employment discrimination, police misconduct, and federal communications regulations, laments the fact that the public bought into the notion of the child murderers.

"I know for a fact that most folks thought those little babies actually did it. It was a foregone conclusion," he says. "Nobody was giving them the benefit of the doubt. Even most of the general Black public had said, 'The kids did it.'

"But they had been victimized. The police had played it off like a fait accompli. If you would've read the press, this was a done deal. The only issue is, 'What are we going to do with these little n _ _ _ _ _?'

"But from the first day we got together, minds began to change and the state's case began to crumble right there in front of them."

In an ironic twist, Myers has trained numerous law enforcement officers in the Chicago area. He served as national deputy director and chief operating officer of the national office of the NAACP, and has taught constitutional law and criminal law procedure. He has represented members of the Black Panther Party, Black Liberation Army and Nation of Islam.

Myers says he has "been at this kind of thing for years. I started out in Mississippi in 1972 and was very involved in the civil rights movement, so this is not new, but this case is really to the extreme because of the age of the kids."

Power: The Red Power Ranger

The youngest member of the Dream Team, Berve Power, is benefiting from his role in the high-profile case, and so soon out of law school. The team is grateful for his researching skills, particularly at the onset of the case.

A Morehouse College alumnus, Power finished at the DePaul University College of Law, and after graduating, began practicing with Myers and Grant, as well as in his uncle's law firm, Power & Dixon.

"The reason we fought like we did is that these were very young children and it hurt to see them with no clue as to what was going on. None," Power says.

"This case only enforces what we already know: that African Americans get the short end of the stick when it comes to police officers. Brothers in Chicago know how the police are. We already start from a position of skepticism."

preface Lewis

Update: Karen Lewis has been president of the 30,000-member Chicago Teachers Union since 2010.

Karen Lewis

By Zondra Hughes & Photography by Victor Powell | *Originally Published September 2, 2010*

n this blackboard jungle, Chicago's teachers – especially African-American teachers – are catching spears on all sides.

The culprit of the classroom chaos, Chicago Teachers Union President Karen Lewis argues, is the corporate education model (i.e., crowding classrooms, closing schools, diverting public funds to private schools), which has resulted in massive teacher firings, and the sudden death – as in school turnarounds – of inner-city schools.

Adding fuel to the corporate education model is successful charter schools, such as Urban Prep, which makes national headlines annually after 100 percent of its male graduates successfully enroll in college.

Urban Prep receives funds from the Board of Education and private donations, as it is a non-profit organization. At issue: public funds that charter schools receive comes from that same pool of money that Chicago public schools rely on.

Nonetheless, Urban Prep's success adds weight to the argument that the public-private model works; and the movement to privatize and turnaround poor performing public schools is going strong.

There has been bad blood between the Chicago Teachers Union and the Board of Education before, but never quite like this.

Truthfully speaking, the Chicago Teachers Union and the Board of Education have never really been into playing nice for the cameras. When there was a dispute, John Q. Public knew about it; the on-camera melee would continue for days, as the teachers dubbed the contract negotiations insulting and the Board of Ed dubbed the teachers spoiled.

But the Chicago Teachers Union always has had a hole card – the threat of a teachers' strike – and sooner or later, disputed issues would be resolved.

As ugly as it used to be, those were the good ole days. These are different times, indeed, and the state's record budget crisis has opened old wounds and inflicted new ones.

These days, the Board of Ed and the Mayor have the hole card.

> **I'm absolutely fearless when it comes to certain things. And it's easy to be fearless when you know you're doing the right thing.**

"What John Q. Public doesn't know is that teachers are terrified," says Lewis. "Everyone is afraid. There was a time that if a principal told you something that was pedagogically incorrect, you would stand up, you would say, 'Are you kidding? No, this isn't going to work; this is what works.'"

Lewis continued, "People do not respect our professional judgment. They don't believe that we know what we're doing, so we've got this setup where principals come in and say, 'It's my way or the highway,' and, 'you need to go.'"

One of society's more degrading sentiments about teachers – 'those who can, do; those who can't, teach,' – is very prevalent, Lewis adds. "Think about how people are rewarded; the farther you are from kids, the greater your salary," she says. "And in 'our' culture, you must be smarter or better if you're making more money and that mentality is there."

Lewis argues that this disrespect of teachers is deeply ingrained in the Chicago Public Schools system.

"We have principals who have been in the classroom for less than three years and they get out because now, to stay in the classroom and to have a career in teaching, or to have a passion for teaching, you're looked down upon," she states. "(The assumption is) you must not be any good because if you were, you would have gotten out of the classroom."

Now, it seems the powers-that-be want to kick teachers out of the classroom – especially the experienced Black teachers.

Last June, the Caucus of Rank and File Educators (CORE) filed charges with the Equal Employment Opportunity Commission (EEOC); the complaint was that African-American teachers suffer a disproportionately adverse impact as a result of the school turnarounds.

"Schools that were closed were primarily in African-American, low socio-economic areas," says Lewis. "The majority of (affected) teachers were older African-American women, and they became the poster child of, 'we've got to get rid of these people.'

"We noticed a sharp decrease in the number of African-American teachers over the age of 40, so we filed an EEOC lawsuit. Age 40 is at least 15 years of experience or maybe more, and is a good indicator of people with experience.

"The other thing we noticed was that the age of experience of the average teacher was dropping significantly," Lewis continued. "So, what we see is that the face of the teacher coming into CPS and being thought of as quality does not look like the student in the areas where they are going to teach. We took this, quite frankly, as an attack."

But the conspiracy is even deeper than race; Lewis believes that the teaching profession, as a whole, is being re-figured with career time limits in place.

"The overall plan is to destroy teaching as a career," Lewis states. "The plan quite frankly is for people to come in and work for five or six years, and then leave because this profession is so hard, you can't do it well for 20 or 30 years. So we should be getting in a fresh crop of young, smart people. This is what we're doing now. This is the plan."

A Feisty One

In June 2010, Karen Lewis had a landslide victory in a runoff election over six-year CTU presidential incumbent Marilyn Stewart, by a vote of 12,080 to 8,326. Lewis headed the slate of candidates from the Caucus of Rank and File Educators.

The former King High School chemistry teacher seemed genetically predisposed to take the helm of the $28 million office and lead the fight for its 30,000 members as her parents, Martha and Geoffrey Jennings, were educators.

But meek schoolgirl she was not. Lewis confesses: "I have just always been feisty, even when I was a little kid."

In the second grade, Karen confronted a classmate, smeared paint over his shirt and was kicked out of school. "They put me out and made me go to Kozminski," she laughs. "So I graduated from Kozminski and then I went to Kenwood."

When Lewis' father, who is on the Hall of Fame at Kenwood, came to teach there, Lewis changed schools again. "He came to Kenwood during my junior year, which had a lot to do with me leaving early," she recalls. Lewis completed high school in Massachusetts, and graduated in 1974 from the prestigious Dartmouth College, the only African-American woman in her class.

Lewis didn't initially plan to become a teacher. "I flunked out of medical school, at the U of I," she says. "So my parents said, 'why don't you sub until you figure out what you're going to do?' And I started

subbing until I got my education hours so that I could teach chemistry, because that's what I loved."

After teaching chemistry at King High School for 22 years, Lewis ran for CTU president.

Once in office, Lewis became the blindside. Out of nowhere, she began demanding answers to the uncomfortable questions and she says that once CTU brought up the Tax Increment Financing (TIF) funds, the news headlines changed.

"Right now, the schools are quite entitled to about $250 million in TIFS; they should just have that money. Mayor Daley must have these TIFs declared surplus, and then that money should revert back to the taxing bodies and the agencies, where it should go," Lewis says.

She continues, "So, when that conversation got started, we started talking to parents and community organizations and broadening the base of support about properly funding public education in Chicago, because that's where the problem is."

"The biggest problem is the state is six to eight months behind on paying its bills," Lewis explains. "They owe us at least $260 million, at last count. The Board of Education asked us for $100 million in concessions, but our members voted not to do that. And they did it on the day that Arne Duncan announced that $106 million would be coming to the state to rehire teachers. Not only did they get the $100 million they were asking for, they got $6 million extra. But they don't want to use that."

A few weeks ago, Karen Lewis and her mother had dinner with other retired schoolteachers. It was an occasion that simultaneously made her feel sad about the current plight of Chicago teachers, and emboldened her to put up a good fight.

"We had an interesting conversation about how education has changed and they were quite shocked – they didn't know how the business end of school is going," Lewis reflected. "They had been CPS teachers and extraordinarily proud of their profession, and they are really appalled at how teachers are being vilified."

Bad press has been about the brunt of threats that Lewis has personally received, but she doesn't focus on that. Lewis vows that she will continue to ask those uncomfortable questions and she will continue to represent her members.

"The one thing I can say about myself is that I'm fearless when it comes to certain things," she says. "Absolutely fearless. And it's easy to be fearless when you know you're doing the right thing."

Karen Lewis

preface
Lewis

Update: The jazz legend still performs live and recently released his 80th album.

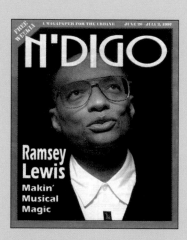

Ramsey Lewis

By Jean A. Williams & Photography by James Hollis | *Originally Published June 19, 1997*

Say what you will about jazz pianist Ramsey Lewis. Over the years, more than a few music critics certainly have. But if you dare speak his name, be prepared to say a mouthful.

After all, if you've got your facts straight, you could be talking for hours about Chicago's native son whose career spans more than four decades, boasts more than 60 albums – five of them gold – and includes three Grammys.

You name the hamlet, he's probably performed in it, bringing him international fame and acclaim. Name the artistic milestone, he's probably reached it. And give back? It seems that nowadays, that concept is built into most of the endeavors he undertakes.

Sure, he's also been dumped on over the years as he went from a true-blue statesman of bona fide jazz to a peddler of more pop-oriented commercial fare, then into a creature baring the fangs of both sides. To be sure, purists, music critics and such have hardly let him live down the success of 1974's *Sun Goddess.*

> We were the darlings of the jazz industry, but then we started to get hit records. The jazz people started to say, 'Whoa, whoa, whoa!'

The title tune – a collaboration with drummer Maurice White of Earth, Wind & Fire fame – and album of the same name went gold and became the impetus of Lewis' decade-plus dance in the mainstream.

Prior to that, he first tasted the pop spotlight as part of his Ramsey Lewis Trio with 1965's *The In Crowd.* That album, his 16th with his trio, was certified gold and earned him his first Grammy.

But it was probably in the mid-'70s and mid-'80s when Lewis turned out his most controversial – read: lightweight – work, such offerings as *Don't It Feel Good* (1975), *Love Notes* (1977), *Routes* (1980) and *Three Piece Suite* (1981).

"The first 17 albums, we were the darlings of the jazz industry, but then we started to get hit records," Lewis says. "And the jazz people started to say, 'Whoa, whoa, whoa! Real jazz artists, you don't have hit records.' So I went through a period where

the critics weren't always kind."

Lewis long ago had his self-reckoning with such times. Today, he remains undaunted by the critical backlash.

"Just so long as they spell the name right," he says wryly. "I long since have learned that everybody has their opinions of what does this taste like, how they liked a play, what they feel about a book. Some of these people are concert reviewers and record reviewers and they must say what they think and feel. And sometimes it agrees with what I think and feel. Sometimes it doesn't."

He does note that, "Fortunately, there have been many more positive critiques and reviews than not."

And at 62, Lewis doesn't seem ready to rest on his laurels – or his thorns. Likely to be a staple of his tomorrows is the state-of-the-art recording studio he owns on North Halsted, where Lewis hopes to make magic for and with other musicians.

Opened in late 1995, his Ivory Pyramid Productions has a deal with Epic Records, which will release projects by its artists. Lewis' son, Frayne, serves as producer and oversaw the logistics of putting the studio together.

Jazz Boy

Jazz is deeply rooted in Lewis' very soul. He was just four when he learned that his parents, Ramsey E. Lewis Sr. and Pauline Richards Lewis, were planning to provide piano lessons for Lewis' oldest sister.

After the determined tot threw a fit for the same privilege, he won lessons, too. That led, in a nutshell, to great things.

In short order, Lewis went on to study piano with Dorothy Mendelsohn at Chicago Musical College, to joining his first band (the Cleffs), to forming his own outfit called the Gentlemen of Swing, predecessors to the Ramsey Lewis Trio.

One of his lifelong jobs has been to bring appreciation for jazz to the masses. The sinewy-built Lewis says that even the unbaptized can become converts.

"If you're a young person and you can get into nightclubs, I would suggest starting to listen there and going to concerts," he says. 'But even before

that, you may want to go to a library with the names of some artists that you've heard about or somebody's told you about, and you can not only read about Duke Ellington, or read about Charlie Parker, but you can go on the next floor, especially in Chicago, and pull the CD out."

The tepid reception of jazz, not just by African Americans, but by the record-buying public, is something that Lewis has done his part to obliterate, even if on the surface it's not what he exactly set out to accomplish.

Sometimes it's just a byproduct of what he does. For instance, his radio program *The Legends of Jazz With Ramsey Lewis* is syndicated nationally.

"Now, there's an educational tool," Lewis says, matter of factly. "I mean, we're not about the business of education, but (we) play the music of the legends. We also play the music of what we refer to as the young lions under age 50 who are carrying on the tradition of the legends and masters."

Then there's his relationship with the Jazz at Ravinia Festival. In 1993, Lewis became artistic director of the Ravinia Park program, an undertaking he continues to this day. From the beginning, Lewis, who is married to business partner Janet and the father of seven children from a previous 35-year marriage, saw his position as an avenue to involve young people in jazz.

One way he gets to do that is by helping administer the Ravinia Mentor Program, which cultivates jazz in city high schools. Also, for over a decade, he has served on the board of Merit, an inner-city music program.

The prolific Lewis appears regularly on BET's *Jazz Central* program and last month released *Urban Nights II*, all-new material on the GRP label. And as is typical of the summer for him, he has been quite itinerant, traveling to play dates nationally and internationally.

"I'm pretty much doing what I want to do," he says. "I want more of it. I want to write more music. I want to have more time to practice the piano."

As successful as he has been, it is hard for him to pinpoint the biggest accomplishment of his storied career, however.

"I don't look at things anymore as biggest," he says. "It's a lot of fun and it's very gratifying to set out to do something and it becomes a reality. And when it becomes a reality, hopefully, you've enjoyed the journey to getting it done."

preface Mac

Update: He actually did get his own network sitcom called *The Bernie Mac Show*, which ran on FOX from 2001 to 2006. Sadly, at the height of his fame, Bernie died in 2008 at the age of 50 from sarcoidosis.

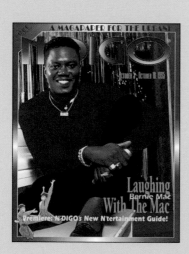

Bernie Mac

By Cheryl Jenkins Richardson & Photography by Paul Mainor | *Originally Published October 5, 1995*

Laughter is indeed healthy. Whether it's derived from pleasure or pain, there is something genuine, something calming, about laughter.

Enter Bernard Jeffery McCullough, better known as Bernie Mac, the Chicago comic who truly has a style all his own, a talent who is quite unpredictable.

Recently, Mac took a few moments from his busy schedule to share his dreams and accomplishments at the place where it all began for him – The Cotton Club on 17th and Michigan.

Sitting across from me, his eyes glistened like a kid who's about to open a Christmas present. When Bernie Mac speaks, you sense the sincerity, the honesty, the openness. You definitely feel the spirituality.

But you'll always feel the laughter. Bernie Mac is what he was destined to be. Comedy is his calling.

Anxiously, as we begin, he points to the spot where the last-minute jokes were pulled together. But first, he starts with his humble beginnings growing up in the Englewood neighborhood on Chicago's South Side.

"I knew I was going to be an entertainer," Mac said. "When I was a kid, everybody would come over to my porch and watch *The Bernie Mac Show*."

Described as almost a vaudeville revue, HBO will air *Midnight Mac*, Fridays (at midnight, of course) throughout the month of October. It will showcase up and coming talent, including celebrity guests and Bernie's very own dancers, the Macaronis.

With a guest roster including stars such as Chicago's own Chaka Kahn, Sheila E., George Duke, Brownstone and Brian McKnight, the future looks very bright for this new half-hour variety show. Mac insists, "These talented local professionals are going to make the celebrity guests work."

> **Comedy pimpslapped him in the face at an early age.**

Sitcom And Stand-up Comics

Host of the tour version of *Def Comedy Jam*, Bernie Mac paid his dues on the road, listing Redd Foxx, Richard Pryor, Bill Cosby, George Carlin, Eddie Murphy and many others as early influences. He also paid homage to the older comedians.

"Red Skelton was so funny he would laugh at his own stuff," Mac says, laughing himself. "He'd laugh so much, he couldn't get the joke out. Jack Benny was also funny to me. He was witty and smooth."

"I take my comedy very seriously and I don't just come out to get paid. I'm not coming out there to be a star," he contends. "I'm coming out there to make you laugh."

As I sat there listening to him talk about the trials by fire it takes to make it in stand-up, I wondered what it must feel like when you bomb.

"If I go out and have a bad night, it goes with the territory," Mac said. "Doctors lose patients, police shoot the wrong people, Michael Jordan has missed a dunk, Walter Payton has fumbled the football. It happens to the best."

Perhaps it's a '90s trend, but it does seem that many comics engage in "attack comedy" – playing the "dozens" and heckling the audience to have a laugh at an audience member's expense. Bernie was quick to defend his particular methods of audience interaction.

"I'm an entertainer. I'm not here to intimidate the audience and I'm not here to talk about their families or talk about their clothes," he said. "People are not paying good money to be insulted."

Early Years

The 37-year-old actor/comedian says comedy pimp-slapped him in the face at an early age.

"I would do anything to make you laugh," he says smiling. "I didn't have any shame when it came to comedy. I didn't mind falling on the floor and making faces. A lot of guys are funny, but they're cool. I didn't care. I just wanted to make you laugh."

Mac has been performing professionally since 1977. He cut his teeth at local clubs like Zanies, The Improv and All Jokes Aside. Noting that Black comedy clubs were rare or non-existent when he started, Bernie said he nonetheless learned the rules of the road to comedy early on.

"You don't run over another comie's time," he said. "That's one thing the White clubs taught me, comedy ethics."

By the time Bernie got his first gig at the Cotton Club, he was penniless and had to borrow a suit from his brother.

"He just opened up his closet door and pointed. And you know he wasn't pointing at the good stuff," Bernie laughs. "So, I don't need to tell you how I was dressed or how I looked. I can only say I hoped my jokes were good."

Mac Attack

I was curious about the way some of his humor appears based on painful experiences. Looking away, Bernie told me of a relative who didn't think he was very funny at all.

"I remember an aunt of mine who never laughed, never smiled," he recalled. "I would perform for the family every once in a while and the first time I made her laugh it was like – an honor. The whole family was thrilled and in-between those laughs, they were embracing one another. My aunt was crying and laughing. She laughed so hard, she was ashamed.

"You bring out the best with laughter," he said, "even when there's nothing to laugh about."

And Mac knows that all too well. By the time he became a young man, he had already lost his parents and three brothers.

Another sensitive issue had to do with his dark-skinned complexion, which had plagued him during his growing years.

"My complexion wasn't happening in the '60s and '70s," Bernie noted. "I was the darkest guy in my neighborhood. I've heard every dark-skinned joke there is. It tore me up as a small boy. I had a complex."

"But I grew out of that complex when I was a sophomore in high school. Then all of a sudden, it just hit me – the hell with it! And I went on with my life."

Coming Full Circle

In spite of the ups and downs of the path he's chosen, there are two things that he has been able to maintain. He has so far kept a stable family life, recently celebrating his 20th wedding anniversary with his wife, Rhonda.

He has also been able to happily witness his daughter Je'niece graduate after her junior year in high school. Currently, she's beginning her freshman year in college.

Another, and certainly not the least factor in his success, is holding onto a spiritual base – the driving force that he feels enabled him to accomplish his dreams.

"I know it's right and I truly know what my role is.

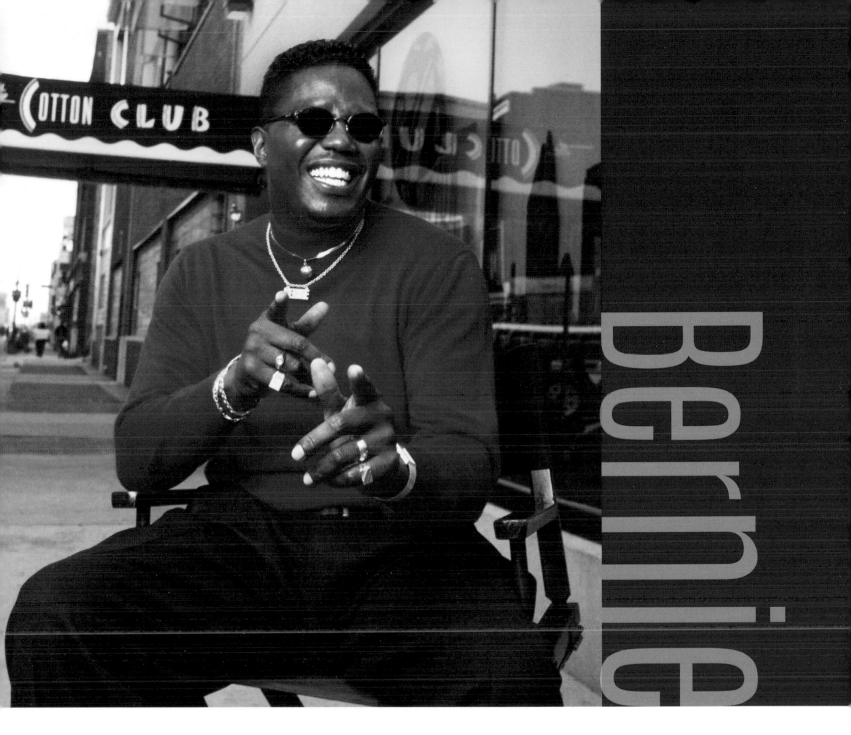

I know God's will. I know that He is real," a somber Bernie declared.

As a veteran of films such as *Mo' Money, Walking Dead,* and the Ice Cube-directed *Friday,* Mac seems confident about finding his place on television.

"I shot a TV pilot called *Pearl's Kitchen* sometime in 1994, a potential sitcom and I'm kinda glad that it never hit the air," he admits. "It wasn't what I wanted; it was diluted and I found out that I was just an actor with no real control."

"I really like shows like *Living Single,*" he emphasized. "It has range and they show a lot of independence. I like that."

Back To Basics

While sitcoms with stand-up comedians are currently all the rage, Mac is betting with HBO that variety shows aren't dead yet. Having *Midnight Mac* originate in Chicago gives him a chance to promote new talent, which is one way he feels that he's giving back to the community.

"I'm tired of hearing about how Black comics can't get on Jay Leno, how they can't get on David Letterman. They will be able to get on my show," Bernie vowed.

As for those Macaronis, I wanted to know how showcasing them would compare to current music videos.

"Every video I see, there's people pumping the air. I wish I could find out what's in that air. I'm afraid to try it. I might get happy. When you get through watching two or three music videos with people gyrating all over the place, you need a cigarette," Mac cracked.

About the role he thought comedy plays in the world today, Mac stated, "I think comedy is important because it cleanses the heart. I want to be the best at what I do, not for personal selfish reasons, but because I have pride. I'm a comedian. I want to bring you joy, I want to see you laugh until tears come out of your eyes."

preface
Madhubuti

Update: In 1998, the Madhubutis established the Betty Shabazz International Charter School, an African-centered network of charter schools comprised of three Chicago campuses : the Betty Shabazz Academy (grades K-8); Barbara Sizemore Academy (grades K-8); and the DuSable Leadership Academy (grades 9-12). The schools instill self-confidence and a strong sense of cultural identity in its students.

Haki & Safisha Madhubuti

By Barbara Kensey & Photography by John Beckett | *Originally Published March 14, 2002*

When you talk about education, literacy, institution building, creation, and the liberation struggle in any kind of serious way – inevitably the names of Haki and Safisha Madhubuti come up.

"Our philosophy," says Haki, "is built on the philosophy of Marcus Garvey, Malcolm X, Elijah Muhammad, Mary McLeod Bethune – people of African descent who decided that we were going to create something. Not only individually, but collectively, so that an institution could come about."

His comrade-in-arms, Safisha, declares, "An educational system that is going to be of the utmost benefit to African Americans, in particular, has to be grounded in ideas that come out of our experience, and therefore we always espoused an African-centered education."

Educators, intellectuals, activists, they represent the best of the good that came out of the 1960s. Well-educated, both formally and informally, in spite of their stints in the Chicago public school system ("We survived it," Safisha says), they are living examples of the principles advocated by their hero/ines – which just happen to also be the principles of Kwanzaa.

Purpose, Unity, Creativity, Self-Determination, Collective Work and Responsibility, and Faith perfectly illustrate their vision and their lives.

Widely known as a writer, educator, lecturer, and the founder and publisher of *Third World Press*, Haki carved his niche in cement as early as 1966 with the publication of his first book of poetry, *Think Black*.

Since then he has authored 18 books, of which the latest *Black Men: Obsolete, Single, Dangerous? The Afrikan American Family in Transition* (1990) has sold more than 100,000 copies. The 1991 recipient of the American Book Award, he is one of the world's bestselling authors of poetry and nonfiction.

In demand internationally as a lecturer, workshop leader, and speaker, at home in Chicago he is the former professor of English and director of the Gwendolyn Brooks Center at Chicago State University, which afforded him the privilege of his extensive travels.

Safisha (the former Carol Easton) is an educator, lecturer, scholar, and co-founder of New Concept Development Center, a fully accredited primary and elementary school located at 7822 South Dobson in a former Catholic school they purchased from the Archdiocese. The school and the adjacent church rectory were purchased with money raised independent of any public or private funding institutions.

The recipient of numerous academic honors, she is widely published and holds a Ph.D. in Education (Curriculum and Instruction) from the University of Chicago, making her Dr. Safisha. Her dissertation was "Signifying as a Scaffold for Literary Interpretation: The Pedagogical Implications of an African American Discourse Genre."

She is assistant professor in the School of Education and Social Policy at Northwestern University. Together, they are a powerful force to be seriously reckoned with.

Humble Beginnings

Both products of humble beginnings – he lived in a tenement, she lived in the projects – neither has to think long or hard to tell you where they're coming from.

When he was about 16 years old, Haki, then Don L. Lee and recently orphaned, said he asked himself three questions, "Why am I so poor?" "Why was my education so deficient?" and "What do conscious people do about that?" The answer became his hallmark. "I felt if we were to survive and to develop in this country, we would have to be institution-based."

> **What we are concerned about is how do we begin to decide our own fate, decide our own destiny.**

And so, armed with Nguzo Saba and the inspiration of Dudley Randall of Broadside Press in Detroit, and Dr. Margaret and Charles Burroughs of the DuSable Museum of African American History, in 1967 Haki founded *Third World Press* in his basement apartment on South Ada Street. He was aided by Johari Amini (Jewel Latimore) and Carolyn Rodgers, two poets of note.

Today, *Third World Press* is the nation's oldest continuously operating Black-owned and managed press, publishing books in all genres. Over 80 titles have been published to date, and with the recent move to the church rectory, *Third World Press* has space to spare for the production, publishing, and shipment of thousands of progressive Black books worldwide.

In 1969, he founded the Institute of Positive Education (IPE), a community-based nonprofit organization, followed in 1972 by the birth of New Concept Development Center. The children's educational wing of IPE, New Concept, began life as a Saturday school for cultural enrichment. In 1974, it became the New Concept School, a pre-school servicing children ages two and a half to five years old.

One of the people who mentored Haki in the early days, Dr. Anderson Thompson, associate professor of African American Studies at Northeastern Illinois University, remembers him as "the prime mover

in our movement."

Thompson says, "He was at the center of the Move- ment. His poems were a moving force that really transformed some of our people. He actually took the perm out of some women's hair! The man has been phenomenal in his principled struggle for liberation."

Joining him in the struggle is his companion of decades. "A brilliant woman," Haki proclaims, pointing out that Safisha already had her Master's degree when they met when he came to speak at the high school where she was teaching. Her thesis had been on the subject of the Black Arts Movement that included his writings.

Married in 1974, they took their vows in the community and remain wedded to the community. It was their work that brought them together, and to a large extent, their work has kept them together.

Safisha has been a teacher throughout her career, beginning in the English Department of Englewood High. As Program Director of New Concept Development Center (NCDC), the institution she co-founded, her commitment is to the liberation of young minds, work that seems to give her great joy.

As an educator she maintains that, "if you can reach children when they're very young and instill in them the pride of being Black, a knowledge of their history and culture, and train them to be critical thinkers, they will look at the world through very different eyes from children who don't have early childhood education.

"One of the things Haki has often said and I think is very much behind what we're trying to do in terms of developing educational institutions, is that ideas run the world, and that our history provides visions for us of what can be."

That thinking has led to the institutionalizing of New Concept, a spacious, bright school – almost like any other school with its blackboards displaying the day's lessons in chalk, its rows of orderly desks and bulletin boards proudly displaying pupil's works, and books.

But there's something different about this school that's apparent just from reading the inside cover of the school's brochure. About the NCDC Philosophy of Education, it reads: "Like Kwame Nkrumah, NCDC believes that 'Knowledge without purpose is blind.' The NCDC curriculum stresses critical thinking, problem solving and application of knowledge in everyday experiences."

It's also apparent in the teacher-student relationship. Here, students refer to all women as Mama, as in "Mama Safisha," and all men are called Baba, the Swahili word for father. Such association, she contends, casts the relationship differently, as one of family rather than just teacher/student.

Creating And Educating

As creators, three of the Madhubutis' proudest creations are their children Laini Nzinga, Bomani Garvey, and Akili Malcolm. When not working or with family, they enjoy a solitary lifestyle, rarely attending receptions or cocktail parties.

For the past 40 years, Haki has been a strict vegetarian, and raised the children with the same diet during their formative years. Occasionally Safisha and the children eat fish and chicken. "We cannot be dogmatic," Haki says. "We do what we feel comfortable in doing."

Although they do not claim a relationship with organized religion, they are spiritual people. "I truly believe there is a supreme force, but I cannot define that force," Haki says. "As far as I'm concerned, what is being said is 'be good, do good work, humble yourself, recognize the life force that goes through all human beings and respect that.'"

It has been 50 years since Haki carried *Third World Press* in his briefcase, selling his books on the road. "I learned from Langston Hughes and Arna Bontemps," he says. The questions he posed to himself at age 16 have resulted in major, significant institutions that impact the lives of millions, and place the Madhubutis in the unique position of being African Americans who are successfully producing, packaging, marketing, distributing knowledge and educating.

Through hard work and dedication and the principles of Kwanzaa, their liberation dreams are coming true. And all of that because in Haki's words, "What we are concerned about is how do we begin to decide our own fate, decide our own destiny?"

preface The McKeevers

Update: Nancy McKeever is a retired Chicago public school teacher, socialite, board president of eta Creative Arts Foundation and on an affiliate board of the Art Institute. Susan has her private law practice handling trusts, wills and estate planning matters. She has served on the boards of the Chicago Police Department, Muntu Dance Theater and WBEZ radio. Steve is still at the helm of his expanded company, Hidden Beach Experiences.

A board director of the Chicago Urban League and People's Energy Corporation, Lester McKeever has a street named after him outside of the deluxe Oglesby Towers apartment high-rise on the South Side that the McKeevers owned and lived in for 40 years. Lester also has an annual award given in his name by the 24,000-member Illinois CPA Association to exceptional leaders who contribute to advancing diversity in the accounting profession.

The McKeevers

By Mark Ruffin & Photography by Victor Powell | *Originally Published September 18, 2003*

Despite the success of his two children, Lester McKeever could never write a how-to book on parenting. Accounting, tax law, the operation of the Federal Reserve and harness racing, maybe, but not child rearing.

"I was just blessed," is the easy answer for the self-effacing man in talking about the accomplishments of his son and daughter, Steve and Susan.

"It was through the good graces of God that to begin with, we had children who didn't give us any problems, and who took the stress off in other areas of experience. But I truly don't know the one key in having successful children."

Lester McKeever is a giant among CPAs in the United States. Starting as a staff accountant in 1959, he has risen to the title of Managing Principal as a partner in the influential Black firm Washington, Pittman & McKeever.

The number of committees, boards, commissions, and prominent memberships that McKeever has been involved with to better our community are numerous, and includes serving on the Finance Committee for the transition teams of both Mayors Harold Washington and Richard M. Daley.

> "You've got to have a strong marital foundation to succeed as a family. We had both hoped to be true role models and disciplinarians of our children, but I truly don't know the one key in having successful children."

McKeever is also one of the leading African Americans involved in horse racing in Illinois, devoting time as board member or chairman of four leading associations in the industry.

For three years, from 1997-99, McKeever was the Chairman of the Board of Directors of the Federal Reserve Bank of Chicago. In the world of finance, being coached by Fed chairman Alan Greenspan is the equivalent of making the all-star team in professional sports.

On the surface it looks like both of his children didn't follow in his footsteps. Susan is a former professional theatrical dancer who now is a lawyer specializing in family estate planning. Steve is the founder and CEO of Hidden Beach Recordings, one of the hottest record companies in America, and home to top acts like Jill Scott, Kindred the Family Soul, and the Unwrapped All-Stars.

The common professional denominator among the three is that all are lawyers. In separate conversations though, the trio concurred that professionally, socially, emotionally and spiritually, the biggest unifying and most influential factor in their lives is the silent partner of the family – wife and mother, Nancy McKeever.

"My wife was very strong in regard to molding the children," McKeever said of his life partner of over 45 years. "You've got to have a strong marital foundation to succeed as a family. We had both hoped to be true role models and disciplinarians of our children, and she has always taken the lead.

"But nothing ever happens without the support and blessing of many, many others," he continued. "Susan and Steve were also influenced tremendously by good teachers, friends, and we've even had some babysitters in their lives that were truly good."

"My parents were good brainwashers," the ridiculously busy record exec, Steve, said by phone from his office in Santa Monica, California.

"We grew up at a very early age knowing that higher education wasn't an option. It was a mandate. We didn't have a choice. We always were led to believe that choices in life started once you got out of grad school with your advanced degree."

"Both my wife and I were very strong on education," agreed the elder McKeever. "An advanced degree was the minimum, after that we told them they could do whatever they wanted. But the advanced degrees that we saw for them wasn't very exciting for my daughter at all."

The Baby Girl

Susan McKeever still isn't sure what she wants to be when she grows up.

"When I was about eight, I thought I was going to be a judge or some kind of international diplomat," Susan explains. "Then I was really interested in being a pediatrician, until I took chemistry in high school.

Steve McKeever

Susan was in the second class of girls who entered St. Ignatius Prep School in the early 1980s. She loved to dance, and had a predilection for languages, particularly French, when she entered Amherst College in Massachusetts.

After studying for a year at the University of Dakar in Senegal, West Africa, the youngest McKeever graduated with honors and a degree in political science and French.

"On the day of her graduation," her father remembers, "she said, 'All you think about is an MBA or a law degree. There's got to be something more to life than that, so I'm going to New York.'

"We didn't know until that day that she wanted to be a dancer," McKeever said laughing. "I knew she'd come around eventually; I just didn't think it would be seven years later. I did learn you have to let them find their own way."

"In law school, I told my husband I was going to go to medical school when I was 40," Susan chuckled because that mark has since passed. "Now with three kids, I've tabled that. My mother said I've been asking myself what I was going to do with my life since I was in the third grade.

"Today, I tell young people they don't have to pick one thing and do it for 60 years straight. No matter what I do, though, it will be working toward making a good contribution to the development of my children and my community.

"Steve is the only person I know who has known exactly what he wanted to do from day one, and has

continued on the exact same path the whole time," Susan continued.

The Musical Son

"Steve did always know what he wanted to do," his father concurred. "Now that he has his own successful business, I really admire him for his own understanding of who he is, what he wanted, and what he had to do for it to materialize.

"Even when he was very young and playing the cello and the piano, he showed that he was going to be in the music business somehow. We didn't know how, but he knew all the time."

Steve first graduated from U of I and then went to Harvard Law School. From there it was on to practicing entertainment law in California before being hired as head of West Coast Business Affairs for Polygram Records. While there, he brought homeboy Robin Harris to the label and produced the late comedian's best-selling album, Bebe's Kids.

Steve then joined Motown as general manager and Senior VP of Artists & Repertoire. Among the artists he signed were Queen Latifah and Shanice. He also had the company diversify, including into the jazz area with the MoJazz label, which introduced the world to smooth jazz guitarist Norman Brown.

Steve helped oversee the sale of Motown, and by the time his five-year contract was up, the company's gross receipts more than doubled, from less than $50 million to $125 million.

At the turn of this century, Steve McKeever achieved his dream by starting his own record company, Hidden Beach. "I'm extremely pleased with the mark and the brand," he said of his growing company. "It is beginning to be really recognized that Hidden Beach means quality, and that really was the ultimate goal. It is that highest level of quality and those same kinds of standards that Susan and I were challenged by our parents to meet growing up."

Lester, The Patriarch

"What did my father say?" Susan wanted to know when asked if her father had mentioned that she was a rebel. "In the context of family, they couldn't have seen me as a rebel because both my parents were rebels."

"To some extent, I agree," Steve added. "I remember in grade school, my mother, who was a lifelong educator, would rip my school books to shreds about what was accurate. I knew in first and second grade that Thomas Jefferson had slaves and so did George Washington.

"I knew that Lincoln wasn't the benevolent African-American loving president who saved the Union. She would tell us really, really young, 'Don't believe this stuff – there are other sides of the story.' They both were incredible trailblazers and unbelievable role models."

There's no question that like his wife, there's a fiery, rebellious side fueled by Black pride in Lester McKeever. Born in Chicago to a mother and father from Georgia and New Jersey respectively, Lester was the first person in his family to graduate from high school. "To my parents, graduating from college was frosting on the cake," he says.

A member of the Wendell Phillips High School Hall of Fame, he went to the school at a time when it was famous for the musicians who attended. Lester pointed out that the academic prowess of the students there was also formidable and many were just as accomplished, but weren't as recognized as their more flamboyant classmates.

The first two years of his higher education were at the University of Illinois when the campus was at Navy Pier in Chicago, and he finished in the very racist Southern Illinois atmosphere of Champaign/Urbana.

Among the indignities Black students suffered was the inability to get their hair cut on campus. McKeever helped organize protests to change the practice, but the close-minded barbers fought back and issued signs in their windows that read, "We do not cut kinky, wooly, or nappy hair regardless of race, color, or creed," McKeever says.

"The whole environment was racist, but it was not a terrible, terrible experience for me because we did fight to try and change things, and the school did show signs of support.

"In fact, I admired the business school at U of I because major accounting firms wouldn't even give African Americans an interview, but U of I insisted that (accounting firm) Arthur Andersen grant me an interview, which they did. But they said they couldn't hire me because their clients would never accept me."

After graduating with a degree in accounting, he came home to work as an accounting supervisor for the Black company, Unity Mutual Life Insurance. He got married and started at the firm he now has full partnership in, which was founded in the '50s by namesake Mary Washington, the first female African-American certified public accountant in the United States.

Nancy, The Matriarch

Nancy McKeever went to Chicago Teachers College, where, among her other extra-curricular activities, she wrote a jazz column for the student newspaper.

While neither parent is an artist, the fact that both of their children are can be squarely blamed on mom. She was the one who exposed them to painting, sculpture, dance, literature, and music.

She taught her children through direct life and academic lessons, but also by example. She instituted three main ingredients into the McKeever family equation that Lester, Steve, and Susan said was a very big part of their growth – travel, spirituality, and community involvement.

"And it wasn't just for our benefit," Susan said. "At the top of my parents' whole notion of service is that you've got to be helping people. My mother did a lot of tangible things for me to see, like taking kids on vacation who may have otherwise never left Chicago. It wasn't like she had money or anything, but she kind of finagled her way."

As a teacher at Carter Woodson elementary school, Nancy tirelessly raised money through bake sales, pancake breakfasts and the like to take her third grade class and her own children on a trip every year. Steve remembers going to Texas, California, Colorado and Canada.

"That the world was a lot bigger than the world we were walking around in was a valuable lesson she wanted us to learn early," Steve says.

Every summer the family went somewhere together. Susan remembered seeing her first opera in Italy around the age of 10, and later being the family interpreter as they toured French-speaking African countries.

"It's amazing what that kind of exposure can do," Susan noted. "But it wasn't just the growth in seeing the world, it was also bonding time for us. It was a strong time to be with my parents – they weren't working, we're not in school, and you have all these things to talk about. Even if the trip wasn't that great, it just gave us a good time to grow together."

Right page:
Lester, Nancy and
Susan McKeever

preface
McSween

Update: Chicagoan Cirilo McSween passed away on November 5, 2008, one day after another Chicagoan, Barack Obama, became the first Black President of the United States. McSween ended up owning 11 McDonald's restaurants and won the Ronald McDonald Award and Golden Arch Award twice each, a feat no one else accomplished before him.

Cirilo McSween

By Derrick K. Baker & Photography by David Jenkins | *Originally Published April, 1991*

f you were to survey his friends, business associates, customers and even his competitors, the consensus would surely be that native West Indian Panamanian Cirilo McSween is an amalgam, one that includes many admirable attributes, not the least of which are successful and conscientious.

McSween is a former collegiate and Olympic track star, life insurance salesman extraordinaire, civil rights activist, banking bigwig and currently owner/operator of four McDonald's franchises in downtown Chicago.

He is a man of many firsts, including:

- the first Black person to own and operate a business on State Street in downtown Chicago;

- the first McDonald's franchisee in company history to sell $3 million in Big Macs, french fries and milk shakes in one year;

- the first Black sales agent for New York Life Insurance Company;

- the first African American to sell $1 million worth of life insurance in one calendar year;

- and the first McDonald's franchisee in the Midwest to operate in a museum – at Chicago's Field Museum of Natural History.

From his tastefully appointed office on east Jackson Boulevard, McSween calls the shots for his four uniquely decorated McDonald's franchises located at 230 South State, 64 East Jackson, the Field Museum of Natural History, and 311 South Wacker. He employs about 350 people and is known – and applauded – for the eye-catching and sometimes controversial motifs at each location.

The Foursome

Patrons at his McDonald's at 311 South Wacker Drive are treated to a mural and photographs featuring more than 100 legends in jazz history, as well as giants in rhythm and blues, rock and roll and jazz. The likes of Duke Ellington, Billie Holliday, Frank Sinatra, Sarah Vaughan, Bing Crosby, Stevie Wonder, Barbara Streisand, Elvis Presley and Quincy Jones, among others, adorn the restaurant's walls.

Visit his first restaurant at 230 South State, and you'll find a spin-off of the United Nations' "Year of the Child" theme with the faces of youth of all races and ethnic backgrounds gracing the walls, along with photos from the Civil Rights Movement and a history of Chicago mural.

The décor of McSween's McDonald's located on the first level of the Field Museum of Natural History features images of underwater and environmental scenes, marble counters and imported Italian tile floors.

Finally, stop by the East Jackson Boulevard franchise located a stone's throw from McSween's office and you will be treated to an exhibition of international sports heroes, more Civil Rights photos and Panamanian Indian textiles.

And if the restaurants' murals aren't enough to divert attention away from your filet of fish sandwich, copies of UCLA basketball coach John Wooden's *Pyramid of Success* are displayed at each McDonald's to give customers an injection of motivation.

What do his customers think of McSween's McDonald's motifs? "The one that people like the best is at Jackson and Wabash. It gives recognition to Blacks; it gives recognition to Indians, too. It gives recognition to everybody who has earned recognition and a place in history," he explains.

"I have really made it a point to exhibit racial harmony in my restaurants. We have made statements about where we are and we continue to make these statements. We have made statements that other McDonald's have not. I think we ought to say 'thank you' to people who have done great as a people."

Before McDonald's

McSween's approach to operating his franchises was shaped in a major way by his outstanding record as a track star. He also credits his prosperity as a fast food franchisee to more than 20 years of service as the first Black life insurance salesman for a major insurer – New York Life Insurance Company.

McSween's introduction to the multi-billion-dollar life insurance business resulted from his stature as the then Big Ten record holder in the quarter-mile run on two curves during his years at the University of Illinois in the mid-1950s. He also distinguished himself by representing Panama at the 1950 Central American and Caribbean Olympics, Bolivian Games, 1950 Pan American Games and as a member of Panama's 1952 Olympic Team.

"When we were through with college, most of the successful athletes at the University of Illinois would sell some life insurance on campus, and I thought of doing the same," McSween said. However, in one of his earliest introductions to racism American style, McSween was advised that Black people didn't represent White insurance companies or large insurance companies at the time.

"When I realized that that was true, I wanted to know why, and that's what threw me into that career. I was at a university in which I was one of the best students there was in terms of my overall activities," says the former finance major. "I didn't think it was okay for me to not be able to do as well in anything that other students had a chance to do."

> When I was growing up, we were poor, but we didn't feel like that because we had goals. People talked to you and you didn't feel trapped.

Therefore, in 1957, McSween moved to Chicago and hit the insurance ground running as a commission-only agent, without the benefit of any formal training in writing insurance.

Not awed by the prospect of asking total strangers to buy a product he was selling, McSween's target market was unlimited. "If a person was alive, I'd try to sell them insurance. I went to fire stations and anywhere else you could name," he says.

As he began to develop a rapport with existing and prospective clients, McSween began to entertain the idea that in his first year he could be the first African American to sell $1 million in life insurance. "I didn't plan it, but I thought it could be possible," he says.

Sure enough, he reached the lofty goal and says his accomplishment "started to change the minds of some insurance people. Before then, it was widely thought that Blacks could never reach that point – even with Black companies. Blacks also had a mental block that we couldn't do it."

McSween became so successful at his new career that he sold $1 million worth of insurance in one month and then went on to sell $2 million. "I was still only dealing with Black people then," he says.

So lucrative was his insurance career that in 1965 he opened McSween Insurance Counselors and Brokers and continued to make a name – and pretty penny – for himself. Moreover, he sold at least $1 million worth of life insurance every year for 28 consecutive years, becoming a Life Member of the Million Dollar Roundtable and the first Black to do so.

What Next?

With a formidable insurance track record to his credit and firm financial footing, McSween collaborated with a group of businessmen and invested in McDonald's. But when the rules changed and simply investing in a franchise was prohibited unless you also operated the outlet, McSween dissolved his interest and "proposed to have one of my own."

With the stage set for his foray into franchising, he acquired the first McDonald's restaurant on South State Street, thereby becoming the first Black person to own a business on that nationally-known thoroughfare.

"I thought it was an opportunity to make a statement. I knew it was a good investment," he says. That investment later paid off to the tune of $3 million in sales for one year, exceeding McSween's expectations and making his the first McDonald's franchise to reach that peak.

In 1984, the corporation named him recipient of its highest honor – The Golden Arch Award, which is presented to five owner/operators worldwide every two years. McSween was also presented with the 1981 Ronald McDonald Award for exemplary contributions to fostering the positive image of McDonald's restaurants in the Midwest.

Cirilo changed McDonald's. He founded the Black McDonald's Association, insisted that there be Black members on McDonald's board, and influenced the corporate structure to hire Black executives.

The Moral McSween

One of the most important and influential people in McSween's life was the Rev. Dr. Martin Luther King Jr. McSween can call himself a true friend of the late civil rights martyr. He served as national treasurer and board member of the Southern Christian Leadership Council during King's presidency and, like many of King's numerous supporters, was there when the going got tough.

"When you were with Martin, you knew the church might blow up, but nobody left to go home. If he called a meeting at two or three in the morning, everyone would be present and accounted for, and we all knew the church might blow up," McSween says. "Martin was free and committed to the freedom of others in a sense that was pure and beyond reproach. Martin's preachings left you spellbound in an irreplaceable way."

McSween's respect for King went beyond showing up at meetings. They were close enough that McSween served as a pallbearer at King's funeral. "Martin taught me that you can be financially successful and be committed to the dignity of man. If I hadn't met Martin, I wouldn't have taken the risks I've taken," says McSween, who also served as chairman of the National

Executive Oversight Committee during Rev. Jesse Jackson's 1988 presidential campaign and provided years of financial leadership for Operation PUSH.

Having developed an even greater sensitivity for the less fortunate as a result of his work in the Civil Rights Movement and his own meager upbringing, McSween has a deep understanding of and commiseration for the plight of the poor.

"Poverty is a situation where your attitude is different," McSween says. "When I was growing up, we were poor, but we didn't feel like that because we had goals. People talked to you and you didn't feel trapped. But now poor people have absolutely no options. They see crime all the time. No one speaks to them without shouting. After a while, everyone around you has been to jail; you're isolated and lonely, and a standard of accomplishment is not available."

What does a man whose previous affiliations include serving as president of the Black McDonald's Owner/Operators Association, board member of the Martin Luther King Jr. Center for Nonviolent Social Change, board member of the Chicago Urban League and national coordinator of the Panama Task Force, organized for the sole purpose of ratifying the Panama Canal Treaty, have in mind for the future?

"I don't have visions of retirement. My lifestyle is such that that's not part of my plan. I see myself working to the conclusion of my life. I would not change my personal life and the way I've lived it," McSween says.

"I could not have asked for any nobler experiences than the ones I've had in my world. They exceed anything that I would have dreamed of. I'm satisfied with my life."

preface Meeks

Update: Today, Salem Baptist is one of the fastest growing megachurches in the United States and the largest African-American church in Illinois with over 15,000 members.

In 2005, Pastor Meeks led Salem in the building of the church's current edifice House of Hope. Located at 752 East 114th Street, it is a $50 million, 10,000-seat community and worship center that is the largest facility in the United States built from the ground up for the purpose of being a worship venue.

In 2002, Rev. Meeks successfully ran for Illinois state senator and served three terms, until 2013, with his major focus on educational equity. During his time in office, he chaired the education committee and was joint chairman of the Illinois Legislative Black Caucus.

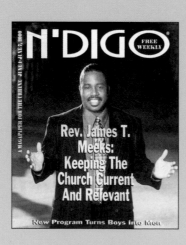

Reverend James Meeks

By Derrick K. Baker & Photography by Reginald Payton | *Originally Published June 1, 2000*

The Reverend James T. Meeks, the charismatic and mentally peripatetic founder and senior pastor of Salem Baptist Church of Chicago, is well known and admired for his incisive and educational sermons. He waxes fiery on the subjects that he interprets and the causes that he espouses.

The very essence of the man who proudly leads what he calls "the greatest church in the world" – and the largest Baptist church in Chicago – is a basic nature that prompts Rev. Meeks to speak the truth as he sees it, whenever and wherever he sees it.

It is that robust and keen sense of what is current and relevant that allows him to connect in the most impressive ways with churchgoers who gain their religious and activist sustenance at Salem Baptist Church in Roseland at 118th Street and Indiana Avenue.

Ranging from the widest mix of blue- and white-collar types, Salem's members are shepherded by a leader who mixes a contemporary religious message with the highest levels of civic, economic, and social activism.

> **There has to be a certain level of activism in the church. We cannot concentrate on the fact that everything is going to be alright in heaven – we've got to make some things right, now!**

These are the responsibilities that come with Rev. Meeks' appointed role as vice president of the Rainbow/PUSH Coalition and as a trusted colleague of Rev. Jesse Jackson.

Whether it's cleaning up vacant lots and boarding up abandoned buildings in the neighborhood, or opening a precedent-setting Christian bookstore in Roseland, or leading voters in ridding the area of excessive liquor stores, Salem Baptist church is more than a church. And the inspirational Rev. Meeks is a bit more than just a Baptist preacher.

A Dose Of Real Religion

Although proud of a litany of ongoing accomplishments, including winning 29,000 souls (introducing a person to Christ) last year, Rev. Meeks speaks candidly about the double-edge sword that is religion in the African-American community, and the significance of people becoming as active outside of the church as they are inside.

"The role of religion in the Black community is central," he begins. "If you take out our churches, I don't think we could measure the impact on the lives of people if they did not have a church to go to.

"The church is the one institution in the community that we own, which means that we are free in our pulpits to address the issues that plague us. It's the place where we get to motivate people to go out and vote. Churches employ people; churches are our meeting place.

"Religion has caused Black people to have hope in the midst of not having money and land. It has given us hope to say that God is going to even this thing out at some point in the end.

"Because the church has been our main source of gathering people to disseminate information, the church has been more instrumental in sending more people to college than any other institution.

"Most people who run for political office come out of one of the churches. The church affords young people so many opportunities that they don't get elsewhere."

But it comes as no surprise that a socially conscious realist like Rev. Meeks acknowledges the "other" effect of the Black church.

"Religion has also hurt us by anesthetizing our pain because we don't own anything. We just get happy in Jesus," he says. "And so we come to church for two or three hours and just get happy and forget about the fact that when we go to work tomorrow we might get fired.

"Religion can make us passive, because for one reason or another the churches can be guilty of not preaching a liberating gospel. When the messages become liberating, that's when we become who we ought to be at our best. When a church becomes passive and just gives people a two-hour fix on Sunday, it can be a detriment to us."

Meeks says, "I would like to see more churches become more involved in what's happening around us. We can't allow these Sunday meetings to just be insignificant gatherings where we never talk about Roseland and Englewood or the problems in the Black community. We can't just talk about Israel and give the

Reverend and Jamilla Meeks

street and let us use their facility that was once a church, but was a daycare center.

"The pastor told me that they would let us use the church for three months. By the time three months were up, he and I had become friends and God had opened his heart toward our ministry and what we were trying to do, and we ended up staying there for five years. I thank God that we were able to go from there to being the largest Baptist church in Chicago today. We did it by being real."

Liquidating Liquor In Roseland

The way Rev. Meeks saw it, a particular set of real numbers painted an ominous and obvious picture that cried out for a new canvas and fresh paint.

What do you do with 60,000 residents in Roseland, 10,000 church members, 59 liquor stores dotting and denigrating the community in five precincts and two wards, and no major retailers anywhere to be found?

If you're Rev. Meeks, you marshal voters and churchgoers to vote dry more than half of the 59 liquor stores in Roseland, whose presence had helped keep mainstream retailers at bay. That is precisely what happened in November 1998 as 30 businesses were forced to stop selling liquor.

Now, on the site of Belcher Drugs & Liquor, formerly the largest liquor store in Roseland, Rev. Meeks' House of Peace Christian Bookcenter sits as the largest Christian bookstore in the Chicagoland area.

Beautifully spread over 11,000-square-feet, and the crown jewel of Salem Baptist Church's ongoing effort to renew the Roseland community, the House of Peace stocks books, music, and church supplies in its impressive facility at 115th Street and Michigan Avenue.

Says Rev. Meeks, "It's a million-dollar store and shows our people what economic development is about. Voting the community dry without the next step of economic development is just half the process. So we put the store there as just the beginning of what all of Roseland could look like.

"We have reached a sad state of affairs when the only businesses in our community are liquor stores," Meeks says. "Many years from now, I hope to still be leading continual fights and showing communities how to do what we're trying to do here.

"How do you bring in a Walmart? A major grocery store?" asks Rev. Meeks, rhetorically. "How do you bring in job training centers and change your community from being a dead spot and a haven for drugs and violence to a community where people are safe on the streets and economic development has happened? How do you do that?"

Roseland is in the 2nd Congressional District, which, according to Meeks, leads the nation in drive

history of the Jewish people and what happened in the Old Testament.

"There has to be a certain level of activism in the church, and if there isn't, then the church becomes a place of celestial gazers – people who stand and just gaze at the heavens.

"I say that we cannot concentrate on the fact that everything is going to be alright in heaven – we've got to make some things right, now! Churches have to find a way to actively change their environment."

A Spiritual Beginning

Change has marked the evolution of Salem Baptist, which has grown from 205 members in 1985 to a current membership of more than 10,000. Change has allowed the church to become the largest employer in Roseland – with 142 on staff – and boast of the largest Sunday school in Chicago with 1,800 parishioners and more than 2,000 in attendance at weekly bible study.

Change has taken this senior pastor to numerous American cities and to Japan, Russia, Rome, South Korea, Indonesia, Israel, Africa, China, Jamaica, Argentina, Sweden, the Czech Republic and Australia.

Change has been the catalyst in Salem hosting youth conferences, married couples retreats, singles summits, children's camping trips, church growth seminars, Christian education seminars, and health and wellness workshops.

The foundation from which this change occurs is what Rev. Meeks calls his most significant personal accomplishment: the origin of Salem Baptist Church.

"We started this church with nothing," he remembers. "We had 200 people, but that's all we had. We used to meet at 8201 South Jeffrey at the Calvary Baptist Church. They built a new church down the

time because "there are no jobs located in our area," he says. "But if we lead the nation in drive time, that means we have cars and we wear clothes. Everything we do, we do outside of this community. We shop outside of the community, we bowl outside of the community. We don't have a pizza place in Roseland that will deliver to my house."

The Real Rev. Meeks

From his former days as a graduate of Bishop College to now leading one of the fastest-growing churches in America, Rev. Meeks remains steadfast in his conviction that while much has changed, he himself has remained true to his word and cause.

"I think that the Rev. Meeks that most people think they know is the real Rev. Meeks. I think that's one of my successes as a preacher and teacher. What you see is what you get," he says.

"I don't have a different demeanor in the pulpit and in public, and then have another one in staff meetings. I never take the time to have another personality. I work hard to be real and not be pretentious. It just doesn't fit me."

preface
Moseley Braun

Update: On November 3, 1992, Carol Moseley Braun became the first African-American woman ever elected to the United States Senate.

Braun served in the Senate for one term, through 1998. Her election marked the first time Illinois elected a Black and a woman as U.S. Senator, and the first time America elected a Black Democrat as a U.S. Senator. She also became the first woman in American history to defeat an incumbent Senator.

Braun was one of two African Americans to serve in the Senate in the 20th Century; the other was Edward Brooke, a Black Republican from Massachusetts, who served from 1966 to 1978.

She was the sole African American in the Senate for her entire term and was also the first woman to serve on the Senate Finance Committee. Her crowning achievement as Senator was directing some $5 billion in funding to the crumbling infrastructure of the nation's schools.

After her Senate stint, for 1999 and 2000, Braun served as the U.S. Ambassador to New Zealand. She then retired to her private law practice and launched a line of natural food products called Ambassador Organics.

Carol Moseley Braun

By Allison J. Keyes and David Smallwood | Photography by Doyle Wicks | *Originally Published January 1992*

When Carol Moseley Braun was a little girl, she wanted to be an adventurer when she grew up. At the moment, she is seeking to become the first African-American female Senator of the United States. That's some adventure.

"While I haven't been able to go out and explore unknown regions of the jungle," Braun says, "I have been able to be an adventurer in another sense altogether."

This 44-year-old native Chicagoan has made a habit of bucking the status quo as a career politician, which is not the most common field chosen by African Americans from Chicago's South Side.

From her days as an assistant U.S. attorney, to her five terms in the Illinois House, to her current job as Cook County Recorder of Deeds and campaign for national office, Braun says she has seen politics as a way to access government for the people.

"My professional endeavors have consistently been in the vanguard for women and for African Americans," Braun explains. "I became a lawyer when there were not many, and I was the only elected African-American Independent in the House of Representatives. My greatest strength is that I can work with people across a lot of lines, whether political, gender-based, racial or ideological."

> "To me, this job as a politician and an advocate for my people is a calling. Every day I ask myself if I am doing what the Lord would have me do."

She grew up in Chicago, in a family of police officers, and never left the city during her educational pursuits. After Parker High School, Braun graduated from the University of Illinois Chicago Circle campus in 1969, then the University of Chicago law school in 1972.

Though her parents' roots are in New Orleans and Alabama, Braun says she is the quintessential Chicagoan. "I make my home as serene an environment as I can manage. It's a place where I can get into my private endeavors," Braun says.

"I have an elderly mother that I am caring for, and a teen-aged son who thinks he's the man of the house. I don't have a large nuclear family, but I have a huge extended family. You know, aunties and uncles all over the place."

Coming from a musical background, she loves jazz and grew up listening to her grandfather play New Orleans ragtime. Braun's father played seven different instruments and had a classical background, but performed with a jazz band. She plays a little piano herself, but laughingly recalls being steered away from the woodwind instruments.

"When I was in high school, I took clarinet in band. I was sitting up trying to practice the clarinet, and my uncle who plays saxophone came in," Braun says. "He listened for a few minutes and said, 'Honey, why don't you take up something else?' I was crushed, but I took piano, and I'm not too bad."

Her musical tastes are rather eclectic. She listens to everything from rap to classical to jazz, and admits to enjoying a little country and western now and then. But she does have one really unusual hobby. "I love woodworking, which makes people nuts," Braun laughs. "I mean making furniture, for real. It's hard to keep fingernails, but I love doing it."

All Things Political

Braun's expertise in working with inflexible materials seemed like a great way to get ready for a political career, especially in 1978 when she was first elected to the 25th District of the Illinois House. Braun's Democratic district included Chatham, South Shore, and East Hyde Park.

Braun says she was the only "voice for the people" in a legislature that was run under strict Democratic Machine rules.

"Everybody else (the other African-American Democrats) in the House at that time was associated with the machine in one way or another," Braun says, adding that she is not putting down former colleagues Richard Newhouse, Earlean Collins or the late Harold Washington for those ties. "It was the beginning of the independent movement as a political force,"

In fact, Braun herself has been accused of both being too independent, and of having too many close ties to the regular Democratic Party.

"I always find it hilarious, those people who want to talk about how I'm not an independent in that my slating for the office of Cook County Recorder of Deeds was the first time I had ever been slated for office," Braun explains, "and that was because of Mayor Harold Washington. So I don't know how that makes me a machine person. If anything, I have kept faith with the people who came behind me in my political career, with my supporters and the voters."

Braun also refuses to play the political games that often mean life or death for legislative programs in a city and state where who you know is often more important than the merits of whatever it is you want passed. She sees herself as someone who puts the people first instead of politics.

"Politics is something you have to deal with in order to effect change. I really don't like political game playing, but I have worked to master the political process. I could do without a lot of the game playing and the back and forth," Braun says.

"And maybe that's what confuses people about my politics. If it's a personality issue, then I don't have interest in that. I do have a passion however, when it comes to the quality of life in this community."

As an example, Braun points to the early 1980s, when she tried to persuade the state's mapmakers to be fair in drawing new legislative districts based on the 1980 census. Braun filed a lawsuit against what she calls gerrymandering, racially unfair maps. Her win resulted in new districts for African-American and Hispanic voters, and created the first Latino state districts.

"Anybody who's ever worked with me knows that's my style," Braun says. "That's what I do. I will go to the wall on behalf of things I believe in. I don't like labels because if anything, they polarize people. So if I have a role in politics or government, it is to find the places where we can agree, to promote cooperation without in any way compromising my principles and my beliefs."

Senate Qualifications

During her time in the state house where she spent five years on the House floor, Braun was floor leader for Mayor Harold Washington, as well as the first female assistant majority leader.

In 1978, Braun was chief sponsor of Illinois's primary and secondary education funding bills. She also worked on the 1988 education reform bill as chief House sponsor and co-chair of the task force that drew up the final version.

Braun says if she wins the U.S senate race, her first priority would be making herself accountable to voters. She envisions a series of town meetings across the state, thinking that would be an excellent way of finding out people's concerns. Education would remain a major focus for her.

She also wants to see Illinois focus more on creating jobs, noting that there are federal policies that could help nurture the manufacturing industry.

"I feel we are on the wrong track in terms of our economy, and we need to get on the right track," Braun says. "Get back to making and producing goods and services that we can sell to somebody else. It does not address the employment needs of the people of Illinois to continue to slip down the slope of service industries, while neglecting our industrial base altogether."

Braun also thinks the country should have a universal health plan, or at least an extensive reform of the existing system.

She scoffs at those who say this nation isn't ready for an African-American female senator. She says before declaring her candidacy, she received scores of letters from places as varied as Chicago's West Side and downstate Canton.

"People are willing to go beyond racism to elect the best candidate," Braun feels and she says she wouldn't expect the same kind of obstructionism from the United States Senate as the late Mayor Washington got from the Chicago City Council during his first term.

The Clarence Thomas Effect

Braun faces incumbent U.S. Senator Alan Dixon (D-Chicago) in the March primary, as well as Loop attorney Albert F. Hofeld. She says she was swept into the race by the call of people furious with Dixon for voting to confirm United States Supreme Court Justice Clarence Thomas.

Braun says the Senate Judiciary hearings over Professor Anita Hill's sexual harassment allegations against Thomas showed Illinoisans that the Senate does not represent the interest of regular Joes and Janes.

Regarding that groundswell push that swept her into the election, Braun laughs, "I feel a little bit like (the late Mayor) Harold Washington must have when he was drafted to run for mayor in 1983."

In addition to the letters, Braun says she received calls from all parts of the state, and three separate groups in Chicago held press conferences urging her to challenge the incumbent senator.

Dixon defended his vote for Clarence Thomas by pointing out that in this country, people are innocent until proven guilty and he accuses both Braun and her fellow challenger of running a single-issue campaign.

But Braun says that trivializes the matter. "Justice Thomas has been confirmed, and I am prepared to give him every respect," she says. "However, the process was a disaster. The issues were appalling and quite frankly, the hearings point to the need for reform in the Senate."

Braun says her previous successful experience in elective office should help negate what she calls a preconceived tendency to expect African Americans entering new arenas to be incompetent. And she says if she wins this election, perhaps her career will be seen by Black children as proof that African Americans can reach for and attain positions of power.

"That's why I'm in this business to begin with – to try to make things better and to hold up the light," Braun explains. "To me, this job as a politician and an advocate for my people is a calling. Every day I ask myself if I am doing what the Lord would have me do. In that regard, I hope my activities make things better for somebody. For lots of somebodies."

preface Moyo

Update: After 28 years, Real Men Cook For Charity has generated more than $1 million in ticket proceeds and donations for worthy causes. Celebrity chefs during the years have included Eddie and Gerald Levert of the O'Jays, former New Orleans Mayor Marc Morial, and former President of the United States Barack Obama, when he was a Senator in Illinois. In addition to her continuing guidance of Real Men Cook, Yvette Moyo is also publisher of several magazines in Chicago, including the *South Shore Current*, under the auspices of her company Binamu Media.

Yvette & Kofi Moyo

By Donna Hodge & Photography by Victor Powell | *Originally Published June 17, 1999*

Real Men Cook For Charity is the Chicago born, now nationwide, longest running and most successful urban Father's Day celebration in the country.

The brainchild of entrepreneurs and marketers Kofi and Yvette Jackson Moyo – owners of the Chicago-based marketing firm Resource Associates International (RAI) – Real Men Cook pays tribute to African-American men by bringing together fathers, sons, uncles, and "brothers" to share their culinary talents.

This year, some 6,000 people are expected to show up at the DuSable Museum for the Chicago portion of this year's event, while close to 20,000 people are expected in total in the six cities across the country participating in Real Men Cook. Those cities include Atlanta, New Orleans, New York, Washington, D.C., and Waukegan, Illinois.

> **We are dedicated to sharing the stories of real men who are undervalued and unheralded in the public, who make contributions everyday. It demonstrates what real men will do, outside of the stereotypes, to care for their families and communities.**

How It All Began

"In 1988, Kofi and I heard about an event in New York called 'Men Who Cook,'" recalls Yvette Moyo. "We were interested in the concept and immediately got in contact with the producer, Lena Turner.

"After a lot of conversations, it was clear that she was not interested in creating a joint business relationship, but gave us her blessings to do something on our own. We did the research and created something unique that reflected the spirit of our community – a Chicago-based event – and gave it a pro-active name, 'Real Men Cook.'"

As marketers and business partners with over 40 years of combined experience, this dynamic husband and wife team created a spirited event that not only spotlights the talents and commitment of African-American men, but also donates proceeds to charities.

Adds Yvette, "Ms. Turner's event no longer takes place in New York, but we carry on her vision and legacy."

The first year, in 1990, the Moyos called upon 10 coordinators that included leading women in Chicago – such as Deborah Crable, Merri Dee, Robin Robinson, and Marti Worrell – to recruit 10 men each to take part in the event. That year's participants included: Bill Campbell, John Davis, Monroe Anderson, Cong. Danny Davis, Stedman Graham, and former Mayor Eugene Sawyer, to name a few.

"This first event was from our hearts," says Yvette. "We wanted to give something back to the community. Of course we wanted to provide for our families financially, but we also wanted to make a social statement and for me, it was putting on an all-male effort to raise money for a good cause."

"Planning this type of event was a challenge," adds Kofi Moyo. "The first three years, our company, small and struggling, took the major responsibility of making this event happen from beginning to end. Like any sizable event that draws 3,000 to 4,000 people, that's quite an undertaking."

Kofi explained that after those first three years, the Moyos came to a crossroads as to whether the company could shoulder the entire event.

"It costs quite a bit to do an event like this if you don't have the right formula," says Kofi, "especially with an African-American effort. We knew full well coming out of the block that first year, that if we didn't give away some money, our credibility would be zero."

So for the first few years, the Moyos reached into their own pockets to make good on their commitment of donating to the charities. Says Kofi, "It was an investment in building the 'brand,' the image, and name of the event."

After three years, they knew there had to be another better way, so Kofi created a moderate partnership with institutions that would benefit financially, beginning with the South Side YMCA, which in the third year of the partnership received $75,000.

Other sites that have hosted Real Men Cook include the Museum of Science and Industry, the State of Illinois building, Chicago State University, New Concept Development Center, and the James Jordan Boys and Girls Center.

However, as the popularity of Real Men Cook For

Yvette & Kofi

Charity grew, so did the need to partner with more sophisticated entities that could manage the growing crowds of about 5,000 people and 200 volunteer cooks for over three hours. So what started off as an indoor event rapidly grew and was forced to expand and become an outdoor one that includes barbecue grills.

The Major Change

This changing of venues was also a part of the ongoing process of finding organizations and beneficiaries who shared the same ideals – grassroots from the heart, not tied up in a corporate structure.

"It was a major change for us. Major in that we created, nurtured and produced it over a number of years. We knew what we wanted it to look like, and knew that institutions might have a different view," says Kofi.

"Ultimately, we managed and produced the event with a staff of other non-for-profit partners in a venue able to accommodate 5,000-plus guests." Kofi notes that "as soon as we created this new partnership, or license model, proceeds to charities doubled."

Last year, Real Men Cook raised over $117,000 dollars, thanks to a matching grant from The Chicago Tribune Charities.

Charitable recipients of Real Men Cook have included: The Greater Chicago Food Depository, The South Side YMCA, The Robert Taylor Boys and Girls Club, The James R. Jordan Boys & Girls Club, The Martin Luther King Boys & Girls Club, and the DuSable Museum of African American History.

This year The Chicago Tribune Charities will match a smaller percentage of the proceeds, but with RAI's marketing model, the Moyos look to surpass last year's totals.

"Usually we select charities based on the ability of the lead charity to live up to their partnership requirements," says Yvette. "We raise all sponsorship dollars and do the marketing. The lead charity sells the tickets, provides staff volunteers and resources daily to maximize the financial results. The secondary charity comes from our volunteer cooks."

This year's line-up of sponsors includes *The Chicago Tribune*; Mobil Oil, which will bring in a NASCAR racing car; Betty Crocker, which is also sponsoring the kids' pavilion and will be bringing in two African American food companies – Michele Foods and Glory Foods; Lawry's Seasoning; South Shore Bank; A1 Steak

Sauce; V103; and NBC-TV/Channel 5.

Their sponsorships give this monumental event the opportunity to give real dollars to charitable organizations. Real Men Cook this year is a part of the Tribune Charities that benefits the DuSable Museum of African American History and the Community Mental Health Council.

What makes this year's Real Men Cook so different is that in New York, Washington, D.C., Atlanta, New Orleans and Waukegan, Illinois, men and their families and friends will partake in what Chicagoans have already experienced – a day of reverence for Black males.

It's fun, laughter, good food, and a venue to see the message that real men work, real men provide, real men care, and "real men cook" – a phrase created by Kofi Moyo.

Coordinators and producers of Real Men Cook in other cities are selected from attendees of RAI's bi-annual marketing symposium, Marketing Opportunities in Black Entertainment (MOBE). They are supplied with a Real Men Cook planning guide of their city, and a video of the Real Men Cook event, as well as a copy of news clippings from previous events, to successfully pull off the affair.

Day Of The Event

The day begins at 6 a.m. as the men prepare their dishes at nearby certified kitchens. The tents start going up at 8 a.m. At 10 a.m., the "grillers" arrive to select their "strategic" spots on the lawn; the cooks from inside the certified kitchens begin to come on out by noon with their food. Then at 2 p.m., a private ceremony is held for sponsors, press, cooks and charity representatives.

"We do a libation and a verbal dedication, then we do a roll call," Kofi explains. "You haven't heard men recognized like this … when you hear these guys, you hear and feel this male spirit. We acknowledge it and wish them Happy Father's Day and thank them for giving up their time to the communities and their families," says Kofi. "From the moment the men arrive, you can feel a connection, a bonding, and a special relationship building."

Men of all ages volunteer to cook, from 10 years old to 80. Some families have had two to three generations working side by side, cooking, serving and doing their thing.

Wives, girlfriends, significant others, sisters, etc., can volunteer to help, but the men do all the work,

Moyo

cooking, serving, answering questions, and naturally media interviews – if there's enough time.

The Moyos estimate that 70 percent of the tickets are purchased by women for themselves as Father's Day gifts, or for their entire family.

It is a family affair. There are lots of things for kids to enjoy, including pony rides, live entertainment, clowns, and face painting. The Black Cowboys will be on hand to demonstrate their talents on the horses, and six museums will offer special activities for kids.

However, for three glorious hours, the men are the stars of the show and attendees are the beneficiaries. You will be able to taste just about every dish imaginable, such as succulent, slowly basted barbecue ribs, homemade pies, melt-in-your-mouth greens, and too rich and decadent desserts.

What's Next?

The Moyos are looking to license this marketing tool to other ethnic communities, such as the Latino community, because it has the same challenges in terms of male role models and images that are presented by the media. Real Men Cook works to dispel those myths.

With their website – www.realmencook.com – up and running, a line of aprons, hats, cookbooks and other items managed by RAI, Yvette and Kofi will continue to tell the stories of real men.

"We are dedicated to sharing the stories of real men who are undervalued and unheralded in the public, who make contributions everyday. We say it demonstrates what real men will do, outside of the stereotypes, to care for their families and communities," says Yvette.

"It's the real intangible. As much as I want it to grow, I hope it never loses its essence," says Kofi. "For many of these guys, they are surrogates to other families and the cohesive healing is very real.

"How you capture that and let the majority feel that – and that this kind of spirit lives in men of character in spite of whatever every day role they might play or are perceived – I would like for that feeling to be as apparent to everyone as it is for us."

preface
Muhammad

Update: Sister Claudette Marie Muhammad serves the Nation of Islam as its national director of fundraising.

Sister Claudette Muhammad

By Tracey Robinson-English & Photography by Victor Powell | *Originally Published March 22, 2007*

Sister Claudette Marie Muhammad is the former Ebony/Jet Fashion Fair model and assistant to U.S. President Lyndon Baines Johnson, and current Chief of Protocol for the Nation of Islam led by the Honorable Minister Louis Farrakhan.

In her eye-opening memoir *Memories*, Sister Muhammad revealed many of her blessings, but she also shared painful ordeals of being molested as a child and later raped, raising a son as a single mother, accepting public assistance, and facing discrimination and domestic violence.

"What I want other men and women to know is that rather than letting the bitterness get the best of you or turning to other vices, you turn to God," she says.

At her Chicago residence recently, Sister Muhammad – statuesque with skin as smooth as shea butter and wise, dark brown eyes – pored over details of yet another work assignment one evening while talking frankly about chapters of her extraordinary life.

Her duties as Chief of Protocol encompass checking that all of the etiquette, courtesies, diplomacy, and travel arrangements bestowed upon most dignitaries are in proper order for Minister Farrakhan.

> All experiences in one's life are indeed a teaching tool, a learning device, to help one get to the next step.

"Some people say I'm a workaholic," Sister Muhammad says, then offers a spunky comeback. "My work is my pleasure, and my pleasure is my work. When I wake up, I can stretch my arms, and touch my feet. I'm continuously working and still turning heads."

Her comments raise an eyebrow, given the public perception that the women of the Nation of Islam are extremely conservative and repressed in many ways. But in the case of Sister Claudette (and many other sisters in the Nation of Islam), she is a confident woman who has risen through the ranks of the Nation to national prominence based on her outstanding performance on the job. She is a world traveler who has worked with leaders and heads of states throughout the still male-dominated Muslim world and African world.

She recently returned from the Nation of Islam's Saviour's Day event in Detroit, which attracted some 70,000 followers who came to hear the riveting message of Minister Farrakhan.

The proud Sister, who exudes regality and often flows into a room in exquisite garments covering her body as required by her faith, brings a wealth of cultural knowledge, political savvy and intelligence to her position, and is known for keeping the Nation on point.

It was Minister Farrakhan who inspired Sister Muhammad to write her book after he realized during one of their many conversations that there was much "I did not know about the person who has been working so closely with me for these many years," he says in her book's foreword.

The eldest of 15 children, Sister Muhammad was molested when she was a child by her paternal grandfather, she writes in a chapter titled, "Little Girl Big Secret." Another chapter, "Beauty Has No Race," unfolds as Sister Muhammad, then enrolled in John Robert Powers School of Modeling in San Diego, California, filed a civil lawsuit with the NAACP in the mid-1950s against a local beauty salon that refused to "do colored people's hair."

"I had actually never faced racism to know it, and was now being slapped in the face with racism," she wrote. "I got their business card, confirmed that I actually had a reservation, and took the manager's name. I then went to the president of the NAACP, who took me to an attorney."

Young and courageous, Sister (then Claudette Johnson) Muhammad won her civil lawsuit, which resulted in the salon hiring a Black beautician to handle Black clients.

Five days prior to her 21st birthday, Sister Muhammad gave birth to her son, Anthony. "Here I was pregnant and no husband," a real taboo at the time, she wrote in a chapter titled "Trusted and Betrayed." Her pregnancy was the result of a one-night stand with an acquaintance, but she later became engaged to her sweetheart, a professional basketball player who promised that they would marry and that

Sister Claudette

he "would take good care of me."

The man was not legally divorced, however. He had a wife and children in Indiana, so the engagement was off. Sister Muhammad moved back in with her mother, and would soon become a single parent.

Good Times, Bad Times

Despite her setbacks, she enjoyed many good times. She became the first Black cheerleader of the "Chargettes," the female team that danced during half-time of the San Diego Chargers football games. She graced the runways as an Ebony Fashion Fair Model and *Jet* cover girl.

While working as a librarian at General Dynamics Astronautics Company, she was appointed the first Black secretary to then Congressman Lionel Van Deerlin in 1962. After years of working for Van Deerlin, she moved on to become a special assistant to the Kerner Commission on Civil Disorders under President Johnson in 1967. She later owned her own public relations firm.

Her share of bad times kept knocking too, however. In 1964, she filed a discrimination charge with the Washington, D.C. Urban League against the Washington Redskins football team for being denied a position as a cheerleader with the female team, the Redskinettes. The charge hit the edition of the *Washington Post* – "Model's brown skin is nixed by the Redskins."

And family tragedies struck when her sister, Margo, was stabbed seven times in the chest by a deranged former boyfriend. Five years later, her mother was brutally murdered at age 55.

"She called me in January, 1975. It was the late evening," Sister Muhammad wrote of her mother. "I couldn't talk with her, because I had just dreamed the night before of myself in a funeral procession, as she had been at my sister's funeral, just five years prior."

Her romantic relationships with several suitors, including Congressman John Conyers Jr., and former heavyweight champion Muhammad Ali are also page-turners. While on Capitol Hill, she dated Conyers and while on tour with Ebony Fashion Fair, she met the heavyweight champion.

"(He) stood beside me and said, 'You could fit well. I'm looking for a wife. I have to get married,' Ali said," Sister Claudette wrote.

"I said to him, 'That is not the way you get a wife. There has to be a relationship.' They all laughed. In several of the cities on the Ebony Fashion Fair Tour, I would walk out on the ramp, look out into the audience, and there would be Muhammad Ali."

A whole new world of opportunity opened to Sister Muhammad during the 1970s and 1980s when connections led her to Africa. With her son now off to college and the responsibilities of parenthood somewhat lifted, she felt free to travel the world, she says. She has visited heads of states in Liberia, Ghana, and many countries in West Africa.

"With my first step on African soil, a feeling of completeness overcame me," she wrote in a chapter titled "The Missing Link." "It was a sensation I had never before experienced. The missing link for the chain of my nice life was finally put into place. I was whole for the first time in my life."

For several years, she would visit and live in Africa for extended periods. After returning to the States, she decided to return to college. Sister Muhammad earned a Bachelor of Arts degree in International Relations and Third World Studies from American University, received a fellowship to Johns Hopkins School of International Law, and studied at the University in Geneva, Switzerland and the United Nations.

Although she was a devout Catholic, she met Minister Farrakhan in 1983 and embraced the teachings of The Most Honorable Elijah Muhammad. In 1988, she became a registered Muslim in the Nation.

As a Sister in the Nation, she describes her work and acquaintance with Minister Farrakhan over the past years as "remarkable. The work for freedom, justice, and equality for our people has brought me much peace, and has allowed me to learn from a diversity of folk from all walks of life," she wrote.

In *Memories*, the reader learns from the lessons of a regal force over the course of her many years of ups and downs. Her beauty, intelligence, and determination opened doors to experiences that celebrate the woman herself.

"All experiences in one's life are indeed a teaching tool, a learning device, to help one get to the next step in life," Sister Muhammad wrote. "I have climbed many ladders, yet I am not tired because I truly believe God is not through with me. No, not yet."

preface Neal

Update: Earl Langdon Neal passed in 2005 at the age of 76. His legal specialty was land acquisition for the city and other public entities for public use. Neal was responsible for acquiring the land for the Dan Ryan Expressway, the Deep Tunnel Project, redevelopment of the near-South Side and near- South Loop, the University of Illinois Chicago campus, Comiskey Park, the White Sox baseball stadium, Stroger Hospital, expansions of McCormick Place, both Midway and O'Hare Airports, and acquisitions that gave rise to the various campuses of the City Colleges of Chicago. He counseled every Chicago mayor for over 50 years.

Isobel Neal retired from her gallery in 1996, but is still an occasional curator of art shows.

Earl and Isobel Neal

By Allison Keyes & Photography by Victor Powell | *Originally Published December 1992*

n 1950, she was a New York debutante whose face in the pages of magazines hailed her arrival on the University of Michigan campus. He was to be a lawyer like his father and grandfather before him.

Bound to carry on a tradition established by her grandfather and an uncle, she enrolled in the undergraduate school of pharmacy. Earl Neal met Isobel Hoskins, as he tells it, in this way: "All of us young men, we awaited her arrival on the campus of the University of Michigan. After I stood in line for an appropriate period of time, three or four months, I managed to get a date...after having been stood up on the first date."

A fairy tale, Isobel counters, but it's easy to imagine. An attractive, diminutive woman, with sparkling eyes, glowing skin, and a warm, sincere personality, Isobel Neal would be right at home on the cover of *Lear's Magazine*.

> **Somebody has to demand something from you, and be interested enough to make sure you produce. It could be a teacher – anybody who says, 'I expect something from you and I know what you can do, so you cannot give anything less.'** — Isobel Neal

Despite an imperfect beginning, they soon began dating casually for about a year, growing more serious as he moved toward graduation. Admittance to the Michigan Bar and a stint in the army for him followed graduation. A return to New York for her, where she changed majors and completed her studies, graduating with a B.A. in history from NYU.

Following his discharge from the army in 1954, he returned home to Chicago where he was admitted to the Illinois Bar and settled down to practice law, part-time, with his father, Earl J. Neal, a native Chicagoan and an established attorney since 1937.

They were married in St. Phillips Church in Brooklyn in 1955, and Mrs. Earl L. Neal joined her young husband in Chicago.

Giving Back Where They Can

Today, Earl Neal is one of Chicago's most prominent attorneys, senior principal of Earl L. Neal & Associates. Isobel Neal is the equally prominent owner of Isobel Neal Gallery, Ltd., a nationally known art gallery that features the works of African-American artists.

Their names appear in the society pages and on all the significant invitation lists. They move in important social and political circles, are frequently asked to chair, sit on, advise, and be ad hoc members of committees and boards...and too often agree.

She fundraises for the United Negro College Fund, the Michael Reese Hospital Crystal Ball, Provident Hospital, and the Museum of Science and Industry's Black Creativity event. He is the recipient of numerous coveted awards, and sits on the boards of major corporations.

Clearly, they are a couple who have earned a place in the power sphere of Chicago. And they did it the old-fashioned way.

"Throughout our lives, we've worked very hard together and have jointly saved and worked toward an objective, a common goal," says Neal. "As I look back on it, we both were very determined. Of course, I was more than driven and Isobel was the perfect partner for the direction I wanted to go."

They are also proud parents and grandparents. Their only son Langdon D. Neal, is an associate of Earl L. Neal & Associates. He is a fourth generation lawyer and longtime member of the Board of Election Commissioners.

Every week Earl devotes time to meeting with young African American entrepreneurs, encouraging the development of their businesses. "My drive is to develop young African-American businesses at a full level of participation, and to open the doors that I can open because I have managed to get inside, and to show others how to do it."

Time Together

With such independently busy schedules, when do they find time to spend with one another?

"We have a boat and that's my passion," says Neal. "We keep the boat in Florida and we try to sneak away every month just for a few days and spend time on the boat alone." That's our quiet time," he says. "We don't go to restaurants. We cook on the boat."

The captain and his first mate have cruised the Bahamas alone, through all of the out islands. Recently, just the two of them went to the Georgia Sea Islands and cruised from island to island, docking at Cumberland Island north of northern Florida, where only 500 people a day are allowed to visit at any given time. The island has 14 miles of beaches with no one on them.

One of their fondest memories is from the 1970s when Isobel took a teaching sabbatical to attend the University of California in Santa Barbara, earning a Master's degree in Anthropology and Archeology.

"It was a good time for both of us," Neal says. "We spent more real time together than we can scratch out today, even though we try harder and we're both here."

The path to prestige and prominence, while paved, was not golden for the Neals. His first full-time position as a salaried employee with the Chicago Land

> **My drive is to develop young African-American businesses at a full level of participation and to open the doors that I can because I have managed to get inside, and to show others how to do it.** — Earl Neal

Clearance Commission earned him $315 a month. Even in 1955, this was not a handsome salary, but the job was providential because it also gained him a specialty in real estate and land acquisition.

She began her career in the Children's Division of the Department of Public Aid, where she supervised foster home children. "I worked there about a year and then applied to the Board of Education to teach," she remembers. Short a few credits to teach high school history, she returned to school at night, where she took elementary education classes.

"My first teaching job was at Mason School at 16th and Keeler," she recalls. "We were on shift in those days and, of course, I started early because the last teacher hired had the first shift. Nobody wanted to start school at 7:30 in the morning, but I was pleased to have a job."

She remained with the Chicago public schools for 20 years, 10 of them in a homebound teaching program for handicapped students. She later taught at Shakespeare and Ludwig Van Beethoven Elementary Schools.

"I'll never forget," she laughs, "at Beethoven we had one teacher for each grade. I had all the 4th graders in the school and I had 60-something students, but there were only 40 seats. Discipline was very simple.

If you couldn't behave, you lost your seat, and nobody wanted to stand up.

"The link to art was there in all those years of teaching," she interjects. "I used art as a project because it was the immediate avenue to attention discipline. I never had a problem because most students wanted to hurry up and get through with their math because they wanted to work on the project we'd started."

Isobel's Gallery

The gallery, a family-owned and financed business, absorbs all of Isobel's time. "Both of us have one common goal," Neal says. "It's to give opportunities to African-American artists who haven't had a chance before to display at a first-rate gallery."

Isobel represents many of the leading African-American artists in the country. Her roster includes a large Chicago contingency that she promotes exhaustively.

She says there is a growing number of young professionals – physicians, lawyers, business people – who have recently acquired property they are now furnishing with art. "They have the sensibility and the awareness that there are African-American artists, and have made a commitment that that's where they want to spend their dollars," Isobel says.

These collectors come from all over the country, in part because the gallery has earned a national reputation for carrying certain artists' work, and also because there are few such Black owned, topnotch galleries in the country. Some people stumble into the gallery quite by accident, and there's also an increased interest among White collectors for work by Black artists because it's the last quality art that is affordable.

Strong Social Consciousness

The Neals rarely socialize unless it's directly related to their broader concerns. They particularly enjoy family gatherings. They're also very selective about their volunteer activities, usually fund-raisers for worthy causes. Throughout their lives, they have nurtured a strong social consciousness.

"I think that one of the most meaningful things Isobel and I have done was to start a swimming program for kids from the Robert Taylor Homes at the Washington Park YMCA," Neal says. He had two reasons for coaching swimming. "The main reason was because I wanted to contribute," he says, "but I also wanted my son to be exposed to all people.

"My father always said, 'You must be as comfortable in the courtroom as you are in a bar. You must be as comfortable on 47th Street as you are downtown.' Taking my son to the "Y" was hard for him at that time," Neal says. "But it was to give him that

sense of comfort with everyone."

What came out of that early experience was priceless, Neal says. "To see the continuing development of these young people that came from just getting a hot dog on Saturday and having someone to talk to who cared about them," he says.

"So many of them finished high school and went on to college. Almost everyone did something. And the very simple thing was that someone cared about them. Someone paid attention. Someone told them that they, too, could achieve, and gave them the opportunity."

Coming from strong family backgrounds steeped in tradition, they recognize the importance of family values in shaping destiny, but Neal is quick to add, "It's harder to do without a family. Someone has to fill in," he says. "I wouldn't talk of family values, but giving value in a person's life. All of us have to give back."

Isobel echoes, "It could be a teacher – anybody who says, 'I expect something from you and I know what you can do, whatever level it is, so you cannot give anything less.' Somebody has to demand something from you, and be interested enough to make sure that you produce."

preface Obama

Update: This was the first major story ever written on Barack Obama. Five years later, in 2008, he was President of the United States. The first Black president was re-elected to a second term in 2012 and Michelle became one of the most popular First Ladies in American history. The Obamas left office in January 2017 to oversee development of the Obama Presidential Library, located on the South Side of Chicago.

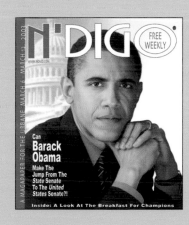

Barack Obama

By Paul Davis & Photography by Victor Powell | *Originally Published March 6, 2003*

His resume beams with the elements that the country's most prestigious law firms and universities yearn for: Harvard graduate, college professor, author, lecturer, and community organizer.

What? Community organizer. This is no tall tale. Barack Obama, state senator from Illinois' 13th District, earned his spurs by toiling in the 'hood.

Obama's surreal odyssey of community service began in New York's legendary Harlem community. From there, he headed to the Midwest, to Chicago's divergent yet politically active Black communities.

Obama says he has spent virtually his entire adult life catering to the needs of people with fragmented hopes, dreams, and aspirations. Now he has readied himself for his greatest career challenge to date: a Democratic primary election run for the United States Senate in March 2004.

The Obama campaign for the U.S. Senate went from a kind of idling position to full-throttle in January after Carol Moseley-Braun announced that she would not seek a rematch with Sen. Peter Fitzgerald (R) for her former Senate seat.

Moving swiftly, Obama officially declared his candidacy for the Senate three days later during an announcement press conference.

My entire adult life has been dedicated to providing opportunities for people in need.

Noticeably absent from Obama's lineup of supporters was Congressman Bobby Rush, whom Obama unsuccessfully challenged for Rush's congressional seat in 2000.

"I've said publicly he gave me a good spanking. That was a good early lesson in my political career – you have to be patient, and it doesn't make sense to divide the African-American base," Obama remarked on his defeat by Rush.

The senatorial candidate said that over the course of the next year, he expects to work with numerous leaders in the African-American community to help communicate his message for change.

The key element for an African-American candidate seeking to run successfully statewide, Obama said,

is to be rooted in the African-American community, recognize it as your base, and yet not be limited by it.

"The nice thing about running statewide is that it gives me the opportunity to recognize that all the issues that African Americans face specifically as a community are issues that also should speak to the broader pool of voters."

Helping To Develop Communities

Obama came from New York to the Chicago in 1985 and worked in low-income neighborhoods on the far South Side of the city with an organization called the Developing Communities Project, a faith-based program that involved about 25 churches.

The group addressed a myriad of problems, Obama says, including improving city services, job training, renovated parks and play lots, and housing and environmental issues. It also helped shape some of the school reform initiatives that produced legislation in 1988.

Obama's work in this area left an indelible mark in his mind about what could be accomplished in the public/political arena.

"It was a terrific education for me, a great experience. It confirmed in my mind that ordinary people can do extraordinary things," he said. "Since then, my entire adult life has been dedicated to providing opportunities for people in need."

Educationally, he earned a B.A. degree from Columbia University in New York, and in 1988, enrolled in Harvard Law School, where he became the first African American to serve as president of the Harvard Law Review. He was a member of the Executive Board of the Black Law Students Association and graduated Magna Cum Laude.

Following his exemplary work at Harvard, Obama could have easily accepted a position with a corporate law firm, but instead his career thirst led him to work at the grassroots level.

In 1992, Obama was tabbed to serve as Illinois Executive Director of Project Vote, a voter registration program that targeted low-income communities of color throughout Cook County. This expansive effort added an astounding 150,000 newly registered voters to the rolls.

Those voters had an immediate impact in the state. They helped Carol Moseley-Braun to be elected the first African-American woman to the United States Senate, and Bill Clinton to be elected President.

Obama describes 1992 as a "watershed year" for Democrats, and says he was proud to be a part of it. The year became even more watershed after the young lawyer/aspiring politician married a work colleague named Michelle Robinson in October 1992.

The Choice He Made

After Project Vote, Obama joined a small civil rights law firm called Miner, Barnhill and Galland. His focus continued to be on civil rights and social justice, and he participated in a voting rights lawsuit against the City of Chicago to insure that African Americans would receive a sufficient number of majority Black wards.

He and his firm also represented clients on employment and discrimination cases, community development corporations that built affordable housing units, and community health clinics.

Shunning the allure of huge corporate dollars and the recognition that would accompany them, Obama's philosophy was grounded in altruism.

"My feeling was I could make a lot of money and not make much of a contribution, or I could make a decent living and be part of the solution. I'm happy with the choice I've made," he says.

Although Obama, still a young 41, was in his youth during the height of the civil rights movement, he says he was inspired by the work of the Student Nonviolent Coordinating Council (SNCC), Fannie Lou Hamer, and Tom Moses. He calls them true American heroes and notes that they opened doors that he was able to walk right through.

In 1992, Obama began teaching constitutional and civil rights law at the University of Chicago Law School, and conducted seminars on race and the law.

Four years later, when State Senator Alice Palmer opted to run for Congress in the 2nd Congressional District, Obama said a number of supporters urged him to run for the state senate office she vacated.

The New State Senator

He did and was elected to the State Senate in 1996, then to a second term in 1998. He said he has maintained a consistent thread of empowering working people and people of color.

In the State Senate, Obama said he has forged working partnerships on tax fairness issues that have passed the earned income tax credit, increased the personal exemption to provide more money in the pockets of working families, and worked on juvenile justice legislation.

Currently, Obama is the lead sponsor in the Senate on issues pertaining to racial profiling, videotaping

interrogations, and death penalty reforms.

The upcoming 2004 U.S. Senate race in Illinois, Obama said, is simply an extension of the path he has traveled his entire adult life, one option of service, and not an attempt by him to simply win another job.

"This U.S. Senate race is an opportunity to help frame the national debate," he says. "I see this as a mission, not just as a way of elevating myself individually."

Obama believes the country is at a crossroads as a nation. With the world becoming increasingly more complex, he said America is faced with important decisions to make, both domestically and internationally.

Americans across the board are facing more and more vulnerabilities in their jobs, and mounting concerns about health insurance.

According to Obama, the economic growth of the 1990s disguised some disturbing trends in this country.

Chief among them, he says, is the growing inequality between the rich and the poor; an ongoing disparity in the mortality rates between African Americans, Hispanics, and their White counterparts; a decline in the quality of public school education; and an enormous rise in the rate of incarceration of African-American youth who are trapped in a drug economy.

The challenge facing the Democratic Party and himself as a U.S. Senator, Obama maintains, is to articulate an alternative plan and alternative vision to challenge the "selfish vision" of President George W. Bush and the Republican Party.

Addressing National Healthcare

At the top of Obama's agenda is healthcare. As a state senator, he chairs the Senate's healthcare committee and has conducted a series of healthcare hearings across Illinois where he's heard countless times about the healthcare crisis and the millions of people who are uninsured.

The discussions range from small businesses that cannot provide health coverage because premiums are too high, to seniors who don't have adequate prescription drug coverage, to hospitals whose reimbursement rates are too low.

"Across the board, you're seeing suburbanites, city folks, Black folks, White folks, Hispanics, businesses, labor unions, all recognizing that the healthcare system is in crisis," Obama says.

The crisis in healthcare, he believes, creates an opportunity nationally to develop a system that every other industrialized country in the world has – basic healthcare coverage for everyone. Obama says he doesn't have any illusion that will happen right away in the Senate, but said the country should begin moving in that direction.

A second priority for Obama is improving the quality of education in Illinois. He says far too many schools are attempting to provide a quality-learning environment in crumbling school buildings that are not wired for the Internet.

Obama also wants to work to make college more affordable in Illinois and is also pushing for, at the state and federal levels, additional funding for early childhood education programs.

He plans to address the federal government's role in promoting economic development and job growth, saying that historically, Illinois has been one of the lowest ranking states in receiving a return on its federal dollars. Part of the reason, he suggests, is that the federal government has failed to direct monies toward transportation, infrastructure, and large-scale projects that would create jobs in the state.

Obama stresses that lawmakers must re-examine drug laws, saying that federal mandatory minimum sentencing for non-violent offenses has been a mistake at both the state and federal levels. He explained that the harsh sentencing guidelines do not take into account the potential for rehabilitation for young people who are involved in non-violent crimes.

Obama also feels that more funding should be provided to educate people who are incarcerated, noting that, "A prisoner who can read is far less likely to land back in jail, because he or she has the opportunity to find a job once they get out."

Affirmative Action And Diversity

Although Obama is a strong supporter of affirmative action, he believes that current programs are inadequate to address the need to open up opportunity to African-American businesses.

A true commitment to diversity, he insists, must be "affirmative" in providing capital opportunities and technical assistance to African-American entrepreneurs and start-up businesses.

"You can have as many affirmative action programs as you want, but if brothers and sisters out here who want to start a business can't get a bank loan, or don't know how to access the latest information in terms of inventory control or marketing techniques, they're going to fail anyway," Obama notes. "We've got to be a lot more aggressive at the federal level in providing capital and technical assistance to entrepreneurs."

Obama said he also supports efforts of businesses of color to compete as general contractors, primes, and to seek senior management roles, not just co-management on projects.

"I've proven at the state level that not only can I open the doors, but I can also help guide these businesses through the process, and insist that they get the full measure of opportunity that's out there economically," he says.

preface
Palmer

Update: Lu Palmer passed away September 12, 2004, at the age of 82. Jorja English Palmer passed away the next year on December 29, 2005, at the age of 75.

Lu and Jorja Palmer

By David Smallwood, Robert Starks, & Photography by Reginald Payton | *Originally Published January 14, 1999*

Put one brilliant advocacy journalist together with one brilliant organizer and strategist – both totally committed to the betterment of the condition of Africans in America – and you have a formidable duo who have helped change and improve the way of life for the Black community in Chicago.

That would be Lu Palmer and his wife Jorja English Palmer, who more than anyone else except the voters, were responsible for putting Chicago's first Black mayor, Harold Washington, into office.

But though that single accomplishment may have been the culmination of the Palmers' community efforts, there have been so many other victories won for Black people along the way since the 1960s that these two were instrumental in bringing about.

Lu became legendary as the strong, unbending, unyielding Black voice in Chicago's majority media – before finally bucking that system in classic Kunta Kinte fashion and becoming a substantial leader in his own right.

> I told them, 'You never understood me. You never understood that I am a Black man first and a reporter second, and my loyalties are to the Black community.'

"This Is Lu Palmer"

These days, Lu hosts the popular *On Target* talk show on WVON radio, and spends time with the organizations he founded, CBUC (Chicago's Black United Communities) and BIPO (the Black Independent Political Organization).

He's a consummate reporter – a veteran of the *Chicago Defender*, and the old *Chicago American* and *Chicago Daily News* newspapers. For 12 years, he hosted the extremely popular radio program, *Lu's Notebook*.

On that show, Lu was raw, "no-bull," unprecedented, and most often used his exceptional reporting skills to inform the Black community on how they were being shafted in some form or fashion. If the situation reported on was bad enough, Lu would end a broadcast with his signature line, "It's enough to make a Negro turn Black."

This program, along with Lu's equally insightful and acerbic *Daily News* columns, made him one of the most respected journalists by the Black community in Chicago media history because of Lu's penchant for telling it like it is. He also became one of the biggest thorns in the paw of the city's White power structure for the very same reason.

A Movement Mother

Jorja English Palmer, whose tongue and tenacity can be as sharp as Lu's typewriter, has been operating group living homes for abused and troubled boys since the early 1980s. She's a nurturer by nature – as much of a mother and caregiver to those in the Movement through the years as she's been a prime organizer.

It extends from her background. Jorja lost her own parents when she was four years old in her hometown of New Madrid, Missouri. Her aunt and uncle brought her to Chicago to live.

Then, when she had her own children, Lu explains, "Jorja's son, our son, Stanford, when he was three years old, got hit by a truck and became developmentally disabled. After he got to be (a young teen), he was very difficult to take care of and Jorja looked for an institution, but couldn't find a Black-run facility for boys in the whole state.

"So she got a bunch of her women together and went to then-Gov. Richard Ogilvie and sold him on backing a Black-run facility for boys."

The result was the Stanford English Home For Boys, the first group home for African American children in Illinois, located on the South Side of Chicago. Jorja spends 10-12 hour days there caring for her "babies," which can number as many as 24 young men at a time.

Active From Early On

Jorja's social activism began in high school, at DuSable, where she graduated as valedictorian. "My teachers were helpful," she explains. "They would have me write stories on situations like the Scottsboro Boys and things like that. They used to send me to the NAACP Youth Council meetings on 51st and South Park. I started writing about these things and trying to raise money."

As a young mother and PTA elementary school president, Jorja was a political activist and community organizer for the West Chatham Improvement Organization when she heard about the efforts of The Woodlawn Organization to fight against "Willis Wagons."

These were cramped modular units designed to handle the overflow at overcrowded Chicago public schools. Named after then school superintendent Benjamin Willis, they were primarily located in Black neighborhoods.

"We'd meet every morning and march to the Board of Education and almost every day we'd get dragged down the steps of the Board, upside down," Jorja recalls. "But in the end, Mayor Daley finally found it more expedient to remove Ben Willis."

The success of that effort led the groups involved to form the Coordinating Council of Community Organizations, headed by Al Raby.

Fighting With King

"We moved from primarily fighting education into other areas," Jorja says. "Rev. James Bevel, one of Dr. King's lieutenants, kept saying the biggest problem besides education was housing, that we (Blacks) were 25 percent of the population, but lived on less than 10 percent of the land.

"We started doing testing of discriminatory real estate practices in White communities and finally Al Raby asked Dr. King to come up and help us. King met with us in the basement of the 50th and Indiana YMCA and we all agreed to join forces with his Southern Christian Leadership Conference (SCLC) to become the Chicago Movement."

Jorja recalls that on the subsequent march to Marquette Park, Whites were literally breaking the ground with pickaxes and coming at the Black marchers with big chunks of sidewalk.

"I got beaten down into a storefront window and Bevel had to call some of the gangbangers he had on the marches with him to pick me up and carry me back to safety," she says. "I couldn't walk for three days and I still have a bad back, but step by step, the Open Housing Agreement came about."

In Chicago, Jorja fought battles involving schools, police brutality, redistricting, women's rights, voting rights and Black political empowerment.

Lu's Journey

In the meantime, Lu's journey found him as an ex-G.I. in his hometown of Newport News, Virginia, where he and a buddy were going into the taxi business until Lu's father said, no way, you're going back to school.

With a degree in sociology from the all-Black Virginia Union University in Richmond, Virginia, Lu had

been put in charge of the camp newspaper in the Army, though he'd never thought about pursuing the field.

But he discovered he could write and that he enjoyed it and one day, Lu's father presented him with a letter of acceptance to Syracuse University's journalism program in New York.

Lu's father was a special guy. He was brought to Newport News to start the first Negro high school. He took a two-room shack, as Lu calls it, and turned it into the renowned Huntington High School, which today still enjoys a stellar national reputation.

Lu says his father was the Black leader in Newport News' Black community, fighting to get the first Black policeman and that kind of thing. But after the elder Palmer led the fight to bring about equal salaries for Black teachers in the state of Virginia, he did not have his annual contract renewed as principal of Huntington, though he had served there for over 20 years.

There was a massive community effort to get his job back, but Lu's father died a year and a half later. "I always say he died of a broken heart," Lu says. "I also say that he was legally lynched by those White folks. After that, I decided I had to do something to try to make up for what they did to my old man."

With A Vengeance

He went to Syracuse, where there were only two Blacks in the journalism program, got all A's, and became a graduate teaching assistant.

"After I got my Master's from Syracuse, I decided I would use my skills as a journalist in the struggle for Black people," Lu says. "That led me to become what I call an 'advocacy journalist'."

He was eventually hired by the *Chicago Defender* to be editor of its *Tri-State Defender* in Memphis, covering the states of Tennessee, Arkansas and Mississippi.

"You talk about a bad town," Lu says. "Memphis was probably one of the five worst Southern cities in the country. I was down there writing about the racism and they burned crosses on my lawn, tried to run me off the road, police beat the hell out of me. Between the Klan and the police, quite likely, had I stayed in Memphis, they would have killed me."

The Defender eventually brought Lu to Chicago, where he worked for a dozen years and quit three times on owner John Sengstacke. A friend arranged a job for him at the *Chicago American*, where there was only one other Black reporter.

But a kindly editor gave Lu enough big stories that his consistent front-page bylines attracted the attention of the *Daily News*, who called him in. The editor was shocked that Lu was Black, but added it was a plus because the paper was looking for a Black columnist, one who would write from the Black perspective.

Major Differences

"I jumped at the chance, but that was my undoing at the *Daily News*," Lu explains. "They just could not countenance what I was writing about and there was constant conflict between me and the editor."

First he was asked to make changes. Then certain of his columns wouldn't run if they were deemed too inflammatory. Finally, Lu wrote a column suggesting that a *Daily News* investigation of then-Malcolm X College president Charles Hurst was crap and explained why.

The editor gave Lu's column to another columnist to rebut and the News ran them side by side. "So I resigned," Lu said. "I told them, 'You never understood me. You never understood that I am a Black man first and a reporter second, and my loyalties are to the Black community and not the *Daily News*.'"

To ensure that he was allowed to remove his vast personal files, which he had collected over the years, Lu had members of the Black Panther Party come to the *Daily News* newsroom dressed in full Panther regalia and escort him out, with his belongings. "Nobody said a damn word," Lu recalls.

After running his own publication, the *Black X-Press Infopaper*, for two years, Lu's community activism stepped up. He had founded CBUC and helped lead the effort to defeat a White candidate of then-Mayor Jane Byrne for Chairman of the Board of Education.

Community Action

That effort helped launch CBUC's campaign to elect Harold Washington as Mayor, and just hours before Harold announced his candidacy, Lu was called in by his radio show sponsor, Illinois Bell, and fired, allegedly for his political activity.

The story goes that Bell had tried to not renew Lu's contract every year, but community groundswell saved him. Finally, it is speculated that there was a $35 million deal between Illinois Bell and the city of Chicago that Jane Byrne threatened to cancel if they didn't yank Lu off the air.

But then came Lu's shining moment – Harold's election. The Palmers were in the eye of the storm from the beginning with the CBUC rallying cry issued by Lu Palmer in 1981, "We Shall See In '83!" and the training of thousands of election workers spearheaded by Jorja.

When asked if it's the biggest disappointment of his life that Harold did not support him in return when Lu sought to fill the 1st District Congressional seat after Harold's election, Lu answered, "If not the biggest, certainly one of the biggest. For years, I never understood it and I'm not sure I still understand it."

Jorja – whom Lu met and courted against the unseemly backdrop of city officers burning food intended for the Black Panthers' Free Breakfast for Children Program, and the aftermath of the murder of Fred Hampton before marrying him in 1975 – said of Harold's slight of her husband of over 20 years: "It hurt Lu tremendously; I don't think he'll ever be the same. Harold was like our brother."

These days, Lu Palmer, jaded and a little depressed, doesn't do a whole lot. "Part of it is certainly disenchantment with the direction in which our movement has gone, the direction in which our people are going," Lu admits.

"I wonder if all the struggle made any difference... our minds have been so manipulated by this American system that we may be worse off than we were. Our minds are controlled, we have lost control over ourselves, we have no institutions, we don't control our communities.

"I am happy to have lived to soon be 77 years old," Lu concluded. "But I'm just so depressed by what's happening to Black people and I'm helpless because I don't know what to do about it."

preface McNeil

Update: Cheryl Grace — formerly Pearson-McNeil; she married in 2016 — is now the Senior Vice President, U.S. Strategic Community Alliances and Consumer Engagement for Nielsen. The Nielsen Company forecasts African-American buying power to reach $1.3 trillion in 2017.

Cheryl Pearson McNeil

By David Smallwood & Photography by Reginald Payton | *Originally Published May 26, 2011*

Earlier in her career, after finishing college, Cheryl Pearson-McNeil thought her destiny lay in the field of journalism and she actually worked as a copy editor for a small paper in a Chicago suburb.

She tried her hand at reporting, but the township meetings she covered and writing about zoning issues put the budding, high-energy reporter to sleep.

One day a press release crossed her desk from the Girl Scouts looking for a public relations director, which prompted her interest.

"That job never made it into the paper," Cheryl recalls, laughing at how the Girl Scouts position she secured transitioned her from journalism to public relations and being a corporate spokesperson.

Today, Cheryl Pearson-McNeil is a dynamic communications strategist who excels at building brand awareness and managing the reputation of major businesses, particularly within diverse communities.

I'm not only helping our company and clients learn more about the African-American community, but helping the community learn about our true economic power as well.

With more than two decades of national corporate and non-profit, television, community, and governmental relations experience, this gregarious, vivacious professional has the know-how and presence to help shape perceptions surrounding a corporation.

Cheryl is the senior vice president of public affairs and government relations for The Nielsen Company, a global information and measurement company that has leading market positions in marketing and consumer information, television and other media measurement, online intelligence, mobile measurement, and trade shows.

Leading The Count At Nielsen

In this role, which she's held since 2009, Cheryl is responsible for widening the scope of Nielsen's corporate, government, community, and social responsibility programs and special initiatives. She's also been tasked with developing and overseeing the company's national diversity advertising strategy.

"Most people aren't aware that Nielsen is the largest marketing research and measurement company in the world and that we're located in more than 100 countries," Cheryl says.

What does that mean exactly? "Well, in a nutshell," Cheryl explains, "Nielsen has its finger on the pulse of what consumers watch and what consumers buy."

"People are familiar with the term 'TV ratings,' and most know that those ratings tell how many people are watching a particular television program," she says. "But that's just one form of how people are watching programming these days."

"The 'watch' side of our business also includes what you're watching on your cell phones, on your computers, what you watch when you go to the movies, which commercials you're paying attention to – we measure all of that!

"And the 'buy' side of our business is where we monitor consumer lifestyle and purchasing behavior as it relates to how you shop at grocery stores, convenience stores, drug stores, big box stores, and even online."

A large part of her job is to raise awareness about the full measurement capabilities Nielsen provides and explain – especially to consumers of color – why they should care about the research and insights Nielsen provides.

Tapping The Marketing Potential of Black America

Getting that information out to the Black community is crucial to The Nielsen Company, as African Americans in the United States have a buying power in excess of $507 billion dollars, according to *Target Market News*, which has tracked Black buying power for years.

"When African Americans and the businesses we spend money with can see our value as consumers from that type of a perspective it should shift the dynamics of the equation somewhat," Cheryl says.

"Marketers and advertisers would never try to market to all people in Greece, for example, using one tactic or strategy. They would try different tactics to appeal to the various demographics of the Greek population. The same concept should hold true for marketing to Black folks here in the United States."

She explained, "My mother Eleanor shops differently than I do because of our age difference, our educational difference, our income difference. What appeals to her in a company or product may not appeal to me.

"A company stands a better chance of getting business from both of us if they approach us by more narrowly defining other demographic subgroups – such as income, family size, and education – than just using a cookie cutter approach based purely on the fact that we're Black," Cheryl says. "Nielsen can provide our clients with that multi-dimensional view of consumers."

A Chicago Fixture

Cheryl joined Nielsen in 2004 as vice president of communications and public affairs for what was then Nielsen Media Research. She helped establish Nielsen's community affairs department, which was not in existence prior to the time she joined.

In 2007, she was promoted to senior vice president of communications for the North American Consumer division of the company, before accepting her current corporate role in 2009.

Prior to joining Nielsen, Cheryl spent four years at WMAQ-TV, the NBC affiliate here in Chicago, where she became a familiar face in the multi-cultural communities in and around the city.

Before that, she led the marketing communications departments at The YWCA of Metropolitan Chicago and Boys and Girls Clubs of Chicago, and worked in City Hall as press secretary for then City Treasurer Miriam Santos.

All these roles helped Cheryl develop a strong community presence and loyal following of people she had worked side by side with to make Chicago a better place to live.

This presence, coupled with her understanding of the television industry, helped her land her position at Nielsen as the company geared up to go beyond their business to business mode of operation, and recognized the need to be supportive of the communities it relied on for participation in its panels and studies.

Cheryl credits the non-profit industry with helping her to first grasp the importance of shaping messages and developing solid branding strategies.

"I started out as the Director of Public Relations at the Girl Scouts of DuPage County, and one of the first 'branding' misperceptions I was asked to erase was that it was an all-White organization," she says. "Here I was in DuPage County of all places, being asked to showcase non-traditional members and volunteers."

She identified Linda Hall, a troop leader who lived in Oak Brook, who was "beautiful, wealthy and Black!" Cheryl recalls. "What a great way to make

our point about pluralism in the suburbs."

Because of Cheryl, Hall and her daughter were subsequently featured on the cover of one of DuPage County's weekly newspapers all decked out in their Girl Scout uniforms. Cheryl admits it is still one of her most "rewarding moments," and reports that she and Linda are still friends to this day.

"Keep in mind, this was back in the 1980s," Cheryl noted. "There were Blacks in the western suburbs, but we were kind of tucked away. Both Linda and I understood that we had accomplished something huge with this cover."

Although it's been two decades since she worked professionally for the Girl Scouts, Cheryl continues her support of the organization because she understands the value it brings to young girls' self-esteem, and how it reaches out to girls of all income brackets. She even became a troop leader for a group of homeless girls at a local shelter.

Bridging The Diversity Chasm

So, how does one go from having campgrounds outside their office window to being the first Black woman named to a senior vice president role at a multi-billion dollar global corporation?

Cheryl holds a Bachelor of Arts degree in public relations from Purdue and a Masters of Business Administration from the Keller Graduate School of Management.

She considers her "translation" skills as one of the primary keys to her success. "I'm good at taking complex information and putting it into laymen's terms so that people are suddenly fascinated by research data," she says.

Cheryl has turned that gift into an asset for Nielsen and pens a bi-weekly column for more than 180 Black newspapers around the country through an alliance with the National Newspaper Publishers Association (NNPA).

"I love sharing Nielsen's information with the public," she says, "and the column gives me a chance to have fun with readers around data and insights and to empower – according to the NNPA – 19 million readers all at the same time."

Finding multiple platform opportunities to connect Nielsen with African-American communities led directly to the Steve Harvey and Tom Joyner syndicated morning radio shows.

"How great is it for millions of listeners to hear Steve or Tom on their respective shows sharing Nielsen information," Cheryl says, "and then driving those listeners to their websites for more stats and an opportunity to win all-expense-paid trips to either the Steve Harvey or Tom Joyner syndicated morning radio shows.

"Alliances like these give me reason to jump out of bed in the morning because I really do believe I'm not only helping our company and our clients learn more about the African-American community, but helping the community learn about their true economic power as well."

Cheryl speaks proudly of the growth The Nielsen Company has achieved in the area of diversity over the last seven years. "Internally we now have employee resource groups and we also have external advisory councils comprised of African-American, Hispanic and Asian industry leaders," she says. "To think I've had a hand in helping shape all of that is really quite personally rewarding.

"It's one of the reasons you see me out in the community so often. I think it's just where I'm supposed to be, spreading the word."

She laughs out loud at that statement, "I know I sound like an evangelist, right? But I honestly do feel inclusion is so important to ensuring empowerment."

Cheryl acknowledges that in many instances in her life she was "the only," or at least, "one of the very few," Blacks in a setting, and credits those early experiences for providing her with the unique ability to seamlessly bridge the diversity chasm.

As a result, Cheryl says, "I feel at home no matter where I am, and from a diversity perspective, that's priceless. I used to joke at NBC that I was Polish one day, Italian the next and Black the day before and after that.

"But it's not just important that I fit in culturally because my role includes ensuring that corporate executives also feel at ease if they suddenly find themselves in the 'minority.' A company's brand identity can be based on something as simple as how people remember you from those experiences.

"And since the face of America is rapidly shifting," Cheryl concludes, "it's important for executives to understand the impact of that shift, and to communicate it in a positive light."

preface Pfleger

Update: Now called The Faith Community of Saint Sabina, the church celebrated its 100th Anniversary in 2016 with Father Pfleger still at its helm. Along the way, he has adopted two Black sons, Lamar and Beronti, and became a foster father to Jarvis Franklin, who tragically was killed in gang crossfire in 1998. Father Pfleger continues to be one of Chicago's and the nation's leading proponents against gun violence and the easy access to guns that is snatching the lives of young people across the country.

He is the subject of a documentary by filmmaker Bob Hercules titled *Radical Disciple: The Story of Father Pfleger* and subject of the book *Radical Disciple: Father Pfleger, St. Sabina Church and the Fight for Social Justice* by Robert McClory.

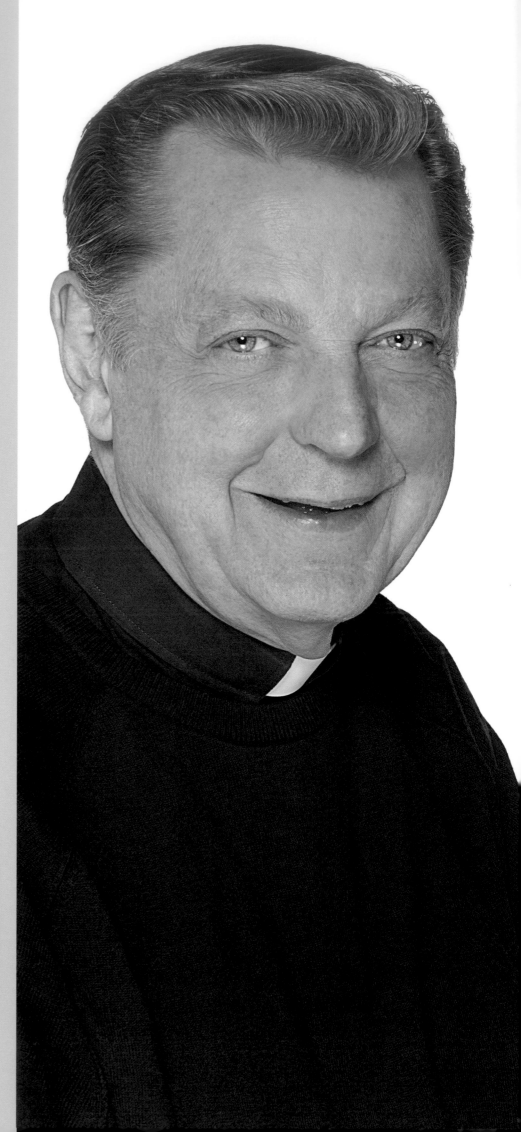

Father Michael Pfleger

By Ken Parish Perkins & Photography by Ernest Collins | *Originally Published October 17, 1996*

Someday the people who love Father Michael Pfleger are going to meet up with the people who hate Father Michael Pfleger, and what a gathering that will be.

Depending on who owns the discussion, the pastor and visionary of Saint Sabina Catholic Church is either a media-hungry, racially-schizoid "nigger lover", as letters to the South Side church are often addressed, or he's a genuine foot soldier fighting for social, political and racial reform within the city's Black and poor enclaves.

When Saint Sabina celebrates its 80th anniversary soon with a benefit concert featuring former Saint Sabina member Chaka Khan, one can't toast the church's longevity without speaking from the vantage point where Father Pfleger is currently perched.

> I firmly believe that the greatest addiction we have in this society is racism. To me, there's nothing that's a greater evil than that.

Saint Sabina was a floundering and disrespected member of the archdiocese preparing for a death march when Pfleger arrived in 1975 as an assistant pastor – a wide-eyed and self-assessed naïve White boy from a racially-intolerant Southwest Side of Chicago. He became Saint Sabina's pastor in 1981 at the age of 31.

The church was on the short list of closures when Father Pfleger's number came up to take over the institution and its academic academy, and repair the church's less than favorable reputation.

The virtually all-Black Saint Sabina, situated in a weary section located at 1210 West 78th Place (near Racine), where guns and gangs mix easily, fluidly and frequently, had a fluctuating worshipping congregation of about 110 – at some services, less than 50 bothered to show up. School enrollment was just as dismal.

The structure was embarrassing; the basement area was locked off. The church looked like what it was: a place you saw on the road to closing.

Tell Him What He Can't Do

"But people who know Father Mike are aware that all you have to do is tell him he can't do something," says parishioner Janice Littlejohn, "and he can kinda go off on you."

Father Pfleger went off all right, by drastically changing the face of the Catholic church, giving Saint Sabina an Afrocentric makeover. Prominently displayed are rows of symbolic red, black and green African-American banners, an altar modeled after an African drum, and a wall mural depicting a Black Christ with superimposed Black hands.

His decision set the church on the healthy (religious, as well as fiscal) path it now enjoys and positioned Father Pfleger as one of the most scrutinized, analyzed and – his parishioners claim – misunderstood men in Chicago.

Adds Littlejohn: "Rarely do I meet people with no feelings for Father Mike – if they know him or have heard of him, they tend to love him to death or despise him immensely, or say he's just an angry man, which in some ways is odd considering the man is a priest."

But Father Pfleger is a different kind of priest for a different kind of parish, a place which can either inspire or incite, depending upon one's socio-political views or their open-mindedness to changes in the Catholic tradition.

Changing To An African-American Church

His office is exactly the kind of lair you would imagine for a man who has spent most of his adult life urging people to effect change by getting involved. On his walls are dozens of serious-looking Black dignitaries, religious and otherwise, smiling entertainment celebs and sports heroes – people who have given support to Saint Sabina by participating in the church's fundraisers or are simply lured to this place by the ever-convincing man in charge.

He's moving his finger across the wall, pointing out Maya Angelou, Arun Gandhi, grandson of the Indian political and spiritual leader Mahatma, Zenani Mandela-Diamini, daughter of Nelson, Jesse Jackson, Shirley Chisholm, Rosa Parks, even Nation of Islam leader Louis Farrakhan.

Father Pfleger stops there, anticipating the next question. "People always say, 'Well, what about his beliefs on this or that,'" he says. "There's no human being on earth whom I agree with on everything, but he's someone I have ultimate respect for. He is not owned by anyone. He says what he believes. He stands for what he believes."

For an angry man, Father Pfleger is surprisingly good company. Slender in a polo shirt and slacks, his smile is warm, his tone mild, his gestures welcoming, even as he talks of the gulf between Blacks and Whites and the often unyielding Catholic Church.

He speaks quietly, quickly, candidly. You think salesman might have been an alternative career. Rarely will his eyes leave yours.

"What used to be here was, basically, a European celebration, a traditional Catholic mass that you would find in any White church in the city," Father Pfleger says. "You could close your eyes and not know the difference. It was a White church, White run, White controlled, with White thinking. And if it was going to survive, it had to become what it was to be, and that was an African-American church."

Saint Sabina would become that African-American church, despite a rocky transition. Angered over the Afrocentric direction of the church, many Black members bailed. Pfleger says, "Some felt it wasn't in the tradition of the church; others said, 'I came to the Catholic Church to escape this color-based stuff.'"

Others switched religious alliances following a biblically rooted approach installed by the pastor. Father Pfleger thinks 25 percent of the congregation changed over a matter of two years. Some left, but more came. Saint Sabina now offers three Sunday services for a congregation of about 2,000.

Enrollment for its educational arm, from kindergarten to eighth grade, is up and graduates move on to academically stringent high schools in and outside the city. Father Pfleger claims that 95 percent of Saint Sabina students end up on college campuses.

The school's success in turning out young minds has defined his work and life about as much as his community involvement, which borders on obsession.

Inside many cookie jars you'll find the church's hands, from businesses – a consortium where people can sell their goods and a food pantry are underway – to retreat centers, job development programs, and a full-service youth center designed to keep children and teenagers off the urban battlefields nearby.

He is noted for his continuous, dogged fight to rid the neighborhood of liquor stores and billboards and halt Black-on-Black crime with Friday night marches and vigils in troubled areas.

Saint Sabina has always been a refuge from the noisy and dangerous concrete world just outside its doors, even for rival neighborhood gangbangers who feel safe to use the church's gymnasium evenings and weekends to play basketball peacefully against each other.

Three Life Lessons

To understand Father Pfleger, it's important to look at his roots. He grew up in a house near 81st and Thomas. That neighborhood is now primarily Black. "Then it was White, middle class, policemen, firemen, city workers," Pfleger says. "Growing up, I thought the whole world was perfect because my block was fine."

His father worked in the bedding business; his mother was a secretary. He often points to three things that changed his life.

The first occurred in the mid-'60s while in high school. He spent two summers on a Native-American reservation in Oklahoma. It was his first encounter with racism. He was going into a store with Native-American children and the store owner refused them.

"I became a maniac," Pfleger recalls. "I remember calling my mother and telling her that I'm moving to Oklahoma because they have problems down there. She sort of laughed at me and said, 'Welcome to America.' I was so naïve."

Life lesson two: he was at Marquette Park during the Dr. Martin Luther King march in 1966. "I watched people I knew, people I went to church with, who lived in my community, throwing rocks, calling the marchers niggers. All this anger and rage and hate," Pfleger recalls.

"Then I saw King walking amid all this in total peace. And I realized it was my first and greatest lesson of nonviolence. He was in control. There were thousands of people screaming in a rage and here he was in total control.

"He wasn't responding to them. I remember thinking to myself, 'I want to get to know this man. Either he's crazy or has some kind of strength I want to know.'"

Pfleger would become obsessed with King. He plastered news clippings of King on the door of his bedroom. Read every King biography he could find. "What I learned about him was that he did what he did out of his faith," Pfleger says.

"He never saw himself as an activist or civil rights leader. He saw himself first as a preacher. That's really what drew me to want to be a minister. He became a mentor of me from a distance."

Life lesson three: While in college, Pfleger started working with the Black Panthers. "Fred Hampton and the Panthers used to meet in the basement of this church where I was living," he says.

"I'd attend the meetings. I realized that everything that was being written about the Panthers was not the

truth. I remember doing quite a lot with the breakfast program, but never hearing anything positive about it in the media. It opened my mind."

Paying The Price

In a matter of eight years, his whole world was turned upside down. "Most of the time, people couldn't understand what I was doing, what I was feeling, and why," he says. "My mother and father, and in particular my sister, kept telling me, 'We don't know what you're doing, we don't understand, but we'll support you.'"

Pfleger always knew he'd pay a price. Whites consider him a traitor. He was cut off from his own extended family. "My greatest hate over the years has been from the White community," he says.

"In the form of hate letters, in terms of threats.

They say, 'Nigger lover, go to Africa.' I've had priests tell me to leave the Catholic Church, that I'm destroying it. My response always is, 'I'm happy here. Why don't you leave if you're not happy?'

"It's interesting because the African-American community has always made me feel welcomed. It was the White community that always made me feel: make a choice. And I knew when I adopted my first son (who is Black) that I would never again live in the White community.

"Because of what I saw there, I would never be able to feel comfortable with him growing up in an all-White community. Obviously there are the Oak Parks and Hyde Parks, but where I come from, I could never go back to," Father Pfleger concludes.

"I firmly believe that the greatest addiction we have in this society is racism. To me, there's nothing that's a greater evil than that."

preface
Preckwinkle

Update: Toni Preckwinkle was elected in 2010 and again in 2014 as President of the Cook County Board. She has reduced the Cook County Jail population from 10,000 to 7,500, with intentions to lower it even further in the coming years.

Toni Preckwinkle

By Robert T. Starks & Photography by Victor Powell | *Originally Published April 8, 2010*

Toni Preckwinkle's rise to the top came after hard work and setbacks. She first ran for alderman of the 4th Ward in 1983, and lost to the incumbent Timothy Evans. In 1987, she ran for a second time and lost to Evans.

However, when she ran in 1991, Preckwinkle defeated Evans and won the Democratic Committeeman seat for that ward and has won every election for alderman since.

Today, Preckwinkle is ready to move from the City Council to Cook County Board President in this year's election.

Cook County has a population of approximately 5.2 million people; it is the second most populous county in the nation behind Los Angeles County; and its population is larger than 29 individual U.S. states, according to the 2015 U.S. census.

> I cannot understand why we cannot have alternative programs for the many young people that are housed in the Cook County jail. We are incarcerating too many young men.

Preckwinkle, a St. Paul, Minnesota native, earned her Bachelor's and Master's degrees in education from the University of Chicago and taught high school history for 10 years. The mother of two and grandmother of three is known for her hands-on involvement in her community; she is oftentimes observed walking the streets of her ward to monitor cleanup crews and to inspect public works projects.

In addition to being a schoolteacher, she has worked as an administrator of a not-for-profit organization, a planner for the Chicago Department of Planning, and Executive Director of the Chicago Jobs Council. Preckwinkle feels that she has amassed the kind of public and private sector experiences that will serve her well if elected to head the Cook County Board.

"I look forward to running a tight ship and practicing fiscal responsibility as President of the Cook County Board," she says.

See Toni Run

Toni Preckwinkle has taken the first step in the direction of securing the Cook County Board Presidency by handily winning the Democratic nomination. She won with 280,947 votes (49 percent) of the vote in the February primary against three other opponents, including the incumbent president Todd Stroger, who came in fourth place with 78,205 votes, or 13 percent.

This has given her added optimism for a win in November because Democrats outnumber Republicans almost 2-to-1 in the county. (In fact, the last Republican Cook County Board President was Richard Ogilvie in 1966).

Preckwinkle tells *N'DIGO* that she believes her hard-earned reputation as a progressive alderman and her ability to negotiate with opponents will allow her to restore some degree of civility to the Cook County Board that, some charge, has been lost.

Todd Stroger supporters were dismayed by Preckwinkle's aggressive run against him in view of the fact that she was given vital support and help by Stroger's father when she began her political career.

"I was indeed supported by President John Stroger in the 1990s and I, in turn, gave him support when he ran both times for the President of Cook County Board," Preckwinkle responds. "I do not consider my running against Todd as revocation of my respect for his father. I am running to reform county government and restore confidence in the Board."

Many voters supported Todd Stroger because of the fact that his father, John Stroger, had built the best county public health care system in the nation and the one-cent tax supported by Todd was not an unbearable burden if it was used to maintain the health care system.

Not so, Preckwinkle says. She argues, "The health care system's independent governing board hired a competent administrator and he has already begun reducing costs to the tune of 19 percent less in 2010 than in 2009. I believe that we can repeal the tax, save the system, and improve it while continuing to reduce costs and save the taxpayers money by instituting sound fiscal management."

Toni Preckwinkle

Platform of Reform

Economic development is a major platform item for her campaign; she intends to focus on increasing the number of green jobs in the county through an aggressive county economic development program.

"Since two of the major responsibilities of the Board are to administer the health care system and the jails, my campaign is focused on these two issues. Therefore, I intend to pay close attention to the jail and make reform of the jail system in this county a priority," Preckwinkle says.

"I cannot understand why we cannot have alternative programs for the many young people that are housed in the Cook County jail. We are incarcerating too many young men. We should have better and more effective drug testing, electronic monitoring, boot camps, and drug treatment."

Given the intense patronage tradition of hiring and promotion in county government, many of the people who were hired during John and Todd Stroger's administrations now fear payback or unemployment in a Preckwinkle administration.

But, "I have no intention of conducting a witch hunt or carrying out revenge firings," she says coolly. "As you know, a new president has the right to bring in his or her own team. We are also obligated to abide by the Shakman Decrees, which prohibits patronage hiring and firings.

"Most county employees are covered by union contracts and rules. So as long as employees and department heads are doing their jobs and serving the citizens of Cook County properly, they will be able to retain their jobs!"

The Critics

Ald. Preckwinkle is an energetic and progressive elected official who is beloved by her constituents in the Hyde Park-Kenwood neighborhood and throughout her ward. After nearly 20 years in the Chicago City Council, she now wants to take on the government of Cook County.

Initially, many critics believed that she could not garner electoral support beyond the South Side because she did not have a citywide or countywide profile. However, she is convinced that her primary vote totals proved that she has appeal across the city and throughout the county.

"I have assembled a winning team to conduct an aggressive campaign. We will spend the rest of the months leading up to the election meeting and communicating with as many voters, elected officials, ministers, business people and civic leaders as possible," Preckwinkle states. "I have not and will not take anyone or anything for granted. We need the support of all of the citizens of this county."

Some critics and progressives were suspicious of her alleged endorsement by Mayor Daley at the beginning of her campaign. After all, Preckwinkle was the lone alderman to vote against Mayor Richard M. Daley's budget in 2005 in a move to protest the city's "insensitivity" toward African Americans when it came to city contracts.

However, Preckwinkle says, "Initially, I asked Daley for his support as I asked every other elected official for his or her support, but he remained non-committed until the end when he did become helpful."

She says that she began immediately after the primary election to meet with people from every area of the county, including many of the ministers that supported Todd Stroger in the primary. Preckwinkle reiterated, "I do not take any voters for granted; I intend to reach out to as many voters in the county as possible."

This legendary alderman from the Hyde Park-Kenwood neighborhood on the South Side of the city is President Barack Obama's alderman. Insiders also know Preckwinkle as the elected official that helped to jumpstart Obama's political career.

She says she has known Obama since the early '90s, when he was doing a voter registration activity, Project Vote, in and around the 1992 election.

The two have maintained a relatively close political relationship since first meeting. She has supported him in every run for political office by offering sage advice, providing him with vital campaign workers, and steering him around political traps.

Her embrace of Obama in the '90s was crucial to his introduction to the Hyde Park-Kenwood community, which is the home of the University of Chicago, and has a long tradition of producing independent voters and elected officials.

So, to put an end to those rumors claiming there is now a strain between Mr. Obama and his alderman, Toni Preckwinkle, she replies, "The President called me the day after the primary to congratulate me on my win."

Perhaps yet another presidential call is in her future after she wins the general election in November.

preface Primo

Update: Mr. Primo has overseen Capri's origination of nearly $10 billion in real estate equity, debt and structured finance transactions since its establishment in 1992. Mrs. Primo is founder and CEO of IntraLink Global, a next generation marketing and content firm that links content strategy, social media, and technology.

Quintin and Diane Primo

By Barbara Samuels & Photography by Chris Griffin | *Originally Published April 25, 2002*

Any discussion of Chicago's power couples would have to include real estate investor Quintin E. Primo III, and his wife Diane, a senior-level marketing executive and management consultant.

The Primos' career paths went in different directions, but each has made major milestones in the 30 years of experience they have in their respective fields.

Their accomplishments are awesome, and their educational backgrounds are impeccable. Both also share an intense interest in community affairs, and they are excellent role models for young people who might want to aspire to follow in their footsteps.

The Primos – introduced to each other in 1981 by Daryl Carter, co-chairman and co-founder of their investment firm, Capri Investment Group – were married in 1983. They are the parents of Francesca Simone and Quintin E. Primo IV. Primo is the son of Bishop Quintin E. Primo, Jr., the first suffragan (assistant) of the Episcopal Diocese of Chicago.

> I advise students to: 1) select a vocation; then 2) Get A Job! An early job might not be in the area you've trained for in college, but find work and build your skills. — Diane Primo

Primo III is the Chairman, CEO and co-founder of Capri Capital Partners, LLC, the nation's largest African American-owned real estate advisory firm. With more than six billion dollars in real estate assets currently under management, and the only corporation advising pension firms, Capri has experienced unprecedented growth over the past decade.

Capri specializes in debt and debt-related investments on behalf of pension funds and other institutional investors, and is a delegated underwriter and service lender for Fannie Mae, Freddie Mac, and HUD/FHA multi-family apartment loans. It is the only minority-owned Fannie Mae-delegated underwriting and servicing lender.

Primo oversees the general business activities of Capri and chairs the firm's global management board. He is Chairman of Capri Select Income, a mezzanine investment fund marketed to pension funds and other institutions.

Headquartered in Chicago, the corporation has offices throughout the United States and also operates in Africa, India, and the Middle East. Capri Capital was co-founded in 1992 by Primo and Carter, his high school friend from Detroit. The company's name was derived by combining the first letters of their last names.

Prior to Capri, Primo was managing director at Q. Primo & Co., a real estate investment banking firm he founded in 1988. He was also a vice president and manager of Citicorp Real Estate, Inc.'s Chicago lending team. Primo received his MBA from Harvard in 1979, and a Bachelor of Science degree in finance from Indiana University.

Telecommunications Wiz

Special thanks are due to Mrs. Diane Primo: she originated the "Privacy Manager" feature that blocks commercial calls – telemarketers included – and holds a U.S. patent for her work in the telecommunications field.

Diane Primo has held senior management and marketing positions with some of the country's largest and most visible corporations. She is a talented specialist in consumer marketing, and is often asked to address industry groups and business publications such as the *Wall Street Journal*.

Diane has been featured in major media, including *Crain's*, the *Chicago Tribune*, *Advertising Age*, and other trade publications, and was selected as one of the "Top 100 Women in Business Under 40" by *Ebony* magazine.

Mrs. Primo received her Master's of Business Administration degree from the Harvard Business School, and a Bachelor of Arts degree in Philosophy from Smith College.

Active in civic and community affairs, she serves as a board member of the Chicago Sinfonietta, and is a member of the Chicago Network and the Economic Club of Chicago, as well as a member of the board of the technology firm, Peopleclick.com.

Mrs. Primo was most recently Chief Executive Officer of WeServeHomes, an economic start-up

Primo
Quintin and Diane

in the home service industry, which was a joint venture between ServiceMaster and the venture capital firm Kleiner Perkins.

As CEO, she was responsible for all aspects of the business, including marketing, technology, business development, call center, program and process management, and finance.

Previously, she was President of Product Marketing with SBC Communications, and held the same position with Ameritech prior to its buyout by SBC in 1999.

Before joining Ameritech in 1997, Mrs. Primo held a series of management positions with The Quaker Oats Company. Prior to this, she was affiliated with Booz Allen & Hamilton, and the Rand McNally Company.

Social Commitment

Next to his family and his business, Mr. Quintin Primo's deep commitment to the Urban Family and Community Services agency is nearest and dearest to his heart.

Co-founded by his father in 1989, the organization provides needed services for women and children. Primo is Chairman of the Board of the social service organization, which is located at 4241 West Washington Street.

> One must demonstrate excellence in the task or career they have chosen. You must distinguish yourself from the pack. Optimum performance is mandatory. — Quintin Primo

In addition, he is a member of the Economic Club of Chicago, a board member of the Ravinia Festival Association, a trustee of the Chicago Community Trust and the Episcopal Church Pension Fund.

He is an honorary board member of the Chicago Sinfonietta, and an officer of the Alliance of Business Leaders and Executives (ABLE). He is a voting member of the Pension Real Estate Association and Urban Land Institute, co-founder and board member of the Real Estate Round Table, the major lobbying

group for the real estate industry. He also serves as an independent trustee of Amli Residential Properties Trust, a real estate investment trust that is traded on the New York Stock Exchange.

Career Advice

When asked what it takes for budding real estate execs to get started in the industry, Primo replied, "First and foremost, one must demonstrate excellence in the task or career they have chosen. At Capri, we look for leadership qualities and self-starters.

"You must distinguish yourself from the pack. Optimum performance is mandatory. Try to build a relationship with a mentor. In this industry, it takes many years to develop relationships. Affirmative action has little impact because the business mainly consists of privately owned properties. Consequently, there is very little outside control. It is critical that excellence is shown early in your career."

Primo pointed out several resources for information. "Seek out real estate clubs, use the library and study trade publications, such as *Real Estate Industry*, *Commercial Property News*, *Real Estate Careers*, and others. Business magazines and newspapers are excellent sources of information. College and university alumni directories are also useful. Find out where alums are employed, then contact them. Call Donald Trump if necessary!"

Mrs. Primo has an extremely practical, direct approach to her industry. "I advise students to: 1) select a vocation; then 2) Get A Job! An early job might not be in the area you've trained for in college, but find work and build your skills.

"Corporations are subjecting job seekers to major psychological testing in order to determine career development. Prepare yourself by talking to people who are successful in your chosen field. Using the library is an excellent way to keep abreast of what's going on in the industry."

She agrees with the idea of researching alumni directories for building industry contacts, mentors, and job opportunities.

The Rands

By Wanda Wright & Photography by Victor Powell | *Originally Published July 10, 2003*

preface

The Rands

Update: Mr. Thomas Rand passed away in 2004 at the age of 85. The family's airport business, now called Mac One Midway, controls 16 of the restaurants at Midway Airport. The family also has food service contracts with McCormick Place and Cook County Jail.

As philanthropists, Tim and Everett have funded construction of homes in a Uganda village for families of children with AIDS. Since 1996, the brothers, along with their friend and founder Larry Huggins, have hosted an annual 'Christmas In The Wards' celebration to bring toys, electronic and educational devices, and warm clothes to thousands of low-income children throughout the city. In 1997 they founded 'The Football Classic' games.

As details unfold, his spirit of enterprise surges forward to capture his listener, charging the air. You can feel it swell up and around you.

Something nearly hypnotic happens as one is transported back to a time when making money required decorum and strategy without pretense. Sitting down talking with Thomas Rand, you begin to understand the meaning behind "survival of the fittest" as an ultimate test.

At nine years old, when other little boys were mastering sticks with stones, Rand worked at a small bakery-candy shop in Little Rock, Arkansas. One day he realized that his meager bakery wage was less than he could make for returning soda pop bottles.

Rising at twilight, he stole past sleeping guard dogs on neighbors' porch steps, gathering empty bottles and cashing them in. Thomas Rand had become a supplier before dawn of the next day.

Today, he is an entrepreneurial giant here in Chicago as a supplier of beverages, as head of Midway Wholesalers.

Opportunity In Unlikely Places

Little Rock, Arkansas might have been anathema to some, but Rand saw opportunity in unlikely places. During a stint as a house detective for a major hotel as a pre-teen, he learned of new opportunities, persistently making mental notes for the future.

In an era where many African Americans were relegated to back room jobs, he got a chance to observe the intricacies of management. His mother, Sadie Washington, set high standards for achievement. She taught school and later ran a small store and post office in Cornerstone, Arkansas.

Following suit, young Thomas eventually held down three jobs. Juggling that load taught him the mechanics of time management, profit, and loss. Thomas graduated from high school in Little Rock and went on to earn a business degree at Philander Smith College.

Being Black in a majority white world never deterred him. "I learned to use opposition to duck or fight enemies," he recalls, "and let that opportunity turn into money."

After working as a porter for New York Central Railroad, he set out to stake his own territory in Chicago. Though married and a father of three small children, he managed to save his checks from the railroad for one year, while buying into a business.

The first venture was a small restaurant and pool hall near the famous Club DeLisa on 55th and State Streets. Down the street, the Jewish owner of a spirits business observed the tenacity of Rand's seven-day, 12-14 hour operation, and persuaded Thomas to manage his liquor store.

Eventually, Rand bought out the aging owner, but when he applied for credit to supply the store with merchandise, he was refused. But impressed by his prompt payment of monthly rent, his realtor stepped in to lend him credibility. As the enterprise grew, the relationship with the realtor faded, so Rand found new resources.

Using southern charm, careful planning, and a cousin who could "pass" (looked White), they collaborated to build business through ardor and adversity. His tenacity and modesty gained so much respect that others sought his council.

Early on, Rand learned that the inequities of society were not due to color barriers so much as they were financial. He developed a passion to live well and help his fellow man do the same.

Filling the merchant needs of small Black companies became a niche for what has become the Rand family's core business, Midway Wholesalers.

Most people haven't got a clue about making money. They just want it.

Thomas Rand was able to craft methods of connecting main channel suppliers to enterprises with limited funds. As a result, small establishments were able to thrive and grow as never before.

His ability to quickly learn by observation and instruction made him a trusted confidant in circles that previously did not, and to some degree still don't, include African Americans.

Meet The Rands

To date, the Rands are the only African-American family to be granted a jurisdictional gambling license in Illinois. Although many others have tried to enter the bidding wars to own casinos, only the Rands passed the critical tests and stringent requirements to win those rights.

A tough resilient team, each one is a stalwart, independent personality. Although this article is primarily about the Rand men, it wouldn't be complete without mentioning their mom, Maud (Mrs. Thomas Rand, now deceased) who taught them humility, compassion and respect for others.

Everett (the older by 30 minutes) fraternal twin of Timothy, says, "When people ask who was the major influence over our lives as children, we credit our mother in instilling strong values and our father for creating the entrepreneurial spirit."

Tyrone, Everett and Timothy were brought into the business as small boys and they worked together as one unit. After school or on weekends, you would find them cleaning bathrooms, washing floors, and stocking shelves beside their father.

Tyrone went on to become a popular attorney and community activist, eventually moving his practice to

Wisconsin. But after a brief illness, he died in his sleep two years ago.

Everett has risen in the community as a thinker, a leader and a harbinger of educational superiority, through his pet project the Chicago Football Classic, which he founded in 1997 along with his brother Tim and construction magnate Larry Huggins.

The Classic has become a huge multi-layered project that annually attracts more than 55,000 African-American families to Soldier Field for the football game and battle of the marching bands between two Black colleges after nearly a week of family-oriented activities.

The proceeds of this effort are reinvested to benefit Historically Black College and University programs, as well as local school program initiatives.

Everett's passion to give back is part of his credo. He actively supports programs of the Chicago Public Schools, and LaRabida, Children's Memorial and Rush Presbyterian Hospitals.

Extremely modest, Everett says, "It is important to reach back. Especially to teach young people the value of customer service in business, to learn to address people with formality, instead of a disinterested familiarity."

"People need to feel important when they patronize your business," Everett says, adding, "Do you know what it feels like to make a purchase, or say a 'hello,' or 'thank you,' and the employer doesn't make the slightest response?" He beams and emphatically points towards himself, "I want to change that!"

Timothy saw an opportunity to expand the family's core business when Midway Airport answered an RFP (Request for Proposal for new business) nearly 10 years ago.

"Everybody laughed at the sleepy little airport in the middle of town," Tim says. Then he smiles with a one-sided grin and shrugs, "Who knew it would become the national and international hub it has grown into?"

Yet, what started out as a grand opportunity turned into a dark episode when Midway Airlines shut down. While some businesses threw up their hands or physically caved in when revenues dropped 70 percent overnight, the Rands stood united in a face-off with disaster.

Contractors refused to cancel more than $500,000 in signed contracts. The family says that they are forever grateful to Mayor Richard M. Daley for negotiating the airport into the grand transportation center it has become today.

The Rands' Midway Concessionaires remains in the game because of their priority towards the highest level of customer service, diversity, and price-conscious offerings. They offer more because they are acutely aware of the competition that may sway consumer purchases before passing through airport doors.

Top: Marc, Everett,
Thomas, Timothy
and Deven Rand

The Next Generation

Marc, Timothy's son, represents the third generation of the Rands, and speaks with deep reverence for the rock solid foundation his grandfather, dad and uncle are still building.

Though his perception is keenly fixed on the trans-cultural shift of a global environment, he does not intend to reinvent the wheel or rock the boat. His concern is to ease the workload for his family, though he works seven-day, 10-hours-a-day work weeks as well.

Marc feels that luck is with him, though he is treated like any other employee that has had to work from the ground up. This includes probation if he breaks the rules. He realizes he is responsible for maintaining the high standards set by the family as they prepare to keep the businesses viable and diversified.

Deven Mauclaire Rand is gorgeous, saucy, strongly opinionated, and full of energy. Wise beyond her years, she is fluent in French, an avid dancer, fashionista, and a buckling percussionist. Her conversation and thought process is advanced far beyond her 13 years, and she is in a rush to join the family initiatives.

Much of the management of Deven's demanding personality falls on the shoulders of her tiny, but tough mom, Sandra, who is Manager of Supplier Diversity for United Airlines. While father Tim tries to hide a proud smile, they both agree that Deven is more than a handful, but wouldn't change one thing about their self-titled "diva!"

The Family Credo

Giving back to the community has been a part of the Rand credo for many, many years. While they aren't "clubby," and remain intensely private, their contributions have led to the success of many cultural, civic, community and business organizations.

Preparation is key for these savvy businessmen. They are diplomatic, but don't have a lot of time or patience for insecure entrepreneurs.

Thomas Rand says, "Most people haven't got a clue about making money. They just want it. There is no way around leadership two or three generations deep."

Timothy offers, "There is no way to avoid working your way up from the bottom either, learning every duty to appreciate how to manage and grow your business."

Everett concludes with, "It is very important to us that development continues to thrive in the minority business environment, but we can't all be the boss in a snap.

"Success requires focus, hard work, long, committed days, and strong external business relationships with accounting, legal, and other professional firms."

When asked about relieving his family, Marc looks as if we have missed the point. Well, wouldn't one think that after such a gleaming track record, relaxation would be the next goal? With a look of disapproval, he nods and gently, but insistently adds, "We do relax … every day together…at work."

preface
Reynolds

Update: Loop Capital today employs more than 175 professionals in 21 offices globally. It has participated in municipal financings totaling over $1 trillion across 49 states, and over $1.5 trillion in corporate debt and equity underwriting since its inception.

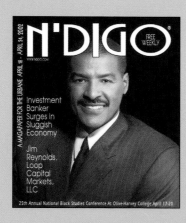

Jim Reynolds

By Derrick K. Baker & Photography by Victor Powell | *Originally Published April 18, 2002*

One conversation with Jim Reynolds is pretty much all it takes to realize that perhaps William Shakespeare had Reynolds in mind when Shakespeare crafted the line, "He was wont to speak plain and to the purpose," for the play *Much Ado About Nothing*.

While that obviously is an exaggeration, the quote is an appropriate description of Reynolds, who with more than 30 years of excellence in the complex and competitive financial services industry, has mastered the intricacies and strategies that fuel the field; an industry that for ages has been defined by such mega-firms as Merrill Lynch and UBS PaineWebber, two of his former employers.

In addition to the Shakespeare analogy, one look at Reynolds' corporate and entrepreneurial careers reveals that he never planned to fail at any of his endeavors – nor has he failed to plan.

> **Money works for you non-stop, 24 hours a day, every single day of your life until you spend it. And when you spend it, it starts to work for the other guy.**

Is it any wonder, then, that the Chicago-based investment banking and brokerage firm Loop Capital Markets, LLC, which Reynolds founded five years ago with six employees and one office, is experiencing triple-digit growth each year and has been Illinois' top-ranked underwriter for issuers over the past two years?

Reynolds understands with great visual acuity that money is an asset that should be treated as such. "Money," he notes, "works 24 hours a day, every single day. It doesn't sleep. You don't have to feed it. You don't have to maintain it. The only thing you have to do is keep it working. And it works for you non-stop, every single day of your life until you spend it. And when you spend it, it starts to work for the other guy."

His ability to literally and figuratively speak English has been the underpinning to his talent for sales, and his talent for identifying talent.

With a belief that he and his 50-plus employees in seven offices around the country "won't be outworked," Reynolds has deftly positioned Loop Capital to not only weather the lingering economic downturn that has caused larger investments firms to downsize thousands of employees, but to also prosper in a fashion and at a pace that would make management guru Peter Drucker proud.

To wit, in 2001, Reynolds, an alumni of Northwestern University's Kellogg Graduate School of Management and the University of Wisconsin-LaCrosse, says Loop Capital was involved in the pricing of more than $300 billion of securities, an eye-popping increase over the $2-$3 billion pricing of securities in the company's first year in 1997.

With an impressive roster of Fortune 500 clients, including General Mills, Sara Lee, General Motors, RR Donnelley & Sons, Peoples Energy, Bank One and ComEd, Loop Capital is expert and active enough to run with the proverbial big dogs, yet nimble enough to satisfy clients' particular needs, which might mean coordinating a stock repurchase for a major corporation, executing trades for more than 100 institutional money managers around the country, or serving as the commission-recapture agent for public and private pension plans.

The firm has served as co-manager or been in the selling group for taxable transactions totaling $100 billion plus, comprising such deals as:

- $3.4 billion in asset-backed securities for Commonwealth Edison;

- $200 million in corporate bonds for RR Donnelley & Sons Company; and

- $2 billion in corporate bonds for Ford Motor Credit.

The Value Of Talent

A chartered financial analyst who holds five securities licenses, Reynolds explains the inverse relationship between the precipitous economy and the fortunes of Loop Capital:

"Right now all the largest firms, including Merrill Lynch, Goldman Sachs and Lehman Brothers, are laying off pretty heavily at the junior levels and at the senior levels just because of the retrenchment in the business. So it's probably not a good time to be at a large firm," Reynolds explains.

"But for me, the converse is true. Having a smaller platform the way I do here at Loop Capital, we're able to begat significant talent in a manner that would have been untouchable for us a year or two ago," says Reynolds, who left Merrill Lynch in 1997 as the company's No. 1 municipal finance salesman in the country.

"We're able to entrench ourselves in some significant business while the big firms are still trying to figure out how they're going to re-shape themselves to go after the business. So for us, (now) is probably as great a time as we've had in our existence.

"The economy here has been good for us. With investment banking, some of the business is very counter-cyclical. We're involved in debt underwriting of corporate and public securities. The slowing of the economy has been incredibly beneficial to us.

"I've been able to grab very good people who have been able to move us deeper into corporate finance. We're able to do a lot more IPOs (initial public offerings) and corporate deals. I've also been able to expand our public finance side by bringing in public finance bankers to further our growth.

"We've been able to secure ourselves as the leading underwriter in the state of municipal issues. We've been able to do that because we have some very significant banking professionals and sales professionals.

"My focus now," Reynolds continues, "is to make sure that as the large firms are shrinking and trying to sort out what they're really going to look like on a long-term basis, I'm grabbing very talented people and we're servicing our accounts very attentively.

"Once the big firms get their ships turned in the right direction, they're going to come out with a vengeance. But if we're already supplying good service to the accounts that they forgot about a little bit, then we'll stay there.

"What I'm focused on now is not necessarily looking at the ups and downs and the whens and what's going to happen in the economic sphere. I'm more focused on the fact that we're providing very focused coverage. We'll be there."

His Kind of Town

Although started in Chicago, Loop Capital Management has offices in Detroit, Houston, Los Angeles, New York, Philadelphia, and San Francisco. Yet, Reynolds still proudly proclaims Chicago as "the best city in the country" for investment banking firms.

"We would not be the firm that we are if we were not in Chicago. If we were in New York or Los Angeles, we would just be another firm," he says. "The city has put its arms around us incredibly. The Mayor (Richard Daley) has given us the opportunity to work as long as we can do a good job with what we have to do.

"The City Council and the aldermen have all been great in making sure that this minority-owned investment company based in Chicago gets a fair opportunity to do business. At the state level, Sen. (Emil) Jones, Speaker (Michael) Madigan, (Sen.) Barack Obama, and various legislators have been awesome in making sure we have an opportunity to participate," he notes.

Wearing another hat, Reynolds is former president of the Alliance of Business Leaders and Entrepreneurs (ABLE), an influential organization of 54 African American business leaders in Chicago.

"I'm a staunch believer that African American businesses need to grow," Reynolds says, referencing ABLE. "It's very important to me that we grow Black business overall because we need to have larger African American-owned corporations."

On other civic and professional fronts, Reynolds is vice chair of the board of the Chicago Urban League, a gubernatorial appointment to the Illinois Business and Economic Development Corporation and is affiliated with the University of Chicago Medical Center and the CFA Institute, to name a few.

Explaining his many involvements, Reynolds says, "Approaching the relationships as a one-way street won't work. As people have helped me, I've tried to find the things they care about.

"For example, we're very much involved in the Chicago Public Schools. When we look at the future of the kids in Chicago, these kids end up not being hired at your Merrill Lynches and Goldman Sachs or your major law firms and major accounting firms; they get hired by minority businesses. Loop Capital is stepping up to its long-term responsibility of making sure this is a better city and a better state."

For example, Reynolds and his staff take on up to 10 high school and college interns each year, and the firm's charitable contributions are a plus for a number of agencies and programs across Chicago.

Why Start A Company?

The core of Reynolds' story of becoming a successful entrepreneur has the feeling of similar stories of ambitious professionals whose dreams exceeded those they accomplished by working for the proverbial "somebody else."

"I just felt that there was a lot more potential that I had, but there wasn't a platform for using it there," Reynolds recalls of his time spent as a director at Merrill Lynch in the Chicago regional office, where he was a leading salesman in the Corporate and Institutional Client Group.

Reynolds managed the municipal sales team responsible for the distribution of all tax-exempt products to institutional investors in the Midwest.

"They needed me to fill one role (at Merrill Lynch), but I felt in addition to that, there were other things I could be doing," he says of his yearn to stretch out. "When I looked at how I was going to satisfy my long-term objective, which was to really see what I can do with the business overall, it was pretty clear that the only way that I was going to do it was to be an entrepreneur.

"I identified several areas where I thought we could do a better job than most of the big firms were doing, and I went after that: keeping the clients' priorities first, and having a small, but very talented, group of people. It worked."

Before joining Merrill Lynch in 1988, Reynolds sharpened his financial teeth as a vice president at PaineWebber, Inc., where he established and headed the Midwest Municipal Bond Sales desk in Chicago. For three years prior, Reynolds was an assistant vice president at Smith Barney, Harrison, Upham Inc. in municipal sales, where he sold tax-exempt securities to institutional investors.

So, has Loop Capital fared as well as Reynolds planned? "It's far exceeded anything I thought we'd be at this time," he answers.

"One of the things that I've grown to learn, particularly as an African-American entrepreneur, (is that) we sometimes tend to not fully appreciate the skills that we have. It's not until you get yourself into an environment with a platform that allows you to use all those skills that you're really able to spread your wings.

"I didn't (anticipate) the response that I've gotten from people who support this firm. That was a wild card. It's been a very pleasant surprise."

With a vision of Loop Capital Markets becoming a "major national investment banking firm – and I think we're well on our way to being that – I'd like to see this be a billion-dollar business," concludes the husband of Sandy, and father of three children.

"I may not be one of the smartest guys; I don't think that's my forte. But most people who know me would probably put me in the group of what they would call, 'the hardest-working and most sincere guys I've ever met.' And that's what's more important to me."

preface
Richardson

Update: Since its beginning, *The History Makers* has recorded nearly 2,700 interviews over 9,000 hours of video footage and has received millions of dollars in grants to continue its work. *History Makers* is America's largest video/oral history on African Americans housed permanently at the Library of Congress and the Chicago Public Library. The collection is also found in top research education institutions like Harvard, Yale, Cornell, University of Chicago, Princeton and others.

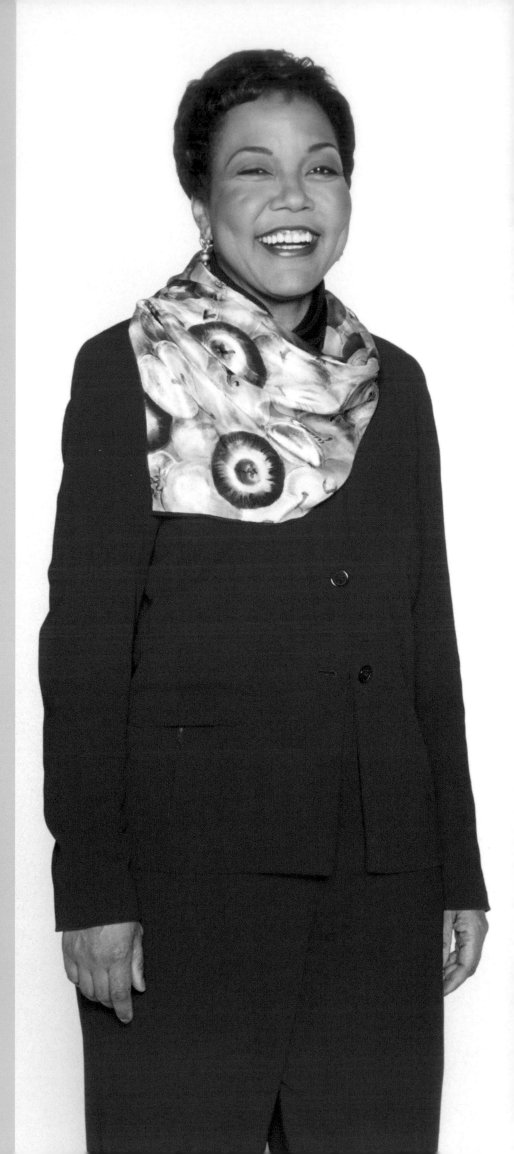

Julieanna Richardson

By Monica DeLeon & Photography by Reginald Payton | *Originally Published March 8, 2001*

On November 2, 2000, the launch of *The History Makers* project was a live interview of performer/activist Harry Belafonte by actor Danny Glover.

The project intends to record the highlights of the lives and careers of such noteworthy people as Etta Moten Barnett, Margaret Burroughs, Vernon Jarrett, Senator Emil Jones, Congressman Bobby Rush and entrepreneur Dempsey Travis.

"What exactly is *The History Makers?*" is a question that has been frequently asked of the project's creator and director Julieanna Richardson.

"I remember when I first had the idea, my friends asked, 'What are you doing? An archive? You must mean a cable channel Julie,' and I'd tell them no, and they'd say, 'A documentary?' and the documentary was absolutely the opposite of what I wanted to do because people already make beautiful documentaries," explains Richardson, describing the meandering road she took that led to *The History Makers'* growing success.

The History Makers at its conclusion will be a compilation of video interviews of well known and unknown leaders in the Black community. Each two-hour interview is structured to present a conversation between the *History Makers* and the viewer.

> **So much of the Black experience has been running away from the past, forgetting.**

The conversation is videotaped, put on audiocassette, sent out for transcription, archived, encoded. Each tape is catalogued with a Library of Congress subject heading and then digitized so that the interview can be sampled at *The History Makers'* website.

The general theme of each interview is, what has really made each person successful. Richardson elaborates, "Success is defined broadly because it doesn't mean people have led perfect lives, but they have made contributions in many ways."

In addition to celebrities, Richardson also looks at people who have played a role in significant organizations like the Pullman Porters, Urban League, NAACP and The Links, Inc. She has already scheduled an interview with the remaining Negro League baseball players.

Newly completed interviews include Alvin Poussaint, Katherine Dunham, Gordon Parks, and a special on the 111 African Americans who have served in the Illinois General Assembly.

Planting The Seed

Richardson planted the seeds for the project over 20 years ago when she was doing independent research on members of the Harlem Renaissance while she was an undergraduate attending Brandeis University.

"In 1973, in doing the research, that's really when I became aware of the Schomburg Center for Research in Black Culture, part of the New York Public Library and its holdings and what a wonderful resource it is," beams Richardson.

"I interviewed people like Thelma "Butterfly" McQueen and Lee Whipple and there were a couple of things that struck me: Butterfly McQueen had made $3,000 when she did *Gone With the Wind*, but she was working at a community center up in Harlem when I met with her, and living a not so good life at that point – but she still had that same voice," Richardson said with a smile.

"The stories struck me, as a young African American person. That, combined with spending time at the Schomburg, listening to tapes of different recordings of different shows that came out during the Harlem Renaissance, made the history really come alive for me."

Poignant personal stories that augment the cold facts and dates of historical events are exactly what made Harry Belefonte's life story come alive the night of the launch of the project.

Tales about his boyhood; detailed descriptions about the stages of his career in the arts; breathtaking accounts of his involvement in the civil rights movement, as well as about the intimate relationships and lifelong bonds formed between him and many of this country's national heroes, brought Belefonte's story alive.

Notably, the historic period during which most of Belafonte's life took place could also be seen on videotape and felt by all who sat captivated and totally immersed in his sharing. The interview that night also aired live on Chicago's *WTTW/Channel 11*.

A Lofty Goal

The project's goal is to complete 5,000 interviews over an initial five-year period. Fortunately Richardson's initial request for support was readily granted by a variety of sources, including the State of Illinois, Northern Trust Bank, the A&E Network, AT&T Broadband, The Playboy Foundation, BET Holdings, and the Chicago, Illinois Chapter of The Links, Inc., among others.

Before embarking upon this project, Richardson was formerly a thespian, lawyer, cable administrator for the City of Chicago, and manager of Chicago cable Channel 25.

"As things happen they stick with you," Richardson says, describing the directions her life took after graduating from Brandeis. "My goal at that time was to go to Yale drama school and pursue a career in theatre, which is the love of my life. Then I got disillusioned. I didn't want to go to New York and drive a taxi, and you know as a Black female the roles available would be really small," Richardson confided.

"I ended up taking a year off because I was trying to decide what I wanted to do. Then I ended up going to law school because I still didn't know what I wanted to do."

After graduating from Harvard Law School, Richardson moved to Chicago to accept a job at a law firm where she was able to do pro bono work for artists. When she began doing more corporate and commercial work, for a change of pace, she accepted a position as the City of Chicago's Cable Administrator. After completing that post, she created her own home shopping program, *Shop Chicago*, on a cable channel.

"I got heavily involved in production, I already had my own equipment, and I was managing a facility that had extra equipment. I also learned how to produce things on a budget," she says.

The paths of her varied careers merged into a meaningful blend of expertise and relationships, all of which provided a network of resources that she used to lay the foundation for *The History Makers* project.

Richardson also credits her college studies that inspired the idea of *The History Makers* project. She explains, "My American Studies background – I have a really diverse background and I want this collection to be academically sound and to be done the right way."

In her pursuit to create *The History Makers*, Richardson took the advice of friends who suggested she do research to determine if such an archive already existed.

"That's where I started out in earnest two years ago," Richardson says. "I checked out the other archives that exist, and all the African American organizations. I wanted to find out what oral histories existed. I started talking to historians, asking if they thought this would be a good idea, and they said yes."

Advancing An Unadvanced Field

Richardson uncovered startling facts about recorded historical data on Blacks in the U.S. Smithsonian Institution has a collection of holdings that mainly covers musical accomplishments, though a few holdings do exist there on slavery and the civil rights movement.

The Library of Congress has a recorded collection of slave narratives, *Remembering Slavery*, which was funded largely by the National Endowment for the Humanities.

Of the 200 Black newspapers that exist in the United States, only three have archives: the *Chicago Defender*, the *Afro American* in Baltimore, Maryland, and the *Philadelphia Tribune*. Richardson attributes the lack of historical collections in part to a belief system that has built upon itself within the community for years.

She explains, "A lot of times, our mentality is that if you were told that you're not worth anything, it's hard to value what you have. So much of the Black experience has been running away from the past, forgetting, and okay, wanting the best for future generations, but cutting off the past because it had no value."

Richardson sought out partnerships with experts in academia, technology, media and community groups, in order to ensure that the information could reach a large percentage of the population and be used in a variety of contexts.

She says, "We have 14 different categories of History Makers and we want to have people assigned who will act as the experts who can help guide us. Similarly, because a lot of this history is not known, or people are not necessarily easily accessible, we felt that through community groups, we could better identify people to profile."

Richardson's experience in cable production helped her to appreciate and develop distribution resources to make the archive accessible and widely used.

She says, "This is what is extremely important to me about *The History Makers*; that it's not going to exist as some dirty old archive for people not to see."

Richardson explains that by making parts of the archive available on the Internet through video streaming, it ensures one method of distribution. She explains, "People can go to the site and hear History Makers talking about different subject matters." The website is (*www.thehistorymakers.com*)

The History Makers' staff is working to make the archive available to Historically Black Colleges and Universities, as well as to African-American museums that are in need of content.

The archives that exist now are either at academic institutions or in public libraries, and while Richardson says, "there's nothing wrong with that," she does add, "I would like this to be controlled by the Black community if possible."

preface Rogers

Update: Desiree Rogers remained president of Peoples Gas until July 2008, when she left to become president of social networking for Allstate Financial until December of 2008.

In January 2009, after the election of her friend Barack Obama as the first Black president of the United States, Desiree served as the White House social secretary for the first 13 months of the Obama presidency. She was the first African American to hold that post.

In 2010, her good friend Linda Johnson Rice asked her to come aboard as the Chief Executive Officer of Johnson Publishing Company, publisher of *Ebony* and *Jet* magazines, the company founded by her father John H. Johnson.

In 2012, Desiree joined the board of the gaming and hospitality company Pinnacle Entertainment and in 2013 accepted the role as chair of the Choose Chicago tourism board. She also sits on the board of the Northwestern Memorial Foundation.

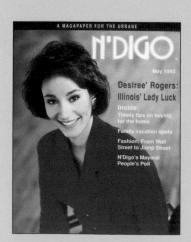

Desiree Rogers

By Kai El' Zabar and Tracey Robinson English | *Originally Published May 1993 & July 29, 2004*

Desireé Glapion Rogers represents a new generation of young, super smart and high-powered corporate African-American women executives equipped with an arsenal of academic, professional and civic achievements.

Even though Black women constitute only 1.2 percent of corporate officers in S&P 500 companies, they have actively played a big league strategy, leveraging professional relationships, good community relations and professional smarts to break through the glass ceiling.

That applies to Desiree Rogers, who says, "If you have a can-do versus a can't-do mentality, everything opens up for you."

She has been a corporate superwoman in Illinois, having served as the first African-American female president of Peoples Gas, North Shore Gas and the Illinois Lottery.

> **Never compromise your goals. You must believe in yourself and then others will begin to believe in you as well. If you push yourself and say, 'I can do, I will do,' soon you will be saying, 'I am doing.'**

Currently, as head of the gas companies, which are divisions of Peoples Energy Corp., she has direct responsibility for the utilities' field operations, customer functions and gas supply management, as well as oversight of external relations. Before her appointment to the post in 2004, she was senior vice president of customer services.

"I'm just thrilled with the opportunity," Rogers says. "I get to work with so many people who are so very good at what they do and to create an environment where people can do their best work – whether we are talking about people answering calls from customers or a group laying new pipes in the ground to provide services to the neighborhoods. This job really allows me to bring together all the teams across the whole business to provide the best service we can for our customers."

Cultivating strong relationships and maintaining a high sense of integrity rank at the top of Rogers' priorities and are reflected in her strategy to get her mission accomplished professionally and personally.

"I've always been the type that's extremely sensitive to being able to follow through on whatever I say I'm going to do, and then get that done. I like to conduct myself in that way," she says.

Today, Rogers is firmly cemented in the inner circle of power. She's listed in *Crain's "Who's Who,"* cited frequently in celebrity columns, and is unarguably one of Chicago's most influential women in business. A well-placed phone call or nod from her goes a long way.

Special Beginnings

Rogers grew up as part of New Orleans Black royalty. Her parents, Joyce and Roy Glapion, were entrepreneurs and city leaders. Her mother owned a lucrative daycare center. Her father was a city councilman, school board president and a key member of the Zulu Social Aid and Pleasure Club, an historic New Orleans Carnival krewe founded by Black laborers in 1916. Desiree has been Zulu Queen twice during Mardi Gras.

Her parents had a healthy respect for education and naturally impressed their values upon her, so it came as no surprise that she chose to attend Wellesley College and Harvard Business School.

Desireé says, "Wellesley was my first opportunity to meet people from all over the country and the world. It brought the element of different perspectives based on geographical location, culture and lifestyle. Yet the competitive, academic environment was not so different from the private girl's high school I attended."

Upon graduation from Wellesley, she accepted a job at Xerox as a marketing rep and then moved on to New England Telephone, where she supervised 12 employees. Although sales was not her primary interest, Desireé expressed, "I wanted to understand the skill and I wanted an introduction to managing people as a way to influence their work production. It was part of my plan."

Then she went to Harvard. "Grad school provided me with a fundamental discipline base, the academic foundation behind those disciplines and principles," she says. "It enabled me to understand marketing and operations, as well as the opportunity

Photo by John Beckett

to gain insight into the people sitting next to me in school. What was their mindset? What was their capitalist vision of the world?"

But Desireé was not the typical Harvard MBA candidate or child of the '80s. Everyone knows that Harvard MBAs go to school to improve their earning potential. They want to manage Fortune 500 companies and make lots of money.

However, Desireé says, "My goal was to come out prepared to run and motivate a group of people to do something well." She accepted a job with AT&T in Chicago, at the central offices in operations.

She says, "The company took a chance on hiring someone with my degree, not knowing whether or not I'd survive. Typically, MBAs do not go into accounting, marketing, or the advertising end of the business. MBAs do not go to the controls or operations offices where people wire equipment. They go to the corporate offices. They do not go out in the field with crews that are actually doing technical work."

But Desireé did, wanting to be involved with the business she works with. For her, it is important to understand the entire process. She explains, "It was essential that I understood and knew how a phone is hooked up, versus just selling or marketing that phone and not knowing how it functions. Learning what I felt was important to know meant I had to be with the people who actually do the technical work."

Her position is that, "Oftentimes companies miss the importance of the integration of operations and marketing. Yes, you can go out and market a product, yet you are dependent upon the people who provide that service internally, or make the product.

"The point is, I can sell anything, but bottom line, I better have sold something that really works or delivers to the consumer, otherwise, over the long term, that company will not be successful. So I wanted to start out in the operations area of the company, where I could learn the product and then move into the more traditional areas where you find MBAs. And that's what I did."

Desireé held three different positions at AT&T. From operations, she went to the engineering department where employees actually engineered the circuits, a very technical aspect of the business; from there to the corporate headquarters, a marketing unit in New Jersey.

She was on the fast track moving full steam ahead in her career, but then got married in 1988 to John Rogers Jr., president of his own financial services firm in Chicago, Ariel Capital Management.

She says of her decision to marry, "The only effect it had on my career was that I knew that Chicago is where I would be making my home. And that was good because, although I enjoy the travel opportunities of some jobs, I was not interested in working for a company that could dictate where I'd live. I prefer that decision to be mine."

So after having moved to New Jersey, Desireé returned to Chicago to join John and went to work for the Levy Organization.

She eventually founded Museum Operations Consulting Associates (MOCA), a firm specializing in operating and providing consulting services to museum retail stores. It was during her stint running MOCA that a member of Illinois Governor Jim Edgar's transition team suggested that she submit her resume and Desiree did, not knowing what she was applying for.

Be In It, To Win It

That's when she became the lady with the big bucks as Illinois Lottery Director, in 1991.

To some she was the fairy godmother, to others, the lady who could make their dreams come true. There's no question she met millionaires regularly. And everybody wanted to know her.

Asked how being director of the Illinois Lottery changed her lifestyle, Rogers quickly asserted: "Time, I had very little personal time. I was constantly trying to maintain a schedule. Simply put, my life was public. I understood that when I went out I represented the Lottery, no matter where I was or what the circumstances were." She chuckled, "So I tried not to look as rough and tumble as I used to when I stepped outside my abode.

"People would come up to me in the theatre, in the parking lot, walking down the street, everywhere, anywhere, and ask me questions pertaining to the Lottery. The moment I exited my home, I was working."

It had a major effect on Desireé's lifestyle. "Of course, I could never say to a potential player – no matter how tired I might have been – 'No, I'm not going to tell you what games we have', or 'I'm not going to talk about that right now.' I had to always be willing to discuss the Lottery, and I was. And I had to be up to date on my products."

She says she ran the Lottery, then a $2 billion state agency, as a corporate entertainment enterprise with her as the CEO. "I ran it like a consumer product company because we had a variety of products that appealed to people," Desiree says. "I was involved in all the decisions from the design of the products to the actual tickets. I participated fully in the entire process."

As a result, in only her second year at the helm, sales were the highest in the history of the Lottery.

One of her major thrusts was the Lottery's decision to give its advertising account to minority-owned firms. Desireé explains, "Oftentimes in advertising, minority-owned firms are asked to develop ad campaigns that relate to a specific group, they are not hired for general market advertisement.

"The Lottery is a very highly visible, highly sought after account and is carefully watched by the industry. By granting qualified minority firms the account, we hoped it would give them the opportunity to do other general marketing advertising."

During her tenure, Rogers worked extensively with more than 8,000 retailers to increase the sales of instant ticket products from $300 million to $600 million. She led the agency until 1997, when she went to work with Peoples Energy.

She's sleek, svelte, polished, and looks like a size six high fashion model. When asked what advice she'd give to aspiring corporate professionals, particularly women, Desireé speaks very authoritatively.

She says, "Never compromise your goals. You must believe in yourself and then others will begin to believe in you as well. If you push yourself and say, 'I can do, I will do,' soon you will be saying, 'I am doing.'"

preface Rogers

Update: Of the roughly 2,290 equity funds in the country, only 200 or so have been around for 30 years, as Ariel has, few with the same manager for all those years, as John Rogers has been. The company currently has over $10 billion in assets under management. John is listed in the book, *The 99 Greatest Investors* and is a board member of the Barack Obama Foundation.

John Rogers Jr.

By David Smallwood & Photography by Warren Browne | *Originally Published July 26, 2001*

That other financial services firm has a bull raging all over the place as their symbol; John Rogers Jr., is content with the image of the tortoise as his – as in slow and steady wins the race.

Only in this case, the tortoise's qualities of patience, deliberation and focus are the keys to building profits for the clients that invest in his Ariel Capital Management Company.

With its inception in 1983, Ariel became the first African-American firm to manage a mutual fund. It offers two, in addition to a bond fund. In those three funds combined, Ariel manages $260 million for nearly 30,000 shareholders and has compounded their investments at a 15-16 percent clip a year over the long term.

Additionally, Ariel's money management division services such clients as McDonald's, Commonwealth Edison, United Airlines, Ameritech and the Chicago Teachers Retirement System. The average account is $18 million.

> I was going to treasurers of Fortune 500 companies saying, 'Let me have some of your pension money to manage.' They had never seen anybody Black before, much less somebody 24 years old.

In total, Ariel has $1.4 billion under management, which is no small change for the company's dedicated, highly skilled staff of 26 and its president, Rogers, who just turned 38 years old.

Rogers is the son of Judge John Rogers Sr. and Jewel Lafontant MANkarious, and former husband of business executive Desiree Rogers. He's a Princeton University graduate who majored in economics and worked as a stockbroker for two years before deciding to open his own firm at the age of 24.

Rogers' interest in the stock market was piqued by his father's habit of buying him stock certificates instead of toys for every birthday and Christmas, beginning at age 12 and letting young John keep the quarterly dividend checks, which grew increasingly larger as the years passed.

John began managing his own portfolio and became adept at maneuvering through the market. It was his belief in his ability to make money for his clients, which he proved as a stockbroker after college, and the marketing opportunity to become the first African-American in America to run a money management firm that led him to open Ariel.

"I looked at the billions of dollars that are out there in big pension funds, corporate America and public funds, and thought there should at least be somebody out there like us to manage some of it," Rogers says.

"I had no money to manage, no clients and I was going to treasurers of Fortune 500 companies saying, 'Let me have some of your pension money to manage.' They had never seen anybody Black before, much less somebody 24 years old. The two together was a pretty deadly combination."

But like the tortoise, John and Ariel persevered, finally getting their first million-dollar account after 18 months. That came thanks to former Chicago city treasurer Cecil Partee, who told Rogers he'd always wanted to invest with a minority firm, but there were none.

Partee introduced John to the Municipal Employees' Annuity and Benefit Fund of Chicago, and though he was petrified, not knowing what to expect, Rogers said the group saw that he enjoyed what he did and that he believed deeply in his investment philosophy. They gave him a chance.

"Their million dollars was a lot of money to me at the time," Rogers says. "I kept thinking, 'If we do a good job with this, they'll give us more.'" They did give him more...the Municipal Employees' Annuity and Benefit Fund of Chicago is now Ariel's largest account at $150 million.

Growing It Slow

Ariel's philosophy is to grow slowly instead of going for the overnight big bang, sticking with what's tried and true companies where there is a well established brand name and consumers who buy that product time and again because they believe in the brand name and the product.

Rogers calls it "patient investing." Patience is a hallmark of Ariel's stock picking. "There are so many companies to invest with that we have to be patient to make sure we find the stock we really, truly believe in," Rogers notes.

Patience and stability pretty much characterize John's personal style. He says he doesn't change much and outside of being president of the Park District, his primary interests next to family are the stock market and basketball.

He was the team captain at Princeton, won the Bulls 3-on-3 contest a few years ago with two other friends, and occasionally plays pickup hoops with his compadre Barack Obama.

A steady, self-effacing man, Rogers says that Ariel is his life's work and he hopes to run the company for 50 years, like his hero, John Johnson, has run his publishing company.

"We're trusted with a lot of people's money that they've put away for retirement and their kids' college expenses," Rogers says. "It's a responsibility that we take seriously to the point that the Ariel team invests our own money in our funds."

While it's well and good to know who John is, good man that he is, it's just as important for *N'DIGO* readers to know what John knows – what we should do with our dollar to make it holler, how to earn the most cash on our stash.

Rogers was kind enough to share – free of charge, thank you – some of the following insights on money management and investments that just might stand you in good stead.

Taxes, Death & Trouble

Marvin Gaye sang that only three things are sure in life; one of them comes around every April 15. What to do about taxes, oh Patient Investor? Rogers says:

1. Pay them. Keep it simple, keep it clean. "Do your job, make as much money as you can, and always maintain a healthy respect for the IRS. If you're going to take care of anybody, take care of them," he advises.

2. Put money into tax-exempt mutual bond funds.

3. Write off the interest deductions you get on your home (and other real estate) mortgages(s).

4. Do not invest in convoluted tax schemes. "90 percent of the time, they come back to haunt you." Rogers says. "I sold tax shelters when I was a stockbroker, but those things never worked. I can tell you horror stories."

Rules Of The Game

"Diversifying your portfolio" is a fancy term for what you should do with your money for it to do you the most good. If you have any income whatsoever, you have a portfolio, and, of course, you want to make the best of it.

Rogers suggests that to attain financial solidity, our portfolio should be diversified approximately according to this formula: a) put money into a home (buy one, upgrade it); b) for the rest of your liquid cash, put 20-25 percent into bonds and money markets (savings accounts, etc.) for safety in the event of that "rainy day;" and c) put the other 75-80 percent into the stock market.

That may seem like a lot to tie up in stocks, but Rogers says, "It's been shown over time that stocks have been the best asset to own over the past 60, 70 years. Stocks have compounded (earnings) between 10-12 percent consistently, while money markets only give you 4-5 percent.

So when you compound that seven percent differential over 20-30 years, the numbers get huge as to what your nest egg is going to be when you decide to retire, or need to break out the money for the kids' college tuition. As a rule of thumb, it's better to have your money in stocks somewhere than sitting in the bank."

But you shouldn't invest in the stock market, Rogers cautions, without following a couple of key rules. The first is that you can't invest if the money you're going to use is what you might need to pay the phone bill next Thursday.

"You need to invest money that you can do without for at least three to five years at a minimum. That's because the market has occasional dips, but in that amount of time, it almost always adjusts itself and comes back performing better," Rogers says.

Which leads to the second caution: You've got to have the attitude of putting that money away and not looking at it for maybe 10 years. Rogers warns that the day-to-day fluctuations of the market might scare you out. "You've got to know you're investing in businesses that are going to draw over time," he assures.

Ms. Blow Brings Ariel A Couple Grand: What Are They Going To Do With It?

Arthaleisha Blow (Joe's daughter), finds a few thousand she forgot she left in her spring jacket last year and wants to invest with Ariel. What are they going to do?

"Put it in our mutual funds," Rogers says. "We've got some stocks we're really excited about right now, which are among our top holdings."

These sizzlers include: Clorox, the bleach company; Hasbro, the toy company; American Media, which owns the *National Inquirer* newpaper and *Star* magazine tabloids; Long's Drug Stores, a major drug store chain in California similar to Walgreens; Her-

man Miller, which makes office furniture; and First Brands, which makes Glad Garbage Bags.

Rogers adds that currently, three of Ariel's favorite stocks are Bob Evans Farms, the restaurant chain ("which does well because they have good sausages"); the Rouse Company, which has built malls in Baltimore, Boston, and New York City ("We're real excited about them because they just bought a bunch of land from Howard Hughes in Las Vegas and Southern California."); and Specialty Equipment, which makes those soft ice cream dispensing machines for McDonald's the world over ("Every time a new McDonald's opens, that's a new ice cream machine.").

Hmmm…after having picked John's brain for these hot tips, why do we still need Ariel as the middle-man?

"Because things change!" Rogers laughs. "We have six of us doing the research, visiting these companies, going to their plants and headquarters, meeting with management, checking the stores to see if their products are still good, still fresh, still work. If they don't we change; we'll sell this one and buy that one. Things go wrong – with the management, the product, or the stock goes up so much you have to take advantage of the profits. So you're paying Ariel to move the stocks around."

To counter the myth that you need big bucks to buy stocks and to encourage those who are skittish and/or unfamiliar about investing in the market, Ariel offers a systematic investment plan for as little as $50 a month through automatic deductions from a person's checking account.

"The money builds up over time and since you're investing on a regular basis, consistent as is, it lets you take advantage of market fluctuations where you can buy low when the market allows," Rogers says. "In fact, the best way to invest successfully is to put money away on a regular basis. That's what I do with my own money," he confides. "Put some away every month. I've been doing it for years."

preface Rush

Update: Bobby Rush has been re-elected to the First Congressional District seat 12 times and during his tenure, has brought more than one billion dollars to his district. He has led efforts to fund major infrastructure projects such as the reconstruction of the Dan Ryan Expressway, the Bronzeville Metra Station, the Englewood Flyover, the CTA Red Line Reconstruction, and the CTA Red Line 95th Street Station Renovation.

Over the years he has obtained millions of dollars in grants for libraries, museums, municipalities, police departments, hospitals, schools and programs that support the arts.

With a Master's Degree in Theology from McCormick Theological Seminary, Rush is an ordained minister. In addition to his congressional responsibilities, he pastors the Beloved Community Christian Church of God in Christ in Chicago.

Bobby Rush

By David Smallwood, Robert Starks & Photography by Reginald Payton | *Originally Published March 9, 2000*

Change. Sometimes it's just natural evolution; sometimes it happens because things might be rotten in Denmark. Whatever the reason, out with the old, in with the new, is an unchangeable fact of life.

When "upstart" Bobby Rush unceremoniously unseated Congressional incumbent Charles Hayes in the March 1992 Democratic primary, it signaled a change that may significantly impact Black leadership in Chicago.

In defeating Hayes, who held the First Congressional District seat for 10 years, Rush won eight of the 12 Black wards in the district and ran close in the four that he lost.

"I think the victory meant that people wanted change," Rush surmised shortly after the election over lunch at Dr. Jam's, where he was continuously approached by well-wishers during his meal.

> **I certainly intend to be one of the focal points of political power in Chicago; I've been working for that all my life.**

"People knew that Hayes had an impressive record in the Civil Rights Movement and as a labor leader – exemplary in both areas – but as a Congressman, he failed to deliver or respond and he became out of touch. He became a captive of the perks and privileges of Congress, rather than a champion who fought to bring resources to bear on the problems that the district is confronted with. People saw that."

Sensing the mood of the voters in his district, Rush took the audacious step of calling out the Black Chicago veteran with long-standing prominence in the community and presented himself as a better alternative.

So who is this young man who would now be king?

Bobby Rush, Alderman of the 2nd Ward since 1983, has been a known quantity in Chicago since he helped found the Illinois Black Panther Party in the 1960s. Born in Albany, Georgia in 1946, his family eventually settled in Chicago.

Bobby attended Marshall High School on the West Side and joined the Army at age 17, serving from 1963 to 1968. After the military, he attended Roosevelt University, where he earned his Bachelor's Degree in Political Science in 1973. He received his Master's Degree in the same field at the University of Illinois at Chicago in 1974.

Rush was elected 2nd Ward Democratic Committeeman in 1984 and again in 1988, selected Democratic State Central Committeeman of the First Congressional District in March 1990, and appointed Deputy Chairman of the Illinois Democratic Party – a newly created position – in April of that year.

As aldermanic chairman of the Committee on Energy and Environmental Protection during the Harold Washington mayoral administration, Rush orchestrated passage of comprehensive toxic waste legislation and called attention to the asbestos problem in Chicago Housing Authority developments.

He was instrumental in the expansion of the Lake Meadows Shopping Center, the conversion of the historic Chicago Bee Building into a public library, the conversion of the Armory into a recreation center, and the improvement of the 35th Street business district.

As a Panther, Rush coordinated the party's free breakfast for children program and free medical clinic, which developed the nation's first mass sickle cell anemia testing program. Before becoming a Panther, he was a member of the Student Non-Violent Coordinating Committee.

Congressional Concerns

Rush has a variety of innovative ideas that he predicts will bear fruit in a "relatively short period of time" if he's elected to Congress. He wants to produce legislation that will speak toward crime in public schools, staggering unemployment levels among high school students, and comprehensive crime prevention programs that could empower local community-based organizations to help prevent crime before it becomes unmanageable.

Rush also quickly intends to address urban issues. "There's a real vacuum that exists in national policy around urban problems," he says. "There have got to be some programmatic responses by the federal government geared toward helping the Black community not only survive, but thrive, and that will help eliminate some of our problems in the areas of crime, housing, education and health care. The federal government has over a trillion dollars that it spends on a lot of things. I say let's spend some on helping urban centers solve their problems."

Immediately on the Rush agenda is addressing the status of Black males in Chicago. "Certainly the large percentage of Black males who are involving themselves in counter-productive activities has to be addressed," he says.

"We've got to find out what can be done to remedy the situation and how we can more effectively deal with the needs and problems of Black males, without coddling them. A key is bringing in institutions at an earlier stage to help them find a right path – other than the law enforcement and penal institutions, which right now are the only agencies addressing this issue."

What the leap portends for Rush from being a Black Panther and having his colleagues gunned down by government forces to representing in Congress the largest Democratic district in the United States is something that only he can feel.

But it comes from deep in his soul and after many wizened years when he says, "I plan to be an instant impact player; I wouldn't have it any other way."

It should be noted that the first organization Bobby Rush belonged to was the Boy Scouts of America when his mother was a den mother operating out of a Cabrini Green church.

He says that evolution and change have been a constant in his life, and notes that while he has discarded some principles of the Black Panther Party, he has kept others, including the notion of organizing power to effectively create solutions, the notion of coalition politics and the notion of aggressive leadership to bring about change.

He believes he will be effective in Congress because of the path that he has walked and embraces the idea of trying to be a powerbroker.

"I certainly intend to be one of the focal points of political power in Chicago; I've been working for that all my life," says Rush, now 46 years old. "You become a leader by over a long period of time demonstrating the fact that you have the intellect, the commitment, the dedication, and are willing to make the extraordinary sacrifices it takes to be a leader.

"I've always accepted the responsibility and sacrifice demanded by leadership and I see myself as being part of the solution. I know I'm going to play a significant role in Congress and a significant role locally in terms of trying to solve problems my district is confronted with."

Mayor Of Chicago

Fast-forward to February 1999 and Rush, who by then had been First District Congressman for six years, was suddenly running for Mayor of Chicago against incumbent Richard M. Daley. Why?

"Because," he told *N'DIGO* before that election, "from my vantage point in Washington, I witnessed Congress sending hundreds of millions of dollars back to Chicago, and I saw how this money was being squandered, in some cases, pilfered. It really upset me that this money was not going to places it was supposed to go or being used for the purposes that it was appropriated for.

"Here we are, the Chicago Democrats in Washington, doing everything we can to send money back to the city and it's not being used as it should, particularly $100 million in empowerment zone money. There was $100 million appropriated, $43 million actually allocated, only $23 million spent and less than 100 jobs actually created. That's horrible. That made me ballistic. That money was supposed to have gone to neighborhoods to create and expand businesses, to build houses and create jobs, not to be squandered."

After Rush lost that 1999 mayoral bid to incumbent Daley in a lopsided defeat, his next big pivotal moment came a scant year later when he was up for re-election for his own seat. Political observers felt that Rush was vulnerable and predicted a strong challenge to arise.

Sure enough, in the 2000 Democratic primary, vying against Rush were two Illinois state senators – Donne Trotter and Barack Obama – both high profile candidates with wide name recognition, well funded campaign chests and good organizations.

Defeating Barack Obama

The First is considered by African Americans as the premier congressional district in the state and a major district in the nation.

Its diverse population includes affluent sections of Hyde Park and Beverly, as well as some of the poorest people in America in Chicago's sprawling CHA housing developments along the State Street corridor.

In the course of the 20th Century, the First District and its Congressmen have played significant and pivotal roles in the shaping of Black politics in America. Oscar DePriest, William Dawson, Ralph Metcalfe, Harold Washington and Charles Hayes have represented the district.

Because of these factors, this three-way primary race received a great deal of attention locally and nationally.

No one was surprised when Trotter and Obama announced their intentions to run. It was clear that Congressman Rush had lost support from some of his base lakefront aldermen since he first ran in 1992. That loss of support was intensified and more widespread after his mayoral election loss in 1999.

State Senator Barack Obama was a 38-year-old civil rights attorney and senior lecturer in Constitutional Law at the University of Chicago Law School, and had begun his career as a community organizer in the Roseland and Altgeld Gardens communities.

In 1992, he led the Illinois Project Vote voter registration drive that added many new voters to the roles and helped assure the victories of Carol Moseley Braun as the nation's first Black female Senator and Bill Clinton as president.

State Senator Donne Trotter was elected to the Illinois House in 1988 and to the 16th Senate district in 1992. Trotter, who attended the Loyola University School of Law and earned his degree while serving in the State Legislature, was an aggressive legislator who honed his skills as a negotiator and fighter.

Those skills were on display in the Senate Appropriations Committee, where Trotter served as the Democratic Party spokesman, and as the Chairman of the Illinois Legislative Black Caucus.

Rush at the time enjoyed a good legislative record in Congress. He served on the Commerce Committee and the Telecommunications, Trade and Consumer Protection, Energy and Power, as well as, Finance and Hazardous Materials sub-committees.

As a member of these powerful committees and sub-committees, he increased funding for education, with an infusion

of $20 million to wire schools for the Internet, $5 million for Chicago State University and $5 million for the Chicago Military Academy. Rush co-sponsored gun legislation and secured some $17 million for South Lake Shore Drive improvements and money to improve the Englewood leg of the CTA Green line.

Among Trotter's biggest supporters were State Representative Connie Howard and high profile activists such as Dr. Conrad Worrill of Northeastern Illinois University and the National Black United Front. Obama's big endorsement was from 4th Ward Ald. Toni Preckwinkle, while Rush was endorsed by President Bill Clinton and Vice President Al Gore, among others.

Despite what was expected to be a close, ferocious fight, Rush bested Obama by almost 30,000 votes and a 2-1 victory margin – winning 60 percent of the vote to Barack's 30 percent (Trotter received seven percent). It was the only loss of Barack Obama's elective career.

Rush went on to defeat his Republican opposition in the November general election, with 88 percent of the vote to retain his prominent position as Congressman from the First Congressional District of Illinois.

preface
Salter

Update: Founded in 1927, the Million Dollar Round Table is a global, independent association of more than 49,500 of the world's leading life insurance and financial service professionals from more than 500 companies in 70 countries.

In 2010, Salter the elder was named to the "Top of the Table" portion of MDRT, the uppermost level of the group — meaning that he is certified as one of the top financial services producers in the world. Roger Salter received an honorary Doctor of Humane Letters from Chicago State University in 2011.

Roger J. Salter the younger is now Vice President of the Sanmar Financial Network.

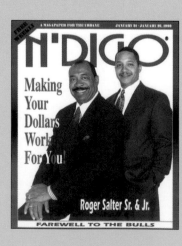

Roger Salter

By Derrick K. Baker & Photography by Reginald Payton | *Originally Published January 21, 1999*

Simply stated, Roger F. Salter is a history-making certified financial planner and achieving entrepreneur who gets as excited, as enthralled, about his industry as Michael Jordan gets making a championship-winning shot.

Put another way, Salter's verbal primer on how his company – Sanmar Financial Planning Corporation – helps people reach their goals is infectious.

So much so that even the most financially destitute person would scrounge up a quarter and turn it over to the Sanmar team of talented professionals with the expectation that the company will help turn that 25 cents into dollars to help the client buy a house, save money for a child's education, or open a new business.

With more than three decades of in-the-trenches, hands-on experience to call on faster than you can say "return on investment," Roger F. Salter *is* financial planning. And with his son, Roger J. Salter – also a certified financial planner – at his side, the West Loop based firm is about the business of serving its over 1,000 clients and policyholders by helping people set goals and reach the dreams they have for themselves and their families.

> **We're trying to bring the Black community into the mainstream of financial planning and break those barriers down. If you're serious about what you want to do, we're serious about talking with you.**

With a 15-20 person, multi-talented, yet specialized team of certified financial planners, accountants, stockbrokers and lawyers among others, the Sanmar Financial Network provides expert advice, consultation and management for its clients on budgeting, taxes, insurance, stocks and bonds, retirement, estate and investment planning, risk management, mutual funds, education funding and pension and legal services, among other areas.

The company routinely puts into force $100 million in life insurance policies each year for its clients, and millions more in mutual funds on behalf of its clients.

With an impressive resume that includes his becoming, in 1965, only the third African American to become a member of the lofty Million Dollar Round Table (MDRT) – meaning he sold $1 million of life insurance in one year – and memberships in the National Association of Securities Dealers and College of Chartered Life Underwriters, Salter is a polished practitioner, sought-after teacher and student of the ever-changing financial planning business.

Teamwork Means A Working Team

"Our strategy is stair-step financial planning. Rome wasn't built in a day," explains Sanmar Chairman and CEO Salter. "We have to build you into new habits. Our approach is to build you on a strong foundation and to gradually add on up the line so you'll have a greater return; a little higher risk, but if anything happens you will stay on solid ground.

"Many people have no idea of the assets they have, so we educate folks about plans. We go into many businesses and they don't have a clue about some of this. Some of them are not at the point where they're struggling, it's just that nobody has brought it to their attention," says Salter, a native of 44th and Wabash and product of Cook County Hospital who often punctuates his remarks with, "Am I making myself clear?"

The combined 150 years plus of experience the Sanmar team brings to the table is precisely how they serve people ranging from the mid-level corporate manager, to the more higher-profile likes of Steve Harvey, Derrick Rose, Merri Dee, Roland Martin, basketball player Kendall Gill and music producer Teddy Riley. Likewise, several lottery winners, Ronald and Ernest Isley of the Isley Brothers, Baldwin Ice Cream President Eric Johnson, and designer Barbara Bates are also Sanmar clients, as was the late Ernie Banks.

Of his team, Salter, who was the first African American to be chosen as the General Agent of the Year by American General Life Insurance Company, notes, "They're all world-class. If you have relationships with people who are talented, it's going to be the best. Our clients aren't doing business with us because we're Black; they're saying, 'these folks know what they're doing.'"

The Business Of Doing Business

Inside Sanmar's office is the younger Roger J. Salter, directing the technical staff in the construction of clients' financial plans and analyzing client data.

Like the captain of a cruise ship, he is a critical cog in Sanmar's daily wheel of operations, maintaining close contact with other team members who work out of their own offices in other parts of the city and country.

Whether crafting or reviewing deferred compensation plans, estate plans or salary continuation plans, the fact that both Salters are two of the only 300 African American certified financial planners in the country is paramount.

The junior Salter, himself a 19-year veteran of the financial planning business, is in most ways a mirror version of his dad when it comes to the business: "We each have different strengths and we complement each other," says Salter, Sanmar's vice president and general manager.

"We have two very different functions in a way. My father is a marketer and a technician of the business. His main function is developing markets. He's creating the image that wealthy folks want to see to feel comfortable. What my position does is force people to do what they say they want to do. Once he brings in the work, the work has to be correct. The contracts

have to be in order. Everything has to be right.

"My job is to tear down the work with my staff like a big jigsaw puzzle. We tear it down and put it back together in the way it's supposed to be. We try to make our plans model plans. After I complete the plan, Dad puts his final touches on it. I'm the technician, working with everybody else on the plan, coordinating everybody's efforts.

"We're trying to say that if you can afford these products and have a need for these products, you should be able to get them. Financial planning has been broken down into a science," continues Salter.

"The recommendations we make are fundamental recommendations that we've learned. I tell my clients, 'This is not my opinion. This is a matter of fact.' We base all of our recommendations, our findings and our analyses on the Internal Revenue Code; interpretations of estate planning laws; investment fundamentals; and all the information that's available."

One Door Opens Another

Selling life insurance door to door was a respectable auspicious way to break into the working world, and that's exactly what the patriarch Salter did on his way to earning membership in the MDRT in 1965.

But before that he says, "I started with a stint in teaching and it didn't move me. In the early 1960s, teachers were starting out making $4,900 a year and you had to work at the post office at night to supplement your income. There were very few people who went into the financial services business.

"In fact, when I first got into insurance," Salter continues, "Whites and Blacks looked at insurance entirely differently. Blacks' insurance businesses were the small debit companies in which you went door to door and collected the premium. But the Whites were doing business on Wall Street, insuring corporate people, establishing pension plans and doing profit sharing plans way back then."

When Salter was named a member of the Million Dollar Roundtable, he says, "It was like, 'Where did you come from?' When I went to the meeting, there were a bunch of White guys looking at the business pretty different from the way I was looking at it, because they were selling $100,000 and $200,000 policies, and million dollar policies in some cases.

"Most Blacks were proud to have $5,000 policies. I saw some things that Blacks knew nothing about. Once I got out and saw what was happening worldwide, it was like a whole different world. I had to bring that world back to African Americans. I had to bring it back to my market.

"We saw a need to have some excellence brought to the community and I did that by forming the agency in 1974," recalls Salter, who in 1969, helped organize the Leo Blackburn Agency of Mutual Benefit Life in Chicago, which was the country's first African-American general agency.

The insurance industry has changed even more today than when Salter jointed the MDRT. "The financial services industry itself is diversified. Now the insurance companies can do stocks, bonds, mutual funds and annuities. It's a different industry," rues Salter, recipient of more than 100 awards for professional and community excellence.

"The financial people that the average businessman or average person sees are either accountants or lawyers. And they are treating the clients as if they studied financial planning."

"What's happening now is everybody wants in," agrees the younger Roger. "A long time ago, there would be a specific market that they would target. The big bank would be trying to get to the people with the big money and big trust funds. Now you look around at all the magazines, and on every page you've got insurance companies and mutual funds advertising.

"What they're saying is, 'You can invest, too.' A lot of folks think, 'Well I need $10,000 to start an investment portfolio.' And the companies are saying, 'Hey, we do $50 a month plans.' People are more educated. People are making more money and with more money, you've got more disposable income. Everybody is forced to deal with a higher level of finance.

"In the old days the employers used to put money away for you. Now they're saying, 'Participate in your own plan.' Sanmar is saying, 'We're going to do business with everybody, it doesn't matter.' We're trying to bring the Black community into the mainstream of financial planning and break those barriers down. If you're serious about what you want to do, we're serious about talking to you."

The senior Salter concludes, "We want to be the Johnnie Cochran of the financial services industry. Period."

preface
Sampson

Update: After 38 years at Fernwood United Methodist Church and 57 years in the ministry total, Rev. Sampson retired on July 12, 2013.

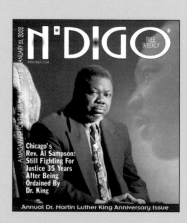

Reverend Al Sampson

By D. Kevin McNeir & Photography by Victor Powell | *Originally Published January 17, 2002*

Controversial is the word that comes to mind for some Chicago residents describing the Rev. Dr. Albert R. Sampson, senior pastor of Fernwood United Methodist Church on the city's South Side, a position he's held since 1975.

But the former "soldier" in Dr. Martin Luther King Jr.'s army of non-violent warriors, who was ordained in 1966 by King himself, says he isn't controversial – just "unpredictable" – and he doesn't plan to change his modus operandi one bit.

"When I make up my mind about getting involved in certain situations, projects, and ministries, I consciously sacrifice my time and focus on those areas where our people are getting ripped off and humiliated," Sampson says. "The system keeps our community in a constant state of destabilization, and in all of the major U.S. cities, you find Blacks being exploited, both by the private and public sectors."

Next week, Sampson will be the keynote speaker in his hometown of Boston, where he'll give the address in the city's annual service honoring the birth of Dr. Martin Luther King, Jr.

In February, he will be one of several dignitaries who will accompany another of Chicago's leading Black religious leaders, the Honorable Minister Louis Farrakhan – who, too, has also often been described as "controversial" – at the World Saviours' Day Conference in Los Angeles.

Sampson's connection to the Black church began in 1956, the year in which he received his license to preach from the Reverend Earl W. Lawson at Emmanuel Baptist Church in Malden, Massachusetts.

Later, Sampson, along with Homer McCall and Albert Brinson (both former assistant ministers at Ebenezer Baptist Church in Atlanta), would become the only three men ordained by Dr. King himself. At that time in 1966, Sampson was a staff member with the Southern Christian Leadership Conference (SCLC).

"I remember going up to Dr. King and simply asking him if he would ordain me, and he said yes," Sampson recalls. "Being right in the heat of the civil rights movement, his willingness to serve as a mentor meant a lot to me. As an adopted child from Boston who never knew his biological father, Dr. King would become both my father and my brother. Certainly, he was one of the strongest Black men in ministry that I have ever known."

Learning The Ropes

Sampson matriculated at Shaw University in Raleigh, North Carolina, where he actively became involved in student government and the civil rights movement. He served as president of both the college's NAACP chapter and the Shaw University student body, and was one of the first students arrested in the Raleigh sit-in demonstrations.

"A lot of people don't know that SNCC (the Student Nonviolent Coordinating Committee) was founded on the Shaw campus," Sampson said. "Many of the rights that some Blacks take for granted were because of the efforts of college students – kids who wanted to be treated fairly. Working with the Greensboro boys, demanding that we be allowed to sit at the food counters in Woolworth's – that was just part of my college experience."

Before receiving his bachelor's degree in religion and social science in 1961, Sampson would lend his assistance in the election of the first Black, John Winters, to the Raleigh City Council, and would serve as a student representative of the North Carolina State Student Legislature, which introduced and passed the first Public Accommodations Bill in the state.

During his senior year, Sampson was introduced to a promising football player and transfer student from the University of Chicago/Champaign-Urbana – a young Jesse Jackson.

"We both wound up being sent to Chicago working for the SCLC," Sampson says. "And those were some lean years for both of us – in fact, for all of the civil rights workers. It wasn't a job for glory seekers or fortune hunters. I remember getting a check for $37.50 for two week's work. But it was never about the money; it was always about helping the people."

As their friendship developed, Sampson would be asked to serve as the godfather for the unborn

> **Dr. King prepared us to go to jail, to protest nonviolently, and if necessary, to die for the cause.**

child who would be named Jesse L. Jackson, Jr. And at Dr. King's request, he would serve on The Woodlawn Organization's (TWO) Chicago staff as an organizer to study the techniques of Saul Alinsky, while Jackson would begin developing a community outreach project called Operation Breadbasket.

After Dr. King's death, Sampson continued his affiliation with the SCLC, which was then led by the Rev. Ralph Abernathy. One of the projects on which he served as an assistant director was an effort by 10 Birmingham, Alabama churches to provide assistance to high school graduates who wanted to attend college. Today that program has become the nationwide model known as Upward Bound.

Political Empowerment And The Soul Slate

Sampson says he has always been interested in empowering people of color, especially in the area where they are often most shut out – politics. But during the late '70s and early '80s, he would receive real on-the-job training as a supporter of Harold Washington, who would eventually become the first African-American Mayor of Chicago.

"The Black community has always had to fight for political and economic power," Sampson muses. "And just as we begin to get more people elected to office and more folks registered to vote, the system seeks a way to destabilize our community by instituting patterns in housing and employment that disperse the Black community.

"Just take a look at the second, third, and fourth wards – they are no longer predominantly African American like they once were. So, no longer do those running for political office or City Hall have to worry about those wards holding the power of swing votes during elections."

When the Task Force for Black Political Empowerment was formed by supporters of Washington, Sampson saw a way to both involve his church members, and to assist in the process of informing citizens about Black candidates, as well as provide information about their credentials and platform.

Professor Robert Starks served as the group's chairperson and Northeastern Illinois University became the site where candidates came to speak to the public and share their platform. According to Sampson, people anticipate the endorsements by the Soul Slate Committee, which developed from the Task Force.

"Previously, Black people in Chicago would endorse every race but their own," Sampson says. "We realized that our people had to become more politically educated and the Soul Slate became one way to do just that. Now when people go to the polls, they know who the Black candidates are, and who we believe will work on our behalf."

The Black Church Revisited

And where is the Black church in all of this? Sampson's response is indicative of why he has been labeled as controversial. But he says he can only respond based on what he believes and has experienced.

"Too many of our city's African American preachers have accepted the offer of bacon and eggs from the mayor, so that they themselves are satisfied," he said.

"But for our people, we should be developing banks and credit unions, opening technical centers and independent schools, and preparing our youth so they will be able to take over the reigns in this new millennium. If we continue with business as usual, the future does not look bright for our children or our community."

Sampson continues to believe in the importance of the Black church and its unique role in improving the overall lives of its members, but says it needs to revisit some of the more crucial issues facing African Americans and revise its strategies, programming, and in some cases, its basic perspective.

"The genius of the Black church is the people take care of their ministers, so we are free enough to move against those systems that seek to destroy our people and make us vulnerable," he said.

"Here in Chicago, ministers have been at the forefront battling against lynchings, neighborhood slums, and the lack of political empowerment. And many of these same issues that we faced during the turbulent 1960s are, unfortunately, still the same."

Influences

In 1979, Sampson opened the doors of his church to Louis Farrakhan, allowing members of the Nation of Islam to temporarily worship and hold meetings there. Since that time, the two men, both from Boston, have developed a personal and professional relationship.

When Farrakhan called for Black men to gather in the nation's capital in 1995, Sampson served as a member of the transportation committee that took Chicagoans to the Million Man March. His church was one of several sites where enthusiastic men — old and young — gathered before making the historic trek to Washington, D.C.

"Minister Farrakhan is to the Honorable Elijah Muhammad what I am to the late Dr. King — we are both disciples," Sampson said. "And both of our teachers were from Atlanta. Minister Farrakhan has keys to our church, with the blessings of our officers, and knows that he and his members are always welcome."

After the march, Sampson was selected as the only Christian minister in a 30-member delegation to travel with Farrakhan to Africa, where they visited 18 countries on an "Atonement-Reconciliation-Responsibility-Peace Tour."

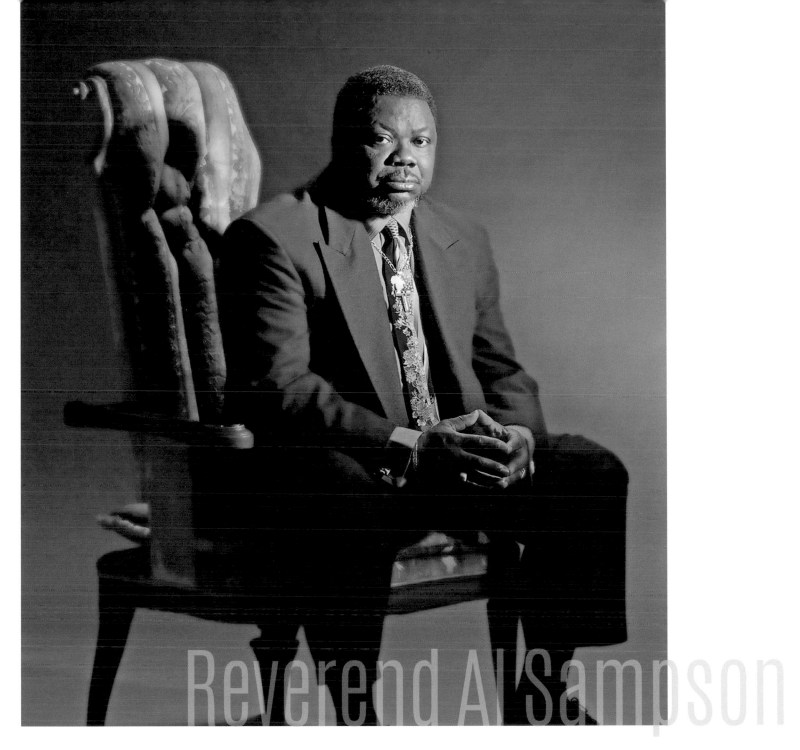

Reverend Al Sampson

Of course, Dr. King is one of Sampson's primary influences from the religious community. He recalls reading the works of Gandhi and supporting the back-to-Africa philosophy of Marcus Garvey, but says that the influence Martin Luther King had on his life remains unparalleled.

"Dr. King prepared us to go to jail, to protest nonviolently, and if necessary, to die for the cause," Sampson said. "People learned to trust him and to believe in him. He was a man of integrity who served a God of liberation. His genius rested in his ability to illustrate the importance of extending the church beyond the walls of its buildings."

Sampson recognizes that the Black church, like any institution that sprang from within the community, does not exist in a vacuum. In fact, given the kinds of ministries they support, he identifies three categories under which he believes most Black churches fall.

"Some churches jump and shout all day, at the encouragement of the pastor, but come Monday morning no transformation has occurred; they're entertainment churches," he said.

"Then there are the containment churches – usually places where many of the educated worship – who tend to stay locked up in the safety of the church instead of organizing members to be productive in their community, moving beyond the church walls.

"Fernwood United Methodist Church is a Martin Luther King church – one that takes its message out into the community and practices what it preaches. Like King, we have continued to challenge the U.S. government and private sector alike, saying there must be ways to include us in this nation's economic initiatives."

Thirty-five years after his ordination as minister by the Rev. Dr. Martin Luther King Jr., Rev. Al Sampson continues to preach, teach, and reach the masses.

preface Saunders

Update: Popular Chicago broadcast journalist Warner Saunders was on the air as a newscaster or public affairs commentator from 1968, when he hosted one of the city's first Black TV talk shows following the death of Martin Luther King, until 2009, when he retired from NBC5.

The Xavier and Northeastern University graduate was a teacher and executive director of the Better Boys Foundation before beginning his television career.

Winner of 19 Emmy Awards throughout that career, as well as numerous other media and community service honors, Warner previously worked for WBBM/Channel 2, where he was one of the most popular hosts in the history of the *Common Ground* public affairs program. He is a member of the Chicago Journalism Hall of Fame.

Nelson Mandela, born July 18, 1918, became South Africa's first Black president on May 10, 1994 and served in that position until 1999. He passed away on December 5, 2013 at the age of 95.

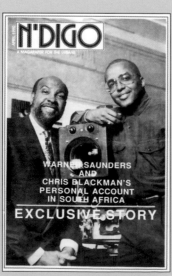

Cover Photo by David Jenkins

Warner Saunders

By Warner Saunders & Chris Blackman (as told to David Smallwood) & Photography by Reginald Payton | *Originally Published April 1990*

The WMAQ/Channel 5 news production team of reporter Warner Saunders and producer Christopher Blackman witnessed history being made in South Africa as they covered the release from prison of Nelson Mandela in February 1990.

In the following exclusive to *N'DIGO*, Warner and Chris tell an informative tale of what they experienced in the strange land of apartheid.

Saunders is an anchor/reporter on Channel 5's daily 4 p.m. newscast and host of *Warner*, an hour-long, weekly public affairs program on the station. Blackman was born along with an identical twin brother in Ghana, West Africa in 1959. After majoring in Communications at Stanford University in California and studying at the Sorbonne in Paris, Chris joined WMAQ/Channel 5 in Chicago as a news writer and producer of the station's noon newscast.

> **Apartheid there is so all-encompassing. It takes over everybody's life. There was a sense of relief, like, 'Please just let him out and let's get on with it and figure out how we can get out of this quagmire we're in.'**

Warner Saunders: Toward the end of 1989, I did a story on three high-wire circus performers from South Africa who talked about it as being a very beautiful, wonderful country. All that we hear on this side about South Africa is the apartheid, violence, police reaction and racial strife.

These guys suggested that we should actually visit South Africa to see what it's like; I talked to Chris and we both thought it would be a pretty good idea. We figured that we could do an overview of South African life – the country, the people, the politics, Black business, sports, culture, the townships, the whole issue of apartheid.

Chris Blackman: We thought it would be wonderful to go over there, get a real look at South Africa through our eyes and then come back and report on this whole process. We wanted to explain to America what South Africa is all about, to remove some of the stereotypes, preconceptions and misconceptions.

Warner: A South Africa trip is an extremely expensive proposition, but we were given the go ahead by station management once the news began to break that Mandela was possibly going to be released.

Upon landing in South Africa, my first impression of Johannesburg was that it looked like "Any Town, USA." The only difference you basically saw was that there were a lot more Black people than whites. That was immediately striking. But there were no signs of segregation, no people telling you to sit over here or stand over there. None of that was apparent at all.

Chris: When you looked closely, though, Blacks were doing all the heavy work – the janitorial type work, the street cleaning and so forth. You expected that because there is such a huge Black population, but you subtly began to take note of the hierarchy. The surprising thing about apartheid in South Africa is that you expect to walk into this situation and feel this racial tension, but it just wasn't there.

Warner: On our crew, we had a white South African cameraman, Carl Schultz, and a Black, a Zulu, Nkosinathi Shange, as our soundman – a Zulu who was well connected in the African National Congress (ANC) and other organizations there. So we had two people working with us who philosophically disagreed about everything.

That literally became a true asset to us because whenever we would do something, you'd see it out of the eyes of the white South African, and then you'd turn to the Zulu and see it out of his eyes. And they did not get along with each other. Their personalities, philosophy on life, their politics – everything was completely different.

On To Cape Town

Warner: Things started happening as soon as we touched down. We were told that we'd better get to Cape Town because there was the great possibility that Mandela was going to be released in a few days.

A mix-up in our schedule caused us to miss our plane, but NBC anchorman Tom Brokaw was there, so we piggybacked with him and took a Lear jet to Cape Town.

We land there and as we're getting off, here comes Rev. Jesse Jackson and Rev. Willie Barrow into the airport with a large entourage. There's this huge crowd of people to receive Jesse and his people from Chicago.

The Africans greeted him like he was a long-lost son. Jesse made a brief speech outside and you literally had to part the waters to get to him. It was an enormously popular thing for him to be there.

We went to Crossroads to film an event. Crossroads is a township outside of Cape Town, a Black shantytown like a squatter's camp. It's one of the worst places you'd ever want to see. We run into Tom Brokaw again there and he says, "I hear there's going to be an announcement today by (South African President) F.W. de Klerk. You better hurry up and get back into town."

We rushed back to Cape Town – and I gotta tell you that Cape Town is absolutely gorgeous; one of the most beautiful cities I've ever seen in my life! – and sure enough, deKlerk made the announcement that Mandela was to be released the next day.

Chris: We spoke to one white gentleman afterwards who was very optimistic about the release and I would say that a majority of whites we talked to, from a solely humanitarian point of view, were happy to see Mandela freed after so long.

They were also hopeful because they see Mandela as one of the beacons of hope for peaceful change in South Africa, as opposed to violent change.

Warner: The pressure has been building so much that the majority of the people in South Africa were very relieved that Mandela was released. They knew that if he did not get released or if something happened to that man while he was in jail, the country would have been up for grabs. There was a sense of relief, like, "Please just let him out and let's get on with it and figure out how we can get out of this quagmire we're in."

You see, apartheid there is so all-encompassing. It takes over everybody's life. It prevents even the white people of goodwill from having any kind of decent relationship with other people they might want to. In many ways, it is even worse than segregation American style.

After the announcement press conference, we went to Victor Verster Prison Farm where Mandela was being held. We wanted to get a standup report outside the jail the night before to be able to say, "Tomorrow morning, Nelson Mandela will walk through these doors and out of prison for the first time in 27 years."

The next day, on February 11, 1990, Mandela is released and we are in downtown Cape Town, about an hour's drive away. But it took Mandela nearly 3-1/2 hours to get downtown because the road was just full of people and well-wishers. It was a hot day at City Hall and there were thousands of people waiting.

Jesse Jackson drove up in this nice Mercedes and parked right in front of City Hall. After he got out and went into the building to wait for Mandela, the crowd jumped on top of the car and smashed it!

And that's just about when the riot started. It was hot, Mandela was late, a window broke, then bottles started being thrown and the police went into action. We were in the middle of all of that. The police started shooting buckshot at the people and the people started throwing things back at them.

The crowd rioted for about an hour and a half, then someone came out and said, "Mandela will speak!" and everybody just calmed down. This was more of a riot of enthusiasm where some young guys decided to break some store windows and do some stuff; it wasn't a riot against the system.

By the time Mandela was set to speak, it was late in the evening. We worked our way up in the pack and got the shot that nobody else in the world had. We followed Mandela onto the balcony and we got a shot looking down on Mandela as he looked over the crowd.

We got that shot because our soundman knew all these ANC people and they kept inching us up to the point where we finally got right behind Mandela as he was walking out. We just followed and filmed him as he went out. We filmed him giving the speech and shot him coming back in. For television people, that's really a coup de grace to have those kinds of shots.

Mandela spoke and the crowd dispersed like nothing happened, but four people had been killed in the riot. During this whole day's events, from both a journalistic perspective and as Black men, it was just incredible being there as history was being made. Objectivity was gone. It was so exciting!

Chris: There was a beautiful moment right at the start of the day. The crowd was packed outside of City Hall and a white photographer climbed up to a perch to get a good vantage point to shoot from.

A Black photographer tried to climb up to the same ledge, but he had a little trouble. The white guy reached over and helped him up and the crowd started cheering and clapping. It was really symbolic of what the whole day was about.

On To Johannesburg

Warner: That night, Mandela went to Johannesburg to prepare for a huge peace rally the next day at Soccer City, which is one of the largest athletic stadiums in the world. We followed him there.

The day of the rally I'll never forget in my life – the kind of day where you just say to yourself, "Yep,

that's the one." It was more emotional even than what had happened at Cape Town.

We're driving over to the Soccer City knowing there would probably be quite a few folks there, but as we approached the place, there's just this tremendous horde of people. It was something to see.

Thousands and thousands of happy people walking, driving, bicycling up to the stadium, chanting, singing and dancing. That's all you heard. It was like a release of all the frustration that had been pent up for all these years.

Chris: Cars were loaded, buses were loaded, people would stop cars and hop in for rides to Soccer City. Buses were going by with people "toi-toi-ing" (a South African dance) on top of the buses. It was like a pilgrimage. There were over 200,000 people inside and outside the stadium, just a sea of Black faces. You've never seen so many Black faces in your life.

Warner: This was the Black celebration. There were some white people, but this was the Black, "Welcome Home Mandela," get-down rally! It was all happy, much better organized than Cape Town, and there was not even a hint of negativity that day.

After this beautiful rally, there was then, finally, our highlight of meeting personally with Nelson Mandela. Jesse Jackson was going to meet him that Thursday and we asked if we could tag along.

We went into the house and met his wife Winnie, who was on the phone telling people that her husband's health was okay. Mandela met with Jesse, then Jesse called us in and we spoke with Mr. Mandela briefly and then again outside of the house, which is really a humble, humble abode.

His wife had this huge home built for them to live in upon his release from prison, but Mandela refused to live in it. His whole belief was that he couldn't come back and do that sort of thing. He had to be among the people.

At home in his backyard, giving interviews with all the media people, Mandela – fresh out of prison – was the calmest person around, just sitting and graciously granting one interview after another. The man is so cool.

When you're around greatness, you know it. And this is a great, great man, without any question. He is South Africa's George Washington, Abraham Lincoln and Martin Luther King all rolled into one.

For the first 15 years of his imprisonment, he had no books, television, radio or newspapers. Imagine what you would be like after 15 years of that. Yet, the man walked in prison with his fist raised, and 27 years later, walked out with the same fist raised.

Nelson and Winnie Mandela in Soccer City on the day after (February 12, 1990) he was released from prison in South Africa.

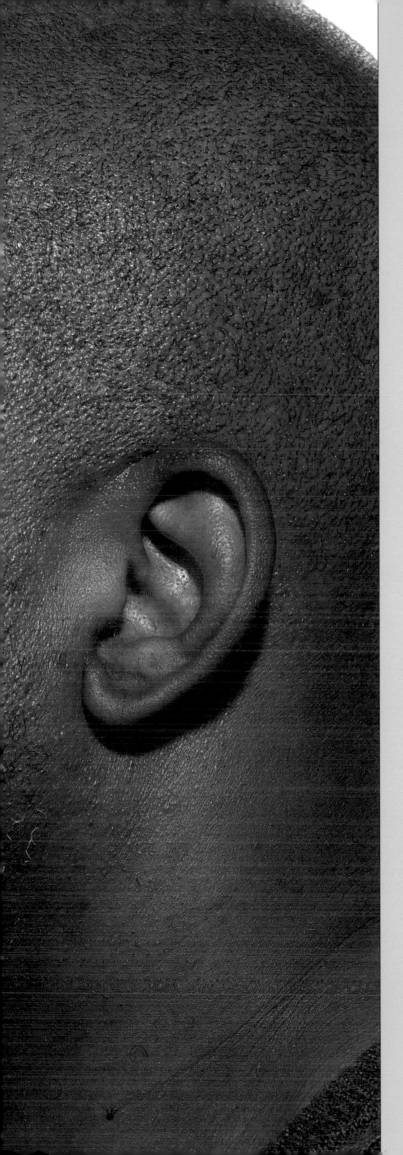

preface Savory

Update: Johnnie Lee Savory was pardoned in January 2015 by then Illinois Governor Pat Quinn. He is still awaiting his Certificate of Innocence from Illinois Governor Bruce Rauner. According to the National Registry of Exonerations, as of the end of 2016, there have been 1,931 exonerations In the United States since 1989, cases in which a wrongly convicted person was cleared of all charges based on new evidence of innocence.

Johnnie Lee Savory

By David Smallwood & Photography by Jason McCoy | *Originally Published August 21, 2014*

Johnnie Lee Savory believes in justice for all, but he's more focused on recognizing injustice all over the world for people like himself who have been wrongly convicted of crimes and have lost their years, their innocence and their human rights because of it.

Savory was convicted of a double murder in Peoria, Illinois in 1977 at the age of 14 and spent 30 years of a 50-100 year bit behind bars for it before being paroled in 2006 because of an overwhelming suggestion of his innocence. Savory has yet to be exonerated, but the results of DNA testing on evidence in his case that is expected to clear his name is forthcoming.

"It only took 30 seconds for me to lose my life when the police snatched me, now it's taken me 30 years to get it back," Savory says. It took his attorneys 15 years to get the courts to even allow the DNA testing, and that was just agreed to in August of last year, 2013.

After school let out on Monday, January 17, 1977, Johnnie Lee Savory visited his classmate James Scopy Robinson's home for the first time. Though the high-schoolers, both 14, had known each other since third grade, they lived several miles from each other in Peoria, Illinois and John's visit to James' place just had never happened.

> **I was supposed to go to high school, graduate, go on to college or whatever my life would have been set up to do, according to my dream. That dream was interfered with. Instead, I was 14 and convicted of double murder.**

"This particular day, James said, 'Man, come on, go home with me,' and I said okay," recalls Savory, now 52 years old. James' mother and stepfather were home, as was his 19-year-old sister, Connie Cooper, a student at Bradley University.

"We ate some hot dogs and corn and played and stuff," says Savory. "We drew some pictures for his mother. We both thought we were artists, so we were asking her which one was the best, you know."

The young boys played on until 10 or 10:30 p.m. before saying good-bye. They had lost track of time and because the buses in Peoria stopped running at 7 p.m.

back then, Johnnie had to walk some miles to get home, and there was already winter snow on the ground.

"But it was alright. It was my friend and we had fun," Savory said. "So we made plans to meet the next day… but it never happened." The next afternoon, January 18, James and his sister Connie were found stabbed to death in their home.

The Nightmare Begins

A week later, on January 25, Peoria police pulled Savory out of school and detained and interrogated him for nearly two days – after he said he didn't want to talk to them, without a lawyer being present, without allowing him to leave even though they said he wasn't a suspect, after he passed an initial polygraph test and after Savory said they plucked hairs from all over his naked body with tweezers – for forensic reasons, they told him – until he gave an oral confession, though he refused to sign any statement.

Savory went to trial in July 1977 and prosecutors asked for the death penalty, at age 14. They contended that Johnnie had been in the home the morning of the murder practicing karate with James, who they say he killed during an argument before blacking out and killing his sister.

The court denied the death penalty, but the all-White jury found Savory guilty in just two hours and the court sentenced him to 50-100 years, the equivalent of life. He had alibis from several people he had been with the day of the murder, but was convicted based on his illegal and coerced confession.

In April 1980, an appellate court unanimously found Savory's confession to be bogus, as it was involuntarily given, and it was a ruling that was upheld by the Illinois and United States Supreme Courts after the state appealed. Johnnie's case was reversed and kicked back to Peoria.

In 1981, the *Peoria Journal Star* newspaper quoted Hon. Michael Mihms, Peoria's State's Attorney in 1977, as saying "Without the confession it's impossible to retry Johnnie Savory, so that's it, he won't be retried."

John Barra, Peoria's State's Attorney in 1981, told the paper, "Without the confession, there is no evidence to tie Savory to the crime, or the scene of the crime."

Aside from the confession, the only evidence was a pair of bloodstained pants several sizes too big for Savory. They belonged to his father. "They took his pants, not my pants," Savory says. "My dad was 250 pounds, 5-foot-10. I was barely 5-feet tall, and weighed 110 pounds."

There was also a small knife with minute traces of blood, considered to be the murder weapon, but which also belonged to Savory's father. And finally, hair was found in both victims' hands, but it didn't match either victim, or Savory, according to a criminologist testifying at the 1977 trial.

Just when it seemed the nightmare was ending for Savory, lo and behold, three witnesses suddenly popped up – siblings from the Ivy family who lived in the community – who swore that Johnnie had made admissions to each of them on separate occasions on the day of the murders regarding the deaths and his involvement in them.

Based on that, a second trial was ordered for Savory, again asking for the death penalty. Largely based on the Ivy's testimony, he was convicted again and sentenced to 40-80 years.

After that second trial, all three Ivy siblings eventually recanted their testimony, saying they lied. But Johnnie Lee Savory remained in prison for 30 years until 2006, when he was finally paroled, thanks to the help of Northwestern University's Center on Wrongful Convictions, after being denied parole 26 times previously.

Railroaded

Savory was in prison from the age of 14 until he was 44 – two-thirds of his life, almost 11,000 days – railroaded by the criminal justice system. What galls him is the role Black people played in throwing him under the bus.

It's believed, and reportedly there was a deathbed confession, that the murders were committed by a member of a prominent Black family in Peoria, and Johnnie was used as a scapegoat to protect them, especially because he was the last person from outside the home to have seen the victims alive the night before and it was easy to pin the rap on him.

Complicit in this frame-up, Savory believes, were Black officers on Peoria's police force, one of whom had personal animosities towards Johnnie's father.

"The police knew I wasn't guilty. My community knew I wasn't guilty because the mothers, the grand-mothers, the big sisters, the aunts – all the women came out in full force to support me, to get me lawyers," says Savory. He says that his godmother Octavia Marie Bu rchett, in particular stood like a beacon in his defense, as did the white Vielburgs, a prominent Peoria family. "But the Black men didn't. The Black men were on the other side, with the police," Savory says.

It was a Black detective, he claims, "who forced the three witnesses – who did not appear at the first trial – to testify falsely that I had made admissions to them about the murder. I have affidavits from all three witnesses saying that two individuals, one being this particular Black cop, forced them into testifying. The juvenile prosecutor at the time testified that these witnesses couldn't have known anything.

"We have never held those accountable in our communities for the lies and things they have done to us," Savory continues. "We're walking around always blaming the White man. The White man didn't do this one, partner. You did this because you disliked the one you saw in the mirror – not me – because I didn't do anything to you. Nothing."

Behind Bars

And yet, there he was, locked up for as long as he could envision.

"Even though I was serving time, I wasn't supposed to be there," Savory says. "I was supposed to finish high school, graduate, go on to college or whatever my life would have been set up to do, according to my dream. That dream was interfered with. And there were not a lot of people in my situation in the country at the time. I was 14 years old and convicted of a double murder."

In prison, Savory completed his GED, started college and earned two vocational education certificates in electronics and auto bodywork. He says so matter-of-factly, seemingly not angry, not bitter, and if you didn't know his story, from outward appearances, you'd never guess his story.

"But I did go through those emotions," Savory says. "I was bitter. I was angry. I couldn't think. I couldn't process what had just happened. So I started reading anything I could get my hands on that had something to do with, or that my life paralleled in some kind of way, to help me to understand what had happened to me.

"I had to go on a new journey. The journey took me to the 1930s, to the Scottsboro Boys and the mothers of those boys. There was no question that they knew they were innocent. They hadn't done anything to those two women. Emmett Till – we were born on the same day in the same month. We both were 14 years old when we suffered a mockery of justice."

The biblical story of Joseph, falsely imprisoned yet showing no anger while being steadily protected and anointed by God, is what Savory most identifies with. "I can only contribute my journey to the grace of God, period. Nothing else," he says. "God communicated with me and sent me good people inside and outside."

Those good people helped Savory build a ground-swell of support that helped lead him to freedom. In prison he worked tirelessly to "let everyone know every day that I was there that I wasn't supposed to be there," in his words.

Savory made videos of his case that he sent to the media and wrote letters about his innocence to people all over the world. And he got one key response, from the late U.S. District Judge Prentice Marshall Sr., who asked his law firm, Jenner & Block, to look into the case.

Their participation snowballed the public support for Johnnie and soon, added to his base of Peoria believers came top names like former Illinois Gov. James Thompson; U.S. Senator Adlai Stevenson III; five former U.S. Attorneys, including Thomas Sullivan, Dan Webb, Sam Skinner, Anton Valukas, and Scott Lassar; Rubin "Hurricane" Carter, and authors John Grisham and Studs Terkel.

Steven Drizin, legal director at the time for Northwestern's Center For Wrongful Convictions of which Rob Warden is executive director, secured Savory's parole and brought him home from jail, with valuable assistance from attorneys Josh Tepfer and Laura Nirider.

Justice and Innocence

Since Savory has been freed, he spends his time volunteering with Northwestern's Center to help those newly released from prison to re-integrate back into society by securing documentation for them and the like.

He also works security for Operation PUSH and is an occasional special aide to Rev. Jesse Jackson Sr. Through the efforts of his long-time friend Jonathan Jackson – they used to play chess together – Savory went to PUSH and has created a

platform to help give the innocent a voice.

He sits on The Reentry Project Committee - Chicago Coalition for the Homeless and spent three years with St. Leonard's Ministries' reentry program on the West Side. Savory attends the Innocence Network Conference every year as a guest of Northwestern and is a welcome fixture as a motivational, inspirational, and authoritative speaker on the exoneration and Innocence Projects scene, even though he's not been exonerated himself…yet. He's spoken at Harvard University about his experiences.

Savory says that when he goes around to various speaking engagements, people often say, "Well, Johnnie, you'll be so happy when you get justice."

"I say, 'Justice from where?' I can't get any justice. If you're innocent but convicted and sentenced to prison, you do not receive justice. I can get truth, but I can't get any justice. Justice is a preventive measure to keep injustice from taking place.

"Anyway, I'm not looking for justice. I'm only looking to make it right. You took 30 years of my life – how do you justify it. You cannot. The only thing that can make it right is by telling the truth, that what we did to him is wrong."

The fruits of his unfortunate labor are already showing. Since the beginning of his ordeal 37 years ago, Savory has sought to clear his name through testing of evidence, but the courts denied him.

When Illinois passed its DNA statute in 1998 offering testing to those who claim wrongful conviction, Johnnie was first in line in the state to seek testing, but he was denied until last year. His case, however, led to a broad interpretation of the DNA statute that enabled hundreds of other wrongfully convicted defendants to get DNA testing, many of whom have been exonerated.

Also, his coerced confession at the age of 14 was among a number of similar cases that led to changes in Illinois law in 2003 and 2013 calling for the electronic recording of juvenile confessions.

"The wheels of justice turn slowly for those waiting in the balance to be exonerated," Savory says. It's clear that his experience has made innocence and exoneration his mission, probably for the rest of his days.

Johnnie Lee
Savory

preface Scott

Update: Scott served as CPS board president for five years until 2006. He was appointed to the position again in February 2009, where he served until his mysterious death nine months later. Michael Scott served multiple public posts appointed by mayors Jane Byrne, Harold Washington, Eugene Sawyer, and Richard Daley.

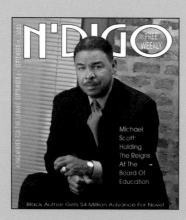

Michael Scott

By Paul Davis & Photography by Victor Powell | *Originally Published September 5, 2002*

t's been over 20 years since Michael W. Scott was first nominated to serve as a member of the Chicago Board of Education in 1982.

A generation later, Scott, 52, is the chief leader of the Board – having survived dynamic changes in Chicago politics in the last two decades – and fiercely dedicated to leaving a stamp of educational achievements in the Chicago Public Schools (CPS).

From the late 1970s through early 1980s, Scott, a lifelong West Side resident of North Lawndale, carved-out an impressive record of community service at the grassroots level.

That community-grown leadership has earned him a number of responsible positions of public trust with three Chicago mayors over the last three decades.

Today, Scott is firmly perched at the highest level of responsibility of the CPS, as President of the Chicago Board of Education, where he is being relied upon to implement educational and management reform for the third largest school district in the nation.

> **When I think about our community and the issues that confront us, the most formidable weapon that we have is education.**

Mayor Richard M. Daley appointed Scott to the Board of Commissioners of the Chicago Park District in 1992. He served as board president for that body for a little over two years, from 1999 to 2001.

Making The Grade

Of his tenure at the Park District, Scott takes pride in the capital improvements he helped oversee at parks on the West and South Sides, as well as on the lakefront.

While Scott has invested in the Community Bank of Lawndale to help spur its growth, he's also assisted in the development of housing on the West Side, and serves on the boards of several civic organizations, including Mount Sinai Hospital, the Chicagoland Chamber of Commerce, the Chicago Urban League, the Museum of Science & Industry, the SAFER Foundation, and the Little City Foundation.

Throughout all his public service, however, Scott has always recognized that schools are the staple and heart of a community.

"If you don't pay attention to that, then all the other stuff does not make sense," Scott insists. "When I think about our community and the issues that confront us, the most formidable weapon that we have is education."

Of his appointment by Daley in June 2001 to school board president, Scott says, "I thought I might have an impact."

In a little over a year, Scott's leadership skills are proving to have just that – a positive impact. Earlier this summer, the board approved a $4.5 billion budget that included over $500 million for capital improvements. It represented the fifth straight balanced budget achieved by the board.

Scott noted that with incremental teachers' costs rising at a rate of $50 million annually and $30 million in state budget cuts, "the fact that we were able to submit a balanced budget is a great testimony to our staff."

The loss of state dollars did require some belt-tightening on the part of the board. As a result, 300 positions were eliminated from the central offices, he said, while the staff in the field was increased by about 300.

Scott is most disturbed by the fact that the state of Illinois ranks 49th in terms of the monies it contributes to grades K-12. "Other states have made education a priority," he says. "It amazes me that in statewide elections, education has not figured more prominently.

"For all those politicians who claim education is valuable (and say) the children are important, for those statistics not to be bouncing off the walls surprises me."

This School Year

A major goal of the current school year, Scott said, is to expand after-school programs and professional development.

He applauds Mayor Daley for having the "courage of his convictions" for taking public responsibility for the schools when his advisors recommended against it.

"Statistically, we've come a long way. We still have

a long way to go," Scott points out while listing the latest student improvements. "Better than 50 percent of our 8th graders are reading at or above the national norms, and better than 50 percent are computing at the national norms.

"Those children were in the 3rd grade when the Mayor took responsibility for the schools. Those children are probably the flagship of our system."

On the issue of minority-owned and women-owned corporations having greater business opportunities with the CPS, Scott said the board is looking to create an MBE/WBE compliance office to assist African-American and other minority businesses with accessing the system.

The Board

Years prior to being named Board President, Scott made a name for himself as a neighborhood leader. As the executive director of the Lawndale People's Planning and Action Conference (LPPAC), he had helped to spur community and commercial development that spawned a senior citizen center, a neighborhood banking facility, a nursing home, and the rehabilitation and construction of 1,500 housing units.

These significant community-based achievements made Scott a hot commodity on the public service and political service levels. He had all the qualities of a future leader. He was bright, articulate, honest, and it didn't hurt that he was good-looking.

In 1980, as Chicago Mayor Jane Byrne was seeking to revamp the board of education in the wake of strident public dissatisfaction with it, she had an eye on Scott.

Scott says that when Byrne contacted him about serving on the board, she indicated that his name appeared on the list of several community groups.

At his first meeting with Mayor Byrne in her office, Scott recalls vividly: "She had two packs of Parliaments in front of her. She was chain-smoking."

Scott and an all-new board were appointed by Byrne, including: Rev. Kenneth Smith, who was president; law professor Joyce Hughes; Rev. Wilfred Reid; and Leon Davis, all of whom were Black, along with six other non-African Americans.

That board faced major immediate challenges, none

less than building a consensus behind a desegregation consent decree, and selecting a new superintendent.

Scott said Professor Hughes spent hour upon hour arming him with information about desegregation, and the impact that busing would have on it. Scott would later be named chairman of the desegregation committee.

The board embarked upon a national search for a new school superintendent, an effort Scott felt was unnecessary. "I didn't think that somebody from outside the city could come and run the Chicago Public Schools," he says. While a majority of the board voted to hire Oakland's Ruth Love as the superintendent, Scott said he voted against her.

Knowing that his and Davis' terms were only for one year, Scott said he contacted Davis to find out if the two of them would be renewed. He and Davis had once stalled a busing contract in favor of two African-American-owned bus companies.

Davis said he had spoken with Mayor Byrne, and that she had reassured him that he and Scott would be reappointed...but a few weeks later, Scott had reason to doubt Byrne's words.

In a letter given to him by a Byrne bodyguard, Scott said the letter essentially was thanking him for his service and for helping her to achieve her campaign goals of electing a Black superintendent. He told Davis, who said he had received a similar letter, that "it sounded like a goodbye note."

The next morning a Chicago newspaper reported that Byrne was dumping Scott and Davis. Scott acknowledged that he was "very hurt" by his removal from the board. But he rebounded.

After Harold Washington's successful mayoral election in 1983, Scott, after working to help a number of independent Democrats defeat machine Democrats, joined the Washington Administration as Deputy Director of Special Events, and later was appointed Director of Special Events.

The Washington years are now part of Scott's storied past and he said he is proud to have contributed in a small way to Harold Washington's success as Mayor of Chicago.

His eyes are now fixed on helping the city's schoolchildren obtain the highest degree of educational success.

Michael Scott

preface
Sengstacke

Update: Mr. John Sengstacke passed away on May 28, 1997. This was Sengstacke's last interview. The *Chicago Defender* is currently owned by Real Times Media, headquartered in Detroit.

John Sengstacke

By Charles Whitaker & Photography by Warren Browne | *Originally Published February 8, 1996*

John H. Sengstacke, publisher of the *Chicago Defender*, is probably the most significant newspaperman in the history of the post-Emancipation era Black press, as he organized the modern Black press to be a real power.

As a young business student at Hampton Institute in the early 1930s, Sengstacke, president and chairman of the Robert S. Abbott Publishing Co., the parent company of the *Chicago Defender*, demonstrated the steely resolve and pioneering instincts that would carry him through life.

Though administrators at Hampton tried to force him into a general curriculum that included a liberal dose of courses like biological science, Sengstacke – whose grandfather founded and edited a newspaper just outside of Savannah, Georgia – had designs on a career in publishing and was bound and determined to take classes more relevant to what he knew would be his life's work.

> **You have to organize and do something if you want change. You can't just sit around and complain.**

"I said, 'Look, I'm going to be in the newspaper business, so I want to know about advertising,'" he recalls. "And that's how the advertising department at Hampton got started. I had the teachers give me what I needed to do what I wanted in the future."

It is a tale that is vintage Sengstacke. The 83-year old business and civic leader has rarely been one to sit back and react to events. He has, throughout the six decades of his magnificent publishing career, been an activist as well as a businessman, and an important player on the national and world stages.

Many journalists and media moguls can boast that they have witnessed and recorded some of the dizzying events and monumental changes that have occurred in the second half of the 20th Century. But few can say, as John Sengstacke can, that they were active participants and important agents for change.

Consider some of the heady achievements and distinctions on the Sengstacke vitae: He has met with and, in some form or other, been asked to counsel every American president since Franklin Roosevelt.

Roosevelt, Harry Truman, John Kennedy and Lyndon Johnson all appointed him to presidential committees and advisory boards. In fact, as a member and secretary of Truman's Committee on Equality of Treatment & Opportunity in the Armed Forces, Sengstacke was among the people directly responsible for the integration of the U.S. military.

He was the founder and seven-time president of the Negro Newspaper Publishers Association, now the National Newspaper Publishers Association (NNPA), a coalition of some 200 newspapers that demonstrated the power of the Black press as a voice in the journalistic marketplace.

But perhaps more importantly, Sengstacke is known as the man who took over an already successful publication – the *Chicago Defender* – and made it the centerpiece of the largest chain of Black newspapers in the country.

Conversation Piece

A conversation with John Sengstacke is like a trek through history. It is a bumpy, but enjoyable ride, with the chain-smoking octogenarian gruffly dropping the names of the rich and powerful people who have curried his favor and advice through the years. In many ways, Sengstacke is a throwback to the stereotype of the newspaperman of old – all brusque and blustery with a voice as smoky as a pack of Marlboros.

But he is clearly no rumpled reporter type. Nattily turned out in a blue, double-breasted blazer, taupe pants and sporty black loafers, it is almost hard to believe that the trim man sitting straight backed in the wood-paneled second floor conference room of the landmark *Defender* building on South Michigan Avenue was born two years before the start of World War I.

But as his stories tumble out in the stream-of-consciousness fashion that is Sengstacke's rhetorical style, it becomes evident that his has indeed been a long and glorious life.

His influence on American politics and race relations has been considerable. Some examples of his clout: In the 1950s, when FBI Chief J. Edgar Hoover had Little Rock, Arkansas school teacher and civil rights activist Daisy Bates under surveillance for publishing a newsletter advocating the integration of the city's public schools, Sengstacke spoke with Hoover on behalf of Bates and all Black publishers, arguing that the government could not infringe on their First Amendment right to free speech. "I think that might have helped in keeping the Black press from being shut down," Sengstacke says.

And in 1940, when the nation's Black publishers – many of them his competitors – were floundering and in need of an organization to represent them collectively, Sengstacke convinced his peers to put aside their petty jealousies and form the NNPA. Similarly, he helped organize Amalgamated Publishers, Inc. to help Black newspapers garner national advertising.

He recalls: "I said to them, 'Look, there's strength in our numbers. If we could just work together, we could be a powerful voice for some good in this country.' And it was because of that and the strength that we represented that we helped to integrate the troops. We showed that the Black press is a very powerful force."

Similarly, when plans were made to wipe out half the housing on the South Side of Chicago to pave way for the Dan Ryan Expressway, Sengstacke was part of the team of influential Black Chicagoans who lobbied for federal funding to build Lake Meadows on an expanse of lakefront territory on the northeast end of the traditional "Black belt."

"You have to organize and do something if you want change," says Sengstacke in an effort to explain his life of civic and professional involvement. "You can't just sit around and complain."

And that, by and large, is the creed by which he has lived his life and run his business. It is a creed, he says, imparted to him by his uncle, legendary *Defender* founder Robert Sengstacke Abbott. "Mr. Abbott told me when I first came here, 'John, I started the business to help my people. Remember, if you help the people, it will pay you.'"

Dogged Instincts

There was never any doubt about the line of work that John Sengstacke would go into. Newspapering had been the family business since before the turn of the century.

Born in Savannah, Sengstacke was inducted into the publishing world as an apprentice on his grandfather's newspaper, the *Woodville* (Georgia) *Times*. It was on this same paper that Robert Abbott got his first taste of publishing.

After earning a degree in business from Hampton and doing some graduate work at Ohio State University in Columbus, Sengstacke headed to Chicago in 1934 to join his now wealthy and famous uncle on what had become the most successful and

influential Black newspaper in the country – the *Chicago Defender*.

Robert Abbott is a legendary figure in the annals of American journalism, noted for his editorial vision and courage. Also a Hampton graduate, Abbott founded the *Defender* in 1905, shortly after moving to Chicago to establish his law practice.

He believed in an activist press and from the outset intended to make his newspaper an important voice in the chorus against the racial oppression and injustice of the day. His mission was to use the power of the press to eliminate prejudice.

Though Chicago already had a number of Black publications at the time of the *Defender*'s founding, the paper quickly became an international success, due in large part to Abbott's strong political and social stands.

So great was Abbott's influence that many historians credit him with instigating the Great Black Migration of the 1920s and '30s, so persuasive were his arguments that Blacks should leave the Jim Crow South.

By 1915, the *Defender* had an international circulation of about 230,000 and Abbott had become one of Chicago's first Black millionaires.

In 1934, fresh from graduate studies at Ohio State, John Sengstacke joined his uncle in Chicago and signed on as vice president and general manager of the *Defender*. Abbott was in poor health, so from the start, the plan was to groom Sengstacke – Abbott's only heir – as his successor.

With his ascension virtually assured, Sengstacke continued to study every aspect of the publishing business so he would be fully equipped to assume the reins of the company.

He took courses in press operation at the Chicago School of Printing and in journalism and business at Northwestern University. All the while, he was slowly taking over day-to-day operations of the *Defender*.

When Abbott died in 1940, Sengstacke was named president of the company. He quickly went about laying the groundwork that would elevate the *Defender* even further above the ranks of popular Black newspapers. Ultimately, it would become the crown jewel in a publishing empire destined to include some of the most influential Black newspapers in the country.

In 1956, Sengstacke converted the *Defender* from a weekly to a daily publication. Throughout the '50s and '60s, the paper continued to attract and cultivate a stable of prize-winning and groundbreaking reporters.

In fact, the list of writers published by the *Defender* through the ages reads like a who's who of Black literature and journalism: Langston Hughes wrote for the *Defender*; the paper also was among the first outlets for the poetry of young Gwendolyn Brooks.

In journalism circles, *Defender* alumni include

retired syndicated columnist and former *Today Show* commentator Chuck Stone, who worked at the *Defender* under Sengstacke; the late foreign correspondent and Washington reporter Ethel Payne, who was the dubbed the "Dean of Black Women Journalists;" and Chicago legends Vernon Jarrett and Lu Palmer.

By the late 1960s, Sengstacke had turned the Abbott Publishing Company into the largest chain of Black newspapers in the country, a publishing empire including such venerable titles as the *Michigan Chronicle* and the *Pittsburgh Courier*. It was the Sengstacke group now, and its president had forged a reputation as one of the most influential entrepreneurs in the country.

Daily Struggles

It is no secret that the *Defender*'s great heyday is, in many respects, behind it. It is back to being a weekly, with circulation hovering in the 16,000 range by most estimates and ad pages are down. Still, it remains a vital source of news and entertainment for the loyal readers who continually turn to it for a view of the Black community not present in other publications.

The man who has led the *Defender* for the past 55 years is determined not to let those people down. He has once again taken hold of the reins after years of being disappointed by the stewardship of others, including relatives he had once hoped would fill his shoes.

Widowed, and with few interests beyond the company he helped to build, Sengstacke is devoting his remaining days to righting this wayward ship. "Retire!" he says, throwing the word back as if it were an epither. "I'm not going to retire until the *Defender* is where it is supposed to be. This was one of the greatest newspapers in the world. I'm not going to stop until it's there again."

preface Smith

Update: Chicago native Chuck Smith has an endless list of credits and accomplishments not only at Goodman Theatre where he is a member of the board of trustees, but also with Victory Gardens Theater, eta, Black Ensemble Theater, the New Federal Theatre in New York, the Oregon Shakespeare Theatre, the Alabama Shakespeare Festival, and the Roby Theater Company in Los Angeles, among others around the country. He is also resident director at the Westcoast Black Theatre Troupe in Sarasota, Florida, and has won and been nominated for several Emmy Awards.

Chuck Smith

By James G. Muhammad, Sergio Mims & Photography by Victor Powell | *Originally Published December 9, 2004 & January 26, 2012*

When Chuck Smith, the Goodman Theatre's legendary resident director, puts his mind to something, watch out. He's going to accomplish it.

Take, for example, the time in 1954 when he vowed as a youth to do something about the fact that he felt DuSable High School was cheated out of a possible state basketball championship in a title game played downstate.

It was the first ever televised finals, and was in black and white, he recalls. "They literally were not letting these Black kids win the game. You could see it."

Through the light-hearted smile that stays with him yet hides a deep-seated determination, Smith continued, "They called bogus fouls and all kinds of stuff. They took it away from them. I vowed as a kid that one day I'd do something about that."

Or take the time in 1970-71 that Smith worked as an understudy at the Goodman Theatre. It's where he earned his first buck in a career that would place him among the elite of the city's theatre community, and a place where he vowed to work full time one day. He accomplished both goals and much more.

> Directing is something I really enjoy because I can sit back and watch my work, and I get a charge out of watching an audience appreciate what I do.

Smith joined the Goodman full time in 1992 as an affiliate artist. Before that, he hooked up with noted playwright Charles Smith (not related) to produce the Emmy Award-winning *Fast Break to Glory*, a teleplay about that DuSable basketball event.

To walk with Smith is not only to walk through the prestigious halls of the Goodman, it is to walk the road of contemporary Chicago theatre history – Black and White.

Book Raises New Voices

It is that theatre community and close friends who celebrate Smith's many accomplishments, particularly the release of *Seven Black Plays*, a book he edited that contains winners of the Theodore Ward Prize for African-American Playwriting. The prize is given every year at Columbia College, where Smith was a professor and facilitator of the national contest of the best new Black plays.

The book, he says, is a resource, so that when he gets any of the many calls he gets from directors inquiring about good Black plays to produce other than the standards, he can respond, "Get my book."

Former Goodman executive director Roche Schulfer noted Smith's determination to institutionalize good Black works at the Tony Award-winning Goodman Theatre. Bringing Smith on, he said, was one of the best moves Goodman made.

"His goal was to institute African-American work as a priority at Goodman. And there's a lot of African-American playwriting out there beyond August Wilson," Schulfer says. "For us, his book validates that."

Shepsu Aakhu's play *Kiwi Black*, a story about father-son relationships, is included in the anthology. Aakhu says the contest is one of the few places that gives recognition for new Black voices, works that are essential to bringing in new audiences. In a sense, Aakhu views Smith as a father to his generation of playwrights and actors.

"Chuck makes a continual effort to stay in touch with anybody Black who's doing anything. He made it through the door and kept it open so others can get in," Aakhu says. "If you are looking for a reason not to quit or not to do what you do, Chuck's the inspiration. He's still there."

Seven Black Plays is another goal of bringing quality to African-American theatre that Smith can check off.

Goodman Board Vice Chairman Les Coney noted Smith's commitment to African-American works in the way the director handled the production of *Proof*.

"Chuck saw the play on Broadway and it was all White. He brought the play here and made it all Black. It became the first production we ever had that was extended even before it opened," Coney says.

But to hear Smith tell it, his determination not to

be pigeonholed simply as a Black director is what has allowed him greater influence to elevate the works of Black playwrights and performers.

"Theodore Ward was my mentor. He showed me how to navigate the waters and told me not to work only with Black companies, but to work with everybody," Smith explains, referencing the man for whom the contest is named. "Theatre is this huge, vast sea of people."

From Humble Beginnings

Born at Cook County Hospital in 1938, Smith graduated from high school and joined the Marine Corps after spending one year at Loop College. He was a Marine for over six years and considers it fortunate that his stint in the military ended just before the Vietnam conflict escalated.

Back home and between jobs at the Spiegel merchandise company, the steel mill and the U.S. Post Office, Smith became bored and considered re-enlisting. That's when he met some guys at the old South Shore Lounge who would change his life. They were with a volunteer group of actors called the Dramatic Arts Guild and performed for patients at Michael Reese Hospital.

One of their actors had dropped out and they asked Smith to take his place. After initially refusing – guys from Smith's neighborhood thought acting was "sissy stuff" – he agreed to at least take a look at the production. But only after the actors told him it was a place he could meet pretty women.

"As soon as I walked into the room, my life changed…and it was not because of the ladies!" Smith says laughing. "It took me many years to figure out why that was.

"It was that everybody was doing something. Everybody was working on a task. They were hanging lights, going over lines, working with the sound. Nobody was just sitting around. I realized that's exactly what happens in the Marine Corps. Everybody is involved in a certain task to complete a mission. The mission here is the play."

Acting in the Michael Reese production wasn't a pleasant experience at first. Smith got plenty of laughs in his role as a preacher. But he thought the audience was laughing at him, so during intermission he complained to other actors that he was quitting after the performance.

His fellow thespians told him the audience wasn't laughing at him, but was responding to the way he portrayed the character. The rousing ovations he received during the curtain call verified that fact, but it still put Smith on the path to doing what he liked better – directing.

"I never really got a charge out of acting," he admits. "Directing is something I really enjoy because I can sit back and watch my work, and I get a charge out of watching an audience appreciate what I do. Acting is very difficult for me. It's easier for me to bring talent out of somebody else because I know exactly what I'm looking for," he says.

"Smart actors can usually solve all your problems – I learned that as a student from one of my old instructors at Loop College, a director by the name of Sydney Daniels. That was sort of his approach – let the actors do their thing within the framework of what I gave them. And if it works and they're not tripping over each other, give them space to create the thing on their own. Then I just fine-tune it."

That first play at Michael Reese was the start of a fascinating theatre career for Smith, although it took him 21 years to quit his 9-5 with the Department of Public Aid. Building on the legacy of the Pekin Theatre, the first Black-owned musical and vaudeville stock theater in Chicago, he helped to form the Chicago Theatre Company (CTC), the city's first Black union-affiliated troupe.

State Of Black Theatre

Smith considers Chicago the capital of Black theatre. With major companies like the eta Creative Arts Foundation, CTC, Black Ensemble, MPAACT (Ma'at Production Association of Afrikan Centered Theatre), Congo Square and other groups springing up across the city, Smith says most good actors don't have to worry about work.

"There's a good appetite for Black theatre and there are more companies producing full seasons in Chicago than any other city in the country," he says. "There may be other cities with more companies, but they're not producing a full season of professional work. In addition, you have companies like the Goodman, Victory Gardens, and Steppenwolf that produce Black theatre on a regular or semi-regular basis.

"What's lacking, especially in the Black theatre community, is backstage talent," he continued. "We really need people like stage managers, lighting designers and costume designers, people who actually want to do this kind of work," he says.

Smith is busy every season. He's directed such heavyweight productions through the years as *The Crucible, The Death of Bessie Smith, Jammin' With Pops, Ma Noah, Proof*, David Mamet's *Race, Pullman Porter Blues, By the Way, Meet Vera Stark, The Good Negro, The Gift Horse, The Amen Corner, Ain't Misbehavin', Knock Me A Kiss, Master Harold…and the Boys, The Meeting*, and many August Wilson plays.

But Smith places the 2001 production of *Ma Rainey's Black Bottom* as one of his best individual moments, as well as being selected as a Chicagoan of

the Year by the *Chicago Tribune,* and being inducted into the Chicago State University Gwendolyn Brooks Center's Literary Hall of Fame.

Ma Rainey's Black Bottom was his first major production on the Goodman stage, and it set a box office record. The play was viewed by then-Vice President Al Gore, Mayor Richard M. Daley, and basketball Hall of Famer Michael Jordan, all of whom spent time with cast members backstage.

"That play put me in a place that I never left in terms of confidence, that I can do this," Smith recalls. And the rest is theatre history.

preface Smith

Update: Bishop Smith has published a book, *Blood Works: The Insights Of A Pastor And Hematologist Into The Wonder And Spiritual Power Of Blood*. He serves on the boards of the historic Wabash YMCA, the Family Institute at Northwestern University and the University of Chicago Cancer Research Center-Community Health Advisory Board and Chicago State University. Apostolic Faith Church opened a new edifice in 2017.

Bishop Horace Smith M.D.

By Ingrid E. Bridges and David Smallwood & Photography by Howard Simmons | *Originally Published April 1, 2010*

Some people believe that God and science don't mix, that faith and medicine are worlds apart. But Horace Smith has successfully treated bodies and souls for more than three decades.

As pastor of Apostolic Faith Church, Bishop Horace E. Smith has preached God's mighty word to the masses as one of the nation's most prominent orators. And as Dr. Horace E. Smith, he also sets out daily to heal God's people medically as a leading pediatrician hematologist-oncologist at Luric Children's Hospital. Both the church and the hospital are located in Chicago.

Apostolic Faith Church, at 3823 South Indiana, has grown by leaps and bounds since Bishop Smith began to preach and teach life into the souls of men, women and children in the very church he grew up in; it welcomes over 4,000 congregants every Sunday to one of three soul-stirring worship services.

The late iconic Bishop Arthur M. Brazier swore Bishop Smith in as pastor of Apostolic Faith in 1980, at a time when the church had fewer than 200 members. Today, thousands of believers can recall when their lives became transformed under Smith's tutelage after hearing his unique, often animated sermons that ultimately led them to surrender their all and follow Christ forever.

Bishop Smith's signature welcoming spirit, his belief that any man of any walk or race can be born again and made new in God's eyes has drawn many into the faith.

> You know, God *will* throw you a curve ball!

Heeding The Call

Smith speaks humbly of his blessed life, of when his view of the world extended as far as State Street and Pershing Road, where he grew up in public housing.

After the sudden death of his mother when Smith was just 10, he and his five siblings were raised by his father Albert Smith and grandmother Alberta Pryor, who trained them spiritually and were responsible for Horace's Christian upbringing through regular attendance at Apostolic Faith Church.

At the same time, young Smith excelled academically. An honor student graduate of Lindblom High School, he went on to earn his Bachelor of Science Degree with honors from Chicago State University in 1971 and his M.D. from the University of Illinois Medical Center in 1975. He met Susan Davenport at the University of Illinois and they wed in 1976.

Smith completed his pediatric residency at University of Illinois Hospital in 1978 and his clinical fellowship in pediatric hematology-oncology at Children's Memorial Hospital/Northwestern University in 1980.

That same year, the presiding pastor of Apostolic Faith Church passed away and Smith was approached to take the position. He was hesitant.

Smith recalls, "I said that this is not the will of God. I did not believe it. I said, 'You must be crazy.' The elders said, 'We are asking that you pray about it.' I thought, this does not make any sense, even though I was a licensed minister.

"I was also beginning my practice, my wife was a clinical pharmacist, and we were only a few years into our marriage. But when I began to pray about this, I knew if it were God's will, it would happen. You know, God *will* throw you a curve ball!"

An Expanding, Busy Ministry

Obviously he accepted the responsibility of shepherding Apostolic and the church has grown ever since – in terms of membership and building expansion.

Each year the ministry provides assistance by way of food and supplies to over 4,000 homeless families around the Chicago area, visitations to nursing homes, outreach to correctional facilities, and a JobSource program that has assisted hundreds of individuals in obtaining employment. Apostolic also broadcasts its *Faithworks Ministry* telecast locally and nationally on The Word Network, providing programming that is enriching and anointed.

"In our ministry we have purposefully preached and planned to become much more intergenerational. Building up and preparing young people must be totally embraced and implemented," Bishop Smith says.

"Our scholarship/educational ministry has become one of the hallmarks of our church." It is a scholarship program that has granted more than $100,000 each

Bishop Smith and his wife Susan.

Apostolic provides resources for the drilling of wells bringing fresh water, which is the number one need in some areas. They also provide food, clothing, education, medical assistance and other goods and services.

The Balancing Act

And still, the Bishop is still a doctor, a concerned and committed pediatrician for critically ill children. He served as director of the Comprehensive Sickle Cell/ Thalassemia Program at Ann & Robert H. Lurie Children's Hospital of Chicago (formerly Children's Memorial Hospital) for over 20 years; is an assistant professor of pediatrics at Northwestern Feinberg School of Medicine; and is recognized worldwide as an outstanding pediatrician in his field.

Managing his life's enormous schedule takes more than a prayer of blessed assurance, but years of organization, focus and discipline instead, Bishop Smith says, and that's no small task.

"In order to do what I do, each staff team – whether at the hospital, university, church or organization – has to embrace the overall vision of ministry and care and the privilege we have to serve others, and then communicate and work together to achieve the various goals and meet the diverse needs of the people."

Actually, Smith finds positivity in the manner in which the various facets of his busy life coexist. He believes, in fact, that ministering and doctoring help him to be more effective at both.

"They mix perfectly," says Smith. "God is the source of all knowledge; then there are the principles of the Bible of helping, healing, supporting and developing people, of impacting people's lives in a positive way. I cannot see a better way to do it."

Still, with his average day consisting of powerful decisions, conversations, procedures and lectures, he often relies on precautionary steps for his own well being. When life becomes somewhat overwhelming, Smith's strong support system of loved ones and friends help him to reboot and focus.

"That is why we must, as high stress leaders, be committed to developing a small but important group of real friends, mentors and colleagues who we give direct permission to speak the truth to us, especially the difficult truth," he advises.

It is written in Psalms 37:23, "The Lord directs the steps of the godly. He delights in every detail of their lives." Looking back over the sacred steps of Bishop Smith that have helped him blossom, many can bear witness that he has a wonderful life – a busy one, but nevertheless, a blessed one.

Bishop Smith sets his sights high to serve the masses, by offering God's gift of healing to the sick and also the gift of salvation to those who will hear and who will obey the Lord.

year for the past 15 years for students to attend college.

Such success, the Bishop says, he ultimately owes to God, and also to his wife, Susan Davenport Smith, and their three lovely daughters whose life force stimulates all that he does for humanity.

"The understanding and cooperation of my wife and children have been indispensable," he says. "Without their support and assistance, I could not do half of what I do."

And what he does is quite a bit. In addition to pastoring and doctoring, from 2004-2010, Smith was the Presiding Bishop of the Pentecostal Assemblies of the World, which has over 1.5 million members worldwide, including in Africa, Asia, Europe, Australia and New Zealand.

As a result, Apostolic Faith has a vast list of overseas missions. "Our church has sponsored more than 2,000 adopted children in South Africa, Liberia, Zimbabwe and the Congo," Smith says. "I went to the Congo to see exactly what was needed. The hospitals there had no aspirin and no running water to sterilize surgical instruments.

"We have no idea what God's people are facing in other countries until we put ourselves there. It put ministry in a whole new perspective for me."

Along with his wife, Sister Susan Smith, the Bishop travels extensively to Africa to view first-hand the devastation of the HIV/AIDS pandemic. In addition,

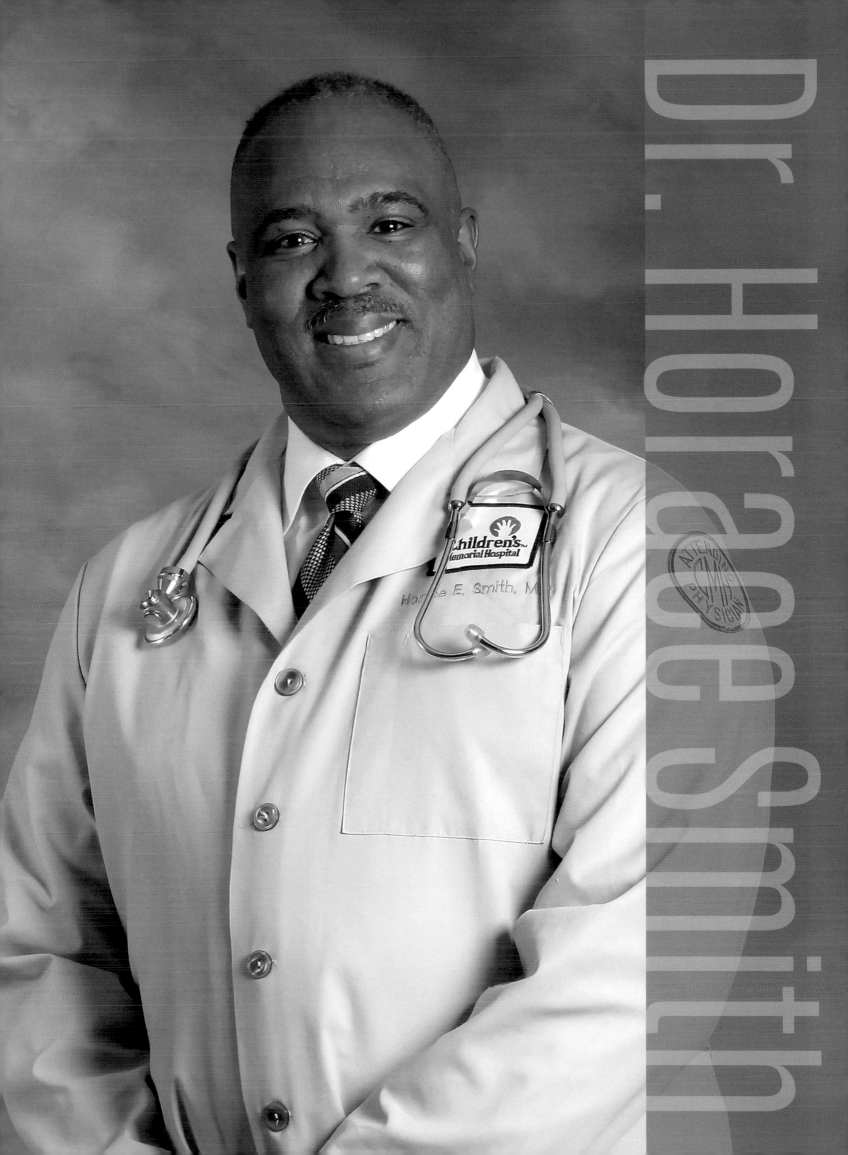

preface Smith

Update: Lovie was named NFL Coach of the Year in 2005 and became the first Black head coach to lead his team to the Superbowl, which the Bears lost in 2006. Lovie remained as Bears coach until 2012, with the third-longest tenure running the team behind George Halas and Mike Ditka.

After coaching the Tampa Bay Buccaneers for one year in 2014, Lovie was named head coach of the University of Illinois in 2016 under a six-year contract. He won his first game coaching his new team by a score of 52-3.

Lovie Smith

By Rod Atkins & Photos Courtesy of the Chicago Bears | *Originally Published February 10, 2005*

With the Super Bowl having just come to an end, it is time for National Football League coaches near and far to begin anew and start preparing for next season. Chicago's own Bears Coach Lovie Smith is already two steps ahead of the game.

"Going into next season, we as coaches have a better understanding of the personnel in place, as well as some areas that we can improve on. Now we as a staff can concentrate on putting our players in the right spots for the team to have success," says Coach Smith.

Since 1920, the Chicago Bears have been one of the cornerstones of the National Football League, providing fans for multiple generations with 26 Hall of Fame Players so far, including Gale Sayers, Dick Butkus, Walter Payton, Mike Ditka, Mike Singletary, and of course, the franchise's first coach and owner, George "Papa Bear" Halas.

The Bears have also won nine championships, including the 1985 Superbowl, which gave them the reputation as the greatest single team – certainly the greatest single defense – in professional football history.

The Bears are hoping to add more championships

> I wanted to be a coach or a teacher as an adult, and everything has worked out well for me in that regard.

to their total, and the man poised to help accomplish that is none other than the Chicago Bears' first African-American head coach and the team's 13th head coach overall...Lovie Smith, who was hired in January 2004.

Smith comes from a pedigree of successful teams, including the Tampa Bay Buccaneers as a linebacker coach under Tony Dungy, whose defenses have consistently ranked high in the league year in and year out.

With the St. Louis Rams, Lovie served as the defensive coordinator. Starting his first year in that role he helped to complement Dont Mike Martz's "Greatest Show on Turf" offense with an attacking defense that forced turnovers and put the team consistently in good scoring field position.

In his last year, Smith assisted the Rams to a

12-4 record. All in all, he has implemented a brand of aggressive football that gets his teams noticed.

While the Bears' record in this, his first year was not so spectacular at 5-11, the team had great moments, such as beating the Green Bay Packers on their home turf – and with the Bears, beating the Packers is always Job Number 1!

This year's team also won back-to-back road games versus the New York Giants and the Tennessee Titans, and somehow contended for a playoff spot in the National Football Conference before injuries to key personnel — safety Mike Brown, starting quarterback Rex Grossman, and middle linebacker Brian Urlacher — eventually took their toll.

"It generally boils down to winning consistently and making steps to achieve the ultimate goal, which is the Super Bowl," Lovie said. "To achieve our goals, we will continue to teach our players and improve upon the first season so we can have a football team that all of Chicago is proud of."

When asked about the injuries or modifying the off-season and training camp regimens, Coach Smith replied, "First off, injuries happen in all areas concerning football. I plan to keep the same tempo that is required for our players to be at their best.

"The players going into the second season will be accustomed to the speed and tempo that is necessary to play football, and are more familiar with what is expected to compete. I've always believed in fast tempos and physical practices."

While the Bears experienced a tailspin of sorts at the end of the season, the defensive side of the ball showed a light at the end of the tunnel with rookies Tommie Harris, Nathan Vasher, and second year linebacker Lance Briggs. Having a healthy nucleus of players creates a boost of optimism for success in the years ahead.

Coming Up

A native of Big Sandy, Texas, Smith's parents and the community instilled in him the work ethic that has served him well...a work ethic that has included coaching at all levels – high school, college, and the National Football League.

Coach Smith describes Big Sandy as, "Typically 'small town U.S.A.' You knew everyone in the town, where you learned the basic fundamentals of life. I was provided a solid base, grew up in church, and was exposed to hard work and effort at all times.

"My parents and other adults instilled in me (certain values) – to pursue my dreams and shoot for the stars, to never look for excuses or place a ceiling on what I could work towards.

"If I wasn't coaching, I could see myself as a teacher, which is similar to my job because the aspects are similar – watching people grow, establishing good quality relationships, and inspiring others to excel in life."

Smith led the Big Sandy Wildcats to three consecutive state championships in high school, and was an all-state player for three years as a defensive end and linebacker.

At Tulsa University, Smith was a two-time all-American, and three-time all-Missouri Conference defensive back.

Says Smith, "Since I wanted to be a coach or a teacher as an adult, everything has worked out well for me in that regard."

It has been almost 20 years since the Bears won a Super Bowl. "Hopefully it won't take that long to bring the city of Chicago another Super Bowl trophy while I'm here," said Smith.

"The tradition is solid. I mean, the Bears are a great organization with the history of being the charter franchise in the National Football League.

"When I walk the halls of the office, I see Virginia McCaskey (daughter of team and league founder George Halas) in the building. Most of the great players for the Bears are still on the scene. The pictures on the wall show the progress of professional football, the trophies won by the team.

"When I see this on a daily basis, I feel blessed to be a part of tradition and history. It really doesn't get any better than that for me."

lovie smith

preface Spann Cooper

Update: In 2006, under the leadership and ingenuity of its president, Melody Spann Cooper (her married name), WVON pulled off one of the most significant coups in Black talk radio history.

It grew from being a 1,000-watt station with 15-hour coverage to 10,000 watts with 24-hour broadcast capability after Spann Cooper engineered a multi-million dollar deal with Clear Channel Communications to lease one of their old, unprofitable stations for five years.

Celebrating its 50th Anniversary in 2013, WVON has continued to carve its unique place in Chicago radio, providing a platform for the concerns of the Black citizenry of Chicago.

Melody Spann Cooper

By David Smallwood and D. Kevin McNeir & Photography by David Jenkins | *Originally Published March 6, 1997*

As head of WVON, Melody Spann is the highest-ranking African-American woman in Chicago radio and one of less than a handful of females running stations in this market.

She is President and General Manager of talk radio station WVON, which is co-owned by her father Pervis Spann and Wesley South, both veteran Chicago broadcasters.

In its long and distinctive history, WVON radio has been two distinctly different entities – but with a common thread and appeal running so deep that it's been interwoven into the fabric of Black Chicago ever since the station first signed on the air.

That happened on April 1, 1963, when the "Voice Of the Negro" began broadcasting as the first full-service, Black-oriented music station in Chicago, to the delight of the city's burgeoning Black population.

WVON started with Polish brothers Leonard and Phil Chess, owners of the successful recording label Chess Records that produced hits for local artists like Muddy Waters and Howling Wolf.

They acquired WHFC/1450AM, a 1,000-watt station licensed to Cicero, Illinois, with the idea of assembling the best radio talent available in order to unify and empower the Black citizens of Chicago.

WVON is a small station, true, but one of the few in the country that Black folks can turn on and hear news about themselves and learn something.

After a change of call letters, WVON hit the airwaves with a group of handpicked radio personalities that included: Franklin McCarthy, E. Rodney Jones, Herb Kent "The Cool Gent," Wesley South, who hosted a talk show called "Hot Line," and Pervis Spann "The Blues Man."

This extraordinary lineup of radio talent that became known as the "Good Guys" eventually added to its roster Ric Ricardo, Bill "Butterball" Crane, Ed Cook, Joe Cobb, Roy Wood, Ed Maloney, Bill "Doc" Lee, Don Cornelius (of Soul Train fame), Richard Pegue, Isabel Joseph Johnson, Cecil Hale, and McKee Fitzhugh.

Under the direction of the station's general manager Lucky Cordell and its "Ambassador of Goodwill" Bernadine C. Washington, the Good Guys held Black Chicago captive for more than a decade and ranked consistently among the top three stations in the Chicago radio market, despite the fact that the station didn't broadcast 24 hours a day and its signal had limited reach, only 250 watts at night.

The Black Giant

But the overarching reach of WVON went far beyond Chicago; in fact, during its heyday, it was the top Black radio station in the country. There was a good reason WVON was commonly referred to as "The Black Giant."

The station was so strong that Motown Records founder Berry Gordy had a special arrangement with WVON that every song he produced would be sent to WVON before any other station in the country.

Rotation on WVON was so powerful that it influenced airplay in other markets, which impacted the overall sales and success of any record. Airplay on WVON was so powerful that a playlist of the top 40 songs the station played was released weekly, and it became a hot, much anticipated commodity among listeners and local record dealers.

WVON's presence also helped to launch the careers of such entertainers as The Jackson 5, Chaka Khan, Gene Chandler, Aretha Franklin, Al Green and the Dells.

But more than just a venue for entertainment, WVON captured the soul of Chicago's Black community. WVON was, and still is, the voice of information for local and national affairs for the Black community, calming its people and lifting their spirits when local and national tragedies threaten our lives and wellbeing. Legendary deejay Herb Kent once said of WVON, "Without it, we wouldn't have hardly any voice at all."

The Good Guys era at the Black Giant ended in the mid-1970s, when the emerging popularity of FM radio absolutely blew WVON and other AM pop music stations out of the water. Station owners decided that the Good Guys were history and fired them all in a painful bloodletting. Like the dinosaurs, the Good Guys became extinct.

After floundering for a while, and following a convoluted process of ownership and frequency changes, WVON as it currently exists ended up in the ownership hands of former Good Guys Pervis Spann and Wesley South, through their company Midwest Broadcasting Corporation. Pervis' daughter, Melody, is in charge of the station today.

Catching The Blues

It's not a first for a Black woman to accede to such a lofty position, as the late Bernadine C. Washington held the title of vice president and general manager of the original WVON in the 1960s and '70s.

But though it was unheard of for a Black woman to function in such a capacity back then, the job descriptions and responsibilities of Bernadine and Melody differ dramatically.

"Bernadine's role was more image, more femme fatale," Spann notes. "She had floats and the Bern Club, her fan club. Bern may have had some say, but her role was more glamour, more of a woman's position.

"I'm out here taking care of the day-to-day operations. I'm out here battling with the men, and that is a very difficult challenge in an industry that is very sexist and very racist."

Those obstacles, while frustrating, are fairly easily handled by Spann compared to the major challenge she has faced during her tenure as WVON president: her own father, Pervis Spann, the legendary Blues Man.

Melody feels that while daddy Pervis wanted to keep the business in the family, he would have preferred to pass it along to her older brother, Darrell, but Darrell apparently wasn't very interested in this station or this market – he's involved now with the family's other radio station in Atlanta.

"With a daughter taking over the business, sometimes it's hard for a father to give her full reign because he envisions her as someone who maybe will get married and stay home and have children like mom did," Melody says. "That was the biggest challenge for my dad – letting go."

Spann says Pervis wanted to give her the title of president and general manager and then have her just sit there "and call him for everything and say,

Pervis Spann

'Daddy, what do you want me to do about this?' But I'm not like that," Spann says. "I hit the ground running. I set goals and started putting people in place I wanted to work with.

"But Pervis didn't seem to want me to be instrumental in this job, he just wanted to dictate to me behind the scenes. Because of that, he and I went at it very often and I mean, we had some big pow-wows."

The Radio Brat

It's not that Melody was unqualified for the position and was just handed the office as entitlement for being the owner's offspring. She grew up as a radio brat during the time when the original WVON radio, her father, and the rest of WVON's Good Guys, were all at the height of their popularity.

"The Good Guys were always around, they were like my godfathers, and my dad promoted concerts, so it was nothing for me to go downstairs and B.B. King or Johnnie Taylor would be in the house or James Brown or Al Green would be on the phone," Spann says.

Melody had also been helping out around the station since she was 15. "During those years, I learned every office, every position. I can turn the station on,

Wesley South

though," Spann explains.

Pervis eventually "cooled out" and has allowed Spann to "do her thing" ever since, Melody says. "But I had to earn that respect from him," she adds. "Now he's developed an unbelievable amount of respect for me as a businesswoman.

"He hardly ever tells me to my face, but he says it to people who come back and tell me how proud he is of me. And dad's largely responsible for what I've become. He and my mother, who was my major influence."

Naming It, Claiming It, Making It Her Own

In 1986, at the height of the Black community's political involvement in Chicago that resulted in the election of Harold Washington as the city's first African-American mayor, WVON's station owners changed the format to talk, making it the first Black station in Chicago to take on that genre. The slogan of the call letters changed from "Voice of the Negro" to "Voice of the Nation."

When Melody purchased Midway Broadcasting's controlling interest in 1999 and became company chairman, as well as WVON president, she joined an elite list of America's female broadcast owners.

Midway's properties include WVON and WRLL/1450AM, a station for Hispanic independent broadcasters to preserve the authentic voice and culture of Chicago's Latino community.

When she assumed the top position, the owners and board were tinkering with the idea of changing WVON's format again, to make it more profitable. "Talk radio is an expensive format compared to some of the other things you could be doing because you need so many people," Spann says.

"But I was determined to keep the format we have. Chicago needs it and I think a certain portion of this town would be kind of silent if it wasn't for WVON. It's a small station, true, but one of the few in the country that Black folks can turn on and hear news about themselves and learn something in addition."

Spann, who sits on several boards and has been honored for her achievements in leadership and business, is hoping that the biggest accomplishment of her presidency will be one day taking WVON to 24-hour broadcasting.

"From my mouth to God's ear," Spann says. "I don't know how, but it's going to happen."

go on the air, do the program, put the log together, cut the commercials and do some of the maintenance and engineering work after the station goes off the air. I grew up there; it was my playground," she laughs.

After graduating from Loyola University as a criminal justice major in 1987, Spann worked as a news anchor for WVON until 1989, when Wesley South needed some assistance in running the station on a day-to-day basis.

"I was the likely person to call," says Spann, who started with South as program director. In 1991, he began teaching her the business side of the operation – payroll taxes, forms filing, the legal aspect, the real nuts and bolts.

"Mr. South allowed me to learn everything I could, and so did so many other Chicago broadcast veterans like Richard Steele, Larry Langford and Wanda Wells," Spann says. "They all helped me and I think they're all proud of me because I'm keeping alive a legacy that these legends and pioneers created."

Which is why she feels her father actually really did want her as president. "He knew that I knew how to operate the station and thought I knew maybe some things he didn't know, too," she guesses.

"And I'm a details person and he's not, so I guess he thought I would be a good person to give a title to… but to still make a secretary out of. I wasn't having it,

preface Stroger

Update: John Stroger was President of the Cook County Board for 12 years from 1994 until 2006. His son Todd succeeded him as board president that year and held the office until 2010. John Stroger passed away on January 18, 2008 at the age of 78.

John Stroger

By Kevin McNeir & Photography by John Beckett | *Originally Published January 23, 2003*

Upon first meeting John H. Stroger Jr., President, Cook County Board of Commissioners, you might be reminded of the old adage, "Walk softly and carry a big stick."

Stroger, never one to mince words, can just as easily stand on the sidelines, where his razor-sharp wit continues to assess the situation at hand, as he can be the keynote speaker at a black-tie event.

But one thing that never changes about Stroger is that he is careful in forming his opinion and once that's done, he refuses to back down.

Maybe that's why having that "big stick" has helped him from time to time in his over 30 years of public service.

> It really boils down to our citizens' life-or-death needs for services and who among the commissioners or aldermen or even mayor, is more attuned to making these needs available to all...no matter what God they may pray to or what color their skin.

New Hospital 100 Years Later

The doors of the old Cook County Hospital first opened in 1914 when the U.S. was facing a number of challenges, both domestic and abroad.

Some older Chicagoans, like Stroger, remember the days when there were separate entrances at the hospital for Blacks and Whites. But they also recall being able to go to the hospital for health care when there was no other alternative.

In 1932 and a dozen times since, efforts to build a new Cook County Hospital met with criticism and apathy – the result being a facility left to deteriorate and unable to meet the needs of continuing changes in health care.

But since first being elected a commissioner of the Cook County Board, Stroger says he has been dreaming about a new hospital.

Now, as president of the board, Stroger has been instrumental in bringing that dream to fruition and proudly sees his name welcoming Cook County residents as they seek medical attention at the John Stroger Jr. Hospital of Cook County.

"Things are running smoothly, but since we've only been in operation for a few months, it's going to take some time to work out all of the bugs," Stroger told *N'DIGO* in an exclusive interview.

"It was phenomenal how quickly we were able to move machines and patients and staff from our former building to this new physical plant, an ultra-modern facility.

"But the real challenge was just persuading voters and other elected officials how important it was for us to move into the new millennium and be prepared to usher in a new era for public hospitals.

"I've been dreaming about a new physical structure since I became a commissioner in 1970, but in reading the history of Chicago and earlier boards, I am reminded that there were those before me who realized we needed a new facility, also.

"Those of us who were like-minded convened a group of citizens to more closely examine the pros and cons of the cost estimates to building a new hospital. That information became known as The Stroger Report, which we completed around 1977," the board president noted.

"But we still had to overcome decades of debate and then four-and-a-half years of construction before opening this new hospital for business on Wednesday, December 11, 2002 – on time and on budget."

Greater Public Health Care Options

The new Stroger Hospital features all-new pristine halls gleaming from daily waxings, skylines that welcome the sunlight in a bitterly cold winter, and bright, comfortable reception areas located on each floor that serve to reduce the apprehension of first-time patients.

"This hospital in particular and the concept of the public health system in general is to care for the medically indigent," Stroger said. "Today we find that among those patients, a high percentage suffer from multiple illnesses that often require long-term treatment. But with this new facility, we can handle many of those cases in an outpatient setting."

In keeping with healthcare trends, approximately 40 percent of the hospital's 1.2 million square feet is designed for specialty outpatient care, diagnosis and treatment.

Stroger says, "When we were planning this hospital, we considered the possibility of a sagging economy and the loss of health benefits by many Americans. That's why this new hospital is so important. It's an anchor for all Cook County residents to know that even in the face of layoffs where they may be without healthcare, they can still have their medical needs addressed."

The new Stroger Hospital features an expanded emergency room and trauma center, a dedicated floor for maternal and child services, robotics technology in the pharmacy, and filmless X-rays and imaging that can be accessed anywhere by physicians at a computer.

The old Cook County Hospital opened the first blood bank in 1937, the first trauma unit in the U.S. in 1966 and the first HIV/AIDS clinic in Chicago in 1983.

The new Stroger Hospital serves as the hub among seven institutions that make up the Cook County Bureau of Health Services, one of the largest public health care systems in the country.

But, overseeing this essential service provider in Cook County is just one of the many tasks that Stroger must handle.

A Typical Day?

Stroger sat back and smiled when asked to describe his "typical day." Apparently, for this wearer of many hats, no day is ever similar to the next.

"I'd like to think that my days follow a pattern of sorts," he said. "But the only thing I know for sure is that they will be very long and complicated. As the president of the Board of Commissioners of Cook County, the buck stops here with me when the issue is of a county nature…just like it does with Mayor Daley when it's a city-related issue. And the hospital, which is getting a lot of attention right now, is only one of the many governmental agencies for which my office is responsible.

"We run juvenile detention centers, support police officers for Cook County Jail and the Circuit Court of Cook County, manage 574 miles of highway that link our city and suburban transportation networks, and are responsible for 68,000 acres of land which make up the County's Forest Preserve Districts.

"Now that I've reached 73 years of age, I don't stay up quite as late as I used to, but then, I no longer seek to avoid those who make up different constituencies. This is my second term as president of the board and along with the hospital, I want to bring some of our programs up to speed before my term expires."

For the record, Stroger became the first African American elected president of the Board and Forest Preserve District of Cook County in November 1994; he was re-elected to a second term in November 1998.

Stroger has always been a man of principle, something he gained through hard work and education during his early years in eastern Arkansas. His family was economically impoverished, but instilled in him the power of education and the importance of moral values, which are the cornerstones of his life's philosophy.

Stroger followed those values as he worked his way through Xavier University in Louisiana, where he earned a B.S. Degree in business administration. Almost 10 years later, married and with a family, he entered and graduated from DePaul Law School.

He and his wife, Yonnie, have remained members of St. Felicitas Church for more than 30 years and still reside in the home where they raised their three children. Sadly, their oldest son died of complications from asthma while a student in college.

Challenges For Black Chicago

As the first African American in his position, it is inevitable that questions are brought to him about the state of Black Chicago. Interestingly enough, Stroger has his own rapid responses to what he believes must occur to improve the quality of life for Chicago's Black citizens.

"Education and healthcare are the two keys, as I see it, to leveling the playing field for Black citizens," Stroger said. "In this 21st Century, we can only compete within the job market if we are educated."

"Today, even a janitor needs a degree. And he needs to be familiar with a computer, too. These are changes in the industry that sometimes African Americans don't know about and which keep us from getting the position."

"I also think it's important to keep our people

healthy, both the young and the old. In most of the statistics of health problems – cancer, HIV/AIDS, you name it – we lead the pack. Part of that means changing the mindset of our people, especially our young.

"Too many of them have gotten caught up in the prison system at early ages. The country is offering practical alternatives to prison for young offenders, but somehow we need to emphasize morality in our young people's learning.

"That's what I held onto myself when faced with making a choice to break the law or to stand firm against peer pressure when I was young," Stroger says. "As a child I dreamed, but I never expected my dreams to become reality. Even though my parents did not have a formal education, they made real sacrifices for their children."

Preparing The Next Generation

Stroger proudly points to a photograph, a picture of his grandson, as he talks about the next generation.

He says that young people, no matter what their race or religion, need to be mentored and trained if they are to successfully carry on the mantle once people like Stroger himself retire from public service.

"I don't plan to sit down just yet," he said. "There are still some things I want to see accomplished. But in the meantime, I believe it's crucial that those young people working around me gain the benefit of my experience. That they learn what it means to be a leader and realize that sometimes leading means standing alone.

"It's not a game that demands popularity. It really boils down to our citizens' life-or-death needs for services and who among the commissioners or aldermen or even mayor, is more attuned to making these needs available to all…no matter what God they may pray to or what color their skin."

"But don't worry," Stroger says with a chuckle and wink of the eye, "I still have some work to do before I can start sleeping in late. Like the poet Robert Frost said, "I've still got many miles to go before I sleep.""

preface Taylor

Update: Black Ensemble Theater moved into its new, gleaming $20 million, 300-seat main stage facility at 4450 North Clark Street in November of 2011. Taylor was honored with a "Jackie Taylor Day in Illinois" in 2009, and received Jeff Awards and League of Chicago Theater Lifetime Achievement Awards for her cultural contributions.

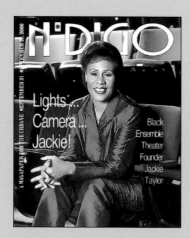

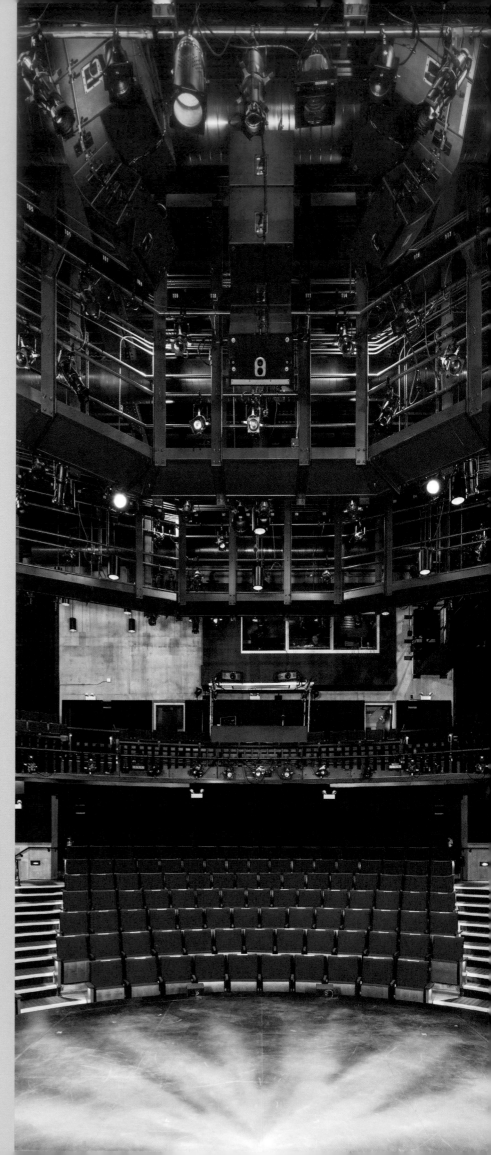

Jackie Taylor

By Rosalind Cummings-Yeates & Photography by Reginald Payton | *Originally Published September 21, 2000*

The name Black Ensemble Theater (BE) carries a long history of noteworthy productions that spring to mind whenever the company's name is mentioned – *The Other Cinderella*; *Muddy Waters: The Hoochie Coochie Man*; *Doo Wop Shoo Bop*; *The Jackie Wilson Story (My Heart Is Crying, Crying)*.

The fine-tuned formula of historical biographies, paired with rousing music that makes many of these productions so memorable, is the creation of the company's founder and artistic director Jackie Taylor.

As lively and dramatic as the plays she writes, directs, produces and sometimes stars in, Taylor embodies the kind of pioneering spirit that it takes to initiate change.

Taylor founded BE 24 years ago when she decided to take control of some of the images that African Americans were being fed. "I wanted to control the images and help people understand who we are. We ain't all dope addicts. We ain't all prostitutes. We have done a lot for this country, and our stories should be heard," she says.

> I wanted to control the images and help people understand who we are. We ain't all dope addicts. We ain't all prostitutes. We have done a lot for this country and our stories should be heard.

From the lives of legends such as Etta James, Dionne Warwick, Ethel Waters, Koko Taylor, Sam Cooke, Thomas Dorsey, Moms Mabley, Jackie Wilson, and Marvin Gaye, Taylor has fashioned stories that are not only heard, but stand as effective challenges to the narrow African-American images that still fill the TV, film, and theatrical landscape. Black Ensemble plays not only entertain, but they educate audiences on the rich, too often overlooked African-American cultural history.

A strong example of this is *The Jackie Wilson Story (My Heart Is Crying, Crying)*, – the open-run musical that has proven so popular that Taylor plans to take it on the road. Filled with riveting details about the life of ground-breaking '50s singer Jackie Wilson, and boasting an awe-inspiring performance by Chester Gregory II as the late singer, the production has single-handedly rekindled local interest in Wilson, drawing seniors who grew up on his music as well as teens who've never heard of him.

"Black Ensemble has certainly found their niche, and it will never run out because our cultural icons in the entertainment field are endless," says Abena Joan Brown, co-founder of eta Creative Arts Foundation, grande dame of Chicago Black theater, as well as mentor to Taylor.

"These stories have never been celebrated, and it's very important because it provides a continuum. It gives young people the opportunity to catch up to our history. We (African Americans) created the musical form as we know it in America today, with *Shuffle Along*, so it's fitting that this is the device that's being used to tell our stories."

A Storyteller Is Born

It seems that telling stories has always been Jackie Taylor's forte. As a child growing up in Cabrini Green in the '60s, she says she was always making up stories and performing.

"I would sit in the closet and talk to hangers and direct them. I used to lie all the time because it was a performance. My parents thought I had a lot of energy and was nutty as a fruitcake. They thought that I would grow out of it one day."

But Taylor realized early on that this was something she was meant to do. "I believe that the Creator gives us all gifts. Mine were writing, performing, and directing. They were always there. I always knew that I would be a performer."

Fortunately for her, her teachers also realized this, and gave her opportunities to write and direct plays in grade school. "I started directing in seventh grade," Taylor says. "My teachers saw that I had a lot of energy. I would perform in class and take over because I loved to make people laugh.

"They said, 'If you keep quiet and keep your grades up, we'll give you the auditorium.' I did a play every month in eighth grade. They wanted to give me a focus. I was lucky they didn't say, 'She needs medication.'

(Instead) they said, 'She's creative, let's nourish it.'"

By the time she was in high school, Taylor had marked a clear path towards the theater. She had written her first play, *The Swingin' Wizard of Oz* at 13, not realizing that Broadway and Hollywood would soon mirror her idea for a Black Wizard of Oz. She majored in theater with an education minor at Loyola, appearing in many of the student theater productions.

"I thought I'd be the first Black actress to win an Academy Award for a lead role. I didn't care if there weren't any roles; I figured I'd write them. I didn't care if they didn't have any movies for us; I figured that I'd produce one. I never saw the boundaries until I got into the business."

Taylor actually entered the professional theater business before she even graduated, accepting a position with Free Street Theater in her last year of college. She mailed in her assignments, and skipped the graduation ceremony so she could work with the integrated theater group.

She stayed with Free Street for two years, then moved on to other theaters, appearing in major productions such as *Young, Gifted and Black* at The Goodman, and *Eden* at Victory Gardens. "I did every theater in town that had a Black play," remembers Taylor.

Playing The Role

In 1974, she read for the part of Johnny Mae, Glynn Turman's girlfriend in the Chicago-filmed classic *Cooley High*, a role that she still gets recognition for.

"I saw that role and I said, 'I know these people. I grew up in Cabrini.' My agent thought I was too old to play the part, but we were all older than what we played." Taylor calls the experience of working with Turman and Lawrence Hilton-Jacobs, "one of the best," outside of working with Sidney Poitier in *To Sir With Love II*. She also acted in *Barbershop 2* and *The Father Clements* story.

The popularity of *Cooley High* created more film offers for Taylor, but they weren't the kind of roles she was interested in doing.

"I kept getting roles that I found demeaning," she says. "They were mostly prostitutes. At the time, Black exploitation was big, and women didn't have much to do, unless you were Pam Grier. I didn't have big breasts, so that was out."

At the time, Taylor was also teaching part-time, and she felt a big contradiction in teaching her students positive methods for alternatives to violence, and portraying violent or amoral characters.

"I decided to shape my own image as a Black woman. There are characters I just will not do," she says. But there's a cost to being selective, and Taylor found herself continuously paying as she got fewer and fewer offers for roles. "When you pick and choose,

you don't get a lot of roles. I had done major film, a couple of TV roles, and I still wasn't working steadily."

Not content to simply accept the situation, Taylor decided that she could do something about it. "Instead of bitching, I thought, what can I do? Well, I can shape the images. I can create the jobs. I said, 'I'm going to start a theater.'"

It was 1976, and Chicago claimed quite a number of Black theaters, from eta to Kuumba, but Taylor saw that they all addressed different groups.

"We all came from different generations," she says. "I was of a different mindset than the others, and there was a place for all of us."

Following the guidance of Abena Joan Brown, Taylor established the Black Ensemble Theater, first on Wells Street in Old Town, then at its present location at 4520 N. Beacon, with the goal of promoting positive African-American images.

"I wanted a theater that would help eradicate racism, a Black theater where everybody came. I thought that seeing the stories of great African Americans would reveal the commonness that all humans share."

Opening the theater with what is now Black Ensemble's signature production, *The Other Cinderella*, Taylor quickly developed an audience for her uplifting plays. To date, the company has produced over 100 plays, including classics such as *A Streetcar Named Desire*, *Julius Caesar*, and *Medea*, all with a Black cultural twist. But the theater is still most famous for its historical musicals, which draw repeat customers from all over the city.

When asked about her rare ability to cast actors who

may not sing and singers who may not act in musicals and coax performances out of them, she explains it this way: "First of all, I'm a teacher. If my actors don't have what they need, I can give it to them. My actors have what they call boot camp. They don't see the script for two weeks. They work out, they dance, they sing, and when I finish with them, they're singers and actors. There are no limitations; it's all in the mind.

"After two weeks, I give them the script and they say, 'I can make the audience think that I can sing.' I believe in total positivity. There are no problems – there are issues, and issues can be solved. When I look at actors, I look at the depth of their talent and if they have the right kind of soul. If they have the right kind of soul and they respect themselves and other people, you can work miracles."

Some would agree that Taylor has indeed performed miracles, rising from Cabrini Green and establishing a successful theater, gaining the honor of having the 4500 block of North Beacon named Jackie Taylor Boulevard, and providing an outlet for preserving African American cultural history.

preface Tillman

Update: Dorothy Tillman, who served as 3rd Ward Alderman for 22 years until 2007, is known for wearing large hats, which has been her trademark.

Dorothy Tillman

By Robert T. Starks & Photography By Victor Powell | *Originally Published February 14, 2002*

Third Ward Alderman Dorothy Tillman was born Dorothy Jean Wright to Edna and James Wright on May 12, 1947 in Montgomery, Alabama. Her father installed shades and Venetian blinds for a rug and shade company and her mother worked as a domestic.

After her parents divorced, her mother married Willie Struggs and the couple moved to Pensacola, Florida. From that time on, Dorothy spent equal time with her mother and stepfather in Pensacola, and her father in Montgomery.

Tillman talks lovingly about her childhood and early life traveling back and forth from Montgomery and Pensacola and growing up with her older brother James, Jr. In spite of the divorce of her parents, she was always confident of the love, support, and protection provided by her parents and grandmother, Julia.

It was this loving and protective home environment that allowed her the freedom to join the civil rights movement at a young age and become a major youth organizer. It was that loving and nurturing grandmother who took Dorothy to church, where at the age of nine she heard for the first time the dynamic minister Dr. Martin Luther King, Jr.

> ## I vowed to do everything that I could to change the condition of my people when I get grown.

Thus, it was clear to Dorothy even at that tender age why Mrs. Rosa Parks had refused to surrender her seat and launched the 1956 Montgomery Bus Boycott that lasted for more than a year.

In the midst of this turmoil, young Dorothy Jean Wright vowed "to do everything that I could to change the condition of my people, when I get grown," Ald. Tillman recalls.

As a natural organizer, she began making good on that promise at age 16, when she was recruited by Rev. James Bevel to become a youth organizer for Dr. King and the Southern Christian Leadership Conference (SCLC).

By then, Tillman was a veteran civil rights participant and organizer. She had participated in boycotts, protests and marches as a member of the Montgomery Improvement Association and the local chapter of the NAACP. In fact, Tillman says, "I can't remember a time when I was not organizing!"

With her determination, energy, and focus, Dorothy was such an effective organizer that after being arrested at a downtown Montgomery lunch counter and being identified by the town sheriff as a student organizer, her high school principal burned Tillman's diploma a month before graduation because she would not agree to call off a student march downtown.

It was courageous acts like this and many others that earned this disciple of Dr. King the nickname, "The Movement Baby."

She was one of the organizers for the SCLC-led march across the Edmund Pettus Bridge in Selma, Alabama on the infamous "Bloody Sunday," and it was during the intense organizing for this march that she first met Stokely Carmichael (a.k.a. Kwame Toure) of SNCC and Malcolm X when he came to Selma in 1965 to speak.

She worked in Selma that summer organizing for the SCLC's community education program with Diane Nash Bevel, Rev. C.T. Vivian, Andrew Young, Rev. Ralph David Abernathy and many others.

Growing up in this environment of hate and hostility, and developing a keen sense of civil rights and wrongs made Tillman vow to fight even harder, and by 1965, the "movement baby" had become the determined "fighter for justice."

Her work and determination was appreciated by Dr. King and the rest of the SCLC staff and, as a result, Rev. Bevel, the head of the SCLC Direct Action Division, asked her to join him and others in trips to Chicago and Cleveland to organize Dr. King's Northern Campaign.

Dorothy Comes To Chicago

On October 31, 1965, Dorothy Jean Wright arrived in Chicago and was given the assignment to organize in Cabrini Green. She met a handsome and talented musician, Jimmy Lee Tillman, in the spring of 1966 in a nightclub.

Jimmy was playing in a band there with Syl Johnson, and she was there to make the announcement that she and others were "preparing to march into Marquette Park that weekend to demonstrate against the segregated housing and public schools," Tillman recalls. This was at the height of the Chicago protests.

Jimmy was immediately fascinated by Dorothy and showed up at the violent Marquette march. While driving Dorothy and other workers home afterward, Jimmy was struck by a rock thrown into his car by a White thug that left a permanent scar on his face.

Dorothy and Jimmy dated and their courtship blossomed into marriage on November 7, 1967. Their first child Jimmy Lee II was born a year later, in December 1968. Ebony, their first daughter, was born in 1969, and three other children were to follow. Tillman is the proud mother of three girls and two boys.

Working out of the SCLC headquarters on 47th and King Drive, Dorothy and her fellow staff members provided the necessary logistical support to Dr. King which made the King campaign in Chicago the success that exposed the raw racism of Chicago to the world.

King had few allies among Chicago's Black elected officials at that time because most of them were "foremen" on the original Mayor Richard J. Daley political plantation. Thus, Dorothy and the staff worked closely with the local civil rights leadership and activists to facilitate the King Movement.

This Chicago movement leadership included Professor Timuel Black, Bob Lucas of CORE, Bill Berry of the Chicago Urban League, Al Raby, Rev. James Mack, and Jorja English Palmer of the Coordinating Council of Community Organizations (CCCO); labor activists Addie Wyatt and Charles Hayes, as well as a small cadre of movement ministers led by Rev. Clay Evans and Rev. A.P. Jackson of Liberty Baptist Church.

Not surprisingly, Tillman was able to hold her own in staff meetings and strategy sessions in this male-dominated and highly charged atmosphere of the movement elite.

The SCLC staff included among others; Rev. Al Sampson, Rev. Jesse L. Jackson, Rev. C.T. Vivian and Rev. James Bevel. In addition to the often-heated debates that occurred in staff and strategy sessions, there was the constant challenge from the other liberation groups like CORE, SNCC, the NAACP, and the Chicago Urban League.

However, because of the commonality of purpose and focus, all of these groups were able to work together to bring about Chicago's first open housing plan and lay the groundwork for the eventual political victory of 1982-83 that elected Chicago's first Black mayor, Harold Washington.

Grabbing Hold Of The Third Ward

In the heat of these historic civil rights and political skirmishes, young Dorothy was busy fighting and absorbing the lessons of battle and sharpening her organizing skills. As a resident of the Third Ward, she became keenly aware of the politics of the ward.

Her children were enrolled in Mollison Elementary School in the Third Ward, but Tillman soon became disenchanted with the quality of education that her children were receiving. It was an environment in which she says, "Black children were not expected to learn because they were deemed to be unteachable."

Tillman organized concerned parents and protested the Continuous Progress Curriculum and the Mastery Learning Program. In a yearlong battle, Tillman and the parents that she had mobilized were able to have the Mastery Learning Program removed from Mollison and the entire Chicago Public Schools system.

As a result of the Mollison School fight, Dorothy and several parents founded the Parent Equalizers of Chicago organization, which had a presence in over 300 schools throughout the city and sparked renewed interest in inner-city school education and a demand for reform.

By 1980, Dorothy had become a familiar face and one that the community trusted to fight for their rights and the rights of their children.

Soon after being elected mayor in 1979, Jane Byrne alienated the Black community, which had been some of her most vigorous supporters. She refused to give African Americans fair and equitable representation on the Chicago Board of Education and the Chicago Housing Authority Board of Commissioners.

Dorothy Tillman and a group of citywide activists, including Lu Palmer, Slim Coleman, Conrad Worrill, and Marion Stamps, challenged Jane Byrne and her policies and their protests set the stage for the election of Harold Washington.

Tillman played a pivotal role in the election of Harold, after having been the coordinator of the Third Ward in Washington's 1982 Congressional Campaign. Soon after the Third Ward aldermanic seat became vacant in 1983, Mayor Washington appointed her to fill the vacancy in the city council.

In the midst of the "Council Wars," Tillman's city council appointment approval was held up by the council's White majority for six months. However, in the 1985 special election, Tillman received 80 percent of the ward vote and became the first woman elected to serve as alderman of the Third Ward.

She is now one of the senior aldermen in the city council, the longest serving woman in the council, and the only woman to serve on Dr. King's staff to be elected to public office.

Aldermanic Achievements

During her tenure, Ald. Tillman organized the African-American Home Builders Association and put together the first African-American showcase of homes in her ward.

For homeless men, she developed the Washington-King Resource Center, an 80-bed shelter that provides a clean and safe environment for those struggling to get back on their feet.

After securing over $4 million in economic development, Tillman constructed the 47th Street Theater and Cultural Center, a multi-purpose facility that includes a 1,000-seat theater, recording studio, restaurant, banquet facility, museum, library, and radio and TV training facility.

Since Tillman has been alderman, the Third Ward has become one of the cleanest and safest wards in the city. The alderman has emphasized the cleanup of abandoned cars, rubbish, and debris, as well as the boarding up and demolition of abandoned buildings. The main thoroughfare of the ward, King Drive, has undergone a major restoration. This is in addition to the millions that have been spent on the upgrading of sewers, streets, and sidewalks throughout the ward.

preface Till-Mobley

Update: Mamie Till-Mobley died January 6, 2003 at the age of 81. She passed away shortly after completing her memoir *The Death of Innocence: The Story of the Hate Crime That Changed America*, with Chicago author and attorney Christopher Benson, which was published later that year. She also co-authored a play with David Barr, *The State of Mississippi vs. Emmett Till*, which was performed in cities around the country from 1999 to 2001.

Emmett Till's cousin Simeon Wright wrote his own book titled *Simeon's Story: An Eyewitness Account of the Kidnapping of Emmett Till*, with author Herb Boyd in 2010. Mr. Wright died September 4, 2017 of bone cancer, 62 years after Till's murder.

During her husband's trial, Carolyn Bryant testified that Emmett had physically and verbally accosted her in the store. In a 2007 interview, she admitted that it never happened.

One hundred days after Emmett Till's murder, Rosa Parks refused to give up her seat on a city bus in Montgomery, Alabama.

Mamie Till-Mobley

By Rosalind Cumings-Yeates, David Smallwood, D. Kevin McNeir & Photography by Brent Jones | *Originally Published August 26, 1999*

Mamie Till-Mobley radiates an inner strength that's difficult to describe. Her luminous, unlined face shines with it. Her formidable spirit rises up out of her septuagenarian body and uses it to challenge anyone and anything.

This quality is not at all unusual for a person of her age, 77, of African descent, who has witnessed many decades of this country's duality, oppression, and brutality toward African Americans.

What is so striking is that Mamie Till-Mobley has been able to maintain this attribute in the face of her staggeringly sad status – as the mother of Emmett Till.

He was the Chicago youth barely turned 14, who was lynched in Mississippi for allegedly flirting with a White woman in 1955. Publicity surrounding the savagery of Till's murder captured the world's attention and ignited the Civil Rights Movement.

Mississippi In '55

In 1955, Mississippi was one of the nation's most segregated states. Since 1882 – when records first started being kept of lynchings in the South – until 1955, Mississippi had officially recorded more than 500 such atrocities, with the likelihood that thousands more murders were never officially reported.

> **Emmett became race hatred so that we can see how it looks...and race hatred is an ugly thing. I didn't have enough tears to cry for Emmett Till. The world would cry for Emmett Till.**

In 1955 in Mississippi, there were three widely reported killings of Black men. The first was the Reverend George Lee, an NAACP organizer who was shot dead in his car on May 7 after leading a voters registration drive in the delta town of Belzoni.

Lee was killed by a shotgun blast to the face, but local police ruled his death a traffic accident. The second murder, a few weeks later, was of NAACP organizer Lamar Smith, who was killed on a Saturday afternoon on the courthouse lawn in the town of Brookhaven. No one was arrested in either murder.

Then there was Emmett Till. Emmett was born July 25, 1941 near Chicago. His mother Mamie, born in Tallahatchie, Mississippi, worked for an Air Force procurement office.

Every African American in Chicago aged 30 and up remembers the story. If you were a child during the mid-'50s, you remember adult whispers of "the Till boy" and photos of the mutilated body in *Jet* Magazine and the *Chicago Defender*.

If you are older, you remember the lines of people that snaked down the streets, numbering tens of thousands, waiting to view Emmett's body at the A.A. Rayner Funeral Home and at his funeral at Roberts Temple Church of God in Christ. If you dared to entertain any equalitarian notions at all about White people, you were slapped down to earth with, "remember what happened to the Till boy."

What Happened To The Till Boy

On August 20, 1955, Mamie Till sent Emmett and a cousin on a train to Leflore County, Mississippi for a summer visit to their 64-year-old great uncle Mose "Preacher" Wright, a sharecropper, and his wife Elizabeth.

On the evening of August 24, Emmett joined a group of several other Black teenagers on a car ride to Money, Mississippi, a nearby town with a population of a hundred people. About 7:30 that night, they pulled up to Bryant's Grocery and Meat Market.

Inside the store was Carolyn Bryant, a 21-year-old who had won several beauty contests. Her husband Roy Bryant, a 24-year-old former soldier, was in Texas on a business trip at the time.

Inside the store, Emmett bought two cents worth of bubblegum. He was alleged to have taken Carolyn Bryant's hand, put his arm around her waist, asked her out on a date and whistled at her.

Four days later, at 2:30 a.m. on August 28, Carolyn Bryant's husband, Roy, and his brother-in-law, J.W. Milam, 36, pulled up to Preacher Wright's cabin where Emmett and his cousin were staying. According to court records, they said they had come to get the "boy who done the talkin'."

Bryant, Milam and their family owned and operated a number of small country stores throughout three Mississippi counties that catered primarily to the Black community there.

Before Preacher's wife Elizabeth could sneak Emmett out the back door, the two men came in and dragged him out into their car and away into the night. Three days later, on August 31, a White boy fishing in the Tallahatchie River found the bloated decomposing body of a human male. It was Emmett Till.

The left side of his head had been caved in. The right side had a bullet hole. The right eye was dislodged. The bridge of the nose had been destroyed. A 75-pound fan was wrapped around his neck with barbed wire. Emmett Till's body was found just 15 miles from where his mother was born.

When Mamie Till received the corpse of her murdered son, she did an amazing thing. Because of the horrific physical condition of the body, Mamie demanded to have an open-casket funeral. She said she wanted "the world to see what they did to my boy." The entire world was shocked and revolted after seeing the famous photographs of the mutilated corpse.

"I didn't have enough tears to cry for Emmett Till. The world would cry for Emmett Till," says Mamie Till-Mobley, her light brown eyes unflinching.

It was true – the world cried out at the atrocious injustice, snapping up newspapers from Chicago to Amsterdam, mourning the 14-year-old boy's murder. After Till's killing, the NAACP's fund to help victims of racial attacks hit record levels and thousands of Blacks began participating in civil rights demonstrations and marches.

Rev. Al Sharpton said of Mamie Till, "Her decision to keep that coffin open put a picture on the conscience of America. She may well have saved thousands of others from suffering a similar fate. Generations unborn owe their gratitude to the mother of Emmett Till. She made America deal with its ugly racial problem."

A Mother's Story

This is how Mamie Till-Mobley tells the story of how her son became a civil rights martyr:

"We were living at 6427 South St. Lawrence, on the second floor of the house that my mother bought for me," she says. "Bo (Emmett) was jolly, he was always smiling. All his buddies liked him. He was the mediator of his group. Despite the fact that he stuttered, they would stop and listen to what he had to say. If Bo was in the crowd, there was no problem. Mothers didn't have to worry."

Leaning back in her chair, Till-Mobley recounts with precise clarity: "My mother's middle sister

Emmett Till and his mother Mamie

Elizabeth married Mose Wright and Papa Mose came up to Chicago to bury a relative. Uncle Mose was taking his grandsons, Curtis and Wheeler, back with him to Mississippi. When Bo found that out, he wanted to be with those boys. My first reaction was no, you boys go down there and get to showing out...

"But Bo persisted. He said, 'I don't see how you can take Papa Mose's and Aunt Lizzie's girls and raise them from third to sixth grade and you won't even let me go with Papa Mose.' That hit a nerve. So I let him go and Papa Mose was never to let those boys out of his sight. We cautioned the boys. I said, 'Bo, if you see a White woman coming toward you, lower your eyes and step off the sidewalk.'

"None of us counted on Papa Mose being such a long-winded preacher. The boys decided to take a little trip uptown while he was preaching a sermon. They figured they would be back by the time he finished and they were. They got back and never mentioned that they had gone uptown.

"Simeon (Wright, a cousin) said that Bo did whistle because someone asked him what he had bought and he said bubblegum. I had taught him to whistle to say what he had to say. Bo's back was to the clerk and she had made no outcry. It happened on a Wednesday and they came and got him Sunday morning.

"They found him in the Tallahatchie River and Uncle Mose identified him by the ring on his finger. To my surprise, people down there called me to say that they had the grave three-fourths dug and they were going to bury him. They had to go to four or five houses because nobody would let them use their phone, because it was dangerous.

"My aunt said, 'Call A.A. Rayner next door.' He said it would cost $3,300 for his body to be brought from Mississippi. In 1955, $10,000 was enough to set you for life. I said, 'If I live, I'll pay it, if I die, I won't have to worry about it.' Mr. Rayner got that body out

Photo by Reginald Payton

waiting for them to bring Emmett back. As it got towards dawn, I knew that he was never coming back.

"When I look back on it, even as they were taking him away, Emmett didn't seem to be afraid. Maybe he didn't think these men would hurt him, much less kill him, for whistling at a white woman."

On August 29, the day after they abducted Emmett Till, Roy Bryant and J.W. Milam were charged with kidnapping and jailed on suspicion of murder. On September 19, they stood trial for murder in a segregated courthouse in Sumner, Mississippi.

On September 23, after deliberating for one hour and seven minutes, an all-White jury found both men not guilty of murder, although Mose Wright had pointed his finger directly at both white men, identifying them as the ones who kidnapped Emmett.

But the jury foreman said the state had not proved the identity of the body and an anonymous juror was quoted as saying deliberations would have been quicker if the jury hadn't stopped to drink some soda pop.

The acquitted murderers hugged their wives, lit cigars and walked out of the courtroom. Both men died without ever expressing remorse, and after admitting in a paid interview with *Look* Magazine, after their acquittal, that they did commit the crimes.

Above:
Simeon Wright-
Till's cousin

of Mississippi and by the time Bo was in the ground, the debt was retired."

A Cousin's Story

Simeon Wright is the son of Preacher Mose Wright, whom young Emmett came to visit. Simeon was 12 at the time and at the store with the group of eight teenagers when the incident happened.

"Emmett never touched her, never asked her out or put his arm around her, never even spoke to her," Simeon recalled in 2007, when at the age of 64, he began to share his memories publicly about his cousin. "But Emmett did whistle at her, wolf-whistled," Simeon admitted.

"We never expected him to do anything like that and we were scared out of our minds. I remember our jumping into the car and just taking off down the road. We couldn't get out of there fast enough."

When Milam and Bryant came to the house to get Till a few days later, Wright recalls, "I was in the bed with Emmett and they told me to put my head down and go back to sleep. My mom offered them money to leave Emmett alone and I think Bryant was willing to accept it, but Milam had other plans. He was calling the shots and said that Emmett had to be whipped.

"After they left with Emmett, no one said a word... nothing. I sat in my bed and kept listening for cars,

"In Their Place"

In May 2004, the FBI re-opened the investigation into Emmett Till's murder to determine if others may have been involved.

Despite its finding that as many as seven people could have taken part in the killing, the FBI confirmed that the five-year statute of limitations had run out for federal prosecution of any potential criminal civil rights violations. It turned its findings over to a Mississippi grand jury, which in February 2007, failed to find any credible evidence to charge anyone else in Till's murder.

Opposite page middle: Carolyn Bryant Left: Emmett's murderers Roy Bryant (left) and J. W. Milam

In the interview *Look* published on January 24, 1956, Bryant and Milam said that they initially planned to "just whip and scare some sense" into Till. But apparently, they saw the same lack of fear that Simeon Wright spoke of Emmett not having when he was abducted from the Wright house earlier that night.

According to the FBI's final report in 2006 after they reopened the investigation into Till's murder, a group of at that point seven men "took Till into a barn and continued to beat him. During the beating, Till was never respectful to the men and did not say 'yes sir' or 'no sir.' Things got out of hand and Till stated something to the effect of 'he was as good as they are.'"

Milam explained it in the *Look* magazine interview this way: "Well, what else could we do? He was hopeless. I'm no bully; I never hurt a nigger in my life. I like niggers – in their place – I know how to work 'em. But I just decided it was time a few people got put on notice.

"As long as I live and can do anything about it, niggers are gonna stay in their place. Niggers ain't gonna vote where I live. If they did, they'd control the government. They ain't gonna go to school with my kids. And when a nigger gets close to mentioning sex with a white woman, he's tired o' livin'. I'm likely to kill him.

"Me and my folks fought for this country, and we got some rights. I stood there in that shed and listened to that nigger throw that poison at me, and I just made up my mind. 'Chicago boy,' I said, 'I'm tired of 'em sending your kind down here to stir up trouble. Goddam you, I'm going to make an example of you – just so everybody can know how me and my folks stand.'"

Message From God

Mamie Till-Mobley is a religious woman who credits God with providing her with the strength to carry on. She was 33 at the time of her son's death, but went back to school to become a teacher and taught elementary school for 25 years.

It was through her church, Evangelistic Crusaders

Church of God In Christ, that "The Emmett Till Players," a program that she founded in 1974 to teach youngsters Dr. Martin Luther King Jr.'s speeches, became widely known.

When asked about the pain of dealing with what happened to her son, she says, "I used to lie in bed, trying to figure out why my baby. I couldn't figure out what we did to be punished so. One night, a white fog came into my room and I recognized it as the presence of the Lord.

"I reached out my hand and I felt the connection. He held onto my hand and let me know that Emmett didn't belong to me. Emmett came here so that people could get political freedom and there would be no more 'strange fruit hanging from the poplar tree,'" she said, referring to Billie Holiday's famous song about Southern lynchings.

"Emmett was beaten for about six hours. Emmett became race hatred so that we can see how it looks… and race hatred is an ugly thing. Over 100,000 people passed by his casket and every fifth person had to be assisted because they were falling out."

Mamie Till-Mobley wants her son's name to represent healing and reconciliation and in fact, his name is carried on 71st Street, from Kedzie to the lake, as Emmett Till Road, the honorary designation being granted in 1991.

"The Lord said that my job was to continue to tell Emmett's story until men's consciences are aroused and justice prevails," Ms. Till-Mobley concluded.

Below: Emmett Till 1941 -1955

preface Tolliver

Update: St. Edmund's Redevelopment Corporation to date has constructed/ rehabbed almost 600 units of housing and a commercial space in 28 buildings at a cost of $72 million. It has plans for two new construction projects costing $28 million more.

St. Edmund's fledgling school has blossomed into the Chicago International Charter School, which has 450 students enrolled in K-8. Rev. Tolliver sits on the boards of Ravinia, Beverly Bank and Trust, St. Paul's College, the Chicago Development Fund and Low Income Housing Trust Fund, the Episcopal Church's Economic Justice Loan Fund, and is a member of Chicago Mayor Rahm Emanuel's Transportation and Infrastructure Committee. Father Tolliver retires in 2017.

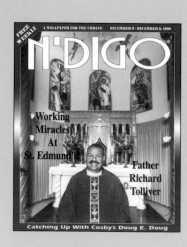

Father Richard Tolliver

By Zondra Hughes & Photography by Brent Jones | *Originally Published December 2, 1998*

To call Father Richard Lamar Tolliver phenomenal is an understatement.

Educationally, he has earned several degrees from some of the finest universities in the nation. Financially, he has initiated an economic boom in one of the poorest communities in Chicago. And spiritually, he has renewed his congregation's faith in miracles, having in 1989 traveled to Chicago to take over the faltering St. Edmund's Episcopal Church.

St. Edmund's Episcopal Church started out as the Washington Park Mission in 1905, and the first services were held in a basement room at 55th Street and Wabash Avenue. In 1906 the name was changed to St. Edmund's Mission, and they moved to the second floor over the Citizen's Trust and Savings Bank at 55th Street (also known as Garfield Boulevard), and State Street. Then in 1908, a new building was built at 5831 South Indiana Avenue.

St. Edmund's began as a White church, with most of its congregation being of Greek and Irish heritage. However, by the mid-1920s, the church had lost a majority of its members, so for the first time in St. Edmund's history, the Episcopal hierarchy sent a young Black priest, Rev. Samuel Martin, to lead the church.

> One of my anti-church critics cynically told me, 'You're determined to make the Black church relevant even if it kills you, aren't you?' I looked at him and said, 'Yes.'

Rev. Martin worked nothing short of a miracle for ailing St. Edmund's, according to Tolliver, who explains, "In 1928, the church's Black population had sprouted in unprecedented numbers, and St. Edmund's quickly became the largest congregation in the entire Episcopal diocese with over 2,000 active members."

In 1948, the church moved to its present address at 6101 South Michigan Avenue, formerly the site of a Greek Orthodox church. St. Edmund's established a successful parochial school and became the church of choice for many of the Black middle- and upper-middle class in Chicago.

No one could have predicted that 40 years later, this center of worship would find itself in need of another miracle.

Challenges

Tolliver was forewarned about St. Edmund's: "One of my friends said, 'Why are you going to that church? You're going to a burial society. The most you're going to have at that church are funerals,'" he recalls.

When Tolliver came in 1989 anyway, he knew he had his work cut out for him. The church's congregation had all but vanished and the building itself was in desperate need of repair. To make matters worse, the surrounding community – once a thriving lifeline for St. Edmund's – was now in a state of decay.

"By the time I got here, this physical plant had severely deteriorated and the congregation was on a decline. The morale was dispirited because all that people saw around them were declining neighborhoods, crime, and an aging congregation," Tolliver says.

Like a bad omen, financial problems also plagued the church. The St. Edmund's Credit Union had folded and in June of 1988, the church was forced to close its parochial school due to financial problems.

"The school had operated for 40 years, so there was a sense of grief and loss in that," Tolliver says. "I knew my first challenge was to revitalize the spirit of the congregation."

Rev. Tolliver understood his mission: he had to rebuild his church, his parishioners and the surrounding community in order to restore the long lost hope in St. Edmund's. He accepted the challenge and proceeded to make progress.

"We started to focus our energy on positive things, but we also established an evangelism and renewal program," Tolliver says. "Our goal was to renew our spirit and to evangelize others. I wanted a dynamic worshipping congregation dedicated to uplifting Christ and our Afrocentric heritage."

Rev. Tolliver's next spiritual hurdle was to physically restore the church, so he organized a renovation committee and orchestrated donation drives to achieve the task. Most donations came from St. Edmund's parishioners and today they have completed over $1.2 million worth of renovations in the church.

It was in this renovation process that Rev. Tolliver realized he had a "problem" — White angels decorating the walls of a Black church.

Behold, The Black Angels

The Greek Orthodox church that was formerly housed in the St. Edmund's edifice had the traditional painting of the Eurocentric Madonna and child behind the altar. There were also Eurocentric murals on the walls, which disturbed some of the younger parishioners.

"Some of the younger members with children would say to me, 'I don't see anything in the art of the church that reflects me and my children, or the heroes that my children could look up to,'" Rev. Tolliver recalls.

"So I looked at the mural behind the altar and I thought, what a wonderful place this would be for art that shows that we (Blacks) played a role in the history of our faith from the beginning of time."

The parishioners formed an art committee that studied various scriptures in the Bible that mention people of African descent. Next, the committee researched top artists in the city and selected Bernard Williams, an instructor at the Art Institute of Chicago. Consequently, the church's new murals illustrate four Biblical characters: Phillip the Evangelist, Simon of Cyrene, and Hagar and her son Ishmael.

Rev. Tolliver also decided to cover the barren walls of the church with Black baby angels.

"The Bible mentions two types of angels, those that are human-like and those that have wings; so we took two baby images and painted examples of each," he says. "The angels are the first thing you see when you walk through the door. Now people are beginning to say, 'When I come to church, I see me.'"

The parishioners also replaced the Eurocentric Christ with a Black Christ carved out of ebony. And Rev. Tolliver had another vision; he wanted to adorn the stained glass windows of the church with Black images.

In May of 1996, the church installed 33 stained glass windows, each depicting people of African, African-American, and Indian descent. The images are of bishops, priests and lay people. St. Edmund's recently drew media attention when civil rights activist Rosa Parks was honored with a stained glass window in her likeness.

The 33 stained glass windows cost $1,000 each and Rev. Tolliver never expected to raise the money in one day – but he did.

"One Sunday I asked the parishioners at the 8 a.m. service for $1,000 donations. By the end of that service we had collected $29,000," he says. "So at the 10:30 service, we only needed four more $1,000 donations, and people got upset because there weren't any windows left. That Sunday we raised $37,000."

Community Contributions

Rev. Tolliver believes that quality housing, education and a sense of security is vital to the church and the community. His primary goal is to unite the community and the church as one "vitally dynamic worshipping congregation."

Faced with a community plagued by inadequate housing, Tolliver formed the St. Edmund's Redevelopment Corporation in 1990. The corporation buys abandoned multi-family buildings and rehabilitates them. To date, the corporation has built a $5 million home for senior citizens and has rehabilitated over 200 units at a price tag of $20 million.

The corporation is now set to purchase the Washington Park scattered homes development from the Chicago Housing Authority and Rev. Tolliver is confident that they will meet the five-year goal of remodeling 500 units of housing.

In addition to housing, crime has been a steady concern of St. Edmund's surrounding community for a long while. In an effort to provide a safer neighborhood, Tolliver and his parishioners formed the Michigan Avenue/Indiana Block Club. It is comprised of residents within a 14-block radius of the church, and its members also participate in the CAPS (Chicago Alternative Policing Strategy) program.

To address the educational needs of the community, Tolliver opened St. Edmund's Academy in 1995, a primary school separate from the church, serving K-4.

Who Is This Guy?

Richard Tolliver grew up in Springfield, Ohio; his father was in the military and his mother was a librarian. After his parents' divorce, Tolliver and his two younger sisters lived with their mother and grandparents. As a young man, Tolliver looked to his grandfather, a Baptist minister, as his male role model.

Most priests vividly remember the circumstances that led them to preach the word of God, commonly referred to as their calling. Initially, Tolliver wasn't attracted to the ministry. For the most part, he had witnessed the pressures that his grandfather experienced as a minister and was afraid to face priesthood.

"I told my grandfather that I had watched the negative things people have said about leaders and all of the demands people had put on him and that I didn't think I could take it," Tolliver recalls.

"He looked me straight in the eye and said, 'The day you decide to stand for something and do something with your life, be prepared to be talked about. If you don't want to be talked about, then don't do anything with your life.'" And through those words of his grandfather, Tolliver heard his calling and enrolled in seminary school.

Rev. Tolliver received his Bachelor's Degree in Religion from Miami University in Oxford, Ohio, and then earned his Master's Degree in Divinity from the Episcopal Divinity School in Cambridge, Massachusetts.

Tolliver went on to complete two Master's degrees simultaneously at Boston University, where he studied Afro-American History and Political Science. He later earned his Ph.D. in Political Science at Howard University.

While he earned his double Master's degrees, Rev. Tolliver worked three part-time jobs to finance his younger sister's college career. However, it wasn't all work and no play for the young man: "I did have quite the social life; I mean, I am a member of Omega Psi Phi Fraternity, Inc.!" he laughs.

Rev. Tolliver has been an ordained priest since 1971 and has traveled widely throughout Africa, Western Europe, the Caribbean and Central America. His dedication has created a new harmonious existence for a church and a community that others had written off long ago.

When asked how he wanted to be remembered, a sweet smile of victory appeared on Tolliver's face.

"When I was in seminary school, one of my anti-church critics cynically told me, 'You're determined to make the Black church relevant even if it kills you, aren't you?' I looked at him and said, 'Yes.' That's what I want to be remembered for — for making the Black church relevant again."

preface Trotter

Update: Donne Trotter has served in the Illinois State Senate, where he is Assistant Majority Leader, since 1993, and is Chairman of the powerful Appropriations Committee.

Donne Trotter

By Paul Davis & Photography By Victor Powell | *Originally Published March 14, 2002*

When Donne E. Trotter takes Interstate 57 from Chicago south to Springfield, as he often must, he tends to be more focused, pays more attention to the details, and is a little less comfortable than most people who regularly traverse the 170 miles to the state's capital.

That's because the state senator's mode of transportation requires that he apply those attributes when riding his motorcycle to his legislative headquarters from Chicago's South Side.

Trotter's road to leadership in the General Assembly has mandated that he draw on those same qualities of focus, attention to details, and never feeling too comfortable about one's achievements, when he's helping to carve up the state's multi-billion dollar annual budget.

Although he was born in little downstate Cairo, Trotter has become quite adept at learning big-city policies and legislative effectiveness.

> **One of the chief responsibilities of an elected official is to enhance and enrich the quality of life of their constituents by bringing home taxpayer dollars to the community.**

First elected a state representative in 1988, Trotter had big shoes to fill – albeit a woman's. But they were not just any woman's shoes. He would go on to replace Carol Moseley-Braun, a popular, bright and articulate representative whose political career was skyrocketing.

Trotter needed to prove himself worthy of following in Moseley-Braun's footsteps immediately. "A lot of women of color were skeptical about me replacing a person as dynamic as Carol," Trotter says. "I made a lot of commitments at the time that I could do anything Carol could do. I wanted to prove that I could work just as hard for everybody."

An early political litmus test for Trotter involved an organized bloc of women in his district who strongly urged him to work to support legislation that would increase the pool of eligible women for Medicaid. His initial efforts to garner sufficient legislative backing were unsuccessful.

Taking Care Of Kids

But years later, one of Trotter's proudest accomplishments is being one of the architects of the KidCare program, which provides low-cost health insurance for uninsured children. The KidCare program, Trotter notes, raised the threshold for eligible children from 100 percent to 185 percent.

The magnitude of KidCare's success took Trotter by surprise. The program has surpassed its original expectations by registering an astonishing 178,000 children for the program.

"KidCare is great. Healthcare is everything," insists Trotter. "If we talk about closing the digital divide, we first have to close the healthcare divide. We can put a computer on every desk, but if you have a child who can't see the screen because he needs glasses, then it makes no difference."

Improving healthcare for people in his district and throughout Illinois is undeniably Trotter's central focus. He's far from a single-issue politician, but enhancing people's access to quality healthcare is among Trotter's major goals. "Healthcare is the beginning and end of everything," he maintains.

With that as his mantra, Trotter says that through the years, he has prepared himself to be a healthcare advocate and a healthcare professional. And, indeed, this bespectacled and handsomely bow tie attired lawmaker equipped himself well for multiple lines of work.

Preparation And Advancement

Trotter received a B.A. degree from Chicago State University in History and Political Science, and he later earned a Master's Degree in Health and Policy of Jurisprudence from Loyola University School of Law in Chicago.

When Trotter's not in the General Assembly attempting to wrest some funding for his constituents in Chicago, he serves as the director of minority health for the Cook County Department of Public Health.

A storied path of political relationships preceded Trotter's ascendancy to the state's leadership perch. He said he was encouraged while in college by members of the Greek fraternity Alpha Phi Alpha that if he wanted to do well in politics, he should become a member. His friends pointed out that elected officials such as Lewis Caldwell, John Stroger Jr., and Tim Evans were all Alphas.

Trotter said he credits the late Michael Smith, who once ran for alderman in Chicago's 4th Ward, with influencing him to get involved with politics. "Smith kept us organized," he recalled. However, Trotter and his band of youthful political neophytes learned an early and sobering lesson about politics back in 1979.

In an aldermanic race that featured Ralph Metcalfe, Jr., the son of the late Cong. Ralph Metcalfe Sr., against Tyrone Kenner, Trotter and his cohorts thought they had pulled off a hard fought victory.

"When we went to bed we were winning the election by 57 votes. However, when we woke up in the morning, we were losing by about 50 votes," a stunned Trotter remembers. "It taught us that you can't take anything for granted and you have to make sure the whole count is in." Kenner's savvy political workers had come up with "phantom votes" from a single precinct overnight, said Trotter.

Political persistence and experience helped bring Trotter and some of his political allies, including activists Harold Lucas and Henry English, one of their first major electoral victories. This young group of independents helped Monica Faith Stewart get elected as a state representative in 1980.

Connections

Lewis Caldwell, a state representative who, prior to serving in elective office was a practicing journalist, reached out to Trotter and became one of his most significant political mentors.

In fact, Caldwell invited Totter to come to Springfield to learn under him. One of Trotter's first jobs in that capacity was serving as the driver for Caldwell and fellow African American lawmakers Charles Gaines and Harold Washington. In Springfield, Trotter came to admire Gaines, who, although a Republican, championed the cause of his community as a "lone ranger."

Trotter credits Cook County Board President John Stroger for helping him to attain new heights. "It's no question that in electoral politics, John Stroger took me to another level," Trotter says. "John Stroger has always given opportunities to young people, unlike a lot of his peers who are threatened by youth coming in," the state senator notes.

Bringing It Back Home

Trotter has effectively drawn upon his political and legislative experiences over the years to help deliver millions of dollars back to his district, and billions of dollars throughout Illinois. Consistent with his advocacy, his priority has been to channel funding to improve the healthcare delivery system in the state.

He helped to bring $1.2 million for a sickle cell anemia program at the University of Illinois. Additionally, Trotter sponsored the first comprehensive screening and treatment program through the Department of Public Health, which is a model for other prostate programs around the country. He sponsored a similar program for women involving breast and cervical cancer screening, research, and public awareness.

Beyond his commitment to increase funding for a variety of healthcare programs, Trotter has also assisted in directing millions of dollars to Chicago for education and capital improvements.

Taking advantage of his position as Democratic spokesman on the Appropriations Committee, Trotter said he is able to "frame the debate" over increasing the funding threshold in an array of areas and adds that he is grateful to State Sen. Emil Jones, Jr., the Senate Democratic Minority Leader, for placing him in a position to have authority over billions of dollars.

About three years ago, Trotter notes, Chicago students were receiving less than $2,000 per student. He said the funding system was flawed and allowed some school districts to provide up to $15,000 per student. "(In Chicago), we've been able to raise the threshold from $2,500 to $3,640," he says. "That may not sound like much, but it's a big change."

Recognizing that the infrastructure of many schools is in desperate need of repair, Trotter said his leadership helped to bring $2.2 billion for capital improvements and argued that while the legislative system is not perfect, he is pleased that the legislature has redirected its focus from building prisons to building up schools.

In that regard, among the litany of projects for which Trotter has obtained funding is a new library and convocation center for Chicago State University, which received $45 million for construction.

Trotter's leadership duties also extend to serving as the chairman of the 27-member Illinois Legislative Black Caucus, which is comprised of minority members from both the House and Senate chambers. As a group, Trotter said the caucus is the largest single ethnic bloc in the Assembly, and when they "work together, we can direct the debate."

As he seeks re-election to a newly drawn 17th Senate District in the coming year, Trotter revealed that $592 million is coming to his district for repair of the Dan Ryan Expressway in jobs and contracts. Trotter said he, Emil Jones, and others are going to make sure that the communities they represent receive their share of the business and jobs on the project.

"We have said to IDOT that some of those jobs and contracts have to come from our community and they've agreed to do that," said Trotter, noting that one of the chief responsibilities of an elected official is to enhance and enrich the quality of life of his/her constituents by bringing home taxpayer dollars to the community.

Politically, Trotter said he is optimistic that Democrats can gain majority control of the Senate after the general election in November, after which Emil Jones would become leader of the Senate. Trotter said that in such a case, with Democrats in control, he'd be able to help the people in his district even more.

Harold

preface Washington

Update: Thanks to this grassroots movement, Harold Washington was elected in 1983 and again in 1987. Dr. Conrad Worrill is the chairman of the National Black United Front and the recently retired director of the Jacob Carruthers Center for Inner City Studies at Northeastern Illinois University, where he taught for 40 years. Robert T. Starks is a retired associate professor of political science at Northeastern Illinois University, and chairman of the Black United Fund of Illinois (BUFI).

Harold Washington

By Dr. Conrad Worrill, Robert Starks, & Photography by Michelle Agins | *Originally Published October 1991*

The 1983 election of Harold Washington as mayor of Chicago was a triumph for the Black community, as the Harold Washington electoral coalition was led and dominated by grassroots organizations and neighborhood associations within the city's Black areas. For the first time in modern history, Chicago's entire African-American community unified and organized in a proactive political movement.

This rare display of unity was evident at every level, as Harold's candidacy was supported organizationally, institutionally and individually by every segment of the Black community. Such unity transformed the movement to elect the city's first Black mayor into a crusade that made participation and voting a moral obligation that bordered on becoming a civic religion.

It is important to understand that this movement was built on the back of grassroots organizational efforts refined in the Black community over a period of nearly 25 years.

> Harold was reluctant to run. He said he would strongly consider it if at least 50,000 new African Americans registered to vote and a substantial war chest would be raised.

During this time, with the existence of a well-entrenched and oppressive political machine, and in the absence of strong economic institutions and a formal independent political apparatus to advance its cause, the Black community in Chicago had little choice but to rely upon its own organizational and institutional network to promote social change.

It was the experience garnered at the grassroots level in organizing and translating political demands during this period that made possible the mass mobilization and organization that eventually elected Harold as mayor.

The idea of a Black person running for mayor in Chicago can be traced back to 1959, when a small group of African Americans led by former Congressman Gus Savage, promoted the candidacy of Lemuel Bentley for City Clerk. Then came the third election of Mayor Richard J. Daley in 1963, but it was an election in which the Black community began to display considerable anti-Machine political behavior.

In the late 1960s, Dick Gregory positioned himself to run for mayor, and in 1971, Rev. Jesse Jackson threw his hat into the ring. After Daley's death in 1976, several Black candidates attempted to run for mayor, including Harold himself, who in 1977 won five wards in his first mayoral bid. The idea was approaching reality.

Education Becomes Political

A public schools crisis in Chicago was one of the major historical events that led to the eventual seating of a Black mayor.

In April of 1980, word leaked out that then-Mayor Mayor Jane Byrne wanted Commonwealth Edison magnate Thomas Ayers to be appointed to and named president of the Chicago public schools board. Several community groups came together to oppose the move.

Research on the part of this group, spearheaded by veteran journalist Lu Palmer and community activist Jorja English Palmer with the assistance of Rev. Al Sampson, revealed that Thomas Ayers did not live in Chicago, which one has to do to serve on the school board. Several community groups came together to oppose Ayers' ascension.

Under the leadership of Lu Palmer, several community groups were called together to discuss strategy. Interestingly enough, this meeting at Bethel AME Church was chaired by Harold Washington, who was a state senator at the time.

The outcome led to two specific strategy formulations. The first was to identify African Americans whom community groups felt were qualified to serve on the Board of Education. It was agreed that African Americans ought to be the majority of the school board representatives because we represented a majority of the school population. Secondly, a strategy unfolded to file suit against Ayers' appointment to the board.

Mass mobilizing of the African-American community around this school board fight became a major issue. There were mass rallies, demonstrations at the board, and letters in support of 35 African-Americans whose names were submitted to Jane Byrne for consideration.

As a result, five African Americans were appointed to the board and Ayers was forced to resign when he was unable to prove he lived in Chicago. This victory was the beginning of a Black unity movement that laid the foundation for the election of Harold Washington.

The mass mobilizing around the school board issue in the Spring of 1980 led to the formation of several new organizations: Chicago Black United Communities (CBUC), the National Black United Front - Chicago Chapter (NBUF), Citizens for Self Determination, the Political Action Conference of Illinois (PACI), and the Parent Equalizers.

During the summer of 1980, the Citizens for Self Determination mobilized for an African-American superintendent to head the Chicago Public Schools, with the consensus candidate being Dr. Manford Byrd. In the final decision, however, Ruth Love, former Superintendent of Schools in Oakland, California was selected.

So, then-Mayor Jayne Byrne and the Board of Education did concede on an African American running the schools, even though they selected one from outside of Chicago and created a School Finance Authority that took away the ability of the new superintendent to control the financial situation of the board.

The Community Mobilized

That fight caused the movement for Black self-determination in Chicago to escalate. On April 4, 1980, the National Black United Front (NBUF) sponsored a conference on "Government Spying and White National Violence" at Quinn Chapel AME Church, which brought together key activists from the Chicago area. Then-Congressman Harold Washington, the late Bobby Wright, Haki Madhubuti, and Minister Louis Farrakhan were keynote speakers. Over 2,000 African Americans attended.

Another important conference, held August 15, 1981, at Malcolm X College, was one of the most prophetic meetings of African-Americans seeking political empowerment. This gathering sought "to examine, to explain, and explore old and new strategies that would enable us to chart new paths toward full political representation and full political empowerment in Black precincts, Black wards, Black congressional districts, Black state legislative districts, in City Hall and throughout the country."

Harold Washington with Jayne Kennedy

In that meeting, "We Shall See in '83!" became the slogan. The keynoter was Rev. Jesse Jackson. One thousand people attended the full day's proceedings.

The Political Action Conference of Illinois (PACI) began to take up the fight in 1981 to preserve three Black Congressional districts. For the first time in Chicago's history, a redistricting map was drawn by African Americans, which became the document that all other groups had to react to. As a result, there are three African-American Congressional districts in Chicago.

In the summer of 1982, "We Shall See In '83!"– popularized by Lu Palmer in his writings and radio broadcasts – was becoming a household slogan in the Black community. The potentiality of electing Chicago's first African-American mayor was becoming more of a reality every day.

Segments of the African-American community fought for a Black Superintendent of Police and backed Sam Nolan, one of the top-ranking policemen in the department. Jane Byrne would have no part of it and instead appointed white Richard Brzeczek. That continued disrespect of the African-American community by Byrne was a focal point in the movement for African-American political empowerment. Byrne became the targeted enemy.

Alderwoman Dorothy Tillman and Marion Stamps kept the issue of the treatment of African-American children in the Chicago public schools a major organizing strategy through their Parent Equalizers group. Through the Chicago Tenant Rights Organization, Stamps led numerous protests in 1982 against the racist actions of the Chicago Housing Authority. An increased demand for greater

African-American representation in the decision-making process of all aspects of government had become the burning issue of the day.

The South African Rugby Team

In the spring of 1982, the South African rugby team, the Springboks, was scheduled to play in Chicago. Immediately, NBUF formed the Black Coalition Against the Rugby Tour. Protests were held at City Hall to challenge the Byrne administration from allowing the Springboks to play on public property.

Alderman Danny Davis presented a resolution against the Springboks using public property. A watered-down version of this resolution was passed. Rev. Jesse Jackson played a key role through Operation PUSH in dramatizing the Springboks' presence in Chicago.

Jackson and Dr. Conrad Worrill, along with other key activists, picketed the Chicago Athletic Club every day the Springboks were in town. Finally, the pressure was so great the team decided to play in Racine, Wisconsin. Only a handful of spectators showed up and the game was met by protestors. The movement won this battle.

During this same period, Alderman Alan Streeter broke from the Machine by not supporting Byrne's school board nominees. CBUC launched its political education training classes in preparation for the fight against the Machine in Streeter's 17th ward.

CBUC mobilized a citywide effort to support the election of Streeter, who did win. The movement defeated the Machine and the excitement was growing to elect Chicago's first African-American mayor.

In early 1982, community organizations united to form a voter registration coalition. Lu Palmer, Tim Black, Zenobia Black, Connie Howard, Oscar Worrill, Nate Clay, Elliot Green and Ivy Montgomery provided the leadership for the People's Movement for Voter Registration.

This organization became the field component of Voter Registration and Vote Community, established by Soft Sheen's Ed Gardner, which led to the great voter registration drive of 1982.

In late June 1982, Mayor Byrne was up to her old tricks again. It was time for appointments at the Chicago Housing Authority. Marion Stamps on the outside and Renault Robinson, a CHA board member, on the inside, had been fighting for over a year to break up the Democratic Party Machine's control of CHA. But Byrne did not want to concede to the community's wishes for fair representation on the CHA board.

Many Black community groups staged a major demonstration at a City Council meeting in late June of 1982 to protest the Byrne administration's policies. Byrne ordered police to lock the Council door after supporters from white ethnic communities filled the Council chambers. This was the "straw that broke the camel's back."

The ChicagoFest Boycott

While Rev. Jesse Jackson was giving his weekly radio report on WBMX (now WVAZ), a caller, who identified herself as a resident of Gary, Indiana, suggested that as a result of Byrne's actions, the African-American community should boycott Jane Byrne's pet project, ChicagoFest.

Rev. Jesse Jackson mobilized the African-American community to do so. On the following Saturday at Operation PUSH, over 2,000 people representing every major Black organization, leader and politician watched Rev. Jackson burn a ChicagoFest ticket.

The audience was highly aroused and left Operation P.U.S.H. that Saturday marching on ChicagoFest.

For 11 days, hundreds of African-Americans walked the picket lines at Navy Pier, the site of the Fest, chanting slogans and carrying signs, "We Shall See in '83!"

The ChicagoFest Boycott was a grand success. Less than one percent that attended was African American. Thus, the boycott became a major mobilizing tool in electing Chicago's first Black mayor.

Harold Washington's name began to emerge as a consensus candidate and Lu Palmer called a meeting with key activists and political leaders to discuss Washington's candidacy. But Harold was reluctant to run. He said he would strongly consider running, if at least 50,000 new African Americans registered to vote and if a substantial war chest would be raised.

Voter registration fever began to catch on in the Black community. Palmer and CBUC distributed a questionnaire for mayor and who would be the people's choice to run. The results were presented at the famous plebiscite meeting at Bethel AME Church.

Over 2,000 cheering and enthusiastic Black people attended the now famous meeting in late August of 1982. The crowd was anxious. Jorja Palmer reported that over 17,000 African-Americans overwhelmingly chose Harold Washington to be the candidate.

Between July 1982 and November 1982, over 150,000 Black people were registered to vote. It was becoming clearer every day that Harold could win. Finally, Harold Washington made his candidacy announcement on November 10, 1982, at the then Hyde Park Hilton Hotel. Thousands of Black people showed up at this historic press conference, showing clearly that we had a new political unity movement in Chicago and triumphantly dispelling the myth of community disorganization.

Left: Harold Washington with
Ed Vrodolyak and Geraldine Ferraro
Below: First Pitch Comiskey Park

Above: Harold Washington
with Bishop Tutu

preface Watson

Update: Wayne Watson's dream of a new Kennedy-King College opened in 2007 as a $263 million state-of-the-art campus in the heart of Englewood.

He capped his 30-year City Colleges career by serving as Chancellor from 1998 to 2009, and then accepted the position of President of Chicago State University that same year. Watson remained at the helm until 2016 and at the time he left Chicago State, he was the longest-serving African-American in Illinois higher education. Watson retired as Chancellor and President Emeritus of both institutions.

Dr. Wayne Watson

By Glenna Ousley & Photography by Reginald Payton | *Originally Published September 16, 1999*

t was 1978 and Wayne Watson was back in Chicago after a stint in the South. In North Carolina, he had been a faculty member at Shaw University and an airlines manager, and in Georgia, a headmaster at a college preparatory school. Now he was looking to resettle in Chicago, having left with a Bachelor's, Master's and Ph.D., all from Northwestern University.

When a friend suggested he check out the City Colleges of Chicago for employment, Watson took his job search right to the top, calling the Chancellor's Office to arrange an interview.

"'Did someone refer you?'" Watson said the secretary inquired.

"No," he responded.

"'Well, send your resume to our Human Resources Office and someone will get back to you,'" Watson recalled being told. "'No one sees the Chancellor.'"

Watson said he was struck by the secretary's tone

> **Part of the game plan is to put this new Kennedy-King College in Englewood, and highlight that neighborhood as a community of heroes and families and roots.**

– right out of the *Wizard of Oz*. "Nobody can see the Great Oz!" he mimicked. "Nor nobody, not nohow!"

Undeterred, Watson sent his resume to the Chancellor, Oscar Shabat, and within two days he received a call from Shabat inviting him to come in for an interview…the next day.

An hour and a half into the interview, in a room filled with City Colleges administrators, Watson said Shabat confessed, "'We were only going to give you a 10-minute courtesy interview; we wanted to see who was bold enough that despite what my secretary told them, would still send me their resume.'"

Shabat hired Watson as Assistant Director of the Advanced Institutional Development Program at Malcolm X College. Today, Watson heads the second largest community college district in the country, as Chancellor himself, with a budget of $340 million.

Watson's 20-year rise through the system came under four chancellors, starting with Shabat, the founding father of the City Colleges system.

"Shabat was the last good chancellor," Watson asserts. "Without a doubt, he was someone who I feel established a foundation for this district."

Musical Chairs

As the first chancellor of the City Colleges of Chicago (CCC), Shabat developed the system from just one building to a collection of seven colleges. Shabat was also the longest-serving chancellor, heading the system from 1966 to 1983.

Salvatore G. Rotella followed Shabat, heading CCC for five years. During his stewardship, it was reported that the City Colleges saw a 23 percent enrollment decline. With just two years remaining on his $95,313-a-year contract, the City Colleges board bought him out, adding an assortment of other benefits to a final tune of $330,000.

Rotella was succeeded by the first African American and the first woman chancellor, Nelvia M. Brady. By all accounts a local success story, she grew up in Chicago's public housing and had a Ph.D. from the University of Michigan.

Brady was a City Colleges board member when she was plucked to head the system on an interim basis, 39 years old at the time. Six months into Brady's tenure, board members abandoned plans for a nationwide search and appointed her chancellor permanently.

But just three years later, City Colleges faculty gave her a "no confidence" vote and recommended to the board that she be terminated. But it was a press conference she called criticizing her bosses that sealed Brady's fate.

She alleged that "demeaning" conditions were put on a one-year contract offered her and she accused Board Chairman Ronald Gidwitz of trying to make her a "princess figurehead leader."

Brady was fired and a national search for her replacement took place. In the meantime, the board appointed a triumvirate of City Colleges presidents – Homer Franklin of Olive-Harvey, Zerrie Campbell of Malcolm X, and Ray LeFevour of Wright – to run the district on an interim basis until a replacement could be found.

That replacement was Ronald Temple, the first

African-American male to lead the district. But Temple's tenure, too, was short-lived. Reportedly dissatisfied with the pace of change at the colleges, the Board voted not to renew his contract.

Temple, like Brady before him, made public the dispute surrounding his job. He, too, bitterly criticized Gidwitz, accusing him of micro-managing the colleges and padding the central administration with his patronage workers.

Unable to negotiate a quick and quiet departure, the board fired Temple and taxpayers continued to pay out his contract – worth an estimated $500,000 – until June 2000.

Watson's Progression

From his start as a program director at Malcolm X, Watson became a dean and a vice president at Malcolm X, a vice chancellor of academic affairs for the district, interim president at Harold Washington College, and later the president of Kennedy-King College.

"Each one of those positions gave me a foundation of understanding a different aspect of the district," says Watson. "And in 1998, all those pieces fit together and established for me a foundation, not so much for me to be a chancellor, but for me to understand this district well enough to run the district as a chancellor."

Though he has both, Watson makes the distinction of the quality of experience winning out over the quantity of experience. When asked about the mistakes of his predecessors, he refused to name names, but described the pitfalls he had witnessed.

"One chancellor thought that this chair was larger than the Mayor's," Watson observed. "Another made the mistake of thinking that the district is run by events. In other words, not setting up sound academic policies and standards, and sound management procedures. Events and parties run out and eventually at the end of the year, they're going to say, what did you accomplish?

"Another chancellor made the mistake of just not running their own district, not making decisions based upon principles – academic principles, principles of both professional and personal integrity, management principles – but making decisions outside of the matrix of integrity, based upon, what do I think an external body wants."

Watson then added, "What I have got to do is make sure the standards are raised, that productivity is increased and that we have a system in place where we pay our bills."

Watson himself is not without critics. They consider him demanding, vindictive, and power hungry. "I am not vindictive," said Watson. "I have regrettably had to terminate some people. But when I terminate somebody it is because you are on (drugs) or because you have been misappropriating funds."

To the charge of being power hungry, he responded, "Do I want the resources in order to solve problems? Yes. If that is power hungry, then I am power hungry. Do I want that type of power for my own personal aggrandizement and advancement, etc.? No, I'm somewhat a student of history and I realize that those people who have used power for that reason have failed."

Perhaps the best insight into Watson's psyche is offered by Watson himself, who was an elite wrestler in college. "In wrestling you have to be aggressive, you have to be creative, you have to be decisive," Watson says.

"If you're going to make a move to do something to someone and to take someone down, you can't have second thoughts about it. You have to make a decision and you execute it. Boom! Same thing in this office."

Warp Speed Changes

Change has occurred within the City Colleges at seemingly warp speed. Within a week of his appointment, Watson met with the President of the University of Illinois, James Stukel, to discuss what educators are calling the K-16 initiative.

Recalls Watson, "I said I'd like to make sure that when my students graduate from the City Colleges, my exit criteria meets what your entrance requirements are for your junior-year level courses."

Watson then proposed the same thing to Paul Vallas, the Chief Executive Officer of the Chicago Public Schools. "Once Paul articulated the course competencies and exit criteria at the senior high school level," Watson said, "he then has to readjust his junior level, the sophomore level and it goes all the way down. That's why it's called K-16."

Watson credits the City Colleges faculty with taking ownership of the initiative, noting that CCC faculty is now looking to work with faculties of other Chicago area universities to align their curricula with them as well.

A major initiative Watson brought before the City Colleges board involved raising standards within the district. Last May, the Trustees approved Watson's recommendation requiring all students to earn a grade of "C" or better in all general education and core requirements in order to graduate. Reportedly, the City Colleges is the first and only district in the state to have such a requirement.

But not all the news surrounding City Colleges under Watson's watch has been positive. He has been criticized for his plan to build a new Kennedy-King College rather than fixing up or even closing the current decrepit facility at 69th and Wentworth, which also has suffered from low enrollments.

Watson, with the backing of Mayor Richard

Daley, has envisioned a new facility to be built at 63rd Street and Halsted as an anchor to help revitalize that Englewood neighborhood.

As a product of Englewood himself, Watson has a deep understanding of the complexities within that community, where 85 percent of residents live below the poverty level.

"I grew up on 63rd Street," Watson says. "There are external economic, political and social forces keeping our children from learning. I had those same forces preying on me as a young man on 63rd Street.

"But I'm where I am because I had goals and I had people who said, 'If that's what you want, we will help you get there.' Students have a fiduciary right to education and someone has to be guardian of that right. That's where I come in.

"Part of the game plan is to put this new Kennedy-King College in Englewood and highlight that neighborhood as a community of heroes and families and roots. You will find families with children who are destined to succeed if given the opportunity.

"The media highlights the mortality rates and crime rates there as the highest in the city. You read about it everyday, but we have to ask ourselves: How do we nullify this so that people begin believing in themselves?"

Providing High Tech Training

On the horizon for the City Colleges of Chicago, Watson says the district plans to play a major role in providing education and trying to meet the needs of high tech companies to make Chicago the Midwest cyberspace capital of the country.

Said Watson, "We're meeting with the mayor's staff and companies that will have a 1,000 to 2,000 jobs. We want to know what the skill sets are that they want. We're gearing ourselves to do more training in those areas," as well as providing customized training for banks and law firms."

Watson added that a big part of his job ahead will simply be to make the public aware of just what the City Colleges are.

"We are not like the University of Illinois where you have just one mission – you take people in and graduate them from college; that is their mission," Watson said.

"The mission of the City Colleges is not only to prepare students for transfer to four-year colleges, but to provide remedial and developmental education, occupational training, and to provide for those who take classes for personal interest or career advancement."

preface White

Update: Jesse White was first elected Secretary of State in 1998 and won landslide victories in 2002, in which he won all 102 counties, and again in 2006 and 2010. On November 4, 2014, White was re-elected to a record-breaking fifth term, winning another landslide victory by a 2-to-1 margin in which he earned over 2.3 million votes statewide — 230,000 votes more than any other statewide constitutional candidate. White became Illinois' longest serving Secretary of State on May 30, 2014.

Since 1959 when he founded the Jesse White Tumbling Team, more than 17,000 young men and women have performed with the group, which he formed to keep young people on the path to success and away from gangs, drugs, alcohol and smoking. The team makes up to 1,500 appearances a year through its seven units of 225 young people a piece.

He has a school — the Jesse White Learning Academy — named after him in Hazel Crest, Illinois.

Jesse White

By Wanda Wright & Photos Courtesy of Jesse White | *Originally Published April 8, 1999*

You would had to have been there on that icebreaker of a winter evening in 1991.

Up the dark staircase and into a chilly room filled with awful old furniture and waiting hopefuls, just to witness the soft spoken gentleman who walked into George Dunne's and Burton Natarus' meeting, past the others, leading two terrified and nervous young adults dressed in business suits.

Waving the political leaders silent, he asked that the young people's issues be placed from the bottom to the top of the priority list. Wincing at first, the sophisticated politicians listened politely, then shook their heads in disbelief.

"What about you? You've waited weeks for this meeting," Dunne said. He raised greyed, bushy eyes with mock suspicion, smiled and continued, "One day I know you're going to ask for something for yourself." Natarus burst with laughter, then bellowed, "Don't count on it, you're talking to Jesse White!"

One Word To Describe Him

Consider the word "superhero." What other adjective might one use to describe someone who jumps from the belly of planes, sleeps an average of four hours per night, never took a day off in 15 years, taught for 33 years, retired, ran and won three successful political campaigns, then spends his weekends counseling families and training kids?

> I have a no-nonsense approach and I mean it. My kids cannot drink, smoke, swear, drop out of school or be unkind to neighbors and friends. They must not dislike anyone because of race, color, and creed or come up with low grades. No matter where they come from.

Whether diving out of the great machines in the sky which bear aloft hurtling bodies that paratroop, or steering a wheel of his own, the 37th elected and first African American in history to become Illinois Secretary of State, Jesse White's class act is "rough and tumble."

Simply speaking, there are two types of politicians in the world – the ones that make promises, and the ones that keep them. White's "Art of Living" has an uncanny similarity to Epictetus of A.D. 55, who was born a slave during the Roman Empire and whose philosophy of self-discipline has lasted nearly 2,000 years.

Much like our political machines, the Romans didn't "let" anyone in, especially minorities, unless they ranked among the razor sharp.

Jesse White's fervor, wit and bedrock wisdom come from his relentless commitment to train children about discipline, character, integrity and achievement.

Totally unstuffy and absolutely passionate about children, Jesse considers himself useful when his ideas are grasped and put to use for other people. With little patience for posturing or pontificating, White's admission into politics has been through high marks and strategic battles.

From Start To "No Time Soon" Finish

After serving as a paratrooper in the United States 101st Airborne Division, White returned to civilian life in a brief professional baseball career with the Chicago Cubs, then continued for 33 years as a teacher and administrator for the Chicago Public Schools.

White's political career began as State Representative of the 1st District in 1974. Skeptics shook their heads at his early campaign promises to fairly represent the most culturally diverse district in Illinois, which contained the Cabrini Green and Henry Horner housing units.

White went on to become well known for his arguments favoring anti-crime measures, education and senior citizen rights. Today, he recruits kids and families for the famous tumbling team that carries his name, while still serving as Committeeman for the 27th Ward.

Where others might entertain thoughts of retirement, Secretary White has just begun the first term of his fifth successful career. A results oriented dogma kept him in the Illinois General Assembly for 16 years, as he garnered a healthy portion of the district's 80 percent White and 12 percent Black vote.

An expanded DePaul campus, artsy River North gallery community and One Magnificent Mile, stand

Secretarial Plans

Illinois' new Secretary of State plans to require having two new license plates on every vehicle, along with a transportation teaching system that caters to all levels of understanding, especially for children.

"Toby Tire" has been created as a walking, talking instructional model for kids to learn the safety rules of boarding and behavior around mobile vehicles.

Soon, school bus drivers will be required to have background checks, Heimlich maneuver training, fingerprint checks and specialized safety instructions before their "classification" license is issued.

As head of the state's libraries, White presides over the Illinois Department of Literacy, a fact that excites many. White's years of volunteerism have amassed an impressive list of "angels" that are anxious to be involved in his projects. Also, he is commissioner of a youth baseball team with over 850 team members, and an army of 250 volunteers that help coordinate the 32 teams.

Says White, "People who have an interest, but not a talent or an inclination, can't wait to work with those that need them!"

He exclaims, "Downstate clubs like the Kiwanis, Rotary, Lions, Masons and Shriners, who are already committed to help kids grow straight and tall, rotate peer tutoring. We are going to mirror their principles with community role models – it's the only way to fill the chasm, to include all the children, to help society."

Speaking of which, White has an enormous amount of energy. Although it's 6 a.m. and most of us are turning over for that important REM sleep, White is somewhere laying down the fourth or fifth mile of his morning run.

He was up until 2 a.m. the night before counseling a single parent, or trying to find housing for a displaced senior. Some things never change.

Those red and white shirts springing about the Chicago Bulls basketball court at half time, known as the Jesse White Tumbling Team, are still tutored and doted upon by their founder.

Currently, the team's reach spans to more than 10 cities beyond the Chicago area and thousands of children are lined up on the waiting list.

Team members must have grades that reflect above C averages and conduct complemented by exemplary behavior. Low achievers are considered, but must attend 90-minute sessions twice a week in specialized one-on-one learning centers.

Transported back to the Solheim Center, an additional hour of tumbling skills is taught. The objective here is to clearly integrate the recreation of tumbling with education and culture. Jesse's team has appeared worldwide: in Japan, Bermuda, Canada, three movies, and 11 McDonald's commercials.

White demands volunteerism, believing that

as testimony to Jesse's incredible ability to redirect negatives, positively.

Deeds that formerly took six months to return, with a 30 percent error rate, now come through to people requesting them in two minutes. Winning the Cook County Recorder of Deeds elections in 1992 and 1996 with an exorbitant number of votes caused local politicos to closely examine what's become known as "White's Methodology."

What they found amazed them.

He introduced office wide automation with state-of-the-art technology, which created faster access and recording processes. Illiterate patronage workers were replaced with qualified employees. A $2.5 million contract held by an outside firm was rescinded, with duties given over to employees.

Today's error rate is presently less than one percent, providing tax savings of over $4 million annually to taxpayers.

nothing creates better success than giving back. His efforts have always been 100 percent involved without remediation. He works with youth, for free.

White's Protégé, Ald. Walter Burnett

White's most famous protégé, perhaps, is Walter Burnett. As a youth, Walter made some mistakes that ended up in him receiving a jail term. White and Burnett's father didn't close the door of hope on Walter, but they didn't excuse his behavior either. Instead, they decided that Burnett would have to work exhaustively to vindicate his past.

And Burnett did work and work, putting in hours at the 1st District and the tumbling team…and eventually becoming White's senior assistant. After his mentor's successful bid for Recorder of Deeds, Burnett approached White about becoming 27th Ward Alderman.

Jesse signed on, watching Walter unseat an incumbent alderman in 1995. Then after feeling his debt to society had been repaid, Walter again asked for White's help to clear the slate of mistakes made in his youth.

But now he wouldn't have to use "clout" or connections. Burnett delivers an impressive record of achievement – there are more condos, small businesses, and multi-cultural residents with new construction than any other section of the city.

Anyone in or around Jesse White's camp must follow his creed. He says, "I have a no-nonsense approach and I mean it. My kids cannot drink, smoke, swear, drop out of school or be unkind to neighbors and friends. They must not dislike anyone because of race, color, and creed or come up with low grades. No matter where they come from."

(It is interesting to note that the majority of children on his teams come from motherless and fatherless families.)

Finally, White is not interested in using the seat of his new office of Secretary of State in the manner of his predecessors, i.e., as a springboard into the governor's mansion.

There will be no pressure for employees or vendors to fill his campaign coffers. Running the state as a business and making its residents proud are White's focuses. His feeling is that a good job will bring overwhelming support.

He has two goals: one is to rewrite history as being the number one advocate for children; the second is being the best Secretary of State in Illinois history.

In a country today where nothing is private or sacred, it's worth noting that someone who could do otherwise cares enough to save all of us through life's most precious legacy…our children.

preface
Williams

Update: Norma J. Williams has literally put thousands of people to work in the last 30 years through her agency. She has completed the Executive Management Program at the Tuck School of Business Administration at Dartmouth College, and the Next One Entrepreneur Program in partnership with Northwestern University's Kellogg School of Management and the Chicago Urban League.

Norma J. Williams

By Marcia A. Reed-Woodard & Photography by Victor Powell | *Originally Published January 9, 2003*

have always been determined to be successful, though I never set out to be CEO of a multi-million dollar company. But I've come to know that your destiny will always seek you out; mine caught up with me in 1986 after being fired for the third and final time," says Norma J. Williams.

Though her last dismissal spurred her on into entrepreneurship, Williams, founder and CEO of NJW Consulting Services, speaks kindly of her last employer. "I don't hold a grudge against the staffing agency that fired me because I know that my termination was not the result of poor performance or behavior, but a part of a bigger plan for my life," she says. "A plan that has set me on the course to be who God intended for me to be all along."

However, Williams is quick to point out that "the plan hasn't always been easy, and the course has never been smooth."

Staffing is about people and relationships; you can't get around that. People relate to people, and the way they relate is in the form of a good or bad relationship.

"I didn't have a business plan, loan, or client when I started NJW on a yellow legal pad at my living room cocktail table," says Williams. "I recruited my first temporary employees while I was standing in line at the unemployment office."

Williams continues to recount her humble beginnings.

"Can you imagine what those unemployed folks had to be thinking?" she asked, placing her manicured hand on her hip.

"I can," she answers. "They were thinking, 'Who is this lady, and how is she offering me a job while she stands in the same unemployment line with me,'" Williams says, rolling her neck a time or two before bursting into infectious laughter. "But I was Norma. I did what I had to do."

On February 1, 1986, Williams founded NJW, now one of Chicago's premiere agencies providing full-service staffing solutions and business consulting, information technology management and professional support services to Fortune 500 companies, as well as local, state and federal government agencies.

NJW's suite of business services includes: administration and regulatory support, requirements analysis, strategic planning, contract administration, document management, financial management, project management, program management, and risk mitigation.

The Preparation

"Starting my own company, and the thought of actually creating my own personal success was a little scary, but the feeling of starting something out of nothing was innately familiar," says Williams. "Once you've lived with having nothing, to be faced with the possibility of losing everything is not a significant fear factor."

Williams, who is the oldest of nine children, was raised by her mother on Chicago's South Side in one of the city's poorest communities.

"Weathering poverty prepared me for entrepreneurship. Having watched my mom improvise made me shrewd," says Williams, who then launched into a discussion of NJW's earlier days.

"My first office was a studio apartment on North Wabash, and the three desks in that apartment were NJW's departments," said Williams, who notes that her childhood love for reading to escape the desperate times had sparked an active imagination.

"As the company grew, I leased larger apartments; five apartments in all," she says, waving her palm for emphasis. "It wasn't until several years after starting that a wonderful gentleman, Ralph G. Moore, heard about my struggles and assisted me in getting the company's first office space."

Williams tells a similar story about obtaining bank credit. "Although NJW grossed more than a million dollars in its first year, it was seven years before a bank agreed to provide my company with a line of credit," she says, with a slight edge in her voice.

"But that's okay…once again, a kind gentleman, Barry Sullivan, the former chairman of Bank One, decided to provide NJW with its first line of credit." Williams confesses that even after securing credit with Bank One, it was another three years before NJW used it.

"At the beginning of my endeavor, I had made God my number one business partner, so not only had I become accustomed to trusting Him to make provision, but I had long since mastered the art of stretching and juggling. I got that from my mom," she says of her financial finesse that allowed her to pay hundreds of temporary employees on a weekly basis without using credit.

It was probably that knack for stretching and juggling that not only helped Williams manage the bills, but also expand the business. Within just 10 years, Williams was able to grow NJW to include six other offices, one in Cleveland, Ohio.

The Purpose

"But with the growth came challenges that even my juggling act couldn't hold together," Williams admits. "When we were small, NJW enjoyed the small business 'boutique experience,' in which I was meeting face-to-face with the companies' representatives, and managing the relationships one-on-one. But as we expanded, I wasn't able to manage the face time or the volume of relationships that NJW had come to have."

She says that in addition to the strain of expansion, employment was at an all-time high. Also, several of the larger staffing firms had started to capture more of the temporary market by hiring more temporary workers at a lower pay rate, and underbidding smaller staffing firms by charging Fortune companies less money per worker.

"It was a melee. Temporaries were treated like numbers, and companies were viewed as just another dollar," Williams explains.

She says that it was during this tumultuous time in the staffing industry that she again was forced to face another turn in her destiny and seek out a niche for her firm's survival.

"I thought long and hard about the situation NJW was in, and I concluded that the best way to stay in the game was to find the soft spot on what had become a porcupine of an industry," says Williams, pausing to laugh. "I had to find the one opportunity that wasn't so apparent to the competition, and NJW had to take advantage of that opportunity to the best of its ability."

The Relationships

Williams says that with much prayer, research and observation, she concluded that the industry was lacking in the area she had excelled in all the time – relationships.

"Staffing is about people and relationships, you can't get around that; not with ID numbers, colorful marketing materials, or tightly executed training programs," says Williams in a matter-of-fact tone.

"People relate to people, and the way they relate is in the form of a good or bad relationship. It was after much soul searching that I realized that NJW has the divinely-appointed opportunity to reach out to people, and create and build good relationships that forever change their lives."

Williams says that during that moment in her life, she realized that NJW was a vehicle to enrich people's lives through employment, training, professional mentoring, and interaction with people they might not otherwise ever get to know.

Inspired by this revelation, Williams says that she revamped the entire way that NJW did business.

"I regret that in the past, NJW had a profile requirement: individuals were screened and hired largely as a result of their appearance and presentation, then to a lesser degree, on their experience and skill set. Presentation was crucial, and more often than not the determining factor," she says.

Williams believes that her experience as a Black woman in White-dominated, corporate America had significantly skewed her perspective on what was essential to getting jobs and getting ahead.

Williams, who admits that colleagues have occasionally referred to her as Norma St. John, after the infamous clothing designer, says, "I had bought into the notion that the only way you could get anywhere in corporate America is if you looked successful and sounded successful."

While Williams still contends that looking and talking professional plays an integral part in securing employment, she no longer makes those factors the deciding prerequisites in assisting people in finding employment.

"Unfortunately, that sentiment was then, but this is now!" she exclaims with a smile that stretches across her face. "Today it's about the person, not the profile or the outer package or simply the presentation."

She adds proudly, "The NJW that exists now screens and hires individuals based on the person they are, and the desire they have to be all that they can be."

The Plan

Williams continues, "NJW has found its purpose in making a daily, life-changing difference in the lives of people, both with our employees and clients. I have come to understand God's plan for my life, and the role that NJW has in that plan."

Although NJW sees hundreds of people on any given day, Williams says that the corporate vision she has written for the company mandates that nobody is going to enter or leave out of NJW's doors with anything less than hope.

She recounts the experience that confirmed her decision to have NJW specialize in changing people's lives.

"An older man, who had just recently been laid off

an industrial job he had worked for more than 22 years, had come in on a Tuesday afternoon because someone had told him I could get him a job," Williams says, her voice breaking with emotion.

"I had never worked with industrial workers, NEVER. But that afternoon, I closed my office door, had my receptionist hold all my phone calls, and sat on the telephone for more than four hours calling and praying that someone would hire that gentleman with his disheveled appearance and broken English."

Williams concludes the memory, "On Thursday, he had a new job, and I had reached another milestone along this course to becoming who God has predestined me to be.

"I have come to truly appreciate the power that I have been invested with – the power to hire and fire individuals, perhaps during one of their most vulnerable times in life," says Williams. "I'm so glad that I'm following this plan to fulfill my destiny, and make a difference in the lives of others through employment and training."

preface Wilson

Update: August Wilson passed away in 2005 at the age of 60 after a battle with liver cancer, but his works live on and he has been celebrated nationally ever since.

Chicago's Goodman Theatre was the first theater in the world to produce Wilson's entire 10-play cycle and two of the Goodman's productions – *Seven Guitars* and *Gem of the Ocean* – were world premieres.

Actor Denzel Washington, who stars in the movie version of *Fences* released in 2016, has a deal with August Wilson's estate to produce all the plays in the cycle for HBO television, one film a year for the next 10 years.

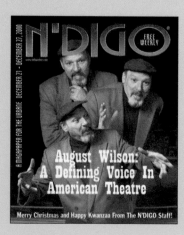

August Wilson

By Rosalind Cummings-Yeates & Photography by Brent Jones | *Originally Published December 21, 2000*

August Wilson speaks with the ease of a preacher, colored with the simplicity and familiarity of your neighbor down the street.

He is unassuming, talking with the young, corn-rowed elevator operator in the Goodman Theatre with as much sincerity as when he's commenting on the themes of his current production at the theatre, *King Hedley II*.

Over the last two decades, Wilson's cycle of plays documenting the 20th Century African-American experience has heralded him as one of the most important voices of American theater.

Two of his plays, *Fences* and *The Piano Lesson*, have earned him Pulitzer Prizes for drama, making him the darling of critics and theater fans alike. It would seem that he's at the pinnacle of his career, with the widely produced, highly acclaimed plays and a TV adaptation to his credit. But Wilson has always been concerned with much more than just critical acclaim.

If you do not know, I will tell you that Black theatre in America is alive. It is vibrant. It is vital. It just isn't funded.

Importance Of Black Theatre

"We need our own theaters," Wilson insisted during a recent interview with *N'DIGO* at the Goodman Theatre. "White theaters do African-American plays, but their mission is European American. We need African-American institutions, then if we want, we can do a few White plays, maybe."

Some view this as a curious position to take, since it comes from a playwright whose plays are generally featured at major White theaters and rarely at Black ones. Indeed, Wilson set off a torrent of criticism when he announced these views in *American Theatre*, in 1996.

Calling himself a "race man" in the Marcus Garvey tradition, the article, which was taken from an address he made to the Theatre Communications Group National Conference at Princeton University, stated:

"Black theatre is a target for cultural imperialists who seek to propagate their ideas about the world as the only valid ideas, and see Blacks as woefully deficient not only in arts and letters, but in the abundant gifts of humanity. If you do not know, I will tell you that Black theatre in America is alive. It is vibrant. It is vital. It just isn't funded."

Sitting back in a chair, his trademark newsboy cap perched above twinkling eyes, Wilson refused to soften his opinion. "We have a growing body of theater artists now that we didn't have 20 years ago," he said. "These artists need places to develop their work, but we don't have the opportunity.

"We haven't worked to build the relationships with funding institutions and we have the tendency to think small," he said, explaining why there is still no major African-American theater with the size and financial resources of the Goodman.

"In order to have these kinds of theaters, you need support, you need strong boards. We tend to leave a lot of things to other people," Wilson added.

Independent Beginning

Leaving things to other people doesn't seem to be a Wilson characteristic, as from his earliest days, he appears to have been a self-sufficient, independent thinker.

Born Frederick August Kittel, Jr. in Pittsburgh in 1945 to a German immigrant father often absent in his childhood and an African-American cleaning woman named Daisy Wilson, he grew up poor in a family of six children. When Wilson grew tired of the racism and low expectations of his teachers, he dropped out of school at 16 and began educating himself at the local library.

This would have been a bold, self-assured move for any teen, but for a Black boy in the 1950s, it was unheard of. Given the oppressive racial climate and limited educational resources of segregation, it's unusual that Wilson had enough confidence in himself to reject what he heard from his White teachers.

"I did quit school, but instead of going to the pool room, I went to the library," he said. "My mother taught us all to read. She always said, if you can read, you can do anything. So I always felt I could know anything. I was always questioning things, but I was told to shut up, sit down."

Wilson points to his mother as the key to his belief in his abilities. He said that she instilled in him a sense of dignity that the times could not diminish.

"My mother was highly principled and demanded respect," he explained. Leaning forward in his chair and briefly sliding off his hat, he recalled an example of this:

"She won a radio contest for Morton Salt. The prize was a brand new Speed Queen washer. When they saw that she was Black, they offered her a certificate for a used washer at the Salvation Army, instead.

"She refused to take it. She said, 'Sometimes, something is not always better than nothing.' She refused to trade in her dignity. She started saving up for the $89 to buy a Speed Queen, and a year later, we got it."

Fortified with his mother's examples of self-worth and respect, Wilson read all of the books he could find by and about Black people. Reveling in the words he read, he became a poet, publishing his poems in various Black publications.

In 1968, with no experience or background, Wilson founded the Black Horizons Theater company with Rob Penny. Calling himself a "cultural nationalist", he set about raising the consciousness of Black Pittsburgh through theater.

In 1978, Wilson moved to St. Paul, Minnesota and seriously began his career as a playwright, producing his first play, *Jitney*. Set in a Pittsburgh taxi station, the drama showcased Wilson's ability to capture the common man, portraying Black urban speech and lifestyles, with appreciative realism. *Jitney* had a well-received run at a small Pittsburgh theater in 1982, foreshadowing Wilson's later theatrical success.

Blues Influence

When discussing his literary influences, he always lists the blues as his primary source of inspiration. After discovering an old Bessie Smith record in the 1960s, Wilson claims that his entire outlook was changed.

"I think that the blues is the best literature we have," he states. "I tapped into it with an anthropological eye; I was able to discover a lot of things. When I first discovered Bessie Smith, the voice literally stunned me. I said, 'This is me! This is mine!'"

Rubbing his beard with enthusiasm, Wilson recalled how it transformed his perceptions. "I was living in a rooming house and I looked at all of the men differently. I saw a history behind them. I began to recognize that there was some value to their lives. It was a profound discovery for me," Wilson said.

Years later, he realized that he could use his discovery about the importance and power of everyday Black life by writing plays about it and exposing it to a larger audience.

Wilson has written a 10-play cycle that documents these vibrant lives through each decade of the 20th Century in America. This collection of work is called Wilson's Century Cycle, or the Pittsburgh Cycle because nine of the 10 plays take place in that city; the other is based in Chicago.

Progression Of A Playwright

Ma Rainey's Black Bottom, Wilson's first play to attract national attention, is set in the 1920s and explores the life of blues musicians. Its production in 1984, bursting with Wilson's lyrical dialog, hailed him as an important new playwright.

His following play, *Fences*, set in the 1950s, portrays a former athlete who discourages his son from accepting an athletic scholarship. The play won the Pulitzer Prize for Drama in 1987 and firmly established Wilson as a dynamic, influential playwright.

The remainder of the Cycle includes the plays: *Gem Of The Ocean* (set in the 1900s); *Joe Turner's Come And Gone* (1910s); *The Piano Lesson* (1930s); *Seven Guitars*

(1940s); *Two Trains Running* (1960s); *Jitney* (1970s); *King Hedley II* (1980s); and *Radio Golf* (1990s).

Wilson includes Black nationalist poet and playwright Amiri Baraka, painter Romare Bearden, and Argentinean short-story writer Jorge Luis Borges, as major influences on his work. He credits Baraka as his primary guide for the process of dramatization. In Bearden, who is famous for rich collages of Black life, he found visual inspiration.

Wilson has said that he tries to translate the grand, colorful images of Black life that Bearden painted on canvas, onto the stage. Borges, an acclaimed short-story writer, influenced Wilson to rethink the way he tells a story. Borges' complex story techniques often appear in the plots of Wilson's plays.

His New Goodman Production

Wilson's current production, *King Hedley II*, displays all of these influences. A tragic tale of forgiveness and redemption, the play is set in 1985, in Pittsburgh. The lead character, King, has just been released from prison.

Facing the harsh reality of Reaganomics and brutal urban violence, King struggles to retain his manhood in a situation filled with hopelessness. Unable to get a job to support his pregnant wife, he returns to his hustler's lifestyle, only to find that it changes nothing.

Filled with both doom and ribald comedy, *King Hedley II* is a blues song personified. Gritty, sullen and yet slightly hopeful, the play captures the vicious cycle of lives crushed by racism, a vanished sense of self, and low expectations. Drawn out and complicated, the production displays a twisted climax worthy of a Borges story, or any Greek tragedy.

Commenting on the violent climate of the 1980s and the legacy that it has bred, Wilson suggests that we are still paying for it.

"We didn't go all the way through slavery to arrive at that point," he said. "We got lost – that connection between our ancestors was broken in some kind of way. We have to start a new connection through redemption and forgiveness.

"Symbolically, in the play, King becomes the messiah and sheds his blood so that the community can be restored. Hopefully, some of us have matured, but a lot of us have abandoned our ancestors and rode off into the sunset in a BMW."

Noted for the way his productions encourage the audience to rethink and analyze history, Wilson sums them up as a simple ode to the lives of everyday Black folks:

"I want people to look and see that these are African people. The contents of their lives are worthy of the highest of accolades," he says.

preface Winston

Update: The Winstons have expanded their ministry to include the Living Word Christian Center-Tuskegee, in Pastor Bill Winston's native Tuskegee, Alabama, where they also own the Washington Plaza mall.

Bill Winston

By Ngina James & Photos Courtesy of Living Word Christian Center | *Originally Published January 18, 2007*

Sitting in one of Pastor Bill Winston's services at Living Word Christian Center in the near-west suburb of Forest Park is like attending a merger of a charismatic college lecture and a comedy club routine.

With Winston's straight-no-chaser style, coupled with an infectious dry wit, he feeds his congregation inspiration, sometimes tinged with a dose of strong medicine, and always leaves them laughing.

Living Word Christian Center has become one of the fastest growing churches in the area, with a membership of some 20,000.

That's a staggering jump from the 50 worshippers who sat in the pews of the humble storefront church in the heart of Chicago's West Side in 1988, when Winston became senior pastor.

In three years, Winston and his wife, Veronica, grew the congregation to 500 and outgrew their location; in 1990, they moved to a larger space in Forest Park.

Less than 10 years after the Winstons began directing the church, membership was over 10,000, and the pastor realized a new location was needed that allowed for additional expansion as the church continued to grow.

> **Part of the ministry's mission is to rebuild people's self-esteem and inner image to conform to God's plan for their success and economic prosperity.**

So, in 1997, in an astute economic move, Living Word purchased the then-declining 33-acre Forest Park Mall, now known as Forest Park Plaza, at 7600 West Roosevelt Road. Winston says the purchase was made with an eye toward redevelopment.

"The goal was captured in the Center's vision to be a place where the integrity of God creates a lasting foundation for success and changes the economic destiny of the people," says Pastor Winston, who had a significant background in corporate America before turning to the ministry.

Providing economic development is as strong a part of Winston's ministry as administering to the spiritual needs of his parishioners.

An Economic Ministry

Living Word took half of the 500,000 square feet of the mall for itself, completely converting a movie cinema complex into a state-of-the-art, multi-million-dollar worship and administrative center.

The other half of the mall's space is allocated for retail, according to Center spokesperson Kim Clay. Existing tenants include Portillo's Hot Dogs, Enterprise, America's Best, Planet Fitness, Ashley Stewart and Taco Bell, among others.

The mall recently brought in full-service grocer Ultra Foods, which takes up 70,000 square feet. "Ultra noted that their opening at our mall was among their most successful new store launches in recent years," Clay says.

The church's business outreach is conducted through the Joseph Business School, founded in 1997. Its mission is to facilitate job and wealth creation through vocational and job readiness training and entrepreneurship workshops.

Living Word also produces *Believers' Walk of Faith*, a radio and TV ministry broadcast hosted by Winston that reaches millions of households nationally and around the world.

In explaining Winston's general philosophy about the church's economic development work, Clay says, "As a successful businessman turned ordained minister, Pastor Winston feels a special calling to bring revitalization to struggling communities.

"He feels that many communities are broken down on the outside because they reflect the condition of the people on the inside, so part of his ministry's mission is to rebuild people's self-esteem and inner image to conform to God's plan for their success and economic prosperity."

In his life prior to heeding the calling of the ministry, William Winston served in the Air Force, where he received awards for superior flying skills, and then became a licensed commercial pilot.

After joining IBM as a marketing representative in the 1970s, his exceptional managerial and relational skills rapidly earned him several promotions at the company.

When he resigned in 1985 to pursue his theological leanings, Winston was a marketing manager in IBM's

Bill

Midwest region and responsible for more than $35 million in sales revenue per year.

A graduate of Tuskegee University, he also attended the prestigious Kellogg Graduate School of Management at Northwestern University here in Chicago.

Childhood Influence

"One of the things that shaped my personality was my environment. I grew up in Tuskegee, Alabama, where there were three dominant professions – medicine, aviation, and education. I was in some way involved in all three," Winston recalls.

His magnet school, sponsored by Tuskegee University, exposed him to many things that are not involved in a standard grade school education.

"We had French in second grade and it was a very advanced curriculum," Winston says. "They would bring in the President of Sierra Leone, Africa, to address us. Tuskegee was where the top veterans' hospital was located, so entertainers such as Roy Rogers and Hop-Along Cassidy would come bring their horses, put on their outfits, perform, and speak to us.

"Most of my friends' parents were in the medical profession, so I would go to the hospital with some of my friends and we would scrub down, go into the operating room because their dad would bring us in and we'd view operations. I wanted to be a doctor."

Education was also a major influence in his early life, partially because his parents were scientists and teachers. "We had renowned educators who used their minds to influence and break down the walls of segregation and color barriers on 'the front lines,' long before leaders such as Dr. Martin Luther King," Winston says.

However, the greatest impact on him was not that of a brilliant doctor or educator, it was a little girl in his second-grade class named Denise James.

"I was in love with Denise. I don't know why, it was just something about her. If I went to the store and bought 10 lollipops, I would give Denise five," Winston recalls.

Denise's father was well-known fighter pilot Daniel "Chappy" James, who eventually became a four-star U.S. general.

"When Chappy came home from overseas, he would pick Denise up from class and I would see him in his uniform. I got my dad to take me out to the airport on Sundays and I would watch the Tuskegee Airmen fly those planes – it excited me like nothing else. So I wanted to be a pilot, too," he says.

Ironically, the only thing that Winston recalls he had no real interest in was being a preacher.

"My family did go to church sometimes, but I wasn't exposed to being a preacher," he explains. "In fact, my ideas about that were not very positive.

"They were actually kind of negative because I knew the preacher at my church got into 'moral difficulties,' so it didn't give me much confidence. I had more confidence in medicine, education, and aviation."

Life Altering Experience

Winston received a B.S. from Tuskegee in premed, then made his pit stop with the Air Force, becoming a fighter pilot in Vietnam and Southeast Asia.

He had gotten married, but because of the enormous demand on pilots to be available at all times, his first marriage ended in divorce. "That was something I said I was never going to do in my life because I had come from a family that was divorced," Winston said.

The divorce from his first wife (not Denise, whom he never saw again after second grade) almost devastated him. The very thing he promised himself he would not do was staring him in the face.

"There was an emptiness I began to feel," he recalls. "My life had taken a negative turn and often the trouble in people's lives is what brings them to a relationship with God. Jesus said the healthy need no physician. What happens is there is a problem that they just can't solve."

Winston says that often, a person does not understand how their life experiences, family, and so much of what they go through are all a part of what God allows to produce the person they will eventually grow into becoming."

Six years after Winston's stint in the military where he reached the level of captain, he took a job in Chicago with IBM, where he met Veronica and married her in 1983.

Winston felt the calling in 1984 and the couple founded their first church in Minneapolis. He eventually attended Lagos Bible School and the Oral Roberts University Graduate School of Theology.

BILL WINSTON MINISTRIES

Winston

"I always wanted to be the best that I could be; I was submerged in excellence," he says. "Being around celebrated doctors, educators, and influential people gave me an image of winning. That is why I could lead a bunch of saints to purchase this mall for our church and build it out. I wanted the most excellent thing, instead of having a limited vision."

Furthermore, Winston says, "You can take a person who hasn't had these environments and put them in a church like this and the Word (in the Bible) will supply everything they need, such as the authority, environment, the experiences. Meditating the Word creates an inner experience.

"So that is what I am doing with this congregation. I'm taking them out of the environments they've come out of and creating brand new experiences in their lives so that they can function on whole new levels that they've never been trained to function on."

Living Word Christian Center members congregate every Sunday morning at 7 a.m., 9 a.m., and 11:15 a.m. at 7600 West Roosevelt Road. They also meet every Wednesday at 6:30 p.m., and as Pastor Winston puts it, "There's always a warm seat awaiting you."

preface
Worrill and Afrik

Update: Baba Hannibal Afrik, born Harold E. Charles, passed in 2011. The former Chicago public school teacher joined with other educators in 1972 to create Shule Ya Watoto, which means "School for Children" in Swahili. A privately funded, independent institution, the African-centered school served West Side kids for more than 30 years, teaching Black history along with traditional disciplines.

Dr. Conrad Worrill retired in 2016 as director of the Jacob H. Carruthers Center for Inner City Studies at Northeastern Illinois University. He was a major contributor to the work, *Should America Pay? Slavery and the Raging Debate on Reparations* published by HarperCollins in 2003. A long-time board member of the Black United Fund of Illinois, Worrill is now focused on writing his memoirs.

Dr. Conrad Worrill & Hannibal Afrik

By David Smallwood & Photography by Calvin Woods | *Originally Published November 27, 1997*

Sometime next summer, the United Nations will ponder whether the United States government has engaged in a systematic pattern of genocide against Black Americans.

At the same time, the American judicial system might be hit with a lawsuit that would force the United States to pay what amounts to trillions of dollars in reparations to African Americans for the harm they suffered from slavery and the discrimination Blacks have endured since.

These startling developments are due in large part to two of Chicago's long-time, hard-core community activists.

Dr. Conrad Worrill – chairman of the National Black United Front (NBUF) and a professor at Northeastern Illinois University's Center for Inner City Studies – is author of the genocide campaign.

We have been left without any compensation for our centuries of free labor. We have never been given any official, legal, or economic consideration for what our ancestors sacrificed and died for in slavery, or for the racial injustice that has existed since slavery.

Helping to lead the charge that seeks to financially compensate Black America for the damage caused by slavery is Baba Hannibal Afrik, co-chair of the National Coalition of Blacks for Reparations in America (N'COBRA). Afrik is also a leader of the Council of Independent Black Institutions, which promotes educational self-reliance.

These men, their organizations, and their actions in helping to cause the above scenarios, are rooted in the philosophy of Pan-African Nationalism. That involves the unity of people of African descent around common goals and objectives, particularly the quest for independence and self-determination.

Whereas Civil Rights was a movement toward equal opportunity and access, the Pan-African Nationalist fight is a struggle or Black liberation. It goes beyond Blacks seeking the legal right to be able to do the same things as White people.

Instead, it involves fighting against the oppression of Whites and their efforts to control and dominate the Black community.

At the same time, it advances the concepts of empowerment of the Black collective and institution-building, with the ultimate aim of nation-building. Therefore, the movement encourages speaking out against and exposing the wrongs that White America perpetrates on Blacks (like the claim of genocide), and promotes the pursuit of financial independence (like the quest for reparations).

We Charge Genocide

Worrill has sought to replicate efforts dating back to 1919 by earlier Black nationalists to bring America up on genocide charges on the world stage. After the United Nations was established in 1945 and the Geneva Genocide Convention Treaty came into existence, William Patterson, Paul Robeson and others mobilized the first formal genocide complaint campaign in 1951.

"They actually compiled a formal complaint, which turned into a book called *We Charge Genocide,*" Worrill says. "We're still working on that, but we have attempted to re-enact that campaign and update it by taking petitions to the streets."

Worrill's delegation officially filed its complaint in Geneva at the United Nations' Human Rights Commission headquarters on May 21, 1997 two days after Malcolm X's birthdate. (In 1964, Malcolm wrote an outline on how to charge the United States government with genocide.) To date, the NBUF has collected more than 200,000 signatures on support petitions.

"According to the way the United Nations defines it," Worrill says, "'genocide' means any of the following acts committed with intent to destroy, in whole or in part, a national, ethnic, racial, or religious group: killing members of the group; causing serious bodily or mental harm to members of the group; deliberately inflicting on the group conditions of life calculated to bring about its physical destruction in whole or in part; imposing measures intended to prevent births within the group; and forcibly transferring the children of one group to another group."

Telling The World

Using those parameters, Worrill's complaint charges the U.S. government with employing a pattern of genocide against Blacks revolving around the CIA/crack cocaine connection in the Black community.

Other acts of genocide mentioned include: cutting back on welfare; privatization of public housing, public education and basic healthcare; racist immigration policies; expanding the prison industry; and environmental discrimination. The petition also accuses the United States of 38 human rights violations.

Worrill explains that five selected experts will deliberate the charges in June 1998. "We want them to tell the world, the 194 nations in the UN, what they think about our complaint," Worrill says. "The reason we decided to go to an international body in the first place is because Blacks sometimes have to go outside the boundaries of this country to seek support from others in the world on the contradictions of how we're being treated inside America.

"This will open up a dialogue with people across the globe about Africans in the world and the conditions they face similar to African Americans. Africans everywhere are up against a world body of ideas called White Supremacy that's at the bottom of all of this."

Worrill noted that a month after the complaint was filed, President Clinton announced his Race Initiative project. "Behind that announcement came the discussion of the U.S. apology for slavery. Behind that was the discussion that an apology without substance is meaningless, so reparations came into it. Now we have a whole new discussion going on," Worrill said.

The Case For Reparations

"Reparations has emerged over the last 15 years or so as an issue of self-determination," Baba Hannibal Afrik continued. "The idea gained in popularity when others in this country began to receive compensation for acts of incarceration and things that don't even approach what Blacks have suffered."

Afrik cited reparations payments made by the American government, including: $1 billion and millions of acres of land to Alaska natives in a land settlement in 1971; $81 million to the Klamaths of Oregon in 1980; $105 million to the Sioux tribe of South Dakota, $12 million to the Seminoles of Florida, and $31 million to the Chippewas of Wisconsin all in 1985; and $32 million to the Ottawas of Michigan in 1986 to honor a treaty made in 1836.

Then there's the $1.2 billion the American government decided to pay Japanese Americans in 1990 for their four-year internment in prison camps during World War II.

"That made more people aware that African Americans are deserving of similar and appropriate compensation," Afrik said. "We thought we would get it with the Emancipation Proclamation through the Freedmen's Bureau and the 40 acres and a mule legislation, but all those efforts were cancelled.

"We have been left without any compensation for our centuries of free labor. We have never been given any official, legal, or economic consideration for what our ancestors sacrificed and died for in slavery, or for the racial injustice that has existed since slavery."

Ten years ago, a group of organizations joined a conference spearheaded by the National Council of Black Lawyers. Out of it came the idea of creating a national organization to specifically address the question of reparations. That was N'COBRA. U.S. Cong. John Conyers heard of the group and asked it to support a reparations bill that he would introduce in 1989.

The focus of N'COBRA since has been to lobby for Congressional support of Conyers' bill; to organize the community around the idea of reparations and mobilize it to pressure the government to address the issue; and to develop a legal strategy to sue the government in court and force reparations.

Reparations How?

Afrik explains that even though some estimates put the compensation amount for Black suffering at nearly $8 trillion, reparations obviously wouldn't come only in the form of direct cash. "It would also involve providing opportunity and access to college scholarships, housing, employment, land technology. There are a lot of ways that every Black person could receive something that would enable them to improve their life and their family's lives based on their needs," Afrik says.

For instance, maybe the 40 acres, farm equipment and enough funds to keep operating for five years could go to families interested in agriculture, Afrik suggested. Those interested in educational advancement could have four-year college scholarships guaranteed for their children.

"Think of the planning those families, who don't know if they have enough money for college, could do. And the child would know there's an opportunity for him to be a doctor or architect," says Afrik.

He suggested that unused government land, spending in the arms and defense industries, and various forms of tax relief, could all be re-directed toward urban renewal, homes, jobs and healthcare for African Americans without affecting the national economy much.

"Basically, reparations would provide the little boost that most Black people in this country need," Afrik says. "There should be an equitable distribution

of reparations to every Black person by their birthright. It's honorable and practical, and it can be worked out. That's the purpose of Conyers' legislation."

Afrik noted that Conyers' bill doesn't ask for reparations, only for the establishment of a commission to study slavery and subsequent racial discrimination against Blacks to determine if the impact of those forces warrants appropriate remedies.

"The precedent was set when a commission studied whether to give reparations to the Japanese," Afrik says. "Conyers is just following suit, so for them to say we are unworthy of study is unthinkable because they've already created the mechanism."

Filing A Historic Suit

Of the lawsuit strategy, Afrik says that N'COBRA has gathered "a black-ribbon committee of some of the most gifted legal minds in this country" to research two options. One is to file in federal court; the second is to pick a specific state for a class-action suit.

"Florida, for instance, has already awarded compensation to the inhabitants of the Rosewood community, so that might be a good state to target, but there are others as well," Afrik says. "Wherever we

file, we will be employing some of the Constitutional strategies used in the Supreme Court desegregation case and we're confident the legal strategy will force the government to acknowledge reparations and begin paying because legally, we're correct.

"We're entitled," he concludes. "It's not a question of whether White folks will grant us reparations, but whether Black folks are going to demand it. It's not a question of morality – depending on White folks to do what's right. It's a question of power – whether Black people can exert enough pressure on their government structure to extract some justice."

Worrill summed up the efforts of these two men who represent a wing of the Black community that would hold America accountable for the injustices it dishes out to African Americans:

"What Brother Hannibal and N'COBRA are doing regarding reparations, what NBUF is doing with the genocide issue, and also with the whole question of African-centered education where we try to reclaim the curriculum, develop Black independent schools – it's all tied in to reclaiming the truth to some extent about our history and legacy as an African people. That's what this thing is really about."

And that's called nation-building.

Dr. Conrad Worrill and Hannibal Afrik

preface Wright

Update: Rev. Jeremiah Wright served as Senior Pastor at Trinity from 1972 through 2008 when he retired to become Pastor Emeritus of Trinity. Rev. Otis Moss III, a graduate of Morehouse College, Yale Divinity School and Chicago Theological Seminary succeeded him.

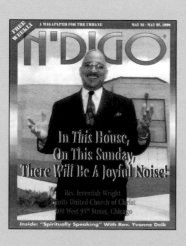

Rev. Dr. Jeremiah A. Wright Jr.

By Donna Gist Coleman & *Originally Published May 21, 1998*

Every Sunday, the faithful flock arrives, sometimes as early as an hour before service, to secure a spot in the 2,200-seat sanctuary of the newly rebuilt Trinity United Church of Christ at 400 West 95th Street.

Three services are held to accommodate Trinity's more than 8,500 members; those who don't make it into the sanctuary spill into two adjacent overflow rooms so that they, too, can be inspired by the spiritual and prophetic words of their senior pastor – formerly the Rev. Dr. Jeremiah A. Wright Jr., and currently the Rev. Otis Moss III.

This is the third time in Trinity's history that the church has expanded to harbor its ever-growing congregation. Trinity's members travel from all over the Chicago area, from Gurnee to Joliet; they represent a full spectrum of the African-American community, from the highly educated to the uneducated, from the wealthy to the economically disadvantaged.

> At Trinity, our titles in the world do not count. Beneath this cross we are all God's children on equal footing; our hands are touching as a symbol and sign of our common humanity.

One of Trinity's most notable members was former President of the United States Barack Obama, who married his wife Michelle there and had his daughters Malia and Natasha baptized there. Oprah Winfrey was a member of the Trinity congregation for a period.

But as Rev. Wright told his congregation one Sunday: "In here, our titles in the world do not count. Beneath this cross we are all God's children on equal footing. Our hands are touching as a symbol and sign of our common humanity in the presence of an uncommon divinity."

"I'm also impressed by the individual attention he gives to members. For instance, when children in the congregation get good grades, he writes personal letters of praise. Last year, when a man tried to snatch one of my daughters, Rev. Wright called her and made her feel so much better. He's a pastor of this huge congregation, yet he can make you feel like he's your individual pastor."

Though the new Trinity facility still has a few odds and ends to complete, the hardest part is over. The new stained-glass windows will depict "the story of the African presence in our faith story" and capture the "brown beauty of God's holiness," Wright says.

Not surprisingly, Trinity UCC, whose motto is "Unashamedly Black and Unapologetically Christian," has the United Church of Christ denomination's largest congregation – an accomplishment in which Wright takes great pride. Last year alone, about 1,400 adults and children joined the congregation, he says.

Wright is also proud of the fact that Trinity is one of the few churches, "Black or White, in this denomination to have built three buildings and two senior citizens homes," adding that the denomination's next largest church membership is about 3,000.

"To have reached national prominence in a denomination that is predominantly White is probably the greatest accomplishment of this church," Wright said. "The denomination sends groups here by the droves every Sunday just to study Trinity. Most churches in the United Church of Christ have about 200 members."

When Trinity began broadcasting its Sunday morning worship service on the radio in 1980, the church's growth in membership "took off in quantum leaps," Wright says. "People often remarked that they had never seen a church that had 'throw-down' music and a sermon you could understand."

The Rev. Dr. Kenneth B. Smith, Trinity's founding pastor, says Wright "has done a phenomenal job of meeting the needs of thousands of people who have joined the church, and he has brought his deep commitment to the Gospel to those thousands.

"His commitment to racial justice is equally impressive. I never would have imagined that something that I had a very slight hand in helping would grow to this size. I think the genius of his preaching style has to do with making religious faith speak culturally to the people who attend or visit the church. Trinity's slogan is his way of making the faith real within a cultural context."

Feeding A Spiritual Hunger

So how has Wright been able to propel the tremendous growth of Trinity's original congregation of just 87 members?

"The short answer is God – and I don't mean that in any esoteric sense," Wright says. "I mean that in addition to God being the spirit that blesses, there's an interest and a burning and a spiritual hunger among African-American folk. Jesus himself said that God draws people. It's the idea of drawing people back home, back to the oldest institution in the African-American community."

That "burning" also has to do with the fact that Trinity "is not just a worship experience on Sunday," Wright says. "It's all the things that take place during the week: 20-plus Bible classes, 60-plus ministries. God draws people because of their hunger, and they're finding fulfillment in the ministries. I'm not responsible for that."

The volunteer ministries, one of which all new members are required to join, include six choirs, a legal counseling ministry, youth dance and drama ministries, an employment ministry, a prison ministry and an HIV/AIDS ministry. The level of commitment, of course, varies with each ministry.

In the HIV/AIDS ministry, for example, participants undergo about 22 hours of intensive training once or twice a year. Two members even took under their wings a man diagnosed with AIDS whose family had abandoned him. When he died, they paid his funeral and burial expenses. "Many members of this ministry have done all kinds of things above and beyond what is required of them," Wright says.

He ensures that his congregation's "hunger" also is satisfied through weekly Bible classes. "A lady once said to me, 'I've never been to a church where you can learn so much, where you have textbooks and such a wide range of teachers and lecturers who come in to speak.' Exposure to minds like that is exciting to people where religion begins to make sense to them," Wright says.

Wright's parents, the Rev. Dr. Jeremiah Wright Sr., and Dr. Mary Wright, instilled the importance of education in their son, who notes with great pride that Trinity has ordained dozens of male and female members of the clergy that are seminary graduates, with dozens more being enrolled in the seminary.

Music, Sweet Music

People also are drawn by the wonderful mix of music – from anthems and spirituals, to contemporary selections such as R. Kelly's inspirational *I Believe I Can Fly* – all rousingly sung by choir members bedecked in colorful African-rooted clothing.

The size of each of the choirs is staggering, ranging from nearly 60 eighth-12th graders who make up Imani Ya Watume (Swahili for "Messengers of Faith"), to the 200-plus adults who compose the sanctuary choir. And the Little Warriors for Christ choir, comprising about 220 children in kindergarten through 7th grade, was growing at such a rapid pace that a sixth choir was formed to join the kindergartners with toddlers and preschoolers.

Wright himself is an accomplished musician, playing the piano and organ by ear. He wrote and composed *God Will Answer Prayer* and *Jesus Is His Name* in the mid-1970s. The latter evolved in an almost supernatural way: Wright was awakened by what he had thought was a beautiful, haunting melody playing on the radio. But when he realized the radio was off, he grabbed a pen and began writing down the words and tune from memory.

"It was like a church service," Wright says. "I could hear the choir singing this song so beautifully and I was singing the tenor line: 'I have a dear savior, He hears when I call, holds my hand lest I stumble, picks me up when I fall.' I woke up and said I was going to call the radio station to request that song – but the radio was off!"

Embracing African Roots and Globalism

Wright is very much committed to teaching people, especially people of color, to love themselves and to know their history. Wright's love for Africa and Black people is reflected in his church's music and in the way he nurtures his congregation spiritually and culturally, and through his sermons, which have given him a reputation in mainstream media as being "controversial."

When the Rev. Dr. Thanda Ngcobo, the first minister and woman to be ordained at Trinity, came to Chicago from South Africa in the early 1970s, she found Trinity to be "like a home in a strange land," she says.

"It was the only United Church of Christ that had a minister who was embracing the spirit of Africa in his music and in his spirituality, and who was open to God, using Him to create such a spiritually penetrating, African healing-kind-of-worship through his music. He did it with such anointing that somehow I knew that there was a mentor for me in him."

Ngcobo, in turn, had a tremendous impact on Wright. "She sensitized me personally to the struggle in Africa," he says, noting that Trinity was the first church in the nation to place a "Free South Africa" sign on its front lawn.

The multilingual Wright continues to answer God's call to minister around the world. He has lectured in Africa and other countries, as well as at seminaries and universities throughout the United States. Considered a top theologian and pastor, he has published four books and numerous articles.

The Philadelphia native holds a doctorate of ministry from United Theological Seminary, master's degrees from Howard University and the University of Chicago, and three honorary doctorates. He received three U.S. Presidential Commendations after serving in the U.S. Marine Corps from 1961-63.

Before Wright accepted the call to become Trinity's third senior pastor in 1972, he was called by two other churches to lead their congregations. But he was attracted by the potential for renewal and reclamation at Trinity.

"These members (at Trinity) were ripe for heading in a new direction," Wright says. "They were ready to break the mold in terms of what the denomination had in its mind when it had started this congregation back in 1961, and where they were at the end of 1971.

"That really sounded exciting, particularly in those years, when so many of our Black churches were moving out of the 'hood. Here was a church saying that it wanted to have roots in the community. That's what led me here."